MACHINE LEARNING
An Algorithmic Perspective

SECOND EDITION

Chapman & Hall/CRC
Machine Learning & Pattern Recognition Series

SERIES EDITORS

Ralf Herbrich
Amazon Development Center
Berlin, Germany

Thore Graepel
Microsoft Research Ltd.
Cambridge, UK

AIMS AND SCOPE

This series reflects the latest advances and applications in machine learning and pattern recognition through the publication of a broad range of reference works, textbooks, and handbooks. The inclusion of concrete examples, applications, and methods is highly encouraged. The scope of the series includes, but is not limited to, titles in the areas of machine learning, pattern recognition, computational intelligence, robotics, computational/statistical learning theory, natural language processing, computer vision, game AI, game theory, neural networks, computational neuroscience, and other relevant topics, such as machine learning applied to bioinformatics or cognitive science, which might be proposed by potential contributors.

PUBLISHED TITLES

BAYESIAN PROGRAMMING
Pierre Bessière, Emmanuel Mazer, Juan-Manuel Ahuactzin, and Kamel Mekhnacha

UTILITY-BASED LEARNING FROM DATA
Craig Friedman and Sven Sandow

HANDBOOK OF NATURAL LANGUAGE PROCESSING, SECOND EDITION
Nitin Indurkhya and Fred J. Damerau

COST-SENSITIVE MACHINE LEARNING
Balaji Krishnapuram, Shipeng Yu, and Bharat Rao

COMPUTATIONAL TRUST MODELS AND MACHINE LEARNING
Xin Liu, Anwitaman Datta, and Ee-Peng Lim

MULTILINEAR SUBSPACE LEARNING: DIMENSIONALITY REDUCTION OF MULTIDIMENSIONAL DATA
Haiping Lu, Konstantinos N. Plataniotis, and Anastasios N. Venetsanopoulos

MACHINE LEARNING: An Algorithmic Perspective, Second Edition
Stephen Marsland

A FIRST COURSE IN MACHINE LEARNING
Simon Rogers and Mark Girolami

MULTI-LABEL DIMENSIONALITY REDUCTION
Liang Sun, Shuiwang Ji, and Jieping Ye

ENSEMBLE METHODS: FOUNDATIONS AND ALGORITHMS
Zhi-Hua Zhou

Chapman & Hall/CRC
Machine Learning & Pattern Recognition Series

MACHINE LEARNING
An Algorithmic Perspective
SECOND EDITION

STEPHEN MARSLAND

CRC Press
Taylor & Francis Group
Boca Raton London New York

CRC Press is an imprint of the
Taylor & Francis Group, an **Informa** business

A CHAPMAN & HALL BOOK

CRC Press
Taylor & Francis Group
6000 Broken Sound Parkway NW, Suite 300
Boca Raton, FL 33487-2742

© 2015 by Taylor & Francis Group, LLC
CRC Press is an imprint of Taylor & Francis Group, an Informa business

No claim to original U.S. Government works

Version Date: 20140826

International Standard Book Number-13: 978-1-4665-8328-3 (Pack - Book and Ebook)

Visit the Taylor & Francis Web site at
http://www.taylorandfrancis.com

and the CRC Press Web site at
http://www.crcpress.com

Again, for Monika

Contents

Prologue to 2nd Edition

There have been some interesting developments in machine learning over the past four years, since the 1st edition of this book came out. One is the rise of Deep Belief Networks as an area of real research interest (and business interest, as large internet-based companies look to snap up every small company working in the area), while another is the continuing work on statistical interpretations of machine learning algorithms. This second one is very good for the field as an area of research, but it does mean that computer science students, whose statistical background can be rather lacking, find it hard to get started in an area that they are sure should be of interest to them. The hope is that this book, focussing on the *algorithms* of machine learning as it does, will help such students get a handle on the ideas, and that it will start them on a journey towards mastery of the relevant mathematics and statistics as well as the necessary programming and experimentation.

In addition, the libraries available for the Python language have continued to develop, so that there are now many more facilities available for the programmer. This has enabled me to provide a simple implementation of the Support Vector Machine that can be used for experiments, and to simplify the code in a few other places. All of the code that was used to create the examples in the book is available at `http://stephenmonika.net/` (in the 'Book' tab), and use and experimentation with any of this code, as part of any study on machine learning, is strongly encouraged.

Some of the changes to the book include:

- the addition of two new chapters on two of those new areas: Deep Belief Networks (Chapter 17) and Gaussian Processes (Chapter 18).

- a reordering of the chapters, and some of the material within the chapters, to make a more natural flow.

- the reworking of the Support Vector Machine material so that there is running code and the suggestions of experiments to be performed.

- the addition of Random Forests (as Section 13.3), the Perceptron convergence theorem (Section 3.4.1), a proper consideration of accuracy methods (Section 2.2.4), conjugate gradient optimisation for the MLP (Section 9.3.2), and more on the Kalman filter and particle filter in Chapter 16.

- improved code including better use of naming conventions in Python.

- various improvements in the clarity of explanation and detail throughout the book.

I would like to thank the people who have written to me about various parts of the book, and made suggestions about things that could be included or explained better. I would also like to thank the students at Massey University who have studied the material with me, either as part of their coursework, or as first steps in research, whether in the theory or the application of machine learning. Those that have contributed particularly to the content of the second edition include Nirosha Priyadarshani, James Curtis, Andy Gilman, Örjan

Ekeberg, and the Osnabrück Knowledge-Based Systems Research group, especially Joachim Hertzberg, Sven Albrecht, and Thomas Wieman.

Stephen Marsland
Ashhurst, New Zealand

Prologue to 1st Edition

One of the most interesting features of machine learning is that it lies on the boundary of several different academic disciplines, principally computer science, statistics, mathematics, and engineering. This has been a problem as well as an asset, since these groups have traditionally not talked to each other very much. To make it even worse, the areas where machine learning methods can be applied vary even more widely, from finance to biology and medicine to physics and chemistry and beyond. Over the past ten years this inherent multi-disciplinarity has been embraced and understood, with many benefits for researchers in the field. This makes writing a textbook on machine learning rather tricky, since it is potentially of interest to people from a variety of different academic backgrounds.

In universities, machine learning is usually studied as part of artificial intelligence, which puts it firmly into computer science and—given the focus on algorithms—it certainly fits there. However, understanding why these algorithms work requires a certain amount of statistical and mathematical sophistication that is often missing from computer science undergraduates. When I started to look for a textbook that was suitable for classes of undergraduate computer science and engineering students, I discovered that the level of mathematical knowledge required was (unfortunately) rather in excess of that of the majority of the students. It seemed that there was a rather crucial gap, and it resulted in me writing the first draft of the student notes that have become this book. The emphasis is on the algorithms that make up the machine learning methods, and on understanding how and why these algorithms work. It is intended to be a practical book, with lots of programming examples and is supported by a website that makes available all of the code that was used to make the figures and examples in the book. The website for the book is: `http://stephenmonika.net/MLbook.html`.

For this kind of practical approach, examples in a real programming language are preferred over some kind of pseudocode, since it enables the reader to run the programs and experiment with data without having to work out irrelevant implementation details that are specific to their chosen language. Any computer language can be used for writing machine learning code, and there are very good resources available in many different languages, but the code examples in this book are written in Python. I have chosen Python for several reasons, primarily that it is freely available, multi-platform, relatively nice to use and is becoming a default for scientific computing. If you already know how to write code in any other programming language, then you should not have many problems learning Python. If you don't know how to code at all, then it is an ideal first language as well. Chapter A provides a basic primer on using Python for numerical computing.

Machine learning is a rich area. There are lots of very good books on machine learning for those with the mathematical sophistication to follow them, and it is hoped that this book could provide an entry point to students looking to study the subject further as well as those studying it as part of a degree. In addition to books, there are many resources for machine learning available via the Internet, with more being created all the time. The Machine Learning Open Source Software website at `http://mloss.org/software/` provides links to a host of software in different languages.

There is a very useful resource for machine learning in the UCI Machine Learning Repository (`http://archive.ics.uci.edu/ml/`). This website holds lots of datasets that can be downloaded and used for experimenting with different machine learning algorithms and seeing how well they work. The repository is going to be the principal source of data for this book. By using these test datasets for experimenting with the algorithms, we do not have to worry about getting hold of suitable data and **preprocessing** it into a suitable form for learning. This is typically a large part of any real problem, but it gets in the way of learning about the algorithms.

I am very grateful to a lot of people who have read sections of the book and provided suggestions, spotted errors, and given encouragement when required. In particular for the first edition, thanks to Zbigniew Nowicki, Joseph Marsland, Bob Hodgson, Patrick Rynhart, Gary Allen, Linda Chua, Mark Bebbington, JP Lewis, Tom Duckett, and Monika Nowicki. Thanks especially to Jonathan Shapiro, who helped me discover machine learning and who may recognise some of his own examples.

Stephen Marsland
Ashhurst, New Zealand

## CHAPTER 1

Introduction

Suppose that you have a website selling software that you've written. You want to make the website more personalised to the user, so you start to collect data about visitors, such as their computer type/operating system, web browser, the country that they live in, and the time of day they visited the website. You can get this data for any visitor, and for people who actually buy something, you know what they bought, and how they paid for it (say PayPal or a credit card). So, for each person who buys something from your website, you have a list of data that looks like (computer type, web browser, country, time, software bought, how paid). For instance, the first three pieces of data you collect could be:

- Macintosh OS X, Safari, UK, morning, SuperGame1, credit card

- Windows XP, Internet Explorer, USA, afternoon, SuperGame1, PayPal

- Windows Vista, Firefox, NZ, evening, SuperGame2, PayPal

Based on this data, you would like to be able to populate a 'Things You Might Be Interested In' box within the webpage, so that it shows software that might be relevant to each visitor, based on the data that you can access while the webpage loads, i.e., computer and OS, country, and the time of day. Your hope is that as more people visit your website and you store more data, you will be able to identify trends, such as that Macintosh users from New Zealand (NZ) love your first game, while Firefox users, who are often more knowledgeable about computers, want your automatic download application and virus/internet worm detector, etc.

Once you have collected a large set of such data, you start to examine it and work out what you can do with it. The problem you have is one of prediction: given the data you have, predict what the next person will buy, and the reason that you think that it might work is that people who seem to be similar often act similarly. So how can you actually go about solving the problem? This is one of the fundamental problems that this book tries to solve. It is an example of what is called supervised learning, because we know what the right answers are for some examples (the software that was actually bought) so we can give the learner some examples where we know the right answer. We will talk about supervised learning more in Section 1.3.

1.1 IF DATA HAD MASS, THE EARTH WOULD BE A BLACK HOLE

Around the world, computers capture and store terabytes of data every day. Even leaving aside your collection of MP3s and holiday photographs, there are computers belonging to shops, banks, hospitals, scientific laboratories, and many more that are storing data incessantly. For example, banks are building up pictures of how people spend their money, hospitals are recording what treatments patients are on for which ailments (and how they respond to them), and engine monitoring systems in cars are recording information about the engine in order to detect when it might fail. The challenge is to do something useful with this data: if the bank's computers can learn about spending patterns, can they detect credit card fraud quickly? If hospitals share data, then can treatments that don't work as well as expected be identified quickly? Can an intelligent car give you early warning of problems so that you don't end up stranded in the worst part of town? These are some of the questions that machine learning methods can be used to answer.

Science has also taken advantage of the ability of computers to store massive amounts of data. Biology has led the way, with the ability to measure gene expression in DNA microarrays producing immense datasets, along with protein transcription data and phylogenetic trees relating species to each other. However, other sciences have not been slow to follow. Astronomy now uses digital telescopes, so that each night the world's observatories are storing incredibly high-resolution images of the night sky; around a terabyte per night. Equally, medical science stores the outcomes of medical tests from measurements as diverse as magnetic resonance imaging (MRI) scans and simple blood tests. The explosion in stored data is well known; the challenge is to do something useful with that data. The Large Hadron Collider at CERN apparently produces about 25 petabytes of data per year.

The size and complexity of these datasets mean that humans are unable to extract useful information from them. Even the way that the data is stored works against us. Given a file full of numbers, our minds generally turn away from looking at them for long. Take some of the same data and plot it in a graph and we can do something. Compare the table and graph shown in Figure 1.1: the graph is rather easier to look at and deal with. Unfortunately, our three-dimensional world doesn't let us do much with data in higher dimensions, and even the simple webpage data that we collected above has four different features, so if we plotted it with one dimension for each feature we'd need four dimensions! There are two things that we can do with this: reduce the number of dimensions (until our simple brains can deal with the problem) or use computers, which don't know that high-dimensional problems are difficult, and don't get bored with looking at massive data files of numbers. The two pictures in Figure 1.2 demonstrate one problem with reducing the number of dimensions (more technically, **projecting it into fewer dimensions**), which is that it can hide useful information and make things look rather strange. This is one reason why **machine learning** is becoming so popular — the problems of our human limitations go away if we can make computers do the dirty work for us. There is one other thing that can help if the number of dimensions is not too much larger than three, which is to use **glyphs** that use other representations, such as size or colour of the datapoints to represent information about some other dimension, but this does not help if the dataset has 100 dimensions in it.

In fact, you have probably interacted with machine learning algorithms at some time. They are used in many of the software programs that we use, such as Microsoft's infamous paperclip in Office (maybe not the most positive example), spam filters, voice recognition software, and lots of computer games. They are also part of automatic number-plate recognition systems for petrol station security cameras and toll roads, are used in some anti-skid braking and vehicle stability systems, and they are even part of the set of algorithms that decide whether a bank will give you a loan.

The attention-grabbing title to this section would only be true if data was very heavy. It is very hard to work out how much data there actually is in all of the world's computers, but it was estimated in 2012 that was about 2.8 zettabytes (2.8×10^{21} bytes), up from about 160 **exabytes** (160×10^{18} bytes) of data that were created and stored in 2006, and projected to reach 40 zettabytes by 2020. However, to make a black hole the size of the earth would

x_1	x_2	Class
0.1	1	1
0.15	0.2	2
0.48	0.6	3
0.1	0.6	1
0.2	0.15	2
0.5	0.55	3
0.2	1	1
0.3	0.25	2
0.52	0.6	3
0.3	0.6	1
0.4	0.2	2
0.52	0.5	3

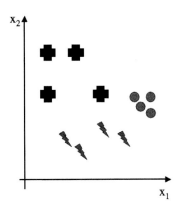

FIGURE 1.1 A set of datapoints as numerical values and as points plotted on a graph. It is easier for us to visualise data than to see it in a table, but if the data has more than three dimensions, we can't view it all at once.

FIGURE 1.2 Two views of the same two wind turbines (Te Apiti wind farm, Ashhurst, New Zealand) taken at an angle of about $30°$ to each other. The two-dimensional projections of three-dimensional objects hides information.

take a mass of about 40×10^{35} grams. So data would have to be so heavy that you couldn't possibly lift a data pen, let alone a computer before the section title were true! However, and more interestingly for machine learning, the same report that estimated the figure of 2.8 zettabytes ('*Big Data, Bigger Digital Shadows, and Biggest Growth in the Far East*' by John Gantz and David Reinsel and sponsored by EMC Corporation) also reported that while a quarter of this data could produce useful information, only around 3% of it was tagged, and less that 0.5% of it was actually used for analysis!

1.2 LEARNING

Before we delve too much further into the topic, let's step back and think about what learning actually is. The key concept that we will need to think about for our machines is **learning from data**, since data is what we have; terabytes of it, in some cases. However, it isn't too large a step to put that into human behavioural terms, and talk about **learning from experience**. Hopefully, we all agree that humans and other animals can display behaviours that we label as intelligent by learning from experience. Learning is what gives us flexibility in our life; the fact that we can adjust and adapt to new circumstances, and learn new tricks, no matter how old a dog we are! The important parts of animal learning for this book are **remembering**, **adapting**, and **generalising**: recognising that last time we were in this situation (saw this data) we tried out some particular action (gave this output) and it worked (was correct), so we'll try it again, or it didn't work, so we'll try something different. The last word, generalising, is about recognising similarity between different situations, so that things that applied in one place can be used in another. This is what makes learning useful, because we can use our knowledge in lots of different places.

Of course, there are plenty of other bits to intelligence, such as **reasoning**, and logical **deduction**, but we won't worry too much about those. We are interested in the most fundamental parts of intelligence—learning and adapting—and how we can model them in a computer. There has also been a lot of interest in making computers reason and deduce facts. This was the basis of most early **Artificial Intelligence**, and is sometimes known as **symbolic processing** because the computer manipulates symbols that reflect the environment. In contrast, machine learning methods are sometimes called **subsymbolic** because no symbols or symbolic manipulation are involved.

1.2.1 Machine Learning

Machine learning, then, is about making computers **modify** or **adapt** their actions (whether these actions are making predictions, or controlling a robot) so that these actions get more accurate, where accuracy is measured by how well the chosen actions reflect the correct ones. Imagine that you are playing Scrabble (or some other game) against a computer. You might beat it every time in the beginning, but after lots of games it starts beating you, until finally you never win. Either you are getting worse, or the computer is learning how to win at Scrabble. Having learnt to beat you, it can go on and use the same strategies against other players, so that it doesn't start from scratch with each new player; this is a form of generalisation.

It is only over the past decade or so that the inherent multi-disciplinarity of machine learning has been recognised. It merges ideas from neuroscience and biology, statistics, mathematics, and physics, to make computers learn. There is a fantastic existence proof that learning is possible, which is the bag of water and electricity (together with a few trace chemicals) sitting between your ears. In Section 3.1 we will have a brief peek inside and see if there is anything we can borrow/steal in order to make machine learning algorithms. It turns out that there is, and **neural networks** have grown from exactly this, although even their own father wouldn't recognise them now, after the developments that have seen them reinterpreted as statistical learners. Another thing that has driven the change in direction of machine learning research is **data mining**, which looks at the extraction of useful information from massive datasets (by men with computers and pocket protectors rather than pickaxes and hard hats), and which requires efficient algorithms, putting more of the emphasis back onto computer science.

The **computational complexity** of the machine learning methods will also be of interest to us since what we are producing is **algorithms**. It is particularly important because we might want to use some of the methods on very large datasets, so algorithms that have high-degree polynomial complexity in the size of the dataset (or worse) will be a problem. The complexity is often broken into two parts: the complexity of training, and the complexity of applying the trained algorithm. Training does not happen very often, and is not usually time critical, so it can take longer. However, we often want a decision about a test point quickly, and there are potentially lots of test points when an algorithm is in use, so this needs to have low computational cost.

1.3 TYPES OF MACHINE LEARNING

In the example that started the chapter, your webpage, the aim was to predict what software a visitor to the website might buy based on information that you can collect. There are a couple of interesting things in there. The first is the data. It might be useful to know what software visitors have bought before, and how old they are. However, it is not possible to get that information from their web browser (even cookies can't tell you how old somebody is), so you can't use that information. Picking the variables that you want to use (which are called **features** in the jargon) is a very important part of finding good solutions to problems, and something that we will talk about in several places in the book. Equally, choosing how to process the data can be important. This can be seen in the example in the time of access. Your computer can store this down to the nearest millisecond, but that isn't very useful, since you would like to spot similar patterns between users. For this reason, in the example above I chose to **quantise** it down to one of the set `morning, afternoon, evening, night`; obviously I need to ensure that these times are correct for their time zones, too.

We are going to loosely define learning as meaning **getting better at some task through practice**. This leads to a couple of vital questions: how does the computer know whether it is getting better or not, and how does it know how to improve? There are several different possible answers to these questions, and they produce different types of machine learning. For now we will consider the question of knowing whether or not the machine is learning. We can tell the algorithm the correct answer for a problem so that it gets it right next time (which is what would happen in the webpage example, since we know what software the person bought). We hope that we only have to tell it a few right answers and then it can 'work out' how to get the correct answers for other problems (**generalise**). Alternatively, we can tell it whether or not the answer was correct, but not how to find the correct answer, so that it has to **search** for the right answer. A variant of this is that we give a score for the answer, according to how correct it is, rather than just a 'right or wrong' response. Finally, we might not have any correct answers; we just want the algorithm to find inputs that have something in common.

These different answers to the question provide a useful way to classify the different algorithms that we will be talking about:

Supervised learning A training set of examples with the correct responses (targets) is provided and, based on this training set, the algorithm generalises to respond correctly to all possible inputs. This is also called learning from exemplars.

Unsupervised learning Correct responses are not provided, but instead the algorithm tries to identify similarities between the inputs so that inputs that have something in common are categorised together. The statistical approach to unsupervised learning is known as density estimation.

Reinforcement learning This is somewhere between supervised and unsupervised learning. The algorithm gets told when the answer is wrong, but does not get told how to correct it. It has to explore and try out different possibilities until it works out how to get the answer right. Reinforcement learning is sometime called learning with a critic because of this monitor that scores the answer, but does not suggest improvements.

Evolutionary learning Biological evolution can be seen as a learning process: biological organisms adapt to improve their survival rates and chance of having offspring in their environment. We'll look at how we can model this in a computer, using an idea of fitness, which corresponds to a score for how good the current solution is.

The most common type of learning is supervised learning, and it is going to be the focus of the next few chapters. So, before we get started, we'll have a look at what it is, and the kinds of problems that can be solved using it.

1.4 SUPERVISED LEARNING

As has already been suggested, the webpage example is a typical problem for supervised learning. There is a set of data (the training data) that consists of a set of input data that has target data, which is the answer that the algorithm should produce, attached. This is usually written as a set of data $(\mathbf{x}_i, \mathbf{t}_i)$, where the inputs are $\mathbf{x}_i$, the targets are $\mathbf{t}_i$, and the i index suggests that we have lots of pieces of data, indexed by i running from 1 to some upper limit N. Note that the inputs and targets are written in boldface font to signify vectors, since each piece of data has values for several different features; the notation used in the book is described in more detail in Section 2.1. If we had examples of every possible piece of input data, then we could put them together into a big look-up table, and there would be no need for machine learning at all. The thing that makes machine learning better than that is generalisation: the algorithm should produce sensible outputs for inputs that weren't encountered during learning. This also has the result that the algorithm can deal with noise, which is small inaccuracies in the data that are inherent in measuring any real world process. It is hard to specify rigorously what generalisation means, but let's see if an example helps.

1.4.1 Regression

Suppose that I gave you the following datapoints and asked you to tell me the value of the output (which we will call y since it is not a target datapoint) when $x = 0.44$ (here, x, t, and y are not written in boldface font since they are scalars, as opposed to vectors).

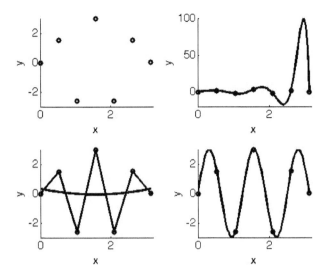

FIGURE 1.3 *Top left:* A few datapoints from a sample problem. *Bottom left:* Two possible ways to predict the values between the known datapoints: connecting the points with straight lines, or using a cubic approximation (which in this case misses all of the points). *Top and bottom right:* Two more complex approximators (see the text for details) that pass through the points, although the lower one is rather better than the top.

x	t
0	0
0.5236	1.5
1.0472	-2.5981
1.5708	3.0
2.0944	-2.5981
2.6180	1.5
3.1416	0

Since the value $x = 0.44$ isn't in the examples given, you need to find some way to **predict** what value it has. You assume that the values come from some sort of function, and try to find out what the function is. Then you'll be able to give the output value y for any given value of x. This is known as a **regression** problem in statistics: fit a mathematical function describing a curve, so that the curve passes as close as possible to all of the datapoints. It is generally a problem of **function approximation** or **interpolation**, working out the value between values that we know.

The problem is how to work out what function to choose. Have a look at Figure 1.3. The top-left plot shows a plot of the 7 values of x and y in the table, while the other plots show different attempts to fit a curve through the datapoints. The bottom-left plot shows two possible answers found by using straight lines to connect up the points, and also what happens if we try to use a cubic function (something that can be written as $ax^3 + bx^2 + cx + d = 0$). The top-right plot shows what happens when we try to match the function using a different polynomial, this time of the form $ax^{10} + bx^9 + \ldots + jx + k = 0$, and finally the bottom-right plot shows the function $y = 3\sin(5x)$. Which of these functions would you choose?

The straight-line approximation probably isn't what we want, since it doesn't tell us much about the data. However, the cubic plot on the same set of axes is terrible: it doesn't get anywhere near the datapoints. What about the plot on the top-right? It looks like it goes through all of the datapoints exactly, but it is very wiggly (look at the value on the y-axis, which goes up to 100 instead of around three, as in the other figures). In fact, the data were made with the sine function plotted on the bottom-right, so that is the correct answer in this case, but the algorithm doesn't know that, and to it the two solutions on the right both look equally good. The only way we can tell which solution is better is to test how well they generalise. We pick a value that is between our datapoints, use our curves to predict its value, and see which is better. This will tell us that the bottom-right curve is better in the example.

So one thing that our machine learning algorithms can do is interpolate between datapoints. This might not seem to be intelligent behaviour, or even very difficult in two dimensions, but it is rather harder in higher dimensional spaces. The same thing is true of the other thing that our algorithms will do, which is classification—grouping examples into different classes—which is discussed next. However, the algorithms are learning by our definition if they adapt so that their performance improves, and it is surprising how often real problems that we want to solve can be reduced to classification or regression problems.

1.4.2 Classification

The classification problem consists of taking input vectors and deciding which of N classes they belong to, based on training from **exemplars** of each class. The most important point about the classification problem is that it is discrete — each example belongs to precisely one class, and the set of classes covers the whole possible output space. These two constraints are not necessarily realistic; sometimes examples might belong partially to two different classes. There are **fuzzy** classifiers that try to solve this problem, but we won't be talking about them in this book. In addition, there are many places where we might not be able to categorise every possible input. For example, consider a vending machine, where we use a neural network to learn to recognise all the different coins. We train the classifier to recognise all New Zealand coins, but what if a British coin is put into the machine? In that case, the classifier will identify it as the New Zealand coin that is closest to it in appearance, but this is not really what is wanted: rather, the classifier should identify that it is not one of the coins it was trained on. This is called **novelty detection**. For now we'll assume that we will not receive inputs that we cannot classify accurately.

Let's consider how to set up a coin classifier. When the coin is pushed into the slot, the machine takes a few measurements of it. These could include the diameter, the weight, and possibly the shape, and are the **features** that will generate our input vector. In this case, our input vector will have three elements, each of which will be a number showing the measurement of that feature (choosing a number to represent the shape would involve an **encoding**, for example that 1=circle, 2=hexagon, etc.). Of course, there are many other features that we could measure. If our vending machine included an atomic absorption spectroscope, then we could estimate the density of the material and its composition, or if it had a camera, we could take a photograph of the coin and feed that image into the classifier. The question of which features to choose is not always an easy one. We don't want to use too many inputs, because that will make the training of the classifier take longer (and also, as the number of input dimensions grows, the number of datapoints required increases

FIGURE 1.4 The New Zealand coins.

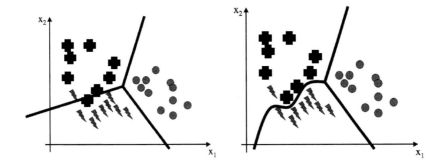

FIGURE 1.5 *Left:* A set of straight line decision boundaries for a classification problem. *Right:* An alternative set of decision boundaries that separate the plusses from the lightening strikes better, but requires a line that isn't straight.

faster; this is known as the curse of dimensionality and will be discussed in Section 2.1.2), but we need to make sure that we can reliably separate the classes based on those features. For example, if we tried to separate coins based only on colour, we wouldn't get very far, because the 20 ¢ and 50 ¢ coins are both silver and the \$1 and \$2 coins both bronze. However, if we use colour and diameter, we can do a pretty good job of the coin classification problem for NZ coins. There are some features that are entirely useless. For example, knowing that the coin is circular doesn't tell us anything about NZ coins, which are all circular (see Figure 1.4). In other countries, though, it could be very useful.

The methods of performing classification that we will see during this book are very different in the ways that they learn about the solution; in essence they aim to do the same thing: find decision boundaries that can be used to separate out the different classes. Given the features that are used as inputs to the classifier, we need to identify some values of those features that will enable us to decide which class the current input is in. Figure 1.5 shows a set of 2D inputs with three different classes shown, and two different decision boundaries; on the left they are straight lines, and are therefore simple, but don't categorise as well as the non-linear curve on the right.

Now that we have seen these two types of problem, let's take a look at the whole process of machine learning from the practitioner's viewpoint.

1.5   THE MACHINE LEARNING PROCESS

This section assumes that you have some problem that you are interested in using machine learning on, such as the coin classification that was described previously. It briefly examines the process by which machine learning algorithms can be selected, applied, and evaluated for the problem.

Data Collection and Preparation   Throughout this book we will be in the fortunate position of having datasets readily available for downloading and using to test the algorithms. This is, of course, less commonly the case when the desire is to learn about some new problem, when either the data has to be collected from scratch, or at the very least, assembled and prepared. In fact, if the problem is completely new, so that appropriate data can be chosen, then this process should be merged with the next step of feature selection, so that only the required data is collected. This can typically be done by assembling a reasonably small dataset with all of the features that you believe might be useful, and experimenting with it before choosing the best features and collecting and analysing the full dataset.

Often the difficulty is that there is a large amount of data that *might* be relevant, but it is hard to collect, either because it requires many measurements to be taken, or because they are in a variety of places and formats, and merging it appropriately is difficult, as is ensuring that it is clean; that is, it does not have significant errors, missing data, etc.

For supervised learning, target data is also needed, which can require the involvement of experts in the relevant field and significant investments of time.

Finally, the quantity of data needs to be considered. Machine learning algorithms need significant amounts of data, preferably without too much noise, but with increased dataset size comes increased computational costs, and the sweet spot at which there is enough data without excessive computational overhead is generally impossible to predict.

Feature Selection   An example of this part of the process was given in Section 1.4.2 when we looked at possible features that might be useful for coin recognition. It consists of identifying the features that are most useful for the problem under examination. This invariably requires prior knowledge of the problem and the data; our common sense was used in the coins example above to identify some potentially useful features and to exclude others.

As well as the identification of features that are useful for the learner, it is also necessary that the features can be collected without significant expense or time, and that they are robust to noise and other corruption of the data that may arise in the collection process.

Algorithm Choice   Given the dataset, the choice of an appropriate algorithm (or algorithms) is what this book should be able to prepare you for, in that the knowledge of the underlying principles of each algorithm and examples of their use is precisely what is required for this.

Parameter and Model Selection   For many of the algorithms there are parameters that have to be set manually, or that require experimentation to identify appropriate values. These requirements are discussed at the appropriate points of the book.

Training Given the dataset, algorithm, and parameters, training should be simply the use of computational resources in order to build a model of the data in order to predict the outputs on new data.

Evaluation Before a system can be deployed it needs to be tested and evaluated for accuracy on data that it was not trained on. This can often include a comparison with human experts in the field, and the selection of appropriate metrics for this comparison.

1.6   A NOTE ON PROGRAMMING

This book is aimed at helping you understand and use machine learning algorithms, and that means writing computer programs. The book contains algorithms in both pseudocode, and as fragments of Python programs based on NumPy (Appendix A provides an introduction to both Python and NumPy for the beginner), and the website provides complete working code for all of the algorithms.

Understanding how to use machine learning algorithms is fine in theory, but without testing the programs on data, and seeing what the parameters do, you won't get the complete picture. In general, writing the code for yourself is always the best way to check that you understand what the algorithm is doing, and finding the unexpected details.

Unfortunately, debugging machine learning code is even harder than general debugging – it is quite easy to make a program that compiles and runs, but just doesn't seem to actually learn. In that case, you need to start testing the program carefully. However, you can quickly get frustrated with the fact that, because so many of the algorithms are stochastic, the results are not repeatable anyway. This can be temporarily avoided by setting the random number seed, which has the effect of making the random number generator follow the same pattern each time, as can be seen in the following example of running code at the Python command line (marked as >>>), where the 10 numbers that appear after the seed is set are the same in both cases, and would carry on the same forever (there is more about the pseudo-random numbers that computers generate in Section 15.1.1):

```
>>> import numpy as np
>>> np.random.seed(4)
>>> np.random.rand(10)
array([ 0.96702984,  0.54723225,  0.97268436,  0.71481599,  0.69772882,
        0.2160895 ,  0.97627445,  0.00623026,  0.25298236,  0.43479153])
>>> np.random.rand(10)
array([ 0.77938292,  0.19768507,  0.86299324,  0.98340068,  0.16384224,
        0.59733394,  0.0089861 ,  0.38657128,  0.04416006,  0.95665297])
>>> np.random.seed(4)
>>> np.random.rand(10)
array([ 0.96702984,  0.54723225,  0.97268436,  0.71481599,  0.69772882,
        0.2160895 ,  0.97627445,  0.00623026,  0.25298236,  0.43479153])
```

This way, on each run the randomness will be avoided, and the parameters will all be the same.

Another thing that is useful is the use of 2D toy datasets, where you can plot things, since you can see whether or not something unexpected is going on. In addition, these datasets can be made very simple, such as separable by a straight line (we'll see more of this in Chapter 3) so that you can see whether it deals with simple cases, at least.

Another way to 'cheat' temporarily is to include the target as one of the inputs, so that the algorithm really has no excuse for getting the wrong answer.

Finally, having a reference program that works and that you can compare is also useful, and I hope that the code on the book website will help people get out of unexpected traps and strange errors.

1.7   A ROADMAP TO THE BOOK

As far as possible, this book works from general to specific and simple to complex, while keeping related concepts in nearby chapters. Given the focus on algorithms and encouraging the use of experimentation rather than starting from the underlying statistical concepts, the book starts with some older, and reasonably simple algorithms, which are examples of supervised learning.

Chapter 2 follows up many of the concepts in this introductory chapter in order to highlight some of the overarching ideas of machine learning and thus the data requirements of it, as well as providing some material on basic probability and statistics that will not be required by all readers, but is included for completeness.

Chapters 3, 4, and 5 follow the main historical sweep of supervised learning using neural networks, as well as introducing concepts such as interpolation. They are followed by chapters on dimensionality reduction (Chapter 6) and the use of probabilistic methods like the EM algorithm and nearest neighbour methods (Chapter 7). The idea of optimal decision boundaries and kernel methods are introduced in Chapter 8, which focuses on the Support Vector Machine and related algorithms.

One of the underlying methods for many of the preceding algorithms, optimisation, is surveyed briefly in Chapter 9, which then returns to some of the material in Chapter 4 to consider the Multi-layer Perceptron purely from the point of view of optimisation. The chapter then continues by considering search as the discrete analogue of optimisation. This leads naturally into evolutionary learning including genetic algorithms (Chapter 10), reinforcement learning (Chapter 11), and tree-based learners (Chapter 12) which are search-based methods. Methods to combine the predictions of many learners, which are often trees, are described in Chapter 13.

The important topic of unsupervised learning is considered in Chapter 14, which focuses on the Self-Organising Feature Map; many unsupervised learning algorithms are also presented in Chapter 6.

The remaining four chapters primarily describe more modern, and statistically based, approaches to machine learning, although not all of the algorithms are completely new: following an introduction to Markov Chain Monte Carlo techniques in Chapter 15 the area of Graphical Models is surveyed, with comparatively old algorithms such as the Hidden Markov Model and Kalman Filter being included along with particle filters and Bayesian networks. The ideas behind Deep Belief Networks are given in Chapter 17, starting from the historical idea of symmetric networks with the Hopfield network. An introduction to Gaussian Processes is given in Chapter 18.

Finally, an introduction to Python and NumPy is given in Appendix A, which should be sufficient to enable readers to follow the code descriptions provided in the book and use the code supplied on the book website, assuming that they have some programming experience in any programming language.

I would suggest that Chapters 2 to 4 contain enough introductory material to be essential for anybody looking for an introduction to machine learning ideas. For an introductory one semester course I would follow them with Chapters 6 to 8, and then use the second half of Chapter 9 to introduce Chapters 10 and 11, and then Chapter 14.

A more advanced course would certainly take in Chapters 13 and 15 to 18 along with the optimisation material in Chapter 9.

I have attempted to make the material reasonably self-contained, with the relevant mathematical ideas either included in the text at the appropriate point, or with a reference to where that material is covered. This means that the reader with some prior knowledge will certainly find some parts can be safely ignored or skimmed without loss.

FURTHER READING

For a different (more statistical and example-based) take on machine learning, look at:

- Chapter 1 of T. Hastie, R. Tibshirani, and J. Friedman. *The Elements of Statistical Learning*, 2nd edition, Springer, Berlin, Germany, 2008.

Other texts that provide alternative views of similar material include:

- Chapter 1 of R.O. Duda, P.E. Hart, and D.G. Stork. *Pattern Classification*, 2nd edition, Wiley-Interscience, New York, USA, 2001.

- Chapter 1 of S. Haykin. *Neural Networks: A Comprehensive Foundation*, 2nd edition, Prentice-Hall, New Jersey, USA, 1999.

## CHAPTER 2

Preliminaries

This chapter has two purposes: to present some of the overarching important concepts of machine learning, and to see how some of the basic ideas of data processing and statistics arise in machine learning. One of the most useful ways to break down the effects of learning, which is to put it in terms of the statistical concepts of bias and variance, is given in Section 2.5, following on from a section where those concepts are introduced for the beginner.

2.1 SOME TERMINOLOGY

We start by considering some of the terminology that we will use throughout the book; we've already seen a bit of it in the Introduction. We will talk about **inputs** and **input vectors** for our learning algorithms. Likewise, we will talk about the **outputs** of the algorithm. The inputs are the data that is fed into the algorithm. In general, machine learning algorithms all work by taking a set of input values, producing an output (answer) for that input vector, and then moving on to the next input. The input vector will typically be several real numbers, which is why it is described as a **vector**: it is written down as a series of numbers, e.g., $(0.2, 0.45, 0.75, -0.3)$. The size of this vector, i.e., the number of elements in the vector, is called the **dimensionality** of the input. This is because if we were to plot the vector as a point, we would need one dimension of space for each of the different elements of the vector, so that the example above has 4 dimensions. We will talk about this more in Section 2.1.1.

We will often write equations in vector and matrix notation, with lowercase boldface letters being used for vectors and uppercase boldface letters for matrices. A vector $\mathbf{x}$ has elements $(x_1, x_2, \ldots, x_m)$. We will use the following notation in the book:

Inputs An input vector is the data given as one input to the algorithm. Written as $\mathbf{x}$, with elements x_i, where i runs from 1 to the number of input dimensions, m.

Weights w_{ij}, are the **weighted connections** between nodes i and j. For neural networks these weights are analogous to the synapses in the brain. They are arranged into a matrix $\mathbf{W}$.

Outputs The output vector is $\mathbf{y}$, with elements y_j, where j runs from 1 to the number of output dimensions, n. We can write $\mathbf{y}(\mathbf{x}, \mathbf{W})$ to remind ourselves that the output depends on the inputs to the algorithm and the current set of weights of the network.

Targets The target vector $\mathbf{t}$, with elements t_j, where j runs from 1 to the number of output dimensions, n, are the extra data that we need for supervised learning, since they provide the 'correct' answers that the algorithm is learning about.

Activation Function For neural networks, $g(\cdot)$ is a mathematical function that describes the firing of the neuron as a response to the weighted inputs, such as the threshold function described in Section 3.1.2.

Error E, a function that computes the inaccuracies of the network as a function of the outputs **y** and targets **t**.

2.1.1 Weight Space

When working with data it is often useful to be able to plot it and look at it. If our data has only two or three input dimensions, then this is pretty easy: we use the x-axis for feature 1, the y-axis for feature 2, and the z-axis for feature 3. We then plot the positions of the input vectors on these axes. The same thing can be extended to as many dimensions as we like provided that we don't actually want to look at it in our 3D world. Even if we have 200 input dimensions (that is, 200 elements in each of our input vectors) then we can try to imagine it plotted by using 200 axes that are all mutually orthogonal (that is, at right angles to each other). One of the great things about computers is that they aren't constrained in the same way we are—ask a computer to hold a 200-dimensional array and it does it. Provided that you get the algorithm right (always the difficult bit!), then the computer doesn't know that 200 dimensions is harder than 2 for us humans.

We can look at projections of the data into our 3D world by plotting just three of the features against each other, but this is usually rather confusing: things can look very close together in your chosen three axes, but can be a very long way apart in the full set. You've experienced this in your 2D view of the 3D world; Figure 1.2 shows two different views of some wind turbines. The two turbines appear to be very close together from one angle, but are obviously separate from another.

As well as plotting datapoints, we can also plot anything else that we feel like. In particular, we can plot some of the parameters of a machine learning algorithm. This is particularly useful for neural networks (which we will start to see in the next chapter) since the parameters of a neural network are the values of a set of weights that connect the neurons to the inputs. There is a schematic of a neural network on the left of Figure 2.1, showing the inputs on the left, and the neurons on the right. If we treat the weights that get fed into one of the neurons as a set of coordinates in what is known as weight space, then we can plot them. We think about the weights that connect into a particular neuron, and plot the strengths of the weights by using one axis for each weight that comes into the neuron, and plotting the position of the neuron as the location, using the value of w_1 as the position on the 1st axis, the value of w_2 on the 2nd axis, etc. This is shown on the right of Figure 2.1.

Now that we have a space in which we can talk about how close together neurons and inputs are, since we can imagine positioning neurons and inputs in the same space by plotting the position of each neuron as the location where its weights say it should be. The two spaces will have the same dimension (providing that we don't use a bias node (see Section 3.3.2), otherwise the weight space will have one extra dimension) so we can plot the position of neurons in the input space. This gives us a different way of learning, since by changing the weights we are changing the location of the neurons in this weight space. We can measure distances between inputs and neurons by computing the Euclidean distance, which in two dimensions can be written as:

$$d = \sqrt{(x_1 - x_2)^2 + (y_1 - y_2)^2}. \tag{2.1}$$

So we can use the idea of neurons and inputs being 'close together' in order to decide

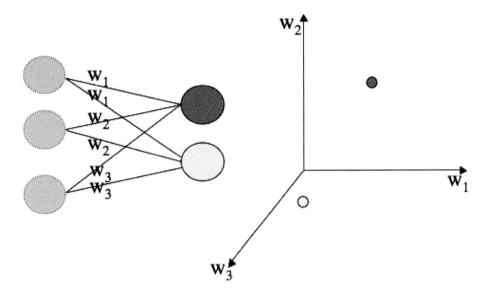

FIGURE 2.1 The position of two neurons in weight space. The labels on the network refer to the dimension in which that weight is plotted, not its value.

when a neuron should fire and when it shouldn't. If the neuron is close to the input in this sense then it should fire, and if it is not close then it shouldn't. This picture of weight space can be helpful for understanding another important concept in machine learning, which is what effect the number of input dimensions can have. The input vector is telling us everything we know about that example, and usually we don't know enough about the data to know what is useful and what is not (think back to the coin classification example in Section 1.4.2), so it might seem sensible to include all of the information that we can get, and let the algorithm sort out for itself what it needs. Unfortunately, we are about to see that doing this comes at a significant cost.

2.1.2 The Curse of Dimensionality

The curse of dimensionality is a very strong name, so you can probably guess that it is a bit of a problem. The essence of the curse is the realisation that as the number of dimensions increases, the volume of the unit hypersphere does not increase with it. The unit hypersphere is the region we get if we start at the origin (the centre of our coordinate system) and draw all the points that are distance 1 away from the origin. In 2 dimensions we get a circle of radius 1 around $(0, 0)$ (drawn in Figure 2.2), and in 3D we get a sphere around $(0, 0, 0)$ (Figure 2.3). In higher dimensions, the sphere becomes a hypersphere. The following table shows the size of the unit hypersphere for the first few dimensions, and the graph in Figure 2.4 shows the same thing, but also shows clearly that as the number of dimensions tends to infinity, so the volume of the hypersphere tends to zero.

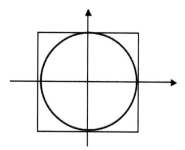

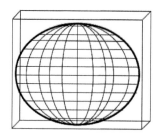

FIGURE 2.2 The unit circle in 2D with its bounding box.

FIGURE 2.3 The unit sphere in 3D with its bounding cube. The sphere does not reach as far into the corners as the circle does, and this gets more noticeable as the number of dimensions increases.

Dimension	Volume
1	2.0000
2	3.1416
3	4.1888
4	4.9348
5	5.2636
6	5.1677
7	4.7248
8	4.0587
9	3.2985
10	2.5502

At first sight this seems completely counterintuitive. However, think about enclosing the hypersphere in a box of width 2 (between -1 and 1 along each axis), so that the box just touches the sides of the hypersphere. For the circle, almost all of the area inside the box is included in the circle, except for a little bit at each corner (see Figure 2.2) The same is true in 3D (Figure 2.3), but if we think about the 100-dimensional hypersphere (not necessarily something you want to imagine), and follow the diagonal line from the origin out to one of the corners of the box, then we intersect the boundary of the hypersphere when all the coordinates are 0.1. The remaining 90% of the line inside the box is outside the hypersphere, and so the volume of the hypersphere is obviously shrinking as the number of dimensions grows. The graph in Figure 2.4 shows that when the number of dimensions is above about 20, the volume is effectively zero. It was computed using the formula for the volume of the hypersphere of dimension n as $v_n = (2\pi/n)v_{n-2}$. So as soon as $n > 2\pi$, the volume starts to shrink.

The curse of dimensionality will apply to our machine learning algorithms because as the number of input dimensions gets larger, we will need more data to enable the algorithm to generalise sufficiently well. Our algorithms try to separate data into classes based on the features; therefore as the number of features increases, so will the number of datapoints we need. For this reason, we will often have to be careful about what information we give to the algorithm, meaning that we need to understand something about the data in advance.

Regardless of how many input dimensions there are, the point of machine learning is to

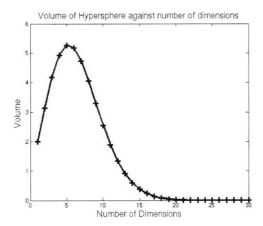

FIGURE 2.4 The volume of the unit hypersphere for different numbers of dimensions.

make predictions on data inputs. In the next section we consider how to evaluate how well an algorithm actually achieves this.

2.2 KNOWING WHAT YOU KNOW: TESTING MACHINE LEARNING ALGO-RITHMS

The purpose of learning is to get better at predicting the outputs, be they class labels or continuous regression values. The only real way to know how successfully the algorithm has learnt is to compare the predictions with known target labels, which is how the training is done for supervised learning. This suggests that one thing you can do is just to look at the error that the algorithm makes on the training set.

However, we want the algorithms to generalise to examples that were not seen in the training set, and we obviously can't test this by using the training set. So we need some different data, a **test set**, to test it on as well. We use this test set of (input, target) pairs by feeding them into the network and comparing the predicted output with the target, but we don't modify the weights or other parameters for them: we use them to decide how well the algorithm has learnt. The only problem with this is that it reduces the amount of data that we have available for training, but that is something that we will just have to live with.

2.2.1 Overfitting

Unfortunately, things are a little bit more complicated than that, since we might also want to know how well the algorithm is generalising as it learns: we need to make sure that we do enough training that the algorithm generalises well. In fact, there is at least as much danger in over-training as there is in under-training. The number of degrees of variability in most machine learning algorithms is huge — for a neural network there are lots of weights, and each of them can vary. This is undoubtedly more variation than there is in the function we are learning, so we need to be careful: if we train for too long, then we will overfit the data, which means that we have learnt about the noise and inaccuracies in the data as well as the actual function. Therefore, the model that we learn will be much too complicated, and won't be able to generalise.

Figure 2.5 shows this by plotting the predictions of some algorithm (as the curve) at

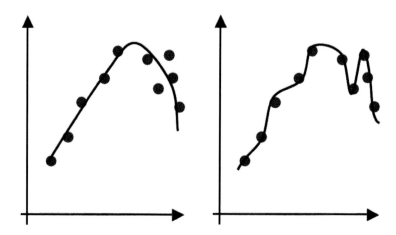

FIGURE 2.5 The effect of overfitting is that rather than finding the generating function (as shown on the left), the neural network matches the inputs perfectly, including the noise in them (on the right). This reduces the generalisation capabilities of the network.

two different points in the learning process. On the left of the figure the curve fits the overall trend of the data well (it has generalised to the underlying general function), but the training error would still not be that close to zero since it passes near, but not through, the training data. As the network continues to learn, it will eventually produce a much more complex model that has a lower training error (close to zero), meaning that it has memorised the training examples, including any noise component of them, so that is has overfitted the training data.

We want to stop the learning process before the algorithm overfits, which means that we need to know how well it is generalising at each timestep. We can't use the training data for this, because we wouldn't detect overfitting, but we can't use the testing data either, because we're saving that for the final tests. So we need a third set of data to use for this purpose, which is called the **validation set** because we're using it to validate the learning so far. This is known as **cross-validation** in statistics. It is part of **model selection**: choosing the right parameters for the model so that it generalises as well as possible.

2.2.2 Training, Testing, and Validation Sets

We now need three sets of data: the **training set** to actually train the algorithm, the **validation set** to keep track of how well it is doing as it learns, and the **test set** to produce the final results. This is becoming expensive in data, especially since for supervised learning it all has to have target values attached (and even for unsupervised learning, the validation and test sets need targets so that you have something to compare to), and it is not always easy to get accurate labels (which may well be why you want to learn about the data). The area of **semi-supervised learning** attempts to deal with this need for large amounts of labelled data; see the Further Reading section for some references.

Clearly, each algorithm is going to need some reasonable amount of data to learn from (precise needs vary, but the more data the algorithm sees, the more likely it is to have seen examples of each possible type of input, although more data also increases the computational time to learn). However, the same argument can be used to argue that the validation and

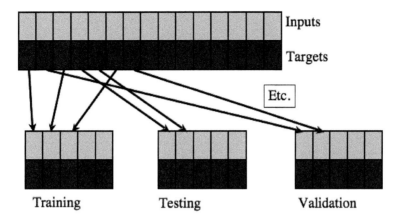

FIGURE 2.6 The dataset is split into different sets, some for training, some for validation, and some for testing.

test sets should also be reasonably large. Generally, the exact proportion of training to testing to validation data is up to you, but it is typical to do something like 50:25:25 if you have plenty of data, and 60:20:20 if you don't. How you do the splitting can also matter. Many datasets are presented with the first set of datapoints being in class 1, the next in class 2, and so on. If you pick the first few points to be the training set, the next the test set, etc., then the results are going to be pretty bad, since the training did not see all the classes. This can be dealt with by randomly reordering the data first, or by assigning each datapoint randomly to one of the sets, as is shown in Figure 2.6.

If you are really short of training data, so that if you have a separate validation set there is a worry that the algorithm won't be sufficiently trained; then it is possible to perform leave-some-out, multi-fold cross-validation. The idea is shown in Figure 2.7. The dataset is randomly partitioned into K subsets, and one subset is used as a validation set, while the algorithm is trained on all of the others. A different subset is then left out and a new model is trained on that subset, repeating the same process for all of the different subsets. Finally, the model that produced the lowest validation error is tested and used. We've traded off data for computation time, since we've had to train K different models instead of just one. In the most extreme case of this there is leave-one-out cross-validation, where the algorithm is validated on just one piece of data, training on all of the rest.

2.2.3 The Confusion Matrix

Regardless of how much data we use to test the trained algorithm, we still need to work out whether or not the result is good. We will look here at a method that is suitable for classification problems that is known as the confusion matrix. For regression problems things are more complicated because the results are continuous, and so the most common thing to use is the sum-of-squares error that we will use to drive the training in the following chapters. We will see these methods being used as we look at examples.

The confusion matrix is a nice simple idea: make a square matrix that contains all the possible classes in both the horizontal and vertical directions and list the classes along the top of a table as the predicted outputs, and then down the left-hand side as the targets. So for example, the element of the matrix at (i, j) tells us how many input patterns were put

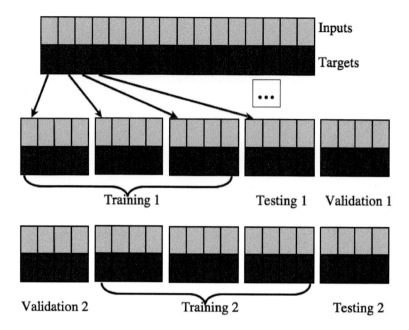

FIGURE 2.7 Leave-some-out, multi-fold cross-validation gets around the problem of data shortage by training many models. It works by splitting the data into sets, training a model on most sets and holding one out for validation (and another for testing). Different models are trained with different sets being held out.

into class i in the targets, but class j by the algorithm. Anything on the leading diagonal (the diagonal that starts at the top left of the matrix and runs down to the bottom right) is a correct answer. Suppose that we have three classes: C_1, C_2, and C_3. Now we count the number of times that the output was class C_1 when the target was C_1, then when the target was C_2, and so on until we've filled in the table:

	Outputs		
	C_1	C_2	C_3
C_1	5	1	0
C_2	1	4	1
C_3	2	0	4

This table tells us that, for the three classes, most examples were classified correctly, but two examples of class C_3 were misclassified as C_1, and so on. For a small number of classes this is a nice way to look at the outputs. If you just want one number, then it is possible to divide the sum of the elements on the leading diagonal by the sum of all of the elements in the matrix, which gives the fraction of correct responses. This is known as the **accuracy**, and we are about to see that it is not the last word in evaluating the results of a machine learning algorithm.

2.2.4 Accuracy Metrics

We can do more to analyse the results than just measuring the accuracy. If you consider the possible outputs of the classes, then they can be arranged in a simple chart like this (where a **true positive** is an observation correctly put into class 1, while a **false positive** is an observation incorrectly put into class 1, while negative examples (both true and false) are those put into class 2):

True Positives	False Positives
False Negatives	True Negatives

The entries on the leading diagonal of this chart are correct and those off the diagonal are wrong, just as with the confusion matrix. Note, however, that this chart and the concepts of false positives, etc., are based on binary classification.

Accuracy is then defined as the sum of the number of true positives and true negatives divided by the total number of examples (where # means 'number of', and TP stands for True Positive, etc.):

$$\text{Accuracy} = \frac{\#TP + \#FP}{\#TP + \#FP + \#TN + \#FN}. \tag{2.2}$$

The problem with accuracy is that it doesn't tell us everything about the results, since it turns four numbers into just one. There are two complementary pairs of measurements that can help us to interpret the performance of a classifier, namely **sensitivity** and **specificity**, and **precision** and **recall**. Their definitions are shown next, followed by some explanation.

$$\text{Sensitivity} = \frac{\#TP}{\#TP + \#FN} \tag{2.3}$$

$$\text{Specificity} = \frac{\#TN}{\#TN + \#FP} \tag{2.4}$$

$$\text{Precision} = \frac{\#TP}{\#TP + \#FP} \tag{2.5}$$

$$\text{Recall} = \frac{\#TP}{\#TP + \#FN} \tag{2.6}$$

Sensitivity (also known as the **true positive rate**) is the ratio of the number of correct positive examples to the number classified as positive, while specificity is the same ratio for negative examples. Precision is the ratio of correct positive examples to the number of actual positive examples, while recall is the ratio of the number of correct positive examples out of those that were classified as positive, which is the same as sensitivity. If you look at the chart again you can see that sensitivity and specificity sum the columns for the denominator, while precision and recall sum the first column and the first row, and so miss out some information about how well the learner does on the negative examples.

Together, either of these pairs of measures gives more information than just the accuracy. If you consider precision and recall, then you can see that they are to some extent inversely related, in that if the number of false positives increases (meaning that the algorithm is using a broader definition of that class), then the number of false negatives often decreases, and vice versa. They can be combined to give a single measure, the F_1 measure, which can be written in terms of precision and recall as:

$$F_1 = 2\frac{\text{precision} \times \text{recall}}{\text{precision} + \text{recall}} \tag{2.7}$$

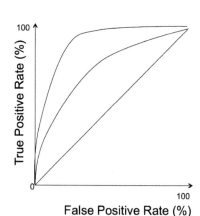

FIGURE 2.8 An example of an ROC curve. The diagonal line represents exactly chance, so anything above the line is better than chance, and the further from the line, the better. Of the two curves shown, the one that is further away from the diagonal line would represent a more accurate method.

and in terms of the numbers of false positives, etc. (from which it can be seen that it computes the mean of the false examples) as:

$$F_1 = \frac{\#TP}{\#TP + (\#FN + \#FP)/2}. \tag{2.8}$$

2.2.5   The Receiver Operator Characteristic (ROC) Curve

Since we can use these measures to evaluate a particular classifier, we can also compare classifiers – either the same classifier with different learning parameters, or completely different classifiers. In this case, the Receiver Operator Characteristic curve (almost always known just as the ROC curve) is useful. This is a plot of the percentage of true positives on the y axis against false positives on the x axis; an example is shown in Figure 2.8. A single run of a classifier produces a single point on the ROC plot, and a perfect classifier would be a point at $(0, 1)$ (100% true positives, 0% false positives), while the anti-classifier that got everything wrong would be at $(1,0)$; so the closer to the top-left-hand corner the result of a classifier is, the better the classifier has performed. Any classifier that sits on the diagonal line from $(0,0)$ to $(1,1)$ behaves exactly at the chance level (assuming that the positive and negative classes are equally common) and so presumably a lot of learning effort is wasted since a fair coin would do just as well.

In order to compare classifiers, or choices of parameters settings for the same classifier, you could just compute the point that is furthest from the 'chance' line along the diagonal. However, it is normal to compute the area under the curve (AUC) instead. If you only have one point for each classifier, the curve is the trapezoid that runs from $(0,0)$ up to the point and then from there to $(1,1)$. If there are more points (based on more runs of the classifier, such as trained and/or tested on different datasets), then they are just included in order along the diagonal line.

The key to getting a curve rather than a point on the ROC curve is to use cross-validation. If you use 10-fold cross-validation, then you have 10 classifiers, with 10 different test sets, and you also have the 'ground truth' labels. The true labels can be used to produce a ranked list of the different cross-validation-trained results, which can be used to specify a curve through the 10 datapoints on the ROC curve that correspond to the results of this classifier. By producing an ROC curve for each classifier it is possible to compare their results.

2.2.6 Unbalanced Datasets

Note that for the accuracy we have implicitly assumed that there are the same number of positive and negative examples in the dataset (which is known as a balanced dataset). However, this is often not true (this can potentially cause problems for the learners as well, as we shall see later in the book). In the case where it is not, we can compute the balanced accuracy as the sum of sensitivity and specificity divided by 2. However, a more correct measure is Matthew's Correlation Coefficient, which is computed as:

$$MCC = \frac{\#TP \times \#TN - \#FP \times \#FN}{\sqrt{(\#TP + \#FP)(\#TP + \#FN)(\#TN + \#FP)(\#TN + \#FN)}} \qquad (2.9)$$

If any of the brackets in the denominator are 0, then the whole of the denominator is set to 1. This provides a balanced accuracy computation.

As a final note on these methods of evaluation, if there are more than two classes and it is useful to distinguish the different types of error, then the calculations get a little more complicated, since instead of one set of false positives and one set of false negatives, you have some for each class. In this case, specificity and recall are not the same. However, it is possible to create a set of results, where you use one class as the positives and everything else as the negatives, and repeat this for each of the different classes.

2.2.7 Measurement Precision

There is a different way to evaluate the accuracy of a learning system, which unfortunately also uses the word precision, although with a different meaning. The concept here is to treat the machine learning algorithm as a measurement system. We feed in inputs and look at the outputs that we get. Even before comparing them to the target values, we can measure something about the algorithm: if we feed in a set of similar inputs, then we would expect to get similar outputs for them. This measure of the variability of the algorithm is also known as precision, and it tells us how repeatable the predictions that the algorithm makes are. It might be useful to think of precision as being something like the variance of a probability distribution: it tells you how much spread around the mean to expect.

The point is that just because an algorithm is precise it does not mean that it is accurate – it can be precisely wrong if it always gives the wrong prediction. One measure of how well the algorithm's predictions match reality is known as trueness, and it can be defined as the average distance between the correct output and the prediction. Trueness doesn't usually make much sense for classification problems unless there is some concept of certain classes being similar to each other. Figure 2.9 illustrates the idea of trueness and precision in the traditional way: as a darts game, with four examples with varying trueness and precision for the three darts thrown by a player.

This section has considered the endpoint of machine learning, looking at the outputs, and thinking about what we need to do with the input data in terms of having multiple datasets, etc. In the next section we return to the starting point and consider how we can start analysing a dataset by dealing with probabilities.

FIGURE 2.9 Assuming that the player was aiming for the highest-scoring triple 20 in darts (the segments each score the number they are labelled with, the narrow band on the outside of the circle scores double and the narrow band halfway in scores triple; the outer and inner 'bullseye' at the centre score 25 and 50, respectively), these four pictures show different outcomes. *Top left:* very accurate: high precision and trueness, *top right:* low precision, but good trueness, *bottom left:* high precision, but low trueness, and *bottom right:* reasonable trueness and precision, but the actual outputs are not very good. *(Thanks to Stefan Nowicki, whose dartboard was used for these pictures.)*

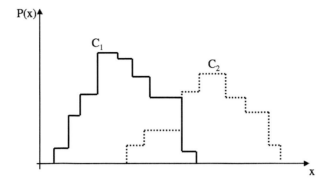

FIGURE 2.10 A histogram of feature values (x) against their probability for two classes.

2.3 TURNING DATA INTO PROBABILITIES

Take a look at the plot in Figure 2.10. It shows the measurements of some feature x for two classes, C_1 and C_2. Members of class C_2 tend to have larger values of feature x than members of class C_1, but there is some overlap between the two classes. The correct class is fairly easy to predict at the extremes of the range, but what to do in the middle is unclear. Suppose that we are trying to classify writing of the letters 'a' and 'b' based on their height (as shown in Figure 2.11). Most people write their 'a's smaller than their 'b's, but not everybody. However, in this example, we have a secret weapon. We know that in English text, the letter 'a' is much more common than the letter 'b' (we called this an unbalanced dataset earlier). If we see a letter that is either an 'a' or a 'b' in normal writing, then there is a 75% chance that it is an 'a.' We are using **prior knowledge** to estimate the **probability** that the letter is an 'a': in this example, $P(C_1) = 0.75, P(C_2) = 0.25$. If we weren't allowed to see the letter at all, and just had to classify it, then if we picked 'a' every time, we'd be right 75% of the time.

However, when we are asked to make a classification we are also given the value of x. It would be pretty silly to just use the value of $P(C_1)$ and ignore the value of x if it might help! In fact, we are given a training set of values of x and the class that each exemplar belongs to. This lets us calculate the value of $P(C_1)$ (we just count how many times out of the total the class was C_1 and divide by the total number of examples), and also another useful measurement: the **conditional probability** of C_1 given that x has value X: $P(C_1|X)$. The conditional probability tells us how likely it is that the class is C_1 given that the value of x is X. So in Figure 2.10 the value of $P(C_1|X)$ will be much larger for small values of X than for large values. Clearly, this is exactly what we want to calculate in order to perform classification. The question is how to get to this conditional probability, since we can't read it directly from the histogram.

The first thing that we need to do to get these values is to **quantise** the measurement x, which just means that we put it into one of a discrete set of values $\{X\}$, such as the bins in a histogram. This is exactly what is plotted in Figure 2.10. Now, if we have lots of examples of the two classes, and the histogram bins that their measurements fall into, we can compute $P(C_i, X_j)$, which is the **joint probability**, and tells us how often a measurement of C_i fell into histogram bin X_j. We do this by looking in histogram bin X_j, counting the number of examples of class C_i that are in it, and dividing by the total number of examples (of any class).

We can also define $P(X_j|C_i)$, which is a different conditional probability, and tells us

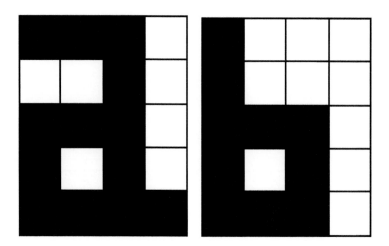

FIGURE 2.11 The letters 'a' and 'b' in pixel form.

how often (in the training set) there is a measurement of X_j given that the example is a member of class C_i. Again, we can just get this information from the histogram by counting the number of examples of class C_i in histogram bin X_j and dividing by the number of examples of that class there are (in any bin). Hopefully, this has just been revision for you from a statistics course at some stage; if not, and you don't follow it, get hold of any introductory probability book.

So we have now worked out two things from our training data: the joint probability $P(C_i, X_j)$ and the conditional probability $P(X_j|C_i)$. Since we actually want to compute $P(C_i|X_j)$ we need to know how to link these things together. As some of you may already know, the answer is **Bayes' rule**, which is what we are now going to derive. There is a link between the joint probability and the conditional probability. It is:

$$P(C_i, X_j) = P(X_j|C_i)P(C_i),\qquad(2.10)$$

or equivalently:

$$P(C_i, X_j) = P(C_i|X_j)P(X_j).\qquad(2.11)$$

Clearly, the right-hand side of these two equations must be equal to each other, since they are both equal to $P(C_i, X_j)$, and so with one division we can write:

$$P(C_i|X_j) = \frac{P(X_j|C_i)P(C_i)}{P(X_j)}.\qquad(2.12)$$

This is Bayes' rule. If you don't already know it, learn it: it is the most important equation in machine learning. It relates the **posterior** probability $P(C_i|X_j)$ with the **prior** probability $P(C_i)$ and **class-conditional** probability $P(X_j|C_i)$. The denominator (the term on the bottom of the fraction) acts to normalise everything, so that all the probabilities sum to 1. It might not be clear how to compute this term. However, if we notice that any observation X_k has to belong to some class C_i, then we can **marginalise** over the classes to compute:

$$P(X_k) = \sum_i P(X_k|C_i)P(C_i).\qquad(2.13)$$

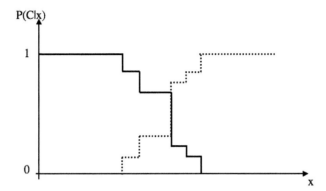

FIGURE 2.12 The posterior probabilities of the two classes C_1 and C_2 for feature x.

The reason why Bayes' rule is so important is that it lets us obtain the posterior probability—which is what we actually want—by calculating things that are much easier to compute. We can estimate the prior probabilities by looking at how often each class appears in our training set, and we can get the class-conditional probabilities from the histogram of the values of the feature for the training set. We can use the posterior probability (Figure 2.12) to assign each new observation to one of the classes by picking the class C_i where:

$$P(C_i|\mathbf{x}) > P(C_j|\mathbf{x}) \quad \forall \ i \neq j, \tag{2.14}$$

where $\mathbf{x}$ is a vector of feature values instead of just one feature. This is known as the **maximum a posteriori** or **MAP** hypothesis, and it gives us a way to choose which class to choose as the output one. The question is whether this is the right thing to do. There has been quite a lot of research in both the statistical and machine learning literatures into what is the right question to ask about our data to perform classification, but we are going to skate over it very lightly.

The MAP question is what is the most likely class given the training data? Suppose that there are three possible output classes, and for a particular input the posterior probabilities of the classes are $P(C_1|\mathbf{x}) = 0.35$, $P(C_2|\mathbf{x}) = 0.45$, $P(C_3|\mathbf{x}) = 0.2$. The MAP hypothesis therefore tells us that this input is in class C_2, because that is the class with the highest posterior probability. Now suppose that, based on the class that the data is in, we want to do something. If the class is C_1 or C_3 then we do action 1, and if the class is C_2 then we do action 2. As an example, suppose that the inputs are the results of a blood test, the three classes are different possible diseases, and the output is whether or not to treat with a particular antibiotic. The MAP method has told us that the output is C_2, and so we will not treat the disease. But what is the probability that it does not belong to class C_2, and so should have been treated with the antibiotic? It is $1 - P(C_2) = 0.55$. So the MAP prediction seems to be wrong: we should treat with antibiotic, because overall it is more likely. This method where we take into account the final outcomes of all of the classes is called the **Bayes' Optimal Classification**. It minimises the probability of misclassification, rather than maximising the posterior probability.

2.3.1 Minimising Risk

In the medical example we just saw it made sense to classify based on minimising the probability of misclassification. We can also consider the risk that is involved in the misclassification. The risk from misclassifying someone as unhealthy when they are healthy is usually smaller than the other way around, but not necessarily always: there are plenty of treatments that have nasty side effects, and you wouldn't want to suffer from those if you didn't have the disease. In cases like this we can create a loss matrix that specifies the risk involved in classifying an example of class C_i as class C_j. It looks like the confusion matrix we saw in Section 2.2, except that a loss matrix always contains zeros on the leading diagonal since there should never be a loss from getting the classification correct! Once we have the loss matrix, we just extend our classifier to minimise risk by multiplying each case by the relevant loss number.

2.3.2 The Naïve Bayes' Classifier

We're now going to return to performing classification, without worrying about the outcomes, so that we are back to calculating the MAP outcome, Equation (2.14). We can compute this exactly as described above, and it will work fine. However, suppose that the vector of feature values had many elements, so that there were lots of different features that were measured. How would this affect the classifier? We are trying to estimate $P(\mathbf{X}_j|C_i) = P(X_j^1, X_j^2, \ldots X_j^n|C_i)$ (where the superscripts index the elements of the vector) by looking at the histogram of all of our training data. As the dimensionality of $\mathbf{X}$ increases (as n gets larger), the amount of data in each bin of the histogram shrinks. This is the curse of dimensionality again (Section 2.1.2), and means that we need much more data as the dimensionality increases.

There is one simplifying assumption that we can make. We can assume that the elements of the feature vector are conditionally independent of each other, given the classification. So given the class C_i, the values of the different features do not affect each other. This is the naïveté in the name of the classifier, since it often doesn't make much sense—it tells us that the features are independent of each other. If we were to try to classify coins it would say that the weight and the diameter of the coin are independent of each other, which clearly isn't true. However, it does mean that the probability of getting the string of feature values $P(X_j^1 = a_1, X_j^2 = a_2, \ldots, X_j^n = a_n|C_i)$ is just equal to the product of multiplying together all of the individual probabilities:

$$P(X_j^1 = a_1|C_i) \times P(X_j^2 = a_2|C_i) \times \ldots \times P(X_j^n = a_n|C_i) = \prod_k P(X_j^k = a_k|C_i), \quad (2.15)$$

which is much easier to compute, and reduces the severity of the curse of dimensionality. So the classifier rule for the naïve Bayes' classifier is to select the class C_i for which the following computation is the maximum:

$$P(C_i) \prod_k P(X_j^k = a_k|C_i). \quad (2.16)$$

This is clearly a great simplification over evaluating the full probability, so it might come as a surprise that the naïve Bayes' classifier has been shown to have comparable results to other classification methods in certain domains. Where the simplification is true, so that the features are conditionally independent of each other, the naïve Bayes' classifier produces exactly the MAP classification.

In Chapter 12 on learning with trees, particularly Section 12.4, there is an example concerned with what to do in the evening based on whether you have an assignment deadline and what is happening. The data, shown below, consists of a set of prior examples from the last few days.

Deadline?	Is there a party?	Lazy?	Activity
Urgent	Yes	Yes	Party
Urgent	No	Yes	Study
Near	Yes	Yes	Party
None	Yes	No	Party
None	No	Yes	Pub
None	Yes	No	Party
Near	No	No	Study
Near	No	Yes	TV
Near	Yes	Yes	Party
Urgent	No	No	Study

In Chapter 12 we will see the results of a decision tree learning about this data, but here we will use the naïve Bayes' classifier. We feed in the current values for the feature variables (deadline, whether there is a party, etc.) and ask the classifier to compute the probabilities of each of the four possible things that you might do in the evening based on the data in the training set. Then we pick the most likely class. Note that the probabilities will be very small. This is one of the problems with the Bayes' classifier: since we are multiplying lots of probabilities, which are all less than one, the numbers get very small.

Suppose that you have deadlines looming, but none of them are particularly urgent, that there is no party on, and that you are currently lazy. Then the classifier needs to evaluate:

- P(Party) × P(Near | Party) × P(No Party | Party) × P(Lazy | Party)

- P(Study) × P(Near | Study) × P(No Party | Study) × P(Lazy | Study)

- P(Pub) × P(Near | Pub) × P(No Party | Pub) × P(Lazy | Pub)

- P(TV) × P(Near | TV) × P(No Party | TV) × P(Lazy | TV)

Using the data above these evaluate to:

$$
\begin{aligned}
P(\text{Party}|\text{near (not urgent) deadline, no party, lazy}) &= \frac{5}{10} \times \frac{2}{5} \times \frac{0}{5} \times \frac{3}{5} \\
&= 0 \qquad (2.17) \\
P(\text{Study}|\text{near (not urgent) deadline, no party, lazy}) &= \frac{3}{10} \times \frac{1}{3} \times \frac{3}{3} \times \frac{1}{3} \\
&= \frac{1}{30} \qquad (2.18) \\
P(\text{Pub}|\text{near (not urgent) deadline, no party, lazy}) &= \frac{1}{10} \times \frac{0}{1} \times \frac{1}{1} \times \frac{1}{1} \\
&= 0 \qquad (2.19) \\
P(\text{TV}|\text{near (not urgent) deadline, no party, lazy}) &= \frac{1}{10} \times \frac{1}{1} \times \frac{1}{1} \times \frac{1}{1} \\
&= \frac{1}{10} \qquad (2.20)
\end{aligned}
$$

So based on this you will be watching TV tonight.

2.4 SOME BASIC STATISTICS

This section will provide a quick summary of a few important statistical concepts. You may well already know about them, but just in case we'll go over them, highlighting the points that are important for machine learning. Any basic statistics book will give considerably more detailed information.

2.4.1 Averages

We'll start as basic as can be, with the two numbers that can be used to characterise a dataset: the mean and the variance. The mean is easy, it is the most commonly used average of a set of data, and is the value that is found by adding up all the points in the dataset and dividing by the number of points. There are two other averages that are used: the median and the mode. The median is the middle value, so the most common way to find it is to sort the dataset according to size and then find the point that is in the middle (of course, if there is an even number of datapoints then there is no exact middle, so people typically take the value halfway between the two points that are closest to the middle). There is a faster algorithm for computing the median based on a randomised algorithm that is described in most textbooks on algorithms. The mode is the most common value, so it just requires counting how many times each element appears and picking the most frequent one. We will also need to develop the idea of variance within a dataset, and of probability distributions.

2.4.2 Variance and Covariance

If we are given a set of random numbers, then we already know how to compute the mean of the set, together with the median. However, there are other useful statistics that can be computed, one of which is the expectation. The name expectation shows the gambling roots of most probability theory, since it describes the amount of money you can expect to win. It consists of multiplying together the payoff for each possibility with the probability of that thing happening, and then adding them all together. So if you are approached in the street by somebody selling raffle tickets for $1 and they tell you that there is a prize of $100,000 and they are selling 200,000 tickets, then you can work out the expected value of your ticket as:

$$E = -1 \times \frac{199,999}{200,000} + 99,999 \times \frac{1}{200,000} = -0.5, \tag{2.21}$$

where the -1 is the price of your ticket, which does not win 199,999 times out of 200,000 and the 99,999 is the prize minus the cost of your ticket. Note that the expected value is not a real value: you will never actually get 50 cents back, no matter what happens. If we just compute the expected value of a set of numbers, then we end up with the mean value.

The variance of the set of numbers is a measure of how spread out the values are. It is computed as the sum of the squared distances between each element in the set and the expected value of the set (the mean, μ):

$$\text{var}(\{\mathbf{x}_i\}) = \sigma^2(\{\mathbf{x}_i\}) = E((\{\mathbf{x}_i\} - \mu)^2) = \sum_{i=1}^{N}(\mathbf{x}_i - \mu)^2. \tag{2.22}$$

The square root of the variance, σ, is known as the standard deviation. The variance looks at the variation in one variable compared to its mean. We can generalise this to look at how two variables vary together, which is known as the covariance. It is a measure of how dependent the two variables are (in the statistical sense). It is computed by:

$$\text{cov}(\{\mathbf{x}_i\}, \{\mathbf{y}_i\}) = E(\{\mathbf{x}_i\} - \boldsymbol{\mu})E(\{\mathbf{y}_i\} - \boldsymbol{\nu}), \tag{2.23}$$

where $\boldsymbol{\nu}$ is the mean of set $\{\mathbf{y}_i\}$. If two variables are independent, then the covariance is 0 (the variables are then known as uncorrelated), while if they both increase and decrease at the same time, then the covariance is positive, and if one goes up while the other goes down, then the covariance is negative.

The covariance can be used to look at the correlation between all pairs of variables within a set of data. We need to compute the covariance of each pair, and these are then put together into what is imaginatively known as the covariance matrix. It can be written as:

$$\boldsymbol{\Sigma} = \begin{pmatrix} E[(\mathbf{x}_1 - \boldsymbol{\mu}_1)(\mathbf{x}_1 - \boldsymbol{\mu}_1)] & E[(\mathbf{x}_1 - \boldsymbol{\mu}_1)(\mathbf{x}_2 - \boldsymbol{\mu}_2)] & \ldots & E[(\mathbf{x}_1 - \boldsymbol{\mu}_1)(\mathbf{x}_n - \mu_n)] \\ E[(\mathbf{x}_2 - \boldsymbol{\mu}_2)(\mathbf{x}_1 - \boldsymbol{\mu}_1)] & E[(\mathbf{x}_2 - \boldsymbol{\mu}_2)(\mathbf{x}_2 - \boldsymbol{\mu}_2)] & \ldots & E[(\mathbf{x}_2 - \boldsymbol{\mu}_2)(\mathbf{x}_n - \mu_n)] \\ \ldots & \ldots & \ldots & \ldots \\ E[(\mathbf{x}_n - \boldsymbol{\mu}_n)(\mathbf{x}_1 - \boldsymbol{\mu}_1)] & E[(\mathbf{x}_n - \boldsymbol{\mu}_n)(\mathbf{x}_2 - \boldsymbol{\mu}_2)] & \ldots & E[(\mathbf{x}_n - \boldsymbol{\mu}_n)(\mathbf{x}_n - \boldsymbol{\mu}_n)] \end{pmatrix} \tag{2.24}$$

where $\mathbf{x}_i$ is a column vector describing the elements of the ith variable, and $\boldsymbol{\mu}_i$ is their mean. Note that the matrix is square, that the elements on the leading diagonal of the matrix are equal to the variances, and that it is symmetric since $\text{cov}(\mathbf{x}_i, \mathbf{x}_j) = \text{cov}(\mathbf{x}_j, \mathbf{x}_i)$. Equation (2.24) can also be written in matrix form as $\boldsymbol{\Sigma} = E[(\mathbf{X} - E[\mathbf{X}])(\mathbf{X} - E[\mathbf{X}])^T]$, recalling that the mean of a variable $\mathbf{X}$ is $E(\mathbf{X})$.

We will see in Chapter 6 that the covariance matrix has other uses, but for now we will think about what it tells us about a dataset. In essence, it says how the data varies along each data dimension. This is useful if we want to think about distances again. Suppose I gave you the two datasets shown in Figure 2.13 and the test point (labelled by the large 'X' in the figures) and asked you if the 'X' was part of the data. For the figure on the left you would probably say yes, while for the figure on the right you would say no, even though the two points are the same distance from the centre of the data. The reason for this is that as well as looking at the mean, you've also looked at where the test point lies in relation to the spread of the actual datapoints. If the data is tightly controlled then the test point has to be close to the mean, while if the data is very spread out, then the distance of the test point from the mean does not matter as much. We can use this to construct a distance measure that takes this into account. It is called the Mahalanobis distance after the person who described it in 1936, and is written as:

$$D_M(\mathbf{x}) = \sqrt{(\mathbf{x} - \boldsymbol{\mu})^T \boldsymbol{\Sigma}^{-1}(\mathbf{x} - \boldsymbol{\mu})}, \tag{2.25}$$

where $\mathbf{x}$ is the data arranged as a column vector, $\boldsymbol{\mu}$ is column vector representing the mean, and $\boldsymbol{\Sigma}^{-1}$ is the inverse of the covariance matrix. If we set the covariance matrix to the identity matrix, then the Mahalanobis distance reduces to the Euclidean distance.

Computing the Mahalanobis distance requires some fairly heavy computational machinery in computing the covariance matrix and then its inverse. Fortunately these are very easy to do in NumPy. There is a function that estimates the covariance matrix of a dataset (`np.cov(x)` for data matrix x) and the inverse is called `np.linalg.inv(x)`. The inverse does not have to exist in all cases, of course.

We are now going to consider a probability distribution, which describes the probabilities of something occurring over the range of possible feature values. There are lots of probability distributions that are common enough to have names, but there is one that is much better known than any other, because it occurs so often; therefore, that is the only one we will worry about here.

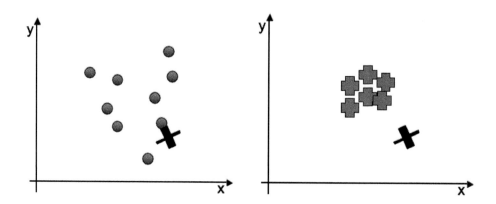

FIGURE 2.13 Two different datasets and a test point.

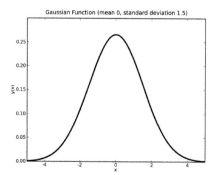

FIGURE 2.14 Plot of the one-dimensional Gaussian curve.

2.4.3 The Gaussian

The probability distribution that is most well known (indeed, the only one that many people know, or even need to know) is the **Gaussian** or **normal distribution**. In one dimension it has the familiar 'bell-shaped' curve shown in Figure 2.14, and its equation in one dimension is:

$$p(x) = \frac{1}{\sqrt{2\pi}\sigma} \exp\left(\frac{-(x-\mu)^2}{2\sigma^2}\right), \tag{2.26}$$

where μ is the mean and σ the standard deviation. The Gaussian distribution turns up in many problems because of the **Central Limit Theorem**, which says that lots of small random numbers will add up to something Gaussian. In higher dimensions it looks like:

$$p(\mathbf{x}) = \frac{1}{(2\pi)^{d/2}|\mathbf{\Sigma}|^{1/2}} \exp\left(-\frac{1}{2}(\mathbf{x}-\boldsymbol{\mu})^T \mathbf{\Sigma}^{-1}(\mathbf{x}-\boldsymbol{\mu})\right), \tag{2.27}$$

where $\mathbf{\Sigma}$ is the $n \times n$ covariance matrix (with $|\mathbf{\Sigma}|$ being its determinant and $\mathbf{\Sigma}^{-1}$ being its inverse). Figure 2.15 shows the appearance in two dimensions of three different cases: when the covariance matrix is the identity; when there are only numbers on the leading diagonal of the matrix; and the general case. The first case is known as a **spherical** covariance matrix, and has only 1 parameter. The second and third cases define ellipses in two dimensions, either aligned with the axes (with n parameters) or more generally, with n^2 parameters.

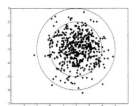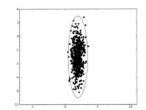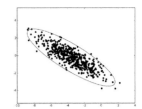

FIGURE 2.15 The two-dimensional Gaussian when (*left*) the covariance matrix is the identity, (*centre*) the covariance matrix has elements on the leading diagonal only, and (*right*) the general case.

2.5 THE BIAS-VARIANCE TRADEOFF

To round off this chapter, we use the statistical ideas of the previous section to look again at the idea of how to evaluate the amount of learning that can be performed, from a theoretical perspective.

Whenever we train any type of machine learning algorithm we are making some choices about a model to use, and fitting the parameters of that model. The more degrees of freedom the algorithm has, the more complicated the model that can be fitted. We have already seen that more complicated models have inherent dangers such as overfitting, and requiring more training data, and we have seen the need for validation data to ensure that the model does not overfit. There is another way to understand this idea that more complex models do not necessarily result in better results. Some people call it the bias-variance dilemma rather than a tradeoff, but this seems to be over-dramatising things a little.

In fact, it is a very simple idea. A model can be bad for two different reasons. Either it is not accurate and doesn't match the data well, or it is not very precise and there is a lot of variation in the results. The first of these is known as the bias, while the second is the statistical variance. More complex classifiers will tend to improve the bias, but the cost of this is higher variance, while making the model more specific by reducing the variance will increase the bias. Just like the Heisenberg Uncertainty Principle in quantum physics, there is a fundamental law at work behind the scenes that says that we can't have everything at once. As an example, consider the difference between a straight line fit to some data and a high degree polynomial, which can go precisely though the datapoints. The straight line has no variance at all, but high bias since it is a bad fit to the data in general. The spline can fit the training data to arbitrary accuracy, but the variance will increase. Note that the variance probably increases by rather less than the bias decreases, since we expect that the spline will give a better fit. Some models are definitely better than others, but choosing the complexity of the model is important for getting good results.

The most common way to compute the error between the targets and the predicted outputs is to sum up the squares of the difference between the two (the reason for squaring them is that if we don't, and just add up the differences, and if we had one example where the target was bigger than the prediction, and one where it was smaller by the same amount, then they would sum to zero). When looking at this sum-of-squares error function we can split it up into separate pieces that represent the bias and the variance. Suppose that the function that we are trying to approximate is $y = f(\mathbf{x}) + \epsilon$, where ϵ is the noise, which is assumed to be Gaussian with 0 mean and variance σ^2. We use our machine learning algorithm to fit a hypothesis $h(\mathbf{x}) = \mathbf{w}^T\mathbf{x} + b$ (where $\mathbf{w}$ is the weight vector from Section 2.1) to the data in order to minimise the sum-of-squares error $\sum_i (y_i - h(\mathbf{x}_i))^2$.

In order to decide whether or not our method is successful we need to consider it on independent data, so we consider a new input $\mathbf{x}^*$ and compute the expected value of the sum-of squares error, which we will assume is a random variable. Remember that $E[x] = \bar{x}$, the mean value. We are now going to do some algebraic manipulation, mostly based on the fact that (where Z is just some random variable):

$$
\begin{aligned}
E[(Z - \bar{Z})^2] &= E[Z^2 - 2Z\bar{Z} + \bar{Z}^2] \\
&= E[Z^2] - 2E[Z]\bar{Z} + \bar{Z}^2 \\
&= E[Z^2] - 2\bar{Z}\bar{Z} + \bar{Z}^2 \\
&= E[Z^2] - \bar{Z}^2.
\end{aligned}
\tag{2.28}
$$

Using this, we can compute the expectation of the sum-of-squares error of a new data-point:

$$
\begin{aligned}
E[(y^* - h(\mathbf{x}^*))^2] &= E[y^{*2} - 2y^*h(\mathbf{x}^*) + h(\mathbf{x}^*)^2] \\
&= E[y^{*2}] - 2E[y^*h(\mathbf{x}^*)] + E[h(\mathbf{x}^*)^2] \\
&= E[(y^{*2} - f(\mathbf{x}^*))^2] + f(\mathbf{x}^*)^2 + E[(h(\mathbf{x}^* - \bar{h}(\mathbf{x}^*))^2] \\
&\quad + \bar{h}(\mathbf{x}^*)^2 - 2f(\mathbf{x}^*)\bar{h}(\mathbf{x}^*) \\
&= E[(y^{*2} - f(\mathbf{x}^*))^2] + E[(h(\mathbf{x}^*) - \bar{h}(\mathbf{x}^*))^2] + (f(\mathbf{x}^*) + \bar{h}(\mathbf{x}^*))^2 \\
&= \text{noise}^2 + \text{variance} + \text{bias}^2.
\end{aligned}
\tag{2.29}
$$

The first of the three terms on the right of the equation is beyond our control. It is the **irreducible error** and is the variance of the test data. The second term is variance, and the third is the square of the bias. The variance tells us how much $\mathbf{x}^*$ changes depending on the particular training set that was used, while the bias tells us about the average error of $h(\mathbf{x}^*)$. It is possible to exchange bias and variance, so that you can have a model with low bias (meaning that on average the outputs are current), but high variance (meaning that the answers wibble around all over the place) or vice versa, but you can't make them both zero – for each model there is a tradeoff between them. However, for any particular model and dataset there is some reasonable set of parameters that will give the best results for the bias and variance together, and part of the challenge of model fitting is to find this point.

This tradeoff is a useful way to see what machine learning is doing in general, but it is time now to go and see what we can actually do with some real machine learning algorithms, starting with neural networks.

FURTHER READING

Any standard statistics textbook gives more detail about the basic probability and statistics introduced here, but for an alternative take from the point of view of machine learning, see:

- Sections 1.2 and 1.4 of C.M. Bishop. *Pattern Recognition and Machine Learning.* Springer, Berlin, Germany, 2006.

For more on the bias-variance tradeoff, see:

- Sections 7.2 and 7.3 of T. Hastie, R. Tibshirani, and J. Friedman. *The Elements of Statistical Learning*, 2nd edition, Springer, Berlin, Germany, 2008.

There are two books on semi-supervised learning that can be used to get an overview of the area:

- O. Chapelle, B. Schölkopf, and A. Zien. *Semi-supervised learning*. MIT Press, Cambridge, MA, USA, 2006.

- X. Zhu and A.B. Goldberg. *Introduction to Semi-Supervised Learning*. Synthesis Lectures on Artificial Intelligence and Machine Learning, 2009.

PRACTICE QUESTIONS

Problem 2.1 Use Bayes' rule to solve the following problem: At a party you meet a person who claims to have been to the same school as you. You vaguely recognise them, but can't remember properly, so decide to work out how likely it is, given that:

- 1 in 2 of the people you vaguely recognise went to school with you
- 1 in 10 of the people at the party went to school with you
- 1 in 5 people at the party you vaguely recognise

Problem 2.2 Consider how using the risk calculation in Section 2.3.1 would change the naïve Bayes classifier.

## CHAPTER 3

Neurons, Neural Networks, and Linear Discriminants

We've spent enough time with the concepts of machine learning, now it is time to actually see it in practice. To start the process, we will return to our demonstration that learning is possible, which is the squishy thing that your skull protects.

3.1 THE BRAIN AND THE NEURON

In animals, learning occurs within the brain. If we can understand how the brain works, then there might be things in there for us to copy and use for our machine learning systems. While the brain is an impressively powerful and complicated system, the basic building blocks that it is made up of are fairly simple and easy to understand. We'll look at them shortly, but it's worth noting that in computational terms the brain does exactly what we want. It deals with noisy and even inconsistent data, and produces answers that are usually correct from very high dimensional data (such as images) very quickly. All amazing for something that weighs about 1.5 kg and is losing parts of itself all the time (neurons die as you age at impressive/depressing rates), but its performance does not degrade appreciably (in the jargon, this means it is robust).

So how does it actually work? We aren't actually that sure on most levels, but in this book we are only going to worry about the most basic level, which is the processing units of the brain. These are nerve cells called neurons. There are lots of them (100 billion $= 10^{11}$ is the figure that is often given) and they come in lots of different types, depending upon their particular task. However, their general operation is similar in all cases: transmitter chemicals within the fluid of the brain raise or lower the electrical potential inside the body of the neuron. If this membrane potential reaches some threshold, the neuron spikes or fires, and a pulse of fixed strength and duration is sent down the axon. The axons divide (arborise) into connections to many other neurons, connecting to each of these neurons in a synapse. Each neuron is typically connected to thousands of other neurons, so that it is estimated that there are about 100 trillion ($= 10^{14}$) synapses within the brain. After firing, the neuron must wait for some time to recover its energy (the refractory period) before it can fire again.

Each neuron can be viewed as a separate processor, performing a very simple computation: deciding whether or not to fire. This makes the brain a massively parallel computer made up of 10^{11} processing elements. If that is all there is to the brain, then we should be able to model it inside a computer and end up with animal or human intelligence inside a computer. This is the view of strong AI. We aren't aiming at anything that grand in this book, but we do want to make programs that learn. So how does learning occur in the brain? The principal concept is **plasticity**: modifying the **strength** of synaptic connections between neurons, and creating new connections. We don't know all of the mechanisms by which the strength of these synapses gets adapted, but one method that does seem to be used was first postulated by Donald Hebb in 1949, and that is what is discussed now.

3.1.1 Hebb's Rule

Hebb's rule says that the changes in the strength of synaptic connections are proportional to the correlation in the firing of the two connecting neurons. So if two neurons consistently fire simultaneously, then any connection between them will change in strength, becoming stronger. However, if the two neurons never fire simultaneously, the connection between them will die away. The idea is that if two neurons both respond to something, then they should be connected. Let's see a trivial example: suppose that you have a neuron somewhere that recognises your grandmother (this will probably get input from lots of visual processing neurons, but don't worry about that). Now if your grandmother always gives you a chocolate bar when she comes to visit, then some neurons, which are happy because you like the taste of chocolate, will also be stimulated. Since these neurons fire at the same time, they will be connected together, and the connection will get stronger over time. So eventually, the sight of your grandmother, even in a photo, will be enough to make you think of chocolate. Sound familiar? Pavlov used this idea, called **classical conditioning**, to train his dogs so that when food was shown to the dogs and the bell was rung at the same time, the neurons for salivating over the food and hearing the bell fired simultaneously, and so became strongly connected. Over time, the strength of the synapse between the neurons that responded to hearing the bell and those that caused the salivation reflex was enough that just hearing the bell caused the salivation neurons to fire in sympathy.

There are other names for this idea that synaptic connections between neurons and assemblies of neurons can be formed when they fire together and can become stronger. It is also known as **long-term potentiation** and **neural plasticity**, and it does appear to have correlates in real brains.

3.1.2 McCulloch and Pitts Neurons

Studying neurons isn't actually that easy. You need to be able to extract the neuron from the brain, and then keep it alive so that you can see how it reacts in controlled circumstances. Doing this takes a lot of care. One of the problems is that neurons are generally quite small (they must be if you've got 10^{11} of them in your head!) so getting electrodes into the synapses is difficult. It has been done, though, using neurons from the giant squid, which has some neurons that are large enough to see. Hodgkin and Huxley did this in 1952, measuring and writing down differential equations that compute the membrane potential based on various chemical concentrations, something that earned them a Nobel prize. We aren't going to worry about that, instead, we're going to look at a mathematical model of a neuron that was introduced in 1943. The purpose of a mathematical model is that it extracts only the bare essentials required to accurately represent the entity being studied, removing all of the extraneous details. McCulloch and Pitts produced a perfect example of this when they modelled a neuron as:

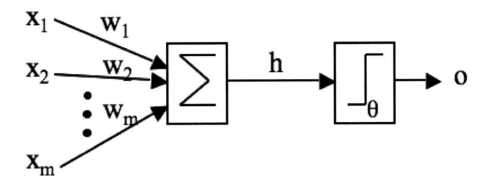

FIGURE 3.1 A picture of McCulloch and Pitts' mathematical model of a neuron. The inputs x_i are multiplied by the weights w_i, and the neurons sum their values. If this sum is greater than the threshold θ then the neuron fires; otherwise it does not.

(1) a set of weighted inputs w_i that correspond to the synapses

(2) an adder that sums the input signals (equivalent to the membrane of the cell that collects electrical charge)

(3) an activation function (initially a threshold function) that decides whether the neuron fires ('spikes') for the current inputs

A picture of their model is given in Figure 3.1, and we'll use the picture to write down a mathematical description. On the left of the picture are a set of input nodes (labelled $x_1, x_2, \ldots x_m$). These are given some values, and as an example we'll assume that there are three inputs, with $x_1 = 1, x_2 = 0, x_3 = 0.5$. In real neurons those inputs come from the outputs of other neurons. So the 0 means that a neuron didn't fire, the 1 means it did, and the 0.5 has no biological meaning, but never mind. (Actually, this isn't quite fair, but it's a long story and not very relevant.) Each of these other neuronal firings flowed along a synapse to arrive at our neuron, and those synapses have strengths, called weights. The strength of the synapse affects the strength of the signal, so we multiply the input by the weight of the synapse (so we get $x_1 \times w_1$ and $x_2 \times w_2$, etc.). Now when all of these signals arrive into our neuron, it adds them up to see if there is enough strength to make it fire. We'll write that as

$$h = \sum_{i=1}^{m} w_i x_i, \qquad (3.1)$$

which just means sum (add up) all the inputs multiplied by their synaptic weights. I've assumed that there are m of them, where $m = 3$ in the example. If the synaptic weights are $w_1 = 1, w_2 = -0.5, w_3 = -1$, then the inputs to our model neuron are $h = 1 \times 1 + 0 \times -0.5 + 0.5 \times -1 = 1 + 0 + -0.5 = 0.5$. Now the neuron needs to decide if it is going to fire. For a real neuron, this is a question of whether the membrane potential is above some threshold. We'll pick a threshold value (labelled θ), say $\theta = 0$ as an example. Now, does our neuron fire? Well, $h = 0.5$ in the example, and $0.5 > 0$, so the neuron does fire, and produces output 1. If the neuron did not fire, it would produce output 0.

The McCulloch and Pitts neuron is a binary threshold device. It sums up the inputs (multiplied by the synaptic strengths or weights) and either fires (produces output 1) or does not fire (produces output 0) depending on whether the input is above some threshold. We can write the second half of the work of the neuron, the decision about whether or not to fire (which is known as an **activation function**), as:

$$o = g(h) = \left\{ \begin{array}{ll} 1 & \text{if } h > \theta \\ 0 & \text{if } h \leq \theta. \end{array} \right. \tag{3.2}$$

This is a very simple model, but we are going to use these neurons, or very simple variations on them using slightly different activation functions (that is, we'll replace the threshold function with something else) for most of our study of neural networks. In fact, these neurons might look simple, but as we shall see, a network of such neurons can perform any computation that a normal computer can, provided that the weights w_i are chosen correctly. So one of the main things we are going to talk about for the next few chapters is methods of setting these weights.

3.1.3 Limitations of the McCulloch and Pitts Neuronal Model

One question that is worth considering is how realistic is this model of a neuron? The answer is: not very. Real neurons are much more complicated. The inputs to a real neuron are not necessarily summed linearly: there may be non-linear summations. However, the most noticeable difference is that real neurons do not output a single output response, but a **spike train**, that is, a sequence of pulses, and it is this spike train that encodes information. This means that neurons don't actually respond as threshold devices, but produce a graded output in a continuous way. They do still have the transition between firing and not firing, though, but the threshold at which they fire changes over time. Because neurons are biochemical devices, the amount of neurotransmitter (which affects how much charge they required to spike, amongst other things) can vary according to the current state of the organism. Furthermore, the neurons are not updated sequentially according to a computer clock, but update themselves randomly (**asynchronously**), whereas in many of our models we will update the neurons according to the clock. There are neural network models that are asynchronous, but for our purposes we will stick to algorithms that are updated by the clock.

Note that the weights w_i can be positive or negative. This corresponds to **excitatory** and **inhibitory** connections that make neurons more likely to fire and less likely to fire, respectively.

Both of these types of synapses do exist within the brain, but with the McCulloch and Pitts neurons, the weights can change from positive to negative or vice versa, which has not been seen biologically—synaptic connections are either excitatory or inhibitory, and never change from one to the other. Additionally, real neurons can have synapses that link back to themselves in a feedback loop, but we do not usually allow that possibility when we make networks of neurons. Again, there are exceptions, but we won't get into them.

It is possible to improve the model to include many of these features, but the picture is complicated enough already, and McCulloch and Pitts neurons already provide a great deal of interesting behaviour that resembles the action of the brain, such as the fact that networks of McCulloch and Pitts neurons can memorise pictures and learn to represent functions and classify data, as we shall see in the next couple of chapters. In the last chapter we saw a simple model of a neuron that simulated what seems to be the most important function of a neuron—deciding whether or not to fire—and ignored the nasty biological things like chemical concentrations, refractory periods, etc. Having this model is only useful if we can use it to understand what is happening when we learn, or use the model in order to solve some kind of problem. We are going to try to do both in this chapter, although the learning that we try to understand will be machine learning rather than animal learning.

3.2 NEURAL NETWORKS

One thing that is probably fairly obvious is that one neuron isn't that interesting. It doesn't do very much, except fire or not fire when we give it inputs. In fact, it doesn't even learn. If we feed in the same set of inputs over and over again, the output of the neuron never varies—it either fires or does not. So to make the neuron a little more interesting we need to work out how to make it learn, and then we need to put sets of neurons together into neural networks so that they can do something useful.

The question we need to think about first is how our neurons can learn. We are going to look at supervised learning for the next few chapters, which means that the algorithms will learn by example: the dataset that we learn from has the correct output values associated with each datapoint. At first sight this might seem pointless, since if you already know the correct answer, why bother learning at all? The key is in the concept of generalisation that we saw in Section 1.2. Assuming that there is some pattern in the data, then by showing the neural network a few examples we hope that it will find the pattern and predict the other examples correctly. This is sometimes known as pattern recognition.

Before we worry too much about this, let's think about what learning is. In the Introduction it was suggested that you learn if you get better at doing something. So if you can't program in the first semester and you can in the second, you have learnt to program. Something has changed (adapted), presumably in your brain, so that you can do a task that you were not able to do previously. Have a look again at the McCulloch and Pitts neuron (e.g., in Figure 3.1) and try to work out what can change in that model. The only things that make up the neuron are the inputs, the weights, and the threshold (and there is only one threshold for each neuron, but lots of inputs). The inputs can't change, since they are external, so we can only change the weights and the threshold, which is interesting since it tells us that most of the learning is in the weights, which aren't part of the neuron at all; they are the model of the synapse! Getting excited about neurons turns out to be missing something important, which is that the learning happens *between* the neurons, in the way that they are connected together.

So in order to make a neuron learn, the question that we need to ask is:

How should we change the weights and thresholds of the neurons so that the network gets the right answer more often?

Now that we know the right question to ask we'll have a look at our very first neural network, the space-age sounding Perceptron, and see how we can use it to solve the problem (it really was space-age, too: created in 1958). Once we've worked out the algorithm and how it works, we'll look at what it can and cannot do, and then see how statistics can give us insights into learning as well.

3.3 THE PERCEPTRON

The Perceptron is nothing more than a collection of McCulloch and Pitts neurons together with a set of inputs and some weights to fasten the inputs to the neurons. The network is shown in Figure 3.2. On the left of the figure, shaded in light grey, are the input nodes. These are not neurons, they are just a nice schematic way of showing how values are fed

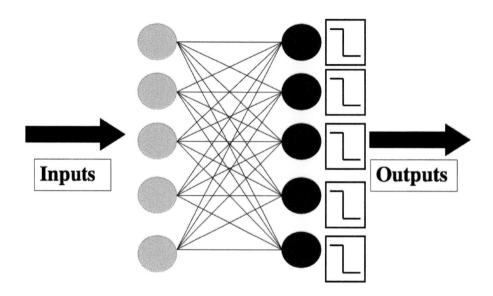

FIGURE 3.2 The Perceptron network, consisting of a set of input nodes (left) connected to McCulloch and Pitts neurons using weighted connections.

into the network, and how many of these input values there are (which is the **dimension** (number of elements) in the input **vector**). They are almost always drawn as circles, just like neurons, which is rather confusing, so I've shaded them a different colour. The neurons are shown on the right, and you can see both the additive part (shown as a circle) and the thresholder. In practice nobody bothers to draw the thresholder separately, you just need to remember that it is part of the neuron.

Notice that the neurons in the Perceptron are completely independent of each other: it doesn't matter to any neuron what the others are doing, it works out whether or not to fire by multiplying together its own weights and the input, adding them together, and comparing the result to its own threshold, regardless of what the other neurons are doing. Even the weights that go into each neuron are separate for each one, so the only thing they share is the inputs, since every neuron sees all of the inputs to the network.

In Figure 3.2 the number of inputs is the same as the number of neurons, but this does not have to be the case — in general there will be m inputs and n neurons. The number of inputs is determined for us by the data, and so is the number of outputs, since we are doing supervised learning, so we want the Perceptron to learn to reproduce a particular **target**, that is, a pattern of firing and non-firing neurons for the given input.

When we looked at the McCulloch and Pitts neuron, the weights were labelled as w_i, with the i index running over the number of inputs. Here, we also need to work out which neuron the weight feeds into, so we label them as w_{ij}, where the j index runs over the number of neurons. So w_{32} is the weight that connects input node 3 to neuron 2. When we make an implementation of the neural network, we can use a two-dimensional array to hold these weights.

Now, working out whether or not a neuron should fire is easy: we set the values of the input nodes to match the elements of an input vector and then use Equations (3.1) and (3.2) for each neuron. We can do this for all of the neurons, and the result is a pattern of firing and non-firing neurons, which looks like a vector of 0s and 1s, so if there are 5 neurons, as in Figure 3.2, then a typical output pattern could be $(0, 1, 0, 0, 1)$, which means that the second and fifth neurons fired and the others did not. We compare that pattern to the target, which is our known correct answer for this input, to identify which neurons got the answer right, and which did not.

For a neuron that is correct, we are happy, but any neuron that fired when it shouldn't have done, or failed to fire when it should, needs to have its weights changed. The trouble is that we don't know what the weights should be—that's the point of the neural network, after all, so we want to change the weights so that the neuron gets it right next time. We are going to talk about this in a lot more detail in Chapter 4, but for now we're going to do something fairly simple to see that it is possible to find a solution.

Suppose that we present an input vector to the network and one of the neurons gets the wrong answer (its output does not match the target). There are m weights that are connected to that neuron, one for each of the input nodes. If we label the neuron that is wrong as k, then the weights that we are interested in are w_{ik}, where i runs from 1 to m. So we know which weights to change, but we still need to work out how to change the values of those weights. The first thing we need to know is whether each weight is too big or too small. This seems obvious at first: some of the weights will be too big if the neuron fired when it shouldn't have, and too small if it didn't fire when it should. So we compute $y_k - t_k$ (the difference between the output y_k, which is what the neuron did, and the target for that neuron, t_k, which is what the neuron should have done. This is a possible error function). If it is negative then the neuron should have fired and didn't, so we make the weights bigger, and vice versa if it is positive, which we can do by subtracting the error value. Hold on, though. That element of the input could be negative, which would switch the values over; so if we wanted the neuron to fire we'd need to make the value of the weight negative as well. To get around this we'll multiply those two things together to see how we should change the weight: $\Delta w_{ik} = -(y_k - t_k) \times x_i$, and the new value of the weight is the old value plus this value.

Note that we haven't said anything about changing the threshold value of the neuron. To see how important this is, suppose that a particular input is 0. In that case, even if a neuron is wrong, changing the relevant weight doesn't do anything (since anything times 0 is 0): we need to change the threshold. We will deal with this in an elegant way in Section 3.3.2. However, before we get to that, the learning rule needs to be finished—we need to decide how much to change the weight by. This is done by multiplying the value above by a parameter called the learning rate, usually labelled as η. The value of the learning rate decides how fast the network learns. It's quite important, so it gets a little subsection of its own (next), but first let's write down the final rule for updating a weight w_{ij}:

$$w_{ij} \leftarrow w_{ij} - \eta(y_j - t_j) \cdot x_i. \tag{3.3}$$

The other thing that we need to realise now is that the network needs to be shown every training example several times. The first time the network might get some of the answers correct and some wrong; the next time it will hopefully improve, and eventually its performance will stop improving. Working out how long to train the network for is not easy (we will see more methods in Section 4.3.3), but for now we will predefine the maximum number of iterations, T. Of course, if the network got all of the inputs correct, then this would also be a good time to stop.

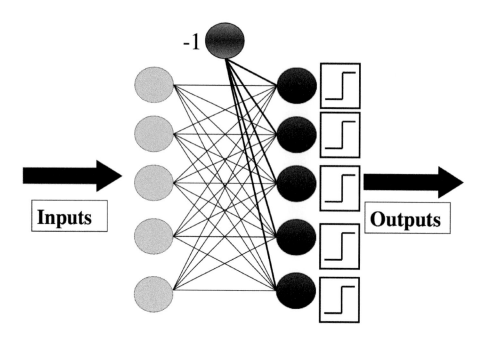

FIGURE 3.3 The Perceptron network again, showing the bias input.

3.3.1 The Learning Rate η

Equation (3.3) above tells us how to change the weights, with the parameter η controlling how much to change the weights by. We could miss it out, which would be the same as setting it to 1. If we do that, then the weights change a lot whenever there is a wrong answer, which tends to make the network **unstable**, so that it never settles down. The cost of having a small learning rate is that the weights need to see the inputs more often before they change significantly, so that the network takes longer to learn. However, it will be more stable and resistant to **noise** (errors) and inaccuracies in the data. We therefore use a moderate learning rate, typically $0.1 < \eta < 0.4$, depending upon how much error we expect in the inputs. It doesn't matter for the Perceptron algorithm, but for many of the algorithms that we will see in the book, the learning rate is a crucial parameter.

3.3.2 The Bias Input

When we discussed the McCulloch and Pitts neuron, we gave each neuron a firing threshold θ that determined what value it needed before it should fire. This threshold should be adjustable, so that we can change the value that the neuron fires at. Suppose that all of the inputs to a neuron are zero. Now it doesn't matter what the weights are (since zero times anything equals zero), the only way that we can control whether the neuron fires or not is through the threshold. If it wasn't adjustable and we wanted one neuron to fire when all the inputs to the network were zero, and another not to fire, then we would have a problem. No matter what values of the weights were set, the two neurons would do the same thing since they had the same threshold and the inputs were all zero.

The trouble is that changing the threshold requires an extra parameter that we need to write code for, and it isn't clear how we can do that in terms of the weight update that we worked out earlier. Fortunately, there is a neat way around this problem. Suppose that we fix the value of the threshold for the neuron at zero. Now, we add an extra input weight to the neuron, with the value of the input to that weight always being fixed (usually the value of $-\pm$ is chosen; in this book I'm going to use -1 to make it stand out, but any non-zero value will do). We include that weight in our update algorithm (like all the other weights), so we don't need to think of anything new. And the value of the weight will change to make the neuron fire—or not fire, whichever is correct—when an input of all zeros is given, since the input on that weight is always -1, even when all the other inputs are zero. This input is called a **bias** node, and its weights are usually given a 0 subscript, so that the weight connecting it to the jth neuron is w_{0j}.

3.3.3   The Perceptron Learning Algorithm

We are now ready to write our first learning algorithm. It might be useful to keep Figure 3.3 in mind as you read the algorithm, and we'll work through an example of using it afterwards. The algorithm is separated into two parts: a **training** phase, and a **recall** phase. The recall phase is used after training, and it is the one that should be fast to use, since it will be used far more often than the training phase. You can see that the training phase uses the recall equation, since it has to work out the activations of the neurons before the error can be calculated and the weights trained.

The Perceptron Algorithm

- **Initialisation**
    - set all of the weights w_{ij} to small (positive and negative) random numbers

- **Training**
    - for T iterations or until all the outputs are correct:
        * for each input vector:
            · compute the activation of each neuron j using **activation function** g:

$$y_j = g\left(\sum_{i=0}^{m} w_{ij}x_i\right) = \begin{cases} 1 & \text{if } \sum_{i=0}^{m} w_{ij}x_i > 0 \\ 0 & \text{if } \sum_{i=0}^{m} w_{ij}x_i \leq 0 \end{cases} \qquad (3.4)$$

            · update each of the weights individually using:

$$w_{ij} \leftarrow w_{ij} - \eta(y_j - t_j) \cdot x_i \qquad (3.5)$$

- **Recall**
    - compute the activation of each neuron j using:

$$y_j = g\left(\sum_{i=0}^{m} w_{ij}x_i\right) = \begin{cases} 1 & \text{if } w_{ij}x_i > 0 \\ 0 & \text{if } w_{ij}x_i \leq 0 \end{cases} \qquad (3.6)$$

Note that the code on the website for the Perceptron has a different form, as will be discussed in Section 3.3.5.

Computing the computational complexity of this algorithm is very easy. The recall phase

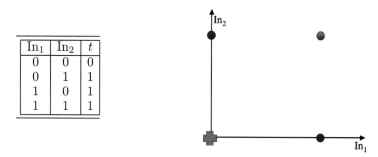

In$_1$	In$_2$	t
0	0	0
0	1	1
1	0	1
1	1	1

FIGURE 3.4 Data for the OR logic function and a plot of the four datapoints.

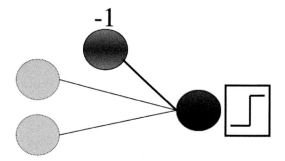

FIGURE 3.5 The Perceptron network for the example in Section 3.3.4.

loops over the neurons, and within that loops over the inputs, so its complexity is $\mathcal{O}(mn)$. The training part does this same thing, but does it for T iterations, so costs $\mathcal{O}(Tmn)$.

It might be the first time that you have seen an algorithm written out like this, and it could be hard to see how it can be turned into code. Equally, it might be difficult to believe that something as simple as this algorithm can learn something. The only way to fix these things is to work through the algorithm by hand on an example or two, and to try to write the code and then see if it does what is expected. We will do both of those things next, first working through a simple example by hand.

3.3.4 An Example of Perceptron Learning: Logic Functions

The example we are going to use is something very simple that you already know about, the logical OR. This obviously isn't something that you actually need a neural network to learn about, but it does make a nice simple example. So what will our neural network look like? There are two input nodes (plus the bias input) and there will be one output. The inputs and the target are given in the table on the left of Figure 3.4; the right of the figure shows a plot of the function with the circles as the **true** outputs, and a cross as the **false** one. The corresponding neural network is shown in Figure 3.5.

As you can see from Figure 3.5, there are three weights. The algorithm tells us to initialise the weights to small random numbers, so we'll pick $w_0 = -0.05, w_1 = -0.02, w_2 = 0.02$. Now we feed in the first input, where both inputs are 0: $(0,0)$. Remember that the input to the bias weight is always -1, so the value that reaches the neuron is $-0.05 \times -1 +$

$-0.02 \times 0 + 0.02 \times 0 = 0.05$. This value is above 0, so the neuron fires and the output is 1, which is incorrect according to the target. The update rule tells us that we need to apply Equation (3.3) to each of the weights separately (we'll pick a value of $\eta = 0.25$ for the example):

$$w_0 \quad : \quad -0.05 - 0.25 \times (1 - 0) \times -1 = 0.2, \qquad (3.7)$$

$$w_1 \quad : \quad -0.02 - 0.25 \times (1 - 0) \times 0 = -0.02, \qquad (3.8)$$

$$w_2 \quad : \quad 0.02 - 0.25 \times (1 - 0) \times 0 = 0.02. \qquad (3.9)$$

Now we feed in the next input $(0, 1)$ and compute the output (check that you agree that the neuron does not fire, but that it should) and then apply the learning rule again:

$$w_0 \quad : \quad 0.2 - 0.25 \times (0 - 1) \times -1 = -0.05, \qquad (3.10)$$

$$w_1 \quad : \quad -0.02 - 0.25 \times (0 - 1) \times 0 = -0.02, \qquad (3.11)$$

$$w_2 \quad : \quad 0.02 - 0.25 \times (0 - 1) \times 1 = 0.27. \qquad (3.12)$$

For the $(1, 0)$ input the answer is already correct (you should check that you agree with this), so we don't have to update the weights at all, and the same is true for the $(1, 1)$ input. So now we've been through all of the inputs once. Unfortunately, that doesn't mean we've finished—not all the answers are correct yet. We now need to start going through the inputs again, until the weights settle down and stop changing, which is what tells us that the algorithm has finished. For real-world applications the weights may never stop changing, which is why you run the algorithm for some pre-set number of iterations, T.

So now we carry on running the algorithm, which you should check for yourself either by hand or using computer code (which we'll discuss next), eventually getting to weight values that settle and stop changing. At this point the weights stop changing, and the Perceptron has correctly learnt all of the examples. Note that there are lots of different values that we can assign to the weights that will give the correct outputs; the ones that the algorithm finds depend on the learning rate, the inputs, and the initial starting values. We are interested in finding a set that works; we don't necessarily care what the actual values are, providing that the network generalises to other inputs.

3.3.5 Implementation

Turning the algorithm into code is fairly simple: we need to design some data structures to hold the variables, then write and test the program. Data structures are usually very basic for machine learning algorithms; here we need an array to hold the inputs, another to hold the weights, and then two more for the outputs and the targets. When we talked about the presentation of data to the neural network we used the term **input vectors**. The vector is a list of values that are presented to the Perceptron, with one value for each of the nodes in the network. When we turn this into computer code it makes sense to put these values into an array. However, the neural network isn't very exciting if we only show it one datapoint: we will need to show it lots of them. Therefore it is normal to arrange the data into a two-dimensional array, with each row of the array being a datapoint. In a language like C or Java, you then write a loop that runs over each row of the array to present the input, and a loop within it that runs over the number of input nodes (which does the computation on the current input vector).

Written this way in Python syntax (Appendix A provides a brief introduction to

Python), the recall code that is used after training for a set of `nData` datapoints arranged in the array `inputs` looks like (this code can be found on the book website):

```
for data in range(nData): # loop over the input vectors
    for n in range(N): # loop over the neurons
        # Compute sum of weights times inputs for each neuron
        # Set the activation to 0 to start
        activation[data][n] = 0
        # Loop over the input nodes (+1 for the bias node)
        for m in range(M+1):
            activation[data][n] += weight[m][n] * inputs[data][m]

        # Now decide whether the neuron fires or not
        if activation[data][n] > 0:
            activation[data][n] = 1
        else
            activation[data][n] = 0
```

However, Python's numerical library NumPy provides an alternative method, because it can easily multiply arrays and matrices together (MATLAB® and R have the same facility). This means that we can write the code with fewer loops, making it rather easier to read, and also means that we write less code. It can be a little confusing at first, though. To understand it, we need a little bit more mathematics, which is the concept of a matrix. In computer terms, matrices are just two-dimensional arrays. We can write the set of weights for the network in a matrix by making an `np.array` that has $m + 1$ rows (the number of input nodes + 1 for the bias) and n columns (the number of neurons). Now, the element of the matrix at location (i, j) contains the weight connecting input i to neuron j, which is what we had in the code above.

The benefit that we get from thinking about it in this way is that multiplying matrices and vectors together is well defined. You've probably seen this in high school or somewhere but, just in case, to be able to multiply matrices together we need the **inner dimensions** to be the same. This just means that if we have matrices $\mathbf{A}$ and $\mathbf{B}$ where $\mathbf{A}$ is size $m \times n$, then the size of $\mathbf{B}$ needs to be $n \times p$, where p can be any number. The n is called the inner dimension since when we write out the size of the matrices in the multiplication we get $(m \times n) \times (n \times p)$.

Now we can compute $\mathbf{AB}$ (but not necessarily $\mathbf{BA}$, since for that we'd need $m = p$, since the computation above would then be $(n \times p) \times (m \times n)$). The computation of the multiplication proceeds by picking up the first **column** of $\mathbf{B}$, rotating it by 90° anti-clockwise so that it is a **row** not a column, multiplying each element of it by the matching element in the first row of $\mathbf{A}$ and then adding them together. This is the first element of the answer matrix. The second element in the first row is made by picking up the second column of $\mathbf{B}$, rotating it to match the direction, and multiplying it by the first row of $\mathbf{A}$, and so on. As an example:

$$\begin{pmatrix} 3 & 4 & 5 \\ 2 & 3 & 4 \end{pmatrix} \times \begin{pmatrix} 1 & 3 \\ 2 & 4 \\ 3 & 5 \end{pmatrix} \tag{3.13}$$

$$= \begin{pmatrix} 3 \times 1 + 4 \times 2 + 5 \times 3 & 3 \times 3 + 4 \times 4 + 5 \times 5 \\ 2 \times 1 + 3 \times 2 + 4 \times 3 & 2 \times 3 + 3 \times 4 + 4 \times 5 \end{pmatrix} \tag{3.14}$$

$$= \begin{pmatrix} 26 & 50 \\ 20 & 38 \end{pmatrix} \tag{3.15}$$

NumPy can do this multiplication for us, using the `np.dot()` function (which is a rather strange name mathematically, but never mind). So to reproduce the calculation above, we use (where `>>>` denotes the Python command line, and so this is code to be typed in, with the answers provided by the Python interpreter shown afterwards):

```
>>> import numpy as np
>>> a = np.array([[3,4,5],[2,3,4]])
>>> b = np.array([[1,3],[2,4],[3,5]])
>>> np.dot(a,b)
array([[26, 50],
       [20, 38]])
```

The `np.array()` function makes the NumPy array, which is actually a matrix here, made up of an array of arrays: each row is a separate array, as you can see from the square brackets within square brackets. Note that we can enter the 2D array in one line of code by using commas between the different rows, but when it prints them out, NumPy puts each row of the matrix on a different line, which makes things easier to see.

This probably seems like a very long way from the Perceptron, but we are getting there, I promise! We can put the input vectors into a two-dimensional array of size $N \times m$, where N is the number of input vectors we have and m is the number of inputs. The weights array is of size $m \times n$, and so we can multiply them together. If we do, then the output will be an $N \times n$ matrix that holds the values of the sum that each neuron computes for each of the N input vectors. Now we just need to compute the activations based on these sums. NumPy has another useful function for us here, which is `np.where(condition,x,y)`, (`condition` is a logical condition and x and y are values) that returns a matrix that has value x where `condition` is true and value y everywhere else. So using the matrix a that was used above,

```
>>> np.where(a>3,1,0)
array([[0, 1, 1],
       [0, 0, 1]])
```

The upshot of this is that the entire section of code for the recall function of the Perceptron can be rewritten in two lines of code as:

```
# Compute activations
activations = np.dot(inputs,self.weights)

# Threshold the activations
return np.where(activations>0,1,0)
```

The training section isn't that much harder really. You should notice that the first part of the training algorithm is the same as the recall computation, so we can put them into a function (I've called it `pcnfwd` in the code because it consists of running **forwards** through the network to get the outputs). Then we just need to compute the weight updates. The weights are in an $m \times n$ matrix, the activations are in an $N \times n$ matrix (as are the targets) and the inputs are in an $N \times m$ matrix. So to do the multiplication `np.dot(inputs,targets - activations)` we need to turn the `inputs` matrix around so that it is $m \times N$. This is done using the `np.transpose()` function, which swaps the rows and columns over (so using matrix a above again) we get:

```
>>> np.transpose(a)
array([[3, 2],
       [4, 3],
       [5, 4]])
```

Once we have that, the weight update for the entire network can be done in one line (where `eta` is the learning rate, η):

```
self.weights -= eta*np.dot(np.transpose(inputs),self.activations-targets)
```

Assuming that you make sure in advance that all your input matrices are the correct size (the `np.shape()` function, which tells you the number of elements in each dimension of the array, is helpful here), the only things that are needed are to add those extra -1's onto the input vectors for the bias node, and to decide what values we should put into the weights to start with. The first of these can be done using the `np.concatenate()` function, making a one-dimensional array that contains -1 as all of its elements, and adding it on to the inputs array (note that `nData` in the code is equivalent to N in the text):

```
inputs = np.concatenate((inputs,-np.ones((self.nData,1))),axis=1)
```

The last thing we need to do is to give initial values to the weights. It is possible to set them all to be zero, and the algorithm will get to the right answer. However, instead we will assign small random numbers to the weights, for reasons that will be discussed in Section 4.2.2. Again, NumPy has a nice way to do this, using the built-in random number generator (with `nin` corresponding to m and `nout` to n):

```
weights = np.random.rand(nIn+1,nOut)*0.1-0.05
```

At this point we have seen all the snippets of code that are required, and putting them together should not be a problem. The entire program is available from the book website as pcn.py. Note that this is a different version of the algorithm because it is a batch version: all of the inputs go forward through the algorithm, and then the error is computed and the weights are changed. This is different to the sequential version that was written down in the first algorithm. The batch version is simpler to write in Python and often works better.

We now move on to seeing the code working, starting with the OR example that was used in the hand-worked demonstration.

Making the OR data is easy, and then running the code requires importing it using its filename (pcn) and then calling the pcntrain function. The print-out below shows the instructions to set up the arrays and call the function, and the output of the weights for 5 iterations of a particular run of the program, starting from random initial points (note that the weights stop changing after the 1st iteration in this case, and that different runs will produce different values).

```
>>> import numpy as np
>>> inputs = np.array([[0,0],[0,1],[1,0],[1,1]])
>>> targets = np.array([[0],[1],[1],[1]])
>>> import pcn_logic_eg
>>>
>>> p = pcn_logic_eg.pcn(inputs,targets)
>>> p.pcntrain(inputs,targets,0.25,6)
Iteration:  0
[[-0.03755646]
 [ 0.01484562]
 [ 0.21173977]]
Final outputs are:
[[0]
 [0]
 [0]
 [0]]
Iteration:  1
[[ 0.46244354]
 [ 0.51484562]
 [-0.53826023]]
Final outputs are:
[[1]
 [1]
 [1]
 [1]]
Iteration:  2
[[ 0.46244354]
 [ 0.51484562]
 [-0.28826023]]
```

```
Final outputs are:
[[1]
 [1]
 [1]
 [1]]
Iteration:  3
[[ 0.46244354]
 [ 0.51484562]
 [-0.03826023]]
Final outputs are:
[[1]
 [1]
 [1]
 [1]]
Iteration:  4
[[ 0.46244354]
 [ 0.51484562]
 [ 0.21173977]]
Final outputs are:
[[0]
 [1]
 [1]
 [1]]
Iteration:  5
[[ 0.46244354]
 [ 0.51484562]
 [ 0.21173977]]
Final outputs are:
[[0]
 [1]
 [1]
 [1]]
```

We have trained the Perceptron on the four datapoints $(0,0), (1,0), (0,1)$, and $(1,1)$. However, we could put in an input like $(0.8, 0.8)$ and expect to get an output from the neural network. Obviously, it wouldn't make any sense from the logic function point-of-view, but most of the things that we do with neural networks will be more interesting than that, anyway. Figure 3.6 shows the **decision boundary**, which shows when the decision about which class to categorise the input as changes from crosses to circles. We will see why this is a straight line in Section 3.4.

Before returning the weights, the Perceptron algorithm above prints out the outputs for the trained inputs. You can also use the network to predict the outputs for other values by using the `pcnfwd` function. However, you need to manually add the -1s on in this case, using:

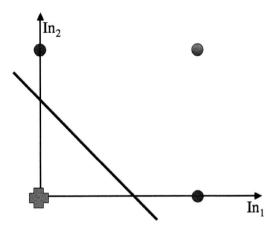

FIGURE 3.6 The decision boundary computed by a Perceptron for the OR function.

```
>>> # Add the inputs that match the bias node
>>> inputs_bias = np.concatenate((inputs,-np.ones((np.shape(inputs)[0],1))),↵
axis=1)
>>> pcn.pcnfwd(inputs_bias,weights)
```

The results on this test data are what you can use in order to compute the accuracy of the training algorithm using the methods that were described in Section 2.2.

In terms of learning about a set of data we have now reached the stage that neural networks were up to in 1969. Then, two researchers, Minsky and Papert, published a book called "Perceptrons." The purpose of the book was to stimulate neural network research by discussing the learning capabilities of the Perceptron, and showing what the network could and could not learn. Unfortunately, the book had another effect: it effectively killed neural network research for about 20 years. To see why, we need to think about how the Perceptron learns in a different way.

3.4 LINEAR SEPARABILITY

What does the Perceptron actually compute? For our one output neuron example of the OR data it tries to separate out the cases where the neuron should fire from those where it shouldn't. Looking at the graph on the right side of Figure 3.4, you should be able to draw a straight line that separates out the crosses from the circles without difficulty (it is done in Figure 3.6). In fact, that is exactly what the Perceptron does: it tries to find a straight line (in 2D, a plane in 3D, and a hyperplane in higher dimensions) where the neuron fires on one side of the line, and doesn't on the other. This line is called the decision boundary or discriminant function, and an example of one is given in Figure 3.7.

To see this, think about the matrix notation we used in the implementation, but consider just one input vector $\mathbf{x}$. The neuron fires if $\mathbf{x} \cdot \mathbf{w}^T \geq 0$ (where $\mathbf{w}$ is the row of $\mathbf{W}$ that connects the inputs to one particular neuron; they are the same for the OR example, since there is only one neuron, and $\mathbf{w}^T$ denotes the transpose of $\mathbf{w}$ and is used to make both of the vectors into column vectors). The $\mathbf{a} \cdot \mathbf{b}$ notation describes the inner or scalar product between two

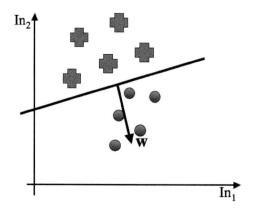

FIGURE 3.7 A decision boundary separating two classes of data.

vectors. It is computed by multiplying each element of the first vector by the matching element of the second and adding them all together. As you might remember from high school, $\mathbf{a} \cdot \mathbf{b} = \|a\|\|b\| \cos\theta$, where θ is the angle between $\mathbf{a}$ and $\mathbf{b}$ and $\|a\|$ is the length of the vector $\mathbf{a}$. So the inner product computes a function of the angle between the two vectors, scaled by their lengths. It can be computed in NumPy using the `np.inner()` function.

Getting back to the Perceptron, the boundary case is where we find an input vector $\mathbf{x}_1$ that has $\mathbf{x}_1 \cdot \mathbf{w}^T = 0$. Now suppose that we find another input vector $\mathbf{x}_2$ that satisfies $\mathbf{x}_2 \cdot \mathbf{w}^T = 0$. Putting these two equations together we get:

$$\mathbf{x}_1 \cdot \mathbf{w}^T = \mathbf{x}_2 \cdot \mathbf{w}^T \tag{3.16}$$
$$\Rightarrow (\mathbf{x}_1 - \mathbf{x}_2) \cdot \mathbf{w}^T = 0. \tag{3.17}$$

What does this last equation mean? In order for the inner product to be 0, either $\|a\|$ or $\|b\|$ or $\cos\theta$ needs to be zero. There is no reason to believe that $\|a\|$ or $\|b\|$ should be 0, so $\cos\theta = 0$. This means that $\theta = \pi/2$ (or $-\pi/2$), which means that the two vectors are at right angles to each other. Now $\mathbf{x}_1 - \mathbf{x}_2$ is a straight line between two points that lie on the decision boundary, and the weight vector $\mathbf{w}^T$ must be perpendicular to that, as in Figure 3.7.

So given some data, and the associated target outputs, the Perceptron simply tries to find a straight line that divides the examples where each neuron fires from those where it does not. This is great if that straight line exists, but is a bit of a problem otherwise. The cases where there is a straight line are called linearly separable cases. What happens if the classes that we want to learn about are not linearly separable? It turns out that making such a function is very easy: there is even one that matches a logic function. Before we have a look at it, it is worth thinking about what happens when we have more than one output neuron. The weights for each neuron separately describe a straight line, so by putting together several neurons we get several straight lines that each try to separate different parts of the space. Figure 3.8 shows an example of decision boundaries computed by a Perceptron with four neurons; by putting them together we can get good separation of the classes.

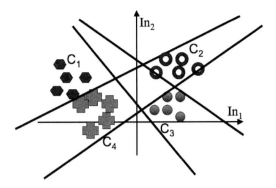

FIGURE 3.8 Different decision boundaries computed by a Perceptron with four neurons.

3.4.1 The Perceptron Convergence Theorem

Actually, it is not quite true that we have reached 1969. There is one more important fact that was known: Rosenblatt's 1962 proof that, given a linearly separable dataset, the Perceptron will converge to a solution that separates the classes, and that it will do it after a finite number of iterations. In fact, the number of iterations is bounded by $1/\gamma^2$, where γ is the distance between the separating hyperplane and the closest datapoint to it. The proof of this theorem only requires some algebra, and so we will work through it here. We will assume that the length of every input vector $\|\mathbf{x}\| \leq 1$, although it isn't strictly necessary provided that they are bounded by some constant R.

First, we know that there is some weight vector $\mathbf{w}^*$ that separates the data, since we have assumed that it is linearly separable. The Perceptron learning algorithm aims to find some vector $\mathbf{w}$ that is parallel to $\mathbf{w}^*$, or as close as possible. To see whether two vectors are parallel we use the inner product $\mathbf{w}^* \cdot \mathbf{w}$. When the two vectors are parallel, the angle between them is $\theta = 0$ and so $\cos\theta = 1$, and so the size of the inner product is a maximum. If we therefore show that at each weight update $\mathbf{w}^* \cdot \mathbf{w}$ increases, then we have nearly shown that the algorithm will converge. However, we do need a little bit more, because $\mathbf{w}^* \cdot \mathbf{w} = \|\mathbf{w}^*\|\|\mathbf{w}\| \cos\theta$, and so we also need to check that the length of $\mathbf{w}$ does not increase too much as well.

Hence, when we consider a weight update, there are two checks that we need to make: the value of $\mathbf{w}^* \cdot \mathbf{w}$ and the length of $\mathbf{w}$.

Suppose that at the tth iteration of the algorithm, the network sees a particular input $\mathbf{x}$ that should have output y, and that it gets this input wrong, so $y\mathbf{w}^{(t-1)} \cdot \mathbf{x} < 0$, where the $(t-1)$ index means the weights at the $(t-1)$st step. This means that the weights need to be updated. This weight update will be $\mathbf{w}^{(t)} = \mathbf{w}^{(t-1)} + y\mathbf{x}$ (where we have set $\eta = 1$ for simplicity, and because it is fine for the Perceptron.

To see how this changes the two values we are interested in, we need to do some computation:

$$
\begin{aligned}
\mathbf{w}^* \cdot \mathbf{w}^{(t)} &= \mathbf{w}^* \cdot \left(\mathbf{w}^{(t-1)} + y\mathbf{x}\right) \\
&= \mathbf{w}^* \cdot \mathbf{w}^{(t-1)} + y\mathbf{w}^* \cdot \mathbf{x} \\
&\geq \mathbf{w}^* \cdot \mathbf{w}^{(t-1)} + \gamma
\end{aligned}
\tag{3.18}
$$

In$_1$	In$_2$	t
0	0	0
0	1	1
1	0	1
1	1	0

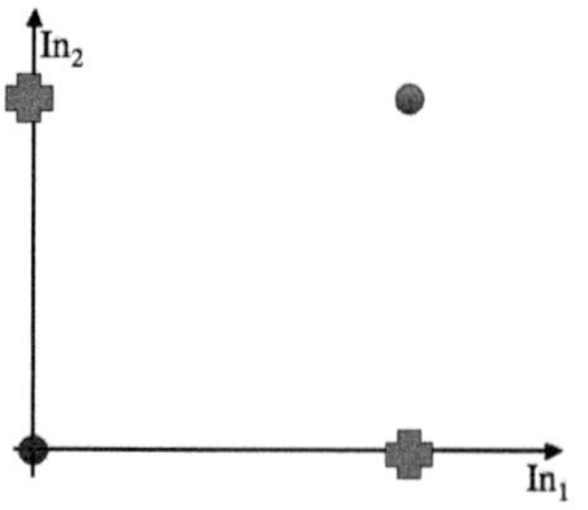

FIGURE 3.9 Data for the XOR logic function and a plot of the four datapoints.

where γ is that smallest distance between the optimal hyperplane defined by $\mathbf{w}^*$ and any datapoint.

This means that at each update of the weights, this inner product increases by at least γ, and so after t updates of the weights, $\mathbf{w}^* \cdot \mathbf{w}^{(t)} \geq t\gamma$. We can use this to put a lower bound on the length of $\|\mathbf{w}^{(t)}\|$ by using the Cauchy–Schwartz inequality, which tells us that $\mathbf{w}^* \cdot \mathbf{w}^{(t)} \leq \|\mathbf{w}^*\|\|\mathbf{w}^{(t)}\|$ and so $\|\mathbf{w}^{(t)}\| \geq t\gamma$.

The length of the weight vector after t steps is:

$$
\begin{aligned}
\|\mathbf{w}^{(t)}\|^2 &= \|\mathbf{w}^{(t-1)} + y\mathbf{x}\|^2 \\
&= \|\mathbf{w}^{(t-1)}\|^2 + y^2\|\mathbf{x}\|^2 + 2y\mathbf{w}^{(t-1)} \cdot \mathbf{x} \\
&\leq \|\mathbf{w}^{(t-1)}\|^2 + 1
\end{aligned}
\tag{3.19}
$$

where the last line follows because $y^2 = 1$, $\|\mathbf{x}\| \leq 1$, and the network made an error, so the $\mathbf{w}^{(t-1)}$ and $\mathbf{x}$ are perpendicular to each other. This tells us that after t steps, $\|\mathbf{w}^{(t)}\|^2 \leq k$.

We can put these two inequalities together to get that:

$$
t\gamma \leq \|\mathbf{w}^{(t-1)}\| \leq \sqrt{t},
\tag{3.20}
$$

and so $t \leq 1/\gamma^2$. Hence after we have made that many updates the algorithm must have converged.

We have shown that if the weights are linearly separable then the algorithm will converge, and that the time that this takes is a function of the distance between the separating hyperplane and the nearest datapoint. This is called the margin, and in Chapter 8 we will see an algorithm that uses this explicitly. Note that the Perceptron stops learning as soon as it gets all of the training data correct, and so there is no guarantee that it will find the largest margin, just that if there is a linear separator, it will find it. Further, we still don't know what happens if the data are not linearly separable. To see that, we will move on to just such an example.

3.4.2 The Exclusive Or (XOR) Function

The XOR has the same four input points as the OR function, but looking at Figure 3.9, you should be able to convince yourself that you can't draw a straight line on the graph that separates true from false (crosses from circles). In our new language, the XOR function is not linearly separable. If the analysis above is correct, then the Perceptron will fail to get the correct answer, and using the Perceptron code above we find:

```
>>> targets = np.array([[0],[1],[1],[0]])
>>> pcn.pcntrain(inputs,targets,0.25,15)
```

which gives the following output (the early iterations have been missed out):

```
Iteration:  11
[[ 0.45946905]
 [-0.27886266]
 [-0.25662428]]
Iteration:  12
[[-0.04053095]
 [-0.02886266]
 [-0.00662428]]
Iteration:  13
[[ 0.45946905]
 [-0.27886266]
 [-0.25662428]]
Iteration:  14
[[-0.04053095]
 [-0.02886266]
 [-0.00662428]]
Final outputs are:
[[0]
 [0]
 [0]
 [0]]
```

You can see that the algorithm does not converge, but keeps on cycling through two different wrong solutions. Running it for longer does not change this behaviour. So even for a simple logical function, the Perceptron can fail to learn the correct answer. This is what was demonstrated by Minsky and Papert in "Perceptrons," and the discovery that the Perceptron was not capable of solving even these problems, let alone more interesting ones, is what halted neural network development for so long. There is an obvious solution to the problem, which is to make the network more complicated—add in more neurons, with more complicated connections between them, and see if that helps. The trouble is that this makes the problem of training the network much more difficult. In fact, working out how to do that is the topic of the next chapter.

3.4.3   A Useful Insight

From the discussion in Section 3.4.2 you might think that the XOR function is impossible to solve using a linear function. In fact, this is not true. If we rewrite the problem in three dimensions instead of two, then it is perfectly possible to find a plane (the 2D analogue of a straight line) that can separate the two classes. There is a picture of this in Figure 3.10. Writing the problem in 3D means including a third input dimension that does not change the data when it is looked at in the (x, y) plane, but moves the point at $(0, 0)$ along a third

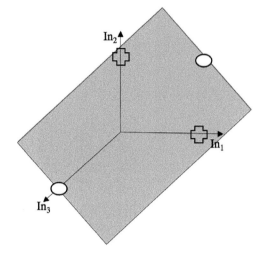

In₁	In₂	In₃	Output
0	0	1	1
0	1	0	0
1	0	0	0
1	1	0	1

FIGURE 3.10 A decision boundary (the shaded plane) solving the XOR problem in 3D with the crosses below the surface and the circles above it.

dimension. So the truth table for the function is the one shown on the left side of Figure 3.10 (where 'In₃' has been added, and only affects the point at $(0,0)$).

To demonstrate this, the following listing uses the same Perceptron code:

```
>>> inputs = np.array([[0,0,1],[0,1,0],[1,0,0],[1,1,0]])
>>> pcn.pcntrain(inputs,targets,0.25,15)
Iteration: 14
[[-0.27757663]
 [-0.21083089]
 [-0.23124407]
 [-0.53808657]]
Final outputs are:
[[0]
 [1]
 [1]
 [0]]
```

In fact, it is always possible to separate out two classes with a linear function, provided that you project the data into the correct set of dimensions. There is a whole class of methods for doing this reasonably efficiently, called kernel classifiers, which are the basis of Support Vector Machines, which are the subject of Chapter 8.

For now, it is sufficient to point out that if you want to make your linear Perceptron do non-linear things, then there is nothing to stop you making non-linear variables. For example, Figure 3.11 shows two versions of the same dataset. On the left side, the coordinates are x_1 and x_2, while on the right side the coordinates are x_1, x_2 and $x_1 \times x_2$. It is now easy to fit a plane (the 2D equivalent of a straight line) that separates the data.

Statistics has been dealing with problems of classification and regression for a long time, before we had computers in order to do difficult arithmetic for us, and so straight

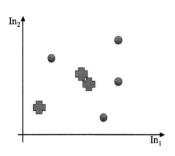 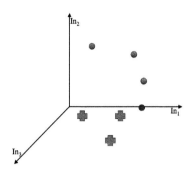

FIGURE 3.11 *Left:* Non-separable 2D dataset. *Right:* The same dataset with third coordinate $x_1 \times x_2$, which makes it separable.

line methods have been around in statistics for many years. They provide a different (and useful) way to understand what is happening in learning, and by using both statistical and computer science methods we can get a good understanding of the whole area. We will see the statistical method of linear regression in Section 3.5, but first we will work through another example of using the Perceptron. This is meant to be a tutorial example, so I will give some of the relevant code and results, but leave places for you to fill in the gaps.

3.4.4 Another Example: The Pima Indian Dataset

The UCI Machine Learning Repository (http://archive.ics.uci.edu/ml/) holds lots of datasets that are used to demonstrate and test machine learning algorithms. For the purposes of testing out the Perceptron and Linear Regressor, we are going to use one that is very well known. It provides eight measurements of a group of American Pima Indians living in Arizona in the USA, and the classification is whether or not each person had diabetes. The dataset is available from the UCI repository (called **Pima**) and there is a file inside the folder giving details of what the different variables mean.

Once you have downloaded it, import the relevant modules (NumPy to use the array methods, PyLab to plot the data, and the Perceptron from the book website) and then load the data into Python. This requires something like the following (where not all of the **import** lines are used immediately, but will be required as more code is developed):

```
>>> import os
>>> import pylab as pl
>>> import numpy as np
>>> import pcn

>>> os.chdir('/Users/srmarsla/Book/Datasets/pima')
>>> pima = np.loadtxt('pima-indians-diabetes.data',delimiter=',')
>>> np.shape(pima)
(768, 9)
```

where the path in the **os.chdir** line will obviously need to be changed to wherever you have saved the dataset. In the **np.loadtxt()** command the **delimiter** specifies which character is used to separate out the datapoints. The **np.shape()** method tells that there are 768

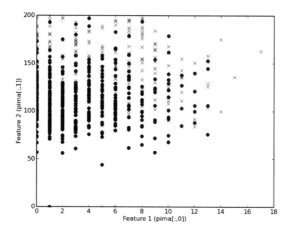

FIGURE 3.12 Plot of the first two dimensions of the Pima Indians dataset showing the two classes as 'x' and 'o'.

datapoints, arranged as rows of the file, with each row containing nine numbers. These are the eight dimensions of data, with the class being the ninth element of each line (indexed as 8 since Python is zero-indexed). This arrangement, with each line of a file (or row of an array) being a datapoint is the one that will be used throughout the book.

You should have a look at the dataset. Obviously, you can't plot the whole thing at once, since that would require being able to visualise eight dimensions. But you can plot any two-dimensional subset of the data. Have a look at a few of them. In order to see the two different classes in the data in your plot, you will have to work out how to use the **np.where** command. Once you have worked that out, you will be able to plot them with different shapes and colours. The **pl.plot** command is in Matplotlib, so you'll need to import that (using **import pylab as pl**) beforehand. Assuming that you have worked out some way to store the indices of one class in **indices0** and the other in **indices1** you can use:

```
pl.ion()
pl.plot(pima[indices0,0],pima[indices0,1],'go')
pl.plot(pima[indices1,0],pima[indices1,1],'rx')
pl.show()
```

to plot the first two dimensions as green circles and red crosses, which (up to colour, of course) should look like Figure 3.12. The **pl.ion()** command ensures that the data is actually plotted, and might not be needed depending upon your precise software setup; this is also true of the **pl.show()** command, which ensures that the graph does not vanish when the program terminates. Clearly, there is no way that you can find a linear separation between these two classes with these features. However, you should have a look at some of the other combinations of features and see if you can find any that are better.

The next thing to do is to try using the Perceptron on the full dataset. You will need to try out different values for the learning rate and the number of iterations for the Perceptron, but you should find that you can get around 50-70% correct (use the confusion matrix method `confmat()` to get the results). This isn't too bad, but it isn't that good, either. The results are quite unstable, too; sometimes the results have only 30% accuracy—worse than chance—which is rather depressing.

```
p = pcn.pcn(pima[:,:8],pima[:,8:9])
p.pcntrain(pima[:,:8],pima[:,8:9],0.25,100)
p.confmat(pima[:,:8],pima[:,8:9])
```

This is, of course, unfair testing, since we are testing the network on the same data we were training it on, and we have already seen that this is unfair in Section 2.2, but we will do something quick now, which is to use even-numbered datapoints for training, and odd-numbered datapoints for testing. This is very easy using the : operator, where we specify the start point, the end point, and the step size. NumPy will fill in any that we leave blank with the beginning or end of the array as appropriate.

```
trainin = pima[::2,:8]
testin = pima[1::2,:8]
traintgt = pima[::2,8:9]
testtgt = pima[1::2,8:9]
```

For now, rather than worrying about training and testing data, we are more interested in working out how to improve the results. And we can do better by preparing the data a little, or **preprocessing** it.

3.4.5 Preprocessing: Data Preparation

Machine learning algorithms tend to learn much more effectively if the inputs and targets are prepared for analysis before the network is trained. As the most basic example, the neurons that we are using give outputs of 0 and 1, and so if the target values are not 0 and 1, then they should be transformed so that they are. In fact, it is normal to scale the targets to lie between 0 and 1 no matter what kind of activation function is used for the output layer neurons. This helps to stop the weights from getting too large unnecessarily. Scaling the inputs also helps to avoid this problem.

The most common approach to scaling the input data is to treat each data dimension independently, and then to either make each dimension have zero mean and unit variance in each dimension, or simply to scale them so that maximum value is 1 and the minimum -1. Both of these scalings have similar effects, but the first is a little bit better as it does not allow outliers to dominate as much. These scalings are commonly referred to as data **normalisation**, or sometimes **standardisation**. While normalisation is not essential for every algorithm, but it is usually beneficial, and for some of the other algorithms that we will see, the normalisation will be essential.

In NumPy it is very easy to perform the normalisation by using the built-in `np.mean()` and `np.var()` functions; the only place where care is needed is along which axis the mean and variance are computed: `axis=0` sums down the columns and `axis=1` sums across the rows. Note that only the input variables are normalised in this code. This is not always true, but here the target variable already has values 0 and 1, which are the possible outputs for the Perceptron, and we don't want to change that.

```
data = (data - data.mean(axis=0))/data.var(axis=0)
targets = (targets - targets.mean(axis=0))/targets.var(axis=0)
```

There is one thing to be careful of, which is that if you normalise the training and testing sets separately in this way then a datapoint that is in both sets will end up being different in the two, since the mean and variance are probably different in the two sets. For this reason it is a good idea to normalise the dataset before splitting it into training and testing.

Normalisation can be done without knowing anything about the dataset in advance. However, there is often useful preprocessing that can be done by looking at the data. For example, in the Pima dataset, column 0 is the number of times that the person has been pregnant (did I mention that all the subjects were female?) and column 7 is the age of the person. Taking the pregnancy variable first, there are relatively few subjects that were pregnant 8 or more times, so rather than having the number there, maybe they should be replaced by an 8 for any of these values. Equally, the age would be better **quantised** into a set of ranges such as 21–30, 31–40, etc. (the minimum age is 21 in the dataset). This can be done using the **np.where** function again, as in this code snippet. If you make these changes and similar ones for the other values, then you should be able to get massively better results.

```
pima[np.where(pima[:,0]>8),0] = 8

pima[np.where(pima[:,7]<=30),7] = 1
pima[np.where((pima[:,7]>30) & (pima[:,7]<=40)),7] = 2
#You need to finish this data processing step
```

The last thing that we can do for now is to perform a basic form of **feature selection** and to try training the classifier with a subset of the inputs by missing out different features one at a time and seeing if they make the results better. If missing out one feature does improve the results, then leave it out completely and try missing out others as well. This is a simplistic way of testing for **correlation** between the output and each of the features. We will see better methods when we look at covariance in Section 2.4.2. We can also consider methods of **dimensionality reduction**, which produce lower dimensionsal representations of the data that still include the relevant information; see Chapter 6 for more details.

Now that we have seen how to use the Perceptron on a better example than the logic functions, we will look at another linear method, but coming from statistics, rather than neural networks.

3.5 LINEAR REGRESSION

As is common in statistics, we need to separate out regression problems, where we fit a line to data, from classification problems, where we find a line that separates out the classes, so that they can be distinguished. However, it is common to turn classification problems into regression problems. This can be done in two ways, first by introducing an **indicator variable**, which simply says which class each datapoint belongs to. The problem is now to use the data to **predict** the indicator variable, which is a regression problem. The second approach is to do repeated regression, once for each class, with the indicator value being 1

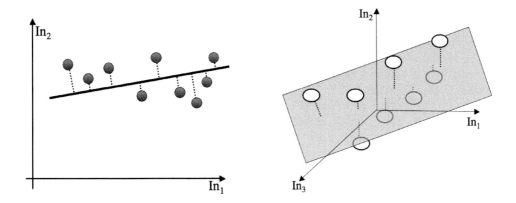

FIGURE 3.13 Linear regression in two and three dimensions.

for examples in the class and 0 for all of the others. Since classification can be replaced by regression using these methods, we'll think about regression here.

The only real difference between the Perceptron and more statistical approaches is in the way that the problem is set up. For regression we are making a prediction about an unknown value y (such as the indicator variable for classes or a future value of some data) by computing some function of known values x_i. We are thinking about straight lines, so the output y is going to be a sum of the x_i values, each multiplied by a constant parameter: $y = \sum_{i=0}^{M} \beta_i x_i$. The β_i define a straight line (plane in 3D, hyperplane in higher dimensions) that goes through (or at least near) the datapoints. Figure 3.13 shows this in two and three dimensions.

The question is how we define the line (plane or hyperplane in higher dimensions) that best fits the data. The most common solution is to try to minimise the distance between each datapoint and the line that we fit. We can measure the distance between a point and a line by defining another line that goes through the point and hits the line. School geometry tells us that this second line will be shortest when it hits the line at right angles, and then we can use Pythagoras' theorem to know the distance. Now, we can try to minimise an error function that measures the sum of all these distances. If we ignore the square roots, and just minimise the sum-of-squares of the errors, then we get the most common minimisation, which is known as least-squares optimisation. What we are doing is choosing the parameters in order to minimise the squared difference between the prediction and the actual data value, summed over all of the datapoints. That is, we have:

$$\sum_{j=0}^{N} \left(t_j - \sum_{i=0}^{M} \beta_i x_{ij} \right)^2 . \tag{3.21}$$

This can be written in matrix form as:

$$(\mathbf{t} - \mathbf{X}\boldsymbol{\beta})^T (\mathbf{t} - \mathbf{X}\boldsymbol{\beta}), \tag{3.22}$$

where $\mathbf{t}$ is a column vector containing the targets and $\mathbf{X}$ is the matrix of input values (even including the bias inputs), just as for the Perceptron. Computing the smallest value of this means differentiating it with respect to the (column) parameter vector $\boldsymbol{\beta}$ and setting the derivative to 0, which means that $\mathbf{X}^T (\mathbf{t} - \mathbf{X}\boldsymbol{\beta}) = 0$ (to see this, expand out the brackets, remembering that $\mathbf{A}\mathbf{B}^T = \mathbf{B}^T\mathbf{A}$ and note that the term $\boldsymbol{\beta}^T \mathbf{X}^t \mathbf{t} = \mathbf{t}^T \mathbf{X}\boldsymbol{\beta}$ since they are both a scalar term), which has the solution $\boldsymbol{\beta} = (\mathbf{X}^T\mathbf{X})^{-1}\mathbf{X}^T\mathbf{t}$ (assuming that the matrix $\mathbf{X}^T\mathbf{X}$ can be inverted). Now, for a given input vector $\mathbf{z}$, the prediction is $\mathbf{z}\boldsymbol{\beta}$. The inverse of a matrix $\mathbf{X}$ is the matrix that satisfies $\mathbf{XX}^{-1} = \mathbf{I}$, where $\mathbf{I}$ is the identity matrix, the matrix that has 1s on the leading diagonal and 0s everywhere else. The inverse of a matrix only exists if the matrix is square (has the same number of rows as columns) and its **determinant** is non-zero.

Computing this is very simple in Python, using the `np.linalg.inv()` function in NumPy. In fact, the entire function can be written as (where the ⟩ symbol denotes a linebreak in the text, so that the command continues on the next line):

```
def linreg(inputs,targets):
        inputs = np.concatenate((inputs,-np.ones((np.shape(inputs)[0],1))),⟩
        axis=1)
        beta = np.dot(np.dot(np.linalg.inv(np.dot(np.transpose(inputs),⟩
        inputs)),np.transpose(inputs)),targets)

        outputs = np.dot(inputs,beta)
```

3.5.1 Linear Regression Examples

Using the linear regressor on the logical OR function seems a rather strange thing to do, since we are performing classification using a method designed explicitly for regression, trying to fit a surface to a set of 0 and 1 points. Worse, we will view it as an error if we get say 1.25 and the output should be 1, so points that are in some sense too correct will receive a penalty! However, we can do it, and it gives the following outputs:

```
[[ 0.25]
 [ 0.75]
 [ 0.75]
 [ 1.25]]
```

It might not be clear what this means, but if we **threshold** the outputs by setting every value less than 0.5 to 0 and every value above 0.5 to 1, then we get the correct answer. Using it on the XOR function shows that this is still a linear method:

```
[[ 0.5]
 [ 0.5]
 [ 0.5]
 [ 0.5]]
```

A better test of linear regression is to find a real regression dataset. The UCI database is useful here, as well. We will look at the **auto-mpg** dataset. This consists of a collection of a number of datapoints about certain cars (weight, horsepower, etc.), with the aim being to predict the fuel efficiency in miles per gallon (mpg). This dataset has one problem. There are missing values in it (labelled with question marks '?'). The `np.loadtxt()` method doesn't like these, and we don't know what to do with them, anyway, so after downloading the dataset, manually edit the file and delete all lines where there is a ? in that line. The linear regressor can't do much with the names of the cars either, but since they appear in quotes (") we will tell `np.loadtxt` that they are comments, using:

```
auto = np.loadtxt('/Users/srmarsla/Book/Datasets/auto-mpg/auto-mpg.data.txt',
comments='"')
```

You should now separate the data into training and testing sets, and then use the training set to recover the β vector. Then you use that to get the predicted values on the test set. However, the confusion matrix isn't much use now, since there are no classes to enable us to analyse the results. Instead, we will use the sum-of-squares error, which consists of computing the difference between the prediction and the true value, squaring them so that they are all positive, and then adding them up, as is used in the definition of the linear regressor. Obviously, small values of this measure are good. It can be computed using:

```
beta = linreg.linreg(trainin,traintgt)

testin = np.concatenate((testin,-np.ones((np.shape(testin)[0],1))),axis=1)
testout = np.dot(testin,beta)
error = np.sum((testout - testtgt)**2)
```

Now you can test out whether normalising the data helps, and perform feature selection as we did for the Perceptron. There are other more advanced linear statistical methods. One of them, Linear Discriminant Analysis, will be considered in Section 6.1 once we have built up the understanding we need.

FURTHER READING

If you are interested in real brains and want to know more about them, then there are plenty of popular science books that should interest you, including:

- Susan Greenfield. *The Human Brain: A Guided Tour*. Orion, London, UK, 2001.

- S. Aamodt and S. Wang. *Welcome to Your Brain: Why You Lose Your Car Keys but Never Forget How to Drive and Other Puzzles of Everyday Life*. Bloomsbury, London, UK, 2008.

If you are looking for something a bit more formal, then the following is a good place to start (particularly the 'Roadmaps' at the beginning):

- Michael A. Arbib, editor. *The Handbook of Brain Theory and Neural Networks*, 2nd edition, MIT Press, Cambridge, MA, USA, 2002.

The original paper by McCulloch and Pitts is:

- W.S. McCulloch and W. Pitts. A logical calculus of ideas imminent in nervous activity. *Bulletin of Mathematics Biophysics*, 5:115–133, 1943.

There is a very nice motivation for neural network-based learning in:

- V. Braitenberg. *Vehicles: Experiments in Synthetic Psychology.* MIT Press, Cambridge, MA, USA, 1984.

If you want to know more about the history of neural networks, then the original paper on the Perceptron and the book that showed the requirement of linear separability (and that some people blame for putting the field back 20 years) still make interesting reads. Another paper that might be of interest is the review article written by Widrow and Lehr, which summarises some of the seminal work:

- F. Rosenblatt. The Perceptron: A probabilistic model for information storage and organization in the brain. *Psychological Review*, 65(6):386–408, 1958.

- M.L. Minsky and S.A. Papert. *Perceptrons: An Introduction to Computational Geometry.* MIT Press, Cambridge MA, 1969.

- B. Widrow and M.A. Lehr. 30 years of adaptive neural networks: Perceptron, madaline, and backpropagation. *Proceedings of the IEEE*, 78(9):1415–1442, 1990.

Textbooks that cover the same material, although from different viewpoints, include:

- Chapter 5 of R.O. Duda, P.E. Hart, and D.G. Stork. *Pattern Classification*, 2nd edition, Wiley-Interscience, New York, USA, 2001.

- Sections 3.1–3.3 of T. Hastie, R. Tibshirani, and J. Friedman. *The Elements of Statistical Learning*, 2nd edition, Springer, Berlin, Germany, 2008.

PRACTICE QUESTIONS

Problem 3.1 Consider a neuron with 2 inputs, 1 output, and a threshold activation function. If the two weights are $w_1 = 1$ and $w_2 = 1$, and the bias is $b = -1.5$, then what is the output for input $(0, 0)$? What about for inputs $(1, 0)$, $(0, 1)$, and $(1, 1)$?

Draw the discriminant function for this function, and write down its equation. Does it correspond to any particular logic gate?

Problem 3.2 Work out the Perceptrons that construct logical NOT, NAND, and NOR of their inputs.

Problem 3.3 The parity problem returns 1 if the number of inputs that are 1 is even, and 0 otherwise. Can a Perceptron learn this problem for 3 inputs? Design the network and try it.

Problem 3.4 Test out both the Perceptron and linear regressor code from the website on the parity problem.

Problem 3.5 The Perceptron code on the website is a batch update algorithm, where the whole of the dataset is fed in to find the errors, and then the weights are updated afterwards, as is discussed in Section 3.3.5. Convert the code to run as sequential updates and then compare the results of using the two versions.

Problem 3.6 Try to think of some interesting image processing tasks that cannot be performed by a Perceptron. (Hint: You need to think of tasks where looking at individual pixels isn't enough to allow classification.)

Problem 3.7 The decision boundary hyperplane found by the Perceptron has equation $y(\mathbf{x}) = \mathbf{w}^T\mathbf{x} + b = 0$. For a point $\mathbf{x}'$, minimise $\|\mathbf{x} - \mathbf{x}'\|^2$ to show that the shortest distance from the point to the hyperplane is $|y(\mathbf{x}')|/\|\mathbf{w}\|$.

Problem 3.8 There is a link to a very large dataset of handwritten figures on the book website (the MNIST dataset). Download it and use a Perceptron to learn about the dataset.

Problem 3.9 For the prostate data available via the website, use both the Perceptron and logistic regressor and compare the results.

Problem 3.10 In the Perceptron Convergence Theorem proof we assumed that $\|\mathbf{x}\| \leq 1$. Modify the proof so that it only assumes that $\|\mathbf{x}\| \leq R$ for some constant R.

## CHAPTER 4

The Multi-layer Perceptron

In the last chapter we saw that while linear models are easy to understand and use, they come with the inherent cost that is implied by the word 'linear'; that is, they can only identify straight lines, planes, or hyperplanes. And this is not usually enough, because the majority of interesting problems are not linearly separable. In Section 3.4 we saw that problems can be made linearly separable if we can work out how to transform the features suitably. We will come back to this idea in Chapter 8, but in this chapter we will instead consider making more complicated networks.

We have pretty much decided that the learning in the neural network happens in the weights. So, to perform more computation it seems sensible to add more weights. There are two things that we can do: add some backwards connections, so that the output neurons connect to the inputs again, or add more neurons. The first approach leads into recurrent networks. These have been studied, but are not that commonly used. We will instead consider the second approach. We can add neurons between the input nodes and the outputs, and this will make more complex neural networks, such as the one shown in Figure 4.1.

We will think about why adding extra layers of nodes makes a neural network more powerful in Section 4.3.2, but for now, to persuade ourselves that it is true, we can check that a prepared network can solve the two-dimensional XOR problem, something that we have seen is not possible for a linear model like the Perceptron. A suitable network is shown in Figure 4.2. To check that it gives the correct answers, all that is required is to put in each input and work through the network, treating it as two different Perceptrons, first computing the activations of the neurons in the middle layer (labelled as C and D in Figure 4.2) and then using those activations as the inputs to the single neuron at the output. As an example, I'll work out what happens when you put in $(1, 0)$ as an input; the job of checking the rest is up to you.

Input $(1, 0)$ corresponds to node A being 1 and B being 0. The input to neuron C is therefore $-1 \times 0.5 + 1 \times 1 + 0 \times 1 = -0.5 + 1 = 0.5$. This is above the threshold of 0, and so neuron C fires, giving output 1. For neuron D the input is $-1 \times 1 + 1 \times 1 + 0 \times 1 = -1 + 1 = 0$, and so it does not fire, giving output 0. Therefore the input to neuron E is $-1 \times 0.5 + 1 \times 1 + 0 \times -1 = 0.5$, so neuron E fires. Checking the result of the inputs should persuade you that neuron E fires when inputs A and B are different to each other, but does not fire when they are the same, which is exactly the XOR function (it doesn't matter that the fire and not fire have been reversed).

So far, so good. Since this network can solve a problem that the Perceptron cannot, it seems worth looking into further. However, now we've got a much more interesting problem to solve, namely how can we train this network so that the weights are adapted to generate the correct (target) answers? If we try the method that we used for the Perceptron we need

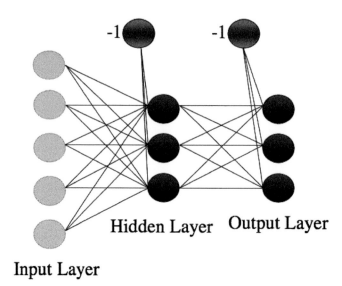

FIGURE 4.1 The Multi-layer Perceptron network, consisting of multiple layers of connected neurons.

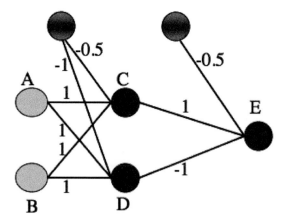

FIGURE 4.2 A Multi-layer Perceptron network showing a set of weights that solve the XOR problem.

to compute the **error** at the output. That's fine, since we know the targets there, so we can compute the difference between the targets and the outputs. But now we don't know which weights were wrong: those in the first layer, or the second? Worse, we don't know what the correct activations are for the neurons in the middle of the network. This fact gives the neurons in the middle of the network their name; they are called the **hidden layer** (or **layers**), because it isn't possible to examine and correct their values directly.

It took a long time for people who studied neural networks to work out how to solve this problem. In fact, it wasn't until 1986 that Rumelhart, Hinton, and McClelland managed it. However, a solution to the problem was already known by statisticians and engineers—they just didn't know that it was a problem in neural networks! In this chapter we are going to look at the neural network solution proposed by Rumelhart, Hinton, and McClelland, the Multi-layer Perceptron (MLP), which is still one of the most commonly used machine learning methods around. The MLP is one of the most common neural networks in use. It is often treated as a 'black box', in that people use it without understanding how it works, which often results in fairly poor results. Getting to the stage where we understand how it works and what we can do with it is going to take us into lots of different areas of statistics, mathematics, and computer science, so we'd better get started.

4.1 GOING FORWARDS

Just as it did for the Perceptron, training the MLP consists of two parts: working out what the outputs are for the given inputs and the current weights, and then updating the weights according to the **error**, which is a function of the difference between the outputs and the targets. These are generally known as going **forwards** and **backwards** through the network. We've already seen how to go forwards for the MLP when we saw the XOR example above, which was effectively the recall phase of the algorithm. It is pretty much just the same as the Perceptron, except that we have to do it twice, once for each set of neurons, and we need to do it layer by layer, because otherwise the input values to the second layer don't exist. In fact, having made an MLP with two layers of nodes, there is no reason why we can't make one with 3, or 4, or 20 layers of nodes (we'll discuss whether or not you might want to in Section 4.3.2). This won't even change our recall (forward) algorithm much, since we just work forwards through the network computing the activations of one layer of neurons and using those as the inputs for the next layer.

So looking at Figure 4.1, we start at the left by filling in the values for the inputs. We then use these inputs and the first level of weights to calculate the activations of the hidden layer, and then we use those activations and the next set of weights to calculate the activations of the output layer. Now that we've got the outputs of the network, we can compare them to the targets and compute the error.

4.1.1 Biases

We need to include a bias input to each neuron. We do this in the same way as we did for the Perceptron in Section 3.3.2, by having an extra input that is permanently set to -1, and adjusting the weights to each neuron as part of the training. Thus, each neuron in the network (whether it is a hidden layer or the output) has 1 extra input, with fixed value.

4.2 GOING BACKWARDS: BACK-PROPAGATION OF ERROR

It is in the backwards part of the algorithm that things get tricky. Computing the errors at the output is no more difficult than it was for the Perceptron, but working out what to do with those errors is more difficult. The method that we are going to look at is called **back-propagation of error**, which makes it clear that the errors are sent backwards through the network. It is a form of **gradient descent** (which is described briefly below, and also given its own section in Chapter 9; in that chapter, in Section 9.3.2, we will see how to use the general gradient descent algorithms for the MLP).

The best way to describe back-propagation properly is mathematically, but this can be intimidating and difficult to get a handle on at first. I've therefore tried to compromise by using words and pictures in the main text, but putting all of the mathematical details into Section 4.6. While you should look at that section and try to understand it, it can be skipped if you really don't have the background. Although it looks complicated, there are actually just three things that you need to know, all of which are from differential calculus: the derivative of $\frac{1}{2}x^2$, the fact that if you differentiate a function of x with respect to some other variable t, then the answer is 0, and the chain rule, which tells you how to differentiate composite functions.

When we talked about the Perceptron, we changed the weights so that the neurons fired when the targets said they should, and didn't fire when the targets said they shouldn't. What we did was to choose an **error function** for each neuron k: $E_k = y_k - t_k$, and tried to make it as small as possible. Since there was only one set of weights in the network, this was sufficient to train the network.

We still want to do the same thing—minimise the error, so that neurons fire only when they should—but, with the addition of extra layers of weights, this is harder to arrange. The problem is that when we try to adapt the weights of the Multi-layer Perceptron, we have to work out which weights caused the error. This could be the weights connecting the inputs to the hidden layer, or the weights connecting the hidden layer to the output layer. (For more complex networks, there could be extra weights between nodes in hidden layers. This isn't a problem—the same method works—but it is more confusing to talk about, so I'm only going to worry about one hidden layer here.)

The error function that we used for the Perceptron was $\sum_{k=1}^{N} E_k = \sum_{k=1}^{N} y_k - t_k$, where N is the number of output nodes. However, suppose that we make two errors. In the first, the target is bigger than the output, while in the second the output is bigger than the target. If these two errors are the same size, then if we add them up we could get 0, which means that the error value suggests that no error was made. To get around this we need to make all errors have the same sign. We can do this in a few different ways, but the one that will turn out to be best is the **sum-of-squares** error function, which calculates the difference between y and t for each node, squares them, and adds them all together:

$$E(\mathbf{t}, \mathbf{y}) = \frac{1}{2} \sum_{k=1}^{N} (y_k - t_k)^2. \tag{4.1}$$

You might have noticed the $\frac{1}{2}$ at the front of that equation. It doesn't matter that much, but it makes it easier when we differentiate the function, and that is the name of the game here: if we differentiate a function, then it tells us the gradient of that function, which is the direction along which it increases and decreases the most. So if we differentiate an error function, we get the gradient of the error. Since the purpose of learning is to minimise the error, following the error function downhill (in other words, in the direction of the negative gradient) will give us what we want. Imagine a ball rolling around on a surface that looks

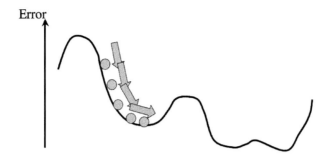

FIGURE 4.3 The weights of the network are trained so that the error goes downhill until it reaches a local minimum, just like a ball rolling under gravity.

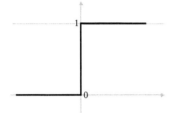

FIGURE 4.4 The threshold function that we used for the Perceptron. Note the discontinuity where the value changes from 0 to 1.

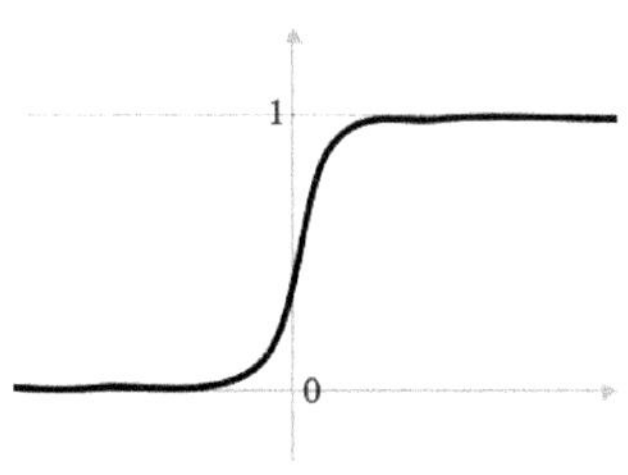

FIGURE 4.5 The sigmoid function, which looks qualitatively fairly similar, but varies smoothly and differentiably.

like the line in Figure 4.3. Gravity will make the ball roll downhill (follow the downhill gradient) until it ends up in the bottom of one of the hollows. These are places where the error is small, so that is exactly what we want. This is why the algorithm is called **gradient descent**. So what should we differentiate with respect to? There are only three things in the network that change: the inputs, the activation function that decides whether or not the node fires, and the weights. The first and second are out of our control when the algorithm is running, so only the weights matter, and therefore they are what we differentiate with respect to.

Having mentioned the activation function, this is a good time to point out a little problem with the threshold function that we have been using for our neurons so far, which is that it is discontinuous (see Figure 4.4; it has a sudden jump in the middle) and so differentiating it at that point isn't possible. The problem is that we need that jump between firing and not firing to make it act like a neuron. We can solve the problem if we can find an activation function that looks like a threshold function, but is differentiable so that we can compute the gradient. If you squint at a graph of the threshold function (for example, Figure 4.4) then it looks kind of S-shaped. There is a mathematical form of S-shaped functions, called **sigmoid functions** (see Figure 4.5). They have another nice property, which is that their derivative also has a nice form, as is shown in Section 4.6.3 for those who know some mathematics. The most commonly used form of this function (where β is some positive parameter) is:

$$a = g(h) = \frac{1}{1 + \exp(-\beta h)}. \tag{4.2}$$

In some texts you will see the activation function given a different form, as:

$$a = g(h) = \tanh(h) = \frac{\exp(h) - \exp(-h)}{\exp(h) + \exp(-h)}, \tag{4.3}$$

which is the hyperbolic tangent function. This is a different but similar function; it is still a sigmoid function, but it **saturates** (reaches its constant values) at ± 1 instead of 0 and 1, which is sometimes useful. It also has a relatively simple derivative: $\frac{d}{dx} \tanh x = (1 - \tanh^2(x))$. We can convert between the two easily, because if the saturation points are (± 1), then we can convert to $(0, 1)$ by using $0.5 \times (x + 1)$.

So now we've got a new form of error computation and a new activation function that decides whether or not a neuron should fire. We can differentiate it, so that when we change the weights, we do it in the direction that is downhill for the error, which means that we know we are improving the error function of the network. As far as an algorithm goes, we've fed our inputs forward through the network and worked out which nodes are firing. Now, at the output, we've computed the errors as the sum-squared difference between the outputs and the targets (Equation (4.1) above). What we want to do next is to compute the gradient of these errors and use them to decide how much to update each weight in the network. We will do that first for the nodes connected to the output layer, and after we have updated those, we will work *backwards* through the network until we get back to the inputs again. There are just two problems:

- for the **output** neurons, we don't know the inputs.

- for the **hidden** neurons, we don't know the targets; for extra hidden layers, we know neither the inputs nor the targets, but even this won't matter for the algorithm we derive.

So we can compute the error at the output, but since we don't know what the inputs were that caused it, we can't update those second layer weights the way we did for the Perceptron. If we use the **chain rule of differentiation** that you all (possibly) remember from high school then we can get around this problem. Here, the chain rule tells us that if we want to know how the error changes as we vary the weights, we can think about how the error changes as we vary the inputs to the weights, and multiply this by how those input values change as we vary the weights. This is useful because it lets us calculate all of the derivatives that we want to: we can write the activations of the output nodes in terms of the activations of the hidden nodes and the output weights, and then we can send the error calculations back through the network to the hidden layer to decide what the target outputs were for those neurons. Note that we can do exactly the same computations if the network has extra hidden layers between the inputs and the outputs. It gets harder to keep track of which functions we should be differentiating, but there are no new tricks needed.

All of the relevant equations are derived in Section 4.6, and you should read that section carefully, since it is quite difficult to describe exactly what is going on here in words. The important thing to understand is that we compute the gradients of the errors with respect to the weights, so that we change the weights so that we go downhill, which makes the errors get smaller. We do this by differentiating the error function with respect to the weights, but we can't do this directly, so we have to apply the chain rule and differentiate with respect to things that we know. This leads to two different update functions, one for each of the

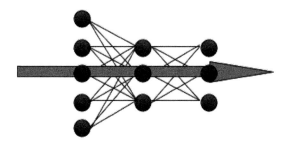

FIGURE 4.6 The forward direction in a Multi-layer Perceptron.

sets of weights, and we just apply these backwards through the network, starting at the outputs and ending up back at the inputs.

4.2.1 The Multi-layer Perceptron Algorithm

We'll get into the details of the basic algorithm here, and then, in the next section, have a look at some practical issues, such as how much training data is needed, how much training time is needed, and how to choose the correct size of network. We will assume that there are L input nodes, plus the bias, M hidden nodes, also plus a bias, and N output nodes, so that there are $(L+1) \times M$ weights between the input and the hidden layer and $(M+1) \times N$ between the hidden layer and the output. The sums that we write will start from 0 if they include the bias nodes and 1 otherwise, and run up to $L, M,$ or N, so that $x_0 = -1$ is the bias input, and $a_0 = -1$ is the bias hidden node. The algorithm that is described could have any number of hidden layers, in which case there might be several values for M, and extra sets of weights between the hidden layers. We will also use i, j, k to index the nodes in each layer in the sums, and the corresponding Greek letters (ι, ζ, κ) for fixed indices.

Here is a quick summary of how the algorithm works, and then the full MLP training algorithm using back-propagation of error is described.

1. an input vector is put into the input nodes

2. the inputs are fed *forward* through the network (Figure 4.6)

    • the inputs and the first-layer weights (here labelled as v) are used to decide whether the hidden nodes fire or not. The activation function $g(\cdot)$ is the sigmoid function given in Equation (4.2) above

    • the outputs of these neurons and the second-layer weights (labelled as w) are used to decide if the output neurons fire or not

3. the *error* is computed as the sum-of-squares difference between the network outputs and the targets

4. this error is fed *backwards* through the network in order to

    • first update the second-layer weights

    • and then afterwards, the first-layer weights

The Multi-layer Perceptron Algorithm

- **Initialisation**

    - initialise all weights to small (positive and negative) random values

- **Training**
    - repeat:
        * for each input vector:
        Forwards phase:

        · compute the activation of each neuron j in the hidden layer(s) using:

$$h_\zeta = \sum_{i=0}^{L} x_i v_{i\zeta} \qquad (4.4)$$

$$a_\zeta = g(h_\zeta) = \frac{1}{1 + \exp(-\beta h_\zeta)} \qquad (4.5)$$

   · work through the network until you get to the output layer neurons, which have activations (although see also Section 4.2.3):

$$h_\kappa = \sum_j a_j w_{j\kappa} \qquad (4.6)$$

$$y_\kappa = g(h_\kappa) = \frac{1}{1 + \exp(-\beta h_\kappa)} \qquad (4.7)$$

   Backwards phase:
   · compute the error at the output using:

$$\delta_o(\kappa) = (y_\kappa - t_\kappa)\, y_\kappa (1 - y_\kappa) \qquad (4.8)$$

   · compute the error in the hidden layer(s) using:

$$\delta_h(\zeta) = a_\zeta (1 - a_\zeta) \sum_{k=1}^{N} w_\zeta \delta_o(k) \qquad (4.9)$$

   · update the output layer weights using:

$$w_{\zeta\kappa} \leftarrow w_{\zeta\kappa} - \eta \delta_o(\kappa) a_\zeta^{\text{hidden}} \qquad (4.10)$$

   · update the hidden layer weights using:

$$v_\iota \leftarrow v_\iota - \eta \delta_h(\kappa) x_\iota \qquad (4.11)$$

   * (if using sequential updating) randomise the order of the input vectors so that you don't train in exactly the same order each iteration
    - until learning stops (see Section 4.3.3)
- **Recall**
    - use the Forwards phase in the training section above

This provides a description of the basic algorithm. As with the Perceptron, a NumPy implementation can take advantage of various matrix multiplications, which makes things easy to read and faster to compute. The implementation on the website is a batch version of the algorithm, so that weight updates are made after all of the input vectors have been presented (as is described in Section 4.2.4). The central weight update computations for the algorithm can be implemented as:

```
deltao = (targets-self.outputs)*self.outputs*(1.0-self.outputs)
deltah = self.hidden*(1.0-self.hidden)*(np.dot(deltao,np.transpose(self.)
weights2)))

updatew1 = np.zeros((np.shape(self.weights1)))
updatew2 = np.zeros((np.shape(self.weights2)))

updatew1 = eta*(np.dot(np.transpose(inputs),deltah[:,:-1]))
updatew2 = eta*(np.dot(np.transpose(self.hidden),deltao))
self.weights1 += updatew1
self.weights2 += updatew2
```

There are a few improvements that can be made to the algorithm, and there are some important things that need to be considered, such as how many training datapoints are needed, how many hidden nodes should be used, and how much training the network needs. We will look at the improvements first, and then move on to practical considerations in Section 4.3. There are lots of details that are given in this section because it is one of the early examples in the book; later on things will be skipped over more quickly.

The first thing that we can do is check that this MLP can indeed learn the logic functions, especially the XOR. We can do that with this code (which is function logic on the website):

```
import numpy as np
import mlp

anddata = np.array([[0,0,0],[0,1,0],[1,0,0],[1,1,1]])
xordata = np.array([[0,0,0],[0,1,1],[1,0,1],[1,1,0]])

p = mlp.mlp(anddata[:,0:2],anddata[:,2:3],2)
p.mlptrain(anddata[:,0:2],anddata[:,2:3],0.25,1001)
p.confmat(anddata[:,0:2],anddata[:,2:3])

q = mlp.mlp(xordata[:,0:2],xordata[:,2:3],2)
q.mlptrain(xordata[:,0:2],xordata[:,2:3],0.25,5001)
q.confmat(xordata[:,0:2],xordata[:,2:3])
```

The outputs that this produces is something like:

```
Iteration:  0  Error:  0.367917569871
Iteration:  1000  Error:  0.0204860723612
Confusion matrix is:
[[ 3.  0.]
 [ 0.  1.]]
Percentage Correct:  100.0
Iteration:  0  Error:  0.515798627074
Iteration:  1000  Error:  0.499568173798
```

```
Iteration:  2000  Error:  0.498271692284
Iteration:  3000  Error:  0.480839047738
Iteration:  4000  Error:  0.382706753191
Iteration:  5000  Error:  0.0537169253359
Confusion matrix is:
[[ 2.   0.]
 [ 0.   2.]]
Percentage Correct:  100.0
```

There are a few things to notice about this. One is that it does work, producing the correct answers, but the other is that even for the AND we need significantly more iterations than we did for the Perceptron. So the benefits of a more complex network come at a cost, because it takes substantially more computational time to fit those weights to solve the problem, even for linear examples. Sometimes, even 5000 iterations are not enough for the XOR function, and more have to be added.

4.2.2 Initialising the Weights

The MLP algorithm suggests that the weights are initialised to small random numbers, both positive and negative. The question is how small is small, and does it matter? One way to get a feeling for this would be to experiment with the code, setting all of the weights to 0, and seeing how well the network learns, then setting them all to large numbers and comparing the results. However, to understand why they should be small we can look at the shape of the sigmoid. If the initial weight values are close to 1 or -1 (which is what we mean by large here) then the inputs to the sigmoid are also likely to be close to ± 1 and so the output of the neuron is either 0 or 1 (the sigmoid has **saturated**, reached its maximum or minimum value). If the weights are very small (close to zero) then the input is still close to 0 and so the output of the neuron is just linear, so we get a linear model. Both of these things can be useful for the final network, but if we start off with values that are inbetween it can decide for itself.

Choosing the size of the initial values needs a little more thought, then. Each neuron is getting input from n different places (either input nodes if the neuron is in the hidden layer, or hidden neurons if it is in the output layer). If we view the values of these inputs as having uniform variance, then the typical input to the neuron will be $w\sqrt{n}$, where w is the initialisation value of the weights. So a common trick is to set the weights in the range $-1/\sqrt{n} < w < 1/\sqrt{n}$, where n is the number of nodes in the input layer to those weights. This makes the total input to a neuron have a maximum size of about 1. Further, if the weights are large, then the activation of a neuron is likely to be at, or close to, 0 or 1 already, which means that the gradients are small, and so the learning is very slow. There is an interplay here with the value of β in the logistic function, which means that small values of β (say $\beta = 3.0$ or less) are more effective. We use random values for the initialisation so that the learning starts off from different places for each run, and we keep them all about the same size because we want all of the weights to reach their final values at about the same time. This is known as **uniform learning** and it is important because otherwise the network will do better on some inputs than others.

4.2.3 Different Output Activation Functions

In the algorithm described above, we used sigmoid neurons in the hidden layer and the output layer. This is fine for classification problems, since there we can make the classes be 0 and 1. However, we might also want to perform regression problems, where the output needs to be from a continuous range, not just 0 or 1. The sigmoid neurons at the output are not very useful in that case. We can replace the output neurons with linear nodes that just sum the inputs and give that as their activation (so $g(h) = h$ in the notation of Equation (4.2)). This does not mean that we change the hidden layer neurons; they stay exactly the same, and we only modify the output nodes. They are not models of neurons anymore, since they don't have the characteristic fire/don't fire pattern. Even so, they enable us to solve regression problems, where we want a real number out, not just a 0/1 decision.

There is a third type of output neuron that is also used, which is the soft-max activation function. This is most commonly used for classification problems where the 1-of-N output encoding is used, as is described in Section 4.4.2. The soft-max function rescales the outputs by calculating the exponential of the inputs to that neuron, and dividing by the total sum of the inputs to all of the neurons, so that the activations sum to 1 and all lie between 0 and 1. As an activation function it can be written as:

$$y_\kappa = g(h_\kappa) = \frac{\exp(h_\kappa)}{\sum_{k=1}^{N} \exp(h_k)}. \tag{4.12}$$

Of course, if we change the activation function, then the derivative of the activation function will also change, and so the learning rule will be different. The changes that need to be made to the algorithm are in Equations (4.7) and (4.8), and are derived in Section 4.6.5. For the linear activation function the first is replaced by:

$$y_\kappa = g(h_\kappa) = h_\kappa, \tag{4.13}$$

while the second is replaced by:

$$\delta_o(\kappa) = (y_\kappa - t_\kappa). \tag{4.14}$$

For the soft-max activation, the update equation that replaces (4.8) is

$$\delta_o(\kappa) = (y_\kappa - t_\kappa)y_\kappa(\delta_{\kappa K} - y_K), \tag{4.15}$$

where $\delta_{\kappa K} = 1$ if $\kappa = K$ and 0 otherwise; see Section 4.6.5 for further details. However, if we modify the error function as well, to have the cross-entropy form (where ln is the natural logarithm):

$$E_{\text{ce}} = -\sum_{k=1}^{N} t_k \ln(y_k), \tag{4.16}$$

then the delta term is Equation (4.14), just as for the linear output; for more details, see Section 4.6.6. Computing these update equations requires computing the error function that is being optimised, and then differentiating it. These additions can be added into the code by allowing the user to specify the type of output activation, which has to be done twice, once in the `mlpfwd` function, and once in the `mlptrain` function. In the former, the new piece of code can be written as:

```
# Different types of output neurons
if self.outtype == 'linear':
        return outputs
elif self.outtype == 'logistic':
    return 1.0/(1.0+np.exp(-self.beta*outputs))
elif self.outtype == 'softmax':
    normalisers = np.sum(np.exp(outputs),axis=1)*np.ones((1,np.shape(outputs))
    [0]))
    return np.transpose(np.transpose(np.exp(outputs))/normalisers)
else:
    print "error"
```

4.2.4 Sequential and Batch Training

The MLP is designed to be a batch algorithm. All of the training examples are presented to the neural network, the average sum-of-squares error is then computed, and this is used to update the weights. Thus there is only one set of weight updates for each **epoch** (pass through all the training examples). This means that we only update the weights once for each iteration of the algorithm, which means that the weights are moved in the direction that most of the inputs want them to move, rather than being pulled around by each input individually. The batch method performs a more accurate estimate of the error gradient, and will thus converge to the local minimum more quickly.

The algorithm that was described earlier was the **sequential** version, where the errors are computed and the weights updated after each input. This is not guaranteed to be as efficient in learning, but it is simpler to program when using loops, and it is therefore much more common. Since it does not converge as well, it can also sometimes avoid local minima, thus potentially reaching better solutions. While the description of the algorithm is sequential, the NumPy implementation on the book website is a batch version, because the matrix manipulation methods of NumPy make that easy. It is, however, relatively simple to modify it to use sequential update (making this change to the code is suggested as an exercise at the end of the chapter). In a sequential version, the order of the weight updates can matter, which is why the pseudocode version of the algorithm include a suggestion about randomising the order of the input vectors at each iteration. This can significantly improve the speed with which the algorithm learns. NumPy has a useful function that assists with this, `np.random.shuffle()`, which takes a list of numbers and reorders them. It can be used like this:

```
np.random.shuffle(change)
inputs = inputs[change,:]
targets = targets[change,:]
```

4.2.5 Local Minima

The driving force behind the learning rule is the minimisation of the network error by gradient descent (using the derivative of the error function to make the error smaller). This

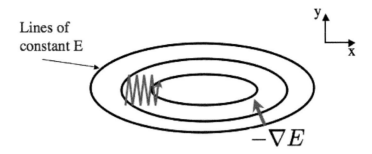

FIGURE 4.7 In 2D, downhill means at right angles to the lines of constant contour. Imagine walking down a hill with your eyes closed. If you find a direction that stays flat, then it is quite likely that perpendicular to that the ground goes uphill or downhill. However, this is not the direction that takes you directly towards the local minimum.

means that we are performing an **optimisation**: we are adapting the values of the weights in order to minimise the error function. As should be clear by now, the way that we are doing this is by approximating the gradient of the error and following it downhill so that we end up at the bottom of the slope. However, following the slope downhill only guarantees that we end up at a **local minimum**, a point that is lower than those close to it. If we imagine a ball rolling down a hill, it will settle at the bottom of a dip. However, there is no guarantee that it will have stopped at the lowest point—only the lowest point **locally**. There may be a much lower point over the next hill, but the ball can't see that, and it doesn't have enough energy to climb over the hill and find the global minimum (have another look at Figure 4.3 to see a picture of this).

Gradient descent works in the same way in two or more dimensions, and has similar (and worse) problems. The problem is that efficient downhill directions in two dimensions and higher are harder to compute locally. Standard contour maps provide beautiful images of gradients in our three-dimensional world, and if you imagine that you are walking in a hilly area aiming to get to the bottom of the nearest valley then you can get some idea of what is going on. Now suppose that you close your eyes, so that you can only feel which direction to go by moving one step and checking if you are higher up or lower down than you were. There will be places where going downwards as steeply as possible at the current point will not take you much closer to the valley bottom. There can be two reasons for this. The first is that you find a nearby local minimum, while the second is that sometimes the steepest direction is effectively across the valley, not towards the global minimum. This is shown in Figure 4.7.

All of these things are true for most of our optimisation problems, including the MLP. We don't know where the global minimum is because we don't know what the error landscape looks like; we can only compute local features of it for the place we are in at the moment. Which minimum we end up in depends on where we start. If we begin near the global minimum, then we are very likely to end up in it, but if we start near a local minimum we will probably end up there. In addition, how long it will take to get to the minimum that we do find depends upon the exact appearance of the landscape at the current point.

We can make it more likely that we find the global minimum by trying out several different starting points by training several different networks, and this is commonly done. However, we can also try to make it less likely that the algorithm will get stuck in local minima. There is a moderately effective way of doing this, which is discussed next.

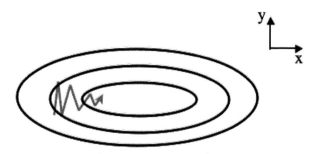

FIGURE 4.8 Adding momentum can help to avoid local minima, and also makes the dynamics of the optimisation more stable, improving convergence.

4.2.6 Picking Up Momentum

Let's go back to the analogy of the ball rolling down the hill. The reason that the ball stops rolling is because it runs out of energy at the bottom of the dip. If we give the ball some weight, then it will generate momentum as it rolls, and so it is more likely to overcome a small hill on the other side of the local minimum, and so more likely to find the global minimum. We can implement this idea in our neural network learning by adding in some contribution from the previous weight change that we made to the current one. In two dimensions it will mean that the ball rolls more directly towards the valley bottom, since on average that will be the correct direction, rather than being controlled by the local changes. This is shown in Figure 4.8.

There is another benefit to momentum. It makes it possible to use a smaller learning rate, which means that the learning is more stable. The only change that we need to make to the MLP algorithm is in Equations (4.10) and (4.11), where we need to add a second term to the weight updates so that they have the form:

$$w_{\zeta\kappa}^t \leftarrow w_{\zeta\kappa}^{t-1} + \eta\delta_o(\kappa)a_\zeta^{\text{hidden}} + \alpha\Delta w_{\zeta\kappa}^{t-1}, \tag{4.17}$$

where t is used to indicate the current update and $t-1$ is the previous one. $\Delta w_{\zeta\kappa}^{t-1}$ is the previous update that we made to the weights (so $\Delta w_{\zeta\kappa}^t = \eta\delta_o(\kappa)a_\zeta^{\text{hidden}} + \alpha\Delta w_{\zeta\kappa}^{t-1}$) and $0 < \alpha < 1$ is the momentum constant. Typically a value of $\alpha = 0.9$ is used. This is a very easy addition to the code, and can improve the speed of learning a lot.

```
updatew1 = eta*(np.dot(np.transpose(inputs),deltah[:,:-1])) + ↵
momentum*updatew1
updatew2 = eta*(np.dot(np.transpose(hidden),deltao)) + momentum*updatew2
```

Another thing that can be added is known as **weight decay**. This reduces the size of the weights as the number of iterations increases. The argument goes that small weights are better since they lead to a network that is closer to linear (since they are close to zero, they are in the region where the sigmoid is increasing linearly), and only those weights that are essential to the non-linear learning should be large. After each learning iteration through all of the input patterns, every weight is multiplied by some constant $0 < \epsilon < 1$. This makes the network simpler and can often produce improved results, but unfortunately, it isn't fail-safe: occasionally it can make the learning significantly worse, so it should be used with care. Setting the value of ϵ is typically done experimentally.

4.2.7 Minibatches and Stochastic Gradient Descent

In Section 4.2.4 it was stated that the batch algorithm converges to a local minimum faster than the sequential algorithm, which computes the error for each input individually and then does a weight update, but that the latter is sometimes less likely to get stuck in local minima. The reason for both of these observations is that the batch algorithm makes a better estimate of the steepest descent direction, so that the direction it chooses to go is a good one, but this just leads to a local minimum.

The idea of a **minibatch** method is to find some happy middle ground between the two, by splitting the training set into random batches, estimating the gradient based on one of the subsets of the training set, performing a weight update, and then using the next subset to estimate a new gradient and using that for the weight update, until all of the training set have been used. The training set are then randomly shuffled into new batches and the next iteration takes place. If the batches are small, then there is often a reasonable degree of error in the gradient estimate, and so the optimisation has the chance to escape from local minima, albeit at the cost of heading in the wrong direction.

A more extreme version of the minibatch idea is to use just one piece of data to estimate the gradient at each iteration of the algorithm, and to pick that piece of data uniformly at random from the training set. So a single input vector is chosen from the training set, and the output and hence the error for that one vector computed, and this is used to estimate the gradient and so update the weights. A new random input vector (which could be the same as the previous one) is then chosen and the process repeated. This is known as **stochastic gradient descent**, and can be used for any gradient descent problem, not just the MLP. It is often used if the training set is very large, since it would be very expensive to use the whole dataset to estimate the gradient in that case.

4.2.8 Other Improvements

There are a few other things that can be done to improve the convergence and behaviour of the back-propagation algorithm. One is to reduce the learning rate as the algorithm progresses. The reasoning behind this is that the network should only be making large-scale changes to the weights at the beginning, when the weights are random; if it is still making large weight changes later on, then something is wrong.

Something that results in much larger performance gains is to include information about the second derivatives of the error with respect to the weights. In the back-propagation algorithm we use the first derivatives to drive the learning. However, if we have knowledge of the second derivatives as well, we can use them as well to improve the network. This will be described in more detail in Section 9.1.

4.3 THE MULTI-LAYER PERCEPTRON IN PRACTICE

The previous section looked at the design and implementation of the MLP network itself. In this section, we are going to look more at choices that can be made about the network in order to use it for solving real problems. We will then apply these ideas to using the MLP to find solutions to four different types of problem: regression, classification, time-series prediction, and data compression.

4.3.1 Amount of Training Data

For the MLP with one hidden layer there are $(L + 1) \times M + (M + 1) \times N$ weights, where L, M, N are the number of nodes in the input, hidden, and output layers, respectively. The extra +1s come from the bias nodes, which also have adjustable weights. This is a potentially huge number of adjustable parameters that we need to set during the training phase. Setting the values of these weights is the job of the back-propagation algorithm, which is driven by the errors coming from the training data. Clearly, the more training data there is, the better for learning, although the time that the algorithm takes to learn increases. Unfortunately, there is no way to compute what the minimum amount of data required is, since it depends on the problem. A rule of thumb that has been around for almost as long as the MLP itself is that you should use a number of training examples that is at least 10 times the number of weights. This is probably going to be a very large number of examples, so neural network training is a fairly computationally expensive operation, because we need to show the network all of these inputs lots of times.

4.3.2 Number of Hidden Layers

There are two other considerations concerning the number of weights that are inherent in the calculation above, which is the choice of the number of hidden nodes, and the number of hidden layers. Making these choices is obviously fundamental to the successful application of the algorithm. We will shortly see a pictorial demonstration of the fact that two hidden layers is the most that you ever need for normal MLP learning. In fact, this result can be strengthened: it is possible to show mathematically that one hidden layer with lots of hidden nodes is sufficient. This is known as the Universal Approximation Theorem; see the Further Reading section for more details. However, the bad news is that there is no theory to guide the choice of the number of hidden nodes. You just have to experiment by training networks with different numbers of hidden nodes and then choosing the one that gives the best results, as we will see in Section 4.4.

We can use the back-propagation algorithm for a network with as many layers as we like, although it gets progressively harder to keep track of which weights are being updated at any given time. Fortunately, as was mentioned above, we will never normally need more than two layers (that is, one hidden layer and the output layer). This is because we can approximate any smooth functional mapping using a linear combination of localised sigmoidal functions. There is a sketchy demonstration that two hidden layers are sufficient using pictures in Figure 4.9. The basic idea is that by combining sigmoid functions we can generate ridge-like functions, and by combining ridge-like functions we can generate functions with a unique maximum. By combining these and transforming them using another layer of neurons, we obtain a localised response (a 'bump' function), and any functional mapping can be approximated to arbitrary accuracy using a linear combination of such bumps. The way that the MLP does this is shown in Figure 4.10. We will use this idea again when we look at approximating functions, for example using radial basis functions in Chapter 5. Note that Figure 4.9 shows that two hidden layers are sufficient. In fact, they aren't necessary: one hidden layer will do, although it may require an arbitrarily large number of hidden nodes. This is known as the Universal Approximation Theorem, and the (mathematical) paper that shows this is provided in the references at the end of the chapter.

Two hidden layers are sufficient to compute these bump functions for different inputs, and so if the function that we want to learn (approximate) is continuous, the network can compute it. It can therefore approximate any decision boundary, not just the linear one that the Perceptron computed.

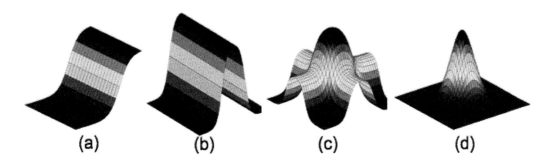

FIGURE 4.9 The learning of the MLP can be shown as the output of a single sigmoidal neuron (a), which can be added to others, including reversed ones, to get a hill shape (b). Adding another hill at 90° produces a bump (c) , which can be sharpened to any extent we want (d), with the bumps added together in the output layer. Thus the MLP learns a local representation of individual inputs.

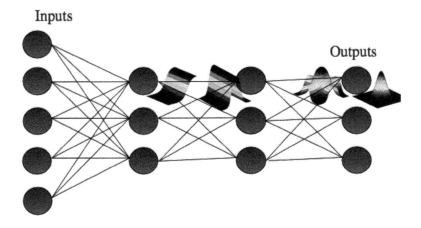

FIGURE 4.10 Schematic of the effective learning shape at each stage of the MLP.

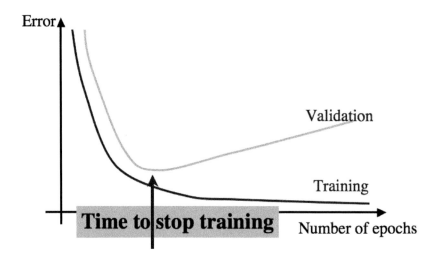

FIGURE 4.11 The effect of overfitting on the training and validation error curves, with the point at which early stopping will stop the learning marked.

4.3.3 When to Stop Learning

The training of the MLP requires that the algorithm runs over the entire dataset many times, with the weights changing as the network makes errors in each iteration. The question is how to decide when to stop learning, and this is a question that we are now ready to answer. It is unfortunate that the most obvious options are not sufficient: setting some predefined number N of iterations, and running until that is reached runs the risk that the network has overfitted by then, or not learnt sufficiently, and only stopping when some predefined minimum error is reached might mean the algorithm never terminates, or that it overfits. Using both of these options together can help, as can terminating the learning once the error stops decreasing.

However, the validation set gives us something rather more useful, since we can use it to monitor the generalisation ability of the network at its current stage of learning. If we plot the sum-of-squares error during training, it typically reduces fairly quickly during the first few training iterations, and then the reduction slows down as the learning algorithm performs small changes to find the exact local minimum. We don't want to stop training until the local minimum has been found, but, as we've just discussed, keeping on training too long leads to overfitting of the network. This is where the validation set comes in useful. We train the network for some predetermined amount of time, and then use the validation set to estimate how well the network is generalising. We then carry on training for a few more iterations, and repeat the whole process. At some stage the error on the validation set will start increasing again, because the network has stopped learning about the function that generated the data, and started to learn about the noise that is in the data itself (shown in Figure 4.11). At this stage we stop the training. This technique is called **early stopping**.

4.4 EXAMPLES OF USING THE MLP

This section is intended to be practical, so you should follow the examples at a computer, and add to them as you wish. The MLP is rather too complicated to enable us to work through the weight changes as we did with the Perceptron.

Instead, we shall look at some demonstrations of how to make the network learn about some data. As was mentioned above, we shall look at the four types of problems that are generally solved using an MLP: regression, classification, time-series prediction, and data compression/data denoising.

4.4.1 A Regression Problem

The regression problem we will look at is a very simple one. We will take a set of samples generated by a simple mathematical function, and try to learn the **generating** function (that describes how the data was made) so that we can find the values of any inputs, not just the ones we have training data for.

The function that we will use is a very simple one, just a bit of a sine wave. We'll make the data in the following way (make sure that you have NumPy imported as **np** first):

```
x = np.ones((1,40))*np.linspace(0,1,40)
t = np.sin(2*np.pi*x) + np.cos(4*np.pi*x) + np.random.randn(40)*0.2
x = x.T
t = t.T
```

The reason why we have to use the `reshape()` method is that NumPy defaults to lists for arrays that are $N \times 1$; compare the results of the `np.shape()` calls below, and the effect of the transpose operator `.T` on the array:

```
>>> x = np.linspace(0,1,40)
>>> np.shape(x)
(40,)
>>> np.shape(x.T)
(40,)
>>>
>>> x = np.linspace(0,1,40).reshape((1,40))
>>> np.shape(x)
(1, 40)
>>> np.shape(x.T)
(40, 1)
```

You can plot this data to see what it looks like (the results of which are shown in Figure 4.12) using:

```
>>> import pylab as pl
>>> pl.plot(x,t,'.')
```

We can now train an MLP on the data. There is one input value, x and one output value t, so the neural network will have one input and one output. Also, because we want the output to be the value of the function, rather than 0 or 1, we will use linear neurons at the output. We don't know how many hidden neurons we will need yet, so we'll have to experiment to see what works.

Before getting started, we need to normalise the data using the method shown in Section 3.4.5, and then separate the data into training, testing, and validation sets. For this example there are only 40 datapoints, and we'll use half of them as the training set, although that isn't very many and might not be enough for the algorithm to learn effectively. We can split the data in the ratio 50:25:25 by using the odd-numbered elements as training data, the even-numbered ones that do not divide by 4 for testing, and the rest for validation:

```
train = x[0::2,:]
test = x[1::4,:]
valid = x[3::4,:]
traintarget = t[0::2,:]
testtarget = t[1::4,:]
validtarget = t[3::4,:]
```

With that done, it is just a case of making and training the MLP. To start with, we will construct a network with three nodes in the hidden layer, and run it for 101 iterations with a learning rate of 0.25, just to see that it works:

```
>>> import mlp
>>> net = mlp.mlp(train,traintarget,3,outtype='linear')
>>> net.mlptrain(train,traintarget,0.25,101)
```

The output from this will look something like:

```
Iteration: 0 Error: 12.3704163654
Iteration: 100 Error: 8.2075961385
```

so we can see that the network is learning, since the error is decreasing. We now need to do two things: work out how many hidden nodes we need, and decide how long to train the network for. In order to solve the first problem, we need to test out different networks and see which get lower errors, but to do that properly we need to know when to stop training. So we'll solve the second problem first, which is to implement early stopping.

We train the network for a few iterations (let's make it 10 for now), then evaluate the validation set error by running the network forward (i.e., the recall phase). Learning should stop when the validation set error starts to increase. We'll write a Python program that does all the work for us. The important point is that we keep track of the validation error and stop when it starts to increase. The following code is a function within the MLP on the book website. It keeps track of the last two changes in validation error to ensure that small fluctuations in the learning don't change it from early stopping to premature stopping:

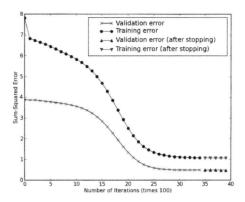

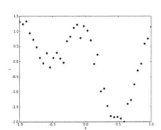

FIGURE 4.12 The data that we will learn using an MLP, consisting of some samples from a sine wave with Gaussian noise added.

FIGURE 4.13 Plot of the error as the MLP learns (top line is total error on the training set; bottom line is on the validation set; it is larger on the training set because there are more datapoints in this set). Early-stopping halts the learning at the point where there is no line, where the crosses become triangles. The learning was continued to show that the error got slightly worse afterwards.

```
old_val_error1 = 100002
old_val_error2 = 100001
new_val_error = 100000

count = 0
while (((old_val_error1 - new_val_error) > 0.001) or ((old_val_error2 - ∤
old_val_error1)>0.001)):
    count+=1
    self.mlptrain(inputs,targets,0.25,100)
    old_val_error2 = old_val_error1
    old_val_error1 = new_val_error
    validout = self.mlpfwd(valid)
    new_val_error = 0.5*np.sum((validtargets-validout)**2)

print "Stopped", new_val_error,old_val_error1, old_val_error2
```

Figure 4.13 gives an example of the output of running the function. It plots the training and validation errors. The point at which early stopping makes the learning finish is the point where there is a missing validation datapoint. I ran it on after that so you could see that the validation error did not improve after that, and so early stopping found the correct point.

We can now return to the problem of finding the right size of network. There is one important thing to remember, which is that the weights are initialised randomly, and so the fact that a particular size of network gets a good solution once does not mean it is the right size, it could have been a lucky starting point. So each network size is run 10 times, and the average is monitored. The following table shows the results of doing this, reporting the sum-of-squares validation error, for a few different sizes of network:

No. of hidden nodes	1	2	3	5	10	25	50
Mean error	2.21	0.52	0.52	0.52	0.55	1.35	2.56
Standard deviation	0.17	0.00	0.00	0.02	0.00	1.20	1.27
Max error	2.31	0.53	0.54	0.54	0.60	3.230	3.66
Min error	2.10	0.51	0.50	0.50	0.47	0.42	0.52

Based on these numbers, we would select a network with a small number of hidden nodes, certainly between 2 and 10 (and the smaller the better, in general), since their maximum error is much smaller than a network with just 1 hidden node. Note also that the error increases once too many hidden nodes are used, since the network has too much variation for the problem. You can also do the same kind of experimentation with more hidden layers.

4.4.2 Classification with the MLP

Using the MLP for classification problems is not radically different once the output encoding has been worked out. The inputs are easy: they are just the values of the feature measurements (suitably normalised). There are a couple of choices for the outputs. The first is to use a single linear node for the output, y, and put some thresholds on the activation value of that node. For example, for a four-class problem, we could use:

$$\text{Class is:} \begin{cases} C_1 & \text{if } y \leq -0.5 \\ C_2 & \text{if } -0.5 < y \leq 0 \\ C_3 & \text{if } 0 < y \leq 0.5 \\ C_4 & \text{if } y > 0.5 \end{cases} \tag{4.18}$$

However, this gets impractical as the number of classes gets large, and the boundaries are artificial; what about an example that is very close to a boundary, say $y = 0.5$? We arbitrarily guess that it belongs to class C_3, but the neural network doesn't give us any information about how close it was to the boundary in the output, so we don't know that this was a difficult example to classify. A more suitable output encoding is called 1-of-N encoding. A separate node is used to represent each possible class, and the target vectors consist of zeros everywhere except for in the one element that corresponds to the correct class, e.g., $(0,0,0,1,0,0)$ means that the correct result is the 4th class out of 6. We are therefore using binary output values (we want each output to be either 0 or 1).

Once the network has been trained, performing the classification is easy: simply choose the element y_k of the output vector that is the largest element of $\mathbf{y}$ (in mathematical notation, pick the y_k for which $y_k > y_j \forall j \neq k$; $\forall$ means for all, so this statement says pick the y_k that is bigger than all other possible values y_j). This generates an unambiguous decision, since it is very unlikely that two output neurons will have identical largest output values. This is known as the hard-max activation function (since the neuron with the highest activation is chosen to fire and the rest are ignored). An alternative is the soft-max function, which we saw in Section 4.2.3, and which has the effect of scaling the output of each neuron according to how large it is in comparison to the others, and making the total output sum to 1. So if there is one clear winner, it will have a value near 1, while if there are several values that are close to each other, they will each have a value of about $\frac{1}{p}$, where p is the number of output neurons that have similar values.

There is one other thing that we need to be aware of when performing classification, which is true for all classifiers. Suppose that we are doing two-class classification, and 90% of our data belongs to class 1. (This can happen: for example in medical data, most tests are negative in general.) In that case, the algorithm can learn to always return the negative class, since it will be right 90% of the time, but still a completely useless classifier! So you should generally make sure that you have approximately the same number of each class in your training set. This can mean discarding a lot of data from the over-represented class, which may seem rather wasteful. There is an alternative solution, known as novelty detection, which is to train the data on the data in the negative class only, and to assume that anything that looks different to that is a positive example. There is a reference about novelty detection in the readings at the end of the chapter.

4.4.3 A Classification Example: The Iris Dataset

As an example we are going to look at another example from the UCI Machine Learning repository. This one is concerned with classifying examples of three types of iris (flower) by the length and width of the sepals and petals and is called `iris`. It was originally worked on by R.A. Fisher, a famous statistician and biologist, who analysed it in the 1930s.

Unfortunately we can't currently load this into NumPy using `loadtxt()` because the class (which is the last column) is text rather than a number, and the `txt` in the function name doesn't mean that it reads text, only numbers in plaintext format. There are two alternatives. One is to edit the data in a text editor using search and replace, and the other is to use some Python code, such as this function:

```python
def preprocessIris(infile,outfile):

    stext1 = 'Iris-setosa'
    stext2 = 'Iris-versicolor'
    stext3 = 'Iris-virginica'
    rtext1 = '0'
    rtext2 = '1'
    rtext3 = '2'

    fid = open(infile,"r")
    oid = open(outfile,"w")

    for s in fid:
        if s.find(stext1)>-1:
            oid.write(s.replace(stext1, rtext1))
        elif s.find(stext2)>-1:
            oid.write(s.replace(stext2, rtext2))
        elif s.find(stext3)>-1:
            oid.write(s.replace(stext3, rtext3))
    fid.close()
    oid.close()
```

You can then load it from the new file using `loadtxt()`. In the dataset, the last column is the class ID, and the others are the four measurements. We'll start by normalising the inputs, which we'll do in the same way as in Section 3.4.5, but using the maximum rather than the variance, and leaving the class IDs alone for now:

```
iris = np.loadtxt('iris_proc.data',delimiter=',')
iris[:,:4] = iris[:,:4]-iris[:,:4].mean(axis=0)
imax = np.concatenate((iris.max(axis=0)*np.ones((1,5)),np.abs(iris.min(↩
axis=0))*np.ones((1,5))),axis=0).max(axis=0)
iris[:,:4] = iris[:,:4]/imax[:4]
```

The first few datapoints will then look like:

```
>>> print iris[0:5,:]
[[-0.36142626  0.33135215 -0.7508489  -0.76741803  0. ]
 [-0.45867099 -0.04011887 -0.7508489  -0.76741803  0. ]
 [-0.55591572  0.10846954 -0.78268251 -0.76741803  0. ]
 [-0.60453809  0.03417533 -0.71901528 -0.76741803  0. ]
 [-0.41004862  0.40564636 -0.7508489  -0.76741803  0. ]]
```

We now need to convert the targets into 1-of-N encoding, from their current encoding as class 1, 2, or 3. This is pretty easy if we make a new matrix that is initially all zeroes, and simply set one of the entries to be 1:

```
# Split into training, validation, and test sets
target = np.zeros((np.shape(iris)[0],3));
indices = np.where(iris[:,4]==0)
target[indices,0] = 1
indices = np.where(iris[:,4]==1)
target[indices,1] = 1
indices = np.where(iris[:,4]==2)
target[indices,2] = 1
```

We now need to separate the data into training, testing, and validation sets. There are 150 examples in the dataset, and they are split evenly amongst the three classes, so the three classes are the same size and we don't need to worry about discarding any datapoints. We'll split them into half training, and one quarter each testing and validation. If you look at the file, you will notice that the first 50 are class 1, the second 50 class 2, etc. We therefore need to randomise the order before we split them into sets, to ensure that there are not too many of one class in one of the sets:

```
# Randomly order the data
order = range(np.shape(iris)[0])
```

```
np.random.shuffle(order)
iris = iris[order,:]
target = target[order,:]

train = iris[::2,0:4]
traint = target[::2]
valid = iris[1::4,0:4]
validt = target[1::4]
test = iris[3::4,0:4]
testt = target[3::4]
```

We're now finally ready to set up and train the network. The commands should all be familiar from earlier:

```
>>> import mlp
>>> net = mlp.mlp(train,traint,5,outtype='softmax')
>>> net.earlystopping(train,traint,valid,validt,0.1)
>>> net.confmat(test,testt)
Confusion matrix is:
[[ 16.   0.   0.]
 [  0.  12.   2.]
 [  0.   1.   6.]]
Percentage Correct:  91.8918918919
```

This tells us that the algorithm got nearly all of the test data correct, misclassifying just two examples of class 2 and one of class 3.

4.4.4 Time-Series Prediction

There is a common data analysis task known as **time-series prediction**, where we have a set of data that show how something varies over time, and we want to predict how the data will vary in the future. It is quite a difficult task, but a fairly important one. It is useful in any field where there is data that appears over time, which is to say almost any field. Most notable (if often unsuccessful) uses have been in trying to predict stock markets and disease patterns. The problem is that even if there is some regularity in the time-series, it can appear over many different scales. For example, there is often seasonal variation—if we plotted average temperature over several years, we would notice that it got hotter in the summer and colder in the winter, but we might not notice if there was a overall upward or downward trend to the summer temperatures, because the summer peaks are spread too far apart in the data.

The other problems with the data are practical. How many datapoints should we look at to make the prediction (i.e., how many inputs should there be to the neural network) and how far apart in time should we space those inputs (i.e., should we use every second datapoint, every 10th, or all of them)? We can write this as an equation, where we are predicting y using a neural network that is written as a function $f(\cdot)$:

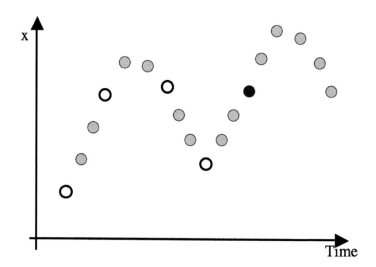

FIGURE 4.14 Part of a time-series plot, showing the datapoints and the meanings of τ and k.

$$y = x(t + \tau) = f(x(t), x(t - \tau), \ldots, x(t - k\tau)), \tag{4.19}$$

where the two questions about how many datapoints and how far apart they should be come down to choices about τ and k.

The target data for training the neural network is simple, because it comes from further up the time-series, and so training is easy. Suppose that $\tau = 2$ and $k = 3$. Then the first input data are elements $1, 3, 5$ of the dataset, and the target is element 7. The next input vector is elements $2, 4, 6$, with target 8, and then $3, 5, 7$ with target 9. You train the network by passing through the time-series (remembering to save some data for testing), and then press on into the future making predictions. Figure 4.14 shows an example of a time-series with $\tau = 3$ and $k = 4$, with a set of datapoints that make up an input vector marked as white circles, and the target coloured black.

The dataset I am going to use is available on the book website. It provides the daily measurement of the thickness of the ozone layer above Palmerston North in New Zealand (where I live) between 1996 and 2004. Ozone thickness is measured in Dobson Units, which are 0.01 mm thickness at 0 degrees Celsius and 1 atmosphere of pressure. I'm sure that I don't need to tell you that the reduction in stratospheric ozone is partly responsible for global warming and the increased incidence of skin cancer, and that in New Zealand we are fairly close to the large hole over Antarctica. What you might not know is that the thickness of the ozone layer varies naturally over the year. This should be obvious in the plot shown in Figure 4.15. A typical time-series problem is to predict the ozone levels into the future and see if you can detect an overall drop in the mean ozone level.

You can load the data using `PNoz = loadtxt('PNOz.dat')` (once you've downloaded it from the website), which will load the data and stick it into an array called PNoz. There are 4 elements to each vector: the year, the day of the year, and the ozone level and sulphur dioxide level, and there are 2855 readings. To just plot the ozone data so that you can see what it looks like, use `plot(arange(shape(PNoz)[0]),PNoz[:,2],'.')`.

The difficult bit is assembling the input vector from the time-series data. The first thing

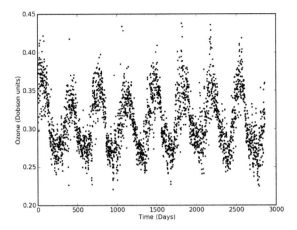

FIGURE 4.15 Plot of the ozone layer thickness above Palmerston North in New Zealand between 1996 and 2004.

is to choose values of τ and k. Then it is just a question of picking k values out of the array with spacing τ, which is a good use for the slice operator, as in this code:

```
test = inputs[-800:,:]
testtargets = targets[-800,:]
train = inputs[:-800:2,:]
traintargets = targets[:-800:2]
valid = inputs[1:-800:2,:]
validtargets = targets[1:-800:2]
```

You then need to assemble training, testing, and validation sets. However, some care is needed here since you need to ensure that they are not picked systematically into each group, (for example, if the inputs are the even-indexed datapoints, but some feature is only seen at odd datapoint times, then it will be completely missed). This can be averted by randomising the order of the datapoints first. However, it is also common to use the datapoints near the end as part of the test set; some possible results from using the MLP in this way are shown in Figure 4.16.

From here you can treat time-series as regression problems: the output nodes need to have linear activations, and you aim to minimise the sum-of-squares error. Since there are no classes, the confusion matrix is not useful. The only extra work is that in addition to testing MLPs with different numbers of input nodes and hidden nodes, you also need to consider different values of τ and k.

4.4.5 Data Compression: The Auto-Associative Network

We are now going to consider an interesting variation of the MLP. Suppose that we train the network to reproduce the inputs at the output layer (called **auto-associative** learning; sometimes the network is known as an **autoencoder**). The network is trained so that whatever

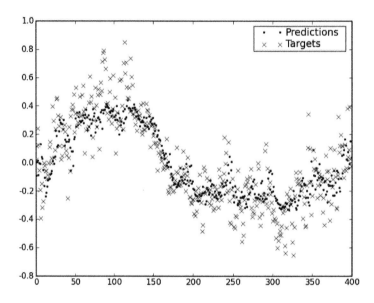

FIGURE 4.16 Plot of 400 predicted and actual output values of the ozone data using the MLP as a time-series predictor with $k = 3$ and $\tau = 2$.

you show it at the input is reproduced at the output, which doesn't seem very useful at first, but suppose that we use a hidden layer that has fewer neurons than the input layer (see Figure 4.17). This **bottleneck** hidden layer has to represent all of the information in the input, so that it can be reproduced at the output. It therefore performs some **compression** of the data, representing it using fewer dimensions than were used in the input. This gives us some idea of what the hidden layers of the MLP are doing: they are finding a different (often lower dimensional) representation of the input data that extracts important components of the data, and ignores the noise.

This auto-associative network can be used to compress images and other data. A schematic of this is shown in Figure 4.18: the 2D image is turned into a 1D vector of inputs by cutting the image into strips and sticking the strips into a long line. The values of this vector are the intensity (colour) values of the image, and these are the input values. The network learns to reproduce the same image at the output, and the activations of the hidden nodes are recorded for each image. After training, we can throw away the input nodes and first set of weights of the network. If we insert some values in the hidden nodes (their activations for a particular image; see Figure 4.19), then by feeding these activations forward through the second set of weights, the correct image will be reproduced on the output. So all we need to store are the set of second-layer weights and the activations of the hidden nodes for each image, which is the compressed version.

Auto-associative networks can also be used to denoise images, since, after training, the network will reproduce the trained image that best matches the current (noisy) input. We don't throw away the first set of weights this time, but if we feed a noisy version of the image into the inputs, then the network will produce the image that is closest to the noisy version at the outputs, which will be the version it learnt on, which is uncorrupted by noise.

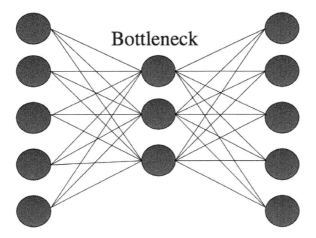

FIGURE 4.17 The auto-associative network. The network is trained to reproduce the inputs at the outputs, passing them through the bottleneck hidden layer that compresses the data.

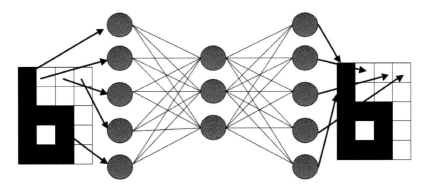

FIGURE 4.18 Schematic showing how images are fed into the auto-associative network for compression.

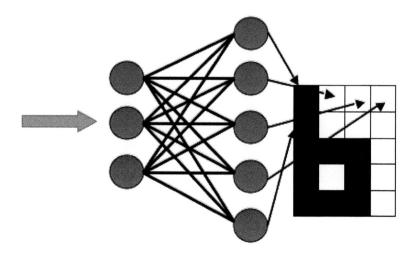

FIGURE 4.19 Schematic showing how the hidden nodes and second layer of weights can be used to regain the compressed images after the network has been trained.

You might be wondering what this representation in the hidden nodes looks like. In fact, if the nodes all have linear activation, then what the network learns to compute are the **Principal Components** of the input data. Principal Components Analysis (PCA) is a useful dimensionality reduction technique, and is described in Section 6.2.

4.5 A RECIPE FOR USING THE MLP

We have covered a lot in this chapter, so I'm going to give you a 'recipe' for how to use the Multi-layer Perceptron when presented with a dataset. This is, by necessity, a simplification of the problem, but it should serve to remind you of many of the important features.

Select inputs and outputs for your problem Before anything else, you need to think about the problem you are trying to solve, and make sure that you have data for the problem, both input vectors and target outputs. At this stage you need to choose what features are suitable for the problem (something we'll talk about more in other chapters) and decide on the output encoding that you will use — standard neurons, or linear nodes. These things are often decided for you by the input features and targets that you have available to solve the problem. Later on in the learning it can also be useful to re-evaluate the choice by training networks with some input feature missing to see if it improves the results at all.

Normalise inputs Rescale the data by subtracting the mean value from each element of the input vector, and divide by the variance (or alternatively, either the maximum or minus the minimum, whichever is greater).

Split the data into training, testing, and validation sets You cannot test the learning ability of the network on the same data that you trained it on, since it will generally fit that data very well (often too well, overfitting and modelling the noise in the data as well as the generating function). We generally split the data into three sets, one for training, one for testing, and then a third set for validation, which is testing how well the network is learning during training. The ratio between the sizes of the three groups depends on how much data you have, but is often around 50:25:25. If you do not have enough data for this, use cross-validation instead.

Select a network architecture You already know how many input nodes there will be, and how many output neurons. You need to consider whether you will need a hidden layer at all, and if so how many neurons it should have in it. You might want to consider more than one hidden layer. The more complex the network, the more data it will need to be trained on, and the longer it will take. It might also be more subject to overfitting. The usual method of selecting a network architecture is to try several with different numbers of hidden nodes and see which works best.

Train a network The training of the neural network consists of applying the Multi-layer Perceptron algorithm to the training data. This is usually run in conjunction with early stopping, where after a few iterations of the algorithm through all of the training data, the generalisation ability of the network is tested by using the validation set. The neural network is very likely to have far too many degrees of freedom for the problem, and so after some amount of learning it will stop modelling the generating function of the data, and start to fit the noise and inaccuracies inherent in the training data. At this stage the error on the validation set will start to increase, and learning should be stopped.

Test the network Once you have a trained network that you are happy with, it is time to use the test data for the first (and only) time. This will enable you to see how well the network performs on some data that it has not seen before, and will tell you whether this network is likely to be usable for other data, for which you do not have targets.

4.6 DERIVING BACK-PROPAGATION

This section derives the back-propagation algorithm. This is important to understand how and why the algorithm works. There isn't actually that much mathematics involved except some slightly messy algebra. In fact, there are only three things that you really need to know. One is the derivative (with respect to x) of $\frac{1}{2}x^2$, which is x, and another is the chain rule, which says that $\frac{dy}{dx} = \frac{dy}{dt}\frac{dt}{dx}$. The third thing is very simple: $\frac{dy}{dx} = 0$ if y is not a function of x. With those three things clear in your mind, just follow through the algebra, and you'll be fine. We'll work in simple steps.

4.6.1 The Network Output and the Error

The output of the neural network (the end of the forward phase of the algorithm) is a function of three things:

- the current input ($\mathbf{x}$)

- the activation function $g(\cdot)$ of the nodes of the network

- the weights of the network ($\mathbf{v}$ for the first layer and $\mathbf{w}$ for the second)

We can't change the inputs, since they are what we are learning about, nor can we change the activation function as the algorithm learns. So the weights are the only things that we can vary to improve the performance of the network, i.e., to make it learn. However, we do need to think about the activation function, since the threshold function that we used for the Perceptron is not differentiable (it has a discontinuity at 0). We'll think about a better one in Section 4.6.3, but first we'll think about the error of the network. Remember that we have run the algorithm **forwards**, so that we have fed the inputs ($\mathbf{x}$) into the algorithm, used the first set of weights ($\mathbf{v}$) to compute the activations of the hidden neurons, then those activations and the second set of weights ($\mathbf{w}$) to compute the activations of the output neurons, which are the outputs of the network ($\mathbf{y}$). Note that I'm going to use i to be an index over the input nodes, j to be an index over the hidden layer neurons, and k to be an index over the output neurons.

4.6.2 The Error of the Network

When we discussed the Perceptron learning rule in the previous chapter we motivated it by minimising the error function $E = \sum_{k=1}^{N} y_k - t_k$. We then invented a learning rule that made this error smaller. We are going to do much better this time, because everything is computed from the principles of **gradient descent**.

To begin with, let's think about the error of the network. This is obviously going to have something to do with the difference between the outputs $\mathbf{y}$ and the targets $\mathbf{t}$, but I'm going to write it as $E(\mathbf{v}, \mathbf{w})$ to remind us that the only things that we can change are the weights $\mathbf{v}$ and $\mathbf{w}$, and that changing the weights changes the output, which in turn changes the error.

For the Perceptron we computed the error as $E = \sum_{k=1}^{N} y_k - t_k$, but there are some problems with this: if $t_k > y_k$, then the sign of the error is different to when $y_k > t_k$, so if we have lots of output nodes that are all wrong, but some have positive sign and some have negative sign, then they might cancel out. Instead, we'll choose the **sum-of-squares** error function, which calculates the difference between y_k and t_k for each node k, squares them, and adds them together (I've missed out the $\mathbf{v}$ in $E(\mathbf{w})$ because we don't use them here):

$$E(\mathbf{w}) \quad = \quad \frac{1}{2} \sum_{k=1}^{N} (y_k - t_k)^2 \tag{4.20}$$

$$= \quad \frac{1}{2} \sum_{k=1}^{N} \left[g \left(\sum_{j=0}^{M} w_{jk} a_j \right) - t_k \right]^2 \tag{4.21}$$

The second line adds in the input from the hidden layer neurons and the second-layer weights to decide on the activations of the output neurons. For now we're going to think about the Perceptron and index the input nodes by i and the output nodes by k, so Equation (4.21) will be replaced by:

$$\frac{1}{2} \sum_{k=1}^{N} \left[g \left(\sum_{i=0}^{L} w_{ik} x_i \right) - t_k \right]^2. \tag{4.22}$$

Now we can't differentiate the threshold function, which is what the Perceptron used for $g(\cdot)$, because it has a discontinuity (sudden jump) at the threshold value. So I'm going to miss it out completely for the moment. Also, for the Perceptron there are no hidden neurons, and so the activation of an output neuron is just $y_\kappa = \sum_{i=0}^{L} w_{i\kappa} x_i$ where x_i is the value of an input node, and the sum runs over the number of input nodes, including the bias node.

We are going to use a **gradient descent algorithm** that adjusts each weight $w_{\iota\kappa}$ for fixed values of ι and κ, in the direction of the negative gradient of $E(\mathbf{w})$. In what follows, the notation ∂ means the **partial derivative**, and is used because there are lots of different functions that we can differentiate E with respect to: all of the different weights. If you don't know what a partial derivative is, think of it as being the same as a normal derivative, but taking care that you differentiate in the correct direction. The gradient that we want to know is how the error function changes with respect to the different weights:

$$\frac{\partial E}{\partial w_{\iota\kappa}} = \frac{\partial}{\partial w_{\iota\kappa}}\left(\frac{1}{2}\sum_{k=1}^{N}(y_k - t_k)^2\right)$$

$$= \frac{1}{2}\sum_{k=1}^{N}2(y_k - t_k)\frac{\partial}{\partial w_{\iota\kappa}}\left(y_k - \sum_{i=0}^{L}w_{i\kappa}x_i\right) \qquad (4.23)$$

$$(4.24)$$

Now t_k is not a function of any of the weights, since it is a value given to the algorithm, so $\frac{\partial t_k}{\partial w_{\iota\kappa}} = 0$ for all values of k, ι, κ, and the only part of $\sum_{i=0}^{L}w_{i\kappa}x_i$ that is a function of $w_{\iota\kappa}$ is when $i = \iota$, that is $w_{\iota\kappa}$ itself, which has derivative 1. Hence:

$$\frac{\partial E}{\partial w_{\iota\kappa}} = \sum_{k=1}^{N}(t_k - y_k)(-x_\iota). \qquad (4.25)$$

Now the idea of the weight update rule is that we follow the gradient **downhill**, that is, in the direction $-\frac{\partial E}{\partial w_{\iota\kappa}}$. So the weight update rule (when we include the learning rate η) is:

$$w_{\iota\kappa} \leftarrow w_{\iota\kappa} + \eta(t_\kappa - y_\kappa)x_\iota, \qquad (4.26)$$

which hopefully looks familiar (see Equation (3.3)). Note that we are computing y_κ differently: for the Perceptron we used the threshold activation function, whereas in the work above we ignored the threshold function. This isn't very useful if we want units that act like neurons, because neurons either fire or do not fire, rather than varying continuously. However, if we want to be able to differentiate the output in order to use gradient descent, then we need a differentiable activation function, so that's what we'll talk about now.

4.6.3 Requirements of an Activation Function

In order to model a neuron we want an activation function that has the following properties:

- it must be differentiable so that we can compute the gradient

- it should saturate (become constant) at both ends of the range, so that the neuron either fires or does not fire

- it should change between the saturation values fairly quickly in the middle

There is a family of functions called **sigmoid functions** because they are S-shaped (see Figure 4.5) that satisfy all those criteria perfectly. The form in which it is generally used is:

$$a = g(h) = \frac{1}{1 + \exp(-\beta h)}, \qquad (4.27)$$

where β is some positive parameter. One happy feature of this function is that its derivative has an especially nice form:

$$g'(h) = \frac{dg}{dh} \quad = \quad \frac{d}{dh}(1 + e^{-\beta h})^{-1} \tag{4.28}$$

$$= \quad -1(1 + e^{-\beta h})^{-2}\frac{de^{-\beta h}}{dh} \tag{4.29}$$

$$= \quad -1(1 + e^{-\beta h})^{-2}(-\beta e^{-\beta h}) \tag{4.30}$$

$$= \quad \frac{\beta e^{-\beta h}}{(1 + e^{-\beta h})^2} \tag{4.31}$$

$$= \quad \beta g(h)(1 - g(h)) \tag{4.32}$$

$$= \quad \beta a(1 - a) \tag{4.33}$$

We'll be using this derivative later. So we've now got an error function and an activation function that we can compute derivatives of. We will consider some other possible activation functions for the output neurons in Section 4.6.5 and an alternative error function in Section 4.6.6. The next thing to do is work out how to use them in order to adjust the weights of the network.

4.6.4 Back-Propagation of Error

It is now that we'll need the chain rule that I reminded you of earlier. In the form that we want, it looks like this:

$$\frac{\partial E}{\partial w_{\zeta\kappa}} = \frac{\partial E}{\partial h_{\kappa}}\frac{\partial h_{\kappa}}{\partial w_{\zeta\kappa}}, \tag{4.34}$$

where $h_{\kappa} = \sum_{j=0}^{M} w_{j\kappa}a_{\zeta}$ is the input to output-layer neuron κ; that is, the sum of the activations of the hidden-layer neurons multiplied by the relevant (second-layer) weights. So what does Equation (4.34) say? It tells us that if we want to know how the error at the output changes as we vary the second-layer weights, we can think about how the error changes as we vary the input to the output neurons, and also about how those input values change as we vary the weights.

Let's think about the second term first (in the third line we use the fact that $\frac{\partial w_{j\kappa}}{\partial w_{\zeta\kappa}} = 0$ for all values of j except $j = \zeta$, when it is 1):

$$\frac{\partial h_{\kappa}}{\partial w_{\zeta\kappa}} \quad = \quad \frac{\partial \sum_{j=0}^{M} w_{j\kappa}a_j}{\partial w_{\zeta\kappa}} \tag{4.35}$$

$$= \quad \sum_{j=0}^{M}\frac{\partial w_{j\kappa}a_j}{\partial w_{\zeta\kappa}} \tag{4.36}$$

$$= \quad a_{\zeta}. \tag{4.37}$$

Now we can worry about the $\frac{\partial E}{\partial h_{\kappa}}$ term. This term is important enough to get its own term, which is the error or delta term:

$$\delta_o(\kappa) = \frac{\partial E}{\partial h_{\kappa}}. \tag{4.38}$$

Let's start off by trying to compute this error for the output. We can't actually compute it directly, since we don't know much about the inputs to a neuron, we just know about its output. That's fine, because we can use the chain rule again:

$$\delta_o(\kappa) = \frac{\partial E}{\partial h_\kappa} = \frac{\partial E}{\partial y_\kappa} \frac{\partial y_\kappa}{\partial h_\kappa}. \tag{4.39}$$

Now the output of output layer neuron κ is

$$y_\kappa = g(h_\kappa^{\text{output}}) = g \left(\sum_{j=0}^{M} w_{j\kappa} a_j^{\text{hidden}} \right), \tag{4.40}$$

where $g(\cdot)$ is the activation function. There are different possible choices for $g(\cdot)$ including the sigmoid function given in Equation (4.27), so for now I'm going to leave it as a function. I've also started labelling whether h refers to an output or hidden layer neuron, just to avoid any possible confusion. We don't need to worry about this for the activations, because we use y for the activations of output neurons and a for hidden neurons. In Equation (4.43) I've substituted in the expression for the error at the output, which we computed in Equation (4.21):

$$\delta_o(\kappa) = \frac{\partial E}{\partial g \left(h_\kappa^{\text{output}} \right)} \frac{\partial g \left(h_\kappa^{\text{output}} \right)}{\partial h_\kappa^{\text{output}}} \tag{4.41}$$

$$= \frac{\partial E}{\partial g \left(h_\kappa^{\text{output}} \right)} g' \left(h_\kappa^{\text{output}} \right) \tag{4.42}$$

$$= \frac{\partial}{\partial g \left(h_\kappa^{\text{output}} \right)} \left[\frac{1}{2} \sum_{k=1}^{N} \left(g(h_k^{\text{output}}) - t_k \right)^2 \right] g' \left(h_\kappa^{\text{output}} \right) \tag{4.43}$$

$$= \left(g(h_\kappa^{\text{output}}) - t_\kappa \right) g'(h_\kappa^{\text{output}}) \tag{4.44}$$

$$= (y_\kappa - t_\kappa) g'(h_\kappa^{\text{output}}), \tag{4.45}$$

where $g'(h_\kappa)$ denotes the derivative of g with respect to h_κ. This will change depending upon which activation function we use for the output neurons, so for now we will write the update equation for the output layer weights in a slightly general form and pick it up again at the end of the section:

$$
\begin{aligned}
w_{\zeta\kappa} &\leftarrow w_{\zeta\kappa} - \eta \frac{\partial E}{\partial w_{\zeta\kappa}} \\
&= w_{\zeta\kappa} - \eta \delta_o(\kappa) a_\zeta.
\end{aligned}
\tag{4.46}
$$

where we are using the minus sign because we want to go downhill to minimise the error.

We don't actually need to do too much more work to get to the first layer weights, v_ι, which connects input ι to hidden node ζ. We need the chain rule (Equation (4.34)) one more time to get to these weights, remembering that we are working **backwards** through the network so that k runs over the output nodes. The way to think about this is that each hidden node contributes to the activation of all of the output nodes, and so we need to consider all of these contributions (with the relevant weights).

$$\delta_h(\zeta) \;=\; \sum_{k=1}^{N} \frac{\partial E}{\partial h_k^{\text{output}}} \frac{\partial h_k^{\text{output}}}{\partial h_\zeta^{\text{hidden}}} \tag{4.47}$$

$$=\; \sum_{k=1}^{N} \delta_o(k) \frac{\partial h_k^{\text{output}}}{\partial h_\zeta^{\text{hidden}}}, \tag{4.48}$$

where we obtain the second line by using Equation (4.38). We now need a nicer expression for that derivative. The important thing that we need to remember is that inputs to the output layer neurons come from the activations of the hidden layer neurons multiplied by the second layer weights:

$$h_\kappa^{\text{output}} = \sum_{j=0}^{M} w_{j\kappa} g\left(h_j^{\text{hidden}}\right), \tag{4.49}$$

which means that:

$$\frac{\partial h_\kappa^{\text{output}}}{\partial h_\zeta^{\text{hidden}}} = \frac{\partial g\left(\sum_{j=0}^{M} w_{j\kappa} h_j^{\text{hidden}}\right)}{\partial h_j^{\text{hidden}}}. \tag{4.50}$$

We can now use a fact that we've used before, which is that $\frac{\partial h_\zeta}{\partial h_j} = 0$ unless $j = \zeta$, when it is 1. So:

$$\frac{\partial h_\kappa^{\text{output}}}{\partial h_\zeta^{\text{hidden}}} = w_{\zeta\kappa} g'(a_\zeta). \tag{4.51}$$

The hidden nodes always have sigmoidal activation functions, so that we can use the derivative that we computed in Equation (4.33) to get that $g'(a_\zeta) = \beta a_\zeta(1 - a_\zeta)$, which allows us to compute:

$$\delta_h(\zeta) = \beta a_\zeta(1 - a_\zeta) \sum_{k=1}^{N} \delta_o(k) w_\zeta. \tag{4.52}$$

This means that the update rule for v_ι is:

$$v_\iota \;\leftarrow\; v_\iota - \eta \frac{\partial E}{\partial v_\iota}$$

$$=\; v_\iota - \eta a_\zeta(1 - a_\zeta) \left(\sum_{k=1}^{N} \delta_o(k) w_\zeta\right) x_\iota. \tag{4.53}$$

Note that we can do exactly the same computations if the network has extra hidden layers between the inputs and the outputs. It gets harder to keep track of which functions we should be differentiating, but there are no new tricks needed.

4.6.5 The Output Activation Functions

The sigmoidal activation function that we have created is aimed at making the nodes act a bit like neurons, either firing or not firing. This is very important in the hidden layer, but earlier in the chapter we have observed two cases where it is not suitable for the output neurons. One was regression, where we want the output to be continuous, and one was multi-class classification, where we want only one of the output neurons to fire. We identified possible activation functions for these cases, and here we will derive the delta term δ_o for them. As a reminder, the three functions are:

Linear $y_\kappa = g(h_\kappa) = h_\kappa$

Sigmoidal $y_\kappa = g(h_\kappa) = 1/(1 + \exp(-\beta h_\kappa))$

Soft-max $y_\kappa = g(h_\kappa) = \exp(h_\kappa)/\sum_{k=1}^{N} \exp(h_k)$

For each of these we need the derivative with respect to each of the output weights so that we can use Equation (4.45).

This is easy for the first two cases, and tells us that for linear outputs $\delta_o(\kappa) = (y_\kappa - t(\kappa))y_\kappa$, while for sigmoidal outputs it is $\delta_o(\kappa) = \beta(y_\kappa - t(\kappa))y_\kappa(1 - y_\kappa)$.

However, we have to do some more work for the soft-max case, since we haven't differentiated it yet. If we write it as:

$$\frac{\partial}{\partial h_K} y_\kappa = \frac{\partial}{\partial h_K}\left(\exp(h_\kappa)\left(\sum_{k=1}^{N}\exp(h_k)\right)^{-1}\right) \tag{4.54}$$

then the problem becomes clear: we have a product of two things to differentiate, and three different indices to worry about. Further, the k index runs over all the output nodes, and so includes K and κ within it. There are two cases: either $K = \kappa$, or it does not. If they are the same, then we can write that $\frac{\partial \exp(h_\kappa)}{\partial h_{kappa}} = \exp(h_\kappa)$ to get (where the last term in the first line comes from the use of the chain rule):

$$\frac{\partial}{\partial h_\kappa}\left(\exp(h_\kappa)\left(\sum_{k=1}^{N}\exp(h_k)\right)^{-1}\right)$$
$$= \exp(h_\kappa)\left(\sum_{k=1}^{N}\exp(h_k)\right)^{-1} - \exp(h_\kappa)\left(\sum_{k=1}^{N}\exp(h_k)\right)^{-2}\exp(h_\kappa)$$
$$= y_\kappa(1 - y_\kappa). \tag{4.55}$$

For the case where $K \neq \kappa$ things are a little easier, and we get:

$$\frac{\partial}{\partial h_K}\exp(h_\kappa)\left(\sum_{k=1}^{N}\exp(h_k)\right)^{-1} = -\exp(h_\kappa)\exp(h_K)\left(\sum_{k=1}^{N}\exp(h_k)\right)^{-2}$$
$$= -y_\kappa y_K. \tag{4.56}$$

Using the **Kronecker delta function** δ_{ij}, which is 1 if $i = j$ and 0 otherwise, we can write the two cases in one equation to get the delta term:

$$\delta_o(\kappa) = (y_\kappa - t_\kappa)y_\kappa(\delta_{\kappa K} - y_K). \tag{4.57}$$

The very last thing to think about is whether or not the sum-of-squares error function is always the best one to use.

4.6.6   An Alternative Error Function

We have been using the sum-of-squares error function throughout this chapter. It is easy to compute and works well in general; we will see another benefit of it in Section 9.2. However, for classification tasks we are assuming that the outputs represent different, independent classes, and this means that we can think of the activations of the nodes as giving us a probability that each class is the correct one.

In this probabilistic interpretation of the outputs, we can ask how likely we are to see each target given the set of weights that we are using. This is known as the likelihood and the aim is to maximise it, so that we predict the targets as well as possible. If we have a 1 output node, taking values 0 or 1, then the likelihood is:

$$p(t|\mathbf{w}) = y_k^{t_k} (1 - y_k)^{1-t_k}. \tag{4.58}$$

In order to turn this into a minimisation function we put a minus sign in front, and it will turn out to be useful to take the logarithm of it as well, which produces the **cross-entropy** error function, which is (for N output nodes):

$$E_{\text{ce}} = -\sum_{k=1}^{N} t_k \ln(y_k), \tag{4.59}$$

where ln is the natural logarithm. This error function has the nice property that when we use the soft-max function the derivatives are very easy because the exponential and logarithm are inverse functions, and so the delta term is simply $\delta_o(\kappa) = y_\kappa - t_\kappa$.

FURTHER READING

The original papers describing the back-propagation algorithm are listed here, along with a well-known introduction to neural networks:

- D.E. Rumelhart, G.E. Hinton, and R.J. Williams. Learning internal representations by back-propagating errors. *Nature*, 323(99):533–536, 1986a.

- D.E. Rumelhart, J.L. McClelland, and the PDP Research Group, editors. *Parallel Distributed Processing*. MIT Press, Cambridge, MA, 1986b.

- R. Lippmann. An introduction to computing with neural nets. *IEEE ASSP Magazine*, pages 4–22, 1987.

For more on the Universal Approximation Theorem, which shows that one hidden layer is sufficient, some references (which are not for the mathematically faint-hearted) are:

- G. Cybenko. Approximations by superpositions of sigmoidal functions. *Mathematics of Control, Signals, and Systems*, 2(4):303–314, 1989.

- Kurt Hornik. Approximation capabilities of multilayer feedforward networks. *Neural Networks*, 4(2):251–257, 1991.

If you are interested in novelty detection, then a review article is:

- S. Marsland. Novelty detection in learning systems. *Neural Computing Surveys*, 3: 157–195, 2003.

The topics in this chapter are covered in any book on machine learning and neural networks. Different treatments are given by:

- Sections 5.1–5.3 of C.M. Bishop. *Pattern Recognition and Machine Learning.* Springer, Berlin, Germany, 2006.

- Section 5.4 of J. Hertz, A. Krogh, and R.G. Palmer. *Introduction to the Theory of Neural Computation.* Addison-Wesley, Redwood City, CA, USA, 1991.

- Sections 4.4–4.7 of T. Mitchell. *Machine Learning.* McGraw-Hill, New York, USA, 1997.

PRACTICE QUESTIONS

Problem 4.1 Work through the MLP shown in Figure 4.2 to ensure that it does solve the XOR problem.

Problem 4.2 Suppose that the local power company wants to predict electricity demand for the next 5 days. They have the data about daily demand for the last 5 years. Typically, the demand will be a number between 80 and 400.

1. Describe how you could use an MLP to make the prediction. What parameters would you have to choose, and what do you think would be sensible values for them?

2. If the weather forecast for the next day, being the estimated temperatures for daytime and nighttime, was available, how would you add that into your system?

3. Do you think that this system would work well for predicting power consumption? Are there demands that it would not be able to predict?

Problem 4.3 Design an MLP that would learn to hyphenate words correctly. You would have a dictionary that shows correct hyphenation examples for lots of words, and you need to choose methods of encoding the inputs and outputs that say whether a hyphen is allowed between each pair of letters. You should also describe how you would perform training and testing.

Problem 4.4 Would the previous system be better than just using the dictionary?

Problem 4.5 Modify the code on the book website to work sequentially rather than in batch mode. Compare the results on the iris dataset.

Problem 4.6 Modify the code so that it performs minibatch optimisation and then stochastic gradient descent (both described in Section 4.2.7) and compare the results with using the standard algorithm on the Pima Indian dataset that was described in Section 3.4.4. Experiment with different sizes for the minibatches.

Problem 4.7 Modify the code to allow another hidden layer to be used. You will have to work out the gradient as well in order to compute the weight updates for the extra layer of weights. Test this new network on the Pima Indian dataset that was described in Section 3.4.4.

Problem 4.8 Modify the code to use the alternative error term in Section 4.6.6 and see what difference it makes for classification problems.

Problem 4.9 A hospital manager wants to predict how many beds will be needed in the geriatric ward. He asks you to design a neural network method for making this prediction. He has data for the last 5 years that cover:

- The number of people in the geriatric ward each week.
- The weather (average day and night temperatures).
- The season of the year (spring, summer, autumn, winter).
- Whether or not there was an epidemic on (use a binary variable: yes or no).

Design a suitable MLP for this problem, considering how you would choose the number of hidden neurons, the inputs (and whether there are any other inputs you need) and the preprocessing, and whether or not you would expect the system to work.

Problem 4.10 Look into the MNIST dataset that is available via the book website. Implement an MLP to learn about them and test different numbers of hidden nodes.

Problem 4.11 A recurrent network has some of its outputs connected to its own inputs, so that the outputs at time t are fed back into the network at time $t + 1$. This can be a different way to deal with time-series data. Modify the MLP code so that it acts as a recurrent network, and test it out on the Palmerston North ozone data on the book website.

Problem 4.12 The alternative activation function that can be used in $\tanh(h)$. Show that $\tanh(h) = 2g(2h) - 1$, where g is given by Equation (4.2). Use this to show that there is an exactly equivalent MLP using the tanh activation function. Modify the code to implement it.

Radial Basis Functions and Splines

In the Multi-layer Perceptron, the activations of the hidden nodes were decided by whether the inputs times the weights were above a threshold that made the neuron fire. While we had to sacrifice some of this ideal to the requirement for differentiability, it was still the case that the product of the inputs and the weights was summed, and if it was well above the threshold then the neuron fired, if it was well below the threshold it did not, and between those values it acted linearly. For any input vector several of the neurons could fire, and the outputs of these neurons times their weights were then summed in the second layer to decide which neurons should fire there. This has the result that the activity in the hidden layer is **distributed** over the neurons there, and it is this pattern of activation that was used as the inputs to the next layer.

In this chapter we are going to consider a different approach, which is to use **local** neurons, where each neuron only responds to inputs in one particular part of the input space. The argument is that if inputs are similar, then the responses to those inputs should also be similar, and so the same neuron should respond. Extending this a little, if an input is between two others, then the neurons that respond to each of the inputs should both fire to some extent. We can justify this by thinking about a typical classification task, since if two input vectors are similar, then they should presumably belong to the same class. In order to understand this better we are going to need two concepts, one from machine learning, **weight space**, and one from neuroscience, **receptive fields**.

5.1 RECEPTIVE FIELDS

In Section 2.1.1 we argued that one way to compute the activations of neurons was to use the concept of **weight space** to abstractly plot them in the same set of dimensions as the inputs, and to have neurons that were 'closer' to the input being more highly activated. To see why this might be a good idea, we need to look at the idea of **receptive fields**.

Suppose that we have a set of 'nodes' (since they are no longer models of neurons in any sense, the terminology changes to call the components of the network 'nodes'). As in Section 2.1.1, these nodes are imagined to be sitting in weight space, and we can change their locations by adjusting the weights. We want to decide how strongly a node matches the current input, so just like in Section 2.1.1 we pretend that input space and weight space are the same, and measure the distance between the input vector position and the position of each node. The activation of these nodes can then be computed according to their distance to the current input, in ways that we'll get to later.

To put this idea of nodes firing when they are 'close' to the input into some sort of context, we are going to have a quick digression into the idea of **receptive fields**. Imagine the back of your eye. Light comes through the pupil and hits the retina, which has light-sensitive cells (rods and cones) spread across it. Now suppose that you look at the night sky with one bright star in it. How will you see the star, or to put it another way, which rods on your retina will detect the light of the star? The obvious answer is that there will be one localised area of your retina that picks up the light, and a few rods that are close together will detect it, while the rest don't see anything except the dark night sky. However, if you looked at the sky again a few hours later, when the position of the star in the sky had changed, then different rods would detect it (assuming that your head is in the same position, of course). So even though the appearance of the star is the same, because the relative position of the star has changed because the earth has rotated, so the rods that you use to detect it have changed. The receptive field of a particular rod within your eye is the area on your retina that it responds to light from. We can extend this to particular sensory neurons as well, so that the response of particular neurons may depend on the location of the stimulus.

We might want to know what shape these receptive fields are, and how the response of the rod (or neuron) changes as the stimulus moves away from the area that matches the rod. If we were equipped with a neuroscience lab with electrodes and measurement devices (and animals, and ethics approval) then we could measure exactly this. We could show pictures of light blobs on dark backgrounds to animals and measure the amount of neuronal activity in particular neurons as the position of the blob moved. And people have done exactly this.

For now, let's just try a **thought experiment**: it's simpler and cheaper, and nothing gets hurt. If we are looking at our star again, then we have already worked out that there is a set of rods that is detecting the light, and plenty of others that aren't. What about a rod that is just at the boundary where the light from the star stops being visible? Let's pick one where its receptive field stops just to the left of this boundary, so that the neuron is not firing. Now move your head slightly to the right, so that it is just inside. What happens? For a real neuron it would start to spike. Assuming that the number of times the neuron spikes says how bright the light that it detects is (which probably isn't exactly true), then it wouldn't spike very often. As you move your head to the right again so that the light on that particular neuron gets brighter and brighter, that neuron will spike more and more often, until once you've moved your head past the light and the spiking slows down, and eventually stops. The left-hand graph of Figure 5.1 shows this, with the points plotted and a smooth curve that goes through them.

Now suppose that you repeat the experiment, but this time you start with the star below your vision and move your head down until you can see it, and then keep on moving your head further down. The exact same thing happens. The graph in the middle of Figure 5.1 shows this. So for this example, it doesn't matter where the point of light is with regard to the neuron, just how far away it is. In other words, if we were to put the star on a wire circle centred on one particular rod within our eye (a bit painful, but that's the good thing about thought experiments), then as we moved the light along the wire the activation of the rod would not change. Only the radius of the circle matters, which is why functions that model this are known as **radial** functions. Mathematically, we say that they only depend on the **two-norm** $\|\mathbf{x}_i - \mathbf{x}\|_2$, that is the Euclidean distance between the point and the centre of the circle.

The main thing that we have not decided yet is how the drop-off should occur from response to maximum brightness to nothing. For real neurons the drop-off has to change

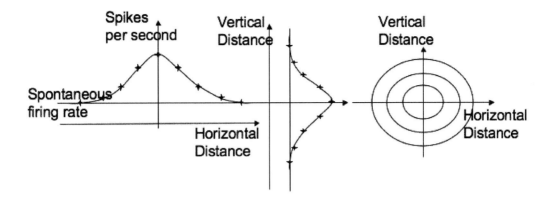

FIGURE 5.1 *Left:* Count of the number of spikes per second as the distance of a rod from the light varies horizontally. Note that it does not go to zero, but to the spontaneous firing rate of the neuron, which is how often it fires without input. *Centre:* The same thing for vertical motion. *Right:* The combination of the two makes a set of circles.

between integer values, but for our mathematical model it doesn't: we can make it decrease smoothly, so that we can use well-behaved (that is, differentiable) mathematical functions. Then we can pick any function that we can differentiate, that decreases symmetrically (in all directions, or radially) from a maximum to zero. There are obviously lots of possible functions with this property that we can pick, but for now we'll go with by far the most common one in statistics, the Gaussian, something that was important enough to get its own section earlier on (Section 2.4.3). It doesn't really go to 0, but if we truncate it a little, then the output value becomes 0 fairly quickly as we move away from the centre. We do not typically use a real Gaussian function for the activation function, ignoring the normalisation to get an approximation to it written as:

$$g(\mathbf{x}, \mathbf{w}, \sigma) = \exp\left(\frac{-\|\mathbf{x} - \mathbf{w}\|^2}{2\sigma^2}\right). \tag{5.1}$$

The choice of σ in this equation is quite important, since it controls the width of the Gaussian. If we make it infinitely large, then the neuron responds to every input. Suppose instead that we make σ smaller and smaller, so that the Gaussian gets thinner and thinner. This means that the receptive field gets narrower and narrower. Eventually, this neuron will respond to exactly one stimulus, and even then, if the input is corrupted by noise, it won't recognise it. This function is sometimes known as an indicator or delta function. Picking the value of σ for each individual node needs to be part of the algorithm.

So, we can use Gaussians to model these receptive fields for neurons so that nodes will fire strongly if the input is close to them, less strongly if the input is further away, and not at all if it is even further away. We are going to see several neural networks in different chapters that use these ideas, mostly for unsupervised learning, but first we will see a supervised one, the radial basis function (RBF) network. Figure 5.2 shows a set of nodes that represent radial bases in weight space. They are often known as centres because they each form the centre of their own circle or ellipse.

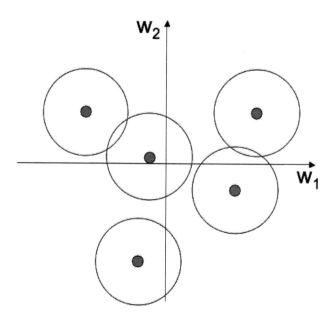

FIGURE 5.2 The effect of radial basis functions in weight space. The points show the position of the RBF in weight space, while the circle around each point shows the receptive field of the node. In higher dimensions these circles become hyperspheres.

5.2 THE RADIAL BASIS FUNCTION (RBF) NETWORK

The argument that started this chapter was that inputs that are close together should generate the same output, whereas inputs that are far apart should not. We have seen that using Gaussian activations, where the output of a neuron is proportional to the distance between the input and the weight, gives us receptive fields. The Gaussian activations mean that normalising the input vectors is very important for the RBF network; Section 14.1.3 will make the reason for this clearer. For any input that we present to a set of these neurons, some of them will fire strongly, some weakly, and some will not fire at all, depending upon the distance between the weights and the particular input in weight space. We can treat these nodes as a hidden layer, just as we did for the MLP, and connect up some output nodes in a second layer. This simply requires adding weights from each hidden (RBF) neuron to a set of output nodes. This is known as an RBF network, and a schematic is shown in Figure 5.3. In the figure, the nodes in both the hidden and output layer are drawn the same, but we haven't decided what kind of nodes to use in the output layer—they don't need to have Gaussian activations. The simplest solution is to use McCulloch and Pitts neurons, in which case this second part of the network is simply a Perceptron network. Note that there is a bias input for the output layer, which deals with the situation when none of the RBF neurons fire. Since we already know exactly how to train the Perceptron, training this second part of the network is easy. The questions that we need to ask are whether or not it is any better than using a Perceptron, and how to train the first layer weights that position the RBF neurons.

A little thought should persuade you that this network is better than just a Perceptron, since the inputs that are given to the Perceptron are non-linear functions of the inputs. In

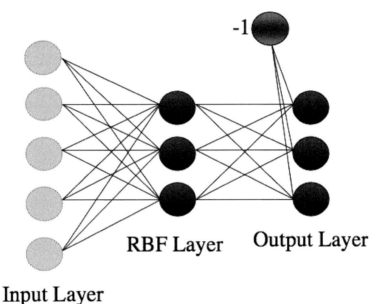

FIGURE 5.3 The Radial Basis Function network consists of input nodes connected by weights to a set of RBF neurons, which fire proportionally to the distance between the input and the neuron in weight space. The activations of these nodes are used as inputs to the second layer, which consists of linear nodes. The schematic looks very similar to the MLP except for the lack of a bias in the hidden layer.

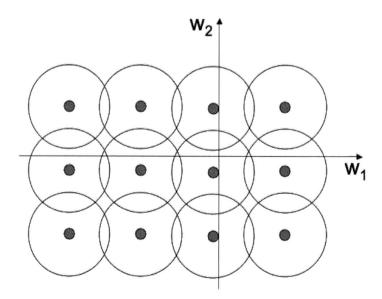

FIGURE 5.4 We can space out RBF nodes to cover the whole of space by continuing this pattern everywhere, so that the network acts as a universal approximator, since there is an output for every possible input.

fact, the RBF network is a universal approximator, just like the MLP. To see this, imagine that we fill the entire space with RBF nodes equally spaced in all directions, so that their receptive fields just overlap, as in Figure 5.4. Now, no matter what the input, there is an RBF node that recognises it and can respond appropriately to it. If we need to make the outputs more finely grained, then we just add more RBFs at the relevant positions and reduce the radius of the receptive fields; and if we don't care, we can just make the receptive fields of each node bigger and use fewer of them.

RBF networks never have more than one layer of non-linear neurons, in contrast to the MLP. However, there are many similarities between the two networks: they are both supervised learning algorithms that form universal approximators. In fact, it turns out that you can turn one into the other because the two types of neuron firing rules (RBFs based on distance and MLPs on inner product) are related. This fact will turn up in another form in Section 14.1.3. The most important difference between them is the fact that the MLP uses the hidden nodes to separate the space using hyperplanes, which are global, while the RBF uses them to match functions locally.

In an RBF network, when we see an input several of the nodes will activate to some degree or other, according to how close they are to the input, and the combination of these activations will enable the network to decide how to respond. Using the analogy we had earlier of looking at a star, suppose that the star is replaced by a torch, and somebody is signalling directions to us. If the torch is high (at 12 o'clock) we go forwards, low (6 o'clock) we go backwards, and left and right (9 and 3 o'clock, respectively) mean that we turn. The RBF network would work in such a way that if the torch was at 2 o'clock or thereabouts, then we would do some of the 12 o'clock action and a bit more of the 3 o'clock action, but none of the 6 or 9 o'clock actions. So we would move forwards and to the right. This adding up of the contributions from the different basis functions according to how active they are means that our responses are local.

5.2.1 Training the RBF Network

In the MLP we used back-propagation of error to adjust first the output layer weights, and then the hidden layer weights. We can do exactly the same thing with the RBF network, by differentiating the relevant activation functions. However, there are simpler and better alternatives for RBF networks. They do not need to compute gradients for the hidden nodes and so they are significantly faster. The important thing to notice is that the two types of node provide different functions, and so they do not need to be trained together. The purpose of the RBF nodes in the hidden layer is to find a non-linear representation of the inputs, while the purpose of the output layer is to find a linear combination of those hidden nodes that does the classification. So we can split the training into two parts: position the RBF nodes, and then use the activations of those nodes to train the linear outputs. This makes things much simpler. For the linear outputs we can use an algorithm that we already know: the Perceptron (Section 3.3).

However, we need to work out something different for the first layer weights, which control the positions of the RBF nodes. One thing that we can do is to avoid the problem of training completely by randomly picking some of the datapoints to act as basis locations. Provided that our training data are representative of the full dataset, this often turns out to be a good solution. The other thing that we can do is to try to position the nodes so that they are representative of typical inputs. This is precisely the problem solved by several unsupervised learning methods, and we are going to see several algorithms for doing this in Chapter 14. For the RBF network, the most common one is the k-means algorithm that is described in Section 14.1. Thus, training an RBF network can be reduced to using two other algorithms that are commonly used in machine learning, one after the other. This is known as a hybrid algorithm, since it combines supervised and unsupervised learning.

The Radial Basic Function Algorithm

- Position the RBF centres by either:

  - using the k-means algorithm to initialise the positions of the RBF centres OR
  - setting the RBF centres to be randomly chosen datapoints

- Calculate the actions of the RBF nodes using Equation (5.1)

- Train the output weights by either:

  - using the Perceptron OR
  - computing the pseudo-inverse of the activations of the RBF centres (this will be described shortly)

To implement this in Python we can simply `import` the other algorithms, and use them directly (if they are in different directories, then you need to add them to the `PYTHONPATH` variable; precisely how to do this varies between programming IDEs). The training is then very simple:

```
def rbftrain(self,inputs,targets,eta=0.25,niterations=100):

    if self.usekmeans==0:
        # Version 1: set RBFs to be datapoints
        indices = range(self.ndata)
        np.random.shuffle(indices)
        for i in range(self.nRBF):
            self.weights1[:,i] = inputs[indices[i],:]
    else:
        # Version 2: use k-means
        self.weights1 = np.transpose(self.kmeansnet.kmeanstrain(inputs))

    for i in range(self.nRBF):
        self.hidden[:,i] = np.exp(-np.sum((inputs - np.ones((1,self.nin))
        *self.weights1[:,i])**2,axis=1)/(2*self.sigma**2))
    if self.normalise:
        self.hidden[:,:-1] /= np.transpose(np.ones((1,np.shape(self.
        hidden)[0]))*self.hidden[:,:-1].sum(axis=1))

    # Call Perceptron without bias node (since it adds its own)
    self.perceptron.pcntrain(self.hidden[:,:-1],targets,eta,niterations)
```

In fact, because of this separation of the two learning parts, we can do better than a Perceptron for training the outputs weights. For each input vector, we compute the activation of all the hidden nodes, and assemble them into a matrix $\mathbf{G}$. So each element of $\mathbf{G}$, say $\mathbf{G}_{ij}$, consists of the activation of hidden node j for input i. The outputs of the network can then be computed as $\mathbf{y} = \mathbf{GW}$ for set of weights $\mathbf{W}$. Except that we don't know what the weights are—that is what we set out to compute—and we want to choose them using the target outputs $\mathbf{t}$.

If we were able to get all of the outputs correct, then we could write $\mathbf{t} = \mathbf{GW}$. Now we just need to calculate the matrix inverse of $\mathbf{G}$, to get $\mathbf{W} = \mathbf{G}^{-1}\mathbf{t}$. Unfortunately, there is a little problem here. The matrix inverse is only defined if a matrix is square, and this one probably isn't—there is no reason why the number of hidden nodes should be the same as the number of training inputs. In fact, we hope it isn't, since that would probably be serious overfitting.

Fortunately, there is a well-defined pseudo-inverse $\mathbf{G}^{+}$ of a matrix, which is $\mathbf{G}^{+} = (\mathbf{G}^{T}\mathbf{G})^{-1}\mathbf{G}^{T}$. Since the point of the inverse $\mathbf{G}^{-1}$ to a matrix $\mathbf{G}$ is that $\mathbf{G}^{-1}\mathbf{G} = \mathbf{I}$, where $\mathbf{I}$ is the identity matrix, the pseudo-inverse is the matrix that satisfies $\mathbf{G}^{+}\mathbf{G} = \mathbf{I}$. If $\mathbf{G}$ is a square, non-singular (i.e., with non-zero determinant) matrix then $\mathbf{G}^{+} = \mathbf{G}^{-1}$. In NumPy the pseudo-inverse is np.linalg.pinv(). This gives us an alternative to the Perceptron network that is even faster, since the training only needs one iteration:

```
self.weights2 = np.dot(np.linalg.pinv(self.hidden),targets)
```

There is one thing that we haven't considered yet, and that is the size of the receptive fields σ for the nodes. We can avoid the problem by giving all of the nodes the same size, and testing lots of different sizes using a validation set to select one that works. Alternatively, we can select it in advance by arguing that the important thing is that the whole space is covered by the receptive fields of the entire set of basis functions, and so the width of the Gaussians should be set according to the maximum distance between the locations of the hidden nodes (d) and the number of hidden nodes. The most common choice is to pick the width of the Gaussian as $\sigma = d/\sqrt{2M}$, where M is the number of RBFs.

There is another way to deal with the fact that there may be inputs that are outside the receptive fields of all nodes, and that is to use **normalised Gaussians**, so that there is always at least one input firing: the node that is closest to the current input, even if that is a long way off. It is a modification of Equation (5.1) and it looks like the soft-max function:

$$g(\mathbf{x}, \mathbf{w}, \sigma) = \frac{\exp(-\|\mathbf{x} - \mathbf{w}\|/2\sigma^2)}{\sum_i \exp(-\|\mathbf{x} - \mathbf{w}_i\|/2\sigma^2)}. \tag{5.2}$$

Using the RBF network on the `iris` dataset that was used in Section 4.4.3 with five RBF centres gives similar results to the MLP, with well over 90% classification accuracy.

With the MLP, one question that we failed to find a nice answer to was how to pick the number of hidden nodes, and we were reduced to training lots of networks with different numbers of nodes and using the one that performed best on the validation set. The same problem occurs with the RBF network.

In the RBF network the activations of the hidden nodes is based on the distance between the current input and the weights. There are various measures of distance that we can use, as will be discussed in Section 7.2.3; we generally use the Euclidean distance. These distances can be computed for any number of dimensions, but as the number of dimensions increases, something rather worrying happens, which is that we start needing more RBF nodes to cover the space. The number of input dimensions has a profound effect on learning, something that has a suitably impressive name that we have already seen—the **curse of dimensionality** (Section 2.1.2). For RBFs, the effect of the curse is that the amount of the space covered by an RBF with a fixed receptive field will decrease, and so we will need many more of them to cover the space.

5.3 INTERPOLATION AND BASIS FUNCTIONS

One of the problems that we looked at in Chapter 1 was that of **function approximation**: given some data, find a function that goes through the data without overfitting to the noise, so that values between the known datapoints can be inferred or **interpolated**. The RBF network solves this problem by each of the basis functions making a contribution to the output whenever the input is within its receptive field. So several RBF nodes will probably respond for each input.

We are now going to make the problem a bit simpler. We won't allow the receptive fields to overlap, and we'll space them out so that they just meet up with each other. Obviously, we won't need the Gaussian part that decides how much each one matches now, either. If the datapoint is within the receptive field of this function then we listen only to this function, otherwise we ignore it and listen to some other function. If each function just returns the average value within its patch, then for one-dimensional data we get a histogram output, as is shown in Figure 5.5. We can extend this a bit further so that the lines are not horizontal, but instead reflect the first derivative of the curve at that point, as is shown in Figure 5.6. This is all right, but we might want the output to be continuous, so that the line within the first bin meets up with the line in the second bin at the boundary, so we can add the extra constraint that the lines have to meet up as well. This gives the curve in Figure 5.7.

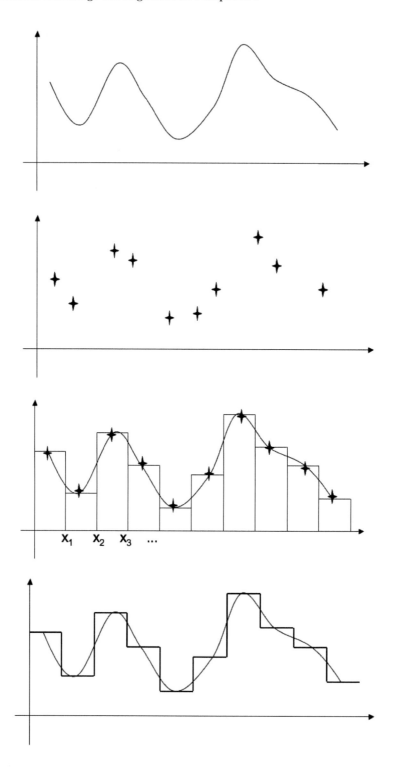

FIGURE 5.5 *Top:* Curve showing a function. *Second:* A set of datapoints from the curve. *Third:* Putting a straight horizontal line through each point creates a histogram that describes an approximation to the curve. *Bottom:* That approximation.

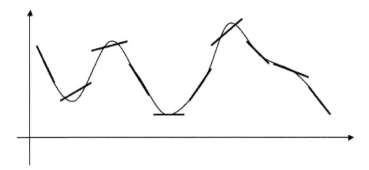

FIGURE 5.6 Representing the points by straight lines that aren't necessarily horizontal (so that their first derivative matches at the point) gives a better approximation.

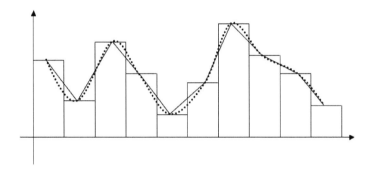

FIGURE 5.7 Making the straight lines meet so that the function is continuous gives a better approximation.

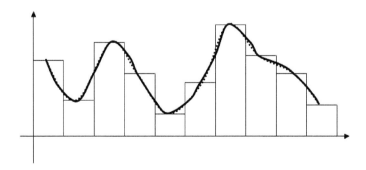

FIGURE 5.8 Using cubic functions to connect the points gives an even better approximation, and the curve is also continuous at the points where the sections join up (known as knotpoints).

Of course, there is no reason why the functions should be linear at all—if we use cubic functions (i.e., polynomials with x^3, x^2, x and constant components) to approximate each piece of data, then we can get results like those shown in Figure 5.8. We can continue to make the functions more complicated, with the important point being how many degrees of continuity we require at the boundaries between the points. These functions are known as **splines**, and the most common one to use is the **cubic spline**. To reach the stage where we can understand it, we need to go back and think about some theory.

5.3.1 Bases and Basis Expansion

Radial basis functions and several other machine learning algorithms can be written in this form:

$$f(\mathbf{x}) = \sum_{i=1}^{n} \alpha_i \Phi_i(\mathbf{x}), \tag{5.3}$$

where $\Phi_i(\mathbf{x})$ is some function of the input value $\mathbf{x}$ and the α_i are the parameters we can solve for in order to make the model fit the data. We will consider the input being scalar values x rather than vector values $\mathbf{x}$ in what follows. The $\Phi_i(x)$ are known as **basis functions** and they are parameters of the model that are chosen. The first thing we need to think about is where each Φ_i is defined. Looking at the third graph of Figure 5.5 we see that the first function should only be defined between 0 and x_1, the next between x_1 and x_2, and so on. These points x_i are called **knotpoints** and they are generally evenly spaced, but choosing how many of them there should be is not necessarily easy. The more knotpoints there are, the more complex the model can be, in which case the model is more likely to overfit, and needs more training data, just like the neural networks that we have seen.

We can choose the Φ_i in any way we like. Suppose that we simply use a **constant function** $\Phi(x) = 1$. Now the model would have value α_1 to the left of x_1, value α_2 between x_1 and x_2, etc. So depending upon how we fit the spline model to the data, the model will have different values, but it will certainly be constant in each region. This is sufficient to make the straight line approximation shown at the bottom of Figure 5.5. However, we might decide that a constant value is not enough, and we use a function that varies linearly (a **linear function** that has value $\Phi(x) = x$ within the region). In this case, we can make Figure 5.6, where each point is represented by a straight line that is not necessarily horizontal. This represents the line close to each point fairly well, but looks messy because the line segments do not meet up.

The question then is how to extend the model to include matching at the **knotpoints**, where one line segment stops and the next one starts. In fact, this is easy. We just insist that the α_i have to be chosen so that at the knotpoint the value of $f(x_1)$ is the same whether we come from the left of x_1 or the right. These are often written as $f(x_1^-)$ and $f(x_1^+)$. Now we just need to work out which α values are involved in the x_1 knotpoint from each side. There are going to be four of them: two for the constant part, and two for the linear part. The ones connected with the constant are obvious: α_1 and α_2. Now suppose that the linear ones are α_{11} and α_{12} (which would mean that there were 10 regions and therefore 9 knotpoints, since then $\alpha_1 \ldots \alpha_{10}$ correspond to the constant functions for each region). In that case, $f(x_1^-) = \alpha_1 + x_1\alpha_{11}$ and $f(x_1^+) = \alpha_2 + x_1\alpha_{12}$. This is an extra constraint that we will need to include when we solve for the values of the α_i.

There is a simpler way to encode this, which is to add some extra basis functions. As well as $\Phi_1(x) = 1$, $\Phi_2(x) = x$, we add some basis functions that insist that the value is 0 at the boundary with x_1: $\Phi_3(x) = (x - x_1)_+$, and the next with the boundary at

x_2: $\Phi_4(x) = (x - x_2)_+$, etc., where $(x)_+ = x$ if $x > 0$ and 0 otherwise. These functions are sufficient to insist that the knotpoint values are enforced, since one is defined on each knotpoint. This is then enough for us to construct the approximation shown in Figure 5.7.

5.3.2 The Cubic Spline

We can carry on adding extra powers of x, but it turns out that the cubic spline is generally sufficient. This has four basic basis functions ($\Phi_1(x) = 1, \Phi_2(x) = x, \Phi_3(x) = x^2, \Phi_4(x) = x^3$), and then as many extras as there are knotpoints, each of the form $\Phi_{4+i}(x) = (x - x_i)_+^3$. This function constrains the function itself and also its first two derivatives to meet at each knotpoint. Notice that while the Φs are not linear, we are simply adding up a weighted sum of them, and so the model is linear in them. We can then produce curves like Figure 5.8, which represent the data very well.

5.3.3 Fitting the Spline to the Data

Having defined the functions, we need to work out how to choose the α_i in order to make the model fit the data. We will continue to define the sum-of-squares error and to minimise that, which is known in the statistical literature as least-squares fitting, and will be described in more detail in Section 9.2. The important point is that everything is linear in the basis functions, so computing the least-squares fit is a linear problem. As with the MLP, the error that we are trying to minimise is:

$$E(y, f(x)) = \sum_{i=1}^{N} (y_i - f(x_i))^2. \tag{5.4}$$

NumPy already has a method defined for computing linear least-squares optimisation: the function `np.linalg.lstsq()`. As a simple example of how to use it we will make some noisy data from a couple of Gaussians and then fit the model parameters, which are 2.5 and 3.2. The final line gives the result, which isn't too far from the correct one, and Figure 5.9 shows the results.

```
import numpy as np
import pylab as pl

x = np.arange(-3,10,0.05)
y =    2.5 *    np.exp(-(x)**2/9)    +    3.2 *    np.exp(-(x-0.5)**2/4)    +
np.random.normal(
0.0, 1.0, len(x))
nParam = 2
A = np.zeros((len(x),nParam), dtype=float)
A[:,0] = np.exp(-(x)**2/9)
A[:,1] = np.exp(-(x-0.5)**2/4)
(p, residuals, rank, s) = np.linalg.lstsq(A,y)

pl.plot(x,y,'.')
pl.plot(x,p[0]*A[:,0]+p[1]*A[:,1],'x')

p
```

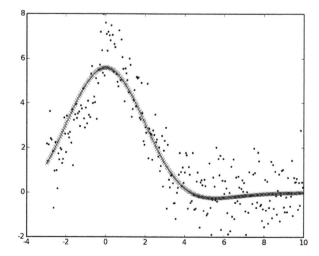

FIGURE 5.9 Using linear least-squares to fit parameters for two Gaussians produces the line from the noisy datapoints plotted as circles.

```
>>> array([ 2.00101406,   3.09626831])
```

5.3.4 Smoothing Splines

The way that we constructed the splines in Section 5.3 was to insist that they went through each knotpoint exactly. This was a good way to describe our constraints, but it is not necessarily realistic: almost all of the data that we ever see will be noisy, and insisting that the data goes through the knotpoints therefore overfits: imagine that the line in Figure 5.9 went through each datapoint. As we try to make the spline model match the data more and more accurately, we will add further knotpoints, which leads to further overfitting. We can deal with this by using **regularisation**. This is a very important idea in optimisation. In essence, it means adding an extra constraint that makes the problem simpler to solve by providing some way to choose from amongst the set of possible solutions.

The most common regulariser that is used for splines is to make the spline model as 'smooth' as possible, where the smoothness is measured by computing the second derivative of the curve at each point, squaring it so that it is always positive, and integrating it along the curve. In this way, a straight line is perfectly smooth, but probably won't be a good match for the data, so we introduce a parameter λ that describes the tradeoff between the two parts. We regain the **interpolating spline** of Section 5.3 for $\lambda = 0$, whereas for $\lambda \to \infty$ we get the least-squares straight line. This type of spline is known as a **smoothing spline**. The cubic smoothing spline is often used. While there are automated methods of choosing λ, it is more normal to use cross-validation to find a value that seems to work well. The form of the optimisation is now:

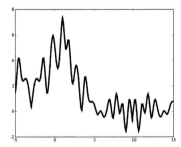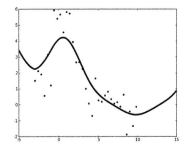

FIGURE 5.10 B-spline fitting of the data shown in Figure 5.9 with *left:* $\lambda = 0$ and *right:* $\lambda = 100$.

$$E(y, f(x), \lambda) = \sum_{i=1}^{N} (y_i - f(x_i))^2 + \lambda \int \left(\frac{d^2 f}{dt^2} \right)^2 dt. \qquad (5.5)$$

SciPy already has functions to perform this in Python, the output of two different values of the smoothing parameter are shown in Figure 5.10.

```
import scipy.signal as sig
# Fit spline
spline = sig.cspline1d(y,100)
xbar = np.arange(-5,15,0.1)
# Evaluate spline
ybar = sig.cspline1d_eval(spline, xbar, dx=x[1]-x[0],x0=x[0])
```

5.3.5 Higher Dimensions

Everything that we have done so far is aimed at one spatial dimension and all of our effort has gone into the cubic spline. However, it is not very clear what to do with higher-dimensional data. One common thing that is done is to take a set of independent basis functions in each different coordinate (x, y, and z in 3D) and then to combine them in all possible combinations ($\Phi_{xi}(x)\Phi_{yj}(y)\Phi_{zk}(z)$). This is known as the **tensor product basis**, and suffers from the curse of dimensionality very quickly, but works well in 2D and 3D, where the **B-spline** is built up in this way. Figure 5.11 shows a grid of knotpoints and a set of points inbetween that can be interpolated in the x_1 and x_2 directions separately.

However, for the smoothing spline there is another problem: what is the higher-dimensional analogue of the curvature measurement that was computed with the second derivative in Equation (5.5)? In two dimensions, one possibility is to consider the **bending energy**. This measures how much energy is required to bend a thin plate so that it passes through a set of points without gravity. It leads to a penalty term that consists of:

$$\int\int_{\mathbb{R}^2} \left(\frac{\partial^2 f}{\partial x_1^2} \right)^2 + 2 \left(\frac{\partial^2 f}{\partial x_1 \partial x_2} \right)^2 + \left(\frac{\partial^2 f}{\partial x_2^2} \right)^2 dx_1 dx_2. \qquad (5.6)$$

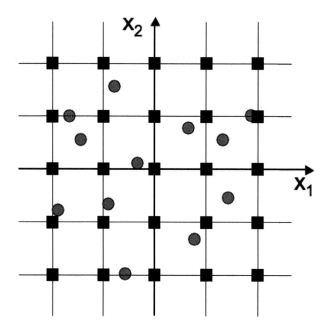

FIGURE 5.11 In 2D the knotpoints (black squares) can be used to interpolate other points (grey circles) in each dimension individually.

Computing the optimal values under this penalty leads to **thin-plate splines**, which are radial basis functions of the form $f(x, y) = f(r) = r^2 \log |r|$, where r is the radial distance between x and y, which was first published by Duchon in 1978, but popularised by Bookstein, who uses it to look at what he calls **morphometrics**, which is the study of how shape changes as animals are growing. The fitting is no different, it is just the basis functions that have changed.

5.3.6 Beyond the Bounds

There is an interesting extra feature to consider. We are fitting our spline to the training data in order to predict the values for other datapoints that we do not know target values for. We assume that our training data are representative of the entire training set, but that does not mean that it contains the lowest possible values, nor the highest. The spline model that we have built has constraints to ensure that the pieces of the spline match up continuously at the knotpoints, but we haven't done anything at all regarding thinking about what happens before the first knotpoint, or after the last. For the polynomials that we are using here, this turns out to be a serious problem, which means that guesses outside the boundaries (**extrapolations**) often turn out to be very inaccurate. Since we don't have any data, it is hard to do much, but one thing that is sometimes done is to insist that outside the boundary knotpoints the function is linear. This is known as the **natural** spline.

FURTHER READING

The original paper on radial basis function neural networks is:

- J. E. Moody and C. Darken. Fast learning in networks of locally-tuned processing units. *Neural Computation*, 1:281–294, 1989.

For more information on splines, not necessarily from the machine learning viewpoint, try:

- C. de Boor. *A Practical Guide to Splines*. Springer, Berlin, Germany, 1978.

- G. Wahba. *Spline Models for Observational Data*. SIAM, Philadelphia, USA, 1990.

- F. Girosi, M. Jones, and T. Poggio. Regularization theory and neural network architectures. *Neural Computation*, 7:219–269, 1995.

- Chapter 5 and Section 6.7 of T. Hastie, R. Tibshirani, and J. Friedman. *The Elements of Statistical Learning*, 2nd edition, Springer, Berlin, Germany, 2008.

- Chapter 5 of S. Haykin. *Neural Networks: A Comprehensive Foundation*, 2nd edition, Prentice-Hall, New Jersey, USA, 1999.

The field of morphometrics, studying how shape changes as organisms grow, is a very interesting one. A possible place to start studying this topic would be:

- F.L. Bookstein. *Morphometric Tools for Landmark Data: Geometry and Biology*. Cambridge University Press, Cambridge, UK, 1991.

PRACTICE QUESTIONS

Problem 5.1 Create an RBF network that solves the XOR function.

Problem 5.2 Apply the RBF network to the Pima Indian dataset and the classification of the MNIST letters. Can you identify differences in the results between the RBF and the MLP?

Problem 5.3 The RBF code that is available on the website uses the hybrid approach. You should be able to change the code so that it uses the fixed centres or full gradient descent method, and then you can experiment with them and see which one works better. In particular, you should be able to find examples where the fixed centres one does not work well if the order of the inputs is poorly chosen.

Problem 5.4 The following function creates some noisy data from a sinusoidal function:

```
def gendata(npoints):
    x = np.arange(0,4*np.pi,1./npoints)

    data = x*np.sin(x) + np.random.normal(0,2,np.size(x))
    print data
    pl.plot(x,x*np.sin(x),'k-',x,data,'k.')
    pl.show()
    return x,data
```

Fit a spline to this data using both the interpolating and smoothing versions of the B-spline. Which makes more sense here? Experiment with different values of the smoothing parameter. Can you work out an algorithm that will attempt to set it based on a validation set?

Problem 5.5 Implement the B-spline in 2D by convolving two 1D cubic splines in orthogonal directions. Can you use it to warp images?

## CHAPTER 6

Dimensionality Reduction

When looking at data and plotting results, we can never go beyond three dimensions in our data, and usually find two dimensions easier to interpret. In addition, we have already seen the curse of dimensionality (Section 2.1.2) means that the higher the number of dimensions we have, the more training data we need. Further, the dimensionality is an explicit factor for the computational cost of many algorithms. These are some of the reasons why **dimensionality reduction** is useful. However, it can also remove noise, significantly improve the results of the learning algorithm, make the dataset easier to work with, and make the results easier to understand. In extreme cases such as the Self-Organising Map that we will see in Section 14.3, where the number of dimensions becomes three or fewer, we can also plot the data, which makes it much easier to understand and interpret.

With this many good things to say about dimensionality reduction, clearly it is something that we need to understand. The importance of the field for machine learning and other forms of data analysis can be seen from the fact that in the year 2000 there were three articles related to dimensionality reduction published together in the prestigious journal *Science*. At the end of the chapter we are going to see two of the algorithms that were described in those papers: Locally Linear Embedding and Isomap.

There are three different ways to do dimensionality reduction. The first is **feature selection**, which typically means looking through the features that are available and seeing whether or not they are actually useful, i.e., **correlated** to the output variables. While many people use neural networks precisely because they don't want to 'get their hands dirty' and look at the data themselves, as we have already seen, the results will be better if you check for correlations and other simple things before using the neural network or other learning algorithm. The second method is **feature derivation**, which means deriving new features from the old ones, generally by applying **transforms** to the dataset that simply change the axes (coordinate system) of the graph by moving and rotating them, which can be written simply as a matrix that we apply to the data. The reason this performs dimensionality reduction is that it enables us to combine features, and to identify which are useful and which are not. The third method is simply to use **clustering** in order to group together similar datapoints, and to see whether this allows fewer features to be used.

To see how choosing the right features can make a problem significantly simpler, have a look at the table on the left of Figure 6.1. It shows the x and y coordinates of 4 points. Looking at the numbers it is hard to see any correlation between the points, and even when they are plotted it simply looks like they might form corners of a rotated rectangle. However, the plot on the right of the figure shows that they are simply a set of four points from a circle, (in fact, the points at $(\pi/6, 4\pi/6, 7\pi/6, 11\pi/6)$) and using this one coordinate, the angle, makes the data a lot easier to understand and analyse.

x	y
2.00	-1.43
2.37	-2.80
1.00	-3.17
0.63	-1.80

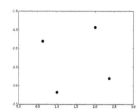 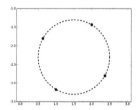

FIGURE 6.1 Three views of the same four points. *Left:* As numbers, where the links are unclear. *Centre:* As four plotted points. *Right:* As four points that lie on a circle.

Once we have worked out how to represent the data, we can suppress dimensions that aren't useful to the algorithm. Even before we get into any form of analysis at all, we can try to perform **feature selection**, looking at the possible inputs that we have for the problem, and deciding which are useful. Many of the methods that we will see in this chapter merge this idea with transformations of the data, so that combinations of the different inputs, rather than the inputs themselves, are used. However, even before using any of the algorithms identified here, input features can be ignored if they do not seem to be useful.

We will see another method of doing feature selection later, since it is inherent to the way that the decision tree (Chapter 12) works: at each stage of the algorithm it decides which feature to add next. This is the **constructive** way to decide on the features: start with none, and then iteratively add more, testing the error at each stage to see whether or not it changed at all when that feature was added. The **destructive** method is to prune the decision tree, lopping off branches and checking whether the error changed at all.

In general, selecting the features is a search problem. We take the best system so far, and then search over the set of possible next features to add. This can be computationally very expensive, since for d features there are $2^d - 1$ possible sets of features to search over, from any individual feature up to the full set. In general, greedy methods (Section 9.4) are employed, although backtracking can also be employed to check whether the search gets stuck.

Many of the algorithms that we will see in this chapter are **unsupervised**. The disadvantage of this is that we are not then able to use the knowledge of their classes in order to reduce the problem further. However, we will start off by considering a method of dimensionality reduction that is aimed at supervised learning, Linear Discriminant Analysis. This method is credited to one of the best-known statisticians of the 20th century, R.A. Fisher, and dates from 1936.

6.1 LINEAR DISCRIMINANT ANALYSIS (LDA)

Figure 6.2 shows a simple two-dimensional dataset consisting of two classes. We can compute various statistics about the data, but we will settle for the means of the two classes in the data, $\boldsymbol{\mu}_1$ and $\boldsymbol{\mu}_2$, the mean of the entire dataset ($\boldsymbol{\mu}$), and the covariance of each class with itself (see Section 2.4.2 for a description of covariance), which is $\sum_j (\mathbf{x}_j - \boldsymbol{\mu})(\mathbf{x}_j - \boldsymbol{\mu})^T$. The question is what we can do with these pieces of data. The principal insight of LDA is that the covariance matrix can tell us about the **scatter** within a dataset, which is the amount of spread that there is within the data. The way to find this scatter is to multiply the covariance by the p_c, the probability of the class (that is, the number of datapoints there are in that class divided by the total number). Adding the values of this for all of the classes gives us a measure of the **within-class scatter** of the dataset:

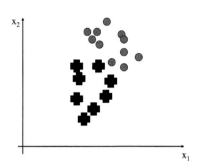

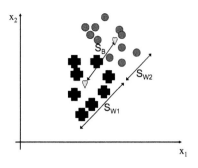

FIGURE 6.2 A set of datapoints in two dimensions, with two classes.

FIGURE 6.3 The meaning of the between-class and within-class scatter. The hearts mark the means of the two classes.

$$S_W = \sum_{\text{classes } c} \sum_{j \in c} p_c(\mathbf{x}_j - \boldsymbol{\mu}_c)(\mathbf{x}_j - \boldsymbol{\mu}_c)^T. \tag{6.1}$$

If our dataset is easy to separate into classes, then this within-class scatter should be small, so that each class is tightly clustered together. However, to be able to separate the data, we also want the distance *between* the classes to be large. This is known as the **between-classes scatter** and is a significantly simpler computation, simply looking at the difference in the means:

$$S_B = \sum_{\text{classes } c} (\boldsymbol{\mu}_c - \boldsymbol{\mu})(\boldsymbol{\mu}_c - \boldsymbol{\mu})^T. \tag{6.2}$$

The meanings of these two measurements is shown in Figure 6.3. The argument about good separation suggests that datasets that are easy to separate into the different classes (i.e., the classes are **discriminable**) should have S_B/S_W as large as possible. This seems perfectly reasonable, but it hasn't told us anything about dimensionality reduction. However, we can say that the rule about making S_B/S_W as large as possible is something that we want to be true for our data when we reduce the number of dimensions. Figure 6.4 shows two **projections** of the dataset onto a straight line. For the projection on the left it is clear that we can't separate out the two classes, while for the one on the right we can. So we just need to find a way to compute a suitable projection.

Remember from Chapter 3 that any line can be written as a vector $\mathbf{w}$ (which we used as our weight vector in Section 3.4; it is one row of weight matrix $\mathbf{W}$). The projection of the data can be written as $z = \mathbf{w}^T \cdot \mathbf{x}$ for datapoint $\mathbf{x}$. This gives us a scalar that is the distance along the $\mathbf{w}$ vector that we need to go to find the projection of point $\mathbf{x}$. To see this, remember that $\mathbf{w}^T \cdot \mathbf{x}$ is the sum of the vectors multiplied together element-wise, and is equal to the size of $\mathbf{w}$ times the size of $\mathbf{x}$ times the cosine of the angle between them. We can make the size of $\mathbf{w}$ be 1, so that we don't have to worry about it, and all that is then described is the amount of $\mathbf{x}$ that lies along $\mathbf{w}$.

So we can compute the projection of our data along $\mathbf{w}$ for every point, and we will have projected our data onto a straight line, as is shown in the two examples in Figure 6.4. Since the mean can be treated as a datapoint, we can project that as well: $\mu'_c = \mathbf{w}^T \cdot \boldsymbol{\mu}_c$. Now we just need to work out what happens to the within-class and between-class scatters.

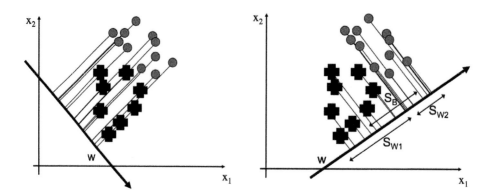

FIGURE 6.4 Two different possible projection lines. The one on the left fails to separate the classes.

Replacing $\mathbf{x}_j$ with $\mathbf{w}^T \cdot \mathbf{x}_j$ in Equations (6.1) and (6.2) we can use some linear algebra (principally the fact that $(\mathbf{A}^T \mathbf{B})^T = \mathbf{B}^T \mathbf{A}^{T^T} = \mathbf{B}^T \mathbf{A}$) to get:

$$\sum_{\text{classes } c} \sum_{j \in c} p_c (\mathbf{w}^T \cdot (\mathbf{x}_j - \boldsymbol{\mu}_c))(\mathbf{w}^T \cdot (\mathbf{x}_j - \boldsymbol{\mu}_c))^T = \mathbf{w}^T S_W \mathbf{w} \qquad (6.3)$$

$$\sum_{\text{classes } c} \mathbf{w}^T (\boldsymbol{\mu}_c - \boldsymbol{\mu})(\boldsymbol{\mu}_c - \boldsymbol{\mu})^T \mathbf{w} = \mathbf{w}^T S_B \mathbf{w}. \qquad (6.4)$$

So our ratio of within-class and between-class scatter looks like $\frac{\mathbf{w}^T S_W \mathbf{w}}{\mathbf{w}^T S_B \mathbf{w}}$.

In order to find the maximum value of this with respect to $\mathbf{w}$, we differentiate it and set the derivative equal to 0. This tells us that:

$$\frac{S_B \mathbf{w}(\mathbf{w}^T S_W \mathbf{w}) - S_W \mathbf{w}(\mathbf{w}^T S_B \mathbf{w})}{(\mathbf{w}^T S_W \mathbf{w})^2} = 0. \qquad (6.5)$$

So we just need to solve this equation for $\mathbf{w}$ and we are done. We start with a little bit of rearranging to get:

$$S_W \mathbf{w} = \frac{\mathbf{w}^T S_W \mathbf{w}}{\mathbf{w}^T S_B \mathbf{w}} S_B \mathbf{w}. \qquad (6.6)$$

If there are only two classes in the data, then we can rewrite Equation (6.2) as $S_B = (\boldsymbol{\mu}_1 - \boldsymbol{\mu}_2)(\boldsymbol{\mu}_1 - \boldsymbol{\mu}_2)^T$. To see this, consider that there are N_1 examples of class 1 and N_2 examples of class 2. Then substitute $(N_1 + N_2)\mu = N_1\mu_1 + N_2\mu_2$ into Equation (6.2). The rewritten $S_B \mathbf{w}$ is in the direction $(\boldsymbol{\mu}_1 - \boldsymbol{\mu}_2)$, and so $\mathbf{w}$ is in the direction of $S_W^{-1}(\boldsymbol{\mu}_1 - \boldsymbol{\mu}_2)$, as can be seen by recalling that the scalar product is independent of order, and so after substituting in the new expression for S_B, the order of the bracketed terms can be changed. Note that we can ignore the ratio of within-class and between-class scatter, since it is a scalar and therefore does not affect the direction of the vector.

Unfortunately, this does not work for the general case. There, finding the minimum is not simple, and requires computing the **generalised eigenvectors** of $S_W^{-1} S_B$, assuming that S_W^{-1} exists. We will be discussing eigenvectors in the next section if you are not sure what they are.

Turning this into an algorithm is very simple. You simply have to compute the between-class and within-class scatters, and then find the value of **w**. In NumPy, the entire algorithm can be written as (where the generalised eigenvectors are computed in SciPy rather than NumPy, which was imported using `from scipy import linalg as la`):

```
C = np.cov(np.transpose(data))

# Loop over classes
classes = np.unique(labels)
for i in range(len(classes)):
    # Find relevant datapoints
    indices = np.squeeze(np.where(labels==classes[i]))
    d = np.squeeze(data[indices,:])
    classcov = np.cov(np.transpose(d))
    Sw += np.float(np.shape(indices)[0])/nData * classcov

Sb = C - Sw
# Now solve for W and compute mapped data
# Compute eigenvalues, eigenvectors and sort into order
evals,evecs = la.eig(Sw,Sb)
indices = np.argsort(evals)
indices = indices[::-1]
evecs = evecs[:,indices]
evals = evals[indices]
w = evecs[:,:redDim]
newData = np.dot(data,w)
```

As an example of using the algorithm, Figure 6.5 shows a plot of the first two dimensions of the iris data (with the classes shown as three different symbols) before and after applying LDA, with the number of dimensions being set to two. While one of the classes (the circles) can already be separated from the others, all three are readily distinguishable after LDA has been applied (and only one dimension, the y one, is required for this).

6.2 PRINCIPAL COMPONENTS ANALYSIS (PCA)

The next few methods that we are going to look at are also involved in computing transformations of the data in order to identify a lower-dimensional set of axes. However, unlike LDA, they are designed for unlabelled data. This does not stop them being used for labelled data, since the learning that takes place in the lower dimensional space can still use the target data, although it does mean that they miss out on any information that is contained in the targets. The idea is that by finding particular sets of coordinate axes, it will become clear that some of the dimensions are not required. This is demonstrated in Figure 6.6, which shows two versions of the same dataset. In the first the data are arranged in an ellipse that runs at 45° to the axes, while in the second the axes have been moved so that the data now runs along the $x-$axis and is centred on the origin. The potential for dimensionality reduction is in the fact that the y dimension does not now demonstrate much variability, and so it might be possible to ignore it and use the x axis values alone

FIGURE 6.5 Plot of the iris data showing the three classes *left:* before and *right:* after LDA has been applied.

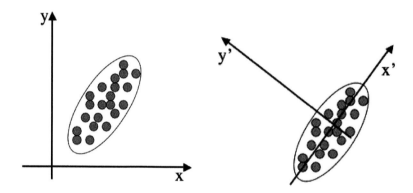

FIGURE 6.6 Two different sets of coordinate axes. The second consists of a rotation and translation of the first and was found using Principal Components Analysis.

without compromising the results of a learning algorithm. In fact, it can make the results better, since we are often removing some of the noise in the data.

The question is how to choose the axes. The first method we are going to look at is Principal Components Analysis (PCA). The idea of a principal component is that it is a direction in the data with the largest variation. The algorithm first centres the data by subtracting off the mean, and then chooses the direction with the largest variation and places an axis in that direction, and then looks at the variation that remains and finds another axis that is orthogonal to the first and covers as much of the remaining variation as possible. It then iterates this until it has run out of possible axes. The end result is that all the variation is along the axes of the coordinate set, and so the covariance matrix is diagonal—each new variable is uncorrelated with every variable except itself. Some of the axes that are found last have very little variation, and so they can be removed without affecting the variability in the data.

Putting this in more formal terms, we have a data matrix $\mathbf{X}$ and we want to rotate it so that the data lies along the directions of maximum variation. This means that we multiply our data matrix by a rotation matrix (often written as $\mathbf{P}^T$) so that $\mathbf{Y} = \mathbf{P}^T\mathbf{X}$, where $\mathbf{P}$ is chosen so that the covariance matrix of $\mathbf{Y}$ is diagonal, i.e.,

$$\text{cov}(\mathbf{Y}) = \text{cov}(\mathbf{P}^T \mathbf{X}) = \begin{pmatrix} \lambda_1 & 0 & 0 & \dots & 0 \\ 0 & \lambda_2 & 0 & \dots & 0 \\ \dots & \dots & \dots & \dots & \dots \\ 0 & 0 & 0 & \dots & \lambda_N \end{pmatrix}. \qquad (6.7)$$

We can get a different handle on this by using some linear algebra and the definition of covariance to see that:

$$
\begin{aligned}
\text{cov}(\mathbf{Y}) &= E[\mathbf{Y}\mathbf{Y}^T] & (6.8) \\
&= E[(\mathbf{P}^T \mathbf{X})(\mathbf{P}^T \mathbf{X})^T] & (6.9) \\
&= E[(\mathbf{P}^T \mathbf{X})(\mathbf{X}^T \mathbf{P})] & (6.10) \\
&= \mathbf{P}^T E(\mathbf{X}\mathbf{X}^T)\mathbf{P} & (6.11) \\
&= \mathbf{P}^T \text{cov}(\mathbf{X})\mathbf{P}. & (6.12)
\end{aligned}
$$

The two extra things that we needed to know were that $(\mathbf{P}^T \mathbf{X})^T = \mathbf{X}^T \mathbf{P}^{T^T} = \mathbf{X}^T \mathbf{P}$ and that $E[\mathbf{P}] = \mathbf{P}$ (and obviously the same for $\mathbf{P}^T$) since it is not a data-dependent matrix. This then tells us that:

$$\mathbf{P}\text{cov}(\mathbf{Y}) = \mathbf{P}\mathbf{P}^T \text{cov}(\mathbf{X})\mathbf{P} = \text{cov}(\mathbf{X})\mathbf{P}, \qquad (6.13)$$

where there is one tricky fact, namely that for a rotation matrix $\mathbf{P}^T = \mathbf{P}^{-1}$. This just says that to invert a rotation we rotate in the opposite direction by the same amount that we rotated forwards.

As $\text{cov}(\mathbf{Y})$ is diagonal, if we write $\mathbf{P}$ as a set of column vectors $\mathbf{P} = [\mathbf{p}_1, \mathbf{p}_2, \dots, \mathbf{p}_N]$ then:

$$\mathbf{P}\text{cov}(\mathbf{Y}) = [\lambda_1 \mathbf{p}_1, \lambda_2 \mathbf{p}_2, \dots, \lambda_N \mathbf{p}_N], \qquad (6.14)$$

which (by writing the λ variables in a matrix as $\boldsymbol{\lambda} = (\lambda_1, \lambda_2, \dots, \lambda_N)^T$ and $\mathbf{Z} = \text{cov}(\mathbf{X})$) leads to a very interesting equation:

$$\boldsymbol{\lambda}\mathbf{p}_i = \mathbf{Z}\mathbf{p}_i \text{ for each } \mathbf{p}_i. \qquad (6.15)$$

At first sight it doesn't look very interesting, but the important thing is to realise that $\boldsymbol{\lambda}$ is a column vector, while $\mathbf{Z}$ is a full matrix, and it can be applied to each of the $\mathbf{p}_i$ vectors that make up $\mathbf{P}$. Since $\boldsymbol{\lambda}$ is only a column vector, all it does is rescale the $\mathbf{p}_i$s; it cannot rotate it or do anything complicated like that. So this tells us that somehow we have found a matrix $\mathbf{P}$ so that for the directions that $\mathbf{P}$ is written in, the matrix $\mathbf{Z}$ does not twist or rotate those directions, but just rescales them. These directions are special enough that they have a name: they are **eigenvectors**, and the amount that they rescale the axes (the λs) by are known as **eigenvalues**.

All eigenvectors of a square symmetric matrix $\mathbf{A}$ are orthogonal to each other. This tells us that the eigenvectors define a space. If we make a matrix $\mathbf{E}$ that contains the (normalised) eigenvectors of a matrix $\mathbf{A}$ as columns, then this matrix will take any vector and rotate it into what is known as the **eigenspace**. Since $\mathbf{E}$ is a rotation matrix, $\mathbf{E}^{-1} = \mathbf{E}^T$, so that rotating the resultant vector back out of the eigenspace requires multiplying it by $\mathbf{E}^T$, where by 'normalised', I mean that the eigenvectors are made unit length. So what should we do between rotating the vector into the eigenspace, and rotating it back out? The answer is that we can stretch the vectors along the axes. This is done by multiplying the vector by a

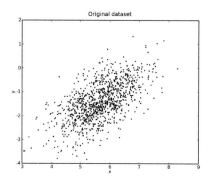
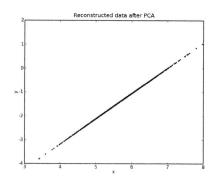

FIGURE 6.7 Computing the principal components of the 2D dataset on the left and using only the first one to reconstruct it produces the line of data shown on the right, which is along the principal axis of the ellipse that the data was sampled from.

diagonal matrix that has the eigenvalues along its diagonal, $\mathbf{D}$. So we can decompose any square symmetric matrix $\mathbf{A}$ into the following set of matrices: $\mathbf{A} = \mathbf{E}\mathbf{D}\mathbf{E}^T$, and this is what we have done to our covariance matrix above. This is called the spectral decomposition.

Before we get on to the algorithm, there is one other useful thing to note. The eigenvalues tell us how much stretching we need to do along their corresponding eigenvector dimensions. The more of this rescaling is needed, the larger the variation along that dimension (since if the data was already spread out equally then the eigenvalue would be close to 1), and so the dimensions with large eigenvalues have lots of variation and are therefore useful dimensions, while for those with small eigenvalues, all the datapoints are very tightly bunched together, and there is not much variation in that direction. This means that we can throw away dimensions where the eigenvalues are very small (usually smaller than some chosen parameter).

It is time to see the algorithm that we need.

The Principal Components Analysis Algorithm

- Write N datapoints $\mathbf{x}_i = (\mathbf{x}_{1i}, \mathbf{x}_{2i}, \dots, \mathbf{x}_{Mi})$ as row vectors

- Put these vectors into a matrix $\mathbf{X}$ (which will have size $N \times M$)

- Centre the data by subtracting off the mean of each column, putting it into matrix $\mathbf{B}$

- Compute the covariance matrix $\mathbf{C} = \frac{1}{N}\mathbf{B}^T\mathbf{B}$

- Compute the eigenvalues and eigenvectors of $\mathbf{C}$, so $\mathbf{V}^{-1}\mathbf{C}\mathbf{V} = \mathbf{D}$, where $\mathbf{V}$ holds the eigenvectors of $\mathbf{C}$ and $\mathbf{D}$ is the $M \times M$ diagonal eigenvalue matrix

- Sort the columns of $\mathbf{D}$ into order of decreasing eigenvalues, and apply the same order to the columns of V

- Reject those with eigenvalue less than some η, leaving L dimensions in the data

---

NumPy can compute the eigenvalues and eigenvectors for us. They are both returned in `evals,evecs = np.linalg.eig(x)`. This makes the entire algorithm fairly easy to implement:

```
def pca(data,nRedDim=0,normalise=1):

    # Centre data
    m = np.mean(data,axis=0)
    data -= m

    # Covariance matrix
    C = np.cov(np.transpose(data))

    # Compute eigenvalues and sort into descending order
    evals,evecs = np.linalg.eig(C)
    indices = np.argsort(evals)
    indices = indices[::-1]
    evecs = evecs[:,indices]
    evals = evals[indices]

    if nRedDim>0:
        evecs = evecs[:,:nRedDim]

    if normalise:
        for i in range(np.shape(evecs)[1]):
            evecs[:,i] / np.linalg.norm(evecs[:,i]) * np.sqrt(evals[i])

    # Produce the new data matrix
    x = np.dot(np.transpose(evecs),np.transpose(data))
    # Compute the original data again
    y=np.transpose(np.dot(evecs,x))+m
    return x,y,evals,evecs
```

Two different examples of using PCA are shown in Figures 6.7 and 6.8. The former shows two-dimensional data from an ellipse being mapped into one principal component, which lies along the principal axis of the ellipse. Figure 6.8 shows the first two dimensions of the iris data, and shows that the three classes are clearly distinguishable after PCA has been applied.

6.2.1 Relation with the Multi-layer Perceptron

We will see (in Section 14.3.2) that PCA can be used in the SOM algorithm to initialise the weights, thus reducing the amount of learning that is required, and that it is very useful for dimensionality reduction. However, there is another reason why people who are interested in neural networks are interested in PCA. We already mentioned it when we talked about the auto-associative MLP in Section 4.4.5. The auto-associative MLP actually computes something very similar to the principal components of the data in the hidden nodes, and this is one of the ways that we can understand what the network is doing. Of course, computing the principal components with a neural network isn't necessarily a good idea. PCA is linear (it just rotates and translates the axes, it can't do anything more complicated). This is clear if we think about the network, since it is the hidden nodes that

FIGURE 6.8 Plot of the first two principal components of the iris data, showing that the three classes are clearly distinguishable.

are computing PCA, and they are effectively a bit like a Perceptron—they can only perform linear tasks. It is the extra layers of neurons that allow us to do more.

So suppose we do just that and use a more complicated MLP network with four layers of neurons instead of two. We still use it as an auto-associator, so that the targets are the same as the inputs. What will the middle hidden layer look like then? A full answer is complicated, but we can speculate that the first layer is computing some non-linear transformation of the data, while the second (bottleneck) layer is computing the PCA of those non-linear functions. Then the third layer reconstructs the data, which appears again in the fourth layer. So the network is still doing PCA, just on a non-linear version of the inputs. This might be useful, since now we are not assuming that the data are linearly separable. However, to understand it better we will look at it from a different viewpoint, thinking of the actions of the first layer as kernels, which are described in Section 8.2.

6.2.2 Kernel PCA

One problem with PCA is that it assumes that the directions of variation are all straight lines. This is often not true. We can use the auto-associator with multiple hidden layers as just discussed, but there is a very nice extension to PCA that uses the kernel trick (which is described in Section 8.2) to get around this problem, just as the SVM got around it for the Perceptron. Just as is done there, we apply a (possibly non-linear) function $\Phi(\cdot)$ to each datapoint $\mathbf{x}$ that transforms the data into the kernel space, and then perform normal linear PCA in that space. The covariance matrix is defined in the kernel space and is:

$$\mathbf{C} = \frac{1}{N} \sum_{n=1}^{N} \Phi(\mathbf{x}_n)\Phi(\mathbf{x}_n)^T, \tag{6.16}$$

which produces the eigenvector equation:

$$\lambda\left(\Phi(\mathbf{x}_i)\mathbf{V}\right) = \left(\Phi(\mathbf{x}_i)\mathbf{C}\mathbf{V}\right) \quad i = 1 \ldots N, \tag{6.17}$$

where $\mathbf{V} = \sum_{j=1}^{N} \boldsymbol{\alpha}_j \Phi(\mathbf{x}_j)$ are the eigenvectors of the original problem and the $\boldsymbol{\alpha}_j$ will turn out to be the eigenvectors of the 'kernelized' problem. It is at this point that we can apply the kernel trick and produce an $N \times N$ matrix $\mathbf{K}$, where:

$$\mathbf{K}_{(i,j)} = (\Phi(\mathbf{x}_i) \cdot \Phi(\mathbf{x}_j)) \,. \tag{6.18}$$

Putting these together we get the equation $N\lambda\mathbf{K}\boldsymbol{\alpha} = \mathbf{K}^2\boldsymbol{\alpha}$, and we left-multiply by $\mathbf{K}^{-1}$ to reduce it to $N\lambda\boldsymbol{\alpha} = \mathbf{K}\boldsymbol{\alpha}$. Computing the projection of a new point $\mathbf{x}$ into the kernel PCA space requires:

$$\left(\mathbf{V}^k \cdot \Phi(\mathbf{x})\right) = \sum_{i=1}^{N} \alpha_i^k \left(\Phi(\mathbf{x}_i) \cdot \Phi(\mathbf{x}_j)\right). \tag{6.19}$$

This is all there is to the algorithm.

The Kernel PCA Algorithm

- Choose a kernel and apply it to all pairs of points to get matrix $\mathbf{K}$ of distances between the pairs of points in the transformed space

- Compute the eigenvalues and eigenvectors of $\mathbf{K}$

- Normalise the eigenvectors by the square root of the eigenvalues

- Retain the eigenvectors corresponding to the largest eigenvalues

---

The only tricky part of the implementation is in the diagonalisation of $\mathbf{K}$, which is generally done using some well-known linear algebra identities, leading to:

```
K = kernelmatrix(data,kernel)

# Compute the transformed data
D = np.sum(K,axis=0)/nData
E = np.sum(D)/nData
J = np.ones((nData,1))*D
K = K - J - np.transpose(J) + E*np.ones((nData,nData))

# Perform the dimensionality reduction
evals,evecs = np.linalg.eig(K)
indices = np.argsort(evals)
indices = indices[::-1]
evecs = evecs[:,indices[:redDim]]
evals = evals[indices[:redDim]]

sqrtE = np.zeros((len(evals),len(evals)))
for i in range(len(evals)):
    sqrtE[i,i] = np.sqrt(evals[i])

newData = np.transpose(np.dot(sqrtE,np.transpose(evecs)))
```

This is a computationally expensive algorithm, since it requires computing the kernel

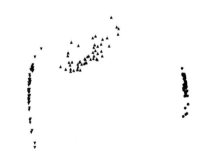

FIGURE 6.9 Plot of the first two non-linear principal components of the iris data, (using the Gaussian kernel) showing that the three classes are clearly distinguishable.

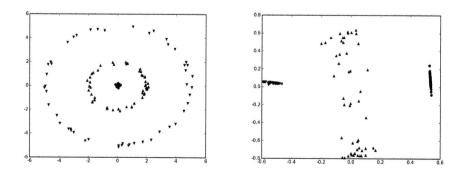

FIGURE 6.10 A very definitely non-linear dataset consisting of three concentric circles, and the (Gaussian) kernel PCA mapping of the iris data, which requires only one component to separate the data.

matrix and then the eigenvalues and eigenvectors of that matrix. The naïve implementation on the algorithm on the website is $\mathcal{O}(n^3)$, but with care it is possible to take advantage of the fact that not all of the eigenvalues are needed, which can lead to an $\mathcal{O}(n^2)$ algorithm.

Figure 6.9 shows the output of kernel PCA when applied to the iris dataset. The fact that it can separate this data well is not very surprising since the linear methods that we have already seen can do it, but it is a useful check of the method. A rather more difficult example is shown in Figure 6.10. Data are sampled from three concentric circles. Clearly, linear PCA would not be able to separate this data, but applying kernel PCA to this example separates the data using only one component.

6.3 FACTOR ANALYSIS

The idea of factor analysis is to ask whether the data that is observed can be explained by a smaller number of uncorrelated **factors** or **latent variables**. The assumption is that the data comes from some underlying data source (or set of data sources) that are not directly known. The problem of factor analysis is to find those independent factors, and the **noise** that is inherent in the measurements of each factor. Factor analysis is commonly used in psychology and other social sciences, and the factors are generally chosen to have some particular meanings: in psychology, they can be related to IQ and other tests.

Suppose that we have a dataset in the usual $N \times M$ matrix $\mathbf{X}$, i.e., each row of $\mathbf{X}$ is an M-dimensional datapoint, and $\mathbf{X}$ has covariance matrix $\boldsymbol{\Sigma}$. As, with PCA, we **centre** the data by subtracting off the mean of each variable (i.e., each column): $\mathbf{b}_j = \mathbf{x}_j - \boldsymbol{\mu}_j$, $j = 1 \ldots M$, so that the mean $E[\mathbf{b}_i] = 0$. Which we've done before, for example for the MLP and many times since.

We can write the model that we are assuming as:

$$\mathbf{X} = \mathbf{WY} + \boldsymbol{\epsilon}, \tag{6.20}$$

where $\mathbf{X}$ are the observations and $\boldsymbol{\epsilon}$ is the noise. Since the factors $\mathbf{b}_i$ that we want to find should be independent, so $\text{cov}(\mathbf{b}_i, \mathbf{b}_j) = 0$ if $i \neq j$. Factor analysis takes explicit notice of the noise in the data, using the variable $\boldsymbol{\epsilon}$. In fact, it assumes that the noise is Gaussian with zero mean and some known variance: $\boldsymbol{\Psi}$, with the variance of each element being $\Psi_i = \text{var}(\epsilon_i)$. It also assumes that these noise measurements are independent of each other, which is equivalent to the assumption that the data come from a set of separate (independent) physical processes, and seems reasonable if we don't know otherwise.

The covariance matrix of the original data, $\boldsymbol{\Sigma}$, can now be broken down into $\text{cov}(\mathbf{Wb} + \boldsymbol{\epsilon}) = \mathbf{WW}^T + \boldsymbol{\Psi}$, where $\boldsymbol{\Psi}$ is the matrix of noise variances and we have used the fact that $\text{cov}(\mathbf{b}) = \mathbf{I}$ since the factors are uncorrelated.

With all of that set up, the aim of factor analysis is to try to find a set of **factor loadings** $\mathbf{W}_{ij}$ and values for the variance of the noise parameters $\boldsymbol{\Psi}$, so that the data in $\mathbf{X}$ can be reconstructed from the parameters, or so that we can perform dimensionality reduction.

Since we are looking at adding additional variables, the natural formulation is an EM algorithm (as described in Section 7.1.1) and this is how the computations are usually performed to produce the maximum likelihood estimate. Getting to the EM algorithm takes some effort. We first define the log likelihood (where $\boldsymbol{\theta}$ is the data we are trying to fit) as:

$$Q(\boldsymbol{\theta}_t | \boldsymbol{\theta}_{t-1}) = \int p(\mathbf{x}|\mathbf{y}, \boldsymbol{\theta}_{t-1}) \log(p(\mathbf{y}|\mathbf{x}, \boldsymbol{\theta}_t) p(\mathbf{x})) d\mathbf{x}. \tag{6.21}$$

We can replace several of the terms in here with values, and we can also ignore any terms that do not depend on $\boldsymbol{\theta}$. The end result of this is a new version of Q, which forms the basis of the E-step:

$$Q(\boldsymbol{\theta}_t | \boldsymbol{\theta}_{t-1}) = \frac{1}{2} \int p(\mathbf{x}|\mathbf{y}, \boldsymbol{\theta}_{t-1}) \log(\det(\boldsymbol{\Psi}^{-1})) - (\mathbf{y} - W\mathbf{x})^T \boldsymbol{\Psi}^{-1} (\mathbf{y} - W\mathbf{x}) \, d\mathbf{x}. \tag{6.22}$$

For the EM algorithm we now have to differentiate this with respect to $\mathbf{W}$ and the individual elements of $\boldsymbol{\Psi}$, and apply some linear algebra, to get update rules:

$$\mathbf{W}_{new} = \left(\mathbf{y}E(\mathbf{x}|\mathbf{y})^T\right)\left(E(\mathbf{x}\mathbf{x}^T|\mathbf{y})\right)^{-1}, \qquad (6.23)$$

$$\Psi_{new} = \frac{1}{N}\text{diagonal}\left(\mathbf{x}\mathbf{x}^T - WE(\mathbf{x}|\mathbf{y})\mathbf{y}^T\right), \qquad (6.24)$$

where diagonal() ensures that the matrix retains values only on the diagonal and the expectations are:

$$E(\mathbf{x}|\mathbf{y}) = \mathbf{W}^T(\mathbf{W}\mathbf{W}^T + \Psi)^{-1}\mathbf{b} \qquad (6.25)$$

$$E(\mathbf{x}\mathbf{x}^T|\mathbf{x}) - E(\mathbf{x}|\mathbf{y})E(\mathbf{x}|\mathbf{y})^T = \mathbf{I} - \mathbf{W}^T(\mathbf{W}\mathbf{W}^T + \Psi)^{-1}W. \qquad (6.26)$$

The only other things that we need to add to the algorithm is some way to decide when to stop, which involves computing the log likelihood and stopping the algorithm when it stops descending. This leads to an algorithm where the basic steps in the loop are:

```
# E-step
A = np.dot(W,np.transpose(W)) + np.diag(Psi)
logA = np.log(np.abs(np.linalg.det(A)))
A = np.linalg.inv(A)

WA = np.dot(np.transpose(W),A)
WAC = np.dot(WA,C)
Exx = np.eye(nRedDim) - np.dot(WA,W) + np.dot(WAC,np.transpose(WA))

# M-step
W = np.dot(np.transpose(WAC),np.linalg.inv(Exx))
Psi = Cd - (np.dot(W,WAC)).diagonal()

tAC = (A*np.transpose(C)).sum()

L = -N/2*np.log(2.*np.pi) -0.5*logA - 0.5*tAC
if (L-oldL)<(1e-4):
    print "Stop",i
    break
```

The output of using factor analysis on the iris dataset are shown in Figure 6.11.

6.4 INDEPENDENT COMPONENTS ANALYSIS (ICA)

There is a related approach to factor analysis that is known as Independent Components Analysis. When we looked at PCA above, the components were chosen so that they were orthogonal and uncorrelated (so that the covariance matrix was diagonal, i.e., so $\text{cov}(\mathbf{b}_i, \mathbf{b}_j) = 0$ if $i \neq j$). If, instead, we require that the components are statistically independent (so that for $E[\mathbf{b}_i, \mathbf{b}_j] = E[\mathbf{b}_i]E[\mathbf{b}_j]$ as well as the $\mathbf{b}_i$ being uncorrelated), then we get ICA.

The common motivation for ICA is the problem of blind source separation. As with factor analysis, the assumption is that the data we see are actually created by a set of underlying

FIGURE 6.11 Plot of the first two factor analysis components of the iris data, showing that the three classes are clearly distinguishable.

physical processes that are independent. The reason why the data we see are correlated is because of the way the outputs from different processes have been mixed together. So given some data, we want to find a transformation that turns it into a mixture of independent **sources** or components.

The most popular way to describe blind source separation is known as **the cocktail party problem**. If you are at a party, then your ears hear lots of different sounds coming from lots of different locations (different people talking, the clink of glasses, background music, etc.) but you are somehow able to focus on the voice of the people you are talking to, and can in fact separate out the sounds from all of the different sources even though they are mixed together. The cocktail party problem is the challenge of separating out these sources, although there is one wrinkle: for the algorithm to work, you need as many ears as there are sources. This is because the algorithm does not have the information we have about what things sound like.

Suppose that we have two sources making noise (s_1^t, s_2^t) where the top index covers the fact that there are lots of datapoints appearing over time, and two microphones that hear things, giving inputs (x_1^t, x_2^t). The sounds that are heard come from the sources as:

$$
\begin{align}
x_1 &= as_1 + bs_2, & (6.27)\\
x_2 &= cs_1 + ds_2, & (6.28)
\end{align}
$$

which can be written in matrix form as:

$$\mathbf{x} = \mathbf{As}, \qquad (6.29)$$

where $\mathbf{A}$ is known as the **mixing matrix**. Reconstructing $\mathbf{s}$ looks easy now: we just compute $\mathbf{s} = \mathbf{A}^{-1}\mathbf{x}$. Except that, unfortunately, we don't know $\mathbf{A}$. The approximation to $\mathbf{A}^{-1}$ that we work out is generally labelled as $\mathbf{W}$, and it is a square matrix since we have the same number of microphones as we do sources.

At this point we need to work out what we actually know about the sources and the signals. There are three things:

- the mixtures are not independent, even though the sources are

- the mixtures will look like normal distributions even if the sources are not (this is because of the **Central Limit Theorem**, something that we won't look at further here)

- the mixtures will look more complicated than the sources

We can use the first fact to say that if we find factors that are independent of each other then they are probably sources, and the second to say that if we find factors that are not Gaussian then they are probably sources. We can measure the amount of independence between two variables by using the **mutual information**, which we will see in Section 12.2.1 when we look at entropy. In fact, the most common approach is to use what is rather uglily known as **negentropy**: $J(y) = H(z) - H(y)$, which maximises the deviations from Gaussianness (where $H(\cdot)$ is the entropy):

$$H(y) = -\int g(y) \log g(y) dy. \tag{6.30}$$

One common approximation is $J(y) = (E[G(y)] - E[G(z)])^2$, where $g(u) = \frac{1}{a} \log \cosh(au)$, so $g'(u) = \tanh(au)$ $1 \leq a \leq 2$. Implementing ICA is actually quite tricky because of some numerical issues, so we won't do it ourselves. There are a few well-used ICA implementations out there, of which the most popular is known as **FastICA**, which is available in Python as part of the MDP package.

6.5 LOCALLY LINEAR EMBEDDING

Two relatively recent methods of computing dimensionality reduction were mentioned in the introduction because they were published in the journal *Science*. Both are non-linear, and both attempt to preserve the neighbourhood relations in the data (as will be discussed for the SOM in Section 14.3) but they use different approaches. The first tries to approximate the data by sticking together sets of locally flat patches that cover the dataset, while the second uses the shortest distances (**geodesics**) on the non-linear space to find a globally optimal solution.

We will look first at the locally linear algorithm, which is called **Locally Linear Embedding** (LLE). It was introduced by Roweis and Saul in 2000. The idea is to say that by making linear approximations we will make some errors, so we should make these errors as small as possible by making the patches small where there is lots of non-linearity in the data. The error is known as the **reconstruction error** and is simply the sum-of-squares of the distance between the original point and its reconstruction:

$$\epsilon = \sum_{i=1}^{N} \left(\mathbf{x}_i - \sum_{j=1}^{N} \mathbf{W}_{ij} \mathbf{x}_j \right)^2. \tag{6.31}$$

The weights $\mathbf{W}_{ij}$ say how much effect the jth datapoint has on the reconstruction of the ith one. The question is which points can be usefully used to reconstruct a particular datapoint. If another point is a long way off, then it probably isn't very useful: only those points that are close to the current datapoint (that are in its **neighbourhood**) are used. There are two common ways to create neighbourhoods:

- Points that are less than some predefined distance d to the current point are neighbours (so we don't know how many neighbours there are, but they are all close)

- The k nearest points are neighbours (so we know how many there are, but some could be far away)

Solving for the weights $\mathbf{W}_{ij}$ is a least-squares problem, which we can simplify by enforcing the constraints that for any point $\mathbf{x}_j$ that is a long way from the current point $\mathbf{x}_i$, $\mathbf{W}_{ij} = 0$, and that $\sum_j \mathbf{W}_{ij} = 1$. This produces a reconstruction of the data, but it does not reduce the dimensionality at all. For this we have to reapply the same basic cost function, but minimise it according to the positions $\mathbf{y}_i$ of the points in some lower dimensional space (dimension L):

$$\mathbf{y}_i = \sum_{i=1}^{N} \left(\mathbf{y}_i - \sum_{j=1}^{L} \mathbf{W}_{ij} \mathbf{y}_j \right)^2 . \tag{6.32}$$

Solving this is rather more complicated, so we won't go into details, but it turns out that the solution is the eigenvalues of the quadratic form matrix $\mathbf{M}_{ij} = \delta_{ij} - \mathbf{W}_{ij} - \mathbf{W}_{ji} + \sum_k \mathbf{W}_{ji} \mathbf{W}_{kj}$, where δ_{ij} is the Kronecker delta function, so $\delta_{ij} = 1$ if $i = j$ and 0 otherwise. This leads to the following algorithm:

The Locally Linear Embedding Algorithm

- Decide on the neighbours of each point (e.g., K nearest neighbours):

  - compute distances between every pair of points
  - find the k smallest distances
  - set $\mathbf{W}_{ij} = 0$ for other points
  - for each point $\mathbf{x}_i$:
    * create a list of its neighbours' locations $\mathbf{z}_i$
    * compute $\mathbf{z}_i = \mathbf{z}_i - \mathbf{x}_i$

- Compute the weights matrix $\mathbf{W}$ that minimises Equation (6.31) according to the constraints:

  - compute local covariance $\mathbf{C} = \mathbf{Z}\mathbf{Z}^T$, where $\mathbf{Z}$ is the matrix of $\mathbf{z}_i$s
  - solve $\mathbf{C}\mathbf{W} = \mathbf{I}$ for $\mathbf{W}$, where $\mathbf{I}$ is the $N \times N$ identity matrix
  - set $\mathbf{W}_{ij} = 0$ for non-neighbours
  - set other elements to $\mathbf{W}/\sum(\mathbf{W})$

- Compute the lower dimensional vectors $\mathbf{y}_i$ that minimise Equation (6.32):

  - create $\mathbf{M} = (\mathbf{I} - \mathbf{W})^T(\mathbf{I} - \mathbf{W})$
  - compute the eigenvalues and eigenvectors of $\mathbf{M}$
  - sort the eigenvectors into order by size of eigenvalue
  - set the qth row of $\mathbf{y}$ to be the $q+1$ eigenvector corresponding to the qth smallest eigenvalue (ignore the first eigenvector, which has eigenvalue 0)

There are a couple of things in there that are a bit tricky to implement, and there is a function that we haven't used before, `np.kron()`, which takes two matrices and multiplies each element of the first one by all the elements of the second, putting all of the results together into one multi-dimensional output array. It is used to construct the set of neighbourhood locations for each point.

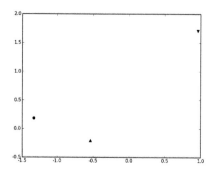

FIGURE 6.12 The Locally Linear Embedding algorithm with $k = 12$ neighbours transforms the iris dataset into three points, separating the data perfectly.

```
for i in range(ndata):
    Z  = data[neighbours[i,:],:] - np.kron(np.ones((K,1)),data[i,:])
    C = np.dot(Z,np.transpose(Z))
    C = C+np.identity(K)*1e-3*np.trace(C)
    W[:,i] = np.transpose(np.linalg.solve(C,np.ones((K,1))))
    W[:,i] = W[:,i]/np.sum(W[:,i])

M = np.eye(ndata,dtype=float)
for i in range(ndata):
    w = np.transpose(np.ones((1,np.shape(W)[0]))*np.transpose(W[:,i]))
    j = neighbours[i,:]
    #print shape(w), np.shape(np.dot(w,np.transpose(w))), np.shape(M[i,j])
    ww = np.dot(w,np.transpose(w))
    for k in range(K):
        M[i,j[k]] -= w[k]
        M[j[k],i] -= w[k]
        for l in range(K):
            M[j[k],j[l]] += ww[k,l]

evals,evecs = np.linalg.eig(M)
ind = np.argsort(evals)
y = evecs[:,ind[1:nRedDim+1]]*np.sqrt(ndata)
```

The LLE algorithm produces a very interesting result on the iris dataset: it separates the three groups into three points (Figure 6.12). This shows that the algorithm works very well on this type of data, but doesn't give us any hints as to what else it can do. Figure 6.13 shows a common demonstration dataset for these algorithms. Known as the **swissroll** for obvious reasons, it is tricky to find a 2D representation of the 3D data because it is rolled up. The right of Figure 6.13 shows that LLE can successfully unroll it.

FIGURE 6.13 A common example used to demonstrate LLE is the swissroll dataset shown on the left. To produce a useful 2D representation of this data requires unrolling the data, which the LLE does successfully, as is shown on the right. The shades are used to identify neighbouring points, and do not have any other purpose.

6.6 ISOMAP

The other algorithm was proposed by Tenenbaum et al., also in 2000. It tries to minimise the global error by looking at all of the pairwise distances and computing global geodesics. It is a variant of the standard multi-dimensional scaling (MDS) algorithm, so we'll talk about that first.

6.6.1 Multi-Dimensional Scaling (MDS)

Like PCA, MDS tries to find a linear approximation to the full dataspace that embeds the data into a lower dimensionality. In the case of MDS the embedding tries to preserve the distances between all pairs of points (however these distances are measured). It turns out that if the space is Euclidean, then the two methods are identical. We use the same notational setup as previously, starting with datapoints $\mathbf{x}_1, \mathbf{x}_2, \dots, \mathbf{x}_N \in \mathbb{R}^M$. We choose a new dimensionality $L < M$ and compute the embedding so that the datapoints are $\mathbf{z}_1, \mathbf{z}_2, \dots \mathbf{z}_N \in \mathbb{R}^L$. As usual, we need a cost function to minimise. There are lots of choices for MDS cost functions, but the more common ones are:

Kruskal–Shephard scaling (also known as least-squares) $S_{KS}(\mathbf{z}_1, \mathbf{z}_2, \dots \mathbf{z}_N) = \sum_{i \neq i'} (d_{ii'} - \|\mathbf{z}_i - \mathbf{z}'_i\|)^2$

Sammon mapping $S_{SM}(\mathbf{z}_1, \mathbf{z}_2, \dots \mathbf{z}_N) = \sum_{i \neq i'} \frac{(d_{ii'} - \|\mathbf{z}_i - \mathbf{z}'_i\|)^2}{d_{ii'}}$. This puts more weight onto short distances, so that neighbouring points stay the correct distance apart.

In either case, gradient descent can be used to minimise the distances. There is another version of MDS called classical MDS that uses similarities between datapoints rather than distances. These can be constructed from a set of distances by using the centred inner product $s_{ii'} = (\mathbf{x}_i - \bar{\mathbf{x}}), (\mathbf{x}'_i - \bar{\mathbf{x}})^T$. By doing this it is possible to construct a direct algorithm that does not have to use gradient descent. The function that needs to be minimised is $\sum_{i \neq i'} \left(s_{ii'} - (\mathbf{z}_i - \bar{\mathbf{z}}), (\mathbf{z}'_i - \bar{\mathbf{z}})^T \right)^2$. The computations that are needed are:

The Multi-Dimensional Scaling (MDS) Algorithm

- Compute the matrix of squared pairwise similarities $\mathbf{D}$, $\mathbf{D}_{ij} = \|\mathbf{x}_i - \mathbf{x}_j\|^2$
- Compute $\mathbf{J} = \mathbf{I}_N - 1/N$ (where $\mathbf{I}_N$ is the $N \times N$ identity function and N is the number of datapoints)
- Compute $\mathbf{B} = -\frac{1}{2}\mathbf{JDJ}^T$
- Find the L largest eigenvalues λ_i of $\mathbf{B}$, together with the corresponding eigenvectors $\mathbf{e}_i$
- Put the eigenvalues into a diagonal matrix $\mathbf{V}$ and set the eigenvectors to be columns of matrix $\mathbf{P}$
- Compute the embedding as $\mathbf{X} = \mathbf{PV}^{1/2}$

This classical MDS algorithm works fine on flat **manifolds** (dataspaces). However, we are interested in manifolds that are not flat, and this is where Isomap comes in. The algorithm has to construct the distance matrix for all pairs of datapoints on the manifold, but there is no information about the manifold, and so the distances can't be computed exactly. Isomap approximates them by assuming that the distances between pairs of points that are close together are good, since over a small distance the non-linearity of the manifold won't matter. It builds up the distances between points that are far away by finding paths that run through points that are close together, i.e., that are neighbours, and then uses normal MDS on this distance matrix:

The Isomap Algorithm

- Construct the pairwise distances between all pairs of points
- Identify the neighbours of each point to make a weighted graph G
- Estimate the geodesic distances d_G by finding shortest paths
- Apply classical MDS to the set of d_G

Floyd's and Dijkstra's algorithms are well-known algorithms for finding shortest paths on graphs. They are of $\mathcal{O}(N^3)$ and $\mathcal{O}(N^2)$ time complexity, respectively. Any good algorithms textbook provides the details if you don't know them.

There is one practical aspect of Isomap, which is that getting the number of neighbours right can be important, otherwise the graph splits into separate **components** (that is, segments of the graph that are not linked to each other), which have infinite distance between them. You then have to be careful to deal only with the largest component, which means that you end up with less data than you started with. Otherwise the implementation is fairly simple.

Figure 6.14 shows the results of applying Isomap to the iris dataset. Here, the default neighbourhood size of 12 produced a largest component that held only one of the three classes, and the other two were deleted. By increasing the neighbourhood size over 50, so that each point had more neighbours than were in its class, the results shown in the figure were produced. On the swissroll dataset shown on the left of Figure 6.13, Isomap produces qualitatively similar results to LLE, as can be seen in Figure 6.15.

FIGURE 6.14 Isomap transforms the iris data in a similar way to factor analysis, provided that the neighbourhood size is large enough to avoid points becoming disconnected.

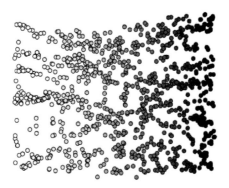

FIGURE 6.15 Isomap also produces a good remapping of the swissroll dataset.

Although the two algorithms produce similar mappings of the swissroll dataset, they are based on different principles. Isomap attempts to find a mapping that preserves the distances between pairs of points within the manifold, no matter how far apart they are, while LLE focuses only on local regions of the manifold. This means that the computational cost of LLE is significantly less, but it can make errors by putting points close together that should be far apart. The choice of which algorithm to use often depends upon the dataset, and trying both of them out for your particular dataset is often a good idea.

FURTHER READING

Surveys of the area of dimensionality reduction include:

- L.J.P. van der Maaten. An introduction to dimensionality reduction using MATLAB. Technical Report MICC 07-07, Maastricht University, Maastricht, the Netherlands, 2007.

- F. Camastra. Data dimensionality estimation methods: a survey. *Pattern Recognition*, 36:2945–2954, 2003.

For more information about many of the methods desribed here, there are books or papers that contain a lot of information. Notable references include:

- (for LDA) Section 4.3 of T. Hastie, R. Tibshirani, and J. Friedman. *The Elements of Statistical Learning*, 2nd edition, Springer, Berlin, Germany, 2008.

- (for PCA) I.T. Jolliffe. *Principal Components Analysis*. Springer, Berlin, Germany, 1986.

- (for kernel PCA) J. Shawe-Taylor and N. Cristianini. *Kernel Methods for Pattern Analysis*. Cambridge University Press, Cambridge, UK, 2004.

- (for ICA) J.V. Stone. *Independent Components Analysis: A Tutorial Introduction*. MIT Press, Cambridge, MA, USA, 2004.

- (for ICA) A. Hyvrinen and E. Oja. Independent components analysis: Algorithms and applications. *Neural Networks*, 13(4–5):411–430, 2000.

- (for LLE) S. Roweis and L. Saul. Nonlinear dimensionality reduction by locally linear embedding. *Science*, 290(5500):2323–2326, 2000.

- (for MDS) T.F. Cox and M.A.A. Cox. *Multidimensional Scaling*. Chapman & Hall, London, UK, 1994.

- (for Isomap) J.B. Tenenbaum, V. de Silva, and J.C. Langford. A global geometric framework for nonlinear dimensionality reduction. *Science*, 290(5500):2319–2323, 2000.

- Chapter 12 of C.M. Bishop. *Pattern Recognition and Machine Learning*. Springer, Berlin, Germany, 2006.

PRACTICE QUESTIONS

Problem 6.1 Use LDA on the iris dataset (which is what Fisher originally tested LDA on).

Problem 6.2 Compare the results with using PCA, which is not supervised and will not therefore be able to find the same space.

Problem 6.3 Compute the eigenvalues and eigenvectors of:

$$\begin{pmatrix} 5 & 7 \\ -2 & -4 \end{pmatrix} \begin{pmatrix} 1 & 0 \\ 0 & 1 \end{pmatrix} \begin{pmatrix} 1 & 2 & 1 \\ 6 & -1 & 0 \\ -1 & -2 & -1 \end{pmatrix} \tag{6.33}$$

Problem 6.4 Compare the algorithms described in this chapter on a variety of different datasets, including the **yeast** dataset and the **wine** dataset. Input the results of the data reduction method to the MLP and SOM. Are the results better than before this preprocessing?

Problem 6.5 Modify the Isomap code to use Dijkstra's algorithm rather than Floyd's algorithm.

Problem 6.6 Another dataset that the Isomap and LLE algorithms are commonly demonstrated on is the 'S' shape that is available on the website. Download it and test various algorithms, not just Isomap and LLE on it. For Isomap and LLE, try different numbers of neighbours to see the effect that this has.

## CHAPTER 7

Probabilistic Learning

One criticism that is often made of neural networks—especially the MLP—is that it is not clear exactly what it is doing: while we can go and have a look at the activations of the neurons and the weights, they don't tell us much. We've already seen some methods that don't have this problem, principally the decision tree in Chapter 12. In this chapter we are going to look at methods that are based on statistics, and that are therefore more transparent, in that we can always extract and look at the probabilities and see what they are, rather than having to worry about weights that have no obvious meaning.

We will look at how to perform classification by using the frequency with which examples appear in the training data, and then we will see how we can deal with our first example of unsupervised learning, when the labels are not present for the training examples. If the data comes from known probability distributions, then we will see that it is possible to solve this problem with a very neat algorithm, the EM algorithm, which we will also see in other guises in later chapters. Finally, we will have a look at a rather different way of using the dataset when we look at nearest neighbour methods.

7.1 GAUSSIAN MIXTURE MODELS

For the Bayes' classifier that we saw in Section 2.3.2 the data had target labels, and so we could do supervised learning, learning the probabilities from the labelled data. However, suppose that we have the same data, but without target labels. This requires unsupervised learning, and we will see lots of ways to deal with this in Chapters 14 and 6, but here we will look at one special case. Suppose that the different classes each come from their own Gaussian distribution. This is known as multi-modal data, since there is one distribution (mode) for each different class. We can't fit one Gaussian to the data, because it doesn't look Gaussian overall.

There is, however, something we can do. If we know how many classes there are in the data, then we can try to estimate the parameters for that many Gaussians, all at once. If we don't know, then we can try different numbers and see which one works best. We will talk about this issue more for a different method (the k-means algorithm) in Section 14.1. It is perfectly possible to use any other probability distribution instead of a Gaussian, but Gaussians are by far the most common choice. Then the output for any particular datapoint that is input to the algorithm will be the sum of the values expected by all of the M Gaussians:

$$f(\mathbf{x}) = \sum_{m=1}^{M} \alpha_m \phi(\mathbf{x}; \boldsymbol{\mu}_m, \boldsymbol{\Sigma}_m), \tag{7.1}$$

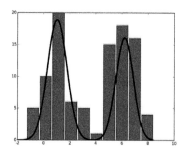 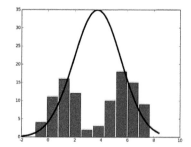

FIGURE 7.1 Histograms of training data from a mixture of two Gaussians and two fitted models, shown as the line plot. The model shown on the left fits well, but the one on the right produces two Gaussians right on top of each other that do not fit the data well.

where $\phi(\mathbf{x}; \boldsymbol{\mu}_m, \boldsymbol{\Sigma}_m)$ is a Gaussian function with mean $\boldsymbol{\mu}_m$ and covariance matrix $\boldsymbol{\Sigma}_m$, and the α_m are weights with the constraint that $\sum\limits_{m=1}^{M} \alpha_m = 1$.

Figure 7.1 shows two examples, where the data (shown by the histograms) comes from two different Gaussians, and the model is computed as a sum or mixture of the two Gaussians together. The figure also gives you some idea of how to use the mixture model once it has been created. The probability that input $\mathbf{x}_i$ belongs to class m can be written as (where a hat on a variable ($\hat{\cdot}$) means that we are estimating the value of that variable):

$$p(\mathbf{x}_i \in c_m) = \frac{\hat{\alpha}_m \phi(\mathbf{x}_i; \hat{\boldsymbol{\mu}}_m; \hat{\boldsymbol{\Sigma}}_m)}{\sum\limits_{k=1}^{M} \hat{\alpha}_m \phi(\mathbf{x}_i; \hat{\boldsymbol{\mu}}_k; \hat{\boldsymbol{\Sigma}}_k)}. \tag{7.2}$$

The problem is how to choose the weights α_m. The common approach is to aim for the **maximum likelihood** solution (the **likelihood** is the conditional probability of the data given the model, and the maximum likelihood solution varies the model to maximise this conditional probability). In fact, it is common to compute the log likelihood and then to maximise that; it is guaranteed to be negative, since probabilities are all less than 1, and the logarithm spreads out the values, making the optimisation more effective. The algorithm that is used is an example of a very general one known as the **expectation-maximisation** (or more compactly, **EM**) algorithm. The reason for the name will become clearer below. We will see another example of an EM algorithm in Section 16.3.3, but here we see how to use it for fitting Gaussian mixtures, and get a very approximate idea of how the algorithm works for more general examples. For more details, see the Further Reading section.

7.1.1 The Expectation-Maximisation (EM) Algorithm

The basic idea of the EM algorithm is that sometimes it is easier to add extra variables that are not actually known (called **hidden** or **latent** variables) and then to maximise the function over those variables. This might seem to be making a problem much more complicated than it needs to be, but it turns out for many problems that it makes finding the solution significantly easier.

In order to see how it works, we will consider the simplest interesting case of the Gaussian mixture model: a combination of just two Gaussian mixtures. The assumption now is that data were created by randomly choosing one of two possible Gaussians, and then creating a sample from that Gaussian. If the probability of picking Gaussian one is p, then the entire model looks like this (where $\mathcal{N}(\boldsymbol{\mu}, \boldsymbol{\sigma}^2)$ specifies a Gaussian distribution with mean $\boldsymbol{\mu}$ and standard deviation $\boldsymbol{\sigma}$):

$$G_1 = \mathcal{N}(\boldsymbol{\mu}_1, \boldsymbol{\sigma}_1^2)$$
$$G_2 = \mathcal{N}(\boldsymbol{\mu}_2, \boldsymbol{\sigma}_2^2)$$
$$y = pG_1 + (1 - p)G_2. \tag{7.3}$$

If the probability distribution of p is written as $\boldsymbol{\pi}$, then the probability density is:

$$P(\mathbf{y}) = \boldsymbol{\pi}\phi(\mathbf{y}; \boldsymbol{\mu}_1, \boldsymbol{\sigma}_1) + (1 - \boldsymbol{\pi})\phi(\mathbf{y}; \boldsymbol{\mu}_2, \boldsymbol{\sigma}_2). \tag{7.4}$$

Finding the maximum likelihood solution (actually the maximum log likelihood) to this problem is then a case of computing the sum of the logarithm of Equation (7.4) over all of the training data, and differentiating it, which would be rather difficult. Fortunately, there is a way around it. The key insight that we need is that if we knew which of the two Gaussian components the datapoint came from, then the computation would be easy. The mean and standard deviation for each component could be computed from the datapoints that belong to that component, and there would not be a problem. Although we don't know which component each datapoint came from, we can pretend we do, by introducing a new variable f. If $f = 0$ then the data came from Gaussian one, if $f = 1$ then it came from Gaussian two.

This is the typical initial step of an EM algorithm: adding latent variables. Now we just need to work out how to optimise over them. This is the time when the reason for the algorithm being called expectation-maximisation becomes clear. We don't know much about variable f (hardly surprising, since we invented it), but we can compute its **expectation** (that is, the value that we 'expect' to see, which is the mean average) from the data:

$$\begin{aligned}\boldsymbol{\gamma}_i(\hat{\boldsymbol{\mu}}_1, \hat{\boldsymbol{\mu}}_2, \hat{\boldsymbol{\sigma}}_1, \hat{\boldsymbol{\sigma}}_2, \hat{\boldsymbol{\pi}}) &= E(f|\hat{\boldsymbol{\mu}}_1, \hat{\boldsymbol{\mu}}_2, \hat{\boldsymbol{\sigma}}_1, \hat{\boldsymbol{\sigma}}_2, \hat{\boldsymbol{\pi}}, D) \\ &= P(f = 1|\hat{\boldsymbol{\mu}}_1, \hat{\boldsymbol{\mu}}_2, \hat{\boldsymbol{\sigma}}_1, \hat{\boldsymbol{\sigma}}_2, \hat{\boldsymbol{\pi}}, D),\end{aligned} \tag{7.5}$$

where D denotes the data. Note that since we have set $f = 1$ this means that we are choosing Gaussian two.

Computing the value of this expectation is known as the **E-step**. Then this estimate of the expectation is maximised over the model parameters (the parameters of the two Gaussians and the mixing parameter $\boldsymbol{\pi}$), the **M-step**. This requires differentiating the expectation with respect to each of the model parameters. These two steps are simply iterated until the algorithm converges. Note that the estimate never gets any smaller, and it turns out that EM algorithms are guaranteed to reach a local maxima.

To see how this looks for the two-component Gaussian mixture, we'll take a closer look at the algorithm:

The Gaussian Mixture Model EM Algorithm

- Initialisation

  - set $\hat{\mu}_1$ and $\hat{\mu}_2$ to be randomly chosen values from the dataset

  - set $\hat{\sigma}_1 = \hat{\sigma}_2 = \sum_{i=1}^{N}(y_i - \bar{y})^2/N$ (where $\bar{y}$ is the mean of the entire dataset)

  - set $\hat{\pi} = 0.5$

- Repeat until convergence:

  - (E-step) $\hat{\gamma}_i = \frac{\hat{\pi}\phi(y_i;\hat{\mu}_1,\hat{\sigma}_1)}{\hat{\pi}\phi(y_i;\hat{\mu}_1,\hat{\sigma}_1)+(1-\hat{\pi})\phi(y_i;\hat{\mu}_2,\hat{\sigma}_2)}$ for $i = 1\ldots N$

  - (M-step 1) $\hat{\mu}_1 = \dfrac{\sum_{i=1}^{N}(1-\hat{\gamma}_i)y_i}{\sum_{i=1}^{N}(1-\hat{\gamma}_i)}$

  - (M-step 2) $\hat{\mu}_2 = \dfrac{\sum_{i=1}^{N}\hat{\gamma}_i y_i}{\sum_{i=1}^{N}\hat{\gamma}_i}$

  - (M-step 3) $\hat{\sigma}_1 = \dfrac{\sum_{i=1}^{N}(1-\hat{\gamma}_i)(y_i-\hat{\mu}_1)^2}{\sum_{i=1}^{N}(1-\hat{\gamma}_i)}$

  - (M-step 4) $\hat{\sigma}_2 = \dfrac{\sum_{i=1}^{N}\hat{\gamma}_i(y_i-\hat{\mu}_2)^2}{\sum_{i=1}^{N}\hat{\gamma}_i}$

  - (M-step 5) $\hat{\pi} = \sum_{i=1}^{N}\dfrac{\hat{\gamma}_i}{N}$

Turning this into Python code does not require any new techniques:

```
while count<nits:
    count = count + 1

    # E-step
    for i in range(N):
        gamma[i] = pi*np.exp(-(y[i]-mu1)**2/(2*s1))/ (pi * np.exp(-(y[i]-
        mu1)**2/(2*s1)) + (1-pi)* np.exp(-(y[i]-mu2)**2/2*s2))

    # M-step
    mu1 = np.sum((1-gamma)*y)/np.sum(1-gamma)
    mu2 = np.sum(gamma*y)/np.sum(gamma)
    s1  = np.sum((1-gamma)*(y-mu1)**2)/np.sum(1-gamma)
```

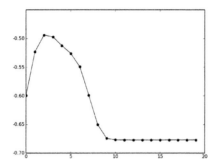

FIGURE 7.2 Plot of the log likelihood changing as the Gaussian Mixture Model EM algorithm learns to fit the two Gaussians shown on the left of Figure 7.1.

```
s2 = np.sum(gamma*(y-mu2)**2)/np.sum(gamma)
pi = np.sum(gamma)/N

ll[count-1] = np.sum(np.log(pi*np.exp(-(y[i]-mu1)**2/(2*s1)) + (1-pi))
*np.exp(-(y[i]-mu2)**2/(2*s2))))
```

Figure 7.2 shows the log likelihood dropping as the algorithm learns for the example on the left of Figure 7.1. The computational costs of this model are very good for classifying a new datapoint, since it is $\mathcal{O}(M)$, where M is the number of Gaussians, which is often of the order of $\log N$ (where N is the number of datapoints). The training is, however, fairly expensive: $\mathcal{O}(NM^2 + M^3)$.

The general algorithm has pretty much exactly the same steps (the parameters of the model are written as $\boldsymbol{\theta}$, $\boldsymbol{\theta}'$ is a dummy variable, D is the original dataset, and D' is the dataset with the latent variables included):

The General Expectation-Maximisation (EM) Algorithm

- Initialisation

  - guess parameters $\hat{\boldsymbol{\theta}}^{(0)}$

- Repeat until convergence:

  - (E-step) compute the expectation $Q(\boldsymbol{\theta}', \hat{\boldsymbol{\theta}}^{(j)}) = E(f(\boldsymbol{\theta}'; D')|D, \hat{\boldsymbol{\theta}}^{(j)})$
  - (M-step) estimate the new parameters $\hat{\boldsymbol{\theta}}^{(j+1)}$ as $\max_{\boldsymbol{\theta}'} Q(\boldsymbol{\theta}', \hat{\boldsymbol{\theta}}^{(j)})$

The trick with applying EM algorithms to problems is in identifying the correct latent variables to include, and then simply working through the steps. They are very powerful methods for a wide variety of statistical learning problems.

We are now going to turn our attention to something much simpler, which is how we can use information about nearby datapoints to decide on classification output. For this we don't use a model of the data at all, but directly use the data that is available.

7.1.2 Information Criteria

The likelihood of the data given the model has another useful function as well. Back in Section 2.2.2 we identified the need to use model selection in order to identify the right time to stop learning. In that section we introduced the idea of a validation set, or using cross-validation if there was not enough data. However, this replaces data with computation time, as many models are trained on different datasets.

An alternative idea is to identify some measure that tells us about how well we can expect this trained model to perform. There are two such information criteria that are commonly used:

Aikake Information Criterium

$$\text{AIC} = \ln(\mathcal{L}) - k \qquad (7.6)$$

Bayesian Information Criterium

$$\text{BIC} = 2\ln(\mathcal{L}) - k\ln N \qquad (7.7)$$

In these equations, k is the number of parameters in the model, N is the number of training examples, and $\mathcal{L}$ is the best (largest) likelihood of the model. In both cases, based on the way that they are written here, the model with the largest value is taken. Both of the measures will favour simple models, which is a form of Occam's razor.

7.2 NEAREST NEIGHBOUR METHODS

Suppose that you are in a nightclub and decide to dance. It is unlikely that you will know the dance moves for the particular song that is playing, so you will probably try to work out what to do by looking at what the people close to you are doing. The first thing you could do would be just to pick the person closest to you and copy them. However, since most of the people who are in the nightclub are also unlikely to know all the moves, you might decide to look at a few more people and do what most of them are doing. This is pretty much exactly the idea behind nearest neighbour methods: if we don't have a model that describes the data, then the best thing to do is to look at similar data and choose to be in the same class as them.

We have the datapoints positioned within input space, so we just need to work out which of the training data are close to it. This requires computing the distance to each datapoint in the training set, which is relatively expensive: if we are in normal Euclidean space, then we have to compute d subtractions and d squarings (we can ignore the square root since we only want to know which points are the closest, not the actual distance) and this has to be done $\mathcal{O}(N^2)$ times. We can then identify the k nearest neighbours to the test point, and then set the class of the test point to be the most common one out of those for the nearest neighbours. The choice of k is not trivial. Make it too small and nearest neighbour methods are sensitive to noise, too large and the accuracy reduces as points that are too far away are considered. Some possible effects of changing the size of k on the decision boundary are shown in Figure 7.3.

This method suffers from the curse of dimensionality (Section 2.1.2). First, as shown above, the computational costs get higher as the number of dimensions grows. This is not as bad as it might appear at first: there are sets of methods such as KD-Trees (see Section 7.2.2 for more details) that compute this in $\mathcal{O}(N\log N)$ time. However, more importantly, as the number of dimensions increases, so the distance to other datapoints tends to increase. In

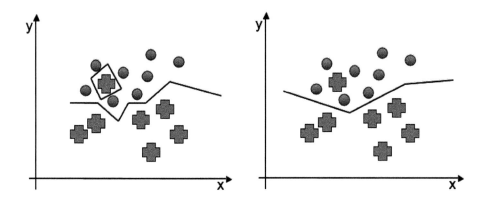

FIGURE 7.3 The nearest neighbours decision boundary with *left:* one neighbour and *right:* two neighbours.

addition, they can be far away in a variety of different directions—there might be points that are relatively close in some dimensions, but a long way in others. There are methods for dealing with these problems, known as **adaptive nearest neighbour** methods, and there is a reference to them in the Further Reading section at the end of the chapter.

The only part of this that requires any care during the implementation is what to do when there is more than one class found in the closest points, but even with that the implementation is nice and simple:

```python
def knn(k,data,dataClass,inputs):

    nInputs = np.shape(inputs)[0]
    closest = np.zeros(nInputs)

    for n in range(nInputs):
        # Compute distances
        distances = np.sum((data-inputs[n,:])**2,axis=1)

        # Identify the nearest neighbours
        indices = np.argsort(distances,axis=0)

        classes = np.unique(dataClass[indices[:k]])
        if len(classes)==1:
            closest[n] = np.unique(classes)
        else:
            counts = np.zeros(max(classes)+1)
            for i in range(k):
                counts[dataClass[indices[i]]] += 1
            closest[n] = np.max(counts)

    return closest
```

We are going to look next at how we can use these methods for regression, before we turn to the question of how to perform the distance calculations as efficiently as possible, something that is done simply but inefficiently in the code above. We will then consider briefly whether or not the Euclidean distance is always the most useful way to calculate distances, and what alternatives there are.

For the k-nearest neighbours algorithm the bias-variance decomposition can be computed as:

$$E((\mathbf{y} - \hat{f}(\mathbf{x}))^2) = \sigma^2 + \left[f(\mathbf{x}) - \frac{1}{k} \sum_{i=0}^{k} f(\mathbf{x}_i) \right]^2 + \frac{\sigma^2}{k}. \tag{7.8}$$

The way to interpret this is that when k is small, so that there are few neighbours considered, the model has flexibility and can represent the underlying model well, but that it makes mistakes (has high variance) because there is relatively little data. As k increases, the variance decreases, but at the cost of less flexibility and so more bias.

7.2.1 Nearest Neighbour Smoothing

Nearest neighbour methods can also be used for regression by returning the average value of the neighbours to a point, or a spline or similar fit as the new value. The most common methods are known as **kernel smoothers**, and they use a **kernel** (a weighting function between pairs of points) that decides how much emphasis (weight) to put onto the contribution from each datapoint according to its distance from the input. We will see kernels in a different context in Section 8.2, but here we shall simply use two kernels that are used for smoothing.

Both of these kernels are designed to give more weight to points that are closer to the current input, with the weights decreasing smoothly to zero as they pass out of the range of the current input, with the range specified by a parameter λ. They are the **Epanechnikov quadratic kernel**:

$$K_{E,\lambda}(x_0, x) = \begin{cases} 0.75 \left(1 - (x_0 - x)^2 / \lambda^2\right) & \text{if } |x - x_0| < \lambda \\ 0 & \text{otherwise} \end{cases}, \tag{7.9}$$

and the **tricube kernel**:

$$K_{T,\lambda}(x_0, x) = \begin{cases} \left(1 - \left|\frac{x_0 - x}{\lambda}\right|^3\right)^3 & \text{if } |x - x_0| < \lambda \\ 0 & \text{otherwise} \end{cases}. \tag{7.10}$$

The results of using these kernels are shown in Figure 7.4 on a dataset that consists of the time between eruptions (technically known as the **repose**) and the duration of the eruptions of Mount Ruapehu, the large volcano in the centre of New Zealand's north island. Values of λ of 2 and 4 were used here. Picking λ requires experimentation. Large values average over more datapoints, and therefore produce lower variance, but at the cost of higher bias.

7.2.2 Efficient Distance Computations: the KD-Tree

As was mentioned above, computing the distances between all pairs of points is very computationally expensive. Fortunately, as with many problems in computer science, designing an efficient data structure can reduce the computational overhead a lot. For the problem of finding nearest neighbours the data structure of choice is the KD-Tree. It has been around since the late 1970s, when it was devised by Friedman and Bentley, and it reduces the cost of finding a nearest neighbour to $\mathcal{O}(\log N)$ for $\mathcal{O}(N)$ storage. The construction of the tree

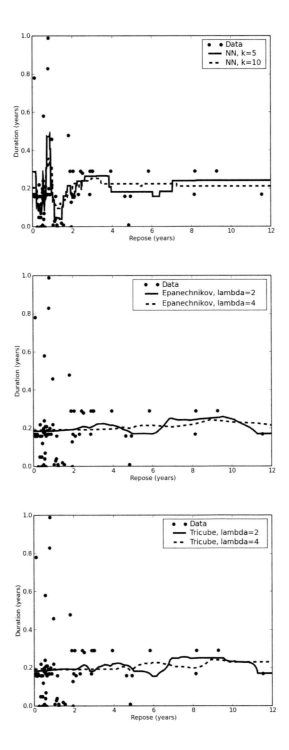

FIGURE 7.4 Output of the nearest neighbour method and two kernel smoothers on the data of duration and repose of eruptions of Mount Ruapehu 1860–2006.

is $\mathcal{O}(N \log^2 N)$, with much of the computational cost being in the computation of the median, which with a naïve algorithm requires a sort and is therefore $\mathcal{O}(N \log N)$, or can be computed with a randomised algorithm in $\mathcal{O}(N)$ time.

The idea behind the KD-tree is very simple. You create a binary tree by choosing one dimension at a time to split into two, and placing the line through the median of the point coordinates of that dimension. Not that different to a decision tree (Chapter 12), really. The points themselves end up as leaves of the tree. Making the tree follows pretty much the same steps as usual for constructing a binary tree: we identify a place to split into two choices, left and right, and then carry on down the tree. This makes it natural to write the algorithm recursively. The choice of what to split and where is what makes the KD-tree special. Just one dimension is split in each step, and the position of the split is found by computing the median of the points that are to be split in that one dimension, and putting the line there. In general, the choice of which dimension to split alternates through the different choices, or it can be made randomly. The algorithm below cycles through the possible dimensions based on the depth of the tree so far, so that in two dimensions it alternates horizontal and vertical splits.

The centre of the construction method is simply a recursive function that picks the axis to split on, finds the median value on that axis, and separates the points according to that value, which in Python can be written as:

```
# Pick next axis to split on
whichAxis = np.mod(depth,np.shape(points)[1])

# Find the median point
indices = np.argsort(points[:,whichAxis])
points = points[indices,:]
median = np.ceil(float(np.shape(points)[0]-1)/2)

# Separate the remaining points
goLeft = points[:median,:]
goRight = points[median+1:,:]

# Make a new branching node and recurse
newNode = node()
newNode.point = points[median,:]
newNode.left = makeKDtree(goLeft,depth+1)
newNode.right = makeKDtree(goRight,depth+1)
return newNode
```

Suppose that we had seven two-dimensional points to make a tree from: $(5, 4), (1, 6), (6, 1), (7, 5), (2, 7), (2, 2), (5, 8)$ (as plotted in Figure 7.5). The algorithm will pick the first coordinate to split on initially, and the median point here is 5, so the split is through $x = 5$. Of those on the left of the line, the median y coordinate is 6, and for those on the right it is 5. At this point we have separated all the points, and so the algorithm terminates with the split shown in Figure 7.6 and the tree shown in Figure 7.7.

Searching the tree is the same as any other binary tree; we are more interested in finding the nearest neighbours of a test point. This is fairly easy: starting at the root of the tree you recurse down through the tree comparing just one dimension at a time until you find a

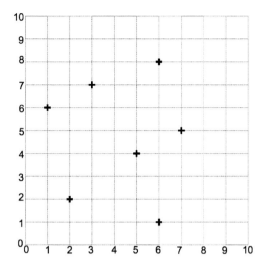

FIGURE 7.5 The initial set of 2D data.

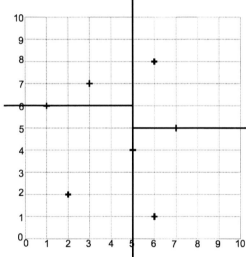

FIGURE 7.6 The splits and leaf points found by the KD-tree.

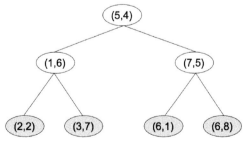

FIGURE 7.7 The KD-tree that made the splits.

leaf node that is in the region containing the test point. Using the tree shown in Figure 7.7 we introduce the test point $(3, 5)$, which finds $(2, 2)$ as the leaf for the box that $(3, 5)$ is in. However, looking at Figure 7.8 we see that this is not the closest point at all, so we need to do some more work.

The first thing we do is label the leaf we have found as a potential nearest neighbour, and compute the distance between the test point and this point, since any other point has to be closer. Now we need to check any other boxes that could contain something closer. Looking at Figure 7.8 you can see that point $(3, 7)$ is closer, and that is the label of the leaf for the sibling box to the one that was returned, so the algorithm also needs to check the sibling box. However, suppose that we used $(4.5, 2)$ as the test point. In that case the sibling is too far away, but another point $(6, 1)$ is closer. So just checking the sibling is not enough — we also need to check the siblings of the parent node, together with its descendants (the cousins of the first point). A look at the figure again should convince you that the algorithm can then terminate in most cases; very occasionally it can be necessary to go even further afield, but it is easy to see which branches to prune. This leads to the following Python program:

```
def returnNearest(tree,point,depth):
  if tree.left is None:
      # Have reached a leaf
      distance = np.sum((tree.point-point)**2)
      return tree.point,distance,0
  else:
      # Pick next axis to split on
      whichAxis = np.mod(depth,np.shape(point)[0])

      # Recurse down the tree
      if point[whichAxis]<tree.point[whichAxis]:
          bestGuess,distance,height = returnNearest(tree.left,point,depth+1)
      else:
          bestGuess,distance,height = returnNearest(tree.right,point,depth+1)

  if height<=2:
      # Check the sibling
      if point[whichAxis]<tree.point[whichAxis]:
          bestGuess2,distance2,height2 =                    returnNearest(tree.right,point,depth+
1)
      else:
          bestGuess2,distance2,height2 =                    returnNearest(tree.left,point,depth+1)

  # Check this node
  distance3 = np.sum((tree.point-point)**2)
  if (distance3<distance2):
      distance2 = distance3
      bestGuess2 = tree.point
```

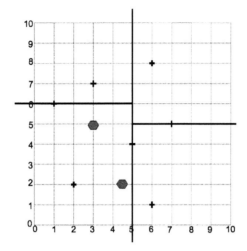

FIGURE 7.8 Two test points for the example KD-tree.

```
if (distance2<distance):
    distance = distance2
    bestGuess = bestGuess2
return bestGuess,distance,height+1
```

7.2.3 Distance Measures

We have computed the distance between points as the Euclidean distance, which is something that you learnt about in high school. However, it is not the only option, nor is it necessarily the most useful. In this section we will look at the underlying idea behind distance calculations and possible alternatives.

If I were to ask you to find the distance between my house and the nearest shop, then your first guess might involve taking a map of my town, locating my house and the shop, and using a ruler to measure the distance between them. By careful application of the map scale you can now tell me how far it is. However, when I set out to buy some milk I'm liable to find that I have to walk rather further than you've told me, since the direct line that you measured would involve walking through (or over) several houses, and some serious fence-scaling. Your 'as the crow flies' distance is the shortest possible path, and it is the straight-line, or Euclidean, distance. You can measure it on the map by just using a ruler, but it essentially consists of measuring the distance in one direction (we'll call it north-south) and then the distance in another direction that is perpendicular to the first (let's call it east-west) and then squaring them, adding them together, and then taking the square root of that. Writing that out, the Euclidean distance that we are all used to is:

$$d_E = \sqrt{(x_1 - x_2)^2 + (y_1 - y_2)^2},\tag{7.11}$$

where (x_1, y_1) is the location of my house in some coordinate system (say by using a GPS tracker) and (x_2, y_2) is the location of the shop.

If I told you that my town was laid out on a grid block system, as is common in towns

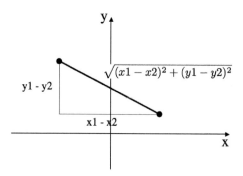

FIGURE 7.9 The Euclidean and city-block distances between two points.

that were built in the interval between the invention of the motor car and the invention of innovative town planners, then you would probably use a different measure. You would measure the distance between my house and the shop in the 'north-south' direction and the distance in the 'east-west' direction, and then add the two distances together. This would correspond to the distance I actually had to walk. It is often known as the city-block or Manhattan distance and looks like:

$$d_C = |x_1 - x_2| + |y_1 - y_2|. \tag{7.12}$$

The point of this discussion is to show that there is more than one way to measure a distance, and that they can provide radically different answers. These two different distances can be seen in Figure 7.9. Mathematically, these distance measures are known as metrics. A metric function or norm takes two inputs and gives a scalar (the distance) back, which is positive, and 0 if and only if the two points are the same, symmetric (so that the distance to the shop is the same as the distance back), and obeys the triangle inequality, which says that the distance from a to b plus the distance from b to c should not be less than the direct distance from a to c.

Most of the data that we are going to have to analyse lives in rather more than two dimensions. Fortunately, the Euclidean distance that we know about generalises very well to higher dimensions (and so does the city-block metric). In fact, these two measures are both instances of a class of metrics that work in any number of dimensions. The general measure is the Minkowski metric and it is written as:

$$L_k(\mathbf{x}, \mathbf{y}) = \left(\sum_{i=1}^{d} |x_i - y_i|^k \right)^{\frac{1}{k}}. \tag{7.13}$$

If we put $k = 1$ then we get the city-block distance (Equation (7.12)), and $k = 2$ gives the Euclidean distance (Equation (7.11)). Thus, you might possibly see the Euclidean metric written as the L_2 norm and the city-block distance as the L_1 norm. These norms have another interesting feature. Remember that we can define different averages of a set of numbers. If we define the average as the point that minimises the sum of the distance to every datapoint, then it turns out that the mean minimises the Euclidean distance (the sum-of-squares distance), and the median minimises the L_1 metric. We met another distance measure earlier: the Mahalanobis distance in Section 2.4.2.

There are plenty of other possible metrics to choose, depending upon the dataspace. We generally assume that the space is flat (if it isn't, then none of these techniques work, and we don't want to worry about that). However, it can still be beneficial to look at other metrics. Suppose that we want our classifier to be able to recognise images, for example of faces. We take a set of digital photos of faces and use the pixel values as features. Then we use the nearest neighbour algorithm that we've just seen to identify each face. Even if we ensure that all of the photos are taken fully face-on, there are still a few things that will get in the way of this method. One is that slight variations in the angle of the head (or the camera) could make a difference; another is that different distances between the face and the camera (scaling) will change the results; and another is that different lighting conditions will make a difference. We can try to fix all of these things in preprocessing, but there is also another alternative: use a different metric that is invariant to these changes, i.e., it does not vary as they do. The idea of invariant metrics is to find measures that ignore changes that you don't want. So if you want to be able to rotate shapes around and still recognise them, you need a metric that is invariant to rotation.

A common invariant metric in use for images is the **tangent distance**, which is an approximation to the Taylor expansion in first derivatives, and works very well for small rotations and scalings; for example, it was used to halve the final error rate on nearest neighbour classification of a set of handwritten letters. Invariant metrics are an interesting topic for further study, and there is a reference for them in the Further Reading section if you are interested.

FURTHER READING

For more on nearest neighbour methods, see:

- T. Hastie and R. Tibshirani. Discriminant adaptive nearest neighbor classification and regression. In David S. Touretzky, Michael C. Mozer, and Michael E. Hasselmo, editors, *Advances in Neural Information Processing Systems*, volume 8, pages 409–415. The MIT Press, 1996.

- N.S. Altman. An introduction to kernel and nearest-neighbor nonparametric regression. *The American Statistician*, 46:175–185, 1992.

The original description of KD-trees is:

- A. Moore. A tutorial on KD-trees. Extract from PhD Thesis, 1991. Available from http://www.cs.cmu.edu/*sim*awm/papers.html.

A reference on the tangent distance is:

- P.Y. Simard, Y.A. Le Cun, J.S. Denker, and B. Victorri. Transformation invariance in pattern recognition: Tangent distance and propagation. *International Journal of Imaging Systems and Technology*, 11:181–194, 2001.

Some of the material in the chapter is covered in:

- Section 9.2 of C.M. Bishop. *Pattern Recognition and Machine Learning*. Springer, Berlin, Germany, 2006.

- Chapter 6 (especially Sections 6.1–6.3) of T. Mitchell. *Machine Learning*. McGraw-Hill, New York, USA, 1997.

- Section 13.3 of T. Hastie, R. Tibshirani, and J. Friedman. *The Elements of Statistical Learning*, 2nd edition, Springer, Berlin, Germany, 2008.

PRACTICE QUESTIONS

Problem 7.1 Extend the Gaussian Mixture Model algorithm to allow for more than two classes in the data. This is not trivial, since it involves modifying the EM algorithm.

Problem 7.2 Modify the KD-tree algorithm so that it works on spheres in the data, rather than rectangles. Since they no longer cover the space you will have to add some cases that fail to return a leaf at all. However, this means that the algorithm will not return points that are far away, which will make the results more accurate. Now modify it so that it does not use the Euclidean distance, but rather the L_1 distance. Compare the results of using these two methods on the iris dataset.

Problem 7.3 Use the small figures of numbers that are available on the book website in order to compute the tangent distance. You will have to write code that rotates the numbers by small amounts in order to check that you have written it correctly. What happens when you make large rotations (particularly of a 6 or 9)? Compare using nearest neighbours with Euclidean distance and the tangent distance to verify the results claimed in the chapter. Extend the experiment to the MNIST dataset.

## CHAPTER 8

Support Vector Machines

Back in Chapter 3 we looked at the Perceptron, a set of McCulloch and Pitts neurons arranged in a single layer. We identified a method by which we could modify the weights so that the network learned, and then saw that the Perceptron was rather limited in that it could only identify straight line classifiers, that is, it could only separate out groups of data if it was possible to draw a straight line (hyperplane in higher dimensions) between them. This meant that it could not learn to distinguish between the two truth classes of the 2D XOR function. However, in Section 3.4.3, we saw that it was possible to modify the problem so that the Perceptron could solve the problem, by changing the data so that it used more dimensions than the original data.

This chapter is concerned with a method that makes use of that insight, amongst other things. The main idea is one that we have seen before, in Section 5.3, which is to modify the data by changing its representation. However, the terminology is different here, and we will introduce kernel functions rather than bases. In principle, it is always possible to transform any set of data so that the classes within it can be separated linearly. To get a bit of a handle on this, think again about what we did with the XOR problem in Section 3.4.3: we added an extra dimension and moved a point that we could not classify properly into that additional dimension so that we could linearly separate the classes. The problem is how to work out which dimensions to use, and that is what kernel methods, which is the class of algorithms that we will talk about in this chapter, do.

We will focus on one particular algorithm, the Support Vector Machine (SVM) , which is one of the most popular algorithms in modern machine learning. It was introduced by Vapnik in 1992 and has taken off radically since then, principally because it often (but not always) provides very impressive classification performance on reasonably sized datasets. SVMs do not work well on extremely large datasets, since (as we shall see) the computations don't scale well with the number of training examples, and so become computationally very expensive. This should be sufficient motivation to master the (quite complex) concepts that are needed to understand the algorithm.

We will develop a simple SVM in this chapter, using cvxopt, a freely available solver with a Python interface, to do the heavy work. There are several different implementations of the SVM available on the Internet, and there are references to some of the more popular ones at the end of the chapter. Some of them include wrappers so that they can be used from within Python.

There is rather more to the SVM than the kernel method; the algorithm also reformulates the classification problem in such a way that we can tell a good classifier from a bad one, even if they both give the same results on a particular dataset. It is this distinction that enables the SVM algorithm to be derived, so that is where we will start.

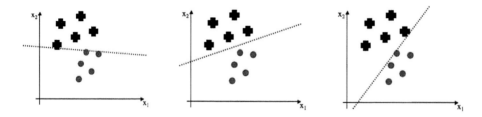

FIGURE 8.1 Three different classification lines. Is there any reason why one is better than the others?

8.1 OPTIMAL SEPARATION

Figure 8.1 shows a simple classification problem with three different possible linear classification lines. All three of the lines that are drawn separate out the two classes, so in some sense they are 'correct', and the Perceptron would stop its training if it reached any one of them. However, if you had to pick one of the lines to act as the classifier for a set of test data, I'm guessing that most of you would pick the line shown in the middle picture. It's probably hard to describe exactly why you would do this, but somehow we prefer a line that runs through the middle of the separation between the datapoints from the two classes, staying approximately equidistant from the data in both classes. Of course, if you were feeling smart, then you might have asked what criteria you were meant to pick a line based on, and why one of the lines should be any better than the others.

To answer that, we are going to try to define why the line that runs halfway between the two sets of datapoints is better, and then work out some way to quantify that so we can identify the 'optimal' line, that is, the best line according to our criteria. The data that we have used to identify the classification line is our training data. We believe that these data are indicative of some underlying process that we are trying to learn, and that the testing data that the algorithm will be evaluated on after training comes from the same underlying process. However, we don't expect to see exactly the same datapoints in the test dataset, and inevitably some of the points will be closer to the classifier line, and some will be further away. If we pick the lines shown in the left or right graphs of Figure 8.1, then there is a chance that a datapoint from one class will be on the wrong side of the line, just because we have put the line tight up against some of the datapoints we have seen in the training set. The line in the middle picture doesn't have this problem; like the baby bear's porridge in Goldilocks, it is 'just right'.

8.1.1 The Margin and Support Vectors

How can we quantify this? We can measure the distance that we have to travel away from the line (in a direction perpendicular to the line) before we hit a datapoint. Imagine that we put a 'no-man's land' around the line (shown in Figure 8.2), so that any point that lies within that region is declared to be too close to the line to be accurately classified. This region is symmetric about the line, so that it forms a cylinder about the line in 3D, and a hyper-cylinder in higher dimensions. How large could we make the radius of this cylinder until we started to put points into a no-man's land, where we don't know which class they are from? This largest radius is known as the **margin**, labelled M. The margin was mentioned briefly in Section 3.4.1, where it affected the speed at which the Perceptron converged. The classifier in the middle of Figure 8.1 has the largest margin of the three. It

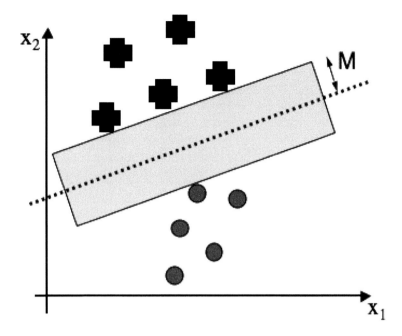

FIGURE 8.2 The margin is the largest region we can put that separates the classes without there being any points inside, where the box is made from two lines that are parallel to the decision boundary.

has the imaginative name of the maximum margin (linear) classifier. The datapoints in each class that lie closest to the classification line have a name as well. They are called support vectors. Using the argument that the best classifier is the one that goes through the middle of no-man's land, we can now make two arguments: first that the margin should be as large as possible, and second that the support vectors are the most useful datapoints because they are the ones that we might get wrong. This leads to an interesting feature of these algorithms: after training we can throw away all of the data except for the support vectors, and use them for classification, which is a useful saving in data storage.

Now that we've got a measurement that we can use to find the optimal decision boundary, we just need to work out how to actually compute it from a given set of datapoints. Let's start by reminding ourselves of some of the things that we worked out in Chapter 3. We have a weight vector (a vector, not a matrix, since there is only one output) and an input vector $\mathbf{x}$. The output we used in Chapter 3 was $y = \mathbf{w} \cdot \mathbf{x} + b$, with b being the contribution from the bias weight. We use the classifier line by saying that any $\mathbf{x}$ value that gives a positive value for $\mathbf{w} \cdot \mathbf{x} + b$ is above the line, and so is an example of the '+' class, while any $\mathbf{x}$ that gives a negative value is in the '∘' class. In our new version of this we want to include our no-man's land. So instead of just looking at whether the value of $\mathbf{w} \cdot \mathbf{x} + b$ is positive or negative, we also check whether the absolute value is less than our margin M, which would put it inside the grey box in Figure 8.2. Remember that $\mathbf{w} \cdot \mathbf{x}$ is the inner or scalar product, $\mathbf{w} \cdot \mathbf{x} = \sum_i w_i x_i$. This can also be written as $\mathbf{w}^T \mathbf{x}$, since this simply means that we treat the vectors as degenerate matrices and use the normal matrix multiplication rules. This notation will turn out to be simpler, and so will be used from here on.

For a given margin value M we can say that any point $\mathbf{x}$ where $\mathbf{w}^T\mathbf{x} + b \geq M$ is a plus, and any point where $\mathbf{w}^T\mathbf{x} + b \leq -M$ is a circle. The actual separating hyperplane is specified by $\mathbf{w}^T\mathbf{x} + b = 0$. Now suppose that we pick a point $\mathbf{x}^+$ that lies on the '+' class boundary line, so that $\mathbf{w}^T\mathbf{x}^+ = M$. This is a support vector. If we want to find the closest point that lies on the boundary line for the 'o' class, then we travel perpendicular to the '+' boundary line until we hit the 'o' boundary line. The point that we hit is the closest point, and we'll call it $\mathbf{x}^-$. How far did we have to travel in this direction? Figure 8.2 hopefully makes it clear that the distance we travelled is M to get to the separating hyperplane, and then M from there to the opposing support vector. We can use this fact to write down the margin size M in terms of $\mathbf{w}$ if we remember one extra thing from Chapter 3, namely that the weight vector $\mathbf{w}$ is perpendicular to the classifier line. If it is perpendicular to the classifier line, then it is obviously perpendicular to the '+' and 'o' boundary lines too, so the direction we travelled from $\mathbf{x}^+$ to $\mathbf{x}^-$ is along $\mathbf{w}$. Now we need to make $\mathbf{w}$ a unit vector $\mathbf{w}/\|w\|$, and so we see that the margin is $1/\|w\|$. In some texts the margin is actually written as the total distance between the support vectors, so that it would be twice the one that we have computed.

So now, given a classifier line (that is, the vector $\mathbf{w}$ and scalar b that define the line $\mathbf{w}^T\mathbf{x} + b$) we can compute the margin M. We can also check that it puts all of the points on the right side of the classification line. Of course, that isn't actually what we want to do: we want to find the $\mathbf{w}$ and b that give us the biggest possible value of M. Our knowledge that the width of the margin is $1/\|w\|$ tells us that making M as large as possible is the same as making $\mathbf{w}^T\mathbf{w}$ as small as possible. If that was the only constraint, then we could just set $\mathbf{w} = \mathbf{0}$, and the problem would be solved, but we also want the classification line to separate out the '+' data from the 'o', that is, actually act as a classifier. So we are going to need to try to satisfy two problems simultaneously: find a decision boundary that classifies well, while also making $\mathbf{w}^T\mathbf{w}$ as small as possible. Mathematically, we can write these requirements as: minimise $\frac{1}{2}\mathbf{w}^T\mathbf{w}$ (where the half is there for convenience as in so many other cases) subject to some constraint that says that the data are well matched. The next thing is to work out what these constraints are.

8.1.2   A Constrained Optimisation Problem

How do we decide whether or not a classifier is any good? Obviously, the fewer mistakes that it makes, the better. So we can write down a set of **constraints** that say that the classifier should get the answer right. To do this we make the target answers for our two classes be ± 1, rather than 0 and 1. We can then write down $t_i \times y_i$, that is, the target multiplied by the output, and this will be positive if the two are the same and negative otherwise. We can write down the equation of the straight line again, which is how we computed y, to see that we require that $t_i(\mathbf{w}^T\mathbf{x} + b) \geq 1$. This means that the constraints just need to check each datapoint for this condition. So the full problem that we wish to solve is:

$$\text{minimise } \frac{1}{2}\mathbf{w}^T\mathbf{w} \text{ subject to } t_i(\mathbf{w}^T\mathbf{x}_i + b) \geq 1 \text{ for all } i = 1, \ldots n. \qquad (8.1)$$

We've put in a lot of effort to write down this equation, but we don't know how to solve it. We could try and use gradient descent, but we would have to put a lot of effort into making it enforce the constraints, and it would be very, very slow and inefficient for the problem. There is a method that is much better suited, which is **quadratic programming**, which takes advantage of the fact that the problem we have described is quadratic and therefore **convex**, and has **linear constraints**. A convex problem is one where if we take any two points on the line and join them with a straight line, then every point on the line will

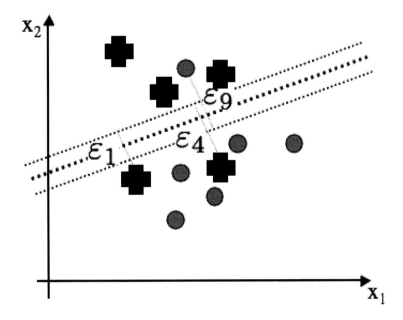

FIGURE 8.3 If the classifier makes some errors, then the distance by which the points are over the border should be used to weight each error in order to decide how bad the classifier is.

be above the curve. Figure 8.4 shows an example of a convex and a non-convex function. Convex functions have a unique minimum, which is fairly easy to see in one dimension, and remains true in any number of dimensions.

The practical upshot of these facts for us is that the types of problem that we are interested in can be solved directly and efficiently (i.e., in polynomial time). There are very effective quadratic programming solvers available, but it is not an algorithm that we will consider writing ourselves. We will, however, work out how to formulate the problem so that it can be presented to a quadratic program solver, and then use one of the programs that other people have been nice enough to prepare and make freely available.

Since the problem is quadratic, there is a unique optimum. When we find that optimal solution, the Karush–Kuhn–Tucker (KKT) conditions will be satisfied. These are (for all values of i from 1 to n, and where the $*$ denotes the optimal value of each parameter):

$$\lambda_i^*(1 - t_i(\mathbf{w}^{*T}\mathbf{x}_i + b^*)) \ = \ 0 \tag{8.2}$$
$$1 - t_i(\mathbf{w}^{*T}\mathbf{x}_i + b^*) \ \leq \ 0 \tag{8.3}$$
$$\lambda_i^* \geq 0, \tag{8.4}$$

where the λ_i are positive values known as Lagrange multipliers, which are a standard approach to solving equations with equality constraints.

The first of these conditions tells us that if $\lambda_i \neq 0$ then $(1 - t_i(\mathbf{w}^{*T}\mathbf{x}_i + b^*)) = 0$. This is only true for the support vectors (the SVMs provide a sparse representation of the data), and so we only have to consider them, and can ignore the rest. In the jargon, the support vectors

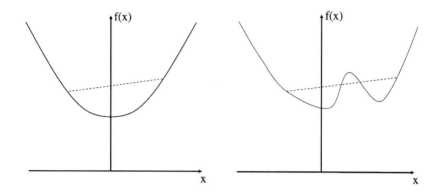

FIGURE 8.4 A function is convex if every straight line that links two points on the curve does not intersect the curve anywhere else. The function on the left is convex, but the one on the right is not, as the dashed line shows.

are those vectors in the **active set** of constraints. For the support vectors the constraints are equalities instead of inequalities. We can therefore solve the **Lagrangian function**:

$$\mathcal{L}(\mathbf{w}, b, \boldsymbol{\lambda}) = \frac{1}{2}\mathbf{w}^T\mathbf{w} + \sum_{i=1}^{n} \lambda_i(1 - t_i(\mathbf{w}^T\mathbf{x}_i + b)), \qquad (8.5)$$

We differentiate this function with respect to the elements of $\mathbf{w}$ and b:

$$\nabla_{\mathbf{w}}\mathcal{L} = \mathbf{w} - \sum_{i=1}^{n} \lambda_i t_i \mathbf{x}_i, \qquad (8.6)$$

and

$$\frac{\partial \mathcal{L}}{\partial b} = -\sum_{i=1}^{n} \lambda_i t_i. \qquad (8.7)$$

If we set the derivatives to be equal to zero, so that we find the saddle points (maxima) of the function, we see that:

$$\mathbf{w}^* = \sum_{i=1}^{n} \lambda_i t_i \mathbf{x}_i, \quad \sum_{i=1}^{n} \lambda_i t_i = 0. \qquad (8.8)$$

We can substitute these expressions at the optimal values of $\mathbf{w}$ and b into Equation (8.5) and, after a little bit of rearranging, we get (where $\boldsymbol{\lambda}$ is the vector of the λ_i):

$$\mathcal{L}(\mathbf{w}^*, b^*, \boldsymbol{\lambda}) = \sum_{i=1}^{n} \lambda_i - \sum_{i=1}^{n} \lambda_i t_i - \frac{1}{2} \sum_{i=1}^{n} \sum_{j=1}^{n} \lambda_i \lambda_j t_i t_j \mathbf{x}_i^T \mathbf{x}_j, \qquad (8.9)$$

and we can notice that using the derivative with respect to b we can treat the middle term as 0. This equation is known as the **dual problem**, and the aim is to maximise it with respect to the λ_i variables. The constraints are that $\lambda_i \geq 0$ for all i, and $\sum_{i=1}^{n} \lambda_i t_i = 0$.

Equation (8.8) gives us an expression for $\mathbf{w}^*$, but we also want to know what b^* is. We know that for a support vector $t_i(\mathbf{w}^T\mathbf{x}_i + b) = 1$, and we can substitute the expression for

$\mathbf{w}^*$ into there and substitute in the $(\mathbf{x}, t)$ of one of the support vectors. However, in case of errors this is not very stable, and so it is better to average it over the whole set of N_s support vectors:

$$b^* = \frac{1}{N_s} \sum_{\text{support vectors } j} \left(t_j - \sum_{i=1}^{n} \lambda_i t_i \mathbf{x}_i^T \mathbf{x}_j \right). \tag{8.10}$$

We can also use Equation (8.8) to see how to make a prediction, since for a new point $\mathbf{z}$:

$$\mathbf{w}^{*T} \mathbf{z} + b^* = \left(\sum_{i=1}^{n} \lambda_i t_i \mathbf{x}_i \right)^T \mathbf{z} + b^*. \tag{8.11}$$

This means that to classify a new point, we just need to compute the inner product between the new datapoint and the support vectors.

8.1.3 Slack Variables for Non-Linearly Separable Problems

Everything that we have done so far has assumed that the datatset is linearly separable. We know that this is not always the case, but if we have a non-linearly separable dataset, then we cannot satisfy the constraints for all of the datapoints. The solution is to introduce some **slack variables** $\eta_i \geq 0$ so that the constraints become $t_i(\mathbf{w}^T \mathbf{x}_i + b) \geq 1 - \eta_i$. For inputs that are correct, we set $\eta_i = 0$.

These slack variables are telling us that, when comparing classifiers, we should consider the case where one classifier makes a mistake by putting a point just on the wrong side of the line, and another puts the same point a long way onto the wrong side of the line. The first classifier is better than the second, because the mistake was not as serious, so we should include this information in our minimisation criterion. We can do this by modifying the problem. In fact, we have to do major surgery, since we want to add a term into the minimisation problem so that we will now minimise $\mathbf{w}^T \mathbf{w} + C \times$ (distance of misclassified points from the correct boundary line). Here, C is a tradeoff parameter that decides how much weight to put onto each of the two criteria: small C means we prize a large margin over a few errors, while large C means the opposite. This transforms the problem into a **soft-margin classifier**, since we are allowing for a few mistakes. Writing this in a more mathematical way, the function that we want to minimise is:

$$L(\mathbf{w}, \boldsymbol{\epsilon}) = \mathbf{w}^T \mathbf{w} + C \sum_{i=1}^{n} \epsilon_i. \tag{8.12}$$

The derivation of the dual problem that we worked out earlier still holds, except that $0 \leq \lambda_i \leq C$, and the support vectors are now those vectors with $\lambda_i > 0$. The KKT conditions are slightly different, too:

$$\lambda_i^* (1 - t_i(\mathbf{w}^{*T} \mathbf{x}_i + b^*) - \eta_i) = 0 \tag{8.13}$$

$$(C - \lambda_i^*)\eta_i = 0 \tag{8.14}$$

$$\sum_{i=1}^{n} \lambda_i^* t_i = 0. \tag{8.15}$$

The second condition tells us that, if $\lambda_i < C$, then $\eta_i = 0$, which means that these are

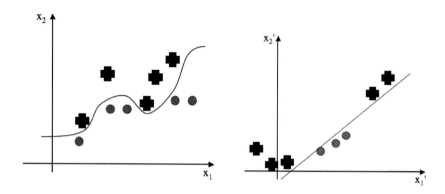

FIGURE 8.5 By modifying the features we hope to find spaces where the data are linearly separable.

the support vectors. If $\lambda_i = C$, then the first condition tells us that if $\eta_i > 1$ then the classifier made a mistake. The problem with this is that it is not as clear how to choose a limited set of vectors, and so most of our training set will be support vectors.

We have now built an optimal linear classifier. However, since most problems are non-linear we seem to have done a lot of work for a case that we could already solve, albeit not as effectively. So while the decision boundary that is found could be better than that found by the Perceptron, if there is not a straight line solution, then the method doesn't work much better than the Perceptron. Not ideal for something that's taken lots of effort to work out! It's time to pull our extra piece of magic out of the hat: transformation of the data.

8.2 KERNELS

To see the idea, have a look at Figure 8.5. Basically, we see that if we modify the features in some way, then we might be able to linearly separate the data, as we did for the XOR problem in Section 3.4.3; if we can use more dimensions, then we might be able to find a linear decision boundary that separates the classes. So all that we need to do is work out what extra dimensions we can use. We can't invent new data, so the new features will have to be derived from the current ones in some way. Just like in Section 5.3, we are going to introduce new functions $\phi(\mathbf{x})$ of our input features.

The important thing is that we are just transforming the data, so that we are making some function $\phi(\mathbf{x}_i)$ from input $\mathbf{x}_i$. The reason why this matters is that we want to be able to use the SVM algorithm that we worked out above, particularly Equation (8.11). The good news is that it isn't any worse, since we can replace $\mathbf{x}_i$ by $\phi(\mathbf{x}_i)$ (and $\mathbf{z}$ by $\phi(\mathbf{z})$) and get a prediction quite easily:

$$\mathbf{w}^T \mathbf{x} + b = \left(\sum_{i=1}^{n} \lambda_i t_i \phi(\mathbf{x}_i) \right)^T \phi(\mathbf{z}) + b. \tag{8.16}$$

We still need to pick what functions to use, of course. If we knew something about the data, then we might be able to identify functions that would be a good idea, but this kind of domain knowledge is not always going to be around, and we would like to automate the algorithm. For now, let's think about a basis that consists of the polynomials of everything up to degree 2. It contains the constant value 1, each of the individual (scalar)

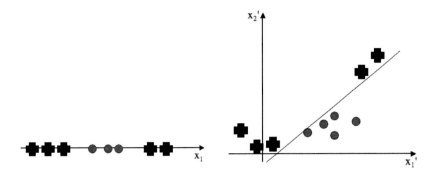

FIGURE 8.6 Using x_1^2 as well as x_1 allows these two classes to be separated.

input elements $x_1, x_2, \ldots, x_d$, and then the squares of each input element $x_1^2, x_2^2, \ldots, x_d^2$, and finally, the products of each pair of elements $x_1 x_2, x_1 x_3, \ldots, x_{d-1} x_d$. The total input vector made up of all these things is generally written as $\Phi(\mathbf{x})$; it contains about $d^2/2$ elements. The right of Figure 8.6 shows a 2D version of this (with the constant term suppressed), and I'm going to write it out for the case $d = 3$, with a set of $\sqrt{2}$s in there (the reasons for them will become clear soon):

$$\Phi(\mathbf{x}) = (1, \sqrt{2}x_1, \sqrt{2}x_2, \sqrt{2}x_3, x_1^2, x_2^2, x_3^2, \sqrt{2}x_1x_2, \sqrt{2}x_1x_3, \sqrt{2}x_2x_3). \qquad (8.17)$$

If there was just one feature, x_1, then we would have changed this from a one-dimensional problem into a three-dimensional one $(1, x_1, x_1^2)$.

The only thing that this has cost us is computational time: the function $\Phi(\mathbf{x}_i)$ has $d^2/2$ elements, and we need to multiply it with another one the same size, and we need to do this many times. This is rather computationally expensive, and if we need to use the powers of the input vector greater than 2 it will be even worse. There is one last piece of trickery that will get us out of this hole: it turns out that we don't actually have to compute $\Phi(\mathbf{x}_i)^T \Phi(\mathbf{x}_j)$. To see how this works, let's work out what $\Phi(\mathbf{x})^T \Phi(\mathbf{y})$ actually is for the example above (where $d = 3$ to match perfectly):

$$\Phi(\mathbf{x})^T \Phi(\mathbf{y}) = 1 + 2\sum_{i=1}^{d} x_i y_i + \sum_{i=1}^{d} x_i^2 y_i^2 + 2 \sum_{i,j=1; i<j}^{d} x_i x_j y_i y_j. \qquad (8.18)$$

You might not recognise that you can factorise this equation, but fortunately somebody did: it can be written as $(1 + \mathbf{x}^T \mathbf{y})^2$. The dot product here is in the original space, so it only requires d multiplications, which is obviously much better—this part of the algorithm has now been reduced from $\mathcal{O}(d^2)$ to $\mathcal{O}(d)$. The same thing holds true for the polynomials of any degree s that we are making here, where the cost of the naïve algorithm is $\mathcal{O}(d^s)$. The important thing is that we remove the problem of computing the dot products of all the extended basis vectors, which is expensive, with the computation of a kernel matrix (also known as the Gram matrix) $\mathbf{K}$ that is made from the dot product of the original vectors, which is only linear in cost. This is sometimes known as the kernel trick. It means that you don't even have to know what $\Phi(\cdot)$ is, provided you know a kernel. These kernels are the fundamental reason why these methods work, and the reason why we went to all that effort to produce the dual formulation of the problem. They produce a transformation of the data so that they are in a higher-dimensional space, but because the datapoints only appear inside those inner products, we don't actually have to do any computations in those higher-dimensional spaces, only in the original (relatively cheap) low-dimensional space.

8.2.1 Choosing Kernels

So how do we go about finding a suitable kernel? Any symmetric function that is positive definite (meaning that it enforces positivity on the integral of arbitrary functions) can be used as a kernel. This is a result of Mercer's theorem, which also says that it is possible to convolve kernels together and the result will be another kernel. However, there are three different types of basis functions that are commonly used, and they have nice kernels that correspond to them:

- polynomials up to some degree s in the elements x_k of the input vector (e.g., x_3^3 or $x_1 \times x_4$) with kernel:

$$\mathbf{K}(\mathbf{x}, \mathbf{y}) = (1 + \mathbf{x}^T \mathbf{y})^s \qquad (8.19)$$

  For $s = 1$ this gives a linear kernel

- sigmoid functions of the x_ks with parameters κ and δ, and kernel:

$$\mathbf{K}(\mathbf{x}, \mathbf{y}) = \tanh(\kappa \mathbf{x}^T \mathbf{y} - \delta) \qquad (8.20)$$

- radial basis function expansions of the x_ks with parameter σ and kernel:

$$\mathbf{K}(\mathbf{x}, \mathbf{y}) = \exp\left(-(\mathbf{x} - \mathbf{y})^2 / 2\sigma^2\right) \qquad (8.21)$$

Choosing which kernel to use and the parameters in these kernels is a tricky problem. While there is some theory based on something known as the Vapnik–Chernik dimension that can be applied, most people just experiment with different values and find one that works, using a validation set as we did for the MLP in Chapter 4.

There are two things that we still need to worry about for the algorithm. One is something that we've discussed in the context of other machine learning algorithms: overfitting, and the other is how we will do testing. The second one is probably worth a little explaining. We used the kernel trick in order to reduce the computations for the training set. We still need to work out how to do the same thing for the testing set, since otherwise we'll be stuck with doing the $\mathcal{O}(d^s)$ computations. In fact, it isn't too hard to get around this problem, because the forward computation for the weights is $\mathbf{w}^T \Phi(\mathbf{x})$, where:

$$\mathbf{w} = \sum_{i \text{ where } \lambda_i > 0} \lambda_i t_i \Phi(\mathbf{x}_i). \qquad (8.22)$$

So we still have the computation of $\Phi(\mathbf{x}_i)^T \Phi(\mathbf{x}_j)$, which we can replace using the kernel as before.

The overfitting problem goes away because of the fact that we are still optimising $\mathbf{w}^T \mathbf{w}$ (remember that from somewhere a long way back?), which tries to keep $\mathbf{w}$ small, which means that many of the parameters are kept close to 0.

8.2.2 Example: XOR

We motivated the SVM by thinking about how we solved the XOR function in Section 3.4.3. So will the SVM actually solve the problem? We'll need to modify the problem to have targets -1 and 1 rather than 0 and 1, but that is not difficult. Then we'll introduce a basis of all terms up to quadratic in our two features: $1, \sqrt{2}x_1, \sqrt{2}x_2, x_1x_2, x_1^2, x_2^2$, where the $\sqrt{2}$ is to keep the multiplications simple. Then Equation (8.9) looks like:

$$\sum_{i=1}^{4} \lambda_i - \sum_{i,j}^{4} \lambda_i \lambda_j t_i t_j \Phi(\mathbf{x}_i)^T \Phi(\mathbf{x}_j), \tag{8.23}$$

subject to the constraints that $\lambda_1 - \lambda_2 + \lambda_3 - \lambda_4 = 0, \lambda_i \geq 0 \ i = 1 \dots 4$. Solving this (which can be done algebraically) tells us that the classifier line is at $x_1 x_2 = 0$. The margin that corresponds to this is $\sqrt{2}$. Unfortunately we can't plot it, since our four points have been transferred into a six-dimensional space. We know that this is not the smallest number that it can be solved in, since we did it in three dimensions in Section 3.4.3, but the dimensionality of the kernel space doesn't matter, as all the computations are in the 2D space anyway.

8.3 THE SUPPORT VECTOR MACHINE ALGORITHM

Quadratic programming solvers tend to be very complex (lots of the work is in identifying the active set), and we would be a long way off topic if we tried to write one. Fortunately, general purpose solvers have been written, and so we can take advantage of this. We will use cvxopt, which is a convex optimisation package that includes a wrapper for Python. There is a link to the relevant website on the book webpage. Cvxopt has a nice and clean interface so we can use this to do the computational heavy lifting for an implementation of the SVM. In essence, the approach is fairly simple: we choose a kernel and then for given data, assemble the relevant quadratic problem and its constraints as matrices, and then pass them to the solver, which finds the decision boundary and necessary support vectors for us. These are then used to build a classifier for that training data. This is given as an algorithm next, and then some parts of the implementation are highlighted, particularly those parts where some speed-up can be achieved by some linear algebra.

The Support Vector Machine Algorithm

- **Initialisation**

  - for the specified kernel, and kernel parameters, compute the kernel of distances between the datapoints
    * the main work here is the computation $\mathbf{K} = \mathbf{X}\mathbf{X}^T$
    * for the linear kernel, return $\mathbf{K}$, for the polynomial of degree d return $\frac{1}{\sigma}\mathbf{K}^d$
    * for the RBF kernel, compute $\mathbf{K} = \exp(-(\mathbf{x} - \mathbf{x}')^2/2\sigma^2)$

- **Training**

  - assemble the constraint set as matrices to solve:

  $$\min_{\mathbf{x}} \frac{1}{2}\mathbf{x}^T t_i t_j \mathbf{K}\mathbf{x} + \mathbf{q}^T\mathbf{x} \text{ subject to } \mathbf{G}\mathbf{x} \leq \mathbf{h}, \mathbf{A}\mathbf{x} = b$$

  - pass these matrices to the solver

- identify the support vectors as those that are within some specified distance of the closest point and dispose of the rest of the training data
- compute b^* using equation (8.10)

- **Classification**

  - for the given test data $\mathbf{z}$, use the support vectors to classify the data for the relevant kernel using:

    * compute the inner product of the test data and the support vectors
    * perform the classification as $\sum_{i=1}^{n} \lambda_i t_i \mathbf{K}(\mathbf{x}_i, \mathbf{z}) + b^*$, returning either the label (hard classification) or the value (soft classification)

8.3.1 Implementation

In order to use the code on the website it is necessary to install the cvxopt package on your computer. There is a link to this on the website. However, we need to work out exactly what we are trying to solve. The key is Equation (8.9), which shows the dual problem, which had constraints $\lambda_i \geq 0$ and $\sum_{i=1}^{n} \lambda_i t_i = 0$. We need to modify it so that we are dealing with the case for slack variables, and using a kernel. Introducing slack variables changes this surprisingly little, basically swapping the first constraint to be $0 \leq \lambda_i \leq C$, while adding the kernel simply turns $\mathbf{x}_i^T \mathbf{x}_j$ into $\mathbf{K}(\mathbf{x}_i, \mathbf{x}_j)$. So we want to solve:

$$\max_{\lambda} \quad = \sum_{i=1}^{n} \lambda_i - \frac{1}{2} \boldsymbol{\lambda}^T \boldsymbol{\lambda} \mathbf{t} \mathbf{t}^T \mathbf{K}(\mathbf{x}_i, \mathbf{x}_j) \boldsymbol{\lambda}, \tag{8.24}$$

$$\text{subject to} \quad 0 \leq \lambda_i \leq C, \sum_{i=1}^{n} \lambda_i t_i = 0. \tag{8.25}$$

The cvxopt quadratic program solver is `cvxopt.solvers.qp()`. This method takes the following inputs `cvxopt.solvers.qp(P, q, G, h, A, b)` and then solves:

$$\min \frac{1}{2} \mathbf{x}^T \mathbf{P} \mathbf{x} + \mathbf{q}^T \mathbf{x} \text{ subject to } \mathbf{G} \mathbf{x} \leq \mathbf{h}, \mathbf{A} \mathbf{x} = \mathbf{b}, \tag{8.26}$$

where $\mathbf{x}$ is the variable we are solving for, which is $\boldsymbol{\lambda}$ for us. Note that this solves minimisation problems, whereas we are doing maximisation, which means that we need to multiply the objective function by -1. To make the equations match we set $\mathbf{P} = t_i t_j \mathbf{K}$ and $\mathbf{q}$ is just a column vector containing -1s. The second constraint is easy, since if $\mathbf{A} = \boldsymbol{\lambda}$ then we get the right equation. However, for the first constraint we need to do a little bit more work, since we want to include two constraints ($0 \leq \lambda_i$ and $\lambda_i \leq C$). To do this, we double up on the number of constraints, multiplying the ones where we want $\geq$ instead of $\leq$ by -1. In order to do this multiplication efficiently, it will also be better to use a matrix with the elements on the diagonal, so that we make the following matrix:

$$
\begin{pmatrix}
t_1 & 0 & \ldots & 0 \\
0 & t_2 & \ldots & 0 \\
& & \ldots & \\
0 & 0 & \ldots & t_n \\
-t_1 & 0 & \ldots & 0 \\
0 & -t_2 & \ldots & 0 \\
& & \ldots & \\
0 & 0 & \ldots & -t_n
\end{pmatrix}
\begin{pmatrix}
\lambda_1 \\
\lambda_2 \\
\ldots \\
\lambda_n
\end{pmatrix}
=
\begin{pmatrix}
C \\
C \\
\ldots \\
C \\
0 \\
0 \\
\ldots \\
0
\end{pmatrix}
\qquad (8.27)
$$

Assembling these, turning them into the matrices expected by the solver, and then calling it can then be written as:

```
# Assemble the matrices for the constraints
P = targets*targets.transpose()*self.K
q = -np.ones((self.N,1))
if self.C is None:
   G = -np.eye(self.N)
   h = np.zeros((self.N,1))
else:
   G = np.concatenate((np.eye(self.N),-np.eye(self.N)))
   h = np.concatenate((self.C*np.ones((self.N,1)),np.zeros((self.N,1))))
A = targets.reshape(1,self.N)
b = 0.0

# Call the quadratic solver
sol = cvxopt.solvers.qp(cvxopt.matrix(P),cvxopt.matrix(q),cvxopt.matrix(G),
cvxopt.matrix(h), cvxopt.matrix(A), cvxopt.matrix(b))
```

There are a couple of novelties in the implementation. One is that the training method actually returns a function that performs the classification, as can be seen here for the polynomial kernel:

```
if self.kernel == 'poly':
   def classifier(Y,soft=False):
      K = (1. + 1./self.sigma*np.dot(Y,self.X.T))**self.degree

      self.y = np.zeros((np.shape(Y)[0],1))
      for j in range(np.shape(Y)[0]):
         for i in range(self.nsupport):
            self.y[j] += self.lambdas[i]*self.targets[i]*K[j,i]
         self.y[j] += self.b

      if soft:
         return self.y
      else:
         return np.sign(self.y)
```

The reason for this is that the classification function has different forms for the different kernels, and so we need to create this function based on the kernel that is specified. A handle for the classifier is stored in the class, and the method can then be called as:

```
output = sv.classifier(Y,soft=False)
```

The other novelty is that some of the computation of the RBF kernel uses some linear algebra to make the computation faster, since NumPy is better at dealing with matrix manipulations than loops. The elements of the RBF kernel are $K_{ij} = \frac{1}{2\sigma} \exp(-\|x_i - x_j\|^2)$. We could go about forming this by using a pair of loops over i and j, but instead we can use some algebra.

The linear kernel has computed $K_{ij} = \mathbf{x}_i^T \mathbf{x}_j$, and the diagonal elements of this matrix are $\|\mathbf{x}_i\|^2$. The trick is to see how to use only these elements to compute the $\|\mathbf{x}_i - \mathbf{x}_j\|^2$ part, and it just requires expanding out the quadratic:

$$(\mathbf{x}_i - \mathbf{x}_j)^2 = \|\mathbf{x}_i\|^2 + \|\mathbf{x}_j^2\| - 2\mathbf{x}_i^T \mathbf{x}_j. \tag{8.28}$$

The only work involved now is to make sure that the matrices are the right shape. This would be easy if it wasn't for the fact that NumPy 'loses' the dimension of some $N \times 1$ matrices, so that they are of size N only, as we have seen before. This means that we need to make a matrix of ones and use the transpose operator a few times, as can be seen in the code fragment below.

```
self.xsquared = (np.diag(self.K)*np.ones((1,self.N))).T
b = np.ones((self.N,1))
self.K -= 0.5*(np.dot(self.xsquared,b.T) + np.dot(b,self.xsquared.T))
self.K = np.exp(self.K/(2.*self.sigma**2))
```

For the classifier we can use the same tricks to compute the product of the kernel and the test data:

```
elif self.kernel == 'rbf':
    def classifier(Y,soft=False):
        K = np.dot(Y,self.X.T)
        c = (1./self.sigma * np.sum(Y**2,axis=1)*np.ones((1,np.shape(Y)[0])))
        .T
        c = np.dot(c,np.ones((1,np.shape(K)[1])))
        aa = np.dot(self.xsquared[self.sv],np.ones((1,np.shape(K)[0]))).T
        K = K - 0.5*c - 0.5*aa
        K = np.exp(K/(2.*self.sigma**2))

        self.y = np.zeros((np.shape(Y)[0],1))
        for j in range(np.shape(Y)[0]):
            for i in range(self.nsupport):
                self.y[j] += self.lambdas[i]*self.targets[i]*K[j,i]
```

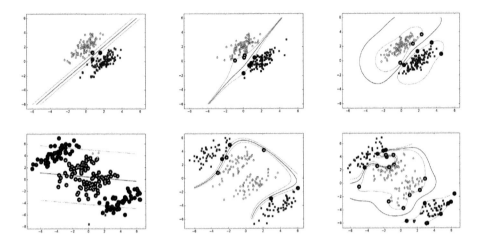

FIGURE 8.7 The SVM learning about a linearly separable dataset (*top row*) and a dataset that needs two straight lines to separate in 2D (*bottom row*) with *left* the linear kernel, *middle* the polynomial kernel of degree 3, and *right* the RBF kernel. $C = 0.1$ in all cases.

```
        self.y[j] += self.b

    if soft:
        return self.y
    else:
        return np.sign(self.y)
```

The first bit of computational work is in computing the kernel (which is $\mathcal{O}(m^2 n)$, where m is the number of datapoints and n is the dimensionality), and the second part is inside the solver, which has to factorise a sum of the kernel matrix and a test matrix at each iteration. Factorisation costs $\mathcal{O}(m^3)$ in general, and this is why the SVM is very expensive to use for large datasets. There are some methods by which this can be improved, and there are some references to this at the end of the chapter.

8.3.2 Examples

In order to see the SVM working, and to identify the differences between the kernels, we will start with some very simple 2D datasets with two classes.

The first example (shown on the top row of Figure 8.7) simply checks that the SVM can learn accurately about data that is linearly separable, which it does successfully. Note that the different kernels produce different decision boundaries, which are not straight lines in the 2D plot for the polynomial kernel (centre) and RBF kernel (right), and that different numbers of support vectors (highlighted in bold) are needed for the different kernels as well.

On the second line of the figure is a dataset that cannot be separated by a single straight line, and which the linear kernel cannot then separate. However, the polynomial and RBF kernels deal with this data successfully with very few support vectors.

For the second example the data come from the XOR dataset with some spread around each of the four datapoints. The dataset is made by making four sets of random Gaussian samples with a small standard deviation, and means of $(0, 0), (0, 1), (1, 0)$, and $(1, 1)$. Figure 8.8 shows a series of outputs from this dataset with the standard deviations of each cluster being 0.1 on the left, 0.3 in the middle, and 0.4 on the right, and with 100 datapoints for training, and 100 datapoints for testing. The training set for the two classes is shown as black and white circles, with the support vectors marked with a thicker outline. The test set are shown as black and white squares.

The top row of the figure shows the polynomial kernel of degree 3 with no slack variables, while the second row shows the same kernel but with $C = 0.1$; the third row shows the RBF kernel with no slack variables, and the last row shows the RBF kernel with $C = 0.1$. It can be seen that where the classes start to overlap, the inclusion of slack variables leads to far simpler decision boundaries and a better model of the underlying data. Both the polynomial and RBF kernels perform well on this problem.

8.4 EXTENSIONS TO THE SVM

8.4.1 Multi-Class Classification

We've talked about SVMs in terms of two-class classification. You might be wondering how to use them for more classes, since we can't use the same methods as we have done to work out the current algorithm. In fact, you can't actually do it in a consistent way. The SVM only works for two classes. This might seem like a major problem, but with a little thought it is possible to find ways around the problem. For the problem of N-class classification, you train an SVM that learns to classify class one from all other classes, then another that classifies class two from all the others. So for N-classes, we have N SVMs. This still leaves one problem: how do we decide which of these SVMs is the one that recognises the particular input? The answer is just to choose the one that makes the strongest prediction, that is, the one where the basis vector input point is the furthest into the positive class region. It might not be clear how to work out which is the strongest prediction. The classifier examples in the code snippets return either the class label (as the sign of y) or the value of y, and this value of y is telling us how far away from the decision boundary it is, and clearly it will be negative if it is a misclassification. We can therefore use the maximum value of this soft boundary as the best classifier.

```
output = np.zeros((np.shape(test)[0],3))
output[:,0] = svm0.classifier(test[:,:2],soft=True).T
output[:,1] = svm1.classifier(test[:,:2],soft=True).T
output[:,2] = svm2.classifier(test[:,:2],soft=True).T

# Make a decision about which class
# Pick the one with the largest margin
bestclass = np.argmax(output,axis=1)
err = np.where(bestclass!=target)[0]
print len(err)/ np.shape(target)[0]
```

Figure 8.9 shows the first two dimensions of the iris dataset and the class decision boundaries for the three classes. It can be seen that using only two dimensions does not

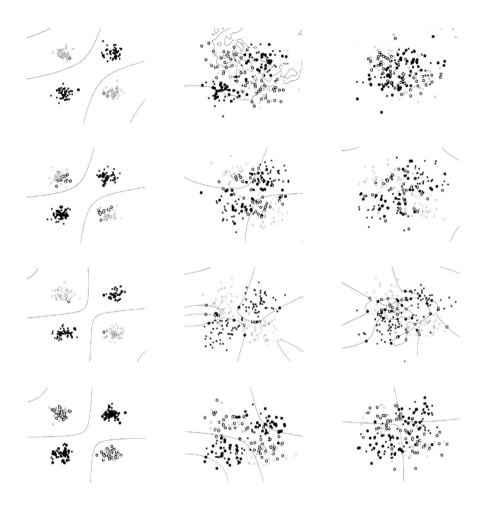

FIGURE 8.8 The effects of different kernels when learning a version of XOR with progressively more overlap (*left* to *right*) between the classes. *Top row:* polynomial kernel of degree 3 with no slack variables, *second row:* polynomial of degree 3 with $C = 0.1$, *third row:* RBF kernel, no slack variables, *bottom row:* RBF kernel with $C = 0.1$. The support vectors are highlighted, and the decision boundary is drawn for each case.

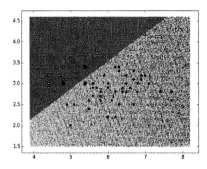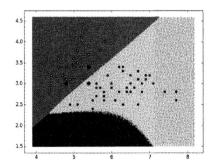

FIGURE 8.9 A linear (*left*) and polynomial, degree 3 (*right*) kernel learning the first two dimensions of the iris dataset, which separates one class very well from the other two, but cannot distinguish between the other two (for good reason). The support vectors are highlighted.

allow good separation of the data, and both kernels get about 33% accuracy, but allowing for all four dimensions, both the RBF and polynomial kernels reliably get about 95% accuracy.

8.4.2 SVM Regression

Perhaps rather surprisingly, it is also possible to use the SVM for regression. The key is to take the usual least-squares error function (with the regulariser that keeps the norm of the weights small):

$$\frac{1}{2}\sum_{i=1}^{N}(t_i - y_i)^2 + \frac{1}{2}\lambda\|\mathbf{w}\|^2,\tag{8.29}$$

and transform it using what is known as an ϵ-insensitive error function (E_ϵ) that gives 0 if the difference between the target and output is less than ϵ (and subtracts ϵ in any other case for consistency). The reason for this is that we still want a small number of support vectors, so we are only interested in the points that are not well predicted. Figure 8.10 shows the form of this error function, which is:

$$\sum_{i=1}^{N}E_\epsilon(t_i - y_i) + \lambda\frac{1}{2}\|\mathbf{w}\|^2.\tag{8.30}$$

You might see this written in other texts with the constant λ in front of the second term replaced by a C in front of the first term. This is equivalent up to scaling. The picture to think of now is almost the opposite of Figure 8.3: we want the predictions to be inside the tube of radius ϵ that surrounds the correct line. To allow for errors, we again introduce slack variables for each datapoint (ϵ_i for datapoint i) with their constraints and follow the same procedure of introducing Lagrange multipliers, transferring to the dual problem, using a kernel function and solving the problem with a quadratic solver.

The upshot of all this is that the prediction we make for test point $\mathbf{z}$ is:

$$f(\mathbf{z}) = \sum_{i=1}^{n}(\mu_i - \lambda_i K(\mathbf{x}_i, \mathbf{z}) + b),\tag{8.31}$$

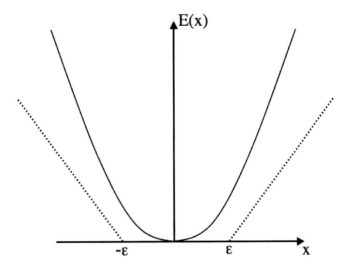

FIGURE 8.10 The ϵ-insensitive error function is zero for any error below ϵ.

where μ_i and λ_i are two sets of constraint variables.

8.4.3 Other Advances

There is a lot of advanced work on kernel methods and SVMs. This includes lots of work on the optimisation, including Sequential Minimal Optimisation, and extensions to compute posterior probabilities instead of hard decisions, such as the Relevance Vector Machine. There are some references in the Further Reading section.

There are several SVM implementations available via the Internet that are more advanced than the implementation on the book website. They are mostly written in C, but some include wrappers to be called from other languages, including Python. An Internet search will find you some possibilities to try, but some common choices are SVMLight, LIBSVM, and scikit-learn.

FURTHER READING

The treatment of SVMs here has only skimmed the surface of the topic. There is a useful tutorial paper on SVMs at:

- C.J. Burges. A tutorial on support vector machines for pattern recognition. *Data Mining and Knowledge Discovery*, 2(2):121–167, 1998.

If you want more information, then any of the following books will provide it (the first is by the creator of SVMs):

- V. Vapnik. *The Nature of Statistical Learning Theory*. Springer, Berlin, Germany, 1995.

- B. Schölkopf, C.J.C. Burges, and A.J. Smola. *Advances in Kernel Methods: Support Vector Learning*. MIT Press, Cambridge, MA, USA, 1999.

- J. Shawe-Taylor and N. Cristianini. *Kernel Methods for Pattern Analysis.* Cambridge University Press, Cambridge, UK, 2004.

If you want to know more about quadratic programming, then a good reference is:

- S. Boyd and L. Vandenberghe. *Convex Optimization.* Cambridge University Press, Cambridge, UK, 2004.

Other machine learning books that give useful coverage of this area are:

- Chapter 12 of T. Hastie, R. Tibshirani, and J. Friedman. *The Elements of Statistical Learning*, 2nd edition, Springer, Berlin, Germany, 2008.

- Chapter 7 of C.M. Bishop. *Pattern Recognition and Machine Learning.* Springer, Berlin, Germany, 2006.

PRACTICE QUESTIONS

Problem 8.1 Suppose that the following are a set of points in two classes:

$$\text{class 1} \quad : \quad \begin{pmatrix} 1 \\ 1 \end{pmatrix} \begin{pmatrix} 1 \\ 2 \end{pmatrix} \begin{pmatrix} 2 \\ 1 \end{pmatrix} \tag{8.32}$$

$$\text{class 2} \quad : \quad \begin{pmatrix} 0 \\ 0 \end{pmatrix} \begin{pmatrix} 1 \\ 0 \end{pmatrix} \begin{pmatrix} 0 \\ 1 \end{pmatrix} \tag{8.33}$$

Plot them and find the optimal separating line. What are the support vectors, and what is the margin?

Problem 8.2 Suppose that the points are now:

$$\text{class 1} \quad : \quad \begin{pmatrix} 0 \\ 0 \end{pmatrix} \begin{pmatrix} 1 \\ 2 \end{pmatrix} \begin{pmatrix} 2 \\ 1 \end{pmatrix} \tag{8.34}$$

$$\text{class 2} \quad : \quad \begin{pmatrix} 1 \\ 1 \end{pmatrix} \begin{pmatrix} 1 \\ 0 \end{pmatrix} \begin{pmatrix} 0 \\ 1 \end{pmatrix} \tag{8.35}$$

Try out the different basis functions that were given in the chapter to see which separate this data and which do not.

Problem 8.3 Apply it to the `wine` dataset, trying out the different kernels. Compare the results to using an MLP. Do the same for the `yeast` dataset.

Problem 8.4 Use an SVM on the MNIST dataset.

Problem 8.5 Verify that introducing the slack variables does not change the dual problem much at all (only changing the constraint to be $0 \leq \lambda_i \leq C$). Start from Equation (8.12) and introduce the Lagrange multipliers and then compare the result to Equations (8.9).

## CHAPTER 9

Optimisation and Search

In almost all of the algorithms that we've looked at in the previous chapters there has been some element of optimisation, generally by defining some sort of error function, and attempting to minimise it. We've talked about gradient descent, which is the optimisation method that forms the basis of many machine learning algorithms. In this chapter, we will look at formalising the gradient descent algorithm and understanding how it works, and then we will look at what we can do when there are no gradients in the problem, and so gradient descent doesn't work.

Whatever method we have used to solve the optimisation problem, the basic methodology has been the same: to compute the derivative of the error function to get the gradient and follow it downhill. What if that derivative doesn't exist? This is actually common in many problems—discrete problems are not defined on continuous functions, and hence can't be differentiated, and so gradient descent can't be used. In theory, it is possible to check all of the cases for a discrete problem to find the optimum, but the computations are infeasible for any interesting problem. We therefore need to think of some other approaches. Some examples of discrete problems are:

Chip design Lay a circuit onto a computer chip so that none of the tracks cross.

Timetabling Given a list of courses and which students are on each course, find a timetable with the minimum number of clashes (or given a number of planes and routes, schedule the planes onto the routes).

The Travelling Salesman Problem Given a set of cities, find a tour (that is, a solution that visits every city exactly once, and returns to the starting point) that minimises the total distance travelled.

One thing that is worth noting is that there is no one ideal solution to the search problem. That is, there is no one search algorithm that is guaranteed to perform the best on every problem that is presented to it—you always have to put some work into choosing the algorithm that will be most effective for your problem, and phrasing your problem to make the algorithm work as efficiently as possible. This is called the No Free Lunch theorem.

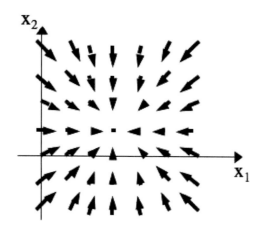

FIGURE 9.1 The downhill gradients to minimise a function. At the solution the gradient is 0. This is a nice example without local minima; they would also have gradient 0.

9.1 GOING DOWNHILL

We will start by trying to derive a better understanding of gradient descent, and seeing the algorithms that can be used for finding local optima for general problems. We will also look at the specific case of solving least-squares optimisation problems, which are the most common examples in machine learning.

The basic idea, as we have already seen, is that we want to minimise a function $f(\mathbf{x})$, where $\mathbf{x}$ is a vector $(x_1, x_2, \ldots, x_n)$ that has elements for each feature value, starting from some initial guess $\mathbf{x}(0)$. We try to find a sequence of new points $\mathbf{x}(i)$ that move downhill towards a solution. The methods that we are going to look at work in any number of dimensions. We will therefore have to take derivatives of the function in each of the different dimensions of $\mathbf{x}$. We write down this whole set of functions as $\nabla f(\mathbf{x})$, which is a vector with elements $(\frac{\partial f}{\partial \mathbf{x}_1}, \frac{\partial f}{\partial \mathbf{x}_2}, \ldots, \frac{\partial f}{\partial \mathbf{x}_n})$, so that it gives us the gradient in each dimension separately. Figure 9.1 shows a set of directions in two dimensions in order to minimise some function.

The first thing to think about is how we know when we have found a solution; in other words, how will we know when to stop? This is relatively easy: it is when $\nabla f = 0$, since then there is no more downhill to go. If you are walking down a hill, then you have reached the bottom when everything is flat around you (which might not be a very large space before things start going up again, but if the function is continuous, as we will assume here, then there must be a point where it is 0 inbetween where it is going down and where it starts going up). So we will know when to terminate the algorithm by checking whether or not $\nabla f = 0$. In practice, the algorithms will always have some numerical inaccuracy, since they are floating point numbers inside the computer, so we usually stop if $|\nabla f| < \epsilon$ where ϵ is some small number, maybe 10^{-5}. There is another concept that it can be useful to think about, which is the places that we can travel to without going up or down, i.e., the places that are at the same level as we are. The full set of places that have the same function value are known as level sets of the function, and some examples are shown in Figure 9.2. Often there will be several discrete parts to a level set, so it is not possible to explore it all without stepping off the set itself.

So from the current point $\mathbf{x}_i$ there are two things that we need to decide: what direction should we move in to go downhill as fast as possible, and how far should we move? Looking

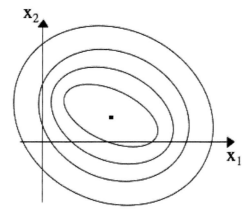

FIGURE 9.2 The lines show contours of equal value (level sets) for a function.

at the second of these questions first, there are two types of methods that can be used to solve it. The simplest approach is a line search: if we know what direction to look in, then we move along it until we reach the minimum in this direction. So this is just a search along the line we are moving along. Writing this down mathematically, if we are currently at $\mathbf{x}_k$ then the next guess will be $\mathbf{x}_{k+1}$, which is:

$$\mathbf{x}_{k+1} = \mathbf{x}_k + \alpha_k \mathbf{p}_k, \tag{9.1}$$

where $\mathbf{p}_k$ is the direction we have chosen to move in and α_k is the distance to travel in that direction, chosen by the line search. Finding a value for α_k can be computationally expensive and inaccurate, so it is generally just estimated.

The other method of choosing how far to move is known as a **trust region**. It is more complex, since it consists of making a local model of the function as a **quadratic form** and finding the minimum of that model. We will see one example of a trust region method in Section 9.2, and more information about general trust region methods is available in the books listed at the end of the chapter.

The direction $\mathbf{p}_k$ can also be chosen in several ways. The left of Figure 9.3 shows the ideal situation, which is that we point directly to the minimum, in which case the line search finds it straight away. Since we don't know the minimum (it is what we are trying to find!) this is virtually impossible. One thing that we can do is to make **greedy** choices and always go downhill as fast as possible at each point. This is known as **steepest descent**, and it means that $\mathbf{p}_k = -\nabla f(\mathbf{x}_k)$. The problem with it can be seen on the right of Figure 9.3, which is that many of the directions that it travels in are not directly towards the centre. In extreme cases they can be very different: across the valley, rather than down towards the global minimum (we saw this in Figure 4.7).

If we don't worry about the stepsize, and just set it as $\alpha_k = 1$, then we can perform the search using Equation (9.1) with a very simple program. All that is needed is to iterate the line search until the solution stops changing (or you decide that there have been too many iterations). The only other thing that you have to compute is the derivative of the function, which is the direction $\mathbf{p}_k$. This is the problem-specific part of the algorithm, and as a small example, we consider a simple three-dimensional function $f(\mathbf{x}) = (0.5x_1^2 + 0.2x_2^2 + 0.6x_3^2)$. We can differentiate once to compute the vector of derivatives, $\nabla f(\mathbf{x}) = (x_1, 0.4x_2, 1.2x_3)$, which is returned by the `gradient()` function in the code below:

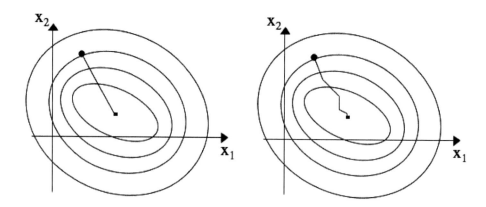

FIGURE 9.3 *Left:* In an ideal world we would know how to go to the minimum directly. In practice, we don't, so we have to approximate it by something like *right:* moving in the direction of steepest descent at each stage.

```
def gradient(x):
    return np.array([x[0], 0.4*x[1], 1.2*x[2]])

def steepest(x0):
    i = 0
    iMax = 10
    x = x0
    Delta = 1
    alpha = 1

    while i<iMax and Delta>10**(-5):
        p = -Jacobian(x)
        xOld = x
        x = x + alpha*p
        Delta = np.sum((x-xOld)**2)
        print x
        i += 1
```

To compute the minimum we now need to pick a start point, for example, $\mathbf{x}(0) = (-2, 2, -2)$, and then we can compute the steepest downhill direction as $(-2, 0.8, -2.4)$. Using the steepest descent method for this example gives fairly poor results, taking several steps before the answer gets close to the correct answer of $(0, 0, 0)$, and even then it is not that close:

```
[ 0. 1.20      0.40]
[ 0. 0.72     -0.08]
[ 0. 0.43      0.01]
[ 0. 0.26     -0.00]
[ 0. 0.16      0.00]
[ 0. 0.09     -0.00]
[ 0. 5.69-02   2.56-05]
```

To see how we can improve on this we need to examine the basics of function approximation.

9.1.1 Taylor Expansion

Steepest descent is based on the Taylor expansion of the function, which is a method of approximating the value of a function at a point in terms of its derivatives: a function $f(\mathbf{x})$ can be approximated by:

$$f(\mathbf{x}) \approx f(\mathbf{x}_0) + \mathbf{J}(f(\mathbf{x}))|_{\mathbf{x}_0}(\mathbf{x} - \mathbf{x}_0) + \frac{1}{2}(\mathbf{x} - \mathbf{x}_0)^T \mathbf{H}(f(\mathbf{x}))|_{\mathbf{x}_0}(\mathbf{x} - \mathbf{x}_0) + \dots, \qquad (9.2)$$

where $\mathbf{x}_0$ is a common, but potentially slightly confusing notation for the initial guess $\mathbf{x}(0)$, the $|_{\mathbf{x}_0}$ notation means that the function is evaluated at that point, and the $\mathbf{J}(\mathbf{x})$ term is the Jacobian, which is the vector of first derivatives:

$$\mathbf{J}(\mathbf{x}) = \frac{\partial f(\mathbf{x})}{\partial \mathbf{x}} = \left(\frac{\partial f(\mathbf{x})}{\partial x_1}, \frac{\partial f(\mathbf{x})}{\partial x_2}, \dots, \frac{\partial f(\mathbf{x})}{\partial x_n} \right) \qquad (9.3)$$

and $\mathbf{H}(\mathbf{x})$ is the Hessian matrix of second derivatives (the Jacobian of the gradient), which for a single function $f(x_1, x_2, \dots x_n)$ is defined as:

$$\mathbf{H}(\mathbf{x}) = \frac{\partial}{\partial \mathbf{x}_i} \frac{\partial}{\partial \mathbf{x}_j} f(\mathbf{x}) = \begin{pmatrix} \frac{\partial^2 f(\mathbf{x})}{\partial x_1^2} & \frac{\partial^2 f(\mathbf{x})}{\partial x_1 \partial x_2} & \cdots & \frac{\partial^2 f(\mathbf{x})}{\partial x_1 \partial x_n} \\ & \cdots & \\ \frac{\partial^2 f(\mathbf{x})}{\partial x_n \partial x_1} & \frac{\partial^2 f(\mathbf{x})}{\partial x_n \partial x_2} & \cdots & \frac{\partial f_n(\mathbf{x})}{\partial x_n^2} \end{pmatrix}. \qquad (9.4)$$

If $f(\mathbf{x})$ is a scalar function (so that it returns just 1 number) then $\mathbf{J}(\mathbf{x}) = \nabla f(\mathbf{x})$ and is a vector and $\mathbf{H}(\mathbf{x}) = \nabla^2 f(\mathbf{x})$ is a two-dimensional matrix. For a vector $\mathbf{f}(\mathbf{x})$ with components $f_1(\mathbf{x}), f_2(\mathbf{x})$, etc., $\mathbf{J}(\mathbf{x})$ is a two-dimensional matrix and $\mathbf{H}(\mathbf{x})$ is three-dimensional.

If we ignore the Hessian term in Equation (9.2), then for scalar $f(\mathbf{x})$ we get precisely the steepest descent step. However, if we choose to minimise Equation (9.2) exactly as it is written (i.e., ignoring third derivatives and higher), then we find the Newton direction at the kth iteration to be: $\mathbf{p}_k = -(\nabla^2 f(\mathbf{x}_k))^{-1} \nabla f(\mathbf{x}_k)$. There is something important to notice about this equation, which is that we actually use the inverse of the Hessian. Computing this is generally of order $\mathcal{O}(N^3)$ (where N is the number of elements in the matrix) which makes this a computationally expensive method. The compensation for this cost is that we don't really have to worry about the stepsize at all; it is always set to 1.

Implementing this requires only 1 line of change to our basic steepest descent algorithm, plus the addition of a function that computes the Hessian. The line to change is the one that computes $\mathbf{p}_k$, which becomes:

```
p = -np.dot(np.linalg.inv(Hessian(x)),Jacobian(x))
```

For this simple example, this algorithm goes straight to the correct answer in one step, which is much better than the steepest descent method that we saw earlier. However, for more complicated functions it won't work as well, because the estimate of the Hessian is not as accurate. There are particular cases where we can, however, do better, as we shall see.

9.2   LEAST-SQUARES OPTIMISATION

For many of the algorithms that we have derived we have used a least-squares error function, such as the error of the MLP and the linear regressor. Least-squares problems turn out to be the most common optimisation problems in many fields, and this means that they have been very well studied and, fortunately, they have special structure in the problem that makes solving them easier than other problems. This leads to a set of special algorithms for solving least-squares problems, although they are mostly special cases of standard methods. One of these has become very well known, the Levenberg–Marquardt method, which is a trust region optimisation algorithm. We will derive the Levenberg–Marquardt algorithm, beginning by identifying why least-squares optimisation is a special case.

9.2.1   The Levenberg–Marquardt Algorithm

For least-squares problems, the objective function that we are optimising is:

$$f(\mathbf{x}) = \frac{1}{2} \sum_{j=1}^{m} r_j^2(\mathbf{x}) = \frac{1}{2} \|\mathbf{r}(\mathbf{x})\|_2^2, \tag{9.5}$$

where the $\frac{1}{2}$ makes the derivative nicer, and $\mathbf{r}(\mathbf{x}) = (r_1(\mathbf{x}), r_2(\mathbf{x}), \ldots, r_m(\mathbf{x}))^T$. In this last version, we can write the (transpose of the) Jacobian of $\mathbf{r}$ as:

$$\mathbf{J}^T(\mathbf{x}) = \left\{ \begin{matrix} \frac{\partial r_1}{\partial x_1} & \frac{\partial r_2}{\partial x_1} & \cdots & \frac{\partial r_m}{\partial x_1} \\ \frac{\partial r_1}{\partial x_2} & \frac{\partial r_2}{\partial x_2} & \cdots & \frac{\partial r_m}{\partial x_2} \\ \cdots & \cdots & \cdots & \cdots \\ \frac{\partial r_1}{\partial x_n} & \frac{\partial r_2}{\partial x_n} & \cdots & \frac{\partial r_m}{\partial x_n} \end{matrix} \right\} = \left[\frac{\partial r_j}{\partial x_i} \right]_{j=1,\ldots,m, \ i=1,\ldots,n}, \tag{9.6}$$

which is useful because the function gradients that we want can mostly be computed directly:

$$\nabla f(\mathbf{x}) = \mathbf{J}(\mathbf{x})^T \mathbf{r}(\mathbf{x}) \tag{9.7}$$

$$\nabla^2 f(\mathbf{x}) = \mathbf{J}(\mathbf{x})^T \mathbf{J}(\mathbf{x}) + \sum_{j=1}^{m} r_j(\mathbf{x}) \nabla^2 r_j(\mathbf{x}). \tag{9.8}$$

The upshot of this is that knowing the Jacobian gives you the first (and usually, most important) part of the Hessian effectively without any additional computational cost, and it is this that special algorithms can exploit to solve least-squares problems efficiently. To see this, remember that, as in all of the other gradient-descent algorithms that we have looked at, we are approximating the function by the Taylor series (Equation (9.2)) up to second-order (Hessian) terms.

If $\|\mathbf{r}(\mathbf{x})\|$ is a linear function of $\mathbf{x}$ (which means that $f(\mathbf{x})$ is quadratic), then the Jacobian is constant and $\nabla^2 r_j(\mathbf{x}) = 0$ for all j. In this case, substituting Equations (9.7) and (9.8) into Equation (9.2) and taking derivatives, we see that at a solution:

$$\nabla f(\mathbf{x}) = \mathbf{J}^T(\mathbf{J}\mathbf{x} + \mathbf{r}) = 0, \tag{9.9}$$

and so:

$$\mathbf{J}^T\mathbf{J}\mathbf{x} = -\mathbf{J}^T\mathbf{r}(\mathbf{x}). \tag{9.10}$$

This is a linear least-squares problem and can be solved. In an ideal world we would be able to see that it is effectively just the statement $\mathbf{A}\mathbf{x} = \mathbf{b}$ (where $\mathbf{A} = \mathbf{J}^T\mathbf{J}$ is a square matrix and $\mathbf{b} = -\mathbf{J}^T\mathbf{r}(\mathbf{x})$ and so solve it directly as:

$$\mathbf{x} = -(\mathbf{J}^T\mathbf{J})^{-1}\mathbf{J}^T\mathbf{r}. \tag{9.11}$$

However, this is computationally expensive and numerically very unstable, so we need to use linear algebra to find $\mathbf{x}$ in a variety of different ways, such as Cholesky factorisation, QR factorisation, or using the Singular Value Decomposition. We will look at the last of these methods, since it uses eigenvectors, which we have already seen in Chapter 6, although we will see the first method in Chapter 18.

The Singular Value Decomposition (SVD) is the decomposition of a matrix $\mathbf{A}$ of size $m \times n$ into:

$$\mathbf{A} = \mathbf{U}\mathbf{S}\mathbf{V}^T, \tag{9.12}$$

where $\mathbf{U}$ and $\mathbf{V}$ are orthogonal matrices (i.e., the inverse of the matrix is its transpose, so $\mathbf{U}^T\mathbf{U} = \mathbf{U}\mathbf{U}^T = \mathbf{I}$, where $\mathbf{I}$ is the identity matrix). $\mathbf{U}$ is of size $m \times m$ and $\mathbf{V}$ is of size $n \times n$. $\mathbf{S}$ is a diagonal matrix of size $m \times n$, with the elements of this matrix, σ_i, being known as singular values.

To apply this to the linear least-squares problem we compute the SVD of $\mathbf{J}^T\mathbf{J}$ and substitute it into Equation (9.11):

$$\begin{align} \mathbf{x} &= \left[(\mathbf{U}\mathbf{S}\mathbf{V}^T)^T(\mathbf{U}\mathbf{S}\mathbf{V}^T)\right]^{-1}(\mathbf{U}\mathbf{S}\mathbf{V}^T)^T\mathbf{J}^T\mathbf{r} \tag{9.13} \\ &= \mathbf{V}\mathbf{S}\mathbf{U}^T\mathbf{J}^T\mathbf{r} \tag{9.14} \end{align}$$

using the fact that $\mathbf{A}\mathbf{B}^T = \mathbf{B}^T\mathbf{A}^T$ and similar linear algebraic identities.

We can actually go a bit further, and deal with the fact that $\mathbf{J}$ is probably not a square matrix. The size of the various matrices will be $m \times m$ for $\mathbf{U}$ and $m \times m$ for the other two (where m and n are defined in Equation (9.6); generally $n < m$). We can split $\mathbf{U}$ into two parts, $\mathbf{U}_1$ of size $m \times n$ and then the last few columns into a second part $\mathbf{U}_2$ of size $(n - m) \times n$. This lets us solve the linear least-squares equation as:

$$\mathbf{x} = \mathbf{V}\mathbf{S}^{-1}\mathbf{U}_1^T\mathbf{J}\mathbf{r}. \tag{9.15}$$

NumPy has an algorithm for linear least-squares in `np.linalg.lstsq()` and can compute the SVD decomposition using `np.linalg.svd()`.

We can now use this derivation to look at the most well-known method for solving non-linear least-squares problems, the Levenberg–Marquardt algorithm. The principal approximation that the algorithm makes is to ignore the residual terms in Equation (9.8), making each iteration a linear least-squares problem, so that $\nabla^2 f(\mathbf{x}) = \mathbf{J}(\mathbf{x})^T\mathbf{J}(\mathbf{x})$. Then the problem to be solved is:

$$\min_{\mathbf{p}} \frac{1}{2}\|\mathbf{J}_k\mathbf{p} + \mathbf{r}_k\|_2^2, \quad \|\mathbf{p}\| \le \Delta_k, \tag{9.16}$$

where Δ_k is the radius of the **trust region**, which is the region where it is assumed that this approximation holds well. In normal trust region methods, the size of the region (Δ_k) is controlled explicitly, but in Levenberg–Marquardt it is used to control a parameter $\nu \ge 0$ that is added to the diagonal elements of the Jacobian matrix and is known as the **damping factor**. The minimum $\mathbf{p}$ then satisfies:

$$(\mathbf{J}^T\mathbf{J} + \nu\mathbf{I})\mathbf{p} = -\mathbf{J}^T\mathbf{r}. \tag{9.17}$$

This is a very similar equation to the one that we solved for the linear least-squares method, and so we can just use that solver here; effectively non-linear least-squares solvers solve a lot of linear problems to find the non-linear solution. There are very efficient Levenberg–Marquardt solvers, since it is possible to avoid computing the $\mathbf{J}^T\mathbf{J}$ term explicitly using the SVD composition that we worked out above.

The basic idea of the trust region method is to assume that the solution is quadratic about the current point, and use that assumption to minimise the current step. You then compute the difference between the actual reduction and the predicted one, based on the model, and make the trust region larger or smaller depending upon how well these two match, and if they do not match at all, then you reject that update. The Levenberg–Marquardt algorithm itself is very general, but it needs to have the function to be minimised, along with its gradient and Jacobian passed into it. The entire algorithm can be written as:

The Levenberg–Marquardt Algorithm

- Given start point $\mathbf{x}_0$

- While $\mathbf{J}^T\mathbf{r}(\mathbf{x})$ >tolerance and maximum number of iterations not exceeded:

   - repeat
      * solve $(\mathbf{J}^T\mathbf{J} + \nu\mathbf{I})\mathbf{dx} = -\mathbf{J}^T\mathbf{r}$ for $\mathbf{dx}$ using linear least-squares
      * set $\mathbf{x}_{\text{new}} = \mathbf{x} + \mathbf{dx}$
      * compute the ratio of the actual and prediction reductions:
         · actual $= \|f(\mathbf{x}) - f(\mathbf{x}_{new})\|$
         · predicted $= \nabla f^T(\mathbf{x}) \times \mathbf{x}_{new} - \mathbf{x}$
         · $\rho = $ actual/predicted
      * if $0 < \rho < 0.25$:
         · accept step: $\mathbf{x} = \mathbf{x}_{\text{new}}$
      * else if $\rho > 0.25$:
         · accept step: $\mathbf{x} = \mathbf{x}_{\text{new}}$
         · increase trust region size (reduce ν)
      * else:
         · reject step
         · reduce trust region (increase ν)
   - until $\mathbf{x}$ is updated or maximum number of iterations is exceeded

---

In SciPy the Levenberg–Marquardt optimiser is in the `optimize` module, and it can be called using `scipy.optimize.leastsq()`. Some general details about using the SciPy optimisers are given in Section 9.3.2.

We will look at two examples of using non-linear least-squares. One is a simple case of finding the minimum of a function that consists of two quadratic terms added together, i.e., a sum-of-squares problem, while the second is to minimise the fitting of a function to data.

The function that we will attempt to minimise is Rosenbrock's function:

$$f(x_1, x_2) = 100(x_2 - x_1^2)^2 + (1 - x_1)^2. \tag{9.18}$$

This is a common problem to try since it has a long narrow valley, so finding the optimal solution is not especially easy (except by hand: if you look at the problem, then guessing that $x_1 = 1, x_2 = 1$ is the minimum is fairly obvious). You need to work out how to encode this in the form required for a sum-of-squares problem, which is basically to write:

$$\mathbf{r} = (10(x_2 - x_1^2), 1 - x_1)^T. \tag{9.19}$$

The Jacobian is then:

$$\mathbf{J} = \begin{pmatrix} -20x_1 & 10 \\ -1 & 0 \end{pmatrix}. \tag{9.20}$$

In this notation, $f(x_1, x_2) = \mathbf{r}^T \mathbf{r}$ and the gradient is $\mathbf{J}^T \mathbf{r}$. All of which can be written as a simple Python function:

```python
def function(p):
    r = np.array([10*(p[1]-p[0]**2),(1-p[0])])
    fp = np.dot(transpose(r),r)
    J = (np.array([[-20*p[0],10],[-1,0]]))
    grad = np.dot(J.T,r.T)
    return fp,r,grad,J
```

Running the algorithm with starting point $(-1.92, 2)$ leads to the following outputs, where the numbers printed on each line are the function value, the parameters that gave it, the gradient, and the value of ν.

f(x)	Params	Grad	nu
292.92	[0.66 -6.22]	672.00	0.001
4421.20	[0.99 0.87]	1099.51	0.0001
1.21	[1.00 1.00]	24.40	1e-05
8.67-07	[1.00 1.00]	0.02	1e-06
6.18-17	[1.00 1.00]	1.57-07	1e-07

The second example is fitting a function to data. The function is a moderately complicated beast that is definitely not amenable to linear least-squares fitting:

$$y = f(p_1, p_2) = p_1 \cos(p_2 x) + p_2 \sin(p_1 x), \tag{9.21}$$

where the p_i are the parameters to be fitted and x is a datapoint from a set that are

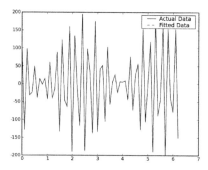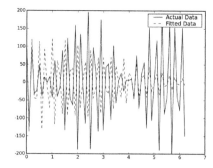

FIGURE 9.4 Using Levenberg–Marquardt for least-squares data fitting of data from Equation (9.21). The example on the left converges to the correct solution, while the one on the right, which still starts from a point close to the correct solution, fails to find it, resulting in significantly different output.

used to construct the function to be fitted. This is a difficult function to fit because it has lots of minima (since sin and cos are periodic, with period 2π). For data fitting problems, the assumption is often that data are generated at regular x points by a noisy process that produces the y values. Then the sum-of-squares error that we wish to minimise is the difference between the data (y) and the current fit (parameter estimates $\hat{p}_1, \hat{p}_2$):

$$\mathbf{r} = y - \hat{p}_1 \cos(\hat{p}_2 x) + \hat{p}_2 \sin(\hat{p}_1 x). \tag{9.22}$$

The Jacobian for this function requires some careful differentiating, and then the whole problem can be left to the optimiser. Figure 9.4 shows two examples of trying to recover values $p_1 = 100, p_2 = 102$. On the left, the starting point is $(100.5, 102.5)$, while on the right it is $(101, 101)$. It can be seen that on this problem, Levenberg–Marquardt is very susceptible to local minima, since while the example on the left works (converging after only 8 iterations), the example on the right, which still starts with parameter values very close to the correct ones, gets stuck and fails, with final parameter values $(100.89, 101.13)$.

9.3 CONJUGATE GRADIENTS

Not every problem that we want to solve is a least-squares problem. The good news is that we can do rather better than steepest descent even when we want to minimise an arbitrary objective function. The key to this is to look again at Figure 9.3, where you can see that there are several of the steepest gradient lines that are in pretty much the same direction. We would only need to go in that direction once if we knew how far to go the first time. And then we would go in a direction **orthogonal** (at right angles) to that one and, in two dimensions, we would be finished, as is shown on the right of Figure 9.5, where one step in the x direction and one in the y direction are enough to complete the minimisation. In n dimensions we would have to take n steps, and then we would have finished. This amazing scenario is the aim of the method of **conjugate gradients**. It manages to achieve it in the linear case, but in most non-linear cases, which are the kind we are usually interested in, it usually requires a few more iterations than it theoretically should, although still many less steps than most other methods for real problems.

It turns out that making the lines be orthogonal is generally impossible, since you don't

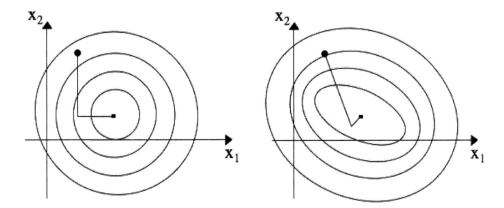

FIGURE 9.5 *Left:* If the directions are orthogonal to each other and the stepsize is correct, then only one step is needed for each dimension in the data, here two. *Right:* The conjugate directions are not orthogonal to each other on the ellipse.

have enough information about the solution space. However, it is possible to make them conjugate or A-orthogonal. Two vectors $\mathbf{p}_i, \mathbf{p}_j$ are conjugate if $\mathbf{p}_i^T \mathbf{A} \mathbf{p}_j = 0$ for some matrix $\mathbf{A}$. Conjugate lines for the ellipse contours in Figure 9.2 are shown on the right of Figure 9.5. Amazingly, the line search that we wrote down in Equation (9.1) is soluble along these directions, since they do not interfere with each other, with solution:

$$\alpha_i = \frac{\mathbf{p}_i^T(-\nabla f(\mathbf{x}_{i-1}))}{\mathbf{p}_i^T \mathbf{A} \mathbf{p}_i}. \tag{9.23}$$

We then need to use a function to find the zeros of this. The Newton–Raphson iteration, which is one method that will do it, is described below. So if we can find conjugate directions, then the line search is much better. The only question that remains is how to find them. This requires a Gram–Schmidt process, which constructs each new direction by taking a candidate solution and then subtracting off any part that lies along any of the directions that have already been used. We start by picking a set of mutually orthogonal vectors $\mathbf{u}_i$ (the basic coordinate axes will do; there are better options, but they are beyond the scope of this book) and then using:

$$\mathbf{p}_k = \mathbf{u}_k + \sum_{i=0}^{k-1} \beta_{ki} \mathbf{p}_i. \tag{9.24}$$

There are two possible β terms that can be used. They are both based on the ratios between the squared Jacobian before and after an update. The Fletcher–Reeves formula is:

$$\beta_{i+1} = \frac{\nabla f(\mathbf{x}_{x+1})^T \nabla f(\mathbf{x}_{i+1})}{\nabla f(\mathbf{x}_i)^T \nabla f(\mathbf{x}_i)}, \tag{9.25}$$

while the Polak–Ribiere formula is:

$$\beta_{i+1} = \frac{\nabla f(\mathbf{x}_{i+1})^T \left(\nabla f(\mathbf{x}_{i+1}) - \nabla f(\mathbf{x})_i \right)}{\nabla f(\mathbf{x}_i)^T \nabla f(\mathbf{x}_i)}. \tag{9.26}$$

The second one is often faster, but sometimes fails to **converge** (reach a stopping point).

We can put these things together to form a complete algorithm. It starts by computing an initial search direction $\mathbf{p}_0$ (steepest descent will do), then finding the α_i that minimises the function $f(\mathbf{x}_i + \alpha_i \mathbf{p}_i)$, and using it to set $\mathbf{x}_{i+1} = \mathbf{x}_i + \alpha_i \mathbf{p}_i$. The next direction is then $\mathbf{p}_{i+1} = -\nabla f(\mathbf{x}_{i+1}) + \beta_{i+1} \mathbf{p}_i$ where β is set by one of the two formulas above.

It is common to **restart** the algorithm every n iterations (where n is the number of dimensions in the problem) because the algorithm has now generated the whole set of conjugate directions. The algorithm will then cycle through the directions again making incremental improvements.

The only thing that we don't know how to do yet is to find the α_is. The usual method of doing that is the Newton–Raphson iteration, which is a method of finding the zero points of a polynomial. It works by computing the Taylor expansion of the function $f(\mathbf{x} + \alpha \mathbf{p})$, which is:

$$f(\mathbf{x}+\alpha\mathbf{p}) \approx f(\mathbf{x})+\alpha\mathbf{p}\left(\frac{d}{d\alpha}f(\mathbf{x}+\alpha\mathbf{p})\right)\bigg|_{\alpha=0} + \frac{\alpha^2}{2}\mathbf{p}\cdot\mathbf{p}\left(\frac{d^2}{d\alpha^2}f(\mathbf{x}+\alpha\mathbf{p})\right)\bigg|_{\alpha=0} +\dots, \quad (9.27)$$

and differentiating it with respect to α, which requires the Jacobian and Hessian matrices (here, these matrices are derivatives of $f(\cdot)$, not $\mathbf{r}$ as they were in Section 9.2):

$$\frac{d}{d\alpha}f(\mathbf{x}+\alpha\mathbf{p}) \approx \mathbf{J}(\mathbf{x})\mathbf{p} + \alpha\mathbf{p}^T\mathbf{H}(\mathbf{x})\mathbf{p}. \quad (9.28)$$

Setting this equal to zero tells us that the minimiser of $f(\mathbf{x} + \alpha\mathbf{p})$ is:

$$\alpha = \frac{\mathbf{J}(\mathbf{x})^T\mathbf{p}}{\mathbf{p}^T\mathbf{H}(\mathbf{x})\mathbf{p}}. \quad (9.29)$$

Unless $f(\mathbf{x})$ is an especially nice function, the second derivative approximation that we have made here won't get us to the bottom in one step, so we will have to iterate this step a few times to find the zero point, which is why it is known as the Newton–Raphson *iteration*, i.e., you have to put it into a loop that runs until the iterate stops changing.

Putting all of those things together gives the entire algorithm, which we'll look at before we work on an example:

The Conjugate Gradients Algorithm

- Given start point $\mathbf{x}_0$, and stopping parameter ϵ, set $\mathbf{p}_0 = -\nabla f(\mathbf{x})$

- Set $\mathbf{p} = \mathbf{p}_0$

- While $\mathbf{p} > \epsilon^2 \mathbf{p}_0$:

    - compute α_k and $\mathbf{x}_{\text{new}} = \mathbf{x} + \alpha_k \mathbf{p}$ using the Newton–Raphson iteration:
        * while $\alpha^2 dp > \epsilon^2$:
            · $\alpha = -(\nabla f(\mathbf{x})^T\mathbf{p})/(\mathbf{p}^T\mathbf{H}(\mathbf{x})\mathbf{p})$
            · $\mathbf{x} = \mathbf{x} + \alpha\mathbf{p}$
            · $dp = \mathbf{p}^T\mathbf{p}$
    - evaluate $\nabla f(\mathbf{x}_{\text{new}})$
    - compute β_{k+1} using Equation (9.25) or (9.26)
    - update $\mathbf{p} \leftarrow \nabla f(\mathbf{x}_{\text{new}}) + \beta_{k+1}\mathbf{p}$
    - check for restarts

9.3.1 Conjugate Gradients Example

Computing the conjugate gradients solution to the function $f(\mathbf{x}) = (0.5x_1^2 + 0.2x_2^2 + 0.6x_3^2)$ makes use of the Jacobian and Hessian again. The first Newton–Raphson step yields an α value of 0.931, so that the next step is:

$$\mathbf{x}(1) = \begin{pmatrix} -2 \\ 2 \\ 0 \end{pmatrix} + 0.931 \times \begin{pmatrix} 2 \\ -0.8 \\ 2.4 \end{pmatrix} = \begin{pmatrix} -0.138 \\ 1.255 \\ 0.235 \end{pmatrix} \tag{9.30}$$

Then $\beta = 0.0337$, so that the direction is:

$$\mathbf{p}(1) = \begin{pmatrix} 0.138 \\ -0.502 \\ -0.282 \end{pmatrix} + 0.0337 \times \begin{pmatrix} 2 \\ -0.8 \\ 2.4 \end{pmatrix} = \begin{pmatrix} 0.205 \\ -0.529 \\ -0.201 \end{pmatrix} \tag{9.31}$$

In the second step, $\alpha = 1.731$,

$$\mathbf{x}(2) = \begin{pmatrix} -0.138 \\ 1.255 \\ 0.235 \end{pmatrix} + 1.731 \times \begin{pmatrix} 0.205 \\ -0.529 \\ -0.201 \end{pmatrix} = \begin{pmatrix} -0.217 \\ -0.136 \\ 0.136 \end{pmatrix} \tag{9.32}$$

and the update is:

$$p(2) = \begin{pmatrix} -0.217 \\ -0.136 \\ 0.136 \end{pmatrix} + 0.240 \times \begin{pmatrix} 0.205 \\ -0.529 \\ -0.201 \end{pmatrix} = \begin{pmatrix} -0.168 \\ -0.263 \\ 0.088 \end{pmatrix} \tag{9.33}$$

A third step then gives the final answer as $(0, 0, 0)$.

9.3.2 Conjugate Gradients and the MLP

The scientific Python libraries SciPy include a set of general purpose optimisation algorithms in `scipy.optimize`, including an interface function (`scipy.optimize.minimize()`) that can call the others. In this section we will investigate using the methods that are provided within that library, particularly the conjugate gradient optimiser, in order to find the weights of the Multi-layer Perceptron (MLP) that was the main algorithm of Chapter 4. In that chapter we derived an algorithm based on gradient descent of the back-propagated error from first principles, but here we can use general methods.

In order to use any gradient descent algorithm we need to work out a function to minimise, an initial guess for where to start searching, and (preferably) the gradient of that function with respect to the variables. The reason for saying 'preferably the gradient' is that many of the algorithms will create a numerical estimate of the gradient if an explicit version is not given. However, since the gradient is fairly easy to compute for the MLP, numerical estimation is not necessary. We used the sum-of-squares error for the MLP, so we just need to work out the derivatives of that function for the three different activation functions that we allow: the normal logistic function, the linear activation that was used for regression problems, and the soft-max activation, and we've already done that in Section 4.6.5.

As was mentioned above, there is an interface function for most of the SciPy optimisers, which has the following form:

```
scipy.optimize.minimize(fun,  x0,  args=(),  method='BFGS',  jac=None,
hess=None,↲
hessp=None, bounds=None, constraints=(), tol=None, callback=None, ↲
options=None)}.
```

The choice of method, which is the actual gradient descent algorithm used can include 'BFGS' (which is the Broyden, Fletcher, Goldfarb, and Shanno algorithm, a variation on Newton's method from Section 9.1.1 that computes an approximation to the Hessian rather than requiring the programmer to supply it) and CG which is the conjugate gradient algorithm.

Looking at the code snippet again we see that we need to pass in an error function and the function to compute the derivatives. Both of these functions take arguments, specifically the inputs to the network, and the targets that those inputs are meant to produce. There is one issue that we have to deal with here, which is that the SciPy optimisers find the minimum value for a vector of parameters, and we currently have two separate weights matrices. We need to reshape these two matrices into vectors and then concatenate them before they can be used, using:

```
w = np.concatenate((self.weights1.flatten(),self.weights2.flatten()))
```

and something similar for the gradients. When the optimiser has run we will need to separate them and put the values back into the weight matrices using:

```
split = (self.nin+1)*self.nhidden
self.weights1 = np.reshape(wopt[:split],(self.nin+1,self.nhidden))
self.weights2 = np.reshape(wopt[split:],(self.nhidden+1,self.nout))
```

The optimiser also needs an initial guess x0 for the weights, but this is not an issue since in the original algorithm they are already set to have small positive and negative values, so we can just use those values.

In fact, there is a numerical detail that we need to deal with as well; technically it could be a problem with the version of the MLP that we implemented in Chapter 4 as well, but it doesn't usually seem to be an issue there. The problem is that when we use the sigmoid function and take the exponential we can get overflow in the floating point number, either from it becoming too large, or too close to 0. This is a particular problem when we use the cross-entropy error function of Section 4.6.6, because we then take the logarithm, and we need to make sure that the input is in the range of the log function. NumPy provides some useful constants to make these checks, and they can be seen in use in the following code snippet, which replaces the error calculation in the original MLP:

```
# Different types of output neurons
if self.outtype == 'linear':
    error = 0.5*np.sum((outputs-targets)**2)
elif self.outtype == 'logistic':
    # Non-zero checks
    maxval = -np.log(np.finfo(np.float64).eps)
    minval = -np.log(1./np.finfo(np.float64).tiny - 1.)
    outputs = np.where(outputs<maxval,outputs,maxval)
    outputs = np.where(outputs>minval,outputs,minval)
    outputs = 1./(1. + np.exp(-outputs))
    error = - np.sum(targets*np.log(outputs) + (1 - targets)*np.log(1 -
    outputs))
elif self.outtype == 'softmax':
    nout = np.shape(outputs)[1]
    maxval = np.log(np.finfo(np.float64).max) - np.log(nout)
    minval = np.log(np.finfo(np.float32).tiny)
    outputs = np.where(outputs<maxval,outputs,maxval)
    outputs = np.where(outputs>minval,outputs,minval)
    normalisers = np.sum(np.exp(outputs),axis=1)*np.ones((1,np.shape(outputs)
    [0]))
    y = np.transpose(np.transpose(np.exp(outputs))/normalisers)
    y[y<np.finfo(np.float64).tiny] = np.finfo(np.float32).tiny
    error = - np.sum(targets*np.log(y));
```

Finally, we need to decide how accurate we want the result to be, and how many iterations we are going to allow the algorithm to run for before calling a halt to the optimisation. When the algorithm has reached a minimum the gradient function will be 0, and so the normal convergence criterium is that the gradient is close to zero. The default value for this parameter is 1×10^{-5} and we will leave this unchanged. We will also specify that the algorithm can run for no more than 10,000 steps. Together, these lead to the following function call to the conjugate gradient optimiser (here the code uses an explicit call to the conjugate gradient method rather than the interface, but there is no real difference):

```
out =       so.fmin_cg(self.mlperror,       w,       fprime=self.mlpgrad,
args=(inputs,targets)
, maxiter=10000, full_output=True, disp=1)
```

The `full_output` and `disp` parameters tell the optimiser to give a report on whether or not it was successful and how much work it did, something like:

```
Warning: Maximum number of iterations has been exceeded.
         Current function value: 7.487182
         Iterations: 10000
         Function evaluations: 250695
```

```
Gradient evaluations: 140930
```

Now all that remains is to extract the new weight values from the values that the optimiser returns, which are in `out[0]`, and we are ready to use the algorithm. The demonstrations that we used in Chapter 4 are all perfectly suitable, of course, and all that needs changing is to import the conjugate gradient version of the MLP instead of the earlier version.

There are other methods of doing gradient descent, some of which are more effective on certain problems (but note that the No Free Lunch theorem tells us that no one solver will be the most effective for every problem). For example, the convex optimisation that was used for the Support Vector Machine in Chapter 8 is a gradient descent method for a particular type of constrained problem. We will next consider what happens when the problems that we wish to solve are discrete, which means that there is no gradient to find.

9.4 SEARCH: THREE BASIC APPROACHES

We are going to discuss three different ways to attempt optimisation without gradients. For each one, we will see how it works on the Travelling Salesman Problem (TSP), which is a classic discrete optimisation problem that consists of trying to find the shortest route through a set of cities that visits each city exactly once and returns to the start. For the first (starting) city we can choose any of the N that are available. For the next, there are $N - 1$ choices, and for the next $N - 2$. Using a brute force search in this way provides a $\mathcal{O}(N!)$ solution, which is obviously infeasible.

In fact, the TSP is an NP-hard problem. The best-known solution that is guaranteed to find the global maximum is using **dynamic programming** and its computational cost is $\mathcal{O}(n^2 2^n)$, but we won't be considering that here—the TSP is an example, not a problem we really want to solve here. The basic search methods are described next.

9.4.1 Exhaustive Search

Try out every solution and pick the best one. While this is obviously guaranteed to find the global optimum, because it checks every single solution, it is impractical for any reasonable size problem. For the TSP it would involve testing out every single possible way of ordering the cities, and calculating the distance for each ordering, so the computational complexity is $\mathcal{O}(N!)$, which is worse than exponential.

It is computationally infeasible to do the computations for more than about $N = 10$ cities. The basic part of the algorithm uses a helper function `permutation()` that computes possible orderings of the cities, but is otherwise fairly obvious:

```
for newOrder in permutation(range(nCities)):
    possibleDistanceTravelled = 0
    for i in range(nCities-1):
        possibleDistanceTravelled += distances[newOrder[i],newOrder[i+1]]
    possibleDistanceTravelled += distances[newOrder[nCities-1],0]

    if possibleDistanceTravelled < distanceTravelled:
```

```
        distanceTravelled = possibleDistanceTravelled
        cityOrder = newOrder
```

9.4.2 Greedy Search

Just make one pass through the system, making the best local choice at each stage. So for the TSP, choose the first city arbitrarily, and then repeatedly pick the city that is closest to where you are now that hasn't been visited yet, until you run out of cities. This is computationally very cheap ($\mathcal{O}(N \log N)$), but it is certainly not guaranteed to find the optimal solution, or even a particularly good one. The code is very simple, though:

```
for i in range(nCities-1):
    cityOrder[i+1] = np.argmin(dist[cityOrder[i],:])
    distanceTravelled  += dist[cityOrder[i],cityOrder[i+1]]
    # Now exclude the chance of travelling to that city again
    dist[:,cityOrder[i+1]] = np.Inf

# Now return to the original city
distanceTravelled += distances[cityOrder[nCities-1],0]
```

9.4.3 Hill Climbing

The basic idea of the hill climbing algorithm is to perform local search around the current solution, choosing any option that improves the result. (It might seem odd to talk about hill *climbing* when we've always talked about minimising a function. Of course, the difference between maximisation and minimisation is just whether you put a minus sign in front of the equation or not, and 'hill climbing' sounds much better than 'hollow descending.') The choice of how to do local search is called the **move-set**. It describes how the current solution can be changed to generate new solutions. So if we were to imagine moving about in 2D Euclidean space, possible moves might be to move 1 step north, south, east, or west.

For the TSP, the hill climbing solution would consist of choosing an initial solution randomly, and then swapping pairs of cities in the tour and seeing if the total length of the tour decreases. The algorithm would stop after some pre-defined number of swaps had occurred, or when no swap improved the result for some pre-defined length of time. As with the greedy search, there is no way to predict how good the solution will be: there is a chance that it will find the global maximum, but no guarantee of it; it could get stuck in the first local maxima. The central loop of the hill climbing algorithm just picks a pair of cities to swap, and keeps the change if it makes the total distance shorter:

```
for i in range(1000):
    # Choose cities to swap
    city1 = np.random.randint(nCities)
    city2 = np.random.randint(nCities)
```

```
if city1 != city2:
    # Reorder the set of cities
    possibleCityOrder = cityOrder.copy()
    possibleCityOrder = np.where(possibleCityOrder==city1,-1,
    possibleCityOrder)
    possibleCityOrder = np.where(possibleCityOrder==city2,city1,
    possibleCityOrder)
    possibleCityOrder = np.where(possibleCityOrder==-1,city2,
    possibleCityOrder)

    # Work out the new distances
    # This can be done more efficiently
    newDistanceTravelled = 0
    for j in range(nCities-1):
        newDistanceTravelled += distances[possibleCityOrder[j],
            possibleCityOrder[j+1]]
    distanceTravelled += distances[cityOrder[nCities-1],0]

    if newDistanceTravelled < distanceTravelled:
        distanceTravelled = newDistanceTravelled
        cityOrder = possibleCityOrder
```

Hill climbing has three particular types of functions that it does badly on. They can all be imagined using the analogy of real hill climbing.

The first is when there are lots of foothills around the optimal solution. In that case the algorithm climbs the local maximum, and may get stuck there; certainly it will take a very long time to reach the optimal solution. The second is on a plateau, where no changes that the algorithm makes affect the solution. In this case the solution will just change randomly, if at all, and the maximum will probably not be found. The third case is when there is a very gently sloping ridge in the data. Most directions that the algorithm looks in will be downhill, and so it may decide that it has already reached the maximum.

9.5 EXPLOITATION AND EXPLORATION

The search methods above can be separated into methods that perform **exploration** of the search space, always trying out new solutions, like exhaustive search, and those performing **exploitation** of the current best solution, by trying out local variations of that current best solution, like hill climbing. Ideally, we would like some combination of the two—we should be trying to improve on the current best solution by local search, and also looking around in case there is an even better solution hiding elsewhere in the search space.

One way to think about this is known as the **n-armed bandit** problem. Suppose that we have a room full of one-armed bandit machines in some tacky Las Vegas casino (for those who don't know, a one-armed bandit is a slot machine with a lever that you pull, as in Figure 9.6). You don't know anything about the machines in advance, such as what the payouts are, and how likely you are to get the payout. You enter the room with a fistful of 50 cent coins from your student loan, aiming to generate enough beer money to get through the year. How do you choose which machine to use?

FIGURE 9.6 A one-armed bandit machine. It has one arm, and it steals your money.

At first, you have no information at all, so you choose randomly. However, as you explore, you pick up information about which machines are good (here, good means that you get a payout more often). You could carry on using them (exploiting your knowledge) or you could try out other machines in the hope of finding one that pays out even more (exploring further). The optimal approach is to trade off the two, always making sure that you have enough money to explore further by exploiting the best machines you know of, but exploring when you can.

One place where this combination of exploration and exploitation can be clearly seen is in evolution. We'll talk about that in the next chapter, but here we will look to physics instead of biology to act as our inspiration.

9.6 SIMULATED ANNEALING

In the field of **statistical mechanics** physicists have to deal with systems that are very large (tens of thousands of molecules and more) so that, while the computations are possible in principle, in practice the computational time is far too large. They have developed **stochastic** methods (that is, based on randomness) in order to get approximate solutions to the problems that, while still expensive, do not require the massive computational times that the full solution would.

The method that we will look at is based on the way in which real-world physical systems can be brought into very low energy states, which are therefore very stable. The system is heated, so that there is plenty of energy around, and each part of the system is effectively random. An **annealing schedule** is applied that cools the material down, allowing it to relax into a low energy configuration. We are going to model the same idea.

We start with an arbitrary temperature T, which is high. We will then randomly choose states and change their values, monitoring the energy of the system before and after. If the energy is lower afterwards, then the system will prefer that solution, so we accept the change. So far, this is similar to gradient descent. However, if the energy is not lower, then we still consider whether or not to accept the solution. We do this by evaluating $E_{\text{before}} - E_{\text{after}}$ and accepting the new solution if the value of $\exp((E_{\text{before}} - E_{\text{after}})/T)$ is bigger than a uniform random value between 0 and 1 (note that the expression is between 0 and 1 since it is the exponential of a negative value). This is called the **Boltzmann distribution**. The rationale behind sometimes accepting poorer states is that we might have found a local minimum, and by allowing this more expensive energy state we can escape from it.

After doing this a few times, the annealing schedule is applied in order to reduce the temperature and the method continues until the temperature reaches 0. As the temperature gets lower, so does the chance of accepting any particular higher energy state. The most common annealing schedule is $T(t + 1) = cT(t)$, where $0 < c < 1$ (more commonly, $0.8 < c < 1$). The annealing needs to be slow to allow for lots of search to happen. For the TSP the best way to include simulated annealing is to modify the hill climbing algorithm above, changing the acceptance criteria for a change in the city ordering to:

```
if newDistanceTravelled < distanceTravelled or (distanceTravelled -
newDistanceTravelled) < T*np.log(np.random.rand()):
    distanceTravelled = newDistanceTravelled
    cityOrder = possibleCityOrder

# Annealing schedule
T = c*T
```

9.6.1 Comparison

Running all four methods above on the TSP for five cities gave the following results, where the best solution found and the distance are given in the first line and the time it took to run (in seconds) on the second:

```
>>> TSP.runAll()
Exhaustive search
((3, 1, 2, 4, 0), 2.65)
0.0036
Greedy search
((0, 2, 1, 3, 4), 3.27)
0.0013
Hill Climbing
((4, 3, 1, 2, 0]), 2.66)
0.1788
Simulated Annealing
((3, 1, 2, 4, 0]), 2.65)
0.0052
```

With ten cities the results were quite different, showing how important good approximations to search are, since even for this fairly small problem the exhaustive search takes a very long time. Note that the greedy search does nearly as well in this case, but this is simply chance.

```
Exhaustive search
((1, 5, 10, 6, 3, 9, 2, 4, 8, 7, 0), 4.18)
```

```
1781.0613
Greedy search
((3, 9, 2, 6, 10, 5, 1, 8, 4, 7, 0]), 4.49)
0.0057
Hill Climbing
((7, 9, 6, 2, 4, 0, 3, 8, 1, 5, 10]), 7.00)
0.4572
Simulated Annealing
((10, 1, 6, 9, 8, 0, 5, 2, 4, 7, 3]), 8.95)
0.0065
```

FURTHER READING

Two books on numerical optimization that provide much more information are:

- J. Nocedal and S.J. Wright. *Numerical Optimization*. Springer, Berlin, Germany, 1999.

- C.T. Kelley. *Iterative Methods for Optimization*. Number 18 in Frontiers in Applied Mathematics. SIAM, Philadelphia, USA, 1999.

A possible reference for the second half of the chapter is:

- J.C. Spall. *Introduction to Stochastic Search and Optimization: Estimation, Simulation, and Control*. Wiley-Interscience, New York, USA, 2003.

Some of the material is covered in:

- Section 6.9 and Sections 7.1–7.2 of R.O. Duda, P.E. Hart, and D.G. Stork. *Pattern Classification*, 2nd edition, Wiley-Interscience, New York, USA, 2001.

PRACTICE QUESTIONS

Problem 9.1 In the discussion after Equation (9.10) it is stated that the direct solution is unstable. Experiment with this and see that it is true.

Problem 9.2 Modify the code in `CG.py` in order to take a general function, together with its Jacobian (and if available its Hessian) and then compute the minimum.

Problem 9.3 Experiment with the Fletcher–Reeves and Polak–Ribiere formulas (Equations (9.25) and (9.26)) when solving Rosenbrock's function using conjugate gradients. Can you find places where one works better than the other?

Problem 9.4 Generate data from the equation $a(1 - \exp(-b(x - c)))$ for choice of parameters a, b, c and x in the range -5 to 5 (with noise). Use Levenberg–Marquardt to fit the parameters.

Problem 9.5 Modify the conjugate gradient version of the MLP to use the other optimisation algorithms provided by SciPy and compare the results. Also, try stopping the optimiser from using the exact computation of the gradient and instead making a numerical estimate of it, and see how that changes the results.

Problem 9.6 By incorporating back-tracking into hill climbing, it is possible to escape from some poor local maxima. Add this into the code and test the results on the Travelling Salesman problem.

Problem 9.7 The logical satisfiability problem is an NP-complete problem that consists of finding truth assignments to sets of logical statements (e.g., $(a_1 \wedge a_2) \vee (\neg a_1 \vee a_3)$) so that they are true. It is an NP-complete problem to find truth assignments. Devise a way to use hill climbing and simulated annealing on the problem.

## CHAPTER 10

Evolutionary Learning

In this chapter we are going to start by treating evolution the same way that we treated neuroscience earlier in the book—by cherry-picking a few useful concepts, and then filling in the gaps with computer science in order to make an effective learning method. To see why this might be interesting, you need to view evolution as a search problem. We don't generally think of it in this way, but animals are competing with each other in all kinds of ways—for example, eating each other—which encourages them to try to find camouflage colours, become toxic to certain predators, etc.

Evolution works on a population through an imaginary fitness landscape, which has an implicit bias towards animals that are 'fitter', i.e., those animals that live long enough to reproduce, are more attractive, and so get more mates, and generate more and healthier offspring. You can find out more from hundreds of books, such as Charles Darwin's *The Origin of Species* (the original book on the topic, still in print and very interesting) and Richard Dawkin's *The Blind Watchmaker*.

The genetic algorithm models the genetic process that gives rise to evolution. In particular, it models sexual reproduction, where both parents give some genetic information to their offspring. As is sketched in Figure 10.1, in biological organisms, each parent passes on one chromosome out of their two, and so there is a 50% chance of any gene making it into the offspring. Of the two versions of each gene (one from each parent) one allele (variation) is selected. Hence, children have similarities with their parents, and there is lots of genetic inheritance. However, there are also random mutations, caused by copying errors when the chromosome material is reproduced, which means that some things do change over time. Real genetics is obviously a lot more complicated than this, but we are taking only the things that we want for our model.

The genetic algorithm shows many of the things that are best and worst about machine learning: it is often, but not always, very effective, it has an array of parameters that are crucial, but hard to set, and it is impossible to guarantee that it will find a result that is any good at all. Having said all that, it often works very well, and it has become a very popular algorithm for people to use when they have no idea of any other way to find a reasonable solution.

In the terms that we saw at the end of the previous chapter, genetic algorithms perform both exploitation and exploration, so that they can make incremental improvements to current good solutions, but also find radically new solutions, some of which may be better than the current best.

We will also look briefly at two other topics in this chapter, a variation of the genetic algorithm that acts on trees that represent computer programs that is known as Genetic

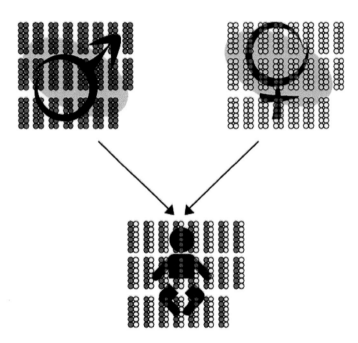

FIGURE 10.1 Each adult in the mating pair passes one of their two chromosomes to their offspring.

Programming, and a set of algorithms that use sampling from a probability distribution rather than an evolving population in order to find better solutions.

10.1 THE GENETIC ALGORITHM (GA)

The Genetic Algorithm is a computational approximation to how evolution performs search, which is by producing modifications of the parent genomes in their offspring and thus producing new individuals with different fitness. Like another mathematical model that we saw earlier in the book—the neuron—it attempts to abstract away everything except the important parts that we need to understand what evolution does. From this principle, the things that we need to model simple genetics inside a computer and solve problems with it are:

- a method for representing problems as chromosomes

- a way to calculate the fitness of a solution

- a selection method to choose parents

- a way to generate offspring by breeding the parents

These items are all described in the following sections, and the basic algorithm is described. We are going to use an example to describe the methods, which is an **NP-complete** problem (if you are not familiar with the term NP-complete, its practical implication is that the problem runs in exponential time or worse in the number of inputs) known as the knapsack problem (a knapsack is a rather old name for a rucksack or bag). Sections 10.3.1 and 10.3.4 provide other examples. The knapsack problem is easy to describe, but difficult to solve in general. Here is the version of it that we will use:

Suppose that you are packing for your holidays. You've bought the biggest and best rucksack that was for sale, but there is still no way that you are going to fit in everything you want to take (camera, money, addresses of friends, etc.) and the things that your mum is insisting you take (spare underwear, phrasebook, stamps to write home with, etc.). As a good computer scientist you decide to measure how much space it takes up and then write a program to work out how to fill as much of the bag as possible, so that you get the best value for your airfare.

This problem, and variations of it, appear in various disguises in cryptography, combinatorics, applied mathematics, logistics, and business, so it is an important problem. Unfortunately, since it is NP-complete, finding the optimal solution for interesting cases (pretty much anything above 10 items) is computationally impossible. There is an obvious greedy algorithm that finds solutions to the knapsack problem. At each stage it takes the largest thing that hasn't been packed yet and that will still fit into the bag, and iterates that rule. This will not necessarily return the optimal solution (unless each thing is larger than the sum of all the ones smaller than it, in which case it will), but it is very quick and simple. So a GA should be getting a much better solution than the greedy rule most of the time to be worth all the effort involved in writing and running it.

10.1.1 String Representation

The first thing that we need is some way to represent the individual solutions, in analogy to the chromosome. GAs use a **string**, with each element of the string (equivalent to the gene) being chosen from some **alphabet**. The different values in the alphabet, which is often just binary, are analogous to the alleles. For the problem we are trying to solve we have to work out a way of encoding the description of a solution as a string. We then create a set of random strings to be our initial population.

It is possible to modify the GA so that the alphabet it uses runs over the real numbers. While purists don't think that this is a GA at all, it is quite popular, because of the number of applications, but it is not as elegant as using a discrete alphabet. It also tends to make the mutation operator that we will see later less useful.

For the knapsack problem the alphabet is very simple, since we can make it binary, since for each item we just need to say whether or not we want to take it. We make the string L units long, where L is the total number of things we would like to take with us, and make each unit a binary digit. We then encode a solution using 0 for the things we will not take and 1 for the things we will. So if there were four things we wanted to take, then $(0, 1, 1, 0)$ would mean that we take the middle two, but not the first or last.

Note that this does not tell us whether or not this string is possible (that is, whether the things that we have said we will take will actually fit into the knapsack), nor whether it is a good string (whether it fills the knapsack). To work these out we need some way to decide how well each string fulfills the problem criteria. This is known as the **fitness** of the string.

10.1.2 Evaluating Fitness

The **fitness function** can be seen as an oracle that takes a string as an argument and returns a value for that string. Together with the string encoding the fitness function forms the problem-specific part of the GA. It is worth thinking about what we want from our fitness function. Clearly, the best string should have the highest fitness, and the fitness should decrease as the strings do less well on the problem. In real evolution, the fitness landscape is not static: there is competition between different species, such as predators and prey, or medical cures for certain diseases, and so the measure of fitness changes over time. We'll ignore that in the genetic algorithm.

For the knapsack problem, we decided that we wanted to make the bag as full as possible. So we would need to know the volume of each item that we want to put into the knapsack, and then for a given string that says which things should be taken, and which should not, we can compute the total volume. This is then a possible fitness function. However, it does not tell us anything about whether they will fit into the bag—with this fitness function the optimal solution is to take everything. So we need to check that they will fit, and if they will not, reduce the fitness of that solution. One option would be to set the fitness to 0 if the things in that string will not all fit. However, suppose that the solution is almost perfect, it is just that there is one thing too many in the knapsack. By setting the fitness to 0 we are reducing the chance of this solution being allowed to evolve and improve during later iterations. For this reason we will make the fitness function be the sum of the values of the items to be taken if they fit into the knapsack, but if they do not we will subtract twice the amount by which they are too big for the knapsack from the size of the knapsack. This allows solutions that are only just over to be considered for improvement, but tries to ensure that they are not the fittest solutions around.

10.1.3 Population

We can now measure the fitness of any string. The GA works on a population of strings, with the first generation usually being created randomly. The fitness of each string is then evaluated, and that first generation is bred together to make a second generation, which is then used to generate a third, and so on. After the initial population is chosen randomly, the algorithm evolves to produce each successive generation, with the hope being that there will be progressively fitter individuals in the populations as the number of generations increases.

To make the initial population for the knapsack problem, we will now create a set of random binary strings of length L by using the random number generator, which is very easy in NumPy using the uniform random number generator and the `np.where()` function:

```
pop = np.random.rand(popSize,stringLength)
pop = np.where(pop<0.5,0,1)
```

We now need to choose parents out of this population, and start breeding them.

10.1.4 Generating Offspring: Parent Selection

For the current generation we need to select those strings that will be used to generate new offspring. The idea here is that average fitness will improve if we select strings that are already relatively fit compared to the other members of the population (following natural selection), which is exploitation of our current population. However, it is also good to allow some exploration in there, which means that we have to allow some possibility of weak strings being considered. If strings are chosen proportionally to their fitness, so that fitter strings are more likely to be chosen to enter the 'mating pool', then this allows for both options. There are three commonly employed ways to do this, although the last one tends to produce better results:

Tournament Selection Repeatedly pick four strings from the population, with replacement and put the fittest two of them into the mating pool.

Truncation Selection Pick some fraction f of the best strings and ignore the rest. For example, $f = 0.5$ is often used, so the best 50% of the strings are put into the mating pool, each twice so that the pool is the right size. The pool is randomly shuffled to make the pairs. This is obviously very easy to implement, but it does limit the amount of exploration that is done, biasing the GA towards exploitation.

Fitness Proportional Selection The better option is to select strings probabilistically, with the probability of a string being selected being proportional to its fitness. The function that is generally used is (for string α):

$$p^\alpha = \frac{F^\alpha}{\sum_{\alpha'} F^{\alpha'}}, \tag{10.1}$$

where F^α is the fitness. If the fitness is not positive then F needs to be replaced by $\exp(sF)$ throughout, where s is the **selection strength**, a parameter, and you might recognise the equation as the soft-max activation from Chapter 4:

$$p^\alpha = \frac{\exp(sF^\alpha)}{\sum_{\alpha'} \exp(sF^{\alpha'})}. \tag{10.2}$$

There is an implementation issue here. We want to pick each string with probability proportional to its fitness, but if we only have one copy of each string, then the probability of picking each string is the same. One way around this is to add more copies of the fitter strings, so that they are more likely to get chosen. This is sometimes called 'roulette selection', because if you imagine that each string gets an area on a roulette wheel, then the larger the area associated to one number, the more likely it is that the ball will land there. You can then just randomly pick strings from this larger set. A method of doing this is shown in the following code snippet, which uses the **np.kron()** function. We've seen this before (in Section 6.5); it is a NumPy function that multiplies each element of its first array argument by every element of the second, putting all of the results together into one multi-dimensional output array. It is useful here in order to populate the new and much larger **newPopulation** array, which contains multiple copies of each string.

```
# Put in repeated copies of each string according to fitness
# Deal with strings with very low fitness
j=0
while np.round(fitness[j])<1:
 j = j+1

newPop = np.kron(np.ones((np.round(fitness[j]),1)),pop[j,:])

# Add multiple copies of strings into the newPop
for i in range(j+1,self.popSize):
 if np.round(fitness[i])>=1:
  newPop = np.concatenate((newPop,np.kron(np.ones((np.round(fitness[i]),1)),)
```

```
      pop[i,:])),axis=0)

      # Shuffle the order (note that there are still too many)
      indices = range(np.shape(newPop)[0])
      np.random.shuffle(indices)
      newPop = newPop[indices[:popSize],:]
      return newPop
```

However we select the strings to put into the mating pool, the next operation is to put them into pairs. Since the order that they are in is random, we can simply pair up the strings so that each even-indexed string takes the following odd-indexed one as its mate.

10.2 GENERATING OFFSPRING: GENETIC OPERATORS

Having selected our breeding pairs, we now need to decide how to combine their two strings to generate the offspring, which is the genetics part of the algorithm. There are two genetic operators that are generally used, and they are discussed now. There are others, but these were the original choices, and are far and away the most common.

10.2.1 Crossover

In biology, organisms have two chromosomes, and each parent donates one of them. Members of our GA population only have one chromosome-equivalent, the string. Thus, we generate the new string as part of the first parent and part of the second. The most common way of doing this is to pick one point at random in the string, and to use parent 1 for the first part of the string, up to the crossover point and parent 2 for the rest. We actually generate two offspring, with the second one consisting of the first part of parent 2 and the second part of parent 1. This scheme is known as single point crossover, and the extension to multi-point crossover is hopefully obvious. The most 'extreme' version is known as uniform crossover and consists of independently selecting each element of the string at random from the two parents. The three types of crossover are shown in Figure 10.2.

Crossover is the operator that performs global exploration, since the strings that are produced are radically different to both parents in at least some places. The hope is that sometimes we will take good parts of both solutions and put them together to make an even better solution. A nice picture example is to imagine a bird that has webbed feet for good swimming, but that cannot fly, breeding with a bird that can fly, but not swim. The offspring? A duck! Obviously, this is not biologically plausible, but it is a good picture of how crossover works. One interesting feature of the GA that obviously isn't true in real genetics is that in addition to the duck the algorithm would produce the bird that can't fly or swim, although it is unlikely to last long since its fitness will presumably not be high. In fact, there are exceptions to this, such as the great New Zealand Kiwi, which can neither swim nor fly, but is happily not extinct.

The following code snippet shows a NumPy implementation of single point crossover. The extension to multi-point and uniform crossover is not particularly difficult.

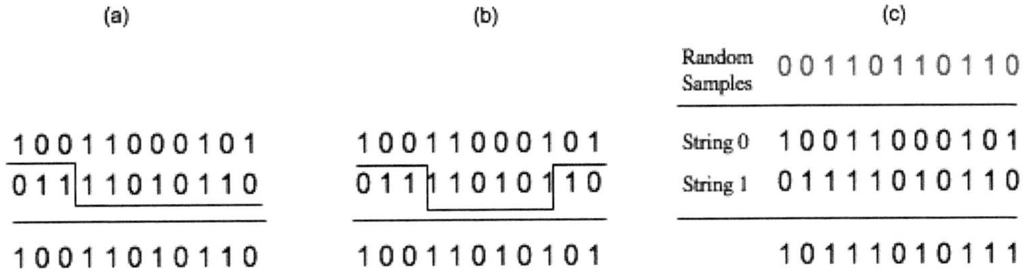

(a)	(b)	(c)

		Random Samples	0 0 1 1 0 1 1 0 1 1 0

1 0 0 1 1 0 0 0 1 0 1   1 0 0 1 1 0 0 0 1 0 1   String 0 1 0 0 1 1 0 0 0 1 0 1
0 1 1|1 1 0 1 0 1 1 0   0 1 1|1 1 0 1 0 1|1 0   String 1 0 1 1 1 1 0 1 0 1 1 0

1 0 0 1 1 0 1 0 1 1 0   1 0 0 1 1 0 1 0 1 0 1   1 0 1 1 1 0 1 0 1 1 1

FIGURE 10.2   The different forms of the crossover operator. (a) Single point crossover. A position in the string is chosen at random, and the offspring is made up of the first part of parent 1 and the second part of parent 2. (b) Multi-point crossover. Multiple points are chosen, with the offspring being made in the same way. (c) Uniform crossover. Random numbers are used to select which parent to take each element from.

```
def spCrossover(pop):
    newPop = np.zeros(shape(pop))
    crossoverPoint = np.random.randint(0,stringLength,popSize)
    for i in range(0,self.popSize,2):
  newPop[i,:crossoverPoint[i]] = pop[i,:crossoverPoint[i]]
  newPop[i+1,:crossoverPoint[i]] = pop[i+1,:crossoverPoint[i]]
  newPop[i,crossoverPoint[i]:] = pop[i+1,crossoverPoint[i]:]
  newPop[i+1,crossoverPoint[i]:] = pop[i,crossoverPoint[i]:]
    return newPop
```

Crossover is not always useful, depending upon the problem; for example, in the Travelling Salesman Problem that we talked about in Chapter 9, the strings that are generated by crossover might not even be valid tours. However, when it is useful, it is often the more powerful of the genetic operators, and has led to the building block hypothesis of how GAs work. The idea is that GAs work well on problems where the solution comes from putting together lots of little solutions, so that different strings assemble each separate building block, and then crossover puts those substrings together to make the final solution.

10.2.2 Mutation

The other genetic operator is mutation, which effectively performs local random search. The value of any element of the string can be changed, governed by some (usually low) probability p. For our binary alphabet in the knapsack problem, mutation causes a bit-flip, as is shown in Figure 10.3. For chromosomes with real values, some random number is generally added or subtracted from the current value. Often, $p \approx 1/L$ where L is the string length, so that there is approximately one mutation in each string. This might seem quite high, but it is often found to be a good choice given that the mutation rate has to trade off doing lots of local search with the risk of disrupting the good solutions.

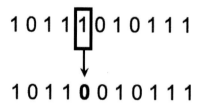

FIGURE 10.3 The effects of mutation on a string.

10.2.3 Elitism, Tournaments, and Niching

At this stage we have taken pairs of parents, and produced pairs of offspring. There is now a choice of what to do with them. The simplest option would be simply replace the parents by their children to make a completely new population, and carry on from there. However, this means that the maximum fitness in each generation can decrease, at least temporarily, and since in the end we are only interested in the 'best' solution, this seems a bit risky: we could potentially lose a really good string that we find early on in the search, and that we never see again.

There is a variety of ways to avoid this, of which the simplest is to use **elitism**, which takes some number of the fittest strings from one generation and puts them directly into the next population, replacing strings that are already there either at random, or by choosing the least fit to replace. Note that at every iteration the population stays the same size, something else that is unlike real evolution. Another solution is to implement a **tournament**, where the two parents and their two offsprings compete, with the two fittest out of the four being put into the new population.

The implementation of these functions continues along the same lines as the previous ones; the **np.argsort()** function returns the indices of the array that sorts them into order, but does not actually sort the array. It returns an array the same size as the one that is sorted, and we only want to extract the first few elite ones. When we do this we will be left with a matrix with a singleton dimension, which is why the **np.squeeze()** function is needed to reduce the array to the right size.

```
def elitism(oldPop,pop,fitness):
    best = np.argsort(fitness)
    best = np.squeeze(oldPop[best[-nElite:],:])
    indices = range(np.shape(pop)[0])
    np.random.shuffle(indices)
    pop = pop[indices,:]
    pop[0:nElite,:] = best
    return pop
```

While elitism and tournaments both ensure that good solutions aren't lost, they both have the problem that they can encourage **premature convergence**, where the algorithm settles down to a constant population that never changes even though it hasn't found an optimum. This happens because the GA favours fitter members of the population, which means that a solution that reaches a local maximum will generally be favoured, and this solution will be exploited. Tournaments and elitism encourage this, because they reduce the amount of diversity in the population by allowing the same individuals to remain over many generations. This means that the exploration aspect of the GA stops occurring. Exploration will be downplayed, making it hard to escape from the local maximum—most strings will have worse fitness, and will therefore be replaced in the population. Eventually, the majority of the strings in the population will be the same, but will represent a local maximum, not the global maximum. The randomness in the GA is a very large part of why it works, and schemes to reduce that randomness often harm the overall results.

One way to solve the problem of premature convergence is through niching (also known as using island populations), where the population is separated into several subpopulations, which all evolve independently for some period of time, so that they are likely to have converged to different local maxima, and a few members of one subpopulation are occasionally injected as 'immigrants' into another subpopulation. Another approach is known as fitness sharing, where the fitness of a particular string is averaged across the number of times that that string appears in the population. This biases the fitness function towards uncommon strings, but can also mean that very common good solutions are selected against.

There are other methods that have been developed to improve the convergence and final results of GAs, but they aren't useful for a basic understanding of how the basic algorithm works, so we'll ignore them. Anybody who wants to know more is directed to one of the books in the references at the end of the chapter.

The complete algorithm for the GA consists of simply putting together the pieces that we have looked at individually. Extending the basic algorithm to include some of the methods mentioned above, such as tournaments and niching, can improve the performance of the algorithm, but does not change the description much. The algorithm is often run for a fixed number of generations. It is a computationally very expensive algorithm, especially if the fitness function is non-trivial to evaluate. After seeing a complete description of the GA, we'll have a look at an example of how the algorithm works by considering the problem of graph colouring, and then look at how to use the GA to solve two sample problems.

The Basic Genetic Algorithm

- **Initialisation**

  – generate N random strings of length L with the chosen alphabet

- **Learning**

  – repeat:
    * create an (initially empty) new population
    * repeat:
      · select two strings from current population, preferably using fitness-proportional selection
      · recombine them in pairs to produce two new strings
      · mutate the offspring
      · either add the two offspring to the population, or use tournaments to put two strings from the four of parents and offspring into the population
    * until N strings for the new population are generated
    * optionally, use elitism to take the fittest strings from the parent generation and replace some others from the child generation

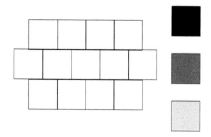

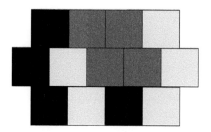

FIGURE 10.4 A sample map that we wish to colour using the three colours shown, without any two adjacent squares having the same colour.

FIGURE 10.5 A possible colouring with several adjacent squares having the same colour.

> > * keep track of the best string in the new population
> > * replace the old population with the new one
> > – until stopping criteria met

10.3 USING GENETIC ALGORITHMS

10.3.1 Map Colouring

Graph colouring is a typical discrete optimisation problem. We want to colour a graph using only k colours, and choose them in such a way that adjacent regions have different colours. It has been mathematically proven that any two-dimensional planar graph can be coloured with four colours, which was the first ever proof that used a computer program to check the cases. Even though it might be impossible, we are going to try to solve the three-colour problem using a genetic algorithm, we just won't be upset if the solution isn't perfect (this is a good idea with a GA anyway, of course). With all problems where you want to apply a genetic algorithm, there are three basic tasks that need to be performed:

Encode possible solutions as strings For this problem, we'll choose our alphabet to consist of the three possible shades (black (b), dark (d), and light (l), say). So for a six-region map, a possible string is $\alpha = \{bdblbb\}$. This says that the first region is black, the second dark grey, etc. We choose an order to record the regions in and stick to it for all the strings, and now we can encode any way of colouring in those six regions. An example problem and a colouring are given in Figures 10.4 and 10.5.

Choose a suitable fitness function The thing that we want to minimise (a **cost** function) is the number of times that two adjacent regions have the same colour. We could count these up fairly simply, but it is not a fitness function, because the best solution has the lowest number, not the highest. One easy way to turn it into a fitness function would be to multiply all the scores by minus one and use Equation (10.2) to turn them into fitnesses, or to count the total number of lines between regions and subtract off the number where the two regions on either side of the line have the same colour.

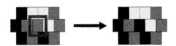 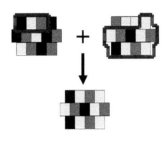

FIGURE 10.6 The way that mutation is performed on a colour, changing it into one of the other colours.

FIGURE 10.7 The effects of crossover on a map.

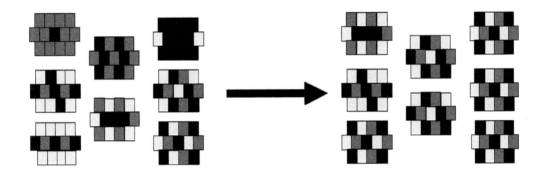

FIGURE 10.8 One generation of the GA working on the map colouring problem.

However, we could also just count the number of correct edges. The example in Figure 10.5 has 16 out of the 26 boundaries correct (where a boundary is the intersection between any two squares), so its fitness is 16.

Choose suitable genetic operators We'll use the standard genetic operators for this, since this example makes the operations of crossover and mutation clear. The way that they are used is shown in Figures 10.6 and 10.7. In general, people just use the standard operators for most problems, but if they don't work well, it can be worth putting some effort into thinking of new ones.

Having made those choices, we can let the GA run on the problem, with a possible population and their offspring shown in Figure 10.8, and look at the best solutions after some preset number of iterations. The GA produces good solutions to this problem, and implementing it for yourself is one of the suggested exercises for this chapter.

10.3.2 Punctuated Equilibrium

For a long time, one thing that creationists and others who did not believe in evolution used as an argument against it was the problem of the lack of intermediate animals in the fossil record. The argument runs that if humans evolved from apes, then there should be some evidence of a whole set of intermediary species that existed during the transition phase, and there aren't. Interestingly, GAs demonstrate one of the explanations why this is not correct, which is that the way that evolution actually seems to work is known as **punctuated**

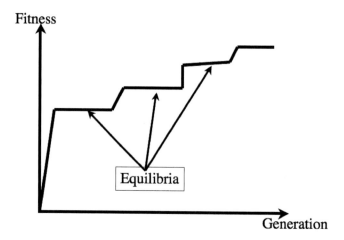

FIGURE 10.9 A graph showing punctuated equilibrium in a genetic algorithm. There is an effectively steady state where fitness does not improve, followed by rapid improvements in fitness until another steady state is reached.

equilibrium. There is basically a steady population of some species for a long time, and then something changes and over a very short (in evolutionary terms... still hundreds or thousands of years) period, there is a big change, and then everything settles down again. So the chance of finding fossils from the intermediary stage is quite small. There is a graph showing this effect in Figure 10.9.

10.3.3 Example: The Knapsack Problem

We used the knapsack problem as an example while we were looking at components of the GA. It is now time to see it being solved. Before we do that, we can use some of the methods from Section 9.4 to solve it. We've already mentioned the greedy algorithm solution, and we can of course use exhaustive search, as well, or any of the other methods we discussed in the last chapter, such as simulated annealing or hillclimbing.

The website has a simple example with 20 different packages, which have a total size of 2436.77 and a maximum knapsack size of 500. The greedy algorithm finds a solution of 487.47, while the optimal solution is eventually found by the exhaustive search as 499.98. The question is how well the GA does on the same problem. We will use the fitness function that was described in Section 10.1.2, where solutions that are too large are penalised by having twice the amount they are over subtracted from the maximum size. Figure 10.10 shows a graph of the output when the GA is run on this problem for 100 iterations. The GA rapidly finds a near-optimal solution (of 499.94) to this relatively simple problem, although in this run it did not find the global optimum.

10.3.4 Example: The Four Peaks Problem

The four peaks is a toy problem (that is, simple problem that isn't useful itself, but is good for testing algorithms) that is quite often used to test out GAs and various developments of them. It is an invented fitness function that rewards strings with lots of consecutive 0s at the start of the string, and lots of consecutive 1s at the end. The fitness consists of counting

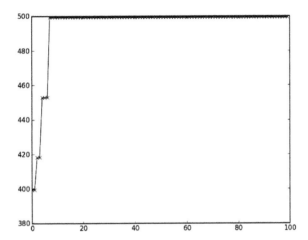

FIGURE 10.10 Evolution of the solution to the knapsack problem. The GA finds a very good solution to this simple problem within a few iterations, but never finds the optimal solution.

the number of 0s at the start, and the number of 1s at the end and returning the maximum of them as the fitness. However, if both the number of 0s and the number of 1s are above some threshold value T then the fitness function gets a bonus of 100 added to it. This is where the name 'four peaks' comes from: there are two small peaks where there are lots of 0s, or lots of 1s, and then there are two larger peaks, where the bonus is included. The GA should find these larger peaks for a successful run.

In NumPy the four peaks fitness function can be written as:

```
def fourpeaks(population,T=15):

    start = np.zeros((np.shape(population)[0],1))
    finish = np.zeros((np.shape(population)[0],1))

    fitness = np.zeros((np.shape(population)[0],1))

    for i in range(np.shape(population)[0]):
        s = np.where(population[i,:]==1)
        f = np.where(population[i,:]==0)
        if np.size(s)>0:
            start = s[0][0]
        else:
            start = 0

        if np.size(f)>0:
            finish = np.shape(population)[1] - f[-1][-1] -1
        else:
```

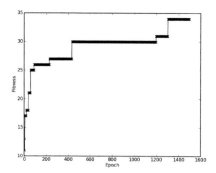

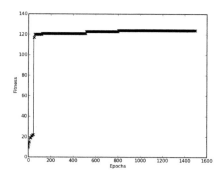

FIGURE 10.11 Evolution of a solution to the four peaks problem. The solution never reaches the bonus score in the fitness function.

FIGURE 10.12 Another solution to the four peaks problem. This solution does reach the bonus score, but does not get the global maximum.

```
          finish = 0

    if start>T and finish>T:
        fitness[i] = np.maximum(start,finish)+100
    else:
        fitness[i] = np.maximum(start,finish)

  fitness = np.squeeze(fitness)
  return fitness
```

Figures 10.11 and 10.12 show the outputs of two runs for a chromosome length of 100 and with $T = 15$. In the second the GA reaches the bonus point, while in the first it does not. Both of these runs used a mutation rate of 0.01, which is $1/L$, and single point crossover. They also used elitism.

10.3.5 Limitations of the GA

There are lots of good things about genetic algorithms, and they work amazingly well a lot of the time. However, they are not without problems, a significant one of which is they can be very slow. The main problem is that once a local maximum has been reached, it can often be a long time before a string is produced that escapes from the local maximum and finds another, higher, maximum. In addition, because we generally do not know anything about the fitness landscape, we can't see how well the GA is doing.

A more basic criticism of genetic algorithms is that it is very hard (read basically impossible) to analyse the behaviour of the GA. We expect that the mean fitness of the population will increase until an equilibrium of some kind is reached. This equilibrium is between the selection operator, which makes the population less diverse, but increases the mean fitness (exploitation), and the genetic operators, which usually reduce the mean fitness, but increase the diversity in the population (exploration). However, proving that this is guaranteed to happen has not been possible so far, which means that we cannot guarantee that the algorithm will converge at all, and certainly not to the optimal solution. This bothers a lot of researchers. That said, genetic algorithms are widely used when other methods do not work, and they are usually treated as a black box—strings are pushed in one end, and eventually an answer emerges. This is risky, because without knowledge of how the algorithm works it is not possible to improve it, nor do you know how cautiously you should treat the results.

10.3.6 Training Neural Networks with Genetic Algorithms

We trained our neural networks, most notably the MLP, using gradient descent. However, we could encode the problem of finding the correct weights as a set of strings, with the fitness function measuring the sum-of-squares error. This has been done, and with good reported results. However, there are some problems with this approach. The first is that we turn all the local information from the targets about the error at each output node of the network into just one number, the fitness, which is throwing away useful information, and the second is that we are ignoring the gradient information, which is also throwing away useful information.

A more sensible use for GAs with neural networks is to use the GA to choose the topology of the network. Previously, we chose the structure in a completely ad hoc way by trying out different structures and choosing the one that worked best. We can use a GA for this problem, although the crossover operator doesn't make a great deal of sense, so we just consider mutation. However, we allow for four different types of mutation: delete a neuron, delete a weight connection, add a neuron, add a connection. The deletion operators bias the learning towards simple networks. Making the GA more complicated by adding extra mutation operators might make you wonder if you can make it more complicated again. And you can; one example of where this can lead is discussed next.

10.4 GENETIC PROGRAMMING

One extension of genetic algorithms that has had a lot of attention is the idea of **genetic programming**. This was introduced by John Koza, and the basic idea is to represent a computer program as a tree (imagine a flow chart of the code). For certain programming languages, notably LISP, this is actually a very natural way to represent a program, but it doesn't work very well in Python, so we will have a quick look at the idea, but not get into writing any explicit algorithms for the method. Tree-based variants on mutation and crossover are defined (replace subtrees by other subtrees, either randomly generated (mutation, Figure 10.13) or swapped from another tree (crossover, Figure 10.14)), and then the genetic program runs just like a normal genetic algorithm, but acting on these program trees rather than strings.

Figure 10.15 shows a set of simple trees that perform arithmetic operations, and some possible developments of them, made using these operators.

Genetic programming has been used for many different tasks, from recognising skin melanomas to circuit design, and lots of very impressive results have been claimed for it. However, the search space is unbelievably large, and the mutation operator not especially useful, and so a lot depends upon the initial population. A set of possibly useful subtrees is usually chosen by the system developer first in order to give the system a head start. There

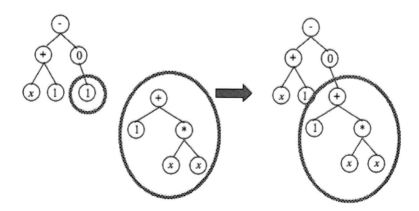

FIGURE 10.13 Example of a mutation in genetic programming.

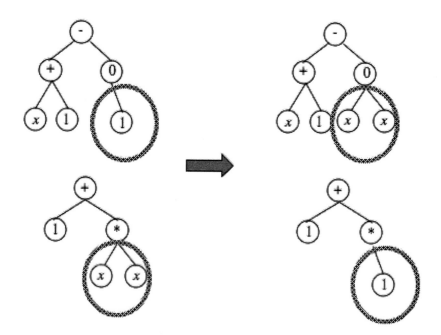

FIGURE 10.14 Example of a crossover in genetic programming.

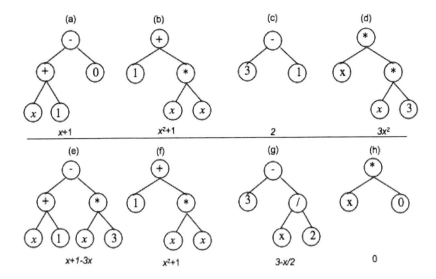

FIGURE 10.15 *Top:* Four arithmetical trees. *Bottom:* Example developments of the four trees: (e) and (h) are a possible crossover of (a) and (d), (f) is a copy of (b), and (g) is a mutation of (c).

are a couple of places where you can find more information on genetic programming in the Further Reading section.

10.5 COMBINING SAMPLING WITH EVOLUTIONARY LEARNING

The last machine learning method in this chapter is an interesting variation on the theme of evolutionary learning, combined with probabilistic models of the type that are described in Chapter 16, namely Bayesian networks. They are often known as estimation of distribution algorithms (EDA).

The most basic version is known as Population-Based Incremental Learning (PBIL), and it is amazingly simple. It works on a binary alphabet, just like the basic GA, but instead of maintaining a population, it keeps a probability vector p that gives the probability of each element being a 0 or 1. Initially, each value of this vector is 0.5, so that each element has equal chance of being 0 or 1. A population is then constructed by sampling from the distribution specified vector, and the fitness of each member of the population is computed. A subset of this population (typically just the two fittest vectors) is chosen to update the probability vector, using a learning rate η, which is often set to 0.005 (where **best** and **second** represent the best and second-best elements of the population):

$$p = p \times (1 - \eta) + \eta(\text{best} + \text{second})/2. \tag{10.3}$$

The population is then thrown away, and a new one sampled from the updated probability vector. The results of using this simple algorithm on the four-peaks problem with $T = 11$ are shown in Figure 10.16 using strings of length 100 with 200 strings in each population. This is directly comparable with Figure 10.12.

The centre of the algorithm is simply the code to find the strings with the two highest fitnesses and use them to update the vector. Everything else is directly equivalent to the genetic algorithm.

```
# Pick best
best[count] = np.max(fitness)
bestplace = np.argmax(fitness)
fitness[bestplace] = 0
secondplace = np.argmax(fitness)

# Update vector
p  = p*(1-eta) + eta*((pop[bestplace,:]+pop[secondplace,:])/2)
```

The probabilistic model that is used in PBIL is very simple: it is assumed that each element of the probability vector is independent, so that there is no interaction. However, there is no reason why more complicated interactions between variables cannot be considered, and several methods have been developed that do exactly this. The first option is to construct a chain, so that each variable depends only on the one to its left. This might involve sorting the order of the probability vector first, but then the algorithm simply needs to measure the mutual information (see Section 12.2.1) between each pair of neighbouring variables. This use of mutual information gives the algorithm its name: MIMIC. There are also more complicated variants using full Bayesian networks, such as the Bayesian Optimisation Algorithm (BOA) and Factorised Distribution Algorithm (FDA).

The power of these developments of the GA is that they use probabilistic models and are therefore more amenable to analysis than normal GAs, which have steadfastly withstood many attempts to better understand their behaviour. They also enable the algorithm to discover correlations between input variables, which can be useful if you want to understand the solution rather than just apply it.

It is important to remember that there is no guarantee that a genetic algorithm will find a good solution, although it often will, and certainly no guarantee that it will find the optimum. The vast majority of applications of genetic algorithms and the other algorithms described in this chapter do not consider this, but use the algorithms as a way to avoid having to understand the problem. Recall the No Free Lunch theorem of the last chapter—there is no universally good solution to the search problem—before using the GA or genetic program as the only search method that you use. Having said that, providing that you are prepared to accept the long running time and the fact that there are no guarantees of a good solution, they are frequently very useful methods.

FURTHER READING

There are entire books written about genetic algorithms, including:

- J.H. Holland. *Adaptation in Natural and Artificial Systems: An Introductory Analysis with Applications to Biology, Control, and Artificial Intelligence.* MIT Press, Cambridge, MA, USA, 1992.

- M. Mitchell. *An Introduction to Genetic Algorithms.* MIT Press, Cambridge, MA, USA, 1996.

- D.E. Goldberg. *Genetic Algorithms in Search, Optimisation, and Machine Learning.* Addison-Wesley, Reading, MA, USA, 1999.

There are also entire books on genetic programming, including:

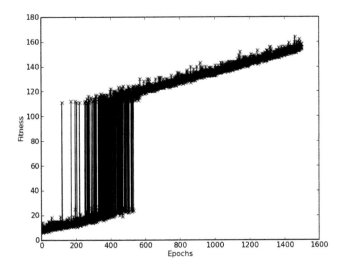

FIGURE 10.16 The evolution of the best fitness using PBIL on the four peaks problem.

- J.R. Koza. *Genetic Programming: On the Programming of Computers by the Means of Natural Selection*. MIT Press, Cambridge, MA, USA, 1992.

- Z. Michalewicz. *Genetic Algorithms + Data Structures = Evolution Programs*, 3rd edition, Springer, Berlin, Germany, 1999.

For more on Estimation of Distribution algorithms, look at:

- S. Baluja and R. Caruana. Removing the genetics from the standard genetic algorithm. In A. Prieditis and S. Russel, editors, *The International Conference on Machine Learning*, pages 38–46, Morgan Kaufmann Publishers, San Mateo, CA, USA, 1995.

- M. Pelikan, D.E. Goldberg, and F. Lobo. A survey of optimization by building and using probabilistic models. *Computational Optimization and Applications*, 21(1):5–20, 2002. Also IlliGAL Report No. 99018.

Details of the two books mentioned about real evolution are:

- C. Darwin. *On the Origin of Species by Means of Natural Selection*, 6th edition, Wordsworth, London, UK, 1872.

- R. Dawkins. *The Blind Watchmaker: Why the Evidence of Evolution Reveals a Universe without Design*. Penguin, London, UK, 1996.

PRACTICE QUESTIONS

Problem 10.1 Suppose that you want to archive your data files, but you have only got one CD, and more data files than will fit on it. You decide to choose the files you will save so as to try to maximise the amount of space you fill on the disk, so that the most data is backed up, but you can't split a data file. Write a greedy algorithm and a hill-climbing algorithm to solve this problem. What guarantees can you make about efficiency of the solutions?

Problem 10.2 (from Jon Shapiro)

In video poker, you are dealt five cards face up. You have one chance to replace any of the cards (or all or none) with cards drawn from the deck. You then get a payout related to the value of your hand as a poker hand. Say your stake is \$1. The lowest hand which pays is pair of jacks or better; this pays \$1 (so your net gain is 0). Two pair pays \$2, three-of-a-kind pays \$3, and so forth. Your goal is to make as much money as possible.

In order to play this game, you need a strategy for deciding which cards to keep and which to replace. For example, if your hand contains two face cards, but is currently worthless, should you hold them both or hold only one? If one is held, there are four chances to match one card; if two are held there are only three chances but there are two cards to match. If the hand contains a pair of low cards, is it better to keep the pair in the hopes of drawing another pair or a card which turns the pair into three-of-a-kind, or is it better to draw five new cards? It is unclear what is the best strategy for replacing cards in losing hands. Devise a way to use a genetic algorithm to search for good strategies for playing this game. Assume that you have a computer version of the game, so that any strategies which the GA proposes can be tested on the computer over many plays. Could an MLP using gradient descent learning be used to learn a good strategy? Why or why not?

Problem 10.3 You have 5000 MP3 files sitting on your computer's hard disk. Unfortunately, the hard disk has started making noises, and you decide that you had better back up the MP3s. Equally unfortunately, you can only burn CDs, not DVDs, on your computer. You need to minimise the number of CDs that you use, so you decide to design a genetic algorithm to choose which MP3s to put onto each CD in order to fill each CD as completely as possible.

Design a genetic algorithm to solve the problem. You will need to consider how you would encode the inputs, which genetic operators are suitable, and how you would make the genetic algorithm deal with the fact that you have multiple CDs, not just one CD.

Problem 10.4 Convert the GA to use real-valued chromosomes and use it to find the minima in Rosenbrock's function (Equation (9.18)).

Problem 10.5 Implement the map colouring fitness function (you will have to design a map first, of course) and see how good the solutions that the GA finds are. Compare maps that are three-colourable with some that are not. Can you think of any other algorithm that could be used to find solutions to this problem?

Problem 10.6 The Royal Road fitness function is designed to test the building block hypothesis, which says that GAs work by assembling small building blocks and then put them together by crossover. The function splits the binary string into l sequential pieces, all b bits long. The fitness of the piece is b for blocks that are all 1s, and 0 for others, and the total fitness is the sum of the fitness for each block. Implement this fitness function and test it on strings of length 16, with blocks of lengths 1, 2, 4, 8. Run your GAs for 10,000 iterations. Compare the results to using PBIL.

## CHAPTER 11

Reinforcement Learning

Reinforcement learning fills the gap between supervised learning, where the algorithm is trained on the correct answers given in the target data, and unsupervised learning, where the algorithm can only exploit similarities in the data to cluster it. The middle ground is where information is provided about whether or not the answer is correct, but not how to improve it. The reinforcement learner has to try out different strategies and see which work best. That 'trying out' of different strategies is just another way of describing search, which was the subject of Chapters 9 and 10. Search is a fundamental part of any reinforcement learner: the algorithm searches over the **state space** of possible inputs and outputs in order to try to maximise a **reward**.

Reinforcement learning is usually described in terms of the interaction between some agent and its environment. The agent is the thing that is learning, and the environment is where it is learning, and what it is learning about. The environment has another task, which is to provide information about how good a strategy is, through some **reward function**.

Think about a child learning to stand up and walk. The child tries out many different strategies for staying upright, and it gets feedback about which work by whether or not it ends up flat on its face. The methods that seem to work are tried over and over again, until they are perfected or better solutions are found, and those that do not work are discarded. This analogy has another useful aspect: it may well not be the last thing that the child does before falling that makes it fall over, but something that happened earlier on (it can take several desperate seconds of waving your arms around before you fall over, but the fall was caused by tripping over something, not by waving your arms about). So it can be difficult to work out which action (or combination of actions) made you fall over, because there are many actions in the chain.

The importance of reinforcement learning for psychological learning theory comes from the concept of **trial-and-error** learning, which has been around for a long time, and is also known as the **Law of Effect**. This is exactly what happens in reinforcement learning, as we'll see, and it was described in a book by Thorndike in 1911 as:

> Of several responses made to the same situation, those which are accompanied or closely followed by satisfaction to the animal will, other things being equal, be more firmly connected with the situation, so that, when it recurs, they will be more likely to recur; those which are accompanied or closely followed by discomfort to the animal will, other things being equal, have their connections with that situation weakened, so that, when it recurs, they will be less likely to occur. The greater the satisfaction or discomfort, the greater the strengthening or weakening of the bond. (E. L. Thorndike, *Animal Intelligence*, page 244.)

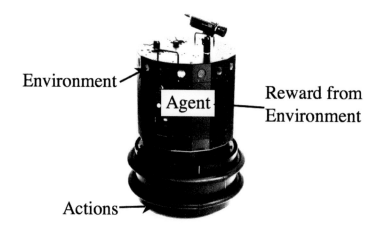

FIGURE 11.1 A robot perceives the current state of its environment through its sensors, and performs actions by moving its motors. The reinforcement learner (agent) within the robot tries to predict the next state and reward.

This is where the name 'reinforcement learning' comes from, since you repeat actions that are reinforced by a feeling of satisfaction. To see how it can be applied to machine learning, we will need some more notation.

11.1 OVERVIEW

Reinforcement learning maps states or situations to actions in order to maximise some numerical reward. That is, the algorithm knows about the current input (the state), and the possible things it can do (the actions), and its aim is to maximise the reward. There is a clear distinction drawn between the agent that is doing the learning and the environment, which is where the agent acts, and which produces the state and the rewards. The most common way to think about reinforcement learning is on a robot. The current sensor readings of the robot, or processed versions of them, could define the state. They are a representation of the environment around the robot in some way. Note that the state doesn't necessarily tell us everything that it would be useful to know (the robot's sensors don't tell it its location, only what it can see about it), and there can be noise and inaccuracies in the state data. The possible ways that the robot can drive its motors are the actions, which move the robot in the environment, and the reward could be how well it does its task without crashing into things. Figure 11.1 shows the idea of state, actions, and environment to a robot, while Figure 11.2 shows how they are linked with each other and with the reward.

In reinforcement learning the algorithm gets feedback in the form of the reward about how well it is doing. In contrast to supervised learning, where the algorithm is 'taught' the correct answer, the reward function evaluates the current solution, but does not suggest how to improve it. Just to make the situation a little more difficult, we need to think about the possibility that the reward can be delayed, which means that you don't actually get the reward until a long time in the future. (For example, think about a robot that is learning to traverse a maze. It doesn't know whether it has found the centre of the maze until it gets there, and it doesn't get the reward until it reaches the centre of the maze.) We therefore need to allow for rewards that don't appear until long after the relevant actions have been

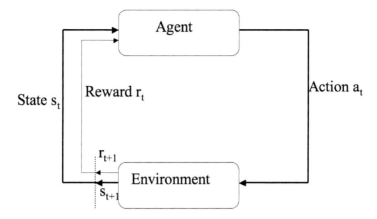

FIGURE 11.2 The reinforcement learning cycle: the learning agent performs action a_t in state s_t and receives reward r_{t+1} from the environment, ending up in state s_{t+1}.

taken. Sometimes we think of the immediate reward and the total expected reward into the future.

Once the algorithm has decided on the reward, it needs to choose the action that should be performed in the current state. This is known as the policy. This is done based on some combination of exploration and exploitation (remember, reinforcement learning is basically a search method), which in this case means deciding whether to take the action that gave the highest reward last time we were in this state, or trying out a different action in the hope of finding something even better.

11.2 EXAMPLE: GETTING LOST

You arrive in a foreign city exhausted after many hours of flying, catch the train into town and stagger into a backpacker's hostel without noticing much of your surroundings. When you wake up it is dark and you are starving, so you set off for a wander around town looking for somewhere to eat. Unfortunately, it is 3 a.m. and, even more unfortunately, you soon realise that you are completely lost. To make matters worse, you discover that you can't remember the name of the backpacker's, or much else about it except that it is in one of the old squares. Of course, that doesn't help much because this part of the city pretty much consists of old squares. There are only two things in your favour: you are fairly sure that you'll recognise the building, and you've studied reinforcement learning and decide to apply it (yes, this book can save your life!).

You are sure that you've only walked through the old part of the city, so you don't need to worry about any street that takes you out of the old part. So at the next bus stop you come to, you have a proper look at the map, and note down the map of the old town squares, which turns out to look like Figure 11.3.

As you finish drawing the map you notice a 24-hour shop and buy as many bags of potato chips as you can fit into your pockets. As a reinforcement learner you decide to reward yourself when you take actions that lead to the backpacker's rather than stuff your face immediately (this is a delayed reward). After thinking about a reward structure you decide that the only one that will work is to eat until you can eat no more when you

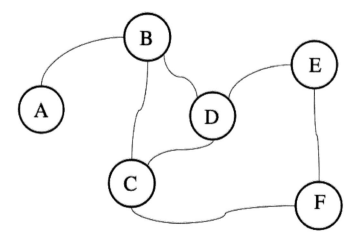

FIGURE 11.3 The old town that you find yourself lost in.

actually get to the backpacker's, and not to reward yourself at all until then. You'll just have to hope that you don't faint from hunger first!

Inspired by the idea of food, you decide that the backpacker's is almost definitely in the square labelled F on the map, because its name seems vaguely familiar. You decide to work out a reward structure so that you can follow a reinforcement learning algorithm to get to the backpacker's. The first thing you work out is that staying still means that you are sleeping on your feet, which is bad. So you assign a reward of −5 for that (while negative reinforcement can be viewed as punishment, it doesn't necessarily correspond clearly, but you might want to imagine it as pinching yourself so that you stay awake). Of course, once you reach state F you are in the backpacker's and will therefore stay there. This is known as an **absorbing state**, and is the end of the problem, when you get the reward of eating all the chips you bought. Now moving between two squares could be good, because it might take you closer to F. But without looking at the map you won't know that, so you decide to just apply a reward when you actually reach F, and leave everything else as neutral. Where there is no direct road between two squares (so that no action takes you from one to the other) there is no reward because it is not a viable action. This results in the reward matrix R shown below (where '-' shows that there is no link) and also in Figure 11.4.

	Next State					
Current State	A	B	C	D	E	F
A	-5	0	-	-	-	-
B	0	-5	0	0	-	-
C	-	0	-5	0	-	100
D	-	0	0	-5	0	-
E	-	-	-	0	-5	100
F	-	-	0	-	0	-

Of course, as a reinforcement learner you don't actually know the reward matrix. That's pretty much what you are trying to discover, but it doesn't make for a very good example. We'll assume that you have now reached a stage of tiredness where you can't even read what is on your paper properly. Having got this set up we've reached the stage where we

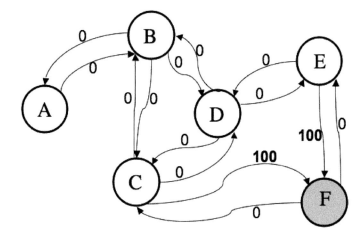

FIGURE 11.4 The *state diagram* if you are correct and the backpacker's is in square (state) F. The connections from each state back into itself (meaning that you don't move) are not shown, to avoid the figure getting too complicated. They are each worth -5 (except for staying in state F, which means that you are in the backpacker's).

need to do some learning, but for now we'll leave you stranded in that foreign city and flesh out a few of the things that we've talked about so far.

11.2.1 State and Action Spaces

Our reinforcement learner is basically a search algorithm, and obviously the larger the number of states that the algorithm has to search through, the longer it will take to find a good solution. The set of all states that are possible for the learner to experience is known as the **state space**. There is a corresponding **action space** that contains all of the possible actions. If we can reduce the size of the state space and action space, then it is almost always a good idea, providing that it does not oversimplify the problem. In the example there are only six states, but still, look at Figure 11.4 and imagine wandering through all of the squares over and over again while we search: it seems like this learning is going to take a long time. And it generally does.

Computing the size of the state space (and the corresponding action space) is relatively simple. For example, suppose that there are five inputs, each an integer between 0 and 100. The size of the state space is then $100 \times 100 \times 100 \times 100 \times 100 = 100^5$, which is incredibly large, so the curse of dimensionality is really kicking in here. However, if we decide that we can **quantize** the data so that instead of 100 numbers there are only two for each input (for example, by assigning every number less than 50 to class 1, and every number 50 and above to class 2), then the size of the state space is a more manageable $2^5 = 32$. Choosing the state space and action space carefully is therefore a crucial part of making a successful reinforcement learner. You want them to be as small as possible without losing accuracy in the results—by reducing the scale of each input from 100 to 2, we have obviously thrown away a lot of information that might have made the quality of the answer better. As is usually the case, there is some element of compromise between the two.

11.2.2 Carrots and Sticks: The Reward Function

The basic idea of the learner is that it will choose the action that gets the maximum expected reward. In the example, we worked out what the rewards would be in a fairly ad hoc way, by saying what we wanted and then thinking about how to get it. That's pretty much the way that it works in practice, too: in Chapter 10 where we looked at genetic algorithms, we had to carefully craft the fitness function to solve the problem that we wanted, and the same thing is true of the **reward function**. In fact, they can be seen as the same thing.

The reward function takes the current state and the chosen action and produces a numerical reward based on them. So in the example, if we are in state A, and choose the action of doing nothing, so that we remain in state A, we get a reward of -5. Note that the reward can be positive or negative, with the latter corresponding to 'punishment', showing that particular actions should be avoided. The reward is generated by the environment around the learner; it is not internal to the learner itself (this is what makes it difficult to describe in our example: the environment doesn't give you rewards in the real world, only when there is a computer (or brain) as part of the environment to help out). In effect, the reward function makes the goal of the learner explicit—the learner is trying to maximise the reward, which means behaving in exactly the way that the reward function expects. The reward tells the learner what the goal is, not how the goal should be achieved, which would be supervised learning. It is therefore usually a bad idea to include **sub-goals** (extra things that the learner should achieve along the way, which are meant to speed up learning), because the learner can find methods of achieving the sub-goals without actually achieving the real goal.

The choice of a suitable reward function is absolutely crucial, with very different behaviours resulting from varying the reward function. For example, consider the difference between these two reward functions for a maze-traversing robot (try to work out the difference before reading the paragraph that follows them):

- receive a reward of 50 when you find the centre of the maze

- receive a reward of -1 for each move and a reward of +50 when you find the centre of the maze

In the first version, the robot will learn to get to the centre of the maze, just as it will in the second version, but the second reward function is biased towards shorter routes through the maze, which is probably a good thing. The maze problem is **episodic**: learning is split into episodes that have a definite endpoint when the robot reaches the centre of the maze. This means that the rewards can be given at the end and then propagated back through all the actions that were performed to update the learner. However, there are plenty of other examples that are not episodic (**continual tasks**), and there is no cut off when the task stops. An example is the child learning to walk that was mentioned at the start of the chapter. A child can walk successfully when it doesn't fall over at all, not when it doesn't fall over for 10 minutes.

Now that the reward has been broken into two parts—an immediate part and a pay-off in the end—we need to think about the learning algorithm a bit more. The thing that is driving the learning is the total reward, which is the expected reward from now until the end of the task (when the learner reaches the **terminal state** or **accepting state**—the backpacker's in our example). At that point there is generally a large pay-off that signals the successful completion of the task. However, the same thing does not work for continual tasks, because there is no terminal state, so we want to predict the reward forever into the infinite future, which is clearly impossible.

11.2.3 Discounting

The solution to this problem is known as **discounting**, and means that we take into account how certain we can be about things that happen in the future: there is lots of uncertainty in the learning anyway, so we should discount our predictions of rewards in the future according to how much chance there is that they are wrong. The rewards that we expect to get very soon are probably going to be more accurate predictions than those a long time in the future, because lots of other things might change. So we add an additional parameter $0 \leq \gamma \leq 1$, and then discount future rewards by multiplying them by γ^t, where t is the number of timesteps in the future this reward is from. As γ is less than 1, so γ^2 is smaller again, and $\gamma^k \to 0$ as $k \to \infty$ (i.e., γ gets smaller and smaller as k gets larger and larger), so that we can ignore most of the future predictions. This means that our prediction of the total future reward is:

$$R_t = r_{t+1} + \gamma r_{t+2} + \gamma^2 r_{t+3} + \ldots + \gamma^{k-1} r_k + \ldots = \sum_{k=0}^{\infty} \gamma^k r_{t+k+1}. \qquad (11.1)$$

Obviously, the closer γ is to zero, the less distance we look into the future, while with $\gamma = 1$ there is no discounting, as in the episodic case above (in fact, discounting is sometimes used for episodic learning as well, since the eventual reward could be a very long way off and we have to deal with that uncertainty in learning somehow). We can apply discounting to the example of learning to walk. When you fall over you give yourself a reward of -1, and otherwise there are no rewards. The -1 reward is discounted into the future, so that a reward k steps into the future has reward $-\gamma^k$. The learner will therefore try to make k as large as possible, resulting in proper walking.

The point of the reward function is that it gives us a way to choose what to do next—our **predictions** of the reward let us exploit our current knowledge and try to maximise the reward we get. Alternatively, we can carry on exploring and trying out new actions in the hope that we find ways to get even larger rewards. The methods of exploration and exploitation that we carry out are the methods of **action selection** that we perform.

11.2.4 Action Selection

At each stage of the reinforcement learning process, the algorithm looks at the actions that can be performed in the current state and computes the **value** of each action; that is, the average reward that is expected for carrying out that action in the current state. The simplest way to do this is to compute the average reward that has been received each time in the past. This is known as $Q_{s,t}(a)$, where s is the state, a is the action, and t is the number of times that the action has been taken before in this state. This will eventually converge to the true prediction of the reward for that action. Based on the current average reward predictions, there are three methods of choosing action a that are worth thinking about for reinforcement learning. We've seen the first and third of them before:

Greedy Pick the action that has the highest value of $Q_{s,t}(a)$, so always choose to exploit your current knowledge.

ϵ-greedy This is similar to the greedy algorithm, but with some small probability ϵ we pick some other action at random. So nearly every time we take the greedy option, but occasionally we try out an alternative in the hope of finding a better action. This throws some exploration into the mix. ϵ-greedy selection finds better solutions over time than the pure greedy algorithm, since it can explore and find better solutions.

Soft-max One refinement of ϵ-greedy is to think about which of the alternative actions to select when the exploration happens. The ϵ-greedy algorithm chooses the alternatives with uniform probability. Another possibility is to use the soft-max function (which we've seen repeatedly, e.g., as Equation (4.12)) to make the selection:

$$P(Q_{s,t}(a)) = \frac{\exp(Q_{s,t}(a)/\tau)}{\sum_b \exp(Q_{s,t}(b)/\tau)}. \tag{11.2}$$

Here, there is a new parameter τ, which is known as the **temperature** because of the link to **simulated annealing**, see Section 9.6. When τ is large, all actions have similar probabilities, and when τ is small, the selection probabilities matter more. In soft-max selection, the current best (greedy) action will be chosen most of the time, but the others will be chosen proportional to their estimated reward, which is updated whenever they are used.

11.2.5 Policy

We have just considered different action selection methods, such as ϵ-greedy and soft-max. The aim of the action selection is to trade off exploration and exploitation in such a way as to maximise the expected reward into the future. Instead, we can make an explicit decision that we are going to always take the optimal choice at each stage, and not do exploration any more. This choice of which action to take in each state in order to get optimal results is known as the **policy**, π. The hope is that we can **learn** a better policy that is specific to the current state s_t. This is the crux of the learning part of reinforcement learning—learn a policy π from states to actions. There is at least one optimal policy that gives the maximum reward, and that is what we want to find. In order to find a policy, there are a few things that we need to worry about. The first is how much information we need to know regarding how we got to the current state, and the second is how we ascribe a **value** to the current state. The first one is important enough both for here and for Chapter 16 that we are going to go into some detail now.

11.3 MARKOV DECISION PROCESSES

11.3.1 The Markov Property

Let's go back to the example. Standing in the square labelled D you need to make a choice of what action to take next. There are four possible options (see Figure 11.4): standing still, or moving to one of B, C, or E. The question is whether or not that is enough information for you to predict the reward accurately and so to choose the best possible action. Or do you also need to know where you have been in the past? Let's say that you know that you came to D from B. In that case, maybe it does not make sense to move back to B, since your reward won't change. However, if you came to D from E then it does actually make sense to go back there, since it moves you closer to F. So in this case, it appears that knowing your previous action doesn't actually help very much, because you don't have enough information to work out what was useful.

Another example where this is usually true is in a game of chess, where the current situation of all the pieces on the board (the state) is enough to predict whether or not the next move is a good one—it does not depend on precisely how each piece got to the current location. Thus, the current state provides enough information. A state that has this property, which is that the current state provides enough information for the reward to be

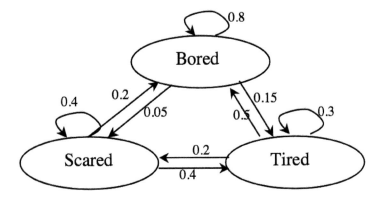

FIGURE 11.5 A simple example of a Markov decision process to decide on the state of your mind tomorrow given your state of mind today.

computed without looking at previous states, is known as a **Markov state**. The importance of this can be seen from the following two equations, the first of which is what is required when the Markov property is **not** true, while for the second one it is true. The equation is the computation of the probability that the next reward is r' and the next state is s'.

$$Pr(r_t = r', s_{t+1} = s' | s_t, a_t, r_{t-1}, s_{t-1}, a_{t-1}, \ldots r_1, s_1, a_1, r_0, s_0, a_0), \qquad (11.3)$$

$$Pr(r_t = r', s_{t+1} = s' | s_t, a_t). \qquad (11.4)$$

Clearly, Equation (11.4), which depends only on where you are now, and what you choose to do now, is much simpler to compute, less likely to suffer from rounding errors, and does not require that the whole history of the learner is stored. In fact, it makes the computation possible, whereas the first is not possible for any interesting problem. A reinforcement learning problem that follows Equation (11.4) (that is, that has the Markov property) is known as a **Markov Decision Process (MDP)**. It means that we can compute the likely next reward, and what the next state will be, from only the current state and action, based on previous experience. We can make decisions (predictions) about the likely behaviour of the learner, and its expected rewards, using just the current state data.

11.3.2 Probabilities in Markov Decision Processes

We have now reduced our reinforcement learning problem to learning about Markov Decision Processes. We will only talk about the case where the number of possible states and actions is finite, because reasoning about the infinite case makes your head hurt. There is a very simple example of an MDP in Figure 11.5, showing predictions for your state-of-mind while preparing for an exam, together with the (**transition probabilities**) for moving between each pair of states shown. This is known as a **Markov chain**. The diagram can be extended into something called a **transition diagram**, which shows the dynamics of a finite Markov Decision Process and usually includes information about the rewards.

We can make a transition diagram for our example, based on Figure 11.4. We'll make the situation a little bit more complicated now by adding in the assumption that you are so tired that even though you are in state B and trying to get to state A, there is a small probability that you will actually take the wrong street and end up in either C or D. We'll

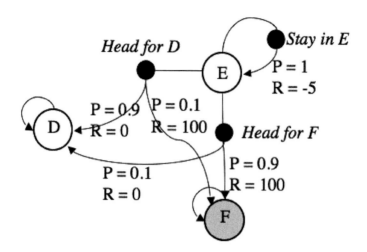

FIGURE 11.6 A small part of the transition diagram for the example. From state E there are three possible actions, and the states in which they end up, together with the rewards, are shown here.

make those probabilities be 0.1 for each extra exit that there is from each state, and we'll assume that you can stand in one place without fear of ending up elsewhere. A very tiny bit of the transition diagram, centred on state E, is shown in Figure 11.6. There are three actions that can be taken in state E (shown by the black circles), with associated probabilities and expected rewards. Learning and using this transition diagram can be seen as the aim of any reinforcement learner.

The Markov Decision Process formalism is a powerful one that can deal with additional uncertainties. For example, it can be extended to deal with the case where the true states are not known, only an observation of the state can be made, which is probabilistically related to the state, and possibly the action. These are known as partially observable Markov Decision Processes (POMDPs), and they are related to the Hidden Markov Models that we will see in Section 16.3. POMDPs are commonly used for robotics, where the sensors of the robots are usually far too inexact and noisy for places the robot visits to be identified with any degree of success. Methods to deal with these problems maintain an estimate of belief of their current state and use that in the reinforcement learning calculations. It is now time to get back to the reinforcement learner and the concept of values.

11.4 VALUES

The reinforcement learner is trying to decide on what action to take in order to maximise the expected reward into the future. This expected reward is known as the value. There are two ways that we can compute a value. We can consider the current state, and average across all of the actions that can be taken, leaving the policy to sort this out for itself (the state-value function, $V(s)$), or we can consider the current state and each possible action that can be taken separately, the action-value function, $Q(s, a)$. In either case we are thinking about what the expected reward would be if we started in state s (where $E(\cdot)$ is the statistical expectation):

$$V(s) = E(r_t|s_t = s) = E\left\{\sum_{i=0}^{\infty} \gamma^i r_{t+i+1}|s_t = s\right\}, \tag{11.5}$$

$$Q(s,a) = E(r_t|s_t = s, a_t = a) = E\left\{\sum_{i=0}^{\infty} \gamma^i r_{t+i+1}|s_t = s, a_t = a\right\}. \tag{11.6}$$

It should be fairly obvious that the second estimate is more accurate in the long run, because we have more information: we know which action we are going to take. However, because of that we need to collect a lot more data, and so it will take a long time to learn. In other words, the action-value function is even more susceptible to the curse of dimensionality than the state-value function. In situations where there are lots of states it will not be possible to store either, and some other method, such as using a parameterised solution space (i.e., having a set of parameters that are controlled by the learner, rather than explicit solutions), will be needed. This is more complicated than we will consider here.

There are now two problems that we need to solve, predicting the value function, and then selecting the optimal policy. We'll think about the second one first. The optimal policy is the one in which the value function is the greatest over all possible states. We label this (not necessarily unique) policy with a star: π^*. The optimal state-value function is then $V^*(s) = \max_\pi V^\pi(s)$ for all possible states s, and the optimal action-value function is $Q^*(s,a) = \max_\pi Q^\pi(s,a)$ for all possible states s and actions a. We can link these two value functions, because the first considers taking the optimal action in each case (since the policy π^* is optimal), while the second considers taking action a this time, and then following the optimal policy from then on. Hence we only need to worry about the current reward and the (discounted) estimate of the future rewards:

$$\begin{aligned} Q^*(s,a) &= E(r_{t+1}) + \gamma \max_{a_{t+1}} Q(s_{t+1}, a_{t+1}) \\ &= E(r_{t+1}) + \gamma V^*(s_{t+1}|s_t = s, a_t = a). \end{aligned} \tag{11.7}$$

Of course, there is no guarantee that we will ever manage to learn the optimal policy. There is bound to be noise and other inaccuracies in the system, and the curse of dimensionality is liable to limit the amount of exploration that we do. However, it will be enough to learn good approximations to the optimal policy. One thing that will work to our advantage is that reinforcement learning operates on-line, in that the learner is exploring the different states as it learns, which means that it is getting more chances to learn about the states that are seen more often, and so will have a better chance of finding the optimal policy for those states.

The question is how you actually update the value function ($V(s)$ or $Q(s,a)$). The idea is to make a look-up table of all the possible states or state-action pairs, and set them all to zero to start with. Then we will use experience to fill them in. Returning to your foreign trip, you wander around until eventually you stumble upon the backpacker's. Gorging yourself on the chips you remember that at the last timestep you were in square E (this remembering is known as a backup). Now you can update the value for E (the reward is $\gamma \times 100$). That is all we do, since your memory is so shot that you can't remember anything else. And there we stop until the next night, when you wake up again and the same thing happens. Except now, you have information about E, although not about any other state. However, when you reach E now, say from D, then you can update the value for D to have reward $\gamma^2 \times 100$. And so it continues, until all of the states (and possibly actions) have values attached.

The obvious problem with this approach is that we have to wait until we reach the goal before we can update the values. Instead, we can use the same trick that we used in Equation (11.7) and use the current reward and the discounted prediction instead, so that the update equation looks like (where μ is the learning rate as usual):

$$V(s_t) \leftarrow V(s_t) + \mu(r_{t+1} + \gamma V(s_{t+1}) - V(s_t)). \tag{11.8}$$

The $Q(s, a)$ version looks very similar, except that we have to include the action information. In both cases we are using the difference between the current and previous estimates, which is why these methods have the name of **temporal difference (TD)** methods. Suppose that we knew rather more about where we had been. In that case, we could have updated more states when we got to the backpacker's, which would have been rather more efficient. The trouble is that we don't know if those states were useful or not—it might have been chance that we visited them. The answer to this is similar to discounting: we introduce another parameter $0 \leq \lambda \leq 1$ that we apply to reduce the amount that being in that particular state matters. The way this works is known as an **eligibility trace**, where an eligible state is one that you have visited recently, and it is computed by setting:

$$e_t(s', a') = \begin{cases} 1 & \text{if } s' = s, a' = s \\ \gamma \lambda e_{t-1}(s', a') & \text{otherwise.} \end{cases} \tag{11.9}$$

If $\lambda = 0$ then you only use the current state, which was the algorithm we had above. For $\lambda = 1$ you retain all the knowledge of where you have been. It can be shown that the TD(0) algorithm (i.e., the TD(λ)indexTD(λ) algorithm with $\lambda = 0$) is optimal, in the sense that it converges to the correct value function V^π for the current policy π. There are some provisos on the values of the parameter μ, which are usually satisfied by incrementally reducing the size of μ as learning progresses. The TD(0) algorithm for Q values is also known as the Q-learning algorithm.

The Q-Learning Algorithm

- **Initialisation**

    - set $Q(s, a)$ to small random values for all s and a

- Repeat:

    - initialise s
    - repeat:
        * select action a using ϵ-greedy or another policy
        * take action a and receive reward r
        * sample new state s'
        * update $Q(s, a) \leftarrow Q(s, a) + \mu(r + \gamma \max_{a'} Q(s', a') - Q(s, a))$
        * set $s \leftarrow s'$
    - For each step of the current episode

- Until there are no more episodes

Note that we can do exactly the same thing for $V(s)$ values instead of $Q(s, a)$ values. There is one thing in this algorithm that is slightly odd, which is in the computation of

$Q(s', a')$. We do not use the policy to find the value of a', but instead choose the one that gives the highest value. This is known as an **off-policy** decision. Modifying the algorithm to work **on-policy** is very easy. It gets an interesting name based on the fact that it uses the set of values $(s_t, a_t, r_{t+1}, s_{t+1}, a_{t+1})$, which reads 'sarsa':

The Sarsa Algorithm

- **Initialisation**

    - set $Q(s, a)$ to small random values for all s and a

- Repeat:

    - initialise s
    - choose action a using the current policy
    - repeat:
        * take action a and receive reward r
        * sample new state s'
        * choose action a' using the current policy
        * update $Q(s, a) \leftarrow Q(s, a) + \mu(r + \gamma Q(s', a') - Q(s, a))$
        * $s \leftarrow s'$, $a \leftarrow a'$
    - for each step of the current episode

- Until there are no more episodes

The two algorithms are very similar. They are both **bootstrap methods**, because they start from poor estimates of the correct answers and iteratively update them as the algorithm progresses. The algorithms work on-line, with the values of Q being updated as soon as r_{t+1} and s_{t+1} are known. In both cases, we are updating the estimates based only on the next state and reward. We could delay our updating for longer, until we knew values of r_{t+n} and s_{t+n}, and then use a TD(λ) algorithm. The only difficulty with this is that there are many different actions a that could be taken between s_t and s_{t+n}.

Once the details of the reward and transition matrices have been sorted out, the implementation of the algorithms doesn't hold many surprises. For example, the central part of the sarsa algorithm using the ϵ-greedy policy can be written in this form:

```
# Stop when the accepting state is reached
while inEpisode:
    r = R[s,a]
    # For this example, new state is the chosen action
    sprime = a

    # epsilon-greedy selection
    if (np.random.rand()<epsilon):
        indices = np.where(t[sprime,:]!=0)
        pick = np.random.randint(np.shape(indices)[1])
        aprime = indices[0][pick]
    else:
```

```
    aprime = np.argmax(Q[sprime,:])

  Q[s,a] += mu * (r + gamma*Q[sprime,aprime] - Q[s,a])
  s = sprime
  a = aprime

  # Check if accepting state reached
  if s==5:
   inEpisode = 0
```

11.5   BACK ON HOLIDAY: USING REINFORCEMENT LEARNING

As an example of how to use the reinforcement algorithms we will finish our example of finding the way to the backpacker's by using the ϵ-greedy policy. The specification of the problem is set up in the reward matrix R and transition matrix t, so the first thing to do is to work out how to describe those, neither of which is very difficult since they were given in Section 11.2. It might not be obvious that t is there, but it is shown in Figure 11.4, and can be written out as (where 1 means that there is a link, and 0 means that there is not):

Current State	Next State					
	A	B	C	D	E	F
A	1	1	0	0	0	0
B	1	1	1	1	0	0
C	0	1	1	1	0	1
D	0	1	1	1	1	0
E	0	0	0	1	1	1
F	0	0	1	0	1	1

It is then just a question of running the algorithm for parameter choices of γ, μ, ϵ, and the number of iterations. A run with $\gamma = 0.4$, $\mu = 0.7$, $\epsilon = 0.1$, and 1,000 iterations (with either sarsa or Q-learning produced the following Q matrix:

1.4	16.0	0	0	0	0
6.4	11.0	40.0	16.0	0	0
0	16.0	35.0	16.0	0	100.0
0	16.0	40.0	11.0	40.0	0
0	0	0	16.0	35.0	100.0
0	0	0	0	0	0

Note that NumPy has a useful np.inf value, so -np.inf can be used as rewards for impossible actions. Some of the 0s can become -np.infs eventually. The question is how to interpret and use this matrix, and the answer is to simply apply the policy at each point, choosing the maximum available Q value for the current state most of the time until you reach the goal state. So from A, the policy will direct you to move to B ($Q = 16$) then on to C ($Q = 40$) and so to F. From D you can go to either C or E ($Q = 40$) and from either of those, directly to F.

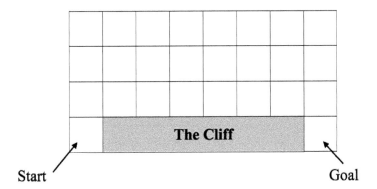

FIGURE 11.7 The example environment.

11.6 THE DIFFERENCE BETWEEN SARSA AND Q-LEARNING

It might not be clear what the difference is between the two algorithms in practice. We're going to consider the little environment that is shown in Figure 11.7, where the agent has to learn a route from the start location on the left to the final location on the right (the example comes from Section 6.5 of Sutton and Barto's book, which is in the readings at the end of the chapter). The reward structure is that every move gets a reward of -1, except for moves that end up on the cliff. These get a reward of -100, and the agent gets put back at the start location. This is clearly an episodic problem, since there is a clear end state.

Both algorithms will start out with no information about the environment, and will therefore explore randomly, using the ϵ-greedy policy. However, over time, the strategies that the two algorithms produce are quite different. The main reason for the difference is that Q-learning always attempts to follow the optimal path, which is the shortest one. This takes it close to the cliff, and the ϵ-greedy part means that inevitably it will sometimes fall over. By way of contrast, the sarsa algorithm will converge to a much safer route that keeps it well away from the cliff, even though it takes longer. The two solutions are shown in Figures 11.8 and 11.9. The sarsa algorithm produces the safe route because it includes information about action selection in its estimates of Q, while Q-learning produces the riskier, but shorter, route. The choice of which is better is up to you, and it depends on how serious the effects of falling off the cliff are.

The reason for the difference between the algorithms is that Q-learning always assumes that the policy will pick the optimal action, and while this is true most of the time, the ϵ-greedy policy does occasionally choose a different action, which can cause problems here. However, the algorithm ignores these dangers because it only focuses on the optimal solution. Sarsa does not take this maximum, and so it will be biased against solutions that take it close to the cliff, because these allow for cases where the agent fell off the cliff, and that therefore have very large negative rewards.

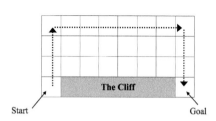

FIGURE 11.8 The sarsa solution is far from optimal, but it is safe.

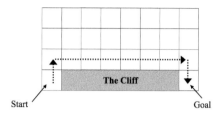

FIGURE 11.9 The Q-learning solution is optimal, but occasionally the random search will tip it over the cliff.

11.7 USES OF REINFORCEMENT LEARNING

Reinforcement learning has been used successfully for many problems, and the results of computer modelling of reinforcement learning have been of great interest to psychologists, as well as computer scientists, because of the close links to biological learning. However, the place where it has been most popular is in intelligent robotics, because of the fact that the robot can be left to attempt to solve the task without human intervention.

For example, reinforcement learning has been used to get robots to learn to clear a room by pushing boxes to the edges. This isn't exactly the most exciting task in the world, but the fact that the robot can learn to do it using reinforcement learning is impressive. Reinforcement learning has been used in other robotic applications, including robots learning to follow each other, travel towards bright lights, and even navigate.

This is not to say that reinforcement learning does not have problems. Since it is, in essence, a search strategy, reinforcement learning suffers from the same difficulties as the search algorithms that we talked about in the last two chapters: it can become stuck in local minima, and if the current search region is effectively flat, then the algorithm does not find any better solution. There are several reports of researchers training robots having the batteries run out before the robot has learnt anything, and even of the researchers giving up and kicking the robot in the right direction to give it a start. In general, reinforcement learning is fairly slow, because it has to build up all of the information through exploration and exploitation in order to find the better solutions. It is also very dependent upon a carefully chosen reward function: get that wrong and the algorithm will do something completely unexpected.

A famous example of reinforcement learning was TD-Gammon, which was produced by Gerald Tesauro. His idea was that reinforcement learning should be very good at learning to play games, because games were clearly episodic—you played until somebody won—and there was a clear reward structure, with a positive reward for winning. There was another benefit, which was that you could set the learner to play against itself. This is actually very important, since the version of TD-Gammon that was actually bundled with the IBM operating system OS/2 Warp had played 1,500,000 games against itself before it stopped improving.

FURTHER READING

A detailed book on reinforcement learning is:

- R.S. Sutton and A.G. Barto. *Reinforcement Learning: An Introduction.* MIT Press, Cambridge, MA, USA, 1998.

An interesting article concerning the use of reinforcement learning is:

- G. Tesauro. Temporal difference learning and TD-gammon. *Communications of the ACM*, 38(3):58–68, 1995.

Alternative treatments are:

- Chapter 13 of T. Mitchell. *Machine Learning.* McGraw-Hill, New York, USA, 1997.

- Chapter 18 of E. Alpaydin. *Introduction to Machine Learning*, 2nd edition, MIT Press, Cambridge, MA, USA, 2009.

PRACTICE QUESTIONS

Problem 11.1 Work through the first few steps of the hill by hand for both sarsa and Q-learning. Then modify the code to run on this example and ensure that they match.

Problem 11.2 Design a Q-learner for playing noughts-and-crosses (also known as Tic-Tac-Toe). Run the algorithm by hand, describing the states, transitions, rewards, and Q-values. Assume that the opponent picks a random (but valid) square for each move. How would your learner change if the opponent played optimally? Would a TD learner behave differently?

Problem 11.3 A robot has 8 range-finding sensors and 2 motors. The range sensors return an integer between 0 and 127 inclusive that represents the distance in centimetres to the nearest object. If the nearest object is further than 127 centimetres away, then 127 is returned. The motors receive an integer input between -100 (full speed backwards) and 100 (full speed forwards).

You want to train the robot to follow the right-hand wall using reinforcement learning. The robot should stay between 15 and 30 centimetres away from the right-hand wall, and if it reaches corners should be able to turn to follow the wall.

Compute the state space, decide if this is a continuous or episodic problem, and then design a suitable reinforcement learner of the problem, considering:

- Any quantisation of the input and output spaces.
- The reward system you choose.
- A description of your chosen learning algorithm.
- Any problems that you anticipate with the system, and what the final result of the learning will be.

Problem 11.4 There are 5 lifts in a 10-storey office building. On each floor there are call buttons for somebody wishing to go up or down, except for the top and bottom floors where there is only 1 call button. When a lift arrives and somebody enters the lift they press the number of the floor on which they wish to stop. Each lift stores the numbers and travels up or down, stopping at each floor that is requested.

Calculate the state and action spaces for the system, and then describe a suitable reinforcement learner for this system. You need to devise a reward function as well as describe the learning method that you believe to be most appropriate. Should the system use delayed rewards? A good reinforcement learning system provides a very effective algorithm for this problem (as compared to standard naïve methods for lift scheduling). Explain why this could be the case, and give possible problems with using a reinforcement learner.

Problem 11.5 It is possible to write a learning Connect-4 player. In case you don't remember Connect-4, the game is played on a grid board of 7×6. Two players take it in turns to drop tokens into the grid where they fill the lowest available spot in the chosen column. The aim is to get four of your coloured tokens in a row. In case that doesn't make sense, or just because you are feeling nostalgic, there are plenty of versions of the game on the Internet.

The state space of Connect-4 is not easy to think about. There is 1 state with no counters on it, 7 states with 1 counter in them (assuming that the same colour counter always starts): one state for the counter being in each row, and 7 again for 2 counters being on the board. However, from there the number of states mushrooms. In the case where the game is a draw, so that all of the squares are full, there is something less than $2^{7\times6} = 2^{42}$ states. I say something less because this counts all the cases that include a line of 4, and also ignores the fact that there are only 21 counters of each colour. The fact remains that the state space is immense, so it is probably going to take a long time to learn.

However, programming the game is relatively simple. There are two absorbing states: when the board is full, and when somebody wins. In either of these cases a reward is given. So you will have to decide on rewards, and write some code that detects when one or the other state has happened. The choice that is made at each turn is simply which column to add the new counter in, so there are only seven possible actions. You need to represent the board, for which I'd recommend a 2D array with 0 meaning empty, 1 meaning contains a red counter, and 2 meaning contains a yellow counter. This should make it easy to detect the absorbing states.

Having set up that lot, you need to make a number of modifications to the Q-learning code. Firstly, you are not going to pass in transition and reward matrices, since making them would be crazy. You are probably going to give a reward of 0 to every move except a win and a loss, so change the code to present those rewards. You then need to change the ϵ-greedy search strategy to simply pick a random (but not full) column, rather than look at the transition matrix. Then that's it; set it running (and be prepared to wait for a very long time. I trained the algorithm for 20,000 games against a purely random player, and at the end of that the Q-learner was winning about 80% of the games).

## CHAPTER 12

Learning with Trees

We are now going to consider a rather different approach to machine learning, starting with one of the most common and powerful data structures in the whole of computer science: the binary tree. The computational cost of making the tree is fairly low, but the cost of using it is even lower: $\mathcal{O}(\log N)$, where N is the number of datapoints. This is important for machine learning, since querying the trained algorithm should be as fast as possible since it happens more often, and the result is often wanted immediately. This is sufficient to make trees seem attractive for machine learning. However, they do have other benefits, such as the fact that they are easy to understand (following a tree to get a classification answer is transparent, which makes people trust it more than getting an answer from a 'black box' neural network).

For these reasons, classification by **decision trees** has grown in popularity over recent years. You are very likely to have been subjected to decision trees if you've ever phoned a helpline, for example for computer faults. The phone operators are guided through the decision tree by your answers to their questions.

The idea of a decision tree is that we break classification down into a set of choices about each feature in turn, starting at the **root** (base) of the tree and progressing down to the **leaves**, where we receive the classification decision. The trees are very easy to understand, and can even be turned into a set of if-then rules, suitable for use in a **rule induction** system.

In terms of optimisation and search, decision trees use a greedy heuristic to perform search, evaluating the possible options at the current stage of learning and making the one that seems optimal at that point. This works well a surprisingly large amount of the time.

12.1 USING DECISION TREES

As a student it can be difficult to decide what to do in the evening. There are four things that you actually quite enjoy doing, or have to do: going to the pub, watching TV, going to a party, or even (gasp) studying. The choice is sometimes made for you—if you have an assignment due the next day, then you need to study, if you are feeling lazy then the pub isn't for you, and if there isn't a party then you can't go to it. You are looking for a nice algorithm that will let you decide what to do each evening without having to think about it every night. Figure 12.1 provides just such an algorithm.

Each evening you start at the top (root) of the tree and check whether any of your friends know about a party that night. If there is one, then you need to go, regardless. Only if there is not a party do you worry about whether or not you have an assignment deadline coming up. If there is a crucial deadline, then you have to study, but if there is nothing that is urgent for the next few days, you think about how you feel. A sudden burst of energy

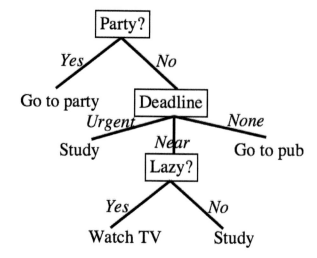

FIGURE 12.1 A simple decision tree to decide how you will spend the evening.

might make you study, but otherwise you'll be slumped in front of the TV indulging your secret love of Shortland Street (or other soap opera of your choice) rather than studying. Of course, near the start of the semester when there are no assignments to do, and you are feeling rich, you'll be in the pub.

One of the reasons that decision trees are popular is that we can turn them into a set of logical disjunctions (if ... then rules) that then go into program code very simply—the first part of the tree above can be turned into:

- if *there is a party* then *go to it*
- if *there is not a party* and *you have an urgent deadline* then *study*
- etc.

That's all that there is to using the decision tree. Compare it to the previous use of this data, with the Naïve Bayes Classifier in Section 2.3.2. The far more interesting part is how to construct the tree from data, and that is the focus of the next section.

12.2 CONSTRUCTING DECISION TREES

In the example above, the three features that we need for the algorithm are the state of your energy level, the date of your nearest deadline, and whether or not there is a party tonight. The question we need to ask is how, based on those features, we can construct the tree. There are a few different decision tree algorithms, but they are almost all variants of the same principle: the algorithms build the tree in a greedy manner starting at the root, choosing the most informative feature at each step. We are going to start by focusing on the most common: Quinlan's ID3, although we'll also mention its extension, known as C4.5, and another known as CART.

There was an important word hidden in the sentence above about how the trees work, which was informative. Choosing which feature to use next in the decision tree can be thought of as playing the game '20 Questions', where you try to elicit the item your opponent is thinking about by asking questions about it. At each stage, you choose a question that gives you the most information given what you know already. Thus, you would ask 'Is it an animal?' before you ask 'Is it a cat?'. The idea is to quantify this question of how much information is provided to you by knowing certain facts. Encoding this mathematically is the task of information theory.

12.2.1 Quick Aside: Entropy in Information Theory

Information theory was 'born' in 1948 when Claude Shannon published a paper called "A Mathematical Theory of Communication." In that paper, he proposed the measure of information *entropy*, which describes the amount of impurity in a set of features. The entropy H of a set of probabilities p_i is (for those who know some physics, the relation to physical entropy should be clear):

$$\text{Entropy}(p) = -\sum_i p_i \log_2 p_i, \qquad (12.1)$$

where the logarithm is base 2 because we are imagining that we encode everything using binary digits (bits), and we define $0 \log 0 = 0$. A graph of the entropy is given in Figure 12.2. Suppose that we have a set of positive and negative examples of some feature (where the feature can only take 2 values: positive and negative). If all of the examples are positive, then we don't get any extra information from knowing the value of the feature for any particular example, since whatever the value of the feature, the example will be positive. Thus, the entropy of that feature is 0. However, if the feature separates the examples into 50% positive and 50% negative, then the amount of entropy is at a maximum, and knowing about that feature is very useful to us. The basic concept is that it tells us how much *extra* information we would get from knowing the value of that feature. A function for computing the entropy is very simple, as here:

```
def calc_entropy(p):

    if p!=0:
        return -p * np.log2(p)
    else:
        return 0
```

For our decision tree, the best feature to pick as the one to classify on now is the one that gives you the most information, i.e., the one with the highest entropy. After using that feature, we re-evaluate the entropy of each feature and again pick the one with the highest entropy.

Information theory is a very interesting subject. It is possible to download Shannon's 1948 paper from the Internet, and also to find many resources showing where it has been applied. There are now whole journals devoted to information theory because it is relevant to so many areas such as computer and telecommunication networks, machine learning, and data storage. Some further readings in the area are given at the end of the chapter.

12.2.2 ID3

Now that we have a suitable measure for choosing which feature to choose next, entropy, we just have to work out how to apply it. The important idea is to work out how much the entropy of the whole training set would decrease if we choose each particular feature for the next classification step. This is known as the *information gain*, and it is defined as

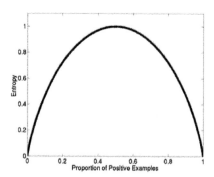

FIGURE 12.2 A graph of entropy, detailing how much information is available from finding out another piece of information given what you already know.

the entropy of the whole set minus the entropy when a particular feature is chosen. This is defined by (where S is the set of examples, F is a possible feature out of the set of all possible ones, and $|S_f|$ is a count of the number of members of S that have value f for feature F):

$$\text{Gain}(S, F) = \text{Entropy}(S) - \sum_{f \in values(F)} \frac{|S_f|}{|S|} \text{Entropy}(S_f). \quad (12.2)$$

As an example, suppose that we have data (with outcomes) $S = \{s_1 = \text{true}, s_2 = \text{false}, s_3 = \text{false}, s_4 = \text{false}\}$ and one feature F that can have values $\{f_1, f_2, f_3\}$. In the example, the feature value for s_1 could be f_2, for s_2 it could be f_2, for s_3, f_3 and for s_4, f_1 then we can calculate the entropy of S as (where $\oplus$ means true, of which we have one example, and $\ominus$ means false, of which we have three examples):

$$
\begin{aligned}
\text{Entropy}(S) &= -p_\oplus \log_2 p_\oplus - p_\ominus \log_2 p_\ominus \\
&= -\frac{1}{4} \log_2 \frac{1}{4} - \frac{3}{4} \log_2 \frac{3}{4} \\
&= 0.5 + 0.311 = 0.811. \quad (12.3)
\end{aligned}
$$

The function $\text{Entropy}(S_f)$ is similar, but only computed with the subset of data where feature F has values f.

If you were trying to follow those calculations on a calculator, you might be wondering how to compute $\log_2 p$. The answer is to use the identity $\log_2 p = \ln p / \ln(2)$, where ln is the natural logarithm, which your calculator can produce. NumPy has the `np.log2()` function.

We now want to compute the information gain of F, so we now need to compute each of the values inside the summation in Equation (12.2), $\frac{|S_f|}{|S|} \text{Entropy}(S)$ (in our example, the features are 'Deadline', 'Party', and 'Lazy'):

$$\frac{|S_{f_1}|}{|S|} \text{Entropy}(S_{f_1}) = \frac{1}{4} \times \left(-\frac{0}{1} \log_2 \frac{0}{1} - \frac{1}{1} \log_2 \frac{1}{1} \right)$$

$$= 0 \tag{12.4}$$

$$\frac{|S_{f_2}|}{|S|} \text{Entropy}(S_{f_2}) = \frac{2}{4} \times \left(-\frac{1}{2} \log_2 \frac{1}{2} - \frac{1}{2} \log_2 \frac{1}{2} \right)$$

$$= \frac{1}{2} \tag{12.5}$$

$$\frac{|S_{f_3}|}{|S|} \text{Entropy}(S_{f_3}) = \frac{1}{4} \times \left(-\frac{0}{1} \log_2 \frac{0}{1} - \frac{1}{1} \log_2 \frac{1}{1} \right)$$

$$= 0 \tag{12.6}$$

The information gain from adding this feature is the entropy of S minus the sum of the three values above:

$$\text{Gain}(S, F) = 0.811 - (0 + 0.5 + 0) = 0.311. \tag{12.7}$$

This can be computed in an algorithm using the following function (where lots of the code is to get the relevant data):

```
def calc_info_gain(data,classes,feature):
  gain = 0
  nData = len(data)
  # List the values that feature can take
  values = []
  for datapoint in data:
      if datapoint[feature] not in values:
          values.append(datapoint[feature])

  featureCounts = np.zeros(len(values))
  entropy = np.zeros(len(values))
  valueIndex = 0
  # Find where those values appear in data[feature] and the corresponding ⤸
  class
  for value in values:
      dataIndex = 0
      newClasses = []
      for datapoint in data:
          if datapoint[feature]==value:
              featureCounts[valueIndex]+=1
              newClasses.append(classes[dataIndex])
          dataIndex += 1

      # Get the values in newClasses
      classValues = []
      for aclass in newClasses:
          if classValues.count(aclass)==0:
              classValues.append(aclass)
```

```
    classCounts = np.zeros(len(classValues))
    classIndex = 0
    for classValue in classValues:
        for aclass in newClasses:
            if aclass == classValue:
                classCounts[classIndex]+=1
        classIndex += 1

    for classIndex in range(len(classValues)):
        entropy[valueIndex] += calc_entropy(float(classCounts[classIndex])
        /sum(classCounts))
        gain += float(featureCounts[valueIndex])/nData * entropy[valueIndex]
        valueIndex += 1
return gain
```

The ID3 algorithm computes this information gain for each feature and chooses the one that produces the highest value. In essence, that is all there is to the algorithm. It searches the space of possible trees in a greedy way by choosing the feature with the highest information gain at each stage. The output of the algorithm is the tree, i.e., a list of nodes, edges, and leaves. As with any tree in computer science, it can be constructed recursively. At each stage the best feature is selected and then removed from the dataset, and the algorithm is recursively called on the rest. The recursion stops when either there is only one class remaining in the data (in which case a leaf is added with that class as its label), or there are no features left, when the most common label in the remaining data is used.

The ID3 Algorithm

- If all examples have the same label:

    - return a leaf with that label

- Else if there are no features left to test:

    - return a leaf with the most common label

- Else:

    - choose the feature $\hat{F}$ that maximises the information gain of S to be the next node using Equation (12.2)
    - add a branch from the node for each possible value f in $\hat{F}$
    - for each branch:
        * calculate S_f by removing $\hat{F}$ from the set of features
        * recursively call the algorithm with S_f, to compute the gain relative to the current set of examples

---

Owing to the focus on classification for real-world examples, trees are often used with text features rather than numeric values. This makes it rather difficult to use NumPy, and so the sample implementation is pretty well pure Python. It uses a feature of Python that is uncommon in other languages, which is the **dictionary** in order to hold the tree, which uses the braces {, }, and which is described next before we look at the decision tree implementation.

12.2.3 Implementing Trees and Graphs in Python

Trees are really just a restricted version of graphs, since they both consist of nodes and edges between the nodes. Graphs are a very useful data structure in many different areas of computer science. There are two reasonable ways to represent a graph computationally. One is as an $N \times N$ matrix, where N is the number of nodes in the network. Each element of the matrix is a 1 if there is a link between the two nodes, and a 0 otherwise. The benefit of this approach is that it is easy to give weights to the links by changing the 1s to the values of the weights. The alternative is to store a list of nodes, following each by a list of nodes that it is linked to. Both are fairly natural in Python, with the second making use of the dictionary, a basic data structure that we have not used much, except for very simply in the decision tree (Chapter 12) that consists of a set of keys and values. For a graph, the key to each dictionary entry is the name of the node, and its value is a list of the nodes that it is connected to, as in this example:

```
graph = {'A': ['B', 'C'],'B': ['C', 'D'],'C': ['D'],'D': ['C'],'E': ['F'],
'F': ['C']}
```

That is all there is to it for creating the dictionary, and using it is not very different, since there are built-in methods to get a list of keys (`keys()`) and check if a key is in a dictionary (`in`). Code to find a path through the graph can then be written as a simple recursive function:

```
def findPath(graph, start, end, pathSoFar):
    pathSoFar = pathSoFar + [start]
    if start == end:
        return pathSoFar
    if start not in graph:
        return None
    for node in graph[start]:
        if node not in pathSoFar:
            newpath = findPath(graph, node, end, pathSoFar)
            return newpath
    return None
```

Using those methods we can now look at a Python implementation of the decision tree, which also has a recursive function call as its basis.

12.2.4 Implementation of the Decision Tree

The `make_tree()` function (which uses the `calc_entropy()` and `calc_info_gain()` functions that were described previously) looks like:

```
def make_tree(data,classes,featureNames):
    # Various initialisations suppressed
```

```
default = classes[np.argmax(frequency)]
if nData==0 or nFeatures == 0:
    # Have reached an empty branch
    return default
elif classes.count(classes[0]) == nData:
    # Only 1 class remains
    return classes[0]
else:
    # Choose which feature is best
    gain = np.zeros(nFeatures)
    for feature in range(nFeatures):
        g = calc_info_gain(data,classes,feature)
        gain[feature] = totalEntropy - g
    bestFeature = np.argmax(gain)
    tree = {featureNames[bestFeature]:{}}
    # Find the possible feature values
    for value in values:
        # Find the datapoints with each feature value
        for datapoint in data:
            if datapoint[bestFeature]==value:
                if bestFeature==0:
                    datapoint = datapoint[1:]
                    newNames = featureNames[1:]
                elif bestFeature==nFeatures:
                    datapoint = datapoint[:-1]
                    newNames = featureNames[:-1]
                else:
                    datapoint = datapoint[:bestFeature]
                    datapoint.extend(datapoint[bestFeature+1:])
                    newNames = featureNames[:bestFeature]
                    newNames.extend(featureNames[bestFeature+1:])
                newData.append(datapoint)
                newClasses.append(classes[index])
            index += 1
        # Now recurse to the next level
        subtree = make_tree(newData,newClasses,newNames)
        # And on returning, add the subtree on to the tree
        tree[featureNames[bestFeature]][value] = subtree
    return tree
```

It is worth considering how ID3 generalises from training examples to the set of all possible inputs. It uses a method known as the inductive bias. The choice of the next feature to add into the tree is the one with the highest information gain, which biases the algorithm towards smaller trees, since it tries to minimise the amount of information that is left. This is consistent with a well-known principle that short solutions are usually better than longer ones (not necessarily true, but simpler explanations are usually easier to remember and understand). You might have heard of this principle as 'Occam's Razor', although I prefer it as an acronym: KISS (Keep It Simple, Stupid). In fact, there is a sound information-theoretic way to write down this principle. It is known as the Minimum Description Length (MDL) and was proposed by Rissanen in 1989. In essence it says that the shortest description of something, i.e., the most compressed one, is the best description.

Note that the algorithm can deal with noise in the dataset, because the labels are assigned to the most common value of the target attribute. Another benefit of decision trees is that they can deal with missing data. Think what would happen if an example has a missing feature. In that case, we can skip that node of the tree and carry on without it, summing over all the possible values that that feature could have taken. This is virtually impossible to do with neural networks: how do you represent missing data when the computation is based on whether or not a neuron is firing? In the case of neural networks it is common to either throw away any datapoints that have missing data, or guess (more technically impute any missing values, either by identifying similar datapoints and using their value or by using the mean or median of the data values for that feature). This assumes that the data that is missing is randomly distributed within the dataset, not missing because of some unknown process.

Saying that ID3 is biased towards short trees is only partly true. The algorithm uses all of the features that are given to it, even if some of them are not necessary. This obviously runs the risk of overfitting, indeed it makes it very likely. There are a few things that you can do to avoid overfitting, the simplest one being to limit the size of the tree. You can also use a variant of early stopping by using a validation set and measuring the performance of the tree so far against it. However, the approach that is used in more advanced algorithms (most notably C4.5, which Quinlan invented to improve on ID3) is pruning.

There are a few versions of pruning, all of which are based on computing the full tree and reducing it, evaluating the error on a validation set. The most naïve version runs the decision tree algorithm until all of the features are used, so that it is probably overfitted, and then produces smaller trees by running over the tree, picking each node in turn, and replacing the subtree beneath every node with a leaf labelled with the most common classification of the subtree. The error of the pruned tree is evaluated on the validation set, and the pruned tree is kept if the error is the same as or less than the original tree, and rejected otherwise.

C4.5 uses a different method called rule post-pruning. This consists of taking the tree generated by ID3, converting it to a set of if-then rules, and then pruning each rule by removing preconditions if the accuracy of the rule increases without it. The rules are then sorted according to their accuracy on the training set and applied in order. The advantages of dealing with rules are that they are easier to read and their order in the tree does not matter, just their accuracy in the classification.

12.2.5 Dealing with Continuous Variables

One thing that we have not yet discussed is how to deal with continuous variables, we have only considered those with discrete sets of feature values. The simplest solution is to discretise the continuous variable. However, it is also possible to leave it continuous and modify the algorithm. For a continuous variable there is not just one place to split it: the variable can be broken between any pair of datapoints, as shown in Figure 12.3. It can, of course, be split in any of the infinite locations along the line as well, but they are no different to this smaller set of locations. Even this smaller set makes the algorithm more expensive for continuous variables than it is for discrete ones, since as well as calculating the information gain of each variable to pick the best one, the information gain of many points within each variable has to be computed. In general, only one split is made to a continuous

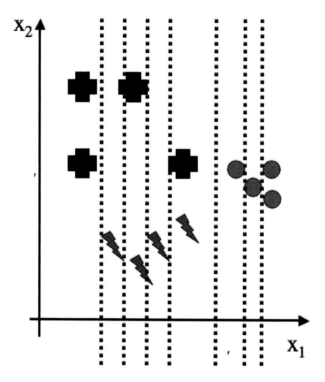

FIGURE 12.3 Possible places to split the variable x_1, between each of the datapoints as the feature value increases.

variable, rather than allowing for threeway or higher splits, although these can be done if necessary.

The trees that these algorithms make are all **univariate** trees, because they pick one feature (dimension) at a time and split according to that one. There are also algorithms that make **multivariate** trees by picking combinations of features. This can make for considerably smaller trees if it is possible to find straight lines that separate the data well, but are not parallel to any axis. However, univariate trees are simpler and tend to get good results, so we won't consider multivariate trees any further. This fact that one feature is chosen at a time provides another useful way to visualise what the decision tree is doing. Figure 12.4 shows the idea. Given a dataset that contains three classes, the algorithm picks a feature and value for that feature to split the remaining data into two. The final tree that results from this is shown in Figure 12.5.

12.2.6 Computational Complexity

The computational cost of constructing binary trees is well known for the general case, being $\mathcal{O}(N \log N)$ for construction and $\mathcal{O}(\log N)$ for returning a particular leaf, where N is the number of nodes. However, these results are for **balanced** binary trees, and decision trees are often not balanced; while the information measures attempt to keep the tree balanced by finding splits that separate the data into two even parts (since that will have the largest entropy), there is no guarantee of this. Nor are they necessarily binary, especially for ID3 and C4.5, as our example shows.

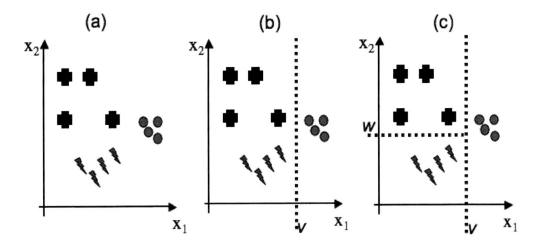

FIGURE 12.4 The effect of decision tree choices. The two-dimensional dataset shown in (a) is split first by choosing feature x_1 (b) and then x_2, (c) which separates out the three classes. The final tree is shown in Figure 12.5.

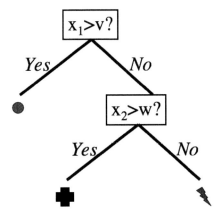

FIGURE 12.5 The final tree created by the splits in Figure 12.4.

If we assume that the tree is approximately balanced, then the cost at each node consists of searching through the d possible features (although this decreases by 1 at each level, that doesn't affect the complexity in the $\mathcal{O}(\cdot)$ notation) and then computing the information gain for the dataset for each split. This has cost $\mathcal{O}(dn \log n)$, where n is the size of the dataset at that node. For the root, $n = N$, and if the tree is balanced, then n is divided by 2 at each stage down the tree. Summing this over the approximately $\log N$ levels in the tree gives computational cost $\mathcal{O}(dN^2 \log N)$.

12.3 CLASSIFICATION AND REGRESSION TREES (CART)

There is another well-known tree-based algorithm, CART, whose name indicates that it can be used for both classification and regression. Classification is not wildly different in CART, although it is usually constrained to construct binary trees. This might seem odd at first, but there are sound computer science reasons why binary trees are good, as suggested in the computational cost discussion above, and it is not a real limation. Even in the example that we started the chapter with, we can always turn questions into binary decisions by splitting the question up a little. Thus, a question that has three answers (say the question about when your nearest assignment deadline is, which is either 'urgent', 'near', or 'none') can be split into two questions: first, 'is the deadline urgent?', and then if the answer to that is 'no', second 'is the deadline near?' The only real difference with classification in CART is that a different information measure is commonly used. This is discussed next, before we look briefly at regression with trees.

12.3.1 Gini Impurity

The entropy that was used in ID3 as the information measure is not the only way to pick features. Another possibility is something known as the Gini impurity. The 'impurity' in the name suggests that the aim of the decision tree is to have each leaf node represent a set of datapoints that are in the same class, so that there are no mismatches. This is known as purity. If a leaf is pure then all of the training data within it have just one class. In which case, if we count the number of datapoints at the node (or better, the fraction of the number of datapoints) that belong to a class i (call it $N(i)$), then it should be 0 for all except one value of i. So suppose that you want to decide on which feature to choose for a split. The algorithm loops over the different features and checks how many points belong to each class. If the node is pure, then $N(i) = 0$ for all values of i except one particular one. So for any particular feature k you can compute:

$$G_k = \sum_{i=1}^{c} \sum_{j \neq i} N(i) N(j), \tag{12.8}$$

where c is the number of classes. In fact, you can reduce the algorithmic effort required by noticing that $\sum_i N(i) = 1$ (since there has to be some output class) and so $\sum_{j \neq i} N(j) = 1 - N(i)$. Then Equation (12.8) is equivalent to:

$$G_k = 1 - \sum_{i=1}^{c} N(i)^2. \tag{12.9}$$

Either way, the Gini impurity is equivalent to computing the expected error rate if the classification was picked according to the class distribution. The information gain can then be measured in the same way, subtracting each value G_i from the total Gini impurity.

The information measure can be changed in another way, which is to add a weight to the misclassifications. The idea is to consider the cost of misclassifying an instance of class i as class j (which we will call the risk in Section 2.3.1) and add a weight that says how important each datapoint is. It is typically labelled as λ_{ij} and is presented as a matrix, with element λ_{ij} representing the cost of misclassifying i as j. Using it is simple, modifying the Gini impurity (Equation (12.8)) to be:

$$G_i = \sum_{j \neq i} \lambda_{ij} N(i) N(j). \tag{12.10}$$

We will see in Section 13.1 that there is another benefit to using these weights, which is to successively improve the classification ability by putting higher weight on datapoints that the algorithm is getting wrong.

12.3.2 Regression in Trees

The new part about CART is its application in regression. While it might seem strange to use trees for regression, it turns out to require only a simple modification to the algorithm. Suppose that the outputs are continuous, so that a regression model is appropriate. None of the node impurity measures that we have considered so far will work. Instead, we'll go back to our old favourite—the sum-of-squares error. To evaluate the choice of which feature to use next, we also need to find the value at which to split the dataset according to that feature. Remember that the output is a value at each leaf. In general, this is just a constant value for the output, computed as the mean average of all the datapoints that are situated in that leaf. This is the optimal choice in order to minimise the sum-of-squares error, but it also means that we can choose the split point quickly for a given feature, by choosing it to minimise the sum-of-squares error. We can then pick the feature that has the split point that provides the best sum-of-squares error, and continue to use the algorithm as for classification.

12.4 CLASSIFICATION EXAMPLE

We'll work through an example using ID3 in this section. The data that we'll use will be a continuation of the one we started the chapter with, about what to do in the evening.

When we want to construct the decision tree to decide what to do in the evening, we start by listing everything that we've done for the past few days to get a suitable dataset (here, the last ten days):

Deadline?	Is there a party?	Lazy?	Activity
Urgent	Yes	Yes	Party
Urgent	No	Yes	Study
Near	Yes	Yes	Party
None	Yes	No	Party
None	No	Yes	Pub
None	Yes	No	Party
Near	No	No	Study
Near	No	Yes	TV
Near	Yes	Yes	Party
Urgent	No	No	Study

To produce a decision tree for this problem, the first thing that we need to do is work out which feature to use as the root node. We start by computing the entropy of S:

$$
\begin{aligned}
\text{Entropy}(S) &= -p_{\text{party}} \log_2 p_{\text{party}} - p_{\text{study}} \log_2 p_{\text{study}} \\
&\quad - p_{\text{pub}} \log_2 p_{\text{pub}} - p_{\text{TV}} \log_2 p_{\text{TV}} \\
&= -\frac{5}{10} \log_2 \frac{5}{10} - \frac{3}{10} \log_2 \frac{3}{10} - \frac{1}{10} \log_2 \frac{1}{10} - \frac{1}{10} \log_2 \frac{1}{10} \\
&= 0.5 + 0.5211 + 0.3322 + 0.3322 = 1.6855
\end{aligned}
\tag{12.11}
$$

and then find which feature has the maximal information gain:

$$
\begin{aligned}
\text{Gain}(S, \text{Deadline}) &= 1.6855 - \frac{|S_{\text{urgent}}|}{10} \text{Entropy}(S_{\text{urgent}}) \\
&\quad - \frac{|S_{\text{near}}|}{10} \text{Entropy}(S_{\text{near}}) - \frac{|S_{\text{none}}|}{10} \text{Entropy}(S_{\text{none}}) \\
&= 1.6855 - \frac{3}{10} \left(-\frac{2}{3} \log_2 \frac{2}{3} - \frac{1}{3} \log_2 \frac{1}{3} \right) \\
&\quad - \frac{4}{10} \left(-\frac{2}{4} \log_2 \frac{2}{4} - \frac{1}{4} \log_2 \frac{1}{4} - \frac{1}{4} \log_2 \frac{1}{4} \right) \\
&\quad - \frac{3}{10} \left(-\frac{1}{3} \log_2 \frac{1}{3} - \frac{2}{3} \log_2 \frac{2}{3} \right) \\
&= 1.6855 - 0.2755 - 0.6 - 0.2755 \\
&= 0.5345
\end{aligned}
\tag{12.12}
$$

$$
\begin{aligned}
\text{Gain}(S, \text{Party}) &= 1.6855 - \frac{5}{10} \left(-\frac{5}{5} \log_2 \frac{5}{5} \right) \\
&\quad - \frac{5}{10} \left(-\frac{3}{5} \log_2 \frac{3}{5} - \frac{1}{5} \log_2 \frac{1}{5} - \frac{1}{5} \log_2 \frac{1}{5} \right) \\
&= 1.6855 - 0 - 0.6855 \\
&= 1.0
\end{aligned}
\tag{12.13}
$$

$$
\begin{aligned}
\text{Gain}(S, \text{Lazy}) &= 1.6855 - \frac{6}{10} \left(-\frac{3}{6} \log_2 \frac{3}{6} - \frac{1}{6} \log_2 \frac{1}{6} - \frac{1}{6} \log_2 \frac{1}{6} - \frac{1}{6} \log_2 \frac{1}{6} \right) \\
&\quad - \frac{4}{10} \left(-\frac{2}{4} \log_2 \frac{2}{4} - \frac{2}{4} \log_2 \frac{2}{4} \right) \\
&= 1.6855 - 1.0755 - 0.4 \\
&= 0.21
\end{aligned}
\tag{12.14}
$$

Therefore, the root node will be the party feature, which has two feature values ('yes' and 'no'), so it will have two branches coming out of it (see Figure 12.6). When we look at the 'yes' branch, we see that in all five cases where there was a party we went to it, so we just put a leaf node there, saying 'party'. For the 'no' branch, out of the five cases there are three different outcomes, so now we need to choose another feature. The five cases we are looking at are:

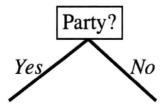

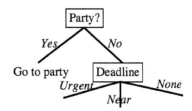

FIGURE 12.6 The decision tree after one step of the algorithm.

FIGURE 12.7 The tree after another step.

Deadline?	Is there a party?	Lazy?	Activity
Urgent	No	Yes	Study
None	No	Yes	Pub
Near	No	No	Study
Near	No	Yes	TV
Urgent	No	Yes	Study

We've used the party feature, so we just need to calculate the information gain of the other two over these five examples:

$$
\begin{aligned}
\text{Gain}(S, \text{Deadline}) &= 1.371 - \frac{2}{5}\left(-\frac{2}{2}\log_2\frac{2}{2}\right) \\
&\quad - \frac{2}{5}\left(-\frac{1}{2}\log_2\frac{1}{2} - \frac{1}{2}\log_2\frac{1}{2}\right) - \frac{1}{5}\left(-\frac{1}{1}\log_2\frac{1}{1}\right) \\
&= 1.371 - 0 - 0.4 - 0 \\
&= 0.971 \hspace{4cm} (12.15) \\
\text{Gain}(S, \text{Lazy}) &= 1.371 - \frac{4}{5}\left(-\frac{2}{4}\log_2\frac{2}{4} - \frac{1}{4}\log_2\frac{1}{4} - \frac{1}{4}\log_2\frac{1}{4}\right) \\
&\quad - \frac{1}{5}\left(-\frac{1}{1}\log_2\frac{1}{1}\right) \\
&= 1.371 - 1.2 - 0 \\
&= 0.1710 \hspace{3.8cm} (12.16)
\end{aligned}
$$

This leads to the tree shown in Figure 12.7. From this point it is relatively simple to complete the tree, leading to the one that was shown in Figure 12.1.

FURTHER READING

For more information about decision trees, the following two books are of interest:

- J.R. Quinlan. *C4.5: Programs for Machine Learning*. Morgan Kaufmann, San Francisco, CA, USA, 1993.

- L. Breiman, J.H. Friedman, R.A. Olshen, and C.J. Stone. *Classification and Regression Trees*. Chapman & Hall, New York, USA, 1993.

If you want to know more about information theory, then there are lots of books on the topic, including:

- T.M. Cover and J.A. Thomas. *Elements of Information Theory*. Wiley-Interscience, New York, USA, 1991.

- F.M. Reza. *An Introduction to Information Theory*. McGraw-Hill, New York, USA, 1961.

The original paper that started the field is:

- C.E. Shannon. A mathematical theory of information. *The Bell System Technical Journal*, 27(3):379–423 and 623–656, 1948.

A book that covers information theory and machine learning is:

- D.J.C. MacKay. *Information Thoery, Inference and Learning Algorithms*. Cambridge University Press, Cambridge, UK, 2003.

Other machine learning textbooks that cover decision trees include:

- Sections 8.2–8.4 of R.O. Duda, P.E. Hart, and D.G. Stork. *Pattern Classification*, 2nd edition, Wiley-Interscience, New York, USA, 2001.

- Chapter 7 of B.D. Ripley. *Pattern Recognition and Neural Networks*. Cambridge University Press, Cambridge, UK, 1996.

- Chapter 3 of T. Mitchell. *Machine Learning*. McGraw-Hill, New York, USA, 1997.

PRACTICE QUESTIONS

Problem 12.1 Suppose that the probability of five events are P(first) = 0.5, and P(second) = P(third) = P(fourth) = P(fifth) = 0.125. Calculate the entropy. Write down in words what this means.

Problem 12.2 Make a decision tree that computes the logical AND function. How does it compare to the Perceptron solution?

Problem 12.3 Turn this politically incorrect data from Quinlan into a decision tree to classify which attributes make a person attractive, and then extract the rules.

Height	Hair	Eyes	Attractive?
Small	Blonde	Brown	No
Tall	Dark	Brown	No
Tall	Blonde	Blue	Yes
Tall	Dark	Blue	No
Small	Dark	Blue	No
Tall	Red	Blue	Yes
Tall	Blonde	Brown	No
Small	Blonde	Blue	Yes

Problem 12.4 When you arrive at the pub, your five friends already have their drinks on the table. Jim has a job and buys the round half of the time. Jane buys the round a quarter of the time, and Sarah and Simon buy a round one eighth of the time. John hasn't got his wallet out since you met him three years ago.

Compute the entropy of each of them buying the round and work out how many questions you need to ask (on average) to find out who bought the round.

Two more friends now arrive and everybody spontaneously decides that it is your turn to buy a round (for all eight of you). Your friends set you the challenge of deciding who is drinking beer and who is drinking vodka according to their gender, whether or not they are students, and whether they went to the pub last night. Use ID3 to work it out, and then see if you can prune the tree.

Drink	Gender	Student	Pub last night
Beer	T	T	T
Beer	T	F	T
Vodka	T	F	F
Vodka	T	F	F
Vodka	F	T	T
Vodka	F	F	F
Vodka	F	T	T
Vodka	F	T	T

Problem 12.5 Use the naïve Bayes classifier from Section 2.3.2 on the datasets that you used for the decision tree (this will involve some effort in turning the textual data into probabilities) and compare the results.

Problem 12.6 The CPU dataset in the UCI repository is a very good regression problem for a decision tree. You will need to modify the decision tree code so that it does regression, as discussed in Section 12.3.2. You will also have to work out the Gini impurity for multiple classes.

Problem 12.7 Modify the implementation to deal with continuous variables, as discussed in Section 12.2.5.

Problem 12.8 The misclassification impurity is:

$$N(i) = 1 - \max_j P(w_j). \tag{12.17}$$

Add this into the code and test the new version on some of the datasets above.

## CHAPTER 13

Decision by Committee: Ensemble Learning

The old saying has it that two heads are better than one. Which naturally leads to the idea that even more heads are better than that, and ends up with decision by committee, which is famously useless for human activities (as in the old joke that a camel is a horse designed by a committee). For machine learning methods the results are rather more impressive, as we'll see in this chapter.

The basic idea is that by having lots of learners that each get slightly different results on a dataset—some learning certain things well and some learning others—and putting them together, the results that are generated will be significantly better than any one of them on its own (provided that you put them together well... otherwise the results could be significantly worse). One analogy that might prove useful is to think about how your doctor goes about performing a diagnosis of some complaint that you visit her with. If she cannot find the problem directly, then she will ask for a variety of tests to be performed, e.g., scans, blood tests, consultations with experts. She will then aggregate all of these opinions in order to perform a diagnosis. Each of the individual tests will suggest a diagnosis, but only by putting them together can an informed decision be reached.

Figure 13.1 shows the basic idea of **ensemble learning**, as these methods are collectively called. Given a relatively simple binary classification problem and some learner that puts an ellipse around a subset of the data, combining the ellipses can provide a considerably more complex decision boundary.

There are then only a couple of questions to ask: which learners should we use, how should we ensure that they learn different things, and how should we combine their results? The methods that we are investigating in this chapter can use any classifier at all. Although in general they only use one type of classifier at a time, they do not have to. A common choice of classifier is the decision tree (see Chapter 12).

Ensuring that the learners see different things can be performed in different ways, and it is the primary difference between the algorithms that we shall see. However, it can also come about naturally depending upon the application area. Suppose that you have lots and lots of data. In that case you could simply randomly partition the data and give different sets of data to different classifiers. Even here there are choices: do you make the partitions separate, or include overlaps? If there is no overlap, then it could be difficult to work out how to combine the classifiers, or it might be very simple: if your doctor always asks for opinions from two colleagues, one specialising in heart problems and one in sports injuries,

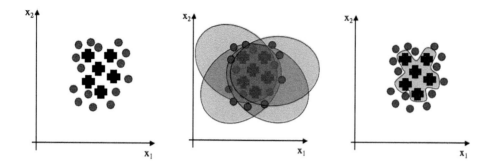

FIGURE 13.1 By combining lots of simple classifiers (here that simply put an elliptical decision boundary onto the data), the decision boundary can be made much more complicated, enabling the difficult separation of the pluses from the circles.

then upon discovering that your leg started hurting after you went for a run she would likely accord more weight to the diagnosis of the sports injury expert.

Interestingly, ensemble methods do very well when there is very little data as well as when there is too much. To see why, think cross-validation (Section 2.2.2). We used cross-validation when there was not enough data to go around, and trained lots of neural networks on different subsets of the data. Then we threw away most of them. With an ensemble method we keep them all, and combine their results in some way. One very simple way to combine the results is to use majority voting — if it's good enough for electing governments in elections, it's good enough for machine learning. Majority voting has the interesting property that for binary classification, the combined classifier will only get the answer wrong if more than half of the classifiers were wrong. Hopefully, this isn't going to happen too often (although you might be able to think of government elections where this has been the case in your view). There are alternative ways to combine the results, as we'll discuss. These things will become clearer as we look at the algorithms, so let's get started.

13.1 BOOSTING

At first sight the claim of the most popular ensemble method, boosting, seems amazing. If we take a collection of very poor (weak in the jargon) learners, each performing only just better than chance, then by putting them together it is possible to make an ensemble learner that can perform arbitrarily well. So we just need lots of low-quality learners, and a way to put them together usefully, and we can make a learner that will do very well.

The principal algorithm of boosting is named AdaBoost, and is described in Section 13.1.1. The algorithm was first described in the mid-1990s by Freund and Shapiro, and while it has had many variations derived from it, the principal algorithm is still one of the most widely used. The algorithm was proposed as an improvement on the original 1990 boosting algorithm, which was rather data hungry. In that algorithm, the training set was split into three. A classifier was trained on the first third, and then tested on the second third. All of the data that was misclassified during that testing was used to form a new dataset, along with an equally sized random selection of the data that was correctly classified. A second classifier was trained on this new dataset, and then both of the classifiers were tested on the final third of the dataset. If they both produced the same output, then that datapoint was ignored, otherwise the datapoint was added to yet another new

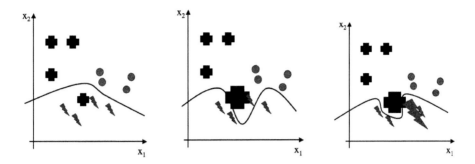

FIGURE 13.2 As points are misclassified, so their weights increase in boosting (shown by the datapoint getting larger), which makes the importance of those datapoints increase, making the classifiers pay more attention to them.

dataset, which formed the training set for a third classifer. Rather than looking further at this version, we will look at the more common algorithm.

13.1.1 AdaBoost

The innovation that AdaBoost (which stands for **adaptive boosting**) uses is to give weights to each datapoint according to how difficult previous classifiers have found to get it correct. These weights are given to the classifier as part of the input when it is trained.

The AdaBoost algorithm is conceptually very simple. At each iteration a new classifier is trained on the training set, with the weights that are applied to the training set for each datapoint being modified at each iteration according to how successfully that datapoint has been classified in the past. The weights are initially all set to the same value, $1/N$, where N is the number of datapoints in the training set. Then, at each iteration, the error (ϵ) is computed as the sum of the weights of the misclassified points, and the weights for incorrect examples are updated by being multiplied by $\alpha = (1 - \epsilon)/\epsilon$. Weights for correct examples are left alone, and then the whole set is normalised so that it sums to 1 (which is effectively a reduction in the importance of the correctly classified datapoints). Training terminates after a set number of iterations, or when either all of the datapoints are classified correctly, or one point contains more than half of the available weight.

Figure 13.2 shows the effect of weighting incorrectly classified examples as training proceeds, with the size of each datapoint being a measure of its importance. As an algorithm this looks like (where $I(y_n \neq h_t(x_n))$ is an **indicator function** that returns 1 if the target and output are not equal, and 0 if they are):

AdaBoost Algorithm

- Initialise all weights to $1/N$, where N is the number of datapoints

- While $0 < \epsilon_t < \frac{1}{2}$ (and $t < T$, some maximum number of iterations):

  - train classifier on $\{S, w^{(t)}\}$, getting hypotheses $h_t(x_n)$ for datapoints x_n

  - compute training error $\epsilon_t = \sum_{n=1}^{N} w_n^{(t)} I(y_n \neq h_t(x_n))$

  - set $\alpha_t = \log\left(\frac{1-\epsilon_t}{\epsilon_t}\right)$

  - update weights using:

  $$w_n^{(t+1)} = w_n^{(t)} \exp(\alpha_t I(y_n \neq h_t(x_n))/Z_t, \tag{13.1}$$

  where Z_t is a normalisation constant

- Output $f(x) = \text{sign}\left(\sum_{t=1}^{T} \alpha_t h_t(x)\right)$

There is nothing too difficult to the implementation, either, as can be seen from the main loop here:

```
for t in range(T):
    classifiers[:,t] = train(data,classes,w[:,t])
    outputs,errors = classify(data,classifiers[0,t],classifiers[1,t])

    index[:,t] = errors
    print "index: ", index[:,t]
    e[t] = np.sum(w[:,t]*index[:,t])/np.sum(w[:,t])

    if t>0 and (e[t]==0 or e[t]>=0.5):
        T=t
        alpha = alpha[:t]
        index = index[:,:t]
        w = w[:,:t]
        break

    alpha[t] = np.log((1-e[t])/e[t])
    w[:,t+1] = w[:,t]* np.exp(alpha[t]*index[:,t])
    w[:,t+1] = w[:,t+1]/np.sum(w[:,t+1])
```

Most of the work of the algorithm is done by the classification algorithm, which is given new weights at each iteration. In this respect, boosting is not quite a stand-alone algorithm: the classifiers need to consider the weights when they perform their classifications. It is not always obvious how to do this for a particular classifier, but we have seen methods of doing it for a few classifiers. For the decision tree we saw a method in Section 12.3.1,

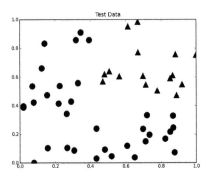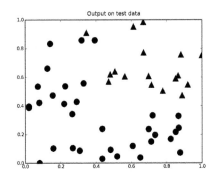

FIGURE 13.3 Boosting learns this simple dataset very successfully, producing an ensemble classifier that is rather more complicated than the simple horizontal or vertical line classifier that the algorithm boosts. On the independent test set shown here, the algorithm gets only 1 datapoint wrong, and that is one that is coincidentally close to one that was misclassified to simulate noise in the training data.

when we looked at the Gini impurity. There, we allowed for a $\boldsymbol{\lambda}$ matrix that encoded the risks associated with misclassification, and these are a perfect place in which to introduce weights. Modification of the decision tree algorithm to deal with these weights is suggested as an exercise for this chapter. A similar argument can be used for the Bayes' classifier; this was discussed in Section 2.3.1.

As a very simple example showing how boosting works, a very simple classifier was created that can only separate data by fitting one either horizontal or vertical line, with it choosing which to fit at the current iteration at random. A two-dimensional dataset was created with data in the top right-hand corner being in one class, and the rest in another, plus a couple of the datapoints were randomly mislabelled to simulate noise. Clearly, this dataset cannot be separated by a single horizontal or vertical decision boundary. However, Figure 13.3 shows the output of the classifier on an independent test set, where the algorithm gets only one datapoint wrong, and that is one that is coincidentally close to one of the 'noisy' datapoints in the training data. Figure 13.4 shows the training data, the error curve on both the training and testing sets, and the first few iterations of the classifier, which can only put in one horizontal or linear classification line.

Clearly, such impressive results require some explanation and understanding. The key to this understanding is to compute the **loss function**, which is simply the measure of the error that is applied (we have been using a sum-of-squares loss function for many algorithms in the book). The loss function for AdaBoost has the form

$$G_t(\alpha) = \sum_{n=1}^{N} \exp\left(-y_n(\alpha h_t(x_n) + f_{t-1}(x_n))\right), \tag{13.2}$$

where $f_{t-1}(x_n)$ is the sum of the hypotheses of that datapoint from the previous iterations:

$$f_{t-1}(x_n) = \sum_{\tau=0}^{t-1} \alpha_\tau h_\tau(x_n). \tag{13.3}$$

Exponential loss functions are well behaved and robust to outliers. The weights $w^{(t)}$

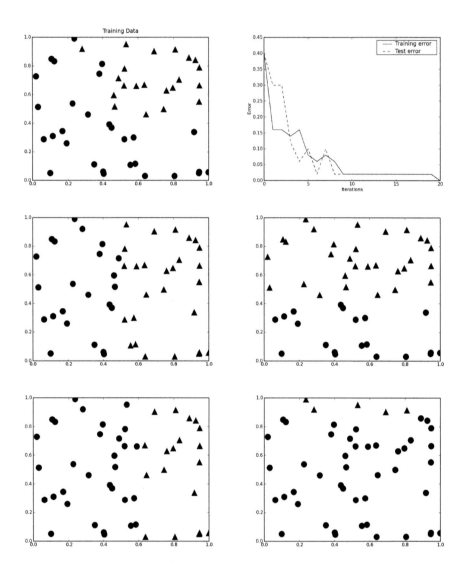

FIGURE 13.4 *Top:* the training data and the error curve. *Middle and bottom:* The first few iterations of the classifier; each plot shows the output of one of the weak classifiers that are boosted by the algorithm.

in the algorithm are nothing more than the second term in Equation (13.2), which can therefore be rewritten as:

$$G_t(\alpha) = \sum_{n=1}^{N} w^{(t)} \exp\left(-y_n \alpha h_t(x_n)\right). \tag{13.4}$$

Deriving the rest of the algorithm from here requires substituting in for the hypotheses h and then solving for α, which produces the full algorithm. Interestingly, this is not the way that AdaBoost was created; this understanding of why it works so well came later. It is possible to choose other loss functions, and providing that they are differentiable they will provide useful boosting-like algorithms, which are collectively known as **arcing** algorithms (for **adaptive reweighting and combining**).

AdaBoost can be modified to perform regression rather than classification (known as **real adaboost**, or sometimes **adaboost.R**). There is another variant on boosting (also called **AdaBoost**, confusingly) that uses the weights to sample from the full dataset, training on a sample of the data rather than the full weighted set, with more difficult examples more likely to be in the training sample. This is more in line with the original boosting algorithm, and is obviously faster, since each training run has fewer data to learn about.

13.1.2 Stumping

There is a very extreme form of boosting that is applied to trees. It goes by the descriptive name of **stumping**. The stump of a tree is the tiny piece that is left over when you chop off the rest, and the same is true here: stumping consists of simply taking the root of the tree and using that as the decision maker. So for each classifier you use the very first question that makes up the root of the tree, and that is it. Often, this is worse than chance on the whole dataset, but by using the weights to sort out when that classifier should be used, and to what extent, as opposed to the other ones, the overall output of stumping can be very successful. In fact, it is pretty much exactly what the simple example that we saw consisted of.

13.2 BAGGING

The simplest method of combining classifiers is known as **bagging**, which stands for **bootstrap aggregating**, the statistical description of the method. This is fine if you know what a **bootstrap** is, but fairly useless if you don't. A bootstrap sample is a sample taken from the original dataset **with replacement**, so that we may get some data several times and others not at all. The bootstrap sample is the same size as the original, and lots and lots of these samples are taken: B of them, where B is at least 50, and could even be in the thousands. The name bootstrap is more popular in computer science than anywhere else, since there is also a bootstrap loader, which is the first program to run when a computer is turned on. It comes from the nonsensical idea of 'picking yourself up by your bootstraps,' which means lifting yourself up by your shoelaces, and is meant to imply starting from nothing.

Bootstrap sampling seems like a very strange thing to do. We've taken a perfectly good dataset, mucked it up by sampling from it, which might be good if we had made a smaller dataset (since it would be faster), but we still ended up with a dataset the same size. Worse, we've done it lots of times. Surely this is just a way to burn up computer time without gaining anything. The benefit of it is that we will get lots of learners that perform slightly differently, which is exactly what we want for an ensemble method. Another benefit is that estimates of the accuracy of the classification function can be made without complicated analytic work, by throwing computer resources at the problem (technically, bagging is a variance reducing algorithm; the meaning of this will become clearer when we talk about bias and variance in Section 2.5). This is a standard technique in modern statistics; we'll see another example in Chapter 15 when we look at Markov Chain Monte Carlo methods. It is sufficiently common to have inspired the comment that "statistics is defined as the discipline where those that think don't count and those that count don't think."

Having taken a set of bootstrap samples, the bagging method simply requires that we fit a model to each dataset, and then combine them by taking the output to be the majority vote of all the classifiers. A NumPy implementation is shown next, and then we will look at a simple example.

```
# Compute bootstrap samples
samplePoints = np.random.randint(0,nPoints,(nPoints,nSamples))
classifiers = []

for i in range(nSamples):
  sample = []
  sampleTarget = []
  for j in range(nPoints):
    sample.append(data[samplePoints[j,i]])
    sampleTarget.append(targets[samplePoints[j,i]])
  # Train classifiers
  classifiers.append(self.tree.make_tree(sample,sampleTarget,features))
```

The example consists of taking the party data that was used in Section 12.4 to demonstrate the decision tree, and restricting the trees to stumps, so that they can make a classification based on just one variable. The output of a decision tree that uses the whole dataset for this is not surprising: it takes the two largest classes, and separates them. However, using just stumps of trees and 20 samples, bagging can separate the data perfectly, as this output shows:

```
Tree Stump Prediction
['Party', 'Party', 'Party', 'Party', 'Pub', 'Party', 'Study', 'Study', ⟩
'Party', 'Study']
Correct Classes
['Party', 'Study', 'Party', 'Party', 'Pub', 'Party', 'Study', 'TV', 'Party', ⟩
'Study']
Bagged Results
['Party', 'Study', 'Party', 'Party', 'Pub', 'Party', 'Study', 'TV', 'Party', ⟩
'Study']
```

13.2.1 Subagging

For some reason, ensemble methods often have good names, such as boosting and bagging (and we will see my choice for best-named, bragging, in Section 13.4). However, the method of subagging wins the prize for the oddest sounding word. It is a combination of 'subsample' and 'bagging,' and it is the fairly obvious idea that you don't need to produce samples that are the same size as the original data. If you make smaller datasets, then it makes sense to sample without replacement, but otherwise the implementation is only very slightly different from the bagging one, except that in NumPy you use `np.random.shuffle()` to produce the samples. It is common to use a dataset size that is half that of the original data, and the results of this can often be comparable to a full bagging simulation.

13.3 RANDOM FORESTS

If there is one method in machine learning that has grown in popularity over the last few years, then it is the idea of random forests. The concept has been around for longer than that, with several different people inventing variations, but the name that is most strongly attached to it is that of Breiman, who also described the CART algorithm that was discussed in Section 12.2, and also gave bagging its name.

The idea is largely that if one tree is good, then many trees (a forest) should be better, provided that there is enough variety between them. The most interesting thing about a random forest is the ways that it creates randomness from a standard dataset. The first of the methods that it uses is the one that we have just seen: bagging. If we wish to create a forest then we can make the trees different by training them on slightly different data, so we take bootstrap samples from the dataset for each tree. However, this isn't enough randomness yet. The other obvious place where it is possible to add randomness is to limit the choices that the decision tree can make. At each node, a random subset of the features is given to the tree, and it can only pick from that subset rather than from the whole set.

As well as increasing the randomness in the training of each tree, it also speeds up the training, since there are fewer features to search over at each stage. Of course, it does introduce a new parameter (how many features to consider), but the random forest does not seem to be very sensitive to this parameter; in practice, a subset size that is the square root of the number of features seems to be common. The effect of these two forms of randomness is to reduce the variance without effecting the bias. Another benefit of this is that there is no need to prune the trees. There is another parameter that we don't know how to choose yet, which is the number of trees to put into the forest. However, this is fairly easy to pick if we want optimal results: we can keep on building trees until the error stops decreasing.

Once the set of trees are trained, the output of the forest is the majority vote for classification, as with the other committee methods that we have seen, or the mean response for regression. And those are pretty much the main features needed for creating a random forest. The algorithm is given next before we see some results of using the random forest.

The Basic Random Forest Training Algorithm

- For each of N trees:
    - create a new bootstrap sample of the training set
    - use this bootstrap sample to train a decision tree
    - at each node of the decision tree, randomly select m features, and compute the information gain (or Gini impurity) only on that set of features, selecting the optimal one
    - repeat until the tree is complete

The implementation of this is very easy: we modify the decision to take an extra parameter, which is m, the number of features that should be used in the selection set at each stage. We will look at an example of using it shortly as a comparison to boosting.

Looking at the algorithm you might be able to see that it is a very unusual machine learning method because it is **embarrassingly parallel**: since the trees do not depend upon each other, you can both create and get decisions from different trees on different individual processors if you have them. This means that the random forest can run on as many processors as you have available with nearly linear speedup.

There is one more nice thing to mention about random forests, which is that with a little bit of programming effort they come with built-in test data: the bootstrap sample will miss out about 35% of the data on average, the so-called out-of-bootstrap examples. If we keep track of these datapoints then they can be used as novel samples for that particular tree, giving an estimated test error that we get without having to use any extra datapoints. This avoids the need for cross-validation.

As a brief example of using the random forest, we start by demonstrating that the random forest gets the correct results on the Party example that has been used in both this and the previous chapters, based on 10 trees, each trained on 7 samples, and with just two levels allowed in each tree:

```
RF prediction
['Party', 'Study', 'Party', 'Party', 'Pub', 'Party', 'Study', 'TV', 'Party', ↵
'Study']
```

As a rather more involved example, the **car evaluation** dataset in the UCI Repository contains 1,728 examples aiming to classify whether or not a car is a good purchase based on six attributes. The following results compare a single decision tree, bagging, and a random forest with 50 trees, each based on 100 samples, and with a maximum depth of five for each tree. It can be seen that the random forest is the most accurate of the three methods.

```
Tree
Number correctly predicted 777.0
Number of testpoints  864
Percentage Accuracy  89.9305555556

Number of cars rated as good or very good 39.0
Number correctly identified as good or very good 18.0
Percentage Accuracy 46.1538461538
-----
Bagger
Number correctly predicted 678.0
Number of testpoints  864
Percentage Accuracy  78.4722222222

Number of cars rated as good or very good 39.0
Number correctly identified as good or very good 0.0
Percentage Accuracy 0.0
-----
```

```
Forest
Number correctly predicted 793.0
Number of testpoints  864
Percentage Accuracy  91.7824074074

Number of cars rated as good or very good 39.0
Number correctly identified as good or very good 20.0
Percentage Accuracy 51.28205128
```

13.3.1 Comparison with Boosting

There are some obvious similarities to boosting (Section 13.1), but it is the differences that are most telling. The most general thing is that boosting is exhaustive, in that it searches over the whole set of features at each stage, and each stage depends on the previous one. This means that boosting has to run sequentially, and the individual steps can be expensive to run. By way of contrast, the parallelism of the random forest and the fact that it only searches over a fairly small set of features at each stage speed the algorithm up a lot.

Since the algorithm only searches a small subset of the data at each stage, it cannot be expected to be as good as boosting for the same number of trees. However, since the trees are cheaper to train, we can make more of them in the same computational time, and often the results are amazingly good even on very large and complicated datasets.

In fact, the most amazing thing about random forests is that they seem to deal very well with really big datasets. It is fairly clear that they should do well computationally, since both the reduced number of features to search over and the ability to parallelise should help there. However, they seem to also produce good outputs based on surprisingly small parts of the problem space seen by each tree.

13.4 DIFFERENT WAYS TO COMBINE CLASSIFIERS

Bagging puts most of its effort into ensuring that the different classifiers see different data, since they see different samples of the data. This is different than boosting, where the data stays the same, but the importance of each datapoint changes for the different classifiers, since they each get different weights according to how well the previous classifiers have performed. Just as important for an ensemble method, though, is how it combines the outputs of the different classifiers. Both boosting and bagging take a vote from amongst the classifiers, although they do it in different ways: boosting takes a weighted vote, while bagging simple takes the majority vote. There are other alternatives to these methods, as well.

In fact, even majority voting is not necessarily simple. Some classification systems will only produce an output where all the classifiers agree, or more than half of them agree, whereas others simply take the most common output, which is what we usually mean by majority voting. The idea of not always producing an output is to ensure that the ensemble does not produce outputs that are contentious, because they are probably difficult datapoints. If the number of classifiers is odd and the classifiers are each independent of each other, then majority voting will return the correct label if more than half of the classifiers agree. Assuming that each individual classifier has a success rate of p, the probability of the ensemble getting the correct answer is a **binomial distribution** of the form:

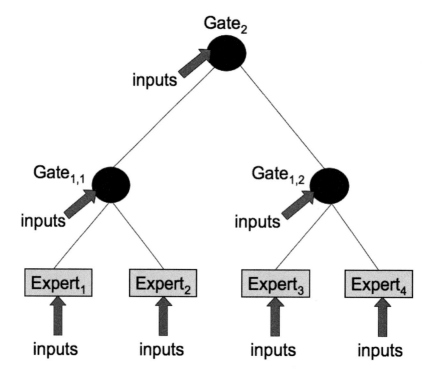

FIGURE 13.5 The Hierarchical Mixture of Networks network, consisting of a set of classifiers (experts) with gating systems that also use the inputs to decide which classifiers to trust.

$$\sum_{k=T/2+1}^{T} \left(\begin{array}{c} T \\ k \end{array} \right) p^k (1 - p)^{T-k}, \tag{13.5}$$

where T is the number of classifiers. If $p > 0.5$, then this sum approaches 1 as $T \to \infty$. This is a lot of the power behind ensemble methods: even if each classifier only gets about half the answers right, if we use a decent number of classifiers (maybe 100), then the probability of the ensemble being correct gets close to 1. In fact, even with less than 50% chance of success for each individual classifier, the ensemble can often do very well indeed.

For regression problems, rather than taking the majority vote, it is common to take the mean of the outputs. However, the mean is heavily affected by outliers, with the result that the median is a more common average to use. It is the use of the median that produces the bragging algorithm, which is meant to imply 'robust bagging'.

There is one more thing that can be done to combine classifiers, and that is to learn how to do it. There is an algorithm that does precisely this, known as the mixture of experts. Inputs are presented to the network, and each individual classifier makes an assessment. These outputs from the classifiers are then weighted by the relevant gate, which produces a weight w using the current inputs, and this is propagated further up the hierarchy. The most common version of the mixture of experts works as follows:

The Mixture of Experts Algorithm

- For each expert:

  - calculate the probability of the input belonging to each possible class by computing (where the $\mathbf{w}_i$ are the weights for that classifier):

$$o_i(\mathbf{x}, \mathbf{w}_i) = \frac{1}{1 + \exp(-\mathbf{w}_i \cdot \mathbf{x})}. \tag{13.6}$$

- For each gating network up the tree:

  - compute:

$$g_i(\mathbf{x}, \mathbf{v}_i) = \frac{\exp(\mathbf{v}_i \mathbf{x})}{\sum_l \exp(\mathbf{v}_l \mathbf{x})}. \tag{13.7}$$

- Pass as input to the next level gates (where the sum is over the relevant inputs to that gate):

$$\sum_k o_j g_j. \tag{13.8}$$

The most common way to train this network is using an **EM algorithm**. This is a general statistical approximation algorithm that is discussed in Section 7.1.1. It is also possible to use gradient descent on the parameters.

There are a couple of other ways to view these mixture of experts methods. One is to regard them as trees, except that the splits are not the **hard** splits that we performed in Chapter 12, but rather **soft**, because they are based on probability. The other is to compare them with radial basis function (RBF) networks (see Section 5.2). Each RBF gave a constant output within its receptive field. If, instead, each node were to give a linear approximation to the data, then the result would be the mixture of experts network.

FURTHER READING

Three papers that cover the three main ensemble methods described in this section are:

- R.E. Schapire. The boosting approach to machine learning: An overview. In D. D. Denison, M. H. Hansen, C. Holmes, B. Mallick, and B. Yu, editors, *Nonlinear Estimation and Classification*, Springer, Berlin, Germany, 2003.

- L. Breiman. Bagging predictors. *Machine Learning*, 26(2):123–140, 1996.

- M.I. Jordan and R.A. Jacobs. Hierarchical mixtures of experts and the EM algorithm. *Neural Computation*, 6(2):181–214, 1994.

An overview of the whole area is provided by:

- L. Kuncheva. *Combining Pattern Classifiers: Methods and Algorithms*. Wiley-Interscience, New York, USA, 2004.

For an alternative viewpoint, see:

- Sections 17.4 and 17.6–17.7 of E. Alpaydin. *Introduction to Machine Learning*, 2nd edition, MIT Press, Cambridge, MA, USA, 2009.

- Section 9.5 of R.O. Duda, P.E. Hart, and D.G. Stork. *Pattern Classification*, 2nd edition, Wiley-Interscience, New York, USA, 2001.

The original paper on Random Forests is still a very useful resource:
Leo Breiman. Random forests. *Machine Learning*, 45(1):5–32, 2001.

PRACTICE QUESTIONS

Problem 13.1 Modify the decision tree implementation to use weights in the computation of the Gini impurity. This is not trivial, since you have to modify the total value of the Gini impurity, too. Once you have done it, use stump trees on the party data.

Problem 13.2 Implement the alternative form of boosting that uses the weights to sample the dataset. Does this make any difference to the outputs?

Problem 13.3 Stumping picks out the single most informative feature in the dataset and uses this. For a binary classification problem this will typically get at least half of the dataset correct. Why? How does this statement generalise to multiple classes?

Problem 13.4 Compare and contrast bagging and cross-validation.

Problem 13.5 The `Breastcancer` dataset in the UCI Machine Learning repository gives ten features and asks for a classification of breast tumours into benign and malignant. It is a difficult dataset, and provides a good comparison of the standard decision tree with boosted and bagged versions. Use all of the methods, using stumping and more advanced trees and see which work better.

Problem 13.6 The Mixture of Experts algorithm works with any kind of expert. Suppose that the experts were each MLPs. Implement this algorithm and see how well it does on the `Breastcancer` dataset above.

Problem 13.7 In Section 13.3 on the random forest, it was mentioned that there exists out-of-bootstrap data that can be used for validation and testing. Modify the code to keep track of this data.

Problem 13.8 Use the boosting code from Problem 13.2 above and compare it with the random forest on the cars dataset from the UCI Repository.

## CHAPTER 14

Unsupervised Learning

Many of the learning algorithms that we have seen to date have made use of a training set that consists of a collection of labelled **target** data, or at least (for evolutionary and reinforcement learning) some scoring system that identifies whether or not a prediction is good or not. Targets are obviously useful, since they enable us to show the algorithm the correct answer to possible inputs, but in many circumstances they are difficult to obtain— they could, for instance, involve somebody labelling each instance by hand. In addition, it doesn't seem to be very biologically plausible: most of the time when we are learning, we don't get told exactly what the right answer should be. In this chapter we will consider exactly the opposite case, where there is no information about the correct outputs available at all, and the algorithm is left to spot some similarity between different inputs for itself.

Unsupervised learning is a conceptually different problem to supervised learning. Obviously, we can't hope to perform regression: we don't know the outputs for any points, so we can't guess what the function is. Can we hope to do classification then? The aim of classification is to identify similarities between inputs that belong to the same class. There isn't any information about the correct classes, but if the algorithm can exploit similarities between inputs in order to **cluster** inputs that are similar together, this might perform classification automatically. So the aim of unsupervised learning is to find clusters of similar inputs in the data without being explicitly told that these datapoints belong to one class and those to a different class. Instead, the algorithm has to discover the similarities for itself. We have already seen some unsupervised learning algorithms in Chapter 6, where the focus was on dimensionality reduction, and hence clustering of similar datapoints together.

The supervised learning algorithms that we have discussed so far have aimed to minimise some external error criterion—mostly the sum-of-squares error—based on the difference between the targets and the outputs. Calculating and minimising this error was possible because we had target data to calculate it from, which is not true for unsupervised learning. This means that we need to find something else to drive the learning. The problem is more general than sum-of-squares error: we can't use any error criterion that relies on targets or other outside information (an **external** error criterion), we need to find something internal to the algorithm. This means that the measure has to be independent of the task, because we can't keep on changing the whole algorithm every time a new task is introduced. In supervised learning the error criterion was task-specific, because it was based on the target data that we provided.

To see how to work out a general error criterion that we can use, we need to go back to some of the important concepts that were discussed in Section 2.1.1: **input space** and **weight space**. If two inputs are close together then it means that their vectors are similar, and so the **distance** between them is small (distance measures were discussed in Section 7.2.3, but here we will stick to Euclidean distance). Then inputs that are close together are identified as being similar, so that they can be clustered, while inputs that are far apart are not clustered together. We can extend this to the nodes of a network by aligning weight space with input space. Now if the weight values of a node are similar to the elements of an input vector then that node should be a good match for the input, and any other inputs that are similar. In order to start to see these ideas in practice we'll look at a simple clustering algorithm, the k-Means Algorithm, which has been around in statistics for a long time.

14.1 THE K-MEANS ALGORITHM

If you have ever watched a group of tourists with a couple of tour guides who hold umbrellas up so that everybody can see them and follow them, then you have seen a dynamic version of the k-means algorithm. Our version is simpler, because the data (playing the part of the tourists) does not move, only the tour guides.

Suppose that we want to divide our input data into k categories, where we know the value of k (for example, we have a set of medical test results from lots of people for three diseases, and we want to see how well the tests identify the three diseases). We allocate k cluster centres to our input space, and we would like to position these centres so that there is one cluster centre in the middle of each cluster. However, we don't know where the clusters are, let alone where their 'middle' is, so we need an algorithm that will find them. Learning algorithms generally try to minimise some sort of error, so we need to think of an error criterion that describes this aim. The idea of the 'middle' is the first thing that we need to think about. How do we define the middle of a set of points? There are actually two things that we need to define:

A distance measure In order to talk about distances between points, we need some way to measure distances. It is often the normal Euclidean distance, but there are other alternatives; we've covered some other alternatives in Section 7.2.3.

The mean average Once we have a distance measure, we can compute the central point of a set of datapoints, which is the mean average (if you aren't convinced, think what the mean of two numbers is, it is the point halfway along the line between them). Actually, this is only true in Euclidean space, which is the one you are used to, where everything is nice and flat. Everything becomes a lot trickier if we have to think about curved spaces; when we have to worry about curvature, the Euclidean distance metric isn't the right one, and there are at least two different definitions of the mean. So we aren't going to worry about any of these things, and we'll assume that space is flat. This is what statisticians do all the time.

We can now think about a suitable way of positioning the cluster centres: we compute the mean point of each cluster, $\boldsymbol{\mu}_{c(i)}$, and put the cluster centre there. This is equivalent to minimising the Euclidean distance (which is the sum-of-squares error again) from each datapoint to its cluster centre.

How do we decide which points belong to which clusters? It is important to decide, since we will use that to position the cluster centres. The obvious thing is to associate each point with the cluster centre that it is closest too. This might change as the algorithm iterates, but that's fine.

We start by positioning the cluster centres randomly through the input space, since we don't know where to put them, and then we update their positions according to the data. We decide which cluster each datapoint belongs to by computing the distance between each datapoint and all of the cluster centres, and assigning it to the cluster that is the closest. Note that we can reduce the computational cost of this procedure by using the KD-Tree algorithm that was described in Section 7.2.2. For all of the points that are assigned to a cluster, we then compute the mean of them, and move the cluster centre to that place. We iterate the algorithm until the cluster centres stop moving. Here is the algorithmic description:

The k-Means Algorithm

- **Initialisation**

    - choose a value for k
    - choose k random positions in the input space
    - assign the cluster centres $\boldsymbol{\mu}_j$ to those positions

- **Learning**

    - repeat
        * for each datapoint $\mathbf{x}_i$:
            · compute the distance to each cluster centre
            · assign the datapoint to the nearest cluster centre with distance

            $$d_i = \min_j d(\mathbf{x}_i, \boldsymbol{\mu}_j). \tag{14.1}$$

        * for each cluster centre:
            · move the position of the centre to the mean of the points in that cluster (N_j is the number of points in cluster j):

            $$\boldsymbol{\mu}_j = \frac{1}{N_j} \sum_{i=1}^{N_j} \mathbf{x}_i \tag{14.2}$$

    - until the cluster centres stop moving

- **Usage**

    - for each test point:
        * compute the distance to each cluster centre
        * assign the datapoint to the nearest cluster centre with distance

        $$d_i = \min_j d(\mathbf{x}_i, \boldsymbol{\mu}_j). \tag{14.3}$$

The NumPy implementation follows these steps almost exactly, and we can take advantage of the `np.argmin()` function, which returns the index of the minimum value, to find the closest cluster. The code that computes the distances, finds the nearest cluster centre, and updates them can then be written as:

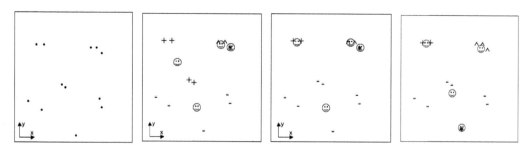

FIGURE 14.1 *Left:* A two-dimensional dataset. *Right:* Three possible ways to position 4 centres (drawn as faces) using the k-means algorithm, which is clearly susceptible to local minima.

```
# Compute distances
distances = np.ones((1,self.nData))*np.sum((data-self.centres[0,:])**2,
axis=1)
for j in range(self.k-1):
    distances = np.append(distances,np.ones((1,self.nData))*np.sum((data-
    self.centres[j+1,:])**2,axis=1),axis=0)

# Identify the closest cluster
cluster = distances.argmin(axis=0)
cluster = np.transpose(cluster*np.ones((1,self.nData)))

# Update the cluster centres
for j in range(self.k):
    thisCluster = np.where(cluster==j,1,0)
    if sum(thisCluster)>0:
        self.centres[j,:] = np.sum(data*thisCluster,axis=0)/np.sum(
        thisCluster)
```

To see how this works in practice, Figures 14.1 and 14.2 show some data and some different ways to cluster that data computed by the k-means algorithm. It should be clear that the algorithm is susceptible to local minima: depending upon where the centres are initially positioned in the space, you can get very different solutions, and many of them look very unlikely to our eyes. Figure 14.2 shows examples of what happens when you choose the number of centres wrongly. There are certainly cases where we don't know in advance how many clusters we will see in the data, but the k-means algorithm doesn't deal with this at all well.

At the cost of significant extra computational expense, we can get around both of these problems by running the algorithm many different times. To find a good local optimum (or even the global one) we use many different initial centre locations, and the solution that minimises the overall sum-of-squares error is likely to be the best one.

By running the algorithm with lots of different values of k, we can see which values give us the best solution. Of course, we need to be careful with this. If we still just measure the sum-of-squares error between each datapoint and its nearest cluster centre, then when

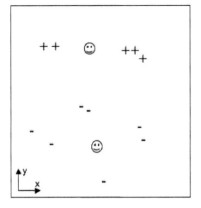 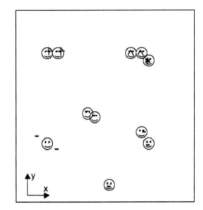

FIGURE 14.2 *Left:* A solution with only 2 classes, which does not match the data well. *Right:* A solution with 11 classes, showing severe overfitting.

we set k to be equal to the number of datapoints, we can position one centre on every datapoint, and the sum-of-squares error will be zero (in fact, this won't happen, since the random initialisation will mean that several clusters will end up coinciding). However, there is no generalisation in this solution: it is a case of serious overfitting. However, by computing the error on a validation set and multiplying the error by k we can see something about the benefit of adding each extra cluster centre.

14.1.1 Dealing with Noise

There are lots of reasons for performing clustering, but one of the more common ones is to deal with noisy data readings. These might be slightly corrupted, or occasionally just plain wrong. If we can choose the clusters correctly, then we have effectively removed the noise, because we replace each noisy datapoint by the cluster centre (we will use this way of representing datapoints for other purposes in Section 14.2). Unfortunately, the mean average, which is central to the k-means algorithm, is very susceptible to outliers, i.e., very noisy measurements. One way to avoid the problem is to replace the mean average with the median, which is what is known as a robust statistic, meaning that it is not affected by outliers (the mean of $(1, 2, 1, 2, 100)$ is 21.2, while the median is 2). The only change that is needed to the algorithm is to replace the computation of the mean with the computation of the median. This is computationally more expensive, as we've discussed previously, but it does remove noise effectively.

14.1.2 The k-Means Neural Network

The k-means algorithm clearly works, despite its problems with noise and the difficulty with choosing the number of clusters. Interestingly, while it might seem a long way from neural networks, it isn't. If we think about the cluster centres that we optimise the positions of as locations in weight space, then we could position neurons in those places and use neural network training. The computation that happened in the k-means algorithm was that each input decided which cluster centre it was closest to by calculating the distance to all of the centres. We could do this inside a neural network, too: the location of each neuron is its position in weight space, which matches the values of its weights. So for each input, we

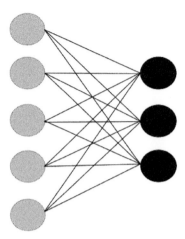

FIGURE 14.3 A single-layer neural network can implement the k-means solution.

just make the activation of a node be the distance between that node in weight space and the current input, as we did for Radial Basis Functions in Chapter 5. Then training is just moving the position of the node, which means adjusting the weights.

So, we can implement the k-means algorithm using a set of neurons. We will use just one layer of neurons, together with some input nodes, and no bias node. The first layer will be the inputs, which don't do any computation, as usual, and the second layer will be a layer of **competitive** neurons, that is, neurons that 'compete' to fire, with only one of them actually succeeding. Only one cluster centre can represent a particular input vector, and so we will choose the neuron with the highest activation h to be the one that fires. This is known as **winner-takes-all** activation, and it is an example of **competitive learning**, since the set of neurons compete with each other to fire, with the winner being the one that **best matches** (i.e., is closest to) the input. Competitive learning is sometimes said to lead to **grandmother** cells, because each neuron in the network will learn to recognise one particular feature, and will fire only when that input is seen. You would then have a specific neuron that was trained to recognise your grandmother (and others for anybody else/anything else that you see often).

We will choose k neurons (for hopefully obvious reasons) and fully connect the inputs to the neurons, as usual. There is a picture of this network in Figure 14.3. We will use neurons with a linear transfer function, computing the activation of the neurons as simply the product of the weights and inputs:

$$h_i = \sum_j w_{ij} x_j. \tag{14.4}$$

Providing that the inputs are **normalised** so that their absolute size is the same (a point that we'll come back to in Section 14.1.3), this effectively measures the distance between the input vector and the cluster centre represented by that neuron, with larger numbers (higher activations) meaning that the two points are closer together.

So the winning neuron is the one that is closest to the current input. The question is how can we then change the position of that neuron in weight space, that is, how do we update its weights? In the k-means algorithm that was described earlier it was easy: we just set the cluster centre to be the mean of all the datapoints that were assigned to that

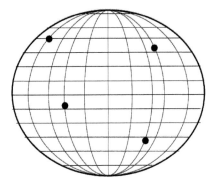

FIGURE 14.4 A set of neurons positioned on the unit sphere in 3D.

centre. However, when we do neural network training, we often feed in just one input vector at a time and change the weights (that is, we use the algorithm on-line, rather than batch). We therefore do not know the mean because we don't know about all the datapoints, just the current one. So we approximate it by moving the winning neuron closer to the current input, making that centre even more likely to be the best match next time that input is seen. This corresponds to:

$$\Delta w_{ij} = \eta x_j. \tag{14.5}$$

However, this is not good enough. To see why not, let's get back to that question of normalisation. This is important enough to need its own subsection.

14.1.3 Normalisation

Suppose that the weights of all the neurons are small (maybe less than 1) except for those to one particular neuron. We'll make those weights be 10 for the example. If an input vector with values $(0.2, 0.2, -0.1)$ is presented, and it happens to be an exact match for one of the neurons, then the activation of that neuron will be $0.2 \times 0.2 + 0.2 \times 0.2 + -0.1 \times -0.1 = 0.09$. The other neurons are not perfect matches, so their activations should all be less. However, consider the neuron with large weights. Its activation will be $10 \times 0.2 + 10 \times 0.2 + 10 \times -0.1 = 3$, and so it will be the winner. Thus, we can only compare activations if we know that the weights for all of the neurons are the same size. We do this by insisting that the weight vector is normalised so that the distance between the vector and the origin (the point $(0, 0, \ldots 0)$) is one. This means that all of the neurons are positioned on the unit hypersphere, which we described in Section 2.1.2 when we talked about the curse of dimensionality: it is the set of all points that are distance one from the origin, so it is a circle in 2D, a sphere in 3D (as shown in Figure 14.4), and a hypersphere in higher dimensions.

Computing this normalisation in NumPy takes a little bit of care because we are normalising the total Euclidean distance from the origin, and the sum and division are row-wise rather than column-wise, which means that the matrix has to be transposed before and after the division:

```
normalisers = np.sqrt(np.sum(data**2,axis=1))*np.ones((1,shape(data)[0]))
data = np.transpose(np.transpose(data)/normalisers)
```

The neuronal activation (Equation (14.4)) can be written as:

$$h_i = \mathbf{W}_i^T \cdot \mathbf{x}, \tag{14.6}$$

where, as usual, $\cdot$ refers to the inner product or scalar product between the two vectors, and $\mathbf{W}_i^T$ is the transpose of the ith row of W. The inner product computes $\|\mathbf{W}_i\|\|\mathbf{x}\|\cos\theta$, where θ is the angle between the two vectors and $\|\cdot\|$ is the magnitude of the vector. So if the magnitude of all the vectors is one, then only the angle θ affects the size of the dot product, and this tells us about the difference between the vector directions, since the more they point in the same direction, the larger the activation will be.

14.1.4   A Better Weight Update Rule

The weight update rule given in Equation (14.5) lets the weights grow without any bound, so that they do not lie on the unit hypersphere any more. If we normalise the inputs as well, which certainly seems reasonable, then we can use the following weight update rule:

$$\Delta w_{ij} = \eta(x_j - w_{ij}), \tag{14.7}$$

which has the effect of moving the weight w_{ij} directly towards the current input. Remember that the only weights that we are updating are those of the winning unit:

```
for i in range(self.nEpochs):
    for j in range(self.nData):
        activation = np.sum(self.weights*np.transpose(data[j:j+1,:]),axis=0)
        winner = np.argmax(activation)
        self.weights[:,winner] += self.eta * data[j,:] - self.weights[:,
        winner]
```

For many of our supervised learning algorithms we minimised the sum-of-squares difference between the output and the target. This was a global error criterion that affected all of the weights together. Now we are minimising a function that is effectively independent in each weight. So the minimisation that we are doing is actually more complicated, even though it doesn't look it. This makes it very difficult to analyse the behaviour of the algorithm, which is a general problem for competitive learning algorithms. However, they do tend to work well.

Now that we have a weight update rule that works, we can consider the entire algorithm for the on-line k-means network:

The On-Line k-Means Algorithm

- **Initialisation**

    - choose a value for k, which corresponds to the number of output nodes
    - initialise the weights to have small random values

- **Learning**

    - normalise the data so that all the points lie on the unit sphere
    - repeat:
        * for each datapoint:
            · compute the activations of all the nodes
            · pick the winner as the node with the highest activation
            · update the weights using Equation (14.7)
        * until number of iterations is above a threshold

- **Usage**

    - for each test point:
        * compute the activations of all the nodes
        * pick the winner as the node with the highest activation

---

14.1.5 Example: The Iris Dataset Again

Now that we have a method of training the k-means algorithm we can use it to learn about data. Except we need to think about how to understand the results. If there aren't any labels in the data, then we can't really do much to analyse the results, since we don't have anything to compare them with. However, we might use unsupervised learning methods to cluster data where we know at least some of the labels. For example, we can use the algorithm on the iris dataset that we looked at in Section 4.4.3, where we classified three types of iris flowers using the MLP. All we need to do is to give some of the data to the algorithm and train it, and then use some more to test the output. However, the output of the algorithm isn't as clear now, because we don't use the labels that come with the data, since we aren't doing supervised learning anymore. To get around that, we need to work out some way of turning the results from the algorithm, which is the index of the cluster that best matches it, into a classification output that we can compare with the labels. This is relatively easy if we used three clusters in the algorithm, since there should hopefully be a one-to-one correspondence between them, but it might turn out that using more clusters gets better results, although this will make the analysis more difficult. You can do this by hand if there are relatively small numbers of datapoints, or you could use a supervised learning algorithm to do it for you, as is discussed next.

To see how the k-means algorithm is used, we can see how it is used on the iris dataset:

```
import kmeansnet
net = kmeansnet.kmeans(3,train)
net.kmeanstrain(train)
cluster = net.kmeansfwd(test)
print cluster
print iris[3::4,4]
```

The output that is produced by this in an example run is (where the top line is the output of the algorithm and the bottom line is the classes from the dataset):

```
[ 0. 0. 0. 0. 0. 1. 1. 1. 1. 2. 1. 2. 2. 2. 0. 1. 2. 1. 0.
  1. 2. 2. 2. 1. 1. 2. 0. 0. 1. 0. 0. 0. 0. 2. 0. 2. 1.]
[ 1. 1. 1. 1. 1. 2. 2. 2. 1. 0. 2. 0. 0. 0. 1. 1. 0. 2. 2.
  2. 0. 0. 0. 2. 2. 0. 1. 2. 1. 1. 1. 1. 1. 0. 1. 0. 2.]
```

and then we can see that cluster 0 corresponds to label 1 and cluster 1 to label 2, in which case the algorithm gets 1 of cluster 0 wrong, 2 of cluster 1, and none of cluster 2.

14.1.6 Using Competitive Learning for Clustering

Deciding which cluster any datapoint belongs to is now an easy task: we present it to the trained algorithm and look what is activated. If we don't have any target data, then the problem is finished. However, for many problems we might want to interpret the best-matching cluster as a class label (alternatively, a set of cluster centres could all correspond to one class). This is fine, since if we have target data we can match the output classes to the targets, provided that we are a bit careful: there is no reason why the order of the nodes in the network should match the order in the data, since the algorithm knows nothing about that order. For that reason, when assigning class labels to the outputs, you need to check which numbers match up carefully, or the results will look a lot worse than they actually are.

There is an alternative solution to this problem of assigning labels, and it is one that we have seen before. In Chapter 5 we considered using the k-means network in order to train the positions of the RBF nodes. It is now possible to see how this works. The k-means part positions the RBFs in the input space, so that they represent the input data well. A Perceptron is then used on top of this in order to provide the match to the outputs in the supervised learning part of the network. Since this is now supervised learning, it ensures that the output categories match the target data classes. It also means that you can use lots of clusters in the k-means network without having to work out which datapoints belong to which cluster, since the Perceptron will do this for you.

We are now going to look at another major algorithm in competitive learning, the Self-Organising Feature Map. As motivation for it, we are going to consider a sample problem for competitive learning, which is a problem in data compression called vector quantisation.

14.2 VECTOR QUANTISATION

We've already discussed using competitive learning for removing noise. There is a related application, data compression, which is used both for storing data and for the transmission of speech and image data. The reason that the applications are related is that both replace the current input by the cluster centre that it belongs to. For noise reduction we do this to replace the noisy input with a cleaner one, while for data compression we do it to reduce the number of datapoints that we send.

Both of these things can be understood by considering them as examples of **data communication**. Suppose that I want to send data to you, but that I have to pay for each data bit I transmit, so I want to keep the amount of data that I send to a minimum. I notice that there are lots of repeated datapoints, so I decide to encode my data before I send it, so that instead of sending the entire set, we agree on a **codebook** of **prototype vectors** together. Now, instead of transmitting the actual data, I can transmit the index of that datapoint in the codebook, which is shorter. All you have to do is take the indices I send you and look them up, and you have the data. We can actually make the code even more efficient by using shorter indices for the datapoints that are more common. This is an important problem in information theory, and every kind of sound and image compression algorithm has a different method of solving it.

There is one problem with the scenario so far, which is that the codebook won't contain every possible datapoint. What happens when I want to send a datapoint and it isn't in the codebook? In that case we need to accept that our data will not look exactly the same, and I send you the index of the prototype vector that is closest to it (this is known as **vector quantisation**, and is the way that **lossy compression** works).

Figure 14.5 shows an interpretation of prototype vectors in two dimensions. The dots at the centre of each cell are the prototype vectors, and any datapoint that lies within a cell is represented by the dot. The name for each cell is the **Voronoi set** of a particular prototype. Together, they produce the **Voronoi tesselation** of the space. If you connect together every pair of points that share an edge, as is shown by the dotted lines, then you get the **Delaunay triangulation**, which is the optimal way to organise the space to perform function approximation.

The question is how to choose the prototype vectors, and this is where competitive learning comes in. We need to choose prototype vectors that are as close as possible to all of the possible inputs that we might see. This application is called **learning vector quantisation** because we are learning an efficient vector quantisation. The k-means algorithm can be used to solve the problem if we know how large we want our codebook to be. However, another algorithm turns out to be more useful, the **Self-Organising Feature Map**, which is described next.

14.3 THE SELF-ORGANISING FEATURE MAP

By far the most commonly used competitive learning algorithm is the **Self-Organising Feature Map** (often abbreviated to SOM), which was proposed by Teuvo Kohonen in 1988. Kohonen was considering the question of how sensory signals get mapped into the cerebral cortex of the brain with an **order**. For example, in the auditory cortex, which deals with the sounds that we hear, neurons that are **excited** (i.e., that are caused to fire) by similar sounds are positioned closely together, whereas two neurons that are excited by very different sounds will be far apart.

There are two novel departures in this for us: firstly, the relative locations of the neurons in the network matters (this property is known as **feature mapping**—nearby neurons

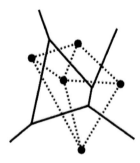

FIGURE 14.5 The Voronoi tesselation of space that performs vector quantisation. Any datapoint is represented by the dot within its cell, which is the prototype vector.

correspond to similar input patterns), and secondly, the neurons are arranged in a grid with connections between the neurons, rather than in layers with connections only between the different layers. In the auditory cortex there appears to be sheets of neurons arranged in 2D, and that is the typical arrangement of neurons for the SOM: a grid of neurons arranged in 2D, as can be seen in Figure 14.6. A 1D line of neurons is also sometimes used. In mathematical terms, the SOM demonstrates relative ordering preservation, which is sometimes known as topology preservation. The relative ordering of the inputs should be preserved by the ordering in the neurons, so that neurons that are close together represent inputs that are close together, while neurons that are far apart represent inputs that are far apart.

This topology preservation is not necessarily possible, because the SOM typically uses a 1D or 2D array of neurons, and most of our input spaces are of much higher dimensionality than that. This means that the ordering cannot be preserved. We have seen this in Figure 1.2, where one view of some wind turbines made it look like they are on top of each other, when they clearly are not, because we used a two-dimensional representation of three-dimensional reality. You've probably seen the same thing in other photos, where trees appear to be growing out of somebody's head. A different way to see the same thing is given in Figure 14.7, where mismatches between the topology of the input space and map lead to changes in the relative ordering. The best that can be said is that SOM is perfectly topology-preserving, which means that if the dimensionality of the input and the map correspond, then the topology of the input space will be preserved. We are going to look at other methods of performing dimensionality reduction in Chapter 6.

The question, then, is how we can implement feature mapping in an unsupervised learning algorithm. The first thing to recognise is that we need some interaction between the neurons in the network, so that when one neuron fires, it affects what happens to those around it. We have seen something like this before, for example, between different layers of the MLP, but now we are thinking about neurons that are within a layer. These are known as lateral connections (i.e., within the layer of the network). How should this interaction work? We are trying to introduce feature mapping, so neurons that are close together in the map should represent similar features. This means that the winning neuron should pull other neurons that are close to it in the network closer to itself in weight space, which means that we need positive connections. Likewise, neurons that are further away should represent different features, and so should be a long way off in weight space, so the winning neuron 'repels' them, by using negative connections to push them away. Neurons that are very far away in the network should already represent different features, so we just ignore them.

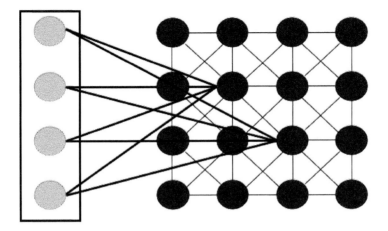

FIGURE 14.6 The Self-Organising Map network. As usual, input nodes (on the left) do no computation, and the weights are modified to change the activations of the neurons (weights are only shown to two nodes for clarity). However, the nodes within the SOM affect each other in that the winning node also changes the weights of neurons that are close to it. Connections are shown in the figure to the eight closest nodes, but this is a parameter of the network.

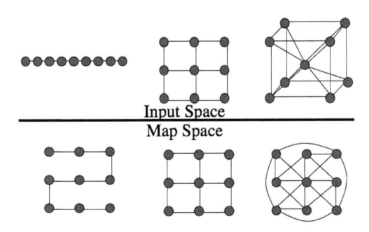

FIGURE 14.7 When inputs in 1D (a straight line), a 2D grid, and a 3D cube are represented by a 2D grid of neurons, the relative ordering is not perfectly preserved. The 1D line is bent, which means that points that used to be a long way apart (such as the first and sixth on the line) are now close together, while the cube becomes very complicated. The lines in the bottom part of the figure represent connections that are meant to be close.

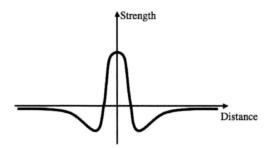

FIGURE 14.8 Graph of the strength of lateral connections for a feature mapping algorithm known as the 'Mexican Hat'.

This is known as the 'Mexican Hat' form of lateral connections, for reasons that should be clear from the picture in Figure 14.8. We can then just use ordinary competitive learning, just like we did for the k-means network in Section 14.1.2. The Self-Organising Map does pretty much exactly this.

14.3.1 The SOM Algorithm

Using the full Mexican hat lateral interactions between neurons is fine, but it isn't essential. In Kohonen's SOM algorithm, the weight update rule is modified instead, so that information about neighbouring neurons is included in the learning rule, which makes the algorithm simpler. The algorithm is a competitive learning algorithm, so that one neuron is chosen as the winner, but when its weights are updated, so are those of its neighbours, although to a lesser extent. Neurons that are not within the neighbourhood are ignored, not repelled.

We will now look at the SOM algorithm before examining some of the details further.

The Self-Organising Feature Map Algorithm

- **Initialisation**

    - choose a size (number of neurons) and number of dimensions d for the map
    - either:
        * choose random values for the weight vectors so that they are all different OR
        * set the weight values to increase in the direction of the first d principal components of the dataset

- **Learning**

    - repeat:
        * for each datapoint:
            · select the best-matching neuron n_b using the minimum Euclidean distance between the weights and the input,

$$n_b = \min_j \|\mathbf{x} - \mathbf{w}_j^T\|. \tag{14.8}$$

        * update the weight vector of the best-matching node using:

$$\mathbf{w}_j^T \leftarrow \mathbf{w}_j^T + \eta(t)(\mathbf{x} - \mathbf{w}_j^T), \tag{14.9}$$

where $\eta(t)$ is the learning rate.

* update the weight vector of all other neurons using:

$$\mathbf{w}_j^T \leftarrow \mathbf{w}_j^T + \eta_n(t)h(n_b, t)(\mathbf{x} - \mathbf{w}_j^T), \qquad (14.10)$$

where $\eta_n(t)$ is the learning rate for neighbourhood nodes, and $h(n_b, t)$ is the neighbourhood function, which decides whether each neuron should be included in the neighbourhood of the winning neuron (so $h = 1$ for neighbours and $h = 0$ for non-neighbours)

* reduce the learning rates and adjust the neighbourhood function, typically by $\eta(t+1) = \alpha \eta(t)^{k/k_{\max}}$ where $0 \leq \alpha \leq 1$ decides how fast the size decreases, k is the number of iterations the algorithm has been running for, and $k_{\max}$ is when you want the learning to stop. The same equation is used for both learning rates (η, η_n) and the neighbourhood function $h(n_b, t)$.

– until the map stops changing or some maximum number of iterations is exceeded

- **Usage**

  – for each test point:

    * select the best-matching neuron n_b using the minimum Euclidean distance between the weights and the input:

$$n_b = \min_j \|\mathbf{x} - \mathbf{w}_j^T\| \qquad (14.11)$$

14.3.2   Neighbourhood Connections

The size of the neighbourhood is thus another parameter that we need to control. How large should the neighbourhood of a neuron be? If we start our network off with random weights, as we did for the MLP, then at the beginning of learning, the network is pretty well unordered (as the weights are random, two nodes that are very close in weight space could be on opposite sides of the map, and vice versa) and so it makes sense that the neighbourhoods should be large, so that we get the rough ordering of the network correct. However, once the network has been learning for a while, the rough ordering has already been created, and the algorithm starts to fine-tune the individual local regions of the network. At this stage, the neighbourhoods should be small, as is shown in Figure 14.9. It therefore makes sense to reduce the size of the neighbourhood as the network adapts. These two phases of learning are also known as **ordering** and **convergence**. Typically, we reduce the neighbourhood size by a small amount at each iteration of the algorithm. We control the learning rate η in exactly the same way, so that it starts off large and decreases over time, as is shown in the algorithm below.

The fact that the size of the neighbourhood changes as the algorithm runs has consequences for an implementation. There is no point using actual connections between nodes, since the number of these will change as the algorithm runs. We therefore set up a matrix that measures the distances between nodes in the network and choose the nodes in the neighbourhood of a particular node as those within a neighbourhood radius that shrinks as the algorithm runs.

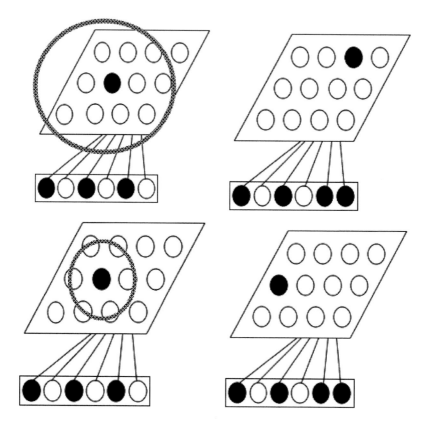

FIGURE 14.9 *Top:* Initially, similar input vectors excite neurons that are far apart, so that the neighbourhood (shown as a circle) needs to be large. *Bottom:* Later on during training the neighbourhood can be smaller, because similar input vectors excite neurons that are close together.

```
# Set up the map distance matrix
mapDist = np.zeros((self.x*self.y,self.x*self.y))
for i in range(self.x*self.y):
    for j in range(i+1,self.x*self.y):
        mapDist[i,j] = np.sqrt((self.map[0,i] - self.map[0,j])**2 + (self.↩
        map[1,i] - self.map[1,j])**2)
 mapDist[j,i] = mapDist[i,j]

# Within the loop, select the neighbours
# Find the neighbours and update their weights
neighbours = np.where(mapDist[best[i]]<=self.nSize,1,0)
neighbours[best[i]] = 0
self.weights += self.eta_n * neighbours*np.transpose((inputs[i,:] - np.↩
transpose(self.weights)))
```

There is another way to initialise the weights in the network, which is to use Principal Components Analysis (which is described in Section 6.2) to find the two (assuming that the map is two-dimensional) largest directions of variation in the data and to initialise the weights so that they increase along these two directions:

```
dummy1,dummy2,evals,evecs = pca.pca(inputs,2)
self.weights = np.zeros((self.nDim,x*y))
for i in range(x*y):
    for j in range(self.mapDim):
        self.weights[:,i] += (self.map[j,i]-0.5)*2*evecs[:,j]
```

This means that the ordering part of the training has already been done in the initialisation, and so the algorithm can be trained with small neighbourhood size from the start. Obviously, this is only possible if the training of the algorithm is in batch mode, so that you have all of the data available for training right from the start. This should be true for the SOM anyway—it is not designed for on-line learning. This can be a bit of a limitation, because there are many cases where we would like to do unsupervised on-line learning.

There are a couple of different things that we can do. One is to ignore that constraint and use the SOM anyway. This is fairly common. However, the size of the map really starts to matter, and there is no guarantee that the SOM will converge to a solution unless batch learning is applied. The alternative is to use one of a variety of networks that are designed to deal with exactly this situation. There are a fair number of these, but Fritzke's "Growing Neural Gas" and Marsland's "Grow When Required" Network are two of the more common ones.

14.3.3 Self-Organisation

You might be wondering what the self-organisation in the name of the SOM is. A particularly interesting aspect of feature mapping is that we get a global ordering of the neurons in the network, despite the fact that the interactions are all local, since neurons that are very far apart do not interact with each other. We thus get a global ordering of the space using only a set of local interactions, which is amazing. This is known as self-organisation, and it appears everywhere. It is part of the growing science of **complexity**. To see how common self-organisation is, consider a flock of birds flying in formation. The birds cannot possibly know exactly where each other are, so how do they keep in formation? In fact, simulations have shown that if each bird just tries to stay diagonally behind the bird to its right, and fly at the same speed, then they form perfect flocks, no matter how they start off and what objects are placed in their way. So the global ordering of the whole flock can arise from the local interactions of each bird looking to the one on its right (or left).

14.3.4 Network Dimensionality and Boundary Conditions

We typically think about applying the SOM algorithm to a 2D rectangular array of neurons (as shown in Figure 14.6), but there is nothing in the algorithm to force this. There are cases where a line of neurons (1D) works better, or where three dimensions are needed. It depends on the dimensionality of the inputs (actually on the **intrinsic** dimensionality, the number of dimensions that you actually need to represent the data), not the number that it is **embedded** in. As an example, consider a set of inputs spread through the room you are in, but all on the plane that connects the bottom of the wall to your left with the top of the wall to your right. These points have intrinsic dimensionality two since they are all on the plane, but they are embedded in your three-dimensional room. Noise and other inaccuracies in data often lead to it being represented in more dimensions than are actually required, and so finding the intrinsic dimensionality can help to reduce the noise.

We also need to consider the boundaries of the network. In some cases, it makes sense that the edges of the map of neurons is strictly defined — for example, if we are arranging sounds from low pitch to high pitch, then the lowest and highest pitches we can hear are obvious endpoints. However, it is not always the case that such boundaries are clearly defined. In this case we might want to remove the boundary conditions. We can do this by removing the boundary by tying the ends together. In 1D this means that we turn a line into a circle, while in 2D we turn a rectangle into a **torus**. To see this, try taking a piece of paper and bend it so that the top and bottom edges line up. You've now got a tube. If you bend the tube round so that the two open ends meet up you have a circle of tube known as a torus. Pictures of these effects are shown in Figure 14.10. In effect, it means that there are no neurons on the edge of the feature map. The choice of the number of dimensions and the boundary conditions depends on the problem that we are considering, but it is usually the case that the torus works better than the rectangle, although it is not always clear why.

The one cost that this has is that the map distances get more complicated to calculate, since we now need to calculate the distances allowing for the wrap around. This can be done using modulo arithmetic, but it is easier to think about taking copies of the map and putting them around the map, so that the original map has copies of itself all around: one above, one below, to the right and left, and also diagonally above and below, as is shown in Figure 14.11. Now we keep one of the points in the original map, and the distance to the second node is the smallest of the distances between the first node and the copies of the second node in the different maps (including the original). By treating the distances in x and y separately, the number of distances that has to be computed can be reduced.

As with the competitive learning algorithm that we considered earlier, the size of the SOM is defined before we start learning. The size of the network (that is, the number of neurons that we put into it) decides how fine-grained the learning is. If there are very few neurons, then the best that the network can do is to find gross generalisations that link the data. However, if there are very large numbers of neurons, then the network can

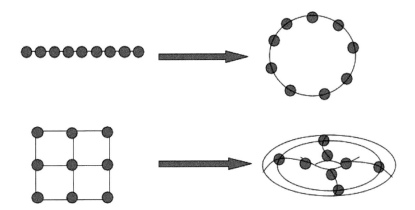

FIGURE 14.10 Using circular boundary conditions in 1D turns a line into a circle, while in 2D it turns a rectangle into a torus.

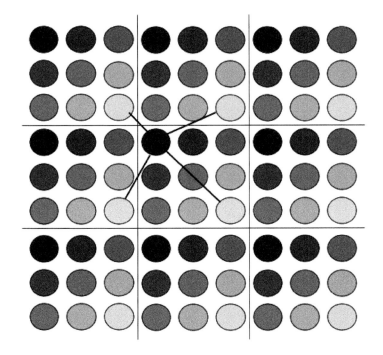

FIGURE 14.11 One way to compute distances between points without any boundary on the map is to imagine copies of the entire map being placed around the original, and picking the shortest of the distances between a node and any of the copies of the other node.

represent every input without ever needing to generalise at all. This is yet another example of overfitting. Clearly, then, choosing the correct size of network is important. The common approach is to test out several different sizes of network, such as 5×5 and 10×10 and see how well the network learns.

14.3.5 Examples of Using the SOM

As a first example of using the SOM, and one that shows the topological ordering of the network, consider training the network on a set of two-dimensional data drawn at random from a uniform distribution in $[-1, 1]$ in both directions. If the network weights are started off randomly, then initially the network is completely disordered (as shown in the top-left picture in Figure 14.12), but after 10 iterations of training the network is ordered so that neighbouring nodes map to data that is close together (bottom-left). Using PCA to initialise the map is not especially useful for this dataset, but it does speed things up: only five iterations through the dataset produce the output shown on the bottom-right of the figure, where it started from the version on the top-right.

For two examples of using the SOM on non-random data, where we can expect to see some actual learning, we will first look at the iris data that we used with the k-means algorithm earlier in this chapter. Figure 14.13 shows a plot of which node of a 5×5 Self-Organising Map was the best match on a set of test data after training for 100 iterations. The three different classes are shown as different shapes (squares, plus triangles pointing up and down), but remember that the network did not receive any information about these target classes. It can be seen that the examples in each of the three classes form different clusters in the map. Looking at the figure, you might be wondering if it is possible to use the plot to identify the different classes by assuming that they are separated in the map. This has been investigated—often by using methods similar to those of Linear Discriminant Analysis that are described in Section 6.1—with some success, and a reference is provided at the end of the chapter.

A more difficult problem is shown in Figure 14.14. The data are the `ecoli` dataset from the UCI Machine Learning repository, and the class is the localisation site of the protein, based on a set of protein measurements. The results with this dataset when testing are not as clearly impressive (but note that the MLP gets about 50% accuracy on this dataset, and that has the target data, which the SOM doesn't). However, the clusters can still be seen to some extent, and they are very clear in the training data. Note that the boundary conditions can make things a little more complicated, since the cluster does not necessarily respect the edges of the map.

FURTHER READING

There is a book by Kohonen, the inventor of the SOM, that provides a very good overview (if rather dated, now) of the area:

- T. Kohonen. *Self-Organisation and Associative Memory*, 3rd edition, Springer, Berlin, Germany, 1989.

The two on-line self-organising networks that were mentioned in the chapter were:

- B. Fritzke. A growing neural gas network learns topologies. In Gerald Tesauro, David S. Touretzky, and Todd K. Leen, editors, *Advances in Neural Information Processing Systems*, volume 7, MIT Press, Cambridge, MA, USA, 1995.

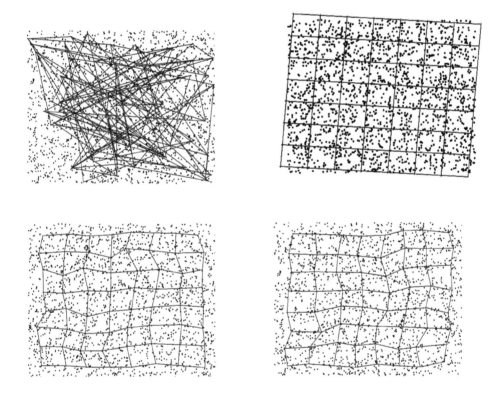

FIGURE 14.12 Training the SOM on a set of uniformly randomly sampled two-dimensional data in the range $[-1, 1]$ in both dimensions. *Top:* Initialisation of the map using *left:* random weights and *right:* PCA (the randomness in the data means that the directions of variation are not necessarily along the obvious directions). *Bottom:* The output after just 10 iterations of training on the left, and 5 on the right, both with typical parameter values.

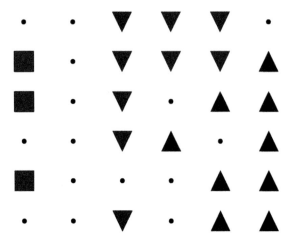

FIGURE 14.13 Plot showing which nodes are the best match according to class, with the three shapes corresponding to three different classes in the iris dataset. The small dots represent nodes that did not fire.

FIGURE 14.14 Plots showing which nodes are the best match according to class, with the three shapes corresponding to three different classes in the *E. coli* dataset, tested on *left:* the training set and *right:* a separate test set. The small dots represent nodes that did not fire.

- S. Marsland, J.S. Shapiro, and U. Nehmzow. A self-organising network that grows when required. *Neural Networks*, 15(8-9):1041–1058, 2002.

A possible reference on processing the data in the map in order to identify clusters is:

- S. Wu and T.W.S. Chow. Self-organizing-map based clustering using a local clustering validity index. *Neural Processing Letters*, 17(3):253–271, 2003.

Books that cover the area include:

- Section 10.14 of R.O. Duda, P.E. Hart, and D.G. Stork. *Pattern Classification*, 2nd edition, Wiley-Interscience, New York, USA, 2001.

- Chapter 9 of S. Haykin. *Neural Networks: A Comprehensive Foundation*, 2nd edition, Prentice-Hall, New Jersey, USA, 1999.

- Section 9.3 of B.D. Ripley. *Pattern Recognition and Neural Networks*. Cambridge University Press, Cambridge, UK, 1996.

PRACTICE QUESTIONS

Problem 14.1 What is the purpose of the neighbourhood function in the SOM? How does it change the learning?

Problem 14.2 A simplistic intruder detection system for a computer network consists of an attempt to categorise users according to (i) the time of day they log in, (ii) the length of time they log in for, (iii) the types of programs they run while logged in, (iv) the number of programs they run while logged in. Suggest how you would train a SOM and the naïve Bayes' classifier to perform the categorisation. What preprocessing of the data would you do, how much data would you need, and how large would you make the SOM? Do you think that such a system would work for intruder detection?

Problem 14.3 The Music Genome Project (http://www.pandora.com) does not work by using a SOM. But it could. Describe how you would implement it.

Problem 14.4 A bank wants to detect fraudulent credit card transactions. They have data for lots and lots of transactions (each transaction is an amount of money, a shop, and the time and date) and some information about when credit cards were stolen, and the transactions that were performed on the stolen card. Describe how you could use a competitive learning method to cluster people's transactions together to identify patterns, so that stolen cards can be detected as changes in pattern. How well do you think this would work? There is much more data of transactions when cards are not stolen, compared to stolen transactions. How does this affect the learning, and what can you do about it?

Problem 14.5 It is possible to use any competitive learning method to position the basis functions of a Radial Basis Function network. The example code used k-means. Modify it to use the SOM instead and compare the results on the wine and yeast datasets.

Problem 14.6 For the wine dataset, experiment with different sizes of map, and boundary conditions. How much difference does it make? Can you use the principal components in order to set the size automatically?

## CHAPTER 15

Markov Chain Monte Carlo (MCMC) Methods

In this chapter we are going to look at a method that has revolutionised statistical computing and statistical physics over the past 20 years. The principal algorithm has been around since 1953, but only when computers became fast enough to be able to perform the computations on real-world examples in hours instead of weeks did the methods become really well known. However, this algorithm has now been cited as one of the most influential ever created.

There are two basic problems that can be solved using these methods, and they are the two that we have been wrestling with for pretty much the entire book: we may want to compute the optimum solution to some objective function, or compute the posterior distribution of a statistical learning problem. In either case the state space may well be very large, and we are only interested in finding the best possible answer—the steps that we go through along the way are not important. We've seen several methods of solving these types of problems during the book, and here we are going to look at one more. We will see a place where MCMC methods are very useful in Section 16.1.

The idea behind everything that we are going to talk about in this chapter is that as we explore the state space, we can also construct samples as we go along in such a way that the samples are likely to come from the most probable parts of the state space. In order to see what this means, we will discuss what Monte Carlo sampling is, and look at Markov chains.

15.1 SAMPLING

We have produced samples from probability distributions in almost all of the algorithms we have looked at, for example, for initialisation of weights. In many cases, the probability distribution we have used has been the uniform one on $[0, 1)$, and we have done it using the `np.random.rand()` function in NumPy, although we have also seen sampling from Gaussian distributions using `np.random.normal()`.

15.1.1 Random Numbers

The basis of all of these sampling methods is in the generation of random numbers, and this is something that computers are not really capable of doing. However, there are plenty of algorithms that produce pseudo-random numbers, the simplest of which is the linear congruential generator. This is a very simple function that is defined by a recurrence relation (i.e., you put one number in to get the second number, and then feed that back in to get the third, and then repeat the cycle):

$$x_{n+1} = (ax_n + c) \mod m, \tag{15.1}$$

where a, c, and m are parameters that have to be chosen carefully. All of them, and the initial input x_0 (which is known as the **seed**), are integers, and so are all of the outputs. The **modulus** function means that the largest number that can be produced is m, and so there are at most m numbers that can be produced by the algorithm. Once one number appears a second time, the whole pattern will repeat again since the equation only uses the current output as input. The length of the sequence between repeats is the **period**, and it should obviously be as long as possible, since it is the most obvious non-randomness in the algorithm. There has been a lot of investigation of choices of the parameters so that the period is length m, so that every integer between 0 and m is produced before the pattern cycles. There are various choices of the parameters that have been selected to work well, including $m = 2^{32}$; $a = 1,664,525$; and $c = 1,013,904,223$. Clearly, just picking numbers at random isn't going to be that useful.

There has been a lot of effort put into different random number generators, since they are important not just for statistical computing, but also cryptography and security. The industry-standard algorithm for generating random samples is the **Mersenne Twister**, which is based on **Mersenne prime numbers**. It is the random number generator used in NumPy. No matter what algorithm generates the numbers, though, it is important to remember that they are not genuinely random, and to genuflect to the wisdom of John von Neumann, one of the fathers of modern computing, who stated:

> Anyone who considers arithmetic methods of producing random digits is, of course, in a state of sin.

The other troublesome thing about random numbers is that it is not actually possible to prove that a sequence of numbers is truly random. There are several tests that can be made of a sequence of numbers to see if they seem to be random. Examples include calculating the **entropy** of the sequence (entropy was described in Section 12.2.1), using a compression algorithm on the sequence (since compression algorithms exploit **redundancy**, i.e., predictability, in the input, if the compression algorithms fail to make the input smaller, then it might be because they are random), and just checking how many numbers are odd compared to even. However, you can never guarantee that a sequence is random, just that it hasn't failed most of the tests yet (but just because it fails one or two of them at some point in the sequence doesn't mean that the sequence isn't random; truly random numbers can look deterministic for a long time... this is part of the joy of randomness!). I'll leave the last word on this to von Neumann again:

> In my experience it was more trouble to test random sequences than to manufacture them.

15.1.2 Gaussian Random Numbers

The Mersenne twister produces uniform random numbers. However, often we might want to produce samples from other distributions, e.g., Gaussian. The usual method of doing this is the **Box–Muller scheme**, which uses a pair of uniformly randomly distributed numbers in order to make two independent Gaussian-distributed numbers with zero mean and unit variance. Let's see how it works.

Suppose that we had two independent zero mean, unit variance normals. Then their product is:

$$f(x, y) = \frac{1}{\sqrt{2\pi}} e^{-x^2/2} \frac{1}{\sqrt{2\pi}} e^{-y^2/2} = \frac{1}{2\pi} e^{-(x^2+y^2)/2}. \tag{15.2}$$

If we use polar coordinates instead (so $x = r\sin(\theta)$ and $y = r\cos(\theta)$) then we would have $r^2 = x^2 + y^2$ and $\theta = \tan^{-1}(y/x)$. Both of these are uniformly distributed random variables ($0 \leq r \leq 1$ and $0 \leq \theta < 2\pi$). In other words, $\theta = 2\pi U_1$ where U_1 is a uniformly distributed random variable. Now we just need a similar expression for r.

We can write that:

$$P(r \leq R) = \int_{r'=0}^{R} \int_{\theta=0}^{2\pi} \frac{1}{2\pi} e^{-r'^2} r' \, dr' \, d\theta = \int_{r'=0}^{r} e^{-r'^2} r' \, dr'. \tag{15.3}$$

If we use the change of variables $\frac{1}{2} r'2 = s$ (so that $r' dr' = ds$) then:

$$P(r \leq R) = \int_{s=0}^{r^2/2} e^{-s} \, ds = 1 - e^{-r^2/2}. \tag{15.4}$$

So to sample r we just need to solve $1 - e^{(-r^2/2)} = 1 - U_2$ where U_2 is another uniformly distributed random variable, and which has solution $r = \sqrt{-2\ln(U_2)}$. So one algorithm to generate the Gaussian variables is:

The Box–Muller Scheme

- Pick two uniformly distributed random numbers $0 \leq U_1, U_2 \leq 1$

- Set $\theta = 2\pi U_1$ and $r = \sqrt{(-2\ln(U_2))}$

- Then $x = r\cos(\theta)$ and $y = r\sin(\theta)$ are independent Gaussian-distributed variables with zero mean and unit variance

---

An alternative approach to computing these random variables is to pick the two uniform random values and scale them to lie between -1 and 1, and to interpret them as describing a point in the plane. If this point is outside the unit circle (so if the variables are U_1 and U_2 as above then if $w^2 = U_1^2 + U_2^2 > 1$) then it is discarded, and another point picked until it is within the circle. Then the transformation $x = U_1 \left(\frac{-2\ln w^2}{w^2}\right)^{\frac{1}{2}}$ and similarly for y with U_2 also provides the variables.

The difference between the methods is that one requires the computation of $\sin(\theta)$, while the other requires that some points are sampled and discarded. Which is faster depends upon the programming language and computer architecture.

A plot of 1,000 samples created by the Box–Muller scheme along with the zero mean, unit variance Gaussian line is shown in Figure 15.1. There is a more efficient algorithm for computing Gaussian-distributed random numbers known as the Ziggurat algorithm that should be investigated further if you require lower computational cost.

There may well be many other distributions that we want to sample from. For common statistical distributions people have worked out schemes like the Box–Muller scheme, but we might want to sample from distributions that we can't describe in those terms. We will see examples of this in Chapter 16. We would like a general method of sampling from any distribution that doesn't have to be tailored to the distribution. There is one important

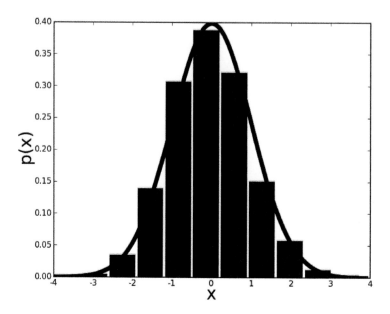

FIGURE 15.1 Histogram of 1,000 Gaussian samples created by the Box–Muller scheme. The line gives the Gaussian distribution with zero mean and unit variance.

concept that can be seen in the Box–Muller scheme, and that is the idea of rejection. When the original samples were not inside the unit circle they were rejected and another one computed to replace them. This is a bit like simulated annealing as we saw it in Section 9.6: we constructed a possible solution and then decided whether or not to use it. Rejection adds computational cost to the procedure, since if we were unlucky this algorithm could run for a long time before it found a pair of numbers that satisfied the criteria. However, it also means that we find samples that satisfy our requirements without having to design any tricky code, and it is generally faster as well, since the computational cost of generating some random numbers is rather less than the cost of doing the complicated transform.

We are going to see rejection used a lot more in this chapter, but before we get there, we should set the idea of sampling onto a proper theoretical footing.

15.2 MONTE CARLO OR BUST

Monte Carlo, a tiny principality on the Mediterranean coast between France and Italy, is famous mostly for its casino and Grand Prix race. As the rich and famous flock to lose money there, they are unlikely to know that the principality also has the dubious honour of having an important statistical principle named after it. The Monte Carlo principle states that if you take independent and identically distributed (i.e., well-behaved) samples $\mathbf{x}^{(i)}$ from an unknown high-dimensional distribution $p(\mathbf{x})$, then as the number of samples gets larger the sample distribution will converge to the true distribution. In other words, sampling works. Written mathematically, this says:

$$p_N(\mathbf{x}) \;=\; \frac{1}{N}\sum_{i=1}^{N}\delta(\mathbf{x}^{(i)} = \mathbf{x})$$

$$\rightarrow \;\lim_{N\to\infty} p_N(\mathbf{x}) = p(\mathbf{x}), \tag{15.5}$$

where $\delta(\mathbf{x}_i = \mathbf{x})$ is the Dirac delta function that is 0 everywhere except at the point $\mathbf{x}_i$ and has $\int \delta(x)dx = 1$. This can be used to compute the expectation as well (where $f(\mathbf{x})$ is some function and $\mathbf{x}$ has discrete values, and the superscript $\cdot^{(i)}$ represents the index of the sample):

$$E_N(f) \;=\; \frac{1}{N}\sum_{i=1}^{N}f(\mathbf{x}^{(i)})$$

$$\rightarrow \;\lim_{N\to\infty} E_N(f) = \sum_{\mathbf{x}} f(\mathbf{x})p(\mathbf{x}). \tag{15.6}$$

The fact that the sample distribution becomes more and more like the true one as we take more and more samples tells us that samples are more likely to be drawn from parts of the distribution that have high probability. This is very useful, since places where there are more samples will allow us to approximate the function well in those regions, and we only really care about the appearance of the function in those places—if the probability is small, then it doesn't matter that the number of samples is small (the area is sparsely covered) since the probability is low there anyway. If we use methods that don't know anything about the probability (such as sampling based on a uniform grid and using splines or something similar), then we have to treat all areas of the space as equally likely, which means that there is going to be a lot of computational resources wasted. There is another benefit, too. In addition to using the samples to approximate the expectation, we can also find a maximum, that is, the most likely outcome, from the samples:

$$\hat{\mathbf{x}} = \arg\max_{\mathbf{x}^{(i)}} p\left(\mathbf{x}^{(i)}\right). \tag{15.7}$$

Allegedly, the idea of Monte Carlo sampling (and the reason that it got its name) first came about when Stan Ulam was considering the probabilities of particular hands of cards. In fact, the whole of probability theory was originally developed by some of the great French mathematicians, such as Fermat, in order to reason about games of chance, so Monte Carlo sampling is in pretty good company. Suppose that you want to do something relatively simple, such as to predict how many times you should expect to win at the patience game that came free with your computer. All you need to do is work out the rules for when you win based on the initial setup, and then look at how many of these setups there are. In a standard deck there are 52 cards, so there are 52! ($\approx 8 \times 10^{67}$) different ways in which the cards can be distributed. So even before we start thinking about the specific rules for the game, we know that the number of different layouts is so large it is basically impossible to think about. Despairing of working it out, you might decide to play a couple of hands of patience and see how well you do. In fact, the Monte Carlo principle tells you that that is exactly what you should be doing. Suppose that you play ten games of patience and six of them come out. You might be able to argue that approximately 60% of the patience games will do well. To believe this, you will have to play far more than ten games with the same success rate, or course; and even then it assumes that you are a good patience player, and don't cheat.

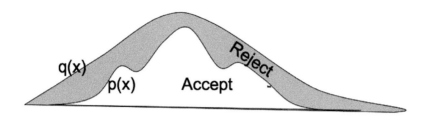

FIGURE 15.2 The proposal distribution method.

15.3 THE PROPOSAL DISTRIBUTION

We now have everything that we need if the distribution $p(\mathbf{x})$ that we are sampling from is easy (that is, not computationally expensive) to sample from. Unfortunately, this is very rarely the case, but fortunately there is a way to get around this problem, which is to cheat by inventing a simpler distribution $q(\mathbf{x})$ that we can sample from easily, and picking samples from there. Obviously we can't just pick any distribution $q(\mathbf{x})$, there has to be some relation between them. So we assume that even though we don't know $p(\mathbf{x})$, we can evaluate some related distribution $\tilde{p}(\mathbf{x})$ for a given $\mathbf{x}$, where:

$$p(\mathbf{x}) = \frac{1}{Z_p}\tilde{p}(\mathbf{x}), \tag{15.8}$$

where Z_p is some normalisation constant that we don't know. This is not usually an unreasonable assumption; we are not saying that we do not know $p(\mathbf{x})$, just that we can't sample from it easily. Now we can pick a number M so that $\tilde{p}(\mathbf{x}) \leq Mq(\mathbf{x})$ for all values of $\mathbf{x}$. We generate a random number $\mathbf{x}^*$ from $q(\mathbf{x})$, and we want this to look like a sample from $p(\mathbf{x})$. We therefore turn to the idea of rejection again, looking at how likely it is that the sample comes from $p(\mathbf{x})$, and discarding it if it turns out to be unlikely.

We make the decision of whether or not to accept the sample by picking a uniformly distributed random number u between 0 and $Mq(\mathbf{x}^*)$. If this random number is less than $\tilde{p}(\mathbf{x}^*)$, then we accept $\mathbf{x}^*$, otherwise we reject it. The reason why this works is known as the **envelope principle**: the pair $(\mathbf{x}^*, u)$ is uniformly distributed under $Mq(\mathbf{x}^*)$, and the rejection part throws away samples that don't match the uniform distribution on $p(\mathbf{x}^*)$, so $Mq(\mathbf{x})$ forms an envelope on $p(\mathbf{x})$. Figure 15.2 shows the idea: we sample from $Mq(\mathbf{x})$ and reject any sample that lies in the grey area. The smaller M is, the more samples we get to keep, but we need to ensure that $\tilde{p}(\mathbf{x}) \leq Mq(\mathbf{x})$. This method is known as **rejection sampling**, and the algorithm can be written as:

The Rejection Sampling Algorithm

- Sample $\mathbf{x}^*$ from $q(\mathbf{x})$ (e.g., using the Box–Muller scheme if $q(\mathbf{x})$ is Gaussian)

- Sample u from uniform$(0, \mathbf{x}^*)$

- If $u < p(\mathbf{x}^*)/Mq(\mathbf{x}^*)$:

  – add $\mathbf{x}^*$ to the set of samples

- Else:

  – reject $\mathbf{x}$ and pick another sample

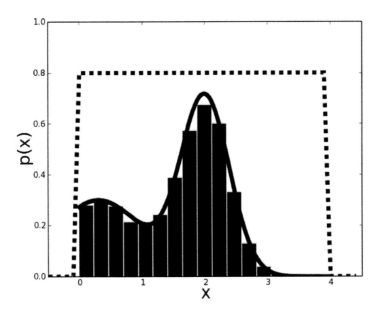

FIGURE 15.3 The histogram shows samples of a mixture of two Gaussians (given by the solid line) as sampled from the uniform box shown as a dotted line by using rejection sampling.

As an example of using rejection sampling, Figure 15.3 shows the results of using it to sample from the mixture of two Gaussians by using the uniform distribution shown by the dotted line. Using $M = 0.8$, as shown in the figure, the algorithm rejects about half of the samples. Using $M = 2$ the algorithm rejects about 85% of samples. So with rejection sampling, you have to throw away samples, and if you don't pick M properly, you will have to reject a lot of them. The curse of dimensionality makes the problem even worse. There are two things that we can do to get over this problem. One is to develop some more sophisticated methods of understanding the space that we are sampling, and the other is to try to ensure that the samples are taken from areas of the space that have high probability.

The reason why we are using these methods at all is that we can't sample from the actual distribution we want, since that is too difficult and/or expensive, but it might be possible to understand it in other ways. In Section 15.4.1 we will look at methods that allow us to travel around within the space by using simple local moves. Before we get to that we will look at a method that tries to ensure that the samples come from regions of high probability. The method is known as importance sampling, because it attaches a weight that says how important each sample is.

Suppose that we want to compute the expectation of a function $f(\mathbf{x})$ for a continuous random variable $\mathbf{x}$ distributed according to unknown distribution $p(\mathbf{x})$. Starting from the expression of the expectation that we wrote out earlier, we can introduce another distribution $q(\mathbf{x})$:

$$E(f) = \int p(\mathbf{x}) f(x) \, d\mathbf{x}$$

$$= \int p(\mathbf{x}) f(\mathbf{x}) \frac{q(\mathbf{x})}{q(\mathbf{x})} d\mathbf{x}$$

$$\approx \frac{1}{N} \sum_{i=1}^{N} \frac{p\left(\mathbf{x}^{(i)}\right)}{q\left(\mathbf{x}^{(i)}\right)} f\left(x^{(i)}\right), \tag{15.9}$$

where we have used the fact that $q(\mathbf{x})$ is the density of a random variable, and so if we perform $\int q(\mathbf{x}) d\mathbf{x}$ over all values of $\mathbf{x}$, then it must equal 1. The ratio $w(\mathbf{x}^{(i)}) = p(\mathbf{x}^{(i)})/q(\mathbf{x}^{(i)})$ is called the importance weight, and it corrects for sampling from the grey region in Figure 15.2 without having to reject samples. While this can be used to estimate the expectation directly, the real benefit of computing the importance weights is that they can be used in order to resample the data. This leads to an algorithm known descriptively as Sampling-Importance-Resampling. In the words of the advert, it 'does exactly what it says on the tin':

The Sampling-Importance-Resampling Algorithm

- Produce N samples $\mathbf{x}^{(i)}$, $i = 1 \ldots N$ from $q(\mathbf{x})$

- Compute normalised importance weights

$$w^{(i)} = \frac{p(\mathbf{x}^{(i)})/q(\mathbf{x}^{(i)})}{\sum_j p(\mathbf{x}^{(j)})/q(\mathbf{x}^{(j)})} \tag{15.10}$$

- Resample from the distribution $\{\mathbf{x}^{(i)}\}$ with probabilities given by the weights $w^{(i)}$

An implementation of this in Python is shown next, and the results of using sampling-importance-resampling on the example in Figure 15.3 are given in Figure 15.4. Note that this method does not reject any samples, but it does involve two separate sampling steps and a relatively expensive loop. Like the other algorithms we have seen, it is sensitive to the quality of the match between the proposal distribution $q(\mathbf{x})$ and the actual distribution $p(\mathbf{x})$.

```
# Sample from q
sample1 = np.random.rand(n)*4

# Compute weights
w = p(sample1)/q(sample1)
w /= np.sum(w)

# Sample from sample1 according to w
cumw = np.zeros(n)
cumw[0] = w[0]
for i in range(1,n):
    cumw[i] = cumw[i-1]+w[i]
```

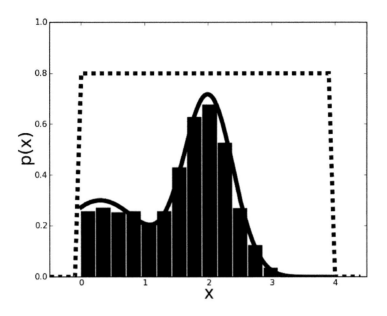

FIGURE 15.4 The histogram shows samples created using sampling-importance-resampling from a mixture of two Gaussians (given by the solid line) as sampled from the uniform box shown as a dotted line.

```
u = np.random.rand(n)

index = 0
for i in range(n):
    indices = np.where(u<cumw[i])
    sample2[index:index+size(indices)] = sample1[i]
    index += np.size(indices)
    u[indices]=2
```

In Section 16.4.2 we will see a method that uses sampling-importance-resampling in an on-line application, known as a particle filter or sequential Monte Carlo method. However, we will first turn our attention to how we can find out more about the sample space. The basic idea is to keep track of the sequence of samples and modify the proposal distribution to take advantage of this, for which we will have to use some more complicated machinery.

15.4 MARKOV CHAIN MONTE CARLO

15.4.1 Markov Chains

In probabilistic terms a chain is a sequence of possible states, where the probability of being in state s at time t is a function of the previous states. A Markov chain is a chain with the Markov property, i.e., the probability at time t depends only on the state at $t - 1$, as discussed in Section 11.3. The set of possible states are linked together by **transition probabilities** that say how likely it is that you move from the current state to each of the others, and they are generally written as a matrix T. They might be constant, or functions of some other variables, but here we will assume that they are constant. Note that, unlike the Markov Decision Processes that we saw in Section 11.3, there is no **action** here that affects the probability of moving into a particular state.

Given a chain, we can perform a **random walk** on the chain by choosing a start state and randomly choosing each successive state according to the transition probabilities. The link to sampling that we need is that if the transition probabilities reflect the distribution that we wish to sample from, then a random walk will explore that distribution. One problem with this is that random walks are very inefficient at exploring space, since they move back towards the start as often as they move away, which means the distance they move from the start scales as $\sqrt{t}$, where t is the number of samples. We therefore want to explore more efficiently than just using a random walk.

We do this by setting up our Markov chain so that it reflects the distribution we wish to sample from, and we want the distribution $p(\mathbf{x}^{(i)})$ to converge to the actual distribution $p(\mathbf{x})$ no matter what state we start from. Since we can start from any state, this tells us that every state is reachable from every other state, which means that the chain is **irreducible** so that the transition matrix can't be cut up into smaller matrices. The chain also has to be **ergodic**, which means that we will revisit every state, so that the probability of visiting any particular state in the future never goes to zero, but is not periodic, which means that we can visit at any time, not just every k iterations for some constant k.

We also want the distribution $p(\mathbf{x})$ to be **invariant** to the Markov chain, which means that the transition probabilities don't change the distribution:

$$p(\mathbf{x}) = \sum_{\mathbf{y}} T(\mathbf{y}, \mathbf{x}) p(\mathbf{y}). \tag{15.11}$$

Finding the transition probabilities to make this true requires that we can move backwards and forwards along the chain with equal probability, so that the chain is **reversible**. This says that the probability of being in an unlikely state s (sampling datapoint $\mathbf{x}$), but heading for a likely state s' (datapoint $\mathbf{x}'$) should be the same as being in the likely state s' and heading for the unlikely state s, so that:

$$p(\mathbf{x})T(\mathbf{x}, \mathbf{x}') = p(\mathbf{x}')T(\mathbf{x}', \mathbf{x}). \tag{15.12}$$

This is known as the **detailed balance** condition and the fact that it leaves the distribution $p(\mathbf{x})$ alone is fairly obvious with a little calculation. If the chain satisfies the detailed balance condition, then it must be ergodic, since $\sum_{\mathbf{y}} T(\mathbf{x}, \mathbf{y}) = 1$, since you must have come from some state, and so:

$$\sum_{\mathbf{y}} p(\mathbf{y})T(\mathbf{y}, \mathbf{x}) = p(\mathbf{x}), \tag{15.13}$$

which means that $p(\mathbf{x})$ must be an invariant distribution of T. So if we can work out how to construct a Markov chain with detailed balance we can sample from it in order to sample from our distribution. This is known as **Markov Chain Monte Carlo (MCMC)** sampling, and the most popular algorithm that is used for MCMC is the **Metropolis–Hastings** algorithm after the two people who were directly involved in its creation.

15.4.2 The Metropolis–Hastings Algorithm

We assume that we have a proposal distribution of the form $q(\mathbf{x}^{(i)}|\mathbf{x}^{(i-1)})$ that we can sample from. The idea of Metropolis–Hastings is similar to that of rejection sampling: we take a sample $\mathbf{x}^*$ and choose whether or not to keep it. Except, unlike rejection sampling, rather than picking another sample if we reject the current one, instead we add another copy of the previous accepted sample. Here, the probability of keeping the sample is $u(\mathbf{x}^*|\mathbf{x}^{(i-1)})$:

$$u(\mathbf{x}^*|\mathbf{x}^{(i)}) = \min\left(1, \frac{\tilde{p}(\mathbf{x}^*)q(\mathbf{x}^{(i)}|\mathbf{x}^*)}{\tilde{p}(\mathbf{x}^{(i)})q(\mathbf{x}^*|\mathbf{x}^{(i)})}\right). \tag{15.14}$$

The Metropolis–Hastings Algorithm

- Given an initial value x_0

- Repeat

    - sample $\mathbf{x}^*$ from $q(\mathbf{x}_i|\mathbf{x}_{i-1})$
    - sample u from the uniform distribution
    - if $u <$ Equation (15.14):
        * set $\mathbf{x}[i+1] = \mathbf{x}^*$
    - otherwise:
        * set $\mathbf{x}[i+1] = \mathbf{x}[i]$

- Until you have enough samples

So why does this algorithm work? Each step involves using the current value to sample from the proposal distribution. These values are accepted if they move the Markov chain towards more likely states, and because the Markov chain is reversible (since it satisfies the detailed balance condition) the algorithm explores states that are proportional to the difficult distribution $p(x)$.

The Python implementation is still very simple:

```
u = np.random.rand(N)
y = np.zeros(N)
y[0] = np.random.normal(mu,sigma)
for i in range(N-1):
    ynew = np.random.normal(mu,sigma)
    alpha = min(1,p(ynew)*q(y[i])/(p(y[i])*q(ynew)))
    if u[i] < alpha:
        y[i+1] = ynew
    else:
        y[i+1] = y[i]
```

The Metropolis–Hastings (and variants of it) are by far the most commonly used MCMC methods, and it is also the most general. It requires that you choose the proposal distribution $q(x^*|x)$ carefully, but it is a very simple algorithm to use. Figure 15.5 shows 5,000

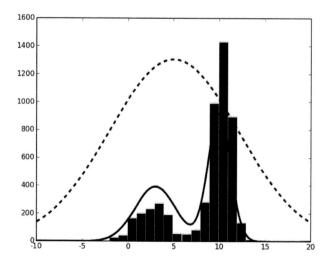

FIGURE 15.5 The results of the Metropolis–Hastings algorithm when the true distribution is a mixture of two Gaussians (shown by the solid line) and the proposal distribution is a single Gaussian (the dotted line).

samples computed using the algorithm on a mixture of two Gaussians based on a proposal distribution that is a single Gaussian.

Note that if the proposal distribution is symmetric, then it drops out of the test in Equation (15.14). This is the original Metropolis algorithm, and it is much closer to the pure random walk. The results of using this algorithm on the same data can be seen in Figure 15.6.

There are other choices of proposal distribution, and they lead to variants on the Metropolis–Hastings algorithm. We will consider the two most common choices next.

15.4.3 Simulated Annealing (Again)

There are lots of times when we might just want to find the maximum of a distribution rather than approximate the distribution itself. We can do this in calculating $\arg\max_{\mathbf{x}^{(i)}} p(\mathbf{x}^{(i)})$ (that is, the $\mathbf{x}^{(i)}$ with the largest probability), but while doing this we will have computed samples from many parts of the space, not just around the maximal region. A possible solution is to use **simulated annealing** as we did in Section 9.6. This changes the Markov chain so that its invariant distribution is not $p(\mathbf{x})$, but rather $p^{1/T_i}(\mathbf{x})$, where $T_i \to 0$ as $i \to \infty$. We need an annealing schedule that cools the system down over time so that we are progressively less likely to accept solutions that are worse over time.

There are only two modifications needed to the Metropolis–Hastings algorithm, and both are trivial: we extend the acceptance criterion to include the temperature and add a line into the loop to include the annealing schedule. The results of using simulated annealing on the example where the true distribution is a mixture of two Gaussians and the proposal distribution is just one is shown in Figure 15.7.

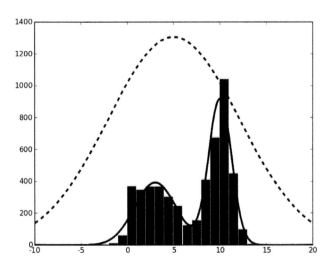

FIGURE 15.6 The results of the Metropolis algorithm when the true distribution is a mixture of two Gaussians (shown by the solid line) and the proposal distribution is a single Gaussian (the dotted line).

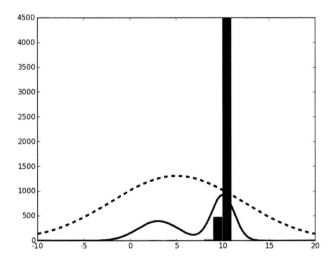

FIGURE 15.7 Using simulated annealing gives the maximum rather than an approximation to the distribution, as is shown here for the same example as in Figures 15.5 and 15.6.

15.4.4 Gibbs Sampling

Another variation on the Metropolis–Hastings algorithm comes when we already know the full conditional probability $p(x_j|x_1, \ldots x_{j-1}, x_{j+1}, \ldots x_n)$ (which is often written as $p(x_j|x_{-j})$ for convenience). We are going to see some examples of this in the next chapter: Bayesian networks. In Section 16.1.2 we will deal with a set of probabilities from a network that looks like:

$$p(\mathbf{x}) = \prod_j p(x_j|x_{\alpha j}), \tag{15.15}$$

where $x_{\alpha j}$ is the parents of x_j (as will become clear in that section).

Given that we know $p(x_j|x_{\alpha j}) \prod_{k \in \beta(j)} p(x_k|x_{\alpha(k)})$ (which is $p(x_j|x_{-j})$), maybe we should try using it as the proposal distribution, giving:

$$q(x^*|x^{(i)}) = \begin{cases} p\left(x_j^*, x_{-j}^{(i)}\right) & \text{if } x_{-j}^* = x_{-j}^{(i)} \\ 0 & \text{otherwise.} \end{cases} \tag{15.16}$$

If we then use Metropolis–Hastings, we find that the acceptance probability P_a is:

$$P_a = \min\left\{1, \frac{p(x^*)p(x_j^{(i)}|x_{-j}^{(i)})}{p(x^{(i)})p(x_j^*|x_{-j}^*)}\right\}, \tag{15.17}$$

and looking carefully at this and expanding out the conditional probabilities we get:

$$P_a = \min\left\{1, \frac{p(x^*)p(x_j^{(i)}, x_{-j}^{(i)})p(x_{-j}^{(i)})}{p(x^{(i)})p(x_j^*, x_{-j}^*)p(x_{-j}^*)}\right\}. \tag{15.18}$$

Since $p(x_j^*, x_{-j}^*) = p(x^*)$, and similarly for $p^{(i)}$, we only have to worry about $\frac{p(x^{(i)})}{p(x_{-j}^*)}$. From the definition of the proposal distribution we know that $x_{*-j} = x_{-j}^{(i)}$, and so the computation is actually $\min 1, 1 = 1$. So we always accept the proposal, which makes things much simpler.

The total algorithm is given by choosing each variable and sampling from its conditional distribution. That's it! The only option that you have is whether to go through the variables in order, or whether to update them in a random order. Rather than running up to some maximum value N, it is not uncommon to run until the joint distribution stops changing. This algorithm is known as the Gibbs sampler and it forms the basis of the software package BUGS (Bayesian Updating with Gibbs Sampling) that is commonly used in statistics. It is also a very useful algorithm for Bayesian networks, as we shall see in the next chapter.

The Gibbs Sampler

- For each variable x_j:

  - initialise $x_j^{(0)}$

- Repeat

  - for each variable x_j:
    * sample $x_1^{(i+1)}$ from $p(x_1|x_2^{(i)}, \ldots x_n^{(i)})$
    * sample $x_2^{(i+1)}$ from $p(x_2|x_1^{(i+1)}, x_3^{(i)}, \ldots x_n^{(i)})$

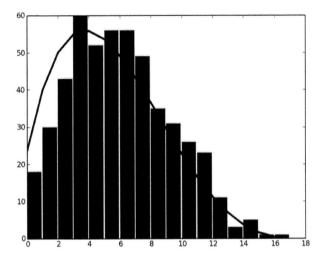

FIGURE 15.8 The Gibbs sampler output for the beta-binomial distribution.

---

    * ...

    * sample $x_n^{(i+1)}$ from $p(x_n | x_1^{(i+1)}, \ldots x_{n-1}^{(i+1)})$

- Until you have enough samples

As an example, suppose that we have a distribution that is made up of two different distributions, a binomial one in x and a beta in y. If you don't know what these distributions are, the combined distribution can be written as:

$$p(x, y, n) = \left(\frac{n!}{x!(n-x)!} \right) y^{x+\alpha-1} + (1-y)^{n-x+\beta-1}. \tag{15.19}$$

The important point is that the overall distribution is a product of two separate ones that can be sampled from separately. Figure 15.8 shows the output of the sampling using the Gibbs sampler, with the line being the correct distribution as usual. There is another example of Gibbs sampling in Section 16.1.2.

FURTHER READING

The historical perspective in this area is provided by:

- N. Metropolis and S. Ulam. The Monte Carlo method. *Journal of the American Statistical Association*, 44(247):335–341, 1949.

Since MCMC is a very useful, but fairly difficult area, there is a good number of review and tutorial articles available. Some that you may find helpful are:

- W.R. Gilks, S. Richardson, and D.J. Spiegelhalter, editors. *Markov Chain Monte Carlo in Practice*. Chapman & Hall, London, UK, 1996.

- C. Andrieu, C. de Freitas, A. Doucet, and M. Jordan. An introduction to MCMC for machine learning. *Machine Learning*, 50:5–43, 2003.

- G. Casella and E.I. George. Explaining the Gibbs sampler. *The American Statistician*, 46(3):167–174, 1992.

- Chib. S. and E. Greenberg. Understanding the Metropolis-Hastings algorithm. *The American Statistician*, 49(4):327–335, 1995.

There is also a more complete treatment of sampling methods in:

- Chapter 11 of C.M. Bishop. *Pattern Recognition and Machine Learning*. Springer, Berlin, Germany, 2006.

PRACTICE QUESTIONS

Problem 15.1 Implement the alternative algorithm for the Box–Muller scheme and compare their times on your computer.

Problem 15.2 Use rejection sampling and importance sampling to sample from a Gaussian distribution using a uniform distribution as the proposal distribution. How many samples do you have to reject with the rejection sampler?

Problem 15.3 The Gibbs sampler can be used in place of the EM algorithm in order to fit the mixtures of a Gaussian Mixture Model (Section 7.1). The idea is to use the samples to introduce the mixing variable π as we did then, and to use the Gibbs sampler to sample from the current estimates of the Gaussians. The algorithm will then look something like:

The Gibbs Sampler for Gaussian Mixtures

- Given some estimates of μ_1, μ_2
- Repeat until the distribution stops changing:
  - for i = 1 to N:
    * sample π according to the E-step of the EM algorithmEM algorithm
    * update:

    $$\hat{\mu}_i = \frac{\sum_{i=1}^{N}(1 - \pi_i^{(t)})x_i}{\sum_{i=1}^{N}(1 - \pi_i^{(t)})}. \tag{15.20}$$

    * sample from the Gaussians with these estimates in order to produce new estimates of the means

---

Implement this and compare the results to using the EM algorithm.

Problem 15.4 Show that the Gibbs sampler satisfies the detailed balance equation.

Problem 15.5 Modify the Metropolis–Hastings algorithm in order to resample when it rejects the current sample. How does it affect the results? Explain the result in terms of the effect on the Markov chain.

## CHAPTER 16

Graphical Models

Throughout this book we have seen that machine learning brings together computer science and statistics. Nowhere is this more clearly shown than in one of the most popular areas of current research in machine learning: **graphical models** (or more completely, **probabilistic graphical models**), which use **graph theory** with all its underlying computational and mathematical machinery in order to explain probabilistic models.

The graphs used in graphical models are the exact ones that are taught in basic algorithms classes: a set of nodes, together with links between them, which can be either **directed** (i.e., have arrows on them so that you can only go one way along them) or not. There are two basic types of graphical models, depending upon whether or not the edges are directed. We will focus primarily on directed graphs, but the undirected kind (known as **Markov Random Fields**) are described in Section 16.2. For such a simple data structure, graphs have turned out to be incredibly powerful in many different parts of computer science, from constructing compilers to managing computer networks. For this reason, there are lots of readily available algorithms for finding **shortest paths** (Floyd's and Djiksta's algorithms, which we've already discussed briefly in Section 6.6), determining cycles, etc. Any good book on algorithms will give details of these and many other graph algorithms.

For our part, we are interested in using graphs to encode probability distributions and so we need to decide what nodes and links are in this context. The nodes are fairly obvious. We generate a node for each **random variable**, and label it accordingly. In this book, we will only consider discrete variables, so that there is a finite number of possible values that the random variable can take. Given a continuous variable we will discretise it into a finite set. While this loses information, it makes the problem much simpler. The alternative is to specify the variable by a probability density function, which can be done, but makes the whole thing harder to describe and understand.

The question is what to make the links represent. Perhaps the best way to think about this is to ask what it means if two nodes are not linked. In this case we are saying that there is no connection between those two variables, which is the same as saying that they are independent. Except it isn't quite as simple as that, because two nodes could be linked through a third node. Have a look at the right of Figure 16.1, where C is not directly linked to B, but there is a link through A. For this reason we have to be careful and talk about **conditional independence**: C is conditionally independent of B, given A.

We use directed links because these relationships are not symmetrical (unless the variables are independent, in which case there is no link). What does the simplest connected graph that we can make, the one on the left of Figure 16.1, mean? There is a rather loose interpretation of the link, which is to say that 'A' causes 'B' (but note that this isn't quite the same semantic usage that we normally have for 'causes', since there may be several

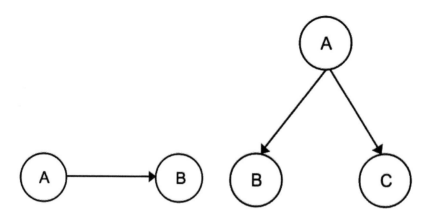

FIGURE 16.1 Two simple graphical models. The arrows denote causal relationships between nodes that represent features.

variables that are all involved in causing B). This is a useful intuition to have, but it is not really correct. More properly, the graph tells us that the probability of A and B is the same as the probability of A times the probability of B conditioned on A: $P(a, b) = P(b|a)P(a)$. If there is no direct link between two nodes then they are conditionally independent of each other.

There is a third thing that we need in order to specify the problem properly, which is the **conditional probability table** for each variable. This specifies what the probabilities are for each of the nodes, conditioned on any nodes that are its parents.

If we wanted to work out a value for $P(a, b)$, then we would need a distribution table for $P(a)$ and one for $P(b|a)$. The nodes are separated into those where we can see their values directly—**observed** nodes—and **hidden** or **latent** nodes, whose values we hope to **infer**, and which may not have clear meanings in all cases.

The basic concept of the graphical model is very simple, which makes it all the more amazing that it produces a powerful set of tools for understanding and creating machine learning algorithms. We will start by looking at the most general model, the **Bayesian Belief Network** or more simply, **Bayesian Network**, and see how they are represented, and the difficulties involved in dealing with them. Following this, we will identify a few places where these difficulties can be overcome, resulting in some very important algorithms that solve a variety of different tasks. In particular, we will look at Markov Random Fields (MRFs), Hidden Markov Models (HMMs), the Kalman Filter, and particle filter.

16.1 BAYESIAN NETWORKS

To start with, we will consider directed graphs, and make one restriction to them, namely that they must not contain **cycles**, that is, there cannot be any loops in the graphs. These graphs go by the rather unlovely name of **DAGs**: directed, acyclic graphs, but for graphical models, when they are paired with the conditional probability tables, they are called Bayesian networks. In order to see what we can do with such a network, we need an example.

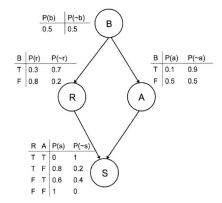

FIGURE 16.2 The sample graphical model. 'B' denotes a node stating whether the exam was boring, 'R' whether or not you revised, 'A' whether or not you attended lectures, and 'S' whether or not you will be scared before the exam.

16.1.1 Example: Exam Fear

Figure 16.2 shows a graph with a full set of distribution tables specified. It is a handy guide to whether or not you will be scared before an exam based on whether or not the course was boring ('B'), which was the key factor you used to decide whether or not to attend lectures ('A') and revise ('R'). We can use it to perform inference in order to decide the likelihood of you being scared before the exam ('S'). There are two kinds of inferences, depending on whether the observations that are made come from the top of the graph or the bottom. If we have a set of observations that can be used to predict an unknown outcome, then we are doing top-down inference or prediction, whereas if the outcome is known, but the causes are hidden, then we are doing bottom-up inference or diagnosis. Either way, we are working out the values of the hidden (unknown) nodes given information about the observed nodes. For the example in Figure 16.2 we will start by predicting whether or not you will be scared before the exam, so it is the outcome that is hidden.

In order to compute the probability of being scared, we need to compute $P(b,r,a,s)$, where the lower-case letters indicate particular values that the upper-case variables can take. The wonderful thing about the graphical model is that we can read the conditional probabilities from the graph—if there is no direct link, then variables are conditionally independent given a node that is already included, so those variables are not needed. For this reason, the computation we need for Figure 16.2 is:

$$
\begin{aligned}
P(s) &= \sum_{b,r,a} P(b,r,a,s) \\
&= \sum_{b,r,a} P(b) \times P(r|b) \times P(a|b) \times P(s|r,a) \\
&= \sum_{b} P(b) \times \sum_{r,a} P(r|b) \times P(a|b) \times P(s|r,a).
\end{aligned} \tag{16.1}
$$

If we know particular values for the three observable nodes, then we can plug them in and work out the probability. In fact, the conditional independence gives us even more: if I know both whether or not you attended lectures and whether or not you revised, then I don't need to know if the course was boring, since there is no direct connection between 'B' and 'S'. Suppose that you didn't attend lectures, but did revise. In that case, the probability of you being scared can be read off the final distribution table as 0.8. The power of the graphical model is when you don't have full information. It is possible to **marginalise** over any of those variables by summing up the values. So suppose that you know that the course was boring, and want to work out how likely it is that you will be scared before the exam. In that case you can ignore the $P(b)$ terms, and just need to sum up the probabilities for r and a using Equation (16.1):

$$
\begin{aligned}
P(s) &= 0.3 \times 0.1 \times 0 + 0.3 \times 0.9 \times 0.8 + 0.7 \times 0.1 \times 0.6 + 0.7 \times 0.9 \times 1 \\
&= 0.328.
\end{aligned}
\tag{16.2}
$$

The backwards inference, or diagnosis, can also be useful. Suppose that I see you looking very scared outside the exam. You look vaguely familiar, but I'm not sure whether or not you came to the lectures. I might want to work out why you are scared—was it because you didn't come to the lectures, or because you didn't revise? To perform this calculation I need to use Bayes' rule to turn the conditional probabilities around, just as was done for the Bayes' classifier in Chapter 7. So the computations that I need are (where $P(s)$ is the normalising constant found by summing over all values of r, a, and b, i.e., Equation (16.2)):

$$
\begin{aligned}
P(r|s) &= \frac{P(s|r)P(r)}{P(s)} \\
&= \frac{\sum_{b,a} P(b,a,r,s)}{P(s)} \\
&= \frac{0.5 \cdot (0.3 \cdot 0.1 \cdot 0 + 0.3 \cdot 0.9 \cdot 0.8) + 0.5 \cdot (0.8 \cdot 0.5 \cdot 0 + 0.8 \cdot 0.5 \cdot 0.8)}{P(s)} \\
&= \frac{0.268}{0.684} = 0.3918. \\
P(a|s) &= \frac{P(s|a)P(a)}{P(s)} \\
&= \frac{0.144}{0.684} = 0.2105.
\end{aligned}
\tag{16.3}
$$

$$
\tag{16.4}
$$

This use of Bayes' rule is the reason why this type of graphical model is known as a Bayesian network. Even in this very simple example, the inference was not trivial, since there were a lot of calculations to do. However, the problem is actually rather worse than that. The computational cost of the simple algorithm we used (start at the root, and follow each link through the graph to perform the computation) is $\mathcal{O}(2^N)$ for a graph with N nodes where each node can be either true or false. In general the problem of exact inference on Bayesian networks is NP-hard (technically, it is actually #P-hard, which is even worse). However, for so-called **polytrees** where there is at most one path between any two nodes, the computational cost is much smaller—linear in the size of the network.

Unfortunately, it is rare to find such polytrees in real examples, so we can either try to turn other networks into polytrees, or consider only approximate inference, which is the most common solution to the problem, and the method that we'll consider next. We can speed things up a little by getting things into the form of Equation (16.1), where the summations were carefully placed as far to the right as possible, so that program loops can be minimised. By doing this the algorithm is as efficient as possible, but it is still NP-hard.

This is sometimes known as the variable elimination algorithm, which is a variation on the bucket elimination algorithm. The idea is to convert the conditional probability tables into what are called λ tables, which simply list all of the possible values for all variables, and which initially contain the conditional probabilities. For example, the λ table for the 'S' variable in Figure 16.2 is:

R	A	S	λ
T	T	T	0
T	T	F	1
T	F	T	0.8
T	F	F	0.2
F	T	T	0.6
F	T	F	0.4
F	F	T	1
F	F	F	0

If I see you looking scared outside the exam (so that S is true), then I can eliminate it from the graph by removing from each table all rows that have S false in them, and deleting the S column. This simplifies things a little, but I have to do rather more in order to compute the probability of you having attended lectures. I don't know whether you revised or not, and I don't know if you found the lectures boring, so I have to marginalise over these variables. The order in which we marginalise doesn't change the correctness (although more advanced algorithms can improve the speed by taking advantage of conditional independence) so we'll pick R first. To eliminate it from the graph, we have to find all of the λ tables that contain it (there will be two of them containing R: the one for R itself and the one that we have just modified to remove S). To remove R, we have to add together the products of the λ values that correspond to places where the other values match. So to complete the entry where B is true and A is false, we have to multiply together the values where B, A, R are respectively true, false, true in the two tables and then add to that the product of where B, A, R are respectively true, false, false. In other words:

$$
\begin{pmatrix}
B & R & \lambda \\
T & T & 0.3 \\
T & F & 0.7 \\
F & T & 0.8 \\
F & F & 0.2
\end{pmatrix}
\times
\begin{pmatrix}
R & A & \lambda \\
T & T & 0 \\
T & F & 0.8 \\
F & T & 0.6 \\
F & F & 1
\end{pmatrix}
\Rightarrow
\begin{pmatrix}
B & A & \lambda \\
T & T & 0.3 \cdot 0 + 0.7 \cdot 0.6 = 0.42 \\
T & F & 0.3 \cdot 0.8 + 0.7 \cdot 1 = 0.94 \\
F & T & 0.8 \cdot 0 + 0.2 \cdot 0.6 = 0.12 \\
F & F & 0.8 \cdot 0.8 + 0.2 \cdot 1 = 0.84
\end{pmatrix}
\quad (16.5)
$$

We can do the same thing in order to eliminate B, which involves all three of the tables, and this will enable the computation of the conditional probability of you attending lectures given that I saw you looking scared before the exam. The benefit of doing things this way is that the whole thing can be written as a general algorithm:

The Variable Elimination Algorithm

- Create the λ tables:
    - for each variable v:
        * make a new table
        * for all possible true assignments x of the parent variables:
            · add rows for $P(v|x)$ and $1 - P(v|x)$ to the table
        * add this table to the set of tables

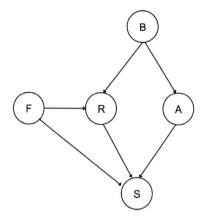

FIGURE 16.3 Adding just one extra node ('F', information about whether or not this is your final year) makes the conditional probability tables significantly more complicated.

- Eliminate known variables v:

  - for each table:

    * remove rows where v is incorrect
    * remove column for v from table

- Eliminate other variables (where x is the variable to keep):

  - for each variable v to be eliminated:

    * create a new table t'
    * for each table t containing v:
      · $v_{\text{true},t} = v_{\text{true},t} \times P(v|x)$
      · $v_{\text{false},t} = v_{\text{false},t} \times P(\neg v|x)$
    * $v_{\text{true},t'} = \sum_t (v_{\text{true},t})$
    * $v_{\text{false},t'} = \sum_t (v_{\text{false},t})$

  - replace tables t with the new one t'

- Calculate conditional probability:

  - for each table:

    * $x_{\text{true}} = x_{\text{true}} \times P(x)$
    * $x_{\text{false}} = x_{\text{false}} \times P(\neg x)$
    * probability is $x_{\text{true}}/(x_{\text{true}} + x_{\text{false}})$

To see that these algorithms do not scale well, consider Figure 16.3, which shows a very simple development of the example in Figure 16.2 by adding just one extra node to the network: whether or not this is your final year ('F'). This makes the network significantly more complicated, since we need another table and extra entries in two of the other tables, and therefore the variable elimination algorithm will take rather longer to run.

16.1.2 Approximate Inference

Since the variable elimination algorithm will only take you so far, for reasonably sized Bayesian networks there is no choice but to perform approximate inference. Fortunately, we have already seen a set of algorithms that are ideally suited to the problem: the Markov Chain Monte Carlo methods that we saw in Chapter 15. There are two other methods of doing approximate inference (loopy belief propagation and mean field approximation), but we will not consider them further; there are references to descriptions of these methods at the end of the chapter.

The basic idea of using MCMC methods in Bayesian networks is to sample from the hidden variables, and then (depending upon the MCMC algorithm employed) weight the samples by their likelihoods. Creating the samples is very easy: for prediction, we start at the top of the graph and sample from each of the known probability distributions. Using Figure 16.2 again, we generate a sample from $P(b)$, and then use that value in the conditional probability tables for 'R' and 'A' to compute $P(r|b = \text{sample value})$ and $P(a|b = \text{sample value})$. These three values are then used to sample from $P(p|b, a, r)$. We can take as many samples as we like in this way, and expect that as the number of samples gets large, so the frequency of specific samples will converge to their expected values.

In this sampling method, we have to work through the graph from top to bottom and select rows from the conditional probability table that match the previous case. This is not what we would do if we were constructing the table by hand. Suppose that you wanted to know how many courses you did not attend the lectures for because the course was boring. You would simply look back through your courses and count the number of boring courses where you didn't go to lectures, ignoring all the interesting courses. We can use exactly this idea if we use rejection sampling (see Section 15.3). The method samples from the unconditional distribution and simply rejects any samples that don't have the correct prior probability. It means that we can sample from each distribution independently, and then throw away any samples that don't match the other variables. This is obviously computationally easier, but we might have to reject a lot of samples.

The solution to this problem is to work out what evidence we already have and use this evidence to assign likelihoods to the other variables that are sampled. Suppose that we sample from $P(b)$ and get value 'true'. If we already know that we did revise, then we weight the observation $P(r|b)$ by the appropriate probability, which is 0.3. We continue through the other variables, sampling where there is no evidence and using the tables to find the probability if we do have evidence. However, we can do rather better than this by using the full MCMC framework. We start by setting values for all of the possible probabilities, based on either evidence or random choices. This gives us an initial state for a Markov chain. Now Gibbs sampling (Section 15.4.4) will find us the maxima of our probability distribution given enough samples.

The probabilities in the network are:

$$p(x) = \prod_j p(x_j|x_{\alpha j}), \tag{16.6}$$

where $x_{\alpha j}$ are the parent nodes of x_j. In a Bayesian network, any given variable is independent of any node that is not their child, given their parents. So we can write:

$$p(x_j|x_{-j}) = p(x_j|x_{\alpha j}) \prod_{k \in \beta(j)} p(x_k|x_{\alpha(k)}), \tag{16.7}$$

where $\beta(j)$ is the set of children of node x_j and x_{-j} signifies all values of x_i except x_j. For

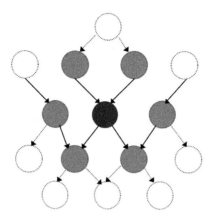

FIGURE 16.4 The Markov blanket of a node is the set of nodes (shaded light grey) that are either parents or children of the node, or other parents of its children (shaded dark grey).

any node we only need to consider its parents, its children, and the other parents of the children, as shown in Figure 16.4. This set is known as the Markov blanket of a node.

Given these calculations, computing the inference on any real Bayesian network generally consists of using Gibbs sampling in order to approximate the inference. For the exam fear example, the algorithm to perform the Gibbs sampling consists of computing the probability distributions (possibly by using parts of the variable elimination algorithm) and then sampling from it:

```
for i in range(nsamples):
    # values contain current samples of b, r, a, s
    values = np.where(np.random.rand(4)<0.5,0,1)
    for j in range(nsteps):
        values=pb__ras(values)
        values=pr__bas(values)
        values=pa__brp(values)
        values=ps__bra(values)
    distribution[values[0]+2*values[1]+4*values[2]+8*values[3]] += 1
distribution /= nsamples
```

For the example, a sample distribution (based on 500 samples, with 10 iterations of each chain) is:

```
b r a s:    dist
1 1 1 1     0.0
1 1 1 0     0.086
1 1 0 1     0.038
1 1 0 0     0.052
1 0 1 1     0.048
```

```
1 0 1 0    0.116
1 0 0 1    0.274
1 0 0 0    0.0
0 1 1 1    0.0
0 1 1 0    0.088
0 1 0 1    0.068
0 1 0 0    0.114
0 0 1 1    0.03
0 0 1 0    0.076
0 0 0 1    0.01
0 0 0 0    0.0
```

16.1.3 Making Bayesian Networks

If we are given the structure and conditional probability tables of the Bayesian network, then we can perform inference on it by using Gibbs sampling or, if the network is simple enough, exactly. However, this raises the important question about where the Bayesian network itself comes from. Unfortunately, the news in this area isn't particularly good: the computational costs of searching over trees are immense, as we shall see. It is not uncommon for people to create the entire network by hand, and only then to use algorithms in order to perform inference on the network. Constructing Bayesian networks by hand is obviously very boring to do, and unless it is based on real data, then it is subjective: putting a whole lot of effort into inference is a waste of time if the data you are inferring about bears no resemblance to reality!

So why is it so difficult to construct Bayesian networks? First, we have already seen that the problem of exact inference on Bayesian networks was NP-hard, which is why we had to use approximate inference. Now let's think about the structure of the graph a little. If there are N nodes (i.e., N random variables in the graph), then how many different graphs are there? For just three nodes ('A', 'B', 'C') we can leave the three unconnected, connect 'A' to 'B' and leave 'C' alone, connect 'B' to 'A' and leave 'C' alone (remember that the links are directional) and lots of variations of that, so that there are seven possible graphs before we have even connected all three nodes to each other. For ten nodes there are $\mathcal{O}(10^{18})$ possible graphs, so we are not going to be searching over all of them. Further, we might want our algorithm to be able to include latent variables, i.e., hidden nodes, which might be a sensible thing to do in terms of explaining the data, but it does make the problem of search even worse.

We've talked about search before: Chapters 9 and 10 are full of search methods. So can we use those methods to solve this problem? The answer is a cautious yes, once we have worked out an objective function to maximise. We want to reward graphs that explain the data well, but we also want to appeal to Occam's razor (which we saw in Section 12.2.2) to ensure that the graphs are as simple as possible. Typical methods are to use an objective function based on the Minimum Description Length (MDL) (which is based on the argument that the solution with the shortest description, i.e., fewest parameters that explains the data, is the best one) or related information-theoretic measures. Then hill climbing or similar algorithms are used to perform local search around a set of random starting graphs. As usual for optimisation problems, getting the scoring function right is critical. You might be wondering why it is not possible to use a genetic algorithm. It is, but given the number of iterations of the GA, each of which would involve constructing hundreds of possible networks, testing them by performing inference, and then combining them, the computational expense rules it out as a practical possibility. As it is such an important problem, there has been a lot of very advanced work on it, which is beyond our scope here. However, there are references at the end of the chapter that contain more information should you want it.

Given that we cannot make the entire graph, we will consider the compromise situation, where we try to compute the conditional probability tables for a known graph based on data. This is quite a sensible compromise: you assume that some expert can put together a network that shows how variables relate to each other, effectively a 'cartoon' of the data generating process, and then you use data in order to compute the conditional probability tables. However, it is still difficult. The idea is to choose the probability distributions to maximise the likelihood of the training data. If there are no hidden nodes, then it is possible to compute the likelihood directly:

$$
\begin{aligned}
L &= \frac{1}{M} \log \prod_{m=1}^{N} P(D_m|G) \\
&= \frac{1}{M} \sum_{n=1}^{N} \sum_{m=1}^{M} \log P(X_n|\text{parents}(X_n), D_m),
\end{aligned}
\tag{16.8}
$$

where M is the number of training data examples D_m, and X_n is one of the N nodes in graph G. Equation (16.8) has broken everything into sums over each node individually, which means that we can compute each separate conditional probability table. To compute the values of the table, you just need to count how often you have been scared before an exam given each of the possible values for having revised and attended lectures, and normalise it to make it into a probability. The danger with this is that with small amounts of data there could be examples that have not happened in training, and that will therefore have probability 0, although this can be dealt with by including prior probabilities and using Bayes' rule to update the estimates using the real data.

Obviously, this doesn't work if there are hidden nodes, since we don't know values for them in the data. Surprisingly, getting around this problem isn't as difficult as might be expected. The key is to see that if we did have values for them, then Equation (16.8) could be used. We can estimate values for them by inference, and then we can iterate these two steps: an estimation step using inference followed by a maximisation step, making this an EM algorithm (Section 7.1.1).

There is lots more work on Bayesian networks, and the references at the end of the chapter include entire books on the topic for anybody wishing to explore more in this area. We will now turn our attention to some other types of graphical models, starting with the variation where the edges are undirected.

16.2 MARKOV RANDOM FIELDS

Bayesian networks are inherently asymmetric, since each edge had an arrow on it. If we remove this constraint, then there is no longer any idea of children and parent nodes. It also makes the idea of conditional independence that we saw for the Bayesian network easier: two nodes in a Markov Random Field (MRF) are conditionally independent of each other, given a third node, if there is no path between the two nodes that doesn't pass through the third node. This is actually a variation on the Markov property, which is how the networks got their name: the state of a particular node is a function only of the states of its immediate neighbours, since all other nodes are conditionally independent given its neighbours. You might think that this fact would make inference on MRFs simpler, but unfortunately it doesn't; in general it is still a #P-hard problem. However, there are particular applications where MRF methods have turned out to be particularly useful, often for images.

The most well-known example is image denoising, something that we have already seen in Section 4.4.5 when we talked about auto-associative learning in the MLP. Suppose that we have a binary image I with pixel values $I_{x_i,x_j} \in \{-1,1\}$. This image is a representation of an 'ideal' image I'_{x_i,x_j} that has no noise in it, which is what we want to recover. If we assume that the amount of noise is small, then there should be a good correlation between the values of each pixel in the two images, so I_{x_i,x_j} and I'_{x_i,x_j} should be correlated. We also assume that within a small 'patch' or region in an image, there is good correlation between pixels (so I_{x_i,x_j} should correlate well with I_{x_i+1,x_j} and its other neighbouring pixels (I_{x_i,x_j-1}, etc.). This assumption says that there are lots of places in the image where all of the pixels are of the same value, and this is (at least approximately) true for most images, and says that the pixels are correlated (and that other pixels in the image are conditionally independent of I_{x_i,x_j} given the neighbours of that pixel, which is the MRF bit).

The original theory of MRFs was worked out by physicists, initially by looking at the Ising model, which is a statistic description of a set of atoms connected in a chain, where each can spin up (+1) or down (-1) and whose spin affects those connected to it in the chain. Physicists tend to think of the energy of such systems, and argue that stable states are those with the lowest energy, since the system needs to get extra energy if it wants to move out of this state. For this reason, the jargon of MRFs is in terms of energies, and we therefore want the energy of our pair of images to be low when the pixels match, and higher when they do not. So we write the energy of the same pixel in two images as $-\eta I_{x_i,x_j} I'_{x_i,x_j}$, where η is a positive constant. Note that if the two pixels have the same sign then the energy is negative, while if they have opposite signs then the energy is positive and therefore larger. The energy of two neighbouring pixels is $-\zeta I_{x_i,x_j} I_{x_i+1,x_j}$, and we can just add these components together to get the total energy:

$$E(I, I') = -\zeta \sum_{i,j}^{N} I_{x_i,x_j} I_{x_i \pm 1, x_j \pm 1} - \eta \sum_{i,j=1}^{N} I_{x_i,x_j} I'_{x_i,x_j}, \qquad (16.9)$$

where the index of the pixels is assumed to run from 1 to N in both the x and y directions in both images and we are only interested in locally flat patches of the image we are changing, which is I.

There is now a simple iterative update algorithm, which is to start with noisy image I and ideal I', and update I so that at each step the energy calculation is lower. So you pick one pixel I_{x_i,x_j} for some values of x_i, x_j at a time, and compute the energies with this pixel being set to -1 and 1, picking the lower one. In probabilistic terms, we are making the probability $p(I, I')$ higher. The algorithm then moves on to another pixel, either choosing a random pixel at each step or moving through them in some pre-determined order, running through the set of pixels until their values stop changing. Figure 16.5 shows an original black and white image, a version corrupted with 10% noise, and the MRF-reconstructed version using parameters $\eta = 2.0, \zeta = 1.5$. This reduces the error from 10% to less than 1%, although it also removes my home country of New Zealand from the map!

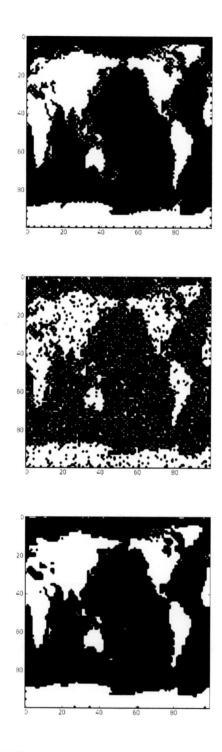

FIGURE 16.5 Using the MRF image denoising algorithm with $\eta = 2.1, \zeta = 1.5$ on a map of the world (*top left*) corrupted by 10% uniformly distributed random noise (*top right*) gives the image below which has about 1% error, although it has smoothed out the edges of all the continents.

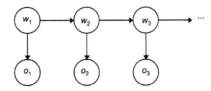

FIGURE 16.6 The Hidden Markov Model is an example of a dynamic Bayesian network. The figure shows the first three states and the related observations unrolled as time progresses.

The Markov Random Field Image Denoising Algorithm

- Given a noisy image I and an original image I', together with parameters η, ζ:

- Loop over the pixels of image I:

    - compute the energies with the current pixel being -1 and 1
    - pick the one with lower energy and set its value in I accordingly

---

We will now focus on a type of graphical model that is in very common use, and that has computationally tractable algorithms for doing exact inference on it.

16.3 HIDDEN MARKOV MODELS (HMMS)

The Hidden Markov Model is one of the most popular graphical models. It is used in speech processing and in a lot of statistical work. The HMM generally works on a set of temporal data. At each clock tick the system moves into a new state, which can be the same as the previous one. Its power comes from the fact that it deals with situations where you have a Markov model, but you do not know exactly which state of the Markov model you are in—instead, you see **observations** that do not uniquely identify the state. This is where the *hidden* in the title comes from. Performing inference on the HMM is not that computationally expensive, which is a big improvement over the more general Bayesian network. The applications that it is most commonly applied to are temporal: a set of measurements made at regular time intervals, which comprise the observations of the state. In fact, the HMM is the simplest **dynamic Bayesian network**, a Bayesian network that deals with **sequential** (often time-series) data. Figure 16.6 shows the HMM as a graphical model.

The example that we will use is this: As a caring teacher I want to know whether or not you are actually working towards the exam. I know from Chapter 12 that there are four things that you do in the evenings (go to the pub, watch TV, go to a party, study) and I want to work out whether or not you are studying. However, I can't just ask you, because you would probably lie to me. So all I can do is try to make observations about your behaviour and appearance. Specifically, I can probably work out if you look tired, hungover, scared, or fine. I want to use these observations to try to work out what you did last night. The problem is that I don't know why you look the way you do, but I can guess by assigning probabilities to those things. So if you look hungover, then I might give probability 0.5 to the guess that you went to the pub last night, 0.25 to the guess that you went to a party, 0.2 to watching TV, and 0.05 to studying. In fact, we will use these the other way round, using the probability that you look hungover given what you did last night. These are known as **observation** or **emission probabilities**.

I don't have access to the other information that was used in Chapter 12, such as what parties are on and what other assignments you have (one of the worst things about stopping being a student is that the number of parties you get invited to drops off), but based on my own experience of being a student I can guess how likely parties are, etc., and knowing what student finances are, I can guess things like the probability of you going to the pub tonight if you went to the pub last night. So now it is just a question of putting these things into a form where I can work with them, and I can prepare my lectures according to how well you are working.

Each day that I see you in lectures I make an observation of your appearance, $o(t)$, and I want to use that observation to guess the state $\omega(t)$. This requires me to build up some kind of probabilities $P(o_k(t)|\omega_j(t))$, which is the probability that I see observation o_k (e.g., you are tired) given that you were in state ω_j (e.g., you went to a party) last night. These are usually labelled as $b_j(o_k)$. The other information that I have, or think I have, is the **transition probability**, which tells me how likely you are to be in state ω_j tonight given that you were in state ω_i last night. So if I think you were at the pub last night I will probably guess that the probability of you being there again tonight is small because your student loan won't be able to handle it. This is written as $P(\omega_j(t+1)|\omega_i(t))$ and is usually labelled as $a_{i,j}$.

I can add one more constraint to each of the probability distributions $a_{i,j}$ and b_i. I know that you did something last night, so $\sum_j a_{i,j} = 1$ and I know that I will make some observation (since if you aren't in the lecture I'll assume you were too tired), so $\sum_k b_j(o_k) = 1$. There is one other thing that is generally assumed, which is that the Markov chain is **ergodic**, something that we saw in Section 15.4.1: it means that there is a non-zero probability of reaching every state eventually, no matter what the starting state.

After a couple of weeks of the course I have made observations about you, and I am ready to sort out my HMM. There are three things that I might want to do with the data:

- see how well the sequence of observations that I've made match my current HMM (Section 16.3.1)

- work out the most probable sequence of states that you've been in based on my observations (Section 16.3.2)

- given several sets of observations (for example, by watching several students) generate a good HMM for the data (Section 16.3.3)

We will start by assuming that I invent a model and want to see how good it is. So I use my own knowledge of being a student to work out the probability distributions and then I can test the observations I make of you against my model. At this point I will probably find out that my student life was different to yours, or things have changed since I was a student, and I will have to generate a new model to match current data. I can then use this improved model to work out what you've been doing each evening. These problems are dealt with in the next three sections.

The HMM itself is made up of the transition probabilities $a_{i,j}$ and the observation probabilities $b_j(o_k)$, and the probability of starting in each of the states, π_i. So these are the things that I need to specify for myself, starting with the transition probabilities (which are also shown in Figure 16.7):

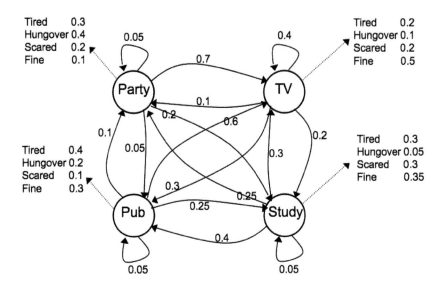

FIGURE 16.7 The example HMM with transition and observation probabilities shown.

| | Previous night | | | |
	TV	Pub	Party	Study
TV	0.4	0.6	0.7	0.3
Pub	0.3	0.05	0.05	0.4
Party	0.1	0.1	0.05	0.25
Study	0.2	0.25	0.2	0.05

and then the observation probabilities:

	TV	Pub	Party	Study
Tired	0.2	0.4	0.3	0.3
Hungover	0.1	0.2	0.4	0.05
Scared	0.2	0.1	0.2	0.3
Fine	0.5	0.3	0.1	0.35

16.3.1 The Forward Algorithm

Suppose that I see the following observations: O = (tired, tired, fine, hungover, hungover, scared, hungover, fine) and I want to work out the likely run of states that generated it. The probability that my observations $O = \{o(1), \ldots, o(T)\}$ come from the model can be computed using simple conditional probability. I know you were doing something last night, so for an observation $o(t)$ =tired (say) I just need to compute the probability that I made that observation given you were in a particular state (say watching TV) and multiply it by the probability that you were in that state given the state I thought you were in the night before (say partying). So for the example, I compute the probability that you were tired given that you were watching TV, which is 0.2, and then multiply it by the probability that you spent last night watching TV given that I thought you were partying the night before, which is 0.1. So this yields probability 0.02 for this particular **state change**. There is one extra thing that we need which is to decide which state you actually start in. I don't know this, so I assign probability 0.25 to each state.

Now I need to do this over every possible sequence of states to find out the most likely one based on what I actually saw. Note that I have used O to denote the whole sequence of observations that I made. In the same way, Ω is an entire sequence of possible states (this is a change in notation from the rest of the methods we have looked at, but it is consistent with the way that other authors describe HMMs). This can be written as:

$$P(O) = \sum_{r=1}^{R} P(O|\Omega_r)P(\Omega_r). \tag{16.10}$$

The r index here describes a possible sequence of states, so Ω_1 is one sequence, Ω_2 another, and so on. We'll consider this in a minute, but first we will use the Markov property to write:

$$P(\Omega_r) = \prod_{t=1}^{T} P(\omega_j(t)|\omega_i(t-1)) = \prod_{t=1}^{T} a_{i,j}, \tag{16.11}$$

and

$$P(O|\Omega_r) = \prod_{t=1}^{T} P(o_k(t)|\omega_j(t)) = \prod_{t=1}^{T} b_j(o_k). \tag{16.12}$$

So Equation (16.10) can be written as:

$$
\begin{aligned}
P(O) &= \sum_{r=1}^{R} \prod_{t=1}^{T} P(o_k(t)|\omega_j(t)) P(\omega_j(t)|\omega_i(t-1)) \\
&= \sum_{r=1}^{R} \prod_{t=1}^{T} b_j(o_k) a_{i,j}.
\end{aligned}
\tag{16.13}
$$

This looks fairly easy now. The only problem is in that sum over r, which runs over all possible sequences of hidden states. If there are N hidden states then there are N^T possible sequences, and for each one we have to compute a product of T probabilities. Not only will these probabilities be incredibly small, but the computational cost of getting them will be astronomical: $\mathcal{O}(N^T T)$.

Fortunately, the Markov property comes to our rescue again. Since the probability of each state only depends on the data at the current and previous timestep $(o(t), \omega(t), \omega(t-1))$ we can build up our computation of $P(O)$ one timestep at a time. This is known as the forward trellis by some people, since it looks like a garden trellis in Figure 16.8. To construct the trellis we introduce a new variable $\alpha_i(t)$ that describes the probability that at time t the state is ω_i and that the first $(t-1)$ steps all matched the observations $o(t)$:

$$
\alpha_j(t) = \begin{cases} 0 & t = 0, j \neq \text{initial state} \\ 1 & t = 0, j = \text{initial state} \\ \sum_i \alpha_i(t-1)a_{i,j}b_j(o_t) & \text{otherwise.} \end{cases}
\tag{16.14}
$$

where $b_j(o_t)$ means the particular emission probability of output o_t. This ensures that only the observation probability that has the index that matches the observation o_t contributes to the sum. Computing $P(O)$ now requires only $\mathcal{O}(N^2 T)$, which is a substantial improvement, in a very simple algorithm, as will be seen shortly.

We will use the following notation: $a_{i,j}$ is the transition probability of going from state i

to state j, so if there are N states, then it is of size $N \times N$; $b_i(o)$ is the transition probability of emitting observation o in state i, so it is of size $N \times O$, where O is the number of different observations that there are (four in the example). It will be useful to introduce four more variables, all of which are probabilities that are conditioned on the observation sequence and the model:

- $\alpha_{i,t}$, which is the probability of getting the observation sequence up to time t and being in state i at time t (size $N \times t$),

- $\beta_{i,t}$, which is the probability of the sequence from $t+1$ to the end given that the state is i at time t,

- $\delta_{i,t}$, which is the highest probability of any path that reaches state i at time t,

- $\xi_{i,j,t}$, which is the probability of being in state i at time t, state j at time $t+1$, and so is an $N \times N \times T$ matrix.

Since $\alpha_{i,t}$ is the probability of getting the observation sequence up to time t and being in state i at time t conditioned on the model and the observations, the probability of the whole observation sequence given the model is just $\sum_{i=1}^{N} \alpha_{i,T}$.

The HMM Forward Algorithm

- Initialise with $\alpha_{i,0} = \pi_i b_i(o_0)$

- For each observation in order o_t, $t = 1, \ldots, T$

  - for each of the N_s possible states s:

    * $\alpha_{s,t+1} = b_s(o_{t+1}) \left(\sum_{i=1}^{N}(\alpha_{i,t} a_{i,s}) \right)$

Let's look at the first two states of our example HMM. In both, the observation is that you were tired, so we need to compute $\alpha_{i,t}$ and so construct the trellis. Figure 16.8 shows the idea, with the initial $\alpha_{i,t=0}$ coming from my guesses about how likely each state is (the π variable), and we just need to run through the set of computations to compute $\alpha_{i,t=2}$ and so on, getting the numbers that are shown in the figure. We then repeat this for the next step and so on until we reach the final state. At this stage we can sum up all of the possible probabilities, which tells me in this case that you were most likely watching TV last night. We will also need to be able to go backwards through the trellis, which is a very similar algorithm that works backwards to compute β values, also based on the transmission probability and observation probability matrices by:

$$\beta_{i,t} = \sum_{j=1}^{N} a_{i,j} b_j(o_{t+1}) \beta_{j,t+1}. \tag{16.15}$$

16.3.2 The Viterbi Algorithm

The next problem that we want to solve is the decoding problem of working out the hidden states: I can use my model of how students are expected to behave and match them with my observations to guess what you have been doing each evening. The algorithm is known as the Viterbi algorithm after its creator, although he actually derived it for error correction, a

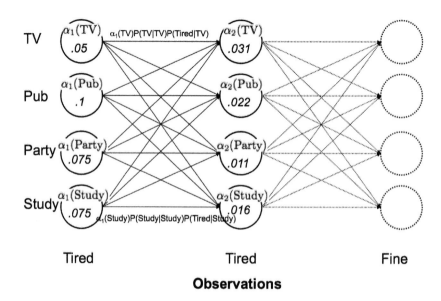

FIGURE 16.8 The forward trellis for the first two observations of the example HMM.

completely different application! We want to work out the $\delta_{i,t}$ variable. This requires finding the maximum probability of any path that gets us to state i at time t that has the right observations for the sequence up to t; apart from being a maximisation instead of a sum, it is pretty similar to the forward algorithm. The initialisation is $\delta_{i,t=0} = \pi_i b_i(o_0)$, since this tells us about the first observations we see, and then we work from there computing each new δ as:

$$\delta_{j,t+1} = \max_i \left(\delta_{i,t} a_{i,j} \right) b_j(o_{t+1}). \tag{16.16}$$

It will also be useful to keep track of which state seems to be the best at each stage: $\phi_{j,t} = \arg\max_i (\delta_{i,t-1} a_{i,j})$, because at the end of the sequence we want to go backwards through the matrix that we have built up and work out the actual most probable path from it.

So once we reach the end, we can work out the most likely state as the one with the highest $q_T^* = \delta_{\cdot, T}$, and then work back through the lattice using $q_t^* = \phi_{q_{t+1}^*, t+1}$ until we reach the start of the sequence. As an algorithm this can be written as:

The HMM Viterbi Algorithm

- Start by initialising $\delta_{i,0}$ by $\pi_i b_i(o_0)$ for each state i, $\phi_0 = 0$

    - run forward in time t:

        * for each possible state s:

            · $\delta_{s,t} = \max_i (\delta_{i,t-1} a_{i,s}) b_s(o_t)$
            · $\phi_{s,t} = \arg\max_i (\delta_{i,t-1} a_{i,s})$

    - set q_T^*, the most likely end hidden state to be $q_T^* = \arg\max_i \delta_{i,T}$

    - run backwards in time computing:

        * $q_{t-1}^* = \phi_{q_t^*, t}$

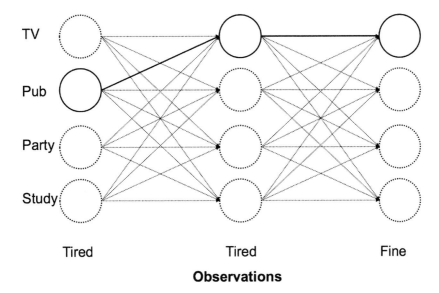

TV

Pub

Party

Study

Tired   Tired   Fine

Observations

FIGURE 16.9   The Viterbi trellis for the first three observations of the example HMM.

Figure 16.9 shows the path for the first three states of the example. Using the numbers from the example, I can use the Viterbi algorithm to find the most likely explanation of a set of observations such as (fine, hungover, hungover, fine, tired, fine, fine, fine, hungover, hungover, tired, scared, scared), which tells me that you seem to have spent a lot of time in the pub. However, even for this most likely sequence, the probability of it is only 7.65×10^{-9}, which doesn't seem very likely. This is one of the problems with HMMs: the state space is so large that the probabilities tend to 0 very quickly. This is both an interpretation problem and a computational one, since we get problems with rounding errors very quickly because the probabilities are so small. This is discussed briefly at the end of this section.

16.3.3   The Baum–Welch or Forward–Backward Algorithm

In the example I had to invent the transition and observation probabilities from my experience, and the result is that the best path is not very likely. It would obviously be better to generate the HMM from sets of observations rather than by making up the transition probabilities. This is a learning process, and it is an unsupervised learning problem since we don't have any target solutions to go on. In fact, finding the optimal probabilities is an NP-complete problem, since we have to search over all the possible sets of probabilities for all the possible sequences. Instead, we will use an EM algorithm known as the Baum–Welch algorithm (see Section 7.1.1 for a previous example of an EM algorithm). This is not quite as good as the previous one in that it is not guaranteed to find even a local optima, but in general it works fairly well.

The key to the algorithm is in its second name: Forward–Backward. We introduced a variable α above that took us forward through the HMM above, and we mentioned that it had a complementary variable β that takes us backwards through the HMM, i.e., $\beta_i(t)$ tells us the probability that at time t we are in state ω_i and the result of the target sequence (times $t+1$ to T) will be generated correctly. So we can now pick any point in the middle of a sequence, and run forwards from the beginning and backwards from the end to see the possible paths.

To see what computations are needed we will work out what the three variables that we are interesting in fitting—π_i, $a_{i,j}$ and $b_i(o_k)$—are, which are respectively the number of times we expect to be in state i at the first observation, the expected number of times we transition from state i to state j divided by the number of times we leave state i, and the expected number of times we see observation o_k when in state i, divided by the number of times we are in state i.

Thinking about the $\xi_{i,j,t}$ variable that we talked about, but haven't used yet, and which is the probability of being in state i at time t, state j at time $t+1$, we can see that (where the $\hat{\ }$ is to make it clear that these are estimates based on the sequences that we see):

$$\hat{\pi}_i = \sum_{j=1}^{N} \xi_{i,j,0} \tag{16.17}$$

$$\hat{a}_{i,j} = \sum_{t=1}^{T-1} \xi_{i,j,t} / \sum_{t=1}^{T-1}\sum_{j=1}^{N} \xi_{i,j,t} \tag{16.18}$$

$$\hat{b}_i(o_k) = \sum_{t=1,o_t=k}^{T}\sum_{j=1}^{N} \xi_{i,j,t} / \sum_{t=1}^{T}\sum_{j=1}^{N} \xi_{i,j,t} \tag{16.19}$$

The notation in the last line means that in the numerator we only include those times t where the observation k was seen, and note that the sums over time in the middle line only go up to $T-1$, since it isn't possible to move on from the last state.

So now the algorithm needs to start by computing $\xi_{i,j,t}$, and then make an estimate of π, a, b, which can then be iterated until the values stop changing. This has the flavour of an EM algorithm: we work out how many times we can **expect** to transition between states, which is the expectation, and then we try to maximise them.

The only thing that we haven't done yet is to work out how to compute $\xi_{i,j,t}$, although looking back at the definitions of the α and β variables, and working out that what we are doing is running forwards until time t, when we get to state i, then transitioning to state j carrying on from there to the end (or equivalently, going backwards from the end to state j at time $t+1$, we see that the form of $\xi_{i,j,t}$ is:

$$\xi_{i,j,t} = \frac{\alpha_{i,t}a_{i,j}b_j(o_{t+1})\beta_{j,t+1}}{\sum_{i=1}^{N}\sum_{j=1}^{N} \alpha_{i,t}a_{i,j}b_j(o_{t+1})\beta_{j,t+1}}, \tag{16.20}$$

where the numerator is simply a normaliser, and the values at T are a little different as there is no b or β then. This leads to the complete Baum–Welch algorithm:

The HMM Baum–Welch (Forward–Backward) Algorithm

- Initialise π to be equal probabilities for all states, and a, b randomly unless you have prior knowledge

- While updates have not converged:

  - **E-step:**
  - use forward and backward algorithms to get α and β
  - for each observation in the sequence $o_t, t = 1 \ldots T$
    * for each state i:
      · for each state j:
      · compute ξ using Equation (16.20)
  - **M-step:**
  - for each state i:
    * compute $\hat{\pi}_i$ using Equation (16.17)
    * for each state j:
      · compute $\hat{a}_{i,j}$ using Equation (16.18)
  - for each different possible observation o:
    * compute $\hat{b}_i(o)$ using Equation (16.19)

Since this is the most important algorithm, here is a Python implementation as well:

```python
def BaumWelch(obs,nStates):

    T = np.shape(obs)[0]
    xi = np.zeros((nStates,nStates,T))

    # Initialise pi, a, b randomly
    pi = 1./nStates*np.ones((nStates))
    a = np.random.rand(nStates,nStates)
    b = np.random.rand(nStates,np.max(obs)+1)

    tol = 1e-5
    error = tol+1
    maxits = 100
    nits = 0
    while ((error > tol) & (nits < maxits)):
            nits += 1
            oldpi = pi.copy()
            olda = a.copy()
            oldb = b.copy()

            # E step
            alpha,c = HMMfwd(pi,a,b,obs)
```

```
            beta = HMMbwd(a,b,obs,c)

            for t in range(T-1):
                    for i in range(nStates):
                            for j in range(nStates):
                                    xi[i,j,t] = alpha[i,t]*a[i,j]*b[j,
                                    obs[t+1]]*beta[j,t+1]
                    xi[:,:,t] /= np.sum(xi[:,:,t])

            # The last step has no b, beta in
            for i in range(nStates):
                    for j in range(nStates):
                            xi[i,j,T-1] = alpha[i,T-1]*a[i,j]
            xi[:,:,T-1] /= np.sum(xi[:,:,T-1])

            # M step
            for i in range(nStates):
                    pi[i] = np.sum(xi[i,:,0])
                    for j in range(nStates):
                            a[i,j] = np.sum(xi[i,j,:T-1])/np.sum(xi[i,:,:
                            T-1])

                    for k in range(max(obs)):
                            found = (obs==k).nonzero()
                            b[i,k] = np.sum(xi[i,:,found])/np.sum(xi[i,:,
                            :])

            error = (np.abs(a-olda)).max() + (np.abs(b-oldb)).max()
            print nits, error, 1./np.sum(1./c), np.sum(alpha[:,T-1])

    return pi, a, b
```

We can't really use this algorithm very well on the simple example, since we would need rather more data to do justice to the training. However, if we do apply it and then compute the Viterbi path, then it gives the same answer as with the invented data.

One final thing to mention with the HMM is that there are ways to deal with the fact that the probabilities get so small, which can cause round-off errors inside the computer. One approach is to renormalise the α values by dividing by the sum of the α values for each time step. If the same values are used in the β calculation as well, then they cancel out beautifully in the final calculations and things work very well. This is the c variable in the following code for the forward algorithm:

```
def HMMfwd(pi,a,b,obs):

    nStates = np.shape(b)[0]
    T = np.shape(obs)[0]
```

```
alpha = np.zeros((nStates,T))
alpha[:,0] = pi*b[:,obs[0]]

for t in range(1,T):
    for s in range(nStates):
        alpha[s,t] = b[s,obs[t]] * np.sum(alpha[:,t-1] * a[:,s])

c = np.ones((T))
if scaling:
    for t in range(T):
        c[t] = np.sum(alpha[:,t])
        alpha[:,t] /= c[t]
return alpha,c
```

That pretty much sums it up for the HMM. It is worth mentioning two limitations of it, which are that the probability distributions are not time dependent, and that the probabilities can get very small. The second of these problems is an implementation detail that needs careful monitoring, while the first can be dealt with by using more general graphical models, although with the additional computational costs that come with that.

16.4 TRACKING METHODS

We will now look at two methods of performing tracking. You perform tracking fairly easily, keeping tabs on where something is and how it is moving. This has an obvious evolutionary benefit, since keeping track of where predators were and whether they were coming towards you could keep you alive. It is also useful for a machine to be able to do this, both for similar reasons to a human or animal (watching something moving and predicting what path it will follow, for example in radar or other imaging method) and to keep track of a changing probability distribution. We will look at two methods of doing it, the Kalman filter and the particle filter.

16.4.1 The Kalman Filter

The Kalman filter (named for E. Kalman; although he was not the original inventor he did do quite a lot of work on it) is a recursive estimator. It makes an estimate of the next step, then computes an error term based on the value that was actually produced in the next step, and tries to correct it. It then uses both of those to make the next prediction, and iterates this procedure. It can be seen as a simple cycle of predict-correct behaviour, where the error at each step is used to improve the estimate at the next iteration. The Kalman filter can be represented by the graphical model shown in Figure 16.10.

Much of the jargon that is associated with the Kalman filter is familiar to us: the state, which is hidden, consists of the variables that we want to know, which we see through noisy observations over time. There is a transition model that tells us how states change from one to another, and an observation model (also called the sensor model here) that tells us how states lead to observations.

The underlying idea is that there is some time-varying process that is generating a set of noisy outputs, where there are two sources of noise: process noise, which represents

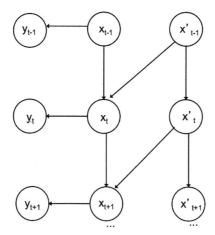

FIGURE 16.10 A representation of the Kalman filter with time derivatives (such as for tracking) as a graphical model.

the fact that the process changes over time, but we don't know how, and observation (or measurement) noise, which is the errors that are made in the readings. Both are assumed to be independent of each other, and zero mean Gaussians. We write the process as a stochastic difference equation in **x**, which has n dimensions:

$$\mathbf{x}_{t+1} = \mathbf{A}\mathbf{x}_t + \mathbf{B}\mathbf{u}_t + \mathbf{w}_t, \tag{16.21}$$

where $\mathbf{A}_t$ is an $n \times n$ matrix that represents the non-driven part of the underlying process, **B** is an $n \times l$ matrix that represents the driving force, and **u** is the l-dimensional driving force. **w** is the process noise, which is assumed to be zero mean with standard deviation **Q**.

The observations that we make are m-dimensional:

$$\mathbf{y}_t = \mathbf{H}\mathbf{x}_t + \mathbf{v}_t, \tag{16.22}$$

where $m \times n$ matrix **H** describes how measurements of the state are measured, and **v** is the measurement noise, which is also assumed to be zero mean, but with standard deviation **R**.

As an example of this, consider a particle moving at a constant speed in one dimension. The state is two dimensional, consisting of the position and velocity of the particle (so $\mathbf{x} = [x, \dot{x}]^T$). Since there is no driving force the next term is $\mathbf{B}\mathbf{u}_t = 0$. The process equation is then derived by using Newton's laws of motion (so $x_{t+1} = x_t + \Delta t \dot{x}_t$, and since we are making indexing by time, $\Delta_t = 1$, and the velocity is constant):

$$\begin{pmatrix} x_{t+1} \\ \dot{x}_{t+1} \end{pmatrix} = \begin{pmatrix} 1 & 1 \\ 0 & 1 \end{pmatrix} \begin{pmatrix} x_t \\ \dot{x}_t \end{pmatrix} + \mathbf{w}_t. \tag{16.23}$$

We can observe the position of the particle, up to measurement noise, but not the velocity, and so the measurement equation is:

$$y_t = \begin{pmatrix} 1 & 0 \end{pmatrix} \begin{pmatrix} x_t \\ \dot{x}_t \end{pmatrix} + \mathbf{v}_t. \tag{16.24}$$

The principal simplifying assumptions of the Kalman filter are that the process is linear and that all of the distributions are Gaussian with constant covariance. Since the convolution of Gaussians is also Gaussian, this means that we can put them together to form new

Gaussians, and so the model stays well behaved. This was a significant advantage over previous methods of tracking, which tended to stop working fairly quickly, since the estimates broke down because the probability distribution stopped being well-defined. We assume that both the transition model and the observation model are Gaussians with means based on the previous observations, and fixed covariances $\mathbf{Q}$ and $\mathbf{R}$ which can be written mathematically as (with the same parameters as the state and measurement update equations):

$$P(\mathbf{x}_{t+1}|\mathbf{x}_t) = \mathcal{N}(\mathbf{x}_{t+1}|\mathbf{A}\mathbf{x}_t, \mathbf{Q}) \tag{16.25}$$
$$P(\mathbf{z}_t|\mathbf{x}_t) = \mathcal{N}(\mathbf{z}_t|\mathbf{H}\mathbf{x}_t, \mathbf{R}). \tag{16.26}$$

Having described the set-up, what do we do? The basic idea is to make a prediction and then correct it when the next observation is available, i.e., at the next timestep. We will use $\hat{\mathbf{x}}$ and $\hat{\mathbf{y}}$ as the estimates, so $\hat{\mathbf{y}}_{t+1} = \mathbf{HA}\hat{\mathbf{x}}_{t+1}$ and so the error is $\mathbf{y}_{t+1} - \hat{\mathbf{y}}_{t+1}$; that is the difference between what was actually observed and what we predicted (without measurement noise). Since this is a probabilistic process with Gaussian distributions, we can also keep a predicted covariance matrix that goes with it: $\hat{\mathbf{\Sigma}}_{t+1} = \mathbf{A}\mathbf{\Sigma}_t\mathbf{A}^T + \mathbf{Q}$ (which is $E[(\mathbf{x}_k - \hat{\mathbf{x}}_k)(\mathbf{x}_k - \hat{\mathbf{x}}_k)^T]$). The Kalman filter weights these error computations by how much trust the filter currently has in its predictions; these weights are known as the Kalman gain and are computed by:

$$\mathbf{K}_{t+1} = \hat{\mathbf{\Sigma}}_{t+1}\mathbf{H}^T \left(\mathbf{H}\hat{\mathbf{\Sigma}}_{t+1}\mathbf{H}^T + \mathbf{R}\right)^{-1}. \tag{16.27}$$

This equation comes from minimising the mean-square error; we will not derive it, but the Further Reading section gives further references for you to follow up if you wish. Using it, the update for the estimate is:

$$\mathbf{x}_{t+1} = \hat{\mathbf{x}}_{t+1} + \mathbf{K}_{t+1}\left(\mathbf{z}_{t+1} - \mathbf{H}\hat{\mathbf{x}}_{t+1}\right), \tag{16.28}$$

All that is then required is to update the covariance estimate:

$$\mathbf{\Sigma}_{t+1} = (\mathbf{I} - \mathbf{K}_{t+1}\mathbf{H})\hat{\mathbf{\Sigma}}_{t+1}, \tag{16.29}$$

where $\mathbf{I}$ is the identity matrix of the relevant size. Putting these equations together leads to a simple algorithm.

The Kalman Filter Algorithm

- Given an initial estimate $\mathbf{x}(0)$

- For each timestep:

  - **predict the next step**
    * predict state as $\hat{\mathbf{x}}_{t+1} = \mathbf{A}\mathbf{x}_t + \mathbf{B}\mathbf{u}_t$
    * predict covariance as $\hat{\mathbf{\Sigma}}_{t+1} = \mathbf{A}\mathbf{\Sigma}_t\mathbf{A}^T + \mathbf{Q}$
  - **update the estimate**
    * compute the error in the estimate, $\boldsymbol{\epsilon} = \mathbf{y}_{t+1} - \mathbf{HA}\mathbf{x}_{t+1}$
    * compute the Kalman gain using Equation (16.27)
    * update the state using Equation (16.28)
    * update the covariance using Equation (16.29)

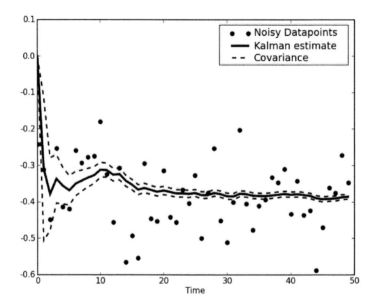

FIGURE 16.11 Estimates of a 1D constant noisy process using a Kalman filter. The filter settles to representing the unchanging mean of the process fairly quickly, and the estimated error (shown as dashed lines) drops accordingly.

Implementing this principally involves repeated use of `np.dot()` to multiply matrices together.

Figure 16.11 shows a simple 1D example of using the Kalman filter, where there is no time variation (so $x_{t+1} = x_t + w_k$). The dots are the noisy data from the process, and the line is the Kalman filter estimate, with the dashed lines representing one standard deviation. It can be seen that the initial estimate was not very good, but the algorithm quickly converges to a good estimate of the mean of the data, and the error drops accordingly.

Now that we have seen the Kalman filter in action, we need to work out how to use it for tracking. We worked out the process in 1D in Equations (16.23) and (16.24), and Figure 16.12 shows an example of 1D tracking, but we will write them in 2D here, to make sure that everything is clear. Again. we will assume that there is no control of the particle, so that it moves at constant velocity (up to noise).

The state of the particle is then:

$$\mathbf{x}_t = (x_1, x2, \dot{x}_1, \dot{x}_2)^T, \quad \mathbf{y}_t = (y_1, y_2)^T, \tag{16.30}$$

$$\mathbf{A} = \begin{pmatrix} 1 & 0 & 1 & 0 \\ 0 & 1 & 0 & 1 \\ 0 & 0 & 1 & 0 \\ 0 & 0 & 0 & 1 \end{pmatrix}, \quad \mathbf{H} = \begin{pmatrix} 1 & 0 & 0 & 0 \\ 0 & 1 & 0 & 0 \end{pmatrix} \tag{16.31}$$

In the absence of any other knowledge, we can assume that $\mathbf{Q}$ and $\mathbf{R}$ are proportional to the 4×4 and 2×2 identity matrices, respectively.

Figure 16.13 shows an example of a point moving in two spatial dimensions, starting at (10,10) and moving to the right at speed 1 for 15 steps, with noise standard deviation 0.1 in

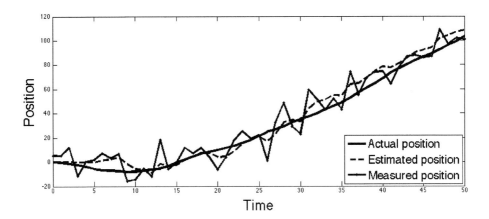

FIGURE 16.12   Demonstration of the Kalman filter tracking an object moving in one spatial dimension.

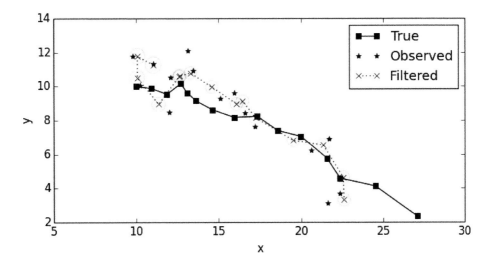

FIGURE 16.13   Demonstration of the Kalman filter tracking an object moving in two spatial dimensions. The grey circles show the covariance around each estimated point.

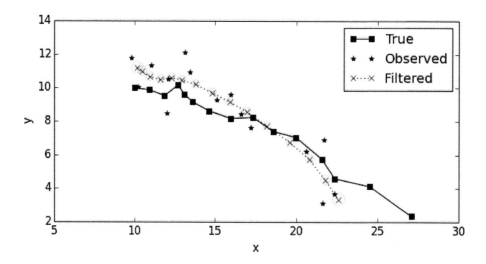

FIGURE 16.14 A smoothed version of the path from Figure 16.13.

both x_1 and x_2, with the grey circles representing the covariance matrix (at one standard deviation). It can be seen that the filter initially tracks the observations, but then learns more of the underlying process. However, the trajectory that is shown is rather 'jumpy' as the high level of noise affects the estimates. One way around this is to use the **Kalman smoother**, which performs a backwards smoothing of the trajectory after the filter has been used to estimate the positions. So the filter is run to predict the points, and then the predictions are updated to be a smoother path along the trajectory of the particle.

There are a variety of ways to do this smoothing, but one option, known as the **Rauch–Tung–Striebel smoother** is to use the following update equations from the endpoint back to the beginning (where the $\hat{(\cdot)}$ variables are the filtered versions):

$$
\begin{aligned}
\mathbf{x}' &= \mathbf{A}\hat{\mathbf{x}} \\
\mathbf{\Sigma}' &= \mathbf{A}\hat{\mathbf{\Sigma}}\mathbf{A}^T + \mathbf{Q} \\
\mathbf{J} &= \hat{\mathbf{\Sigma}}\mathbf{A}\mathbf{\Sigma}' \\
\mathbf{x}_s &= \hat{\mathbf{x}} + \mathbf{J}(\hat{\mathbf{x}} - \mathbf{x}') \\
\mathbf{\Sigma}_s &= \hat{\mathbf{\Sigma}} + \mathbf{J}(\hat{\mathbf{\Sigma}} - \mathbf{\Sigma}')\mathbf{J}^T
\end{aligned}
\tag{16.32}
$$

Figure 16.14 shows the smoothed trajectory from Figure 16.13.

One of the main assumptions of the Kalman filter was that the process was linear. There are many cases where this is not true. One option to deal with non-linearity is to linearise about the current estimate $(\mathbf{x}_t, \mathbf{\Sigma}_t)$ and this leads to the **Extended Kalman Filter**. There are a lot of similarities with the original Kalman filter, so let's try and pick out the differences.

We start with some non-linear stochastic difference equation:

$$
\mathbf{x}_{t+1} = f(\mathbf{x}_t, \mathbf{u}_t, \mathbf{w}_t),
\tag{16.33}
$$

where the variables are the same as for the Kalman filter, except that we have a non-linear function $f(\cdot)$ in place of the nice linear matrix, and we also have a measurement function:

$$
\mathbf{y}_t = h(\mathbf{x}_t, \mathbf{v}_t).
\tag{16.34}
$$

If we have a current estimate $\hat{\mathbf{x}}_t$ then we can evaluate the function at that point by computing $\tilde{\mathbf{x}} = f(\hat{\mathbf{x}}, \mathbf{u}_t, 0)$, where we are assuming that the mean of the noise is 0. We now linearise about this point as:

$$x_{t+1} \approx \tilde{\mathbf{x}}_{t+1} + \mathbf{J}_{f,x}(\hat{\mathbf{x}}_t, \mathbf{u}_t, 0)(\mathbf{x}_t - \hat{\mathbf{x}}_t) + \mathbf{J}_{f,w}(\hat{\mathbf{x}}_t, \mathbf{u}_t, 0)\mathbf{w}_t), \qquad (16.35)$$

and similarly for $h(\cdot)$ to get:

$$y_t \approx \tilde{\mathbf{y}}_{t+1} + \mathbf{J}_{h,x}(\tilde{\mathbf{x}}_t, 0)(\mathbf{x}_t - \tilde{\mathbf{x}}_t) + \mathbf{J}_{h,v}(\tilde{\mathbf{x}}_t, \mathbf{v}_t). \qquad (16.36)$$

In both of these equations $\mathbf{J}$ refers to the Jacobian of the subscripted function with regard to the variable in the second subscript, so:

$$\mathbf{J}_{f,x}|_{i,j} = \frac{\partial f_i}{\partial \mathbf{x}_j}(\hat{\mathbf{x}}_t, \mathbf{u}_t, 0). \qquad (16.37)$$

So providing that we can compute these two functions and their derivatives, we can use them to make an estimate of the error, which is a linear function and so can be estimated using the normal Kalman filter. This leads to the following algorithm:

The Extended Kalman Filter Algorithm

- Given an initial estimate $\mathbf{x}(0)$

- For each timestep:

  - **predict the next step**
    * predict state as $\hat{\mathbf{x}}_{t+1} = f(\hat{\mathbf{x}}_t, \mathbf{u}_t, 0$
    * compute the Jacobians $\mathbf{J}_{f,x}$ and $\mathbf{J}_{f,w}$
    * predict covariance as $\hat{\mathbf{\Sigma}}_{t+1} = \mathbf{J}_{f,x}\mathbf{\Sigma}_t\mathbf{J}_{f,x}^T + \mathbf{J}_{f,w}\mathbf{Q}\mathbf{J}_{f,w}^T$
  - **update the estimate**
    * compute the error in the estimate, $\boldsymbol{\epsilon} = \mathbf{y}_t - h(\hat{\mathbf{x}}_t, 0)$
    * compute the Jacobians $\mathbf{J}_{h,x}$ and $\mathbf{J}_{h,w}$
    * compute the Kalman gain using $\mathbf{K} = \mathbf{J}_{f,x}\mathbf{J}_{h,x}^T(\mathbf{J}_{h,x}\mathbf{J}_{f,x}\mathbf{J}_{h,x}^T + \mathbf{J}_{h,w}\mathbf{R}\mathbf{J}_{h,w}^T)^{-1}$
    * update the state using $\hat{\mathbf{x}} = \hat{\mathbf{x}} + \mathbf{K}\boldsymbol{\epsilon}$
    * update the covariance using $(\mathbf{I} - \mathbf{K}\mathbf{J}_{h,x})\mathbf{J}_{f,x}$

Figure 16.15 shows an example of the extended Kalman filter tracking the function $h(x, y, z) = x + y$ with $f(x, y, z) = (y, z, -.5x(y + z))$.

The Extended Kalman Filter is not an optimal estimator. Further, if the assumptions about local linearity that underlie the linearisation are not true, then the estimate is very poor, and even where it is good, it requires the computation of the Jacobians, which is potentially difficult. There have been various attempts to improve upon it; one method that may be of interest is to choose a set of points that represent the statistics of the data and to transform them by passing them through the non-linear functions ($f(\cdot)$ and $h(\cdot)$), and then to compute the statistics of those points in order to estimate the statistics of the transformed data. This has the great name of the **unscented transform**, and can be used to produce an **Unscented Kalman Filter**. For more information on this, see the Further Reading section; instead we will look at a common MCMC algorithm for performing tracking, the **particle filter**.

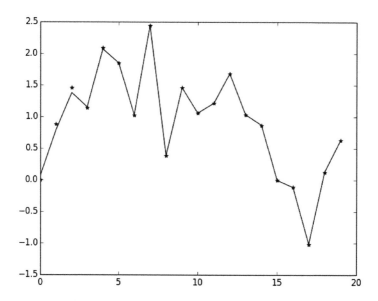

FIGURE 16.15 The extended Kalman filter tracking the function $h(x, y, z) = x + y$ with $f(x, y, z) = (y, z, -.5x(y + z))$.

16.4.2 The Particle Filter

As well as the linearity of the function, the Kalman filter also assumes that the distributions are Gaussian, so that they can be convolved and stay as Gaussians. In order to get around this problem, we return to the methods that have underpinned many of the algorithms in this chapter: sampling. The particular sampling technique that we will use is the sampling-importance-resampling algorithm of Section 15.3, which forms the basis of the **particle filter,** or **condensation** method. This is a relatively recent development, and has been finding many successful applications in tracking, including in image and signal analysis. The idea is to use sampling to keep track of the **state** of the probability distribution. This is known as **sequential sampling,** since we are using a set of samples for time t to estimate the process at time $t + 1$, and then resampling from there.

One benefit of sampling methods is that we don't have to hold on to the Markov assumption. In tracking, prior history can be useful, which means that the Markov assumption is a bad one. The proposal distribution is generally written as $q(\mathbf{x}_{t+1}|\mathbf{x}_{0:t}, \mathbf{y}_{0:t})$ to make this dependence clear, and the proposal distribution that is generally used in the estimated transition probabilities $p(\hat{\mathbf{x}}_{t+1}|\mathbf{x}_{0:t}, \mathbf{y}_{01:t})$, since it is a simple distribution that is related to the process. With this decided, there is very little else to the basic particle filter: a schematic of one iteration of the particle filter is shown in Figure 16.16. The basic algorithm is given next, followed by some points about the implementation and some examples.

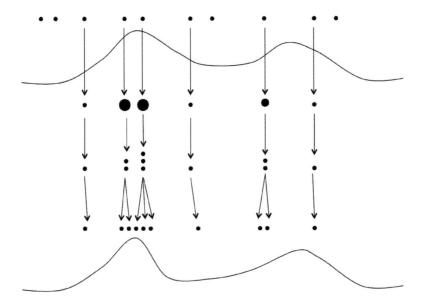

FIGURE 16.16 A schematic of one iteration of a particle filter. A set of random particle positioned have importance weights computed according to the distribution, and then new particles are created and modified based on these weights, and the estimated distribution is updated.

The Particle Filter Algorithm

- Sample $\mathbf{x}_0^{(i)}$ from $p(\mathbf{x}_0$ for $i = 1 \ldots N$

- For each timestep:

  - **importance sample**
  - for each datapoint:
    * sample $\hat{\mathbf{x}}_t^{(i)}$ from $q(\mathbf{x}_t^{(i)}|\mathbf{x}_{0:t-1}^{(i)}, \mathbf{y}_{1:t})$
    * add $\hat{\mathbf{x}}_t^{(i)}$ onto the list of samples to get $\mathbf{x}_{0:t}^{(i)}$ from $\mathbf{x}_{0:t-1}^{(i)}$
    * compute the importance weights:

$$w_t^{(i)} = w_{t-1}^{(i)} \frac{p(\mathbf{y}_t|\hat{\mathbf{x}}_t^{(i)})p(\mathbf{x}_t^{(i)}|\hat{\mathbf{x}}_{t-1}^{(i)})}{q(\mathbf{x}_t^{(i)}|\mathbf{x}_{0:t-1}^{(i)}, \mathbf{y}_{1:t})} \tag{16.38}$$

  - normalise the importance weights by dividing by their sum
  - **resample the particles**
    * retain particles according to their importance weights, so that there might be several copies of some particles, and none of others to get the same number of particles approximately sampled from $p(\mathbf{x}_{0:t}^{(i)}|\mathbf{y}_{1:t})$

The resampling part of this algorithm deserves a little more consideration, because there are several ways in which it can be done, and they differ in their computational time and the variance of the estimates. The code on the website provides two implementations: systematic resampling and residual resampling. The basic idea of systematic resampling is to use the cumulative sum of the weights (which will be 1 at the very end by definition) and a set of uniform random numbers $\tilde{u}_k$, put together so that they are in order using $u_k = (k = 1 + \tilde{u}_k)/N$ and put n_i copies of particles i into the next set, where n_i is the number of u_k for which $\sum_{s=1}^{i-1} w_s \leq u_k < \sum_{s=1}^{i} w_s$. One way to implement this is using the following code:

```
def systematic(w,N):
    # Systematic resampling
    N2 = np.shape(w)[0]
    # One too many to make sure it is >1
    samples = np.random.rand(N+1)
    indices = np.arange(N+1)
    u = (samples+indices)/(N+1)
    cumw = np.cumsum(w)
    keep = np.zeros((N))
    # ni copies of particle xi where ni = number of u between ws[i-1] and ws[
i]
    j = 0
    for i in range(N2):
        while((u[j]<cumw[i]) & (j<N)):
            keep[j] = i
            j+=1

    return keep
```

Residual sampling tries to speed this up (although it is an $\mathcal{O}(n)$ algorithm, it is called often, and so making it fast is a very good idea) by first using the integer part of Nw_i as an idea of how many copies of each particle i to keep, and then using stratified samples for the rest.

Figure 16.17 shows the particle filter keeping track of a distribution that changes at $t = 30$. The positions of the particles are shown as dots, the underlying state process is shown as the dashed line, and the observations are shown as pluses. The solid line is the hypothesised observation based on the mean of the particles. It can be seen that this tracks the observations very well.

As an example of using the Particle Filter for tracking, Figure 16.18 shows an object moving at constant speed being tracked in 2D. The weights are computed based on the Euclidean distance between each particle and the object, and the particles are resampled if the average distance between them grows too large.

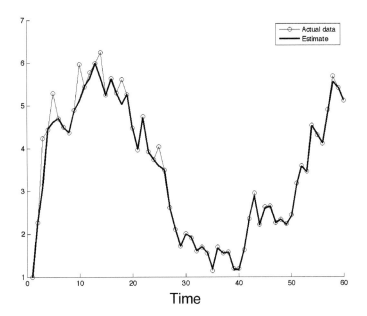

FIGURE 16.17 A particle filter tracking a 1D distribution that changes at $t = 30$. The observations are marked as pluses, the underlying state is shown by the dashed line, the particles at each iteration are shown as dots, and the hypothesised observation based on the mean of the particles is shown as a solid line.

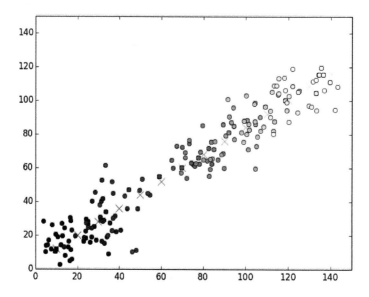

FIGURE 16.18 A particle filter tracking an object moving at a constant speed upwards and to the right in 2D. The crosses show the position of the object, and the circles show 15 particles at each iteration, starting at black $(t = 0)$ and fading to white $(t = 10)$. It can be seen that the particles track the object successfully.

FURTHER READING

Graphical models are a growth area at the moment, with lots of interesting research being done in the area. The original work in the area, and the motivations for it, are described in:

- J. Pearl. *Probabilistic Reasoning in Intelligent Systems: Networks of Plausible Inference*. Morgan Kaufmann, San Mateo, CA, USA, 1988.

Alternative overviews of Bayesian networks can be found in the following papers and books, the last of which is a collection of papers that provides a good overview of the area:

- W.L. Buntine. Operations for learning with graphical models. *Journal of Artificial Intelligence Research*, 2:159–225, 1994.

- D. Husmeier. Introduction to learning Bayesian networks from data. In D. Husmeier, R. Dybowski, and S. Roberts, editors, *Probabilistic Modelling in Bioinformatics and Medical Informatics*, Springer, Berlin, Germany, 2005.

- Chapters 8 and 13 of C.M. Bishop. *Pattern Recognition and Machine Learning.* Springer, Berlin, Germany, 2006.

- M.I. Jordan, editor. *Learning in Graphical Models*. MIT Press, Cambridge, MA, USA, 1999.

In the area of Markov Random Fields, the image denoising example comes from:

- S. Geman and D. Geman. Stochastic relaxation, Gibbs distributions and the Bayesian restoration of images. *IEEE Transactions on Pattern Analysis and Machine Intelligence*, 6:721–741, 1984.

Markov Random Fields are most commonly used in imaging. There are good overviews in:

- P. Pèrez. Markov random fields and images. *CWI Quarterly*, 11(4):413–437, 1998.

- R. Kindermann and J.L. Snell. *Markov Random Fields and Their Applications*. American Mathematical Society, Providence, RI, USA, 1980.

For more details on the Hidden Markov Model, the Kalman filter and the particle filter, you might want to look at:

- L.R. Rabiner. A tutorial on hidden Markov models and selected applications in speech recognition. *Proceedings of the IEEE*, 77(2):257–268, 1989.

- Z. Ghahramani. An introduction to Hidden Markov Models and Bayesian networks. *International Journal of Pattern Recognition and Artificial Intelligence*, 15:9–42, 2001.

- G. Welch and G. Bishop. An introduction to the Kalman filter, 1995. URL `http://www.cs.unc.edu/~welch/kalman/`. Technical Report TR 95-041, Department of Computer Science, University of North Carolina at Chapel Hill, USA.

- M.S. Arulampalam, S. Maskell, N. Gordon, and T. Clapp. A tutorial on particle filters for online nonlinear/non-Gaussian Bayesian tracking. *IEEE Transactions on Signal Processing*, 50(2):174–188, 2002.

- S.J. Julier and J.K. Uhlmann. A new method for the nonlinear transformation of means and covariances in nonlinear filters. *IEEE Transactions on Automatic Control*, 45(3):477–482, 2000.

- R. van der Merwe, A. Doucet, N. de Freitas, and E. Wan. The unscented particle filter. In *Advances in Neural Information Processing Systems*, 2000. (the technical report version of this paper is particularly helpful).

A more detailed treatment is given in:

- Chapters 8 and 13 of C.M. Bishop. *Pattern Recognition and Machine Learning*. Springer, Berlin, Germany, 2006.

PRACTICE QUESTIONS

Problem 16.1 Compute the probability of taking notes (N) in the Bayesian network shown in Figure 16.19. The problem describes the chance of you taking notes in the lecture or sleeping (S) according to whether or not the course was boring (B) based on whether or not the professor is boring (L) and the content is dull (C). Compute the chance of falling asleep in a lecture given that both the professor and the course are boring.

Problem 16.2 Use MCMC in order to compute the chance of taking notes in a lecture given only that you know the lecture is interesting.

Problem 16.3 Compute the most likely path through the HMM shown in Figure 16.20 using the Viterbi algorithm.

Problem 16.4 Suppose that you notice a fairground show where the showman demonstrates that a coin is fair, but then makes it turn up heads many times in a row. You notice that he actually has two coins, and swaps between them with sleight-of-hand. Watching, you start to see that he sticks to the fair coin with probability 0.4, and to the biased coin with probability 0.1, and that the biased coin seems to come up heads about 85% of the time. Make a hidden Markov model for this problem, construct an observation sequence, and use the Viterbi algorithm to estimate the states.

Problem 16.5 On the website are a series of robot sensor readings. The aim is to predict the next reading from the current one by using a Perceptron, and then monitor the output of the Perceptron by using a Kalman filter in order to identify problem places where the prediction does not work.

Problem 16.6 Figure 16.18 performs tracking of an object in 2D using the Euclidean distance between each particle and the object to set the weights. Modify the code to compare this to using a binary weight based on proximity to the object where you will need to set a threshold to define proximity.

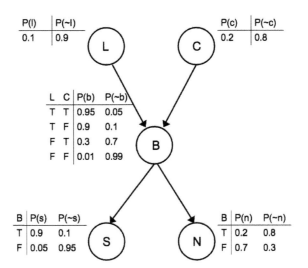

<table>
<tr><td>P(l)</td><td>P(~l)</td></tr>
<tr><td>0.1</td><td>0.9</td></tr>
</table>

<table>
<tr><td>P(c)</td><td>P(~c)</td></tr>
<tr><td>0.2</td><td>0.8</td></tr>
</table>

L	C	P(b)	P(~b)
T	T	0.95	0.05
T	F	0.9	0.1
F	T	0.3	0.7
F	F	0.01	0.99

B	P(s)	P(~s)
T	0.9	0.1
F	0.05	0.95

B	P(n)	P(~n)
T	0.2	0.8
F	0.7	0.3

FIGURE 16.19 The Bayesian Network example for Problem 16.1.

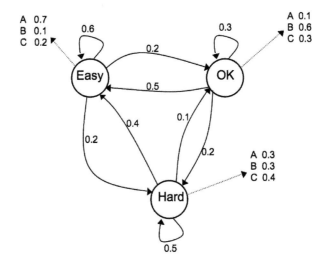

FIGURE 16.20 The Hidden Markov Model example for Problem 16.3.

## CHAPTER 17

Symmetric Weights and Deep Belief Networks

Let's return to the model of the neuron that was the basis for the neural network algorithms such as the Perceptron in Chapter 3 and the multi-layer Perceptron in Chapter 4. These algorithms were based on what are effectively an integrate-and-fire model of a neuron, where the product of the inputs and the weights was compared with a threshold (generally zero when a bias node was also used) and the neuron produced a continuous approximation to firing (output one) or not firing (output zero) for each input. The approximation was typically the logistic function. The algorithms based on neurons that we have seen have been asymmetric in the sense that the values of the inputs and weights made the (hidden) neurons fire, or not, but the values of the neurons would never affect the inputs (in fact, these input nodes were never considered as neurons).

If we were to think of these networks as graphs, the edges would be directed, with the arrowhead pointing at the neurons from the inputs. This is shown on the left of Figure 17.1, where the shading suggests that the two sets of nodes are different, since the light-coloured nodes affect the firing of the dark-coloured nodes (based on the direction arrows on the links), but not vice-versa. On the right of the figure, the links are not directed, and so the nodes are all the same colour, since the firing of the nodes in the top layer, together with the weights on the edges, can be used to decide if the nodes in the lower layer fire or not, as well as the other way round.

However, the first learning rule that we saw (Hebb's rule in Section 3.1.1) was entirely symmetrical. It said that if two neurons fire at the same time then the synaptic connection between them gets stronger, while if they do not fire at the same time then the connection gets weaker. As we saw in that section, this means that if we only see one of two neurons with a connection between them, then we can decide what the other one does: if they are positively connected, then if the first one fires, so does the second one, and if they are negatively connected, then if the first one fires, the second does not. It doesn't matter which of the two neurons we see, since the connection between them is symmetric — if we use the usual notation of writing w_{mn} for the weight (strength) of the connection between neuron m and neuron n, then $w_{mn} = w_{nm}$, and so the weight matrix is symmetric.

In this chapter we explore a series of algorithms that are based on learning and using these symmetric weights. While in general such networks are potentially very complicated and hard to train, there are certain cases that are tractable and that turn out to be useful. The first network that we look into is an early—and conceptually very simple—network,

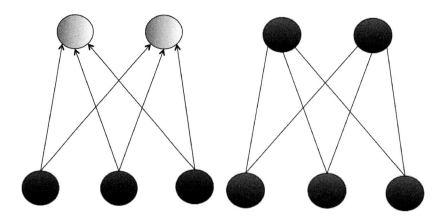

FIGURE 17.1 Two neural networks made up of two layers of nodes. On the *left* the weighted links are directional so that whether or not the lighter-coloured nodes fire affects the firing of the darker-coloured nodes, but not vice-versa, while on the *right* the two layers are symmetric, so that the firing of the upper layer can change the firing of the lower layer in the same way as from bottom to top.

which was described by John Hopfield in 1982. However, before seeing the network we will look at what it does.

17.1 ENERGETIC LEARNING: THE HOPFIELD NETWORK

17.1.1 Associative Memory

One thing that we know our brains are very good at is remembering things. This is clearly a crucial part of learning: recognising things that we have seen before. There are many different types of memory, but one of the most useful is **associative memory**. An associative memory, also known as a **context-addressable memory**, works by learning a set of patterns in such a way that if you see a new pattern, the memory reproduces whichever of the stored patterns most closely resembles it. We use this all the time — for example, when we recognise the letters of the alphabet that are written in some font that we haven't seen before, or when we recognise a person when we see them from an unusual angle, or decide that one person looks like another. It can be thought of as completing or correcting inputs (depending upon whether there are missing values, or incorrect values in the input).

So it would be worth studying context-addressable memories just because they are clearly important in the brain. However, there are some more practical applications of them, too. For example, we can use them to remove the noise from images, or reconstruct the full image. We train the memory by showing it the complete pictures, and then, when we show the memory a noisy (i.e., corrupted with some errors), or partial (with missing values) version it will reproduce the original version.

As an example of the things that you can do with an associative memory, suppose that we learn a list of pairs of words that are associated together, such as:
Humphrey - Bogart
Ingrid - Bergman
Paul - Henreid

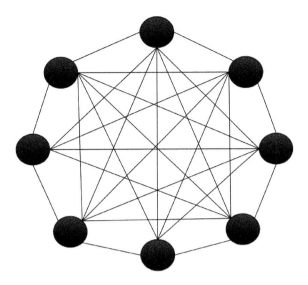

FIGURE 17.2 Schematic of the Hopfield network, which is a fully connected set of neurons with symmetric weights.

```
Claude - Rains
Omar - Sharif
Julie - Christie
```
The two things that we can do with an associative memory are pattern completion, so that if we saw 'Ingrid' then the memory can provide 'Bergman', and pattern denoising, so that if we saw 'Hungry – Braggart' then the memory can correct it to 'Humphrey – Bogart'. Of course, we can confuse it by adding memories that overlap. So if
```
Paul - Newman
```
was added to the memory, then looking for 'Paul' would produce one of the two ('Henreid' or 'Newman') arbitrarily.

Having understood what the memory does, let's work out how to make one.

17.1.2 Making an Associative Memory

The Hopfield network consists of a set of McCulloch and Pitts neurons that are fully connected with symmetric weights, so that every neuron is connected to every other neuron, except for itself (so that $w_{ii} = 0$). In the brain there are cases where neurons have synapses that connect back to themselves, but we'll ignore that here. There is a picture of the Hopfield network in figure 17.2.

McCulloch and Pitts neurons are binary, they either fire or don't fire, but rather than using 1 and 0 to encode these outputs, it is more convenient to use 1 and -1 instead. One reason for this is that it gives us Hebb's rule very simply. If $s_i^{(t)}$ is the activation of neuron i at time t, then we can write Hebb's rule as:

$$\frac{dw_{ij}^t}{dt} = s_i^{(t)} s_j^{(t)}, \tag{17.1}$$

so that if two neurons have the same behaviour (firing or not firing) then the weight increases, while if they have opposite behaviour then the weight decreases.

Note the time superscripts in Equation (17.1), which imply that the weight update is based on the activations of the neurons at the current time. However, things are not as clear when we consider the update of each neuron to decide whether or not it is firing. The reason for this is that the weights are symmetric, and so there is no pre-defined order in which the neurons should be updated. For a directed network, we start at the inputs, and use those values and the weights to decide whether or not the next layer fire, and so on until we get to the outputs. However, for symmetric weights there is no clearly defined order. This means that there are two different ways in which we can do the update, and they can sometimes produce different output behaviours. One method is to use:

$$s_i^{(t)} = \text{sign}\left(\sum_j w_{ij} s_j^{(t-1)}\right), \tag{17.2}$$

which describes **synchronous update** where effectively every neuron has its value updated at the same time; imagine all of the neurons making a simultaneous decision about whether or not to fire at the next time step. The second version is **asynchronous**, each neuron makes a decision about when to fire based on the current values — either $s_j^{(t-1)}$ or $s_j^{(t)}$ depending which is available — of all of the other neurons. The order in which the neurons are updated could be either random or in some fixed sequence. In either case, it can be necessary to run the update for several steps to ensure that the network **settles** into a steady state. This is sufficient to enable the network to recall previous inputs.

Regardless of which form of update is used, it is still normal to set the threshold for each neuron to fire at 0, so that the decision about whether or not each will fire is:

$$s_i = \text{sign}\left(\sum_j w_{ij} s_j\right), \tag{17.3}$$

where sign($\cdot$) is a function that returns 1 if the input is greater than 0, and -1 otherwise. It is possible to include a bias node (which is a node with a constant value, usually ± 1) to change this value in the normal way if required.

We give an input to the Hopfield network by setting the activations of the neurons (the s_i) and then running the update equation until the neurons stop changing values. So once the weights are set, the remembering is very simple. The learning is also simple: the Hopfield network learns the weights using Hebb's rule:

$$w_{ij} = \frac{1}{N} \sum_{n=1}^{N} s_i(n) s_j(n), \tag{17.4}$$

where N is the number of patterns that we want the network to learn and $s_i(n)$ is the activation of neuron i for input pattern n. There is no t superscript since we are setting the values of the neurons, not waiting for them to update.

The $\frac{1}{N}$ takes the place of the learning rate η in previous learning algorithms. It doesn't have much effect for the Hopfield network, since learning is effectively **one-shot**, but by using $\frac{1}{N}$ the maximum size of the weights is independent of N.

Suppose that we are learning to reproduce binary images, as in Section 4.4.5. We have one neuron for each pixel of the picture, and we equate $s_i = 1$ with black pixels and $s_i = -1$ with white pixels. By considering the case of one input pattern, we can now see that the

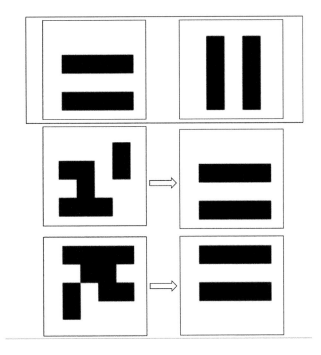

FIGURE 17.3 The Hopfield network is trained on the top two images. When the first image on the second row is presented it settles back to the first image on the top row. However, when the second image is presented, it settles to the third image, which is the inverse of the first input pattern.

Hopfield network does perform image correction. If we set the weights based on an image and then present a noisy version of that image to the network, then each of the neurons will have its activity updated by all of the other neurons. Many of the neurons will change state from 1 to -1 and back again several times until the network settles into its final state (stabilises). So what will the network stabilise to? Well, providing that more than half of the initial bits are correct, on average the total input to each neuron will be more than half correct, and this will overwhelm the errors. This means that the correct pattern is an attractor: if we let the network settle into its final state, that final state will correspond to the pattern that the network learned.

What if more than half of the inputs are incorrect? That means that black pixels are white, and white pixels are black. In this case, the network will settle to the inverse of the pattern, i.e., the pattern where black and white have been swapped throughout the image (we will see an example of this in Figure 17.3). If we label the first, correct pattern as x, this second pattern is $-x$. This is also an attractor.

Of course, the network actually learns about many input patterns (N of them) and so there will be many attractors. For this reason, it is not guaranteed to find the 'correct' answer, since the noisy input may actually be closer to another of the trained patterns that the one you expect. This suggests a question that we need to consider, which is: how many memories can the Hopfield network hold; that is, how many different patterns can the network remember?

However, before analysing the network further, and answering this question, we will need a sidetrack, so first here is the complete algorithm:

The Hopfield Algorithm

- **Learning**

  - take a training set of N d-dimensional inputs $\mathbf{x}(1), \mathbf{x}(2), \ldots, \mathbf{x}(N)$ with elements ± 1
  - create a set of d neurons (or $d + 1$ including a bias node that is permanently set to 1) and set the weights to:

$$
w_{ij} = \begin{cases} \frac{1}{N} \sum_{n=1}^{N} x_i(n) x_j(n) & \forall i \neq j \\ 0 & \forall i = j \end{cases} \tag{17.5}
$$

- **Recall**

  - present the new input $\mathbf{x}$ by setting the states s_i of the neurons to x_i
  - **repeat**
    * update the neurons using:

$$
s_i^{(t)} = \text{sign}\left(\sum_j w_{ij} s_j^* \right), \tag{17.6}
$$

    where s_j^* is $s_j^{(t)}$ if that neuron has been updated already, and $s_j^{(t-1)}$ if it has not. This means that for synchronous update $s_j^* = s_j^{(t-1)}$ for every node, while for asynchronous update it could be either value.
  - **until** the network stabilises
  - read off the states s_i of the neurons as the output

One way to implement the different forms of update is shown in the following code snippet, which makes clear the difference between the synchronous and asynchronous versions:

```
def update_neurons(self):
    if self.synchronous:
        act = np.sum(self.weights*self.activations,axis=1)
        self.activations = np.where(act>0,1,-1)
    else:
        order = np.arange(self.nneurons)
        if self.random:
            np.random.shuffle(order)
            for i in order:
                if np.sum(self.weights[i,:]*self.activations)>0:
                    self.activations[i] = 1
                else:
                    self.activations[i] = -1
    return self.activations
```

Figure 17.4 shows an example of a Hopfield network being used. The network is trained on an image of each of the digits 0 to 9 taken from the 'Binary Alphadigits' dataset (a web link is provided on the book website). These are 20×16 binary images, of the digits '0' to '9' and 'A' to 'Z' and the images used are shown in the top row of the figure.

Following the setting of the weights, the network was presented with the corrupted version of the image of the '2', as shown in the next line, and then performed asynchronous random updating to settle back to the original, trained, image.

17.1.3 An Energy Function

We will return to the question of the capacity of the network shortly, but first let's investigate one of the major contributions that Hopfield made, which was to write down an **energy** **function** for his network. Energy functions are used in physics to compute how much energy a system has, with the idea that systems relax into low energy states, for example the way that sets of chemicals mix together to form stable compounds. The energy function for the Hopfield network with d neurons (where d may or may not include a bias node) is (using the usual matrix notation in the second line):

$$
\begin{aligned}
H &= -\frac{1}{2} \sum_{i=1}^{d} \sum_{j=1}^{d} w_{ij} s_i s_j \\
&= -\frac{1}{2} \mathbf{s} \mathbf{W} \mathbf{s}^T
\end{aligned}
\tag{17.7}
$$

The reason for the $\frac{1}{2}$ is that each weight is counted twice in the double sum, since $w_{ij} s_i s_j$ is the same as $w_{ji} s_j s_i$, and the negative signs are because we consider that finding lower energies is better. Note that in the Hopfield network nodes are not connected to themselves, and so $w_{ii} = 0$.

To see what the energy function computes, consider the case where the network has learnt one training example, and it sees it again. In this case, $w_{ij} = s_i s_j$, and since $s_i^2 = 1$ no matter whether $s_i = -1$ or $s_i = 1$:

$$
\begin{aligned}
H &= -\frac{1}{2} \sum_{i=1}^{d} \sum_{j=1}^{d} w_{ij} s_i s_j \\
&= -\frac{1}{2} \sum_{i=1}^{d} \sum_{j=1, j \neq i}^{d} s_i s_j s_i s_j \\
&= -\frac{1}{2} \sum_{i=1}^{d} \sum_{j=1, j \neq i}^{d} s_i^2 s_j^2 \\
&= -\frac{1}{2} \sum_{i=1}^{d} \sum_{j=1, j \neq i}^{d} 1 \\
&= -\frac{d(d-1)}{2}.
\end{aligned}
\tag{17.8}
$$

Note the insistence that the second sum is only over $j \neq i$ from the second line on to account for the fact that $w_{ii} = 0$.

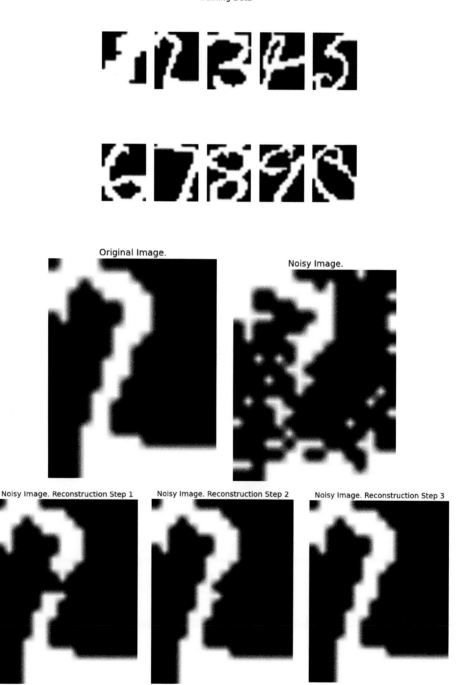

FIGURE 17.4 Example of the Hopfield Network reconstructing a noisy version of an image. The network was trained on the images at the top. It was then presented with the image on the right of the second row, which is the image on the left of that row, but with 50 bits corrupted by being inverted (so black becomes white and vice-versa). Three iterations of the algorithm running are shown in the third row.

Clearly, any place where the weights and the neurons disagree will give a contribution with +1 instead of -1, and so the total sum will have a higher (less negative) value. Thus, the energy function describes the amount of mismatch between the values of the neurons and what the weights say they should be.

An energy function sets the neural activity of the network into terms that physicists have used for a long time, and indeed, physicists immediately recognised this equation – it is (a slight variation of) the energy of the Ising Spin Glasses, which are a simple model of magnetic materials, and have been very well studied. Once we have an energy function, we can watch how it changes as the network stabilises.

We have just seen that once the network is stable so that the weights and neuron activations agree, the energy is at a minimum, and while we wait for it to stabilise, the energy is higher. This means that the attractors (stable patterns) are local minima of the error function, just as in previous discussions about such functions. We can imagine the change in energy as the network learns as an energy landscape (for the example shown in Figure 17.4 the energy went from -1119.0 to -6447.8). If we think about a ball bearing rolling around on this landscape under gravity, then the ball will roll downhill until it gets to the bottom of some hollow, where it will stop. If there are lots of hollows, then which hollow it will end up in depends on where it starts in the landscape. This is what happens when many images are stored in the network — there are many different hollows relating to each of the different images. The area around an attractor, from where the ball bearing will roll into that hollow, is called the basin of attraction.

Another benefit of having an energy function is that we can see that the network will eventually reach a stable state at a local minimum. (In fact, this is only true for asynchronous update; for synchronous update there are cases that never converge.) To see that the network will reach a local minima, we need to consider an update step where the value of bit i changes. In this case, the network has gone from state $\mathbf{s} = (s_1, \ldots s_i, \ldots s_d)$ to state $\mathbf{s}' = (s_1, \ldots s_i', \ldots s_d)$ and the energy has gone from $H(\mathbf{s})$ to $H(\mathbf{s}')$. If we consider this difference, we get:

$$H(\mathbf{s}) - H(\mathbf{s}') = -\frac{1}{2} \sum_{j=1}^{d} w_{ij} s_i s_j + \frac{1}{2} \sum_{j=1}^{d} w_{ij} s_i' s_j \qquad (17.9)$$

$$= -\frac{1}{2}(s_i - s_i') \sum_{j=1}^{d} w_{ij} s_j \qquad (17.10)$$

The reason that the bit flipped is because the combination of the weights and the values of the other neurons disagreed with its current value, so s_i and $\sum_{j=1}^{d} w_{ij} s_j$ must have opposite signs. Likewise, s_i and s_i' have opposite signs since the bit flipped. Hence, $H(\mathbf{s}) - H(\mathbf{s}')$ must be positive, and so the total energy of the network has decreased. This means that while the energy of the network continues to change, it will decrease towards a minimum. There is no guarantee that the network will reach a global optimum, though.

17.1.4 Capacity of the Hopfield Network

The question of how many different memories the Hopfield network can store is obviously an important one. Fortunately, it is fairly simple to answer by considering the stability of a single neuron in the network, which we will label as the ith one. Suppose that the network has learnt about input $\mathbf{x}(n)$ already. If that input is presented to the network again, then the output of neuron i will be (using Equation 17.4 and ignoring the $\frac{1}{N}$ throughout since it is just a scaling factor):

$$
\begin{aligned}
s_i &= \sum_{j=1}^{d} w_{ij} x_j(n) \\
&= \sum_{j=1, j \neq i}^{d} \left((x_i(n) x_j(n)) \, x_j(n) + \left(\sum_{m=1, m \neq n}^{N} x_i(m) x_j(m) \right) x_j(n) \right) \\
&= x_i(n)(d-1) + \sum_{j=1, j \neq i}^{d} \sum_{m=1, m \neq n}^{N} x_i(m) x_j(m) x_j(n) \tag{17.11}
\end{aligned}
$$

The output that we want is $s_i = x_i(n)$, which is the ($d-1$ times) the value of the first term, and so we ideally want the second term to be zero. Note that there are $(d-1) \times (N-1)$ terms to be summed up.

The possible values for each x_i are ± 1, and we assume that each neuron has an equal chance of either value, which means that we can model them as random binary variables with zero mean and unit variance. Thus, the total sum has mean $(d-1)x_i(n)$ (that is, either $-(d-1)$ or $d-1$) and variance $(d-1) \times (N-1)$ (and hence standard deviation $\sqrt{(d-1)(N-1)}$) and it is approximately Gaussian distributed. So what is the probability that bit i flips state? This happens in the tails of the Gaussian distribution, and we can compute it using the **Gaussian cumulative distribution function** (where $t = \frac{-(d-1)}{\sqrt{(d-1)(N-1)}}$) as:

$$
P(\text{bit } i \text{ flips}) = \frac{1}{\sqrt{2\pi}} \int_{-\infty}^{t} e^{-t^2/2} dt \tag{17.12}
$$

This means that it is the ratio of $d-1$ and $N-1$ that is of interest, which is not surprising since more neurons should be able to hold more memories. There is always a chance that a bit will flip. If we are prepared to accept a 1% chance of this, then Equation (17.12) tells us that we can store about $N \approx 0.18d$ patterns. However, we aren't quite finished. The computation we just did was about the probability of the bit flipping on the first iteration of the update rule. A more involved analysis eventually tells us that with that same error rate of 1% the network can store about $N \approx 0.138d$ patterns. So for the 20×16 images that are learnt in the example dataset, there are 320 neurons, so it should be able to hold around 44 images.

17.1.5 The Continuous Hopfield Network

There is a continuous version of the Hopfield network, which can be adapted to deal with more interesting data, such as grayscale images. The basic difference is that the neurons need to have an activation function that runs between -1 and 1. This could be done with a scaled version of the **logistic (sigmoidal)** function that was used in earlier chapters, but instead it is convenient to use the **hyperbolic tangent** function, which is already in that range. In NumPy this is computed with `np.tanh()`. Changing the Hopfield network to use these neurons is one of the exercises for this chapter.

In the continuous Hopfield network we make the same type of transformation as we did for the MLP, using a continuous activation function instead of the binary threshold. This changes the function of the network so that instead of minimising the energy function

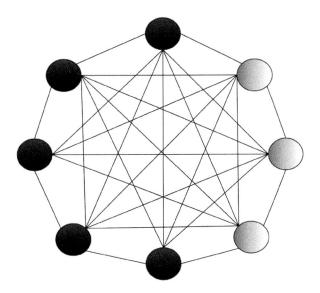

FIGURE 17.5   A schematic of a BM network. All the nodes are fully connected, but there are visible nodes (in dark grey) and hidden nodes.

in Equation (17.7), it approximates the probability distribution that matches that energy function:

$$p(\mathbf{x}|\mathbf{W}) = \frac{1}{Z(\mathbf{W})} \exp\left[\frac{1}{2}\mathbf{x}^T\mathbf{W}\mathbf{x}\right],\qquad(17.13)$$

where $Z(\mathbf{W}) = \sum_{\mathbf{x}} \exp\left(\frac{1}{2}\mathbf{x}^T\mathbf{W}\mathbf{x}\right)$ is a normalising function.

We can actually compute the distribution in Equation (17.13) directly if we transform the neuron activations to lie between 0 and 1 instead of -1 and 1, and then interpret them as the probability of the neuron firing, so that 0 means that the neuron does not fire and 1 means that it definitely does. This means that we have a stochastic neuron, which fires with probability $1/(1 + e^{-x})$. A network based on stochastic neurons like this is known as a **Boltzmann machine**. It produces **Gibbs samples** (see Section 15.4.4) of precisely this probability distribution, and it is described next.

17.2   STOCHASTIC NEURONS — THE BOLTZMANN MACHINE

The original Boltzmann machine is fully connected just like the Hopfield network. However, in addition to the neurons where the input can be specified (and the output read off), which are termed **visible neurons**, there are also **hidden neurons**, which are free to take on any role in the computational model. Figure 17.5 shows a schematic of a possible Boltzmann machine, which is fully connected, with a set of visible neurons and a set of hidden nodes.

In order to see how to train a Boltzmann machine, let's start with a stochastic Hopfield network, where there are no hidden nodes. We will label the states of these visible nodes as **v**. We know that the network is sampling from:

$$P(\mathbf{v}|\mathbf{W}) = \frac{1}{Z(\mathbf{W})} \exp\left(\frac{1}{2}\mathbf{v}^T\mathbf{W}\mathbf{v}\right),\qquad(17.14)$$

Therefore, learning consists of modifying the weight matrix $\mathbf{W}$ so that the generative model in Equation 17.14 matches the training data $(\mathbf{x}^n)$ well. We want to maximise the likelihood of this, which we can do by computing the derivative of the log of it with respect to each weight w_{ij}:

$$\frac{\partial}{\partial w_{ij}} \log \prod n = 1^N P(\mathbf{x}^n|\mathbf{W}) \quad = \quad \frac{\partial}{\partial w_{ij}} \sum_{n=1}^{N} \frac{1}{2}(\mathbf{x}^n)^T \mathbf{W}\mathbf{x}^n - \log Z(\mathbf{W}) \quad (17.15)$$

$$= \quad \sum_{n=1}^{N} \left(x_i^n x_j^n - x_i^n x_j^n P(\mathbf{x}|\mathbf{W}) \right) \quad (17.16)$$

$$= \quad N\langle x_i x_j \rangle_{\text{data}} - \langle x_i x_j \rangle_{P(\mathbf{x}|\mathbf{W})}, \quad (17.17)$$

where in the last line the $\langle , \rangle$ notation means the average, so that the first term is the average over the data, and the second term is the average over samples from the probability distribution.

This means that the gradient with respect to each weight is proportional to the difference between two correlations: the correlation between two values in the data (the empirical correlation) and the correlation between them in the current model. Clearly, the first of these is easy to calculate, but the second isn't easy to evaluate directly. However, it can be estimated by sampling from the model as the Boltzmann machine iterates.

Hinton, who first described the Boltzmann machine, describes the algorithm for computing these two parts as a 'wake-sleep' algorithm. Initially the algorithm is awake, so it computes the correlation in the data. The network then falls asleep and 'dreams' about the data that it has seen, which lets it estimate the correlations in the model.

We can extend this derivation to a network with hidden neurons as well. We will label the states of the set of hidden neurons as $\mathbf{h}$, so that the state of the whole network is $\mathbf{y} = (\mathbf{v}, \mathbf{h})$. Remember that the hidden states are unknown. The likelihood of the weight matrix $\mathbf{W}$ given a data example $\mathbf{x}^n$ is (where Z now has to sum over the hidden nodes $\mathbf{h}$ as well as the visible nodes):

$$P(\mathbf{x}^n|\mathbf{W}) = \sum_{h} P(\mathbf{x}^n, \mathbf{h}|\mathbf{W}) = \sum_{\mathbf{h}} \frac{1}{Z(\mathbf{W})} \exp\left(\frac{1}{2}(\mathbf{y}^n)^T \mathbf{W}\mathbf{y}^n\right). \quad (17.18)$$

Computing the derivative of the log likelihood as before, the gradient with respect to a weight w_{ij} has a similar form of the difference between two terms that are found while the network is asleep and awake:

$$\frac{\partial}{\partial w_{ij}} \log P(\{\mathbf{x}^n\}|\mathbf{W}) = \sum_{n} \left(\langle y_i y_j \rangle_{P(\mathbf{h}|\mathbf{x}^n, \mathbf{W})} - \langle y_i y_j \rangle_{P(\mathbf{v}, \mathbf{h}|\mathbf{W})} \right). \quad (17.19)$$

Unfortunately, now both of these correlations have to be sampled by running the network for many iterations, where each iteration has two stages: in the first, awake, stage the visible neurons have the values clamped to the input (that is, they are held fixed), while the hidden nodes are allowed to take any values under their model, while in the second, asleep, stage both sets are sampled from the model.

In Chapter 15 we saw one possible way to get around problems like this, by setting up a Markov chain that converges to the correct probability distribution. If we let the chain run until equilibrium then the result will be samples from the distribution, and so we can approximate the average over the distribution by an average over these samples.

Unfortunately, this is still computationally very expensive since it will take lots of steps for the Markov chain to converge at each stage.

However, using this, training the algorithm consists of clamping the visible nodes to the input, and then using Gibbs sampling (see Section 15.4.4) until the network settles, then computing the first of the two terms in Equation (17.19). Following this, the visible nodes are allowed to go free as well and the whole distribution is sampled from, first the visible nodes and then the hidden nodes, up and down through the network, until it converges again, and then computing the second term. The weights can then be trained by using Equation (17.19).

The Boltzmann machine is a very interesting neural network, particularly because it produces a generative probabilistic model (which is what is sampled from for the weight updates). However, it is computationally very expensive since every learning step involves Monte Carlo sampling from the two distributions. In fact, since it is based on symmetric connections the Boltzmann machine is actually a Markov Random Field (MRF) (see Section 16.2). The computational expense has meant that the normal Boltzmann machine has never been popular in practical use, which is why we haven't examined an implementation of it. However, a simplification of it has, and we will consider that next.

17.2.1 The Restricted Boltzmann Machine

The main computational expense in the algorithm above is that both of the correlations have to be found by sampling, which means that the algorithm has to run for lots of iterations so that it converges at each step of the learning. This is progressively more expensive as the number of nodes grows, so that the algorithm scales very badly. However, some of this sampling was unnecessary for the machine that didn't have hidden nodes, where it is possible to compute the first term from the data alone. Ideally, we would like to find some simplification of the machine that allows for this to happen, and that also makes the number of sampling steps required to estimate the second correlation reasonably small.

It turns out that it is the interconnections *within* each layer that cause some of the problems. Without these interconnections, the nodes in a layer are conditionally independent of each other, given that the nodes in the other layer are held constant. In other words, by treating each hidden neuron as an individual 'expert' and multiplying together their distributions for each visible neuron (or taking logs and adding them) it is possible to compute the probability distribution for each visible neuron. Similarly, the distribution over the hidden nodes can be computed given the visible nodes.

So the restricted Boltzmann machine (RBM) consists of two layers of nodes, the visible ones (which are clamped to the inputs during the 'awake' training) and the hidden ones. There are no interconnections within either of the two layers, but they are fully connected between them using the symmetric weights. This is known as a bipartite graph and an example for three input nodes and two hidden nodes is shown in Figure 17.6. This machine was originally known by the delightful name of Harmonium, but the RBM name has stuck, not least because the tractable training algorithm is conceptually very similar to that for the full Boltzmann machine.

The algorithm that is used to train RBMs is known as the Contrastive Divergence (CD) algorithm, and it was created by Hinton and colleagues, who also first proposed the Boltzmann machine. The algorithm is a wake-sleep algorithm, and it will be given shortly, before we consider a numerical example, derive the update equations, and consider some implementation issues.

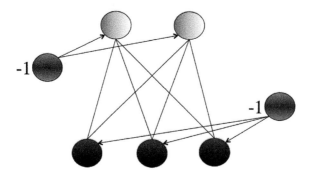

FIGURE 17.6   A schematic of the RBM network. There are two layers of nodes (the visible ones and the hidden ones) that are connected with symmetric weights.

The Restricted Boltzmann Machine

- **Initialisation**

    - initialise all weights to small (positive and negative) random values, usually with zero means and standard deviation about 0.01

- **Contrastive Divergence Learning**

    - take a training set of d-dimensional inputs $\mathbf{x}(1), \mathbf{x}(2), \ldots, \mathbf{x}(N)$ with elements ± 1
    - for some number of training epochs or until the error gets small:
        * Awake phase
        * clamp the visible nodes to the values of one of the input vectors
        * compute the probability of each hidden node j firing as (where b_j is the bias input to hidden node h_j):

$$p(h_j = 1 | \mathbf{v}, \mathbf{W}) = 1/(1 + \exp(-b_j - \sum_{i=1}^{d} v_i w_{ij})) \qquad (17.20)$$

        * create a random sample to decide if each hidden node h_j fires
        * compute CDpos $= \frac{1}{N} \sum_i \sum_j v_i h_j$
        * Asleep phase
        * for some number of CD steps:
            · re-estimate v_i using (where a_i is the bias input to hidden node h_i):

$$p(v_i' = 1 | \mathbf{h}, \mathbf{W}) = 1/(1 + \exp(-a_i - \sum_{j=1}^{n} w_{ij} h_j)) \qquad (17.21)$$

            · create a random sample to decide if each visible node v_i fires

· re-estimate h_j using:

$$p(h'_j = 1|\mathbf{v}, \mathbf{W}) = 1/(1 + \exp(-\sum_{i=1}^{d} v'_i w_{ij})) \qquad (17.22)$$

· create a random sample to decide if each hidden node h_j fires

  ∗ use the current values of v_i and h_j to compute CDneg = $\frac{1}{N} \sum_i \sum_j v_i h_j$

− **Weight Update**

− update the weights with (where η is the learning rate, m is the momentum size, and τ is the current step and $\tau - 1$ is the previous one):

$$\Delta w_{ij}^\tau = \eta(CDpos - CDneg) + m\Delta w_{ij}^{\tau-1} \qquad (17.23)$$
$$w_{ij} \leftarrow \Delta w_{ij}^\tau \qquad (17.24)$$

− update the bias weights with the same learning rule, but based on (where $\mathbf{v}^n$ is the vector of visible values for the nth input, and similarly for $\mathbf{h}^n$):

$$CDpos_{\text{visible bias}} = \sum_{n=1}^{N} \mathbf{x}(n) \qquad (17.25)$$

$$CDneg_{\text{visible bias}} = \sum_{n=1}^{N} \mathbf{v}^n \qquad (17.26)$$

$$CDpos_{\text{hidden bias}} = \sum_{n=1}^{N} \mathbf{x}(n) \qquad (17.27)$$

$$CDneg_{\text{hidden bias}} = \sum_{n=1}^{N} \mathbf{h}^n \qquad (17.28)$$

$$(17.29)$$

− compute an error term (such as the **reconstruction error** $\sum_i (v_i - v'_i)^2$)

· **Recall**

− clamp an input $\mathbf{x}$ by setting the states of the nodes v_i to x_i

  ∗ compute the activation of each hidden node j as:

$$p(h_j = 1|\mathbf{v}, \mathbf{W}) = 1/(1 + \exp(-\sum_{i=1}^{d} v_i w_{ij})) \qquad (17.30)$$

  ∗ create a random sample to decide if each hidden node h_j fires
  ∗ re-estimate v_i using:

$$p(v'_i = 1|\mathbf{h}, \mathbf{W}) = 1/(1 + \exp(-\sum_{j=1}^{n} w_{ij} h_j)) \qquad (17.31)$$

  ∗ create a random sample to decide if each visible node v_i fires

This is a pretty complicated algorithm, so let's consider a simple example of using an RBM to illustrate it. Suppose that students need to choose three out of five possible courses for a particular part of their degree. The courses are Software Engineering (SE), Machine Learning (ML), Human-Computer Interaction (HCI), Discrete Maths (DM), and Databases (DB). If a tutor wants to help students by recommending which courses would suit them better, then it could be useful to separate the students according to whether they prefer programming or information technology. Looking at a few examples from previous years, the tutor might see examples like: (ML, DM, DB) and (SE, ML, DB) for the more programming-orientated students and (SE, HCI, DB) for those that prefer IT. There will, of course, be students who like both types of courses, and their choices would look more mixed.

Given only the list of which courses students took, the RBM can be used to identify the clusters in the data and then, given the information about what kind of student they are, it can suggest which courses they might choose.

		Courses		
SE	ML	HCI	DM	DB
0	1	0	1	1
1	1	0	1	0
1	1	0	0	1
1	1	0	0	1
1	0	1	0	1
1	1	1	0	0

On a very simple, small example like this we can see the effects of the computations very simply. The wake phase of the algorithm uses these inputs to compute the probabilities, and then sample activations, for the hidden layer, initially based on random weights. It then works out the number of times that a visible node and hidden node fired at the same time, which is an approximation to the expectation of the data. So if for our particular inputs the computed activations of the hidden nodes were:

Hidden Node 1	Hidden Node 2
1	0
0	1
1	1
0	1
0	1
0	0

then for each of the five courses the CDpos values will be:

Course	Hidden Node 1	Hidden Node 2
SE	1	4
ML	2	3
HCI	0	1
DB	1	1
DB	2	3

There are also similar computations for the bias nodes.

The algorithm then takes some small number of update steps sampling the visible nodes and then the hidden nodes, and makes the same estimation to get CDneg values, which are compared in order to get the weight updates, which consist of subtracting these two matrices and including any momentum term to keep the weights moving in the same direction.

After a few iterations of learning the probabilities start to be significantly different to 0.5 as the algorithm identifies the appropriate structure. For example, after 10 iterations with the dataset, the probabilities could be (to 2 decimal places):

Courses				
SE	ML	HCI	DM	DB
0.78	0.63	0.23	0.29	0.49
0.90	0.76	0.19	0.22	0.60
0.90	0.76	0.19	0.22	0.60
0.90	0.76	0.19	0.22	0.60
0.89	0.75	0.34	0.30	0.63
0.89	0.75	0.34	0.30	0.63

At this point we can look at either the probabilities or activations of the hidden nodes when the visible nodes are clamped to the inputs, or to new test data, or we can clamp the hidden nodes to particular values and look at the probabilities or activations of the visible nodes.

If we look at the hidden node activations for the training inputs, then we might well see something like:

Hidden Node 1	Hidden Node 2
0	1
0	1
1	1
1	1
1	0
1	0

This suggests that the algorithm has identified the same categories that were used to generate the data, and also seen that the two students in the middle chose a mixture of the courses.

We can also feed in a new student to the visible nodes, who took (SE, ML, DB) and the algorithm will turn on both of the hidden nodes. Further, if we turn on only the first of the two hidden nodes, and sample a few times from the visible nodes we will see outputs like $(1, 1, 1, 0, 1)$ and $(1, 1, 1, 0, 0)$, since the algorithm does not know to only choose three courses.

17.2.2 Deriving the CD Algorithm

Having seen the algorithm and a small example of using it, it is now time to look at the derivation of it. In order to understand the ideas behind this algorithm, let's recap a little about what we are doing, which is trying to compute the probability distribution $p(\mathbf{y}, \mathbf{W})$, which can be written as:

$$p(\mathbf{y}, \mathbf{W}) = \frac{1}{Z(\mathbf{W})} \exp(\mathbf{y}^T \mathbf{W} \mathbf{y}). \tag{17.32}$$

In order to find the maximum likelihood solution to this equation, as we did previously, we would use a training set, compute the derivative of the log likelihood based on this training set, and use gradient ascent. We saw what this derivative looked like in Equation (17.15), but we will write it in a slightly different way here.

The log likelihood based on N training inputs is:

$$
\begin{aligned}
\mathcal{L} &= \frac{1}{N} \sum_{n=1}^{N} \log p(\mathbf{x}^n, \mathbf{W}) \\
&= \langle \log p(\mathbf{x}, \mathbf{W}) \rangle_{\text{data}} \\
&= -\frac{1}{2} \langle (\mathbf{x}^n)^T \mathbf{W} \mathbf{x}^n \rangle_{\text{data}} - \log Z(\mathbf{W})
\end{aligned}
\tag{17.33}
$$

When we compute the derivative of this with respect to the weights the second term goes away and we get:

$$
\frac{\partial \mathcal{L}}{\partial \mathbf{W}} = -\langle \frac{\partial \mathcal{L}}{\partial \mathbf{W}} \rangle_{\text{data}} + \langle \frac{\partial \mathcal{L}}{\partial \mathbf{W}} \rangle_{p(\mathbf{x}, \mathbf{W})}
\tag{17.34}
$$

Looking at it in this form it is clear what the problem is: the second term is averaged over the full probability distribution, which includes the normalisation term $Z(\mathbf{W})$, which is a sum over all of the possible values of $\mathbf{x}$, and so it is very expensive to compute.

The last insight we need is to see an alternative description of what maximising the likelihood computes. This is that it minimises what is known as the Kullback–Leibler (KL) divergence, which is a measure of the difference between two probability distributions. In fact, it is precisely the information gain that we used in Chapter 12. The KL divergence between two probability distributions p and q is defined as:

$$
KL(p||q) = \int p(x) \log \frac{p(x)}{q(x)} dx
\tag{17.35}
$$

Note that it is asymmetric, in that $KL(p||q) \neq KL(q||p)$ in general.

To see that minimising this is equivalent to maximising the log likelihood we just need to write it out:

$$
\begin{aligned}
KL(p(\mathbf{x}, \mathbf{W})_{\text{data}} || p(\mathbf{x}, \mathbf{W})_{\text{model}}) &= \sum_{n=1}^{N} p_{\text{data}} \log \frac{p_{\text{data}}}{p_{\text{model}}} dx \\
&= \sum_{n=1}^{N} p_{\text{data}} \log p_{\text{data}} - \sum_{n=1}^{N} p_{\text{data}} \log p_{\text{model}} \\
&= \sum_{n=1}^{N} p_{\text{data}} \log p_{\text{data}} - \frac{1}{N} \sum_{n=1}^{N} \log p(\mathbf{x}^n | \mathbf{W})
\end{aligned}
\tag{17.36}
$$

Since the first term is independent of the weights it can be ignored for the optimisation, and the second term is the definition of the log likelihood.

Hinton's insight was that if, instead of minimising the KL divergence, the difference between two different KL divergences $(KL(p_{\text{data}}||p_{\text{model}}) - KL(p_{\text{MCMC}(n)}||p_{\text{model}})$ was minimised, then the expensive term in Equation 17.34 would cancel out. The term $p_{\text{MCMC}(n)}$ denotes the probability distribution after n samples of the Markov chain; often $n = 1$.

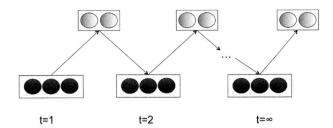

t=1   t=2   t=∞

FIGURE 17.7 The form of alternating Gibbs sampling. The initial values of the visible nodes are used (with the weights) to compute the probability distribution for the hidden nodes, and then these are used to re-estimate the values of the visible nodes, and the process iterates.

That is the idea of the contrastive divergence algorithm: we compute the expectation of the data, and then use Gibbs sampling starting at the data distribution for a small number of steps to get the next term. In the terms of a wake-sleep algorithm, we don't allow the network to dream for long before we wake it up and demand to know what it was dreaming about.

In order to see what the difference is between them, consider the (non-restricted) Boltzmann machine that had only visible nodes. In that case we worked out the full computation using maximum likelihood, and the resulting weight update equation is:

$$w_{ij} \leftarrow w_{ij} + \eta(\langle v_i v_j \rangle_{\text{data}} - \langle v_i v_j \rangle_{p(\mathbf{x}, \mathbf{W})}) \qquad (17.37)$$

Using the CD algorithm instead doesn't change things much:

$$w_{ij} \leftarrow w_{ij} + \eta(\langle v_i v_j \rangle_{\text{data}} - \langle v_i v_j \rangle_{\text{MCMC}(n)}) \qquad (17.38)$$

For the restricted Boltzmann machine the CD weight update is:

$$w_{ij} \leftarrow w_{ij} + \eta(\langle v_i h_j \rangle_{p(\mathbf{h}|\mathbf{v}, \mathbf{W})} - \langle v_i h_j \rangle_{\text{MCMC}(n)}) \qquad (17.39)$$

The first term estimates the distribution of the hidden nodes based on the training data, while the second runs a few steps of the Markov chain to estimate the distribution. This running of the Markov chain is in the form of alternating Gibbs sampling, where the values of the visible nodes and the weights are used to estimate the hidden nodes, and then these are used to estimate the visible nodes, and the process iterates. This is shown in Figure 17.7. As with other algorithms based on gradient ascent (or descent), such as the MLP, it can be very helpful to include a momentum term in the weight update, and this is included in the description of the RBM algorithm that is given below. Following that are a few notes about the implementation of the RBM.

Looking at this algorithm you might notice that the bias weights are kept separate to the others, and have their own update rules. This is because there are two sets of bias weights: separate ones for the visible nodes and the hidden nodes. These are not symmetrical weights for the simple reason that they aren't really weights like the other connections, but just a convenient way of encoding the different activation thresholds for each neuron.

Most of the computational steps are simple to compute in NumPy. However, one particular step justifies a little bit of thought, which is the decision about whether a neuron actually fires or not, based on a random sample. The probability computation for a neuron is something like:

```
sumin = self.visiblebias + np.dot(hidden,self.weights.T)
self.visibleprob = 1./(1. + np.exp(-sumin))
```

and so the problem is to decide whether or not the neuron actually fires. The simplest way to do it is to sample a uniform random number between 0 and 1, and then check whether or not that is bigger. Two possible ways to do that are shown in the next code snippet:

```
self.visibleact1 = (self.visibleprob>np.random.rand(np.shape(self.↲
visibleprob)[0],self.nvisible)).astype('float')
self.visibleact2 = np.where(self.visibleprob>np.random.rand(self.visibleprob.↲
shape[0],self.visibleprob.shape[1]),1.,0.)
```

There is no difference between the output of these two lines, so at first glance there is nothing to choose between them. However, there is a difference. To see it we need to explore the tools that Python provides to time things, with the `TimeIt` module. This can be used in different ways, but as a demonstration, we will just use it at the Python command line. The TimeIt module runs a command (or set of commands) a specified number of times, and returns information about how long that took.

The next few lines show the results of running this on my computer, where the first argument to the `timeit` method is the command to time, the second is the setup to do (which is not included in the time), and the last one is the number of times to run it. So this code makes a fairly small array of random numbers and uses the two approaches to turn them into binary firing values, performing it 1,000 times.

```
>>> import timeit
>>> timeit.timeit("h = (probs > np.random.rand(probs.shape[0],probs.shape[1])↲
).astype('float')",setup="import numpy as np; probs =
np.random.rand(1000,↲
100)",number=1000)
2.2446439266204834
>>> timeit.timeit("h= np.where(probs>np.random.rand(probs.shape[0],probs.↲
shape[1]),1.,0.)",setup="import numpy as np; probs =
np.random.rand(1000,100)↲
",number=1000)
5.140886068344116
```

It can be seen that the second method takes more than twice as long as the first method, although neither of them is that fast. Since this is a computation that will be performed many, many times when the RBM runs, it is definitely worth using the first version rather than the second.

You might be wondering why the truth values are cast as floats rather than ints. We have seen the reason for this type of casting before which is that NumPy tends to cast things as the lowest complexity type, and so if the activations are cast as integers, then the whole calculation of the probabilities that are based on this input at the next layer can also be cast as integers, which obviously causes large errors.

Using this code to compute the activations of the two layers, the steps for simple contrastive divergence in Python match the algorithm description very clearly:

```python
def contrastive_divergence(self,inputs,labels=None,dw=None,dwl=None,
dwvb=None,dwhb=None,dwlb=None,silent=False):
    # Clamp input into visible nodes
    visible = inputs
    self.labelact = labels

    for epoch in range(self.nepochs):
    # Awake Phase
    # Sample the hidden variables
    self.compute_hidden(visible,labels)

    # Compute <vh>_0
    positive = np.dot(inputs.T,self.hiddenact)
    positivevb = inputs.sum(axis=0)
    positivehb = self.hiddenprob.sum(axis=0)

    # Asleep Phase
    # Do limited Gibbs sampling to sample from the hidden distribution
    for j in range(self.nCDsteps):
        self.compute_visible(self.hiddenact)
        self.compute_hidden(self.visibleact,self.labelact)

    # Compute <vh>_n
    negative = np.dot(self.visibleact.T,self.hiddenact)
    negativevb = self.visibleact.sum(axis=0)
    negativehb = self.hiddenprob.sum(axis=0)

    # Learning rule (with momentum)
    dw = self.eta * ((positive - negative) / np.shape(inputs)[0] - self.
    decay*self.weights) + self.momentum*dw
    self.weights += dw
    dwvb = self.eta * (positivevb - negativevb) / np.shape(inputs)[0] + self.
    momentum*dwvb
    self.visiblebias += dwvb
    dwhb = self.eta * (positivehb - negativehb) / np.shape(inputs)[0] + self.
    momentum*dwhb
    self.hiddenbias += dwhb
    error = np.sum((inputs - self.visibleact)**2)

    visible = inputs
```

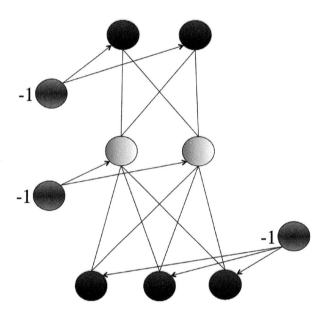

FIGURE 17.8 An RBM for supervised learning, with an extra layer of 'label' nodes, also connected with symmetric weights. However, these nodes use soft-max activation instead of logistic activation.

```
self.labelact = labels
```

17.2.3 Supervised Learning

The RBM performs pattern completion, just like the Hopfield network, so that after training, when a corrupted or partial input is shown to the network (by putting them into the visible units) the network relaxes to a lower energy trained state. However, it is possible to extend the RBM so that it performs classification. This is done by adding an additional layer of **soft-max** units (for a reminder about soft-max, see Section 4.2.3) that also have symmetric weights (see Figure 17.8).

The activation of these nodes is soft-max rather than logistic, so that there is only one neuron (one class) activated for each input. The training rule for this extra set of weights (and the corresponding bias weights) is also based on contrastive divergence.

The additions that this makes to an implementation of the RBM are fairly simple, with the most obvious difference in the sampling of the visible nodes, since there are now two sets of them: the input nodes and the label nodes ($\mathbf{l}$), so we are computing $p(\mathbf{v}|\mathbf{h}, \mathbf{W})$ and $p(\mathbf{l}|\mathbf{h}, \mathbf{W}')$, where $\mathbf{W}'$ are the extra weights connecting the hidden nodes to the label nodes; these weights are not included in the conditioning of each other since they are independent given the hidden nodes. However, the probabilities of the hidden nodes are conditioned on both of them (and both sets of weights): $p(\mathbf{h}|\mathbf{v}, \mathbf{l}, \mathbf{W}, \mathbf{W}')$.

Since the label nodes are soft-max units, the activation of them is different, as was described in Section 4.2.3. However, the implementation can be a little awkward in that if we use the soft-max equation as it stands, then the numbers get very large (since we are calculating e^x for quite large values of x). One simple solution to this is to subtract off the largest value so that the numbers are all 0 or below. This does make for quite complicated code, unfortunately:

```
# Compute label activations (softmax)
if self.nlabels is not None:
  sumin = self.labelbias + np.dot(hidden,self.labelweights.T)
  summax = sumin.max(axis=1)
  summax = np.reshape(summax,summax.shape+(1,)).repeat(np.shape(sumin)[1],
  axis=-1)
  sumin -= summax
normalisers = np.exp(sumin).sum(axis=1)
  normalisers = np.reshape(normalisers,normalisers.shape+(1,)).repeat(np.
  shape(sumin)[1],axis=-1)
  self.labelact = np.exp(sumin)/normalisers
```

Figure 17.9 shows the outputs of a RBM with 50 hidden nodes learning about 3 letters ('A', 'B', and 'S') from the Binary Alphadigits dataset without knowing about the labels, while Figure 17.10 shows the same examples, but with a labelled RBM. The algorithm had 1,000 epochs of learning. The top row shows the training set (with 20 examples of each letter) and the reconstructed version of each member of the training set, while the bottom row shows the test set of the remaining 57 examples (19 of each) and their reconstructions. It can be seen that the reconstructions are mostly pretty good. The labelled algorithm got 0 training examples wrong, and 5 of the test examples wrong, whereas the unlabelled version got 0 training examples wrong, but 7 test examples wrong.

17.2.4 The RBM as a Directed Belief Network

We have just seen that the RBM does a pretty good job of learning about a fairly complex dataset, and that the fact that we can use the network as a generative model helps us to see what it is learning. One way to understand the power of the RBM is to see that it is equivalent to a directed network that has an infinite number of layers, all consisting of the same stochastic neurons as the RBM, and with the same weight matrix connecting each pair of sequential layers, as is shown in Figure 17.11.

For a given set of weights we can use this network to generate possible inputs that were used in training by putting a random configuration into the nodes of an infinitely deep layer. The activations of the previous layer can then be inferred using the weights, and choosing the binary state of each neuron from a probability distribution based on the parents. This procedure can be iterated until the visible nodes are reached, and this gives us a reconstruction of a possible input.

It is also possible to go 'up' the network, from the visible nodes through the layers, by using the transpose of the weight matrix that is used for going from top to bottom. This enables us to infer the factorial distribution (that is, just the product of independent distributions) over a hidden layer by setting values for the visible layer below it. This is a factorial distribution since the nodes in the hidden layer are independent of each other. We can follow this process up the layers, and it enables us to sample from the posterior distribution over the hidden layers.

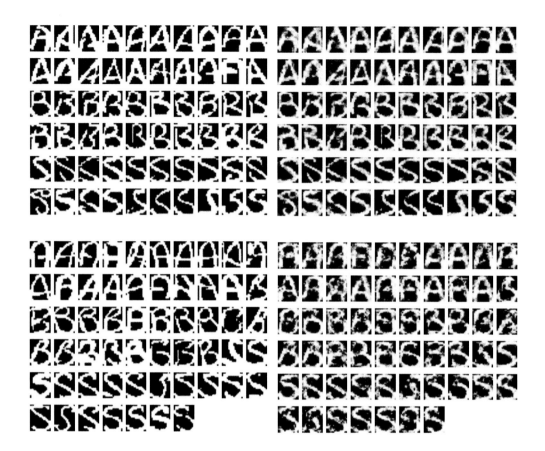

FIGURE 17.9 Training with an unlabelled RBM. *Top left:* Training set, *top right:* reconstructed versions of the training set, *bottom left:* Test set, *bottom right:* reconstructed versions of the test set. A few errors can be seen in this last set, such as the last picture on the 5th line, where an 'S' has been reconstructed as a 'B'.

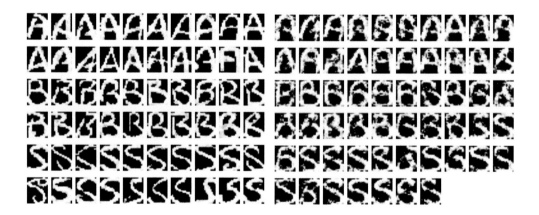

FIGURE 17.10 Training with a labelled RBM. *Left:* reconstructed versions of the training set, *right:* reconstructed versions of the test set.

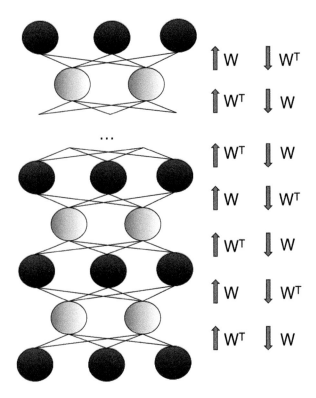

FIGURE 17.11 A Directed Belief Network with infinite layers.

Since we can sample from the posterior distribution, we can also compute derivatives of the probability of the data (and more pertinently, the log probability of the data):

$$\frac{\partial \log p(\mathbf{v}^0)}{\partial w_{ij}} = \langle h_j^0(v_i^0 - \hat{v}_i^0)\rangle, \tag{17.40}$$

where $\mathbf{v}^0$ denotes the vector of values in visible layer 0, and $\hat{v}_i$ is the probability that neuron i is firing if the visible vector is reconstructed from the sampled hidden values. Since the weight matrix is the same between each pair of layers, $\hat{v}_i^0 = v_i^1$.

Since we have the same weight matrix at each layer, the full derivative of the weight needs to have the contribution of all of the layers included in it:

$$\frac{\partial \log p(\mathbf{v}^0)}{\partial w_{ij}} = \langle h_j^0(v_i^0 - v_i^1)\rangle + \langle v_i^1(h_j^0 - h_j^1)\rangle + \langle h_j^1(v_i^1 - v_i^2)\rangle + \langle v_i^2(h_j^1 - h_j^2)\rangle + \ldots \tag{17.41}$$

If you look at this carefully, you will notice that most of the terms cancel out, and the final result is:

$$\frac{\partial \log p(\mathbf{v}^0)}{\partial w_{ij}} = \langle v_i^0 h_j^0 \rangle - \langle v_i^\infty h_j^\infty \rangle, \tag{17.42}$$

which is exactly the same as the full Boltzmann machine. Since the two networks minimise the same gradient and are based on the same sampling steps, they are equivalent.

This actually lets us see something important, which is the RBM seems to cancel out some of the need for **explaining away** when performing inference. Explaining away is one of the main challenges with performing inference in a belief network. We want to be able to choose between possible competing reasons for something happening, so that if we see that a visible node is on, and there are two competing hidden nodes that could have caused it, they don't both get switched on automatically.

To see why explaining away matters, suppose that you are sitting a multiple-choice exam for a topic that you know nothing about (hopefully not machine learning any more!). If you were to get a passing grade for that exam, then the possible reasons could be that you got very lucky with your guesses, or that the examiner mixed up your exam paper with somebody who did understand the material.

Both of these reasons are quite unlikely, and they are independent of each other. So if you see the class genius looking shocked when she collects her result, then you can deduce that your exam papers have been swapped over, and stop thinking about buying a lottery ticket on the way home. In other words, although the two explanations are independent of each other, they are made conditionally dependent by the fact that they are both explanations for your exam success.

Explaining away was not a problem in the infinite belief network that we have just seen, but it would be for a finite one. Consider a single hidden layer, with a data vector clamped on the visible inputs. The nodes in the hidden layer would have a distribution that includes conditional dependencies between them, based on the data vector. In the infinite version this doesn't happen, since the other hidden layers cancel them out. These cancelling-out terms are sometimes known as **complementary priors**.

The RBM is of interest in itself, but it is what you can build it up into that is even more interesting, and this fact of equivalence with the infinite directed belief network will help with the required algorithm, as we shall see in the next section.

17.3 DEEP LEARNING

We saw in Chapter 4 that an MLP can learn any arbitrary decision surface. However, the fact that it can do it only tells part of the story of learning. It might very well need lots and lots of nodes in order to learn some interesting function, and that means even more weights, and even more training data, and even more learning time, and even more local minima to get stuck in. So while it is true in theory, it doesn't mean that the MLP is the last word in learning, not even supervised learning.

One way to view all of the algorithms that we have talked about in this book is that they are *shallow* in the sense that they take a set of inputs and produce (linear or nonlinear) combinations of those inputs, but nothing more than that. Even the methods that are based on trees only consider one input at a time, and so are effectively just a weighted combination of the inputs.

This doesn't seem to be the way that the brain works, since it has columns built up of several layers of neurons, and it also isn't the way that we seem to do things like analysing images. For example, Figure 17.12 shows an image and different representations and sets of features that can be derived from the image. If we want to perform image recognition then we can't just feed in the pixel values into our machine learning algorithm, since all that this will do is find combinations of these pixel values and try to perform classification based on that. Instead, we derive sets of features of interest from the images, and feed those into the learning algorithm. We choose the features that seem to be useful according to our knowledge of the problem that we wish to solve and the appearance of the images; for example, if we are looking at the shape of objects, then edges are more useful than textures. It might also be useful to know how circular objects are, etc. Further, if the intensity of lighting in the images change, so that some are dark and some are light, then pixel intensities are not very useful, but edges and other features based on derivatives of the image intensity might well be.

All of this knowledge is put into the choice of the inputs features by the human investigator, and then the derived features are fed into the machine learning algorithm, with the hope that combinations of these derived features will be enough to enable the recognition.

However, when we look at an image we appear to perform several different recognition problems, looking at shape, texture, colour, etc., both independently and together. It seems that we split the recognition problem up into lots of sub-problems, and solve those and combine the results of those sub-problems to make our decision. We go from the colour of individual parts of the image (sort-of like pixels) through progressively more abstract representations until we combine them all to recognise the whole image.

We can make **deep** networks, where there are progressively more combinations of derived features from the inputs with the MLP, since we can just add more layers and then use the back-propagation algorithm to update the weights. But the search space that the algorithm is trying to find a minimum of gets massively larger as we do this, and the estimates of the gradients in that space that the back-propagation algorithm is making get noisier and noisier. So making deep networks isn't so hard, but training them is. In fact, they should actually need less training overall than a shallow network that has the equivalent expressivity, for reasons that I won't go into here, but that doesn't make them easier to train.

The first experiments that people performed into deep learning were mostly with **autoencoders**, which we saw in Section 4.4.5. These were MLPs where the inputs and outputs were clamped together, so that the (smaller number of) hidden nodes produced a lower dimensional representation of the inputs. We also saw that this could be used to perform pattern completion.

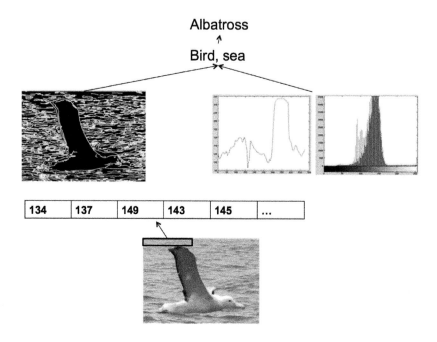

FIGURE 17.12 The idea of deep learning is that initial analysis of an image such as the bird at the bottom can only deal with the pixel values. The learners at different levels can produce higher-order correlations of the data, so that eventually the whole system can learn more complicated functions.

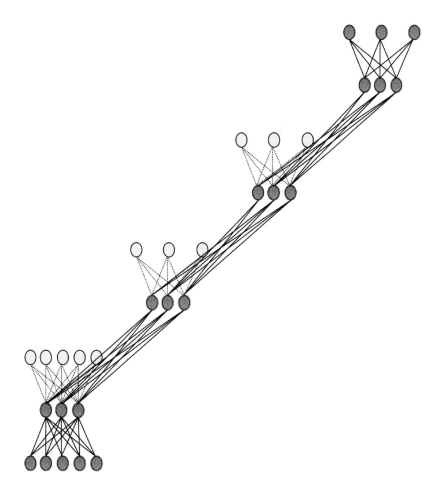

FIGURE 17.13 A schematic of a deep network built up of a set of autoencoders. The hidden layer of one autoencoder, which provides a representation of the input data it sees, is used as the input to the next one. The second half of each autoencoder, which is the reconstruction of the inputs, is shown in lighter grey and with dotted weight lines.

The idea is fairly simple: we train a single autoencoder, and then use the hidden layer of that network as the input to another one. This second network learns a higher-order representation of the initial inputs, that are based on the activations of the hidden nodes of the original network. Progressively more autoencoders can be trained and stacked on top of one another, and if the purpose is to do classification or regression, then a Perceptron can be added at the top, to take the activations of the final set of hidden nodes and perform supervised learning on them. Figure 17.13 shows a schematic of this kind of learning architecture.

The simplicity of the scheme is also the problem with it. Each autoencoder is trained in a pretty much unsupervised way; it is normal back-propagation learning, but the input and the desired output are the same, so there is no real information about what the hidden layer should be learning. There is some real supervised learning in the Perceptron at the final layer of the network, but this network has to deal with what it gets as the inputs, there is no error signal that informs the weights in all of the lower-down autoencoders and enables them to be trained further to produce more useful representations of the inputs.

There is some similarity between autoencoders and RBMs; they perform the same job, but the autoencoder is directional in that the weights run from input to hidden node to output, while the RBM weights are symmetrical. This means that we can run the RBM backwards: we can take samples of the hidden nodes and infer the values of the visible nodes that gave rise to them. This is a **generative model** of the type of inputs that the network sees. And this means that we can get information from the top of a stack of RBMs and push it back down through the RBMs all the way back to the input visible units, which gives us a chance of actually changing the weights of these RBMs, and so the representations that they find.

Deep learning is a very popular area for research at the moment, and various companies like Google obviously believe it is important, since they are employing a large number of deep learning researchers, and buying up companies that have been successful in developing applications based upon these ideas.

A set of stacked RBMs is known as a **Deep Belief Network (DBN)** and it is the topic of the next section.

17.3.1 Deep Belief Networks (DBN)

Conceptually, the DBN is pretty much the same thing that we have just seen with autoencoders. It consists of a series of unlabelled RBMs stacked together, with a labelled RBM at the very top. However, while creating the architecture is simple, we need to do some work to work out how to train it.

The first hope would be that we set up our stack of RBMs, and then use CD learning to train all of the weights in the network at the same time. However, it turns out that it takes a very long time for the network to settle to a distribution, and this involves lots of sampling steps up and down the network.

Instead, we will start greedily, by sequentially training the series of RBMs, just as we discussed doing for the autoencoders above. We clamp an input onto the visible nodes, and train this RBM, which will learn a set of symmetric weights that describe a generative model of the inputs. We then sample the hidden nodes of the RBM, and sequentially train a series of these RBMs, each unlabelled, with the visible nodes for layer i being clamped to samples of the hidden nodes for layer $i-1$. At the top layer we use an RBM with labels, and train that. This is the complete greedy learning algorithm for the DBN, and it is exactly the same as we could do with an autoencoder. However, we haven't finished yet.

At this stage we can recognise that there are two purposes to the network: to recognise inputs (that is, to do normal classification) based on the visible nodes and to generate samples that look like the inputs based on the hidden nodes. The RBM is fully symmetric and so the same weight matrix is used for these two purposes. However, once we start to add extra layers of RBMs above and below, with success training of each RBM based on the training of the one below it, things get a bit out of sync between working upwards from the visible nodes at the bottom to perform recognition, and working downwards from the output nodes to generate samples, principally because in the generative model the weights were set assuming that the hidden node probabilities came from the recognition model, and this is no longer true, since they come from the layers above the current one, and therefore will be different to the values that they were trained on.

For these reasons, there are two parts to the training. In the first, greedy, part there is only one set of weights, and so the training is precisely that of a set of autoencoders, while in the second part the **recognition weights** and **generative weights** are decoupled, except for the labelled RBM at the top layer (since there the weights are still actually the same since there are no layers above to confuse things). We can now use a variant of the wake-sleep algorithm that we saw earlier. Starting at the visible layer with a clamped input, we use the recognition weights to pick a state for each hidden variable, and then adjust the generative weights using Equation (17.40). Once we have reached the associative memory RBM at the top, we train this normally and then create samples of the hidden units using (truncated) Gibbs sampling. These are then used to sample the visible nodes at the top-most unlabelled RBM, and a similar update rule (with the role of hidden and visible nodes switched) is used to train the recognition weights.

So initially there is only one set of weights, and these are cloned at the appropriate point in the learning, and then modified from there. The following code snippet shows one way to implement this in NumPy.

```python
def updown(self,inputs,labels):

    N = np.shape(inputs)[0]

    # Need to untie the weights
    for i in range(self.nRBMs):
        self.layers[i].rec = self.layers[i].weights.copy()
        self.layers[i].gen = self.layers[i].weights.copy()

    old_error = np.iinfo('i').max
    error = old_error
    self.eta = 0
    for epoch in range(11):
        # Wake phase

        v = inputs
        for i in range(self.nRBMs):
            vold = v
            h,ph = self.compute_hidden(v,i)
            v,pv = self.compute_visible(h,i)

            # Train generative weights
            self.layers[i].gen += self.eta * np.dot((vold-pv).T,h)/N
            self.layers[i].visiblebias += self.eta * np.mean((vold-pv),axis=0)

            v=h

        # Train the labelled RBM as normal
        self.layers[self.nRBMs].contrastive_divergence(v,labels,silent=True)

        # Sample the labelled RBM
        for i in range(self.nCDsteps):
            h,ph = self.layers[self.nRBMs].compute_hidden(v,labels)
            v,pv,pl = self.layers[self.nRBMs].compute_visible(h)
```

```
# Compute the class error
#print (pl.argmax(axis=1) != labels.argmax(axis=1)).sum()

# Sleep phase

# Initialise with the last sample from the labelled RBM
h = v
for i in range(self.nRBMs-1,-1,-1):
    hold = h
    v, pv = self.compute_visible(h,i)
    h, ph = self.compute_hidden(v,i)

    # Train recognition weights
    self.layers[i].rec += self.eta * np.dot(v.T,(hold-ph))/N
    self.layers[i].hiddenbias += self.eta * np.mean((hold-ph),axis=0)

    h=v

old_error2 = old_error
old_error = error
error = np.sum((inputs - v)**2)/N
if (epoch%2==0):
        print epoch, error
if (old_error2 - old_error)<0.01 and (old_error-error)<0.01:
    break
```

This combination of a greedy and wake-sleep algorithm trains the RBN. It is possible to show that if the full maximum likelihood training (rather than CD learning) is used then this training regime will never reduce the log probability of the data under the generative model. However, in practice CD learning is always used since it gives good results in a reasonable time.

Both classification and generative modelling simply consist of choosing values for the appropriate nodes and then sampling your way up or down the set of layers of the network. The entire algorithm is given next.

The Deep Belief Network Algorithm

- **Initialisation**

    - create a set of unlabelled RBMs with pre-defined numbers of hidden nodes in each, and the corresponding number of visible nodes in the layer above; finish with a single labelled RBM.

    - initialise all weights to small (positive and negative) random values, usually with zero mean and 0.01 standard deviation

- **Greedy learning**

    - clamp the input vector on the visible units of the first RBM and train it using the CD learning algorithm in Section 17.2.1

- – sample the hidden nodes of this RBM and use these values to set the visible units of the next RBM
- – repeat up the stack until you reach the RBM with labels; train this one with supervised learning using the hidden layer of the topmost RBM as the input visible units and the labels as the output visible units
- – **Wake-sleep**
  - * for some pre-determined number of epochs, or until learning stops improving:
  - * for each of the unlabelled RBMs (k):
    - · create a copy of the weight matrix, separating those for recognition and for generation
    - · set the visible nodes to the relevant inputs (the inputs or the hidden nodes of the network below)
    - · sample the hidden nodes and use those samples to reconstruct the visible nodes
    - · update the generative weights with:

$$w_{ij}^{g,(k)} \leftarrow w_{ij}^{g,(k)} + \eta h_j (v_i - \hat{v}_i) \qquad (17.43)$$

    where v_i is the input value of visible node i, $\hat{v}_i$ is the reconstructed version, and (k) indexes the RBMs
    - · update the biases with:

$$w_{\text{visible},ij} \leftarrow w_{\text{visible},ij} + \eta \text{mean}(v_i - \hat{v}_i) \qquad (17.44)$$

  - * train the labelled RBM as normal with CD learning
  - * use alternating Gibbs' sampling for a small number of iterations to get samples for hidden and visible nodes of the labelled RBM
  - * for each of the unlabelled RBMs (k), starting at the top:
    - · initialise the hidden nodes with the samples from the visible nodes of the layer above
    - · sample the visible nodes and use those samples to reconstruct the hidden nodes
    - · update the recognition weights with:

$$w_{ij}^{r,(k)} \leftarrow w_{ij}^{r,(k)} + \eta v_i (h_j - \hat{h}_j) \qquad (17.45)$$

    where h_j is the input value of hidden node j and $\hat{h}_j$ is the reconstructed version
    - · update the biases with:

$$w_{\text{hidden},ij} \leftarrow w_{\text{hidden},ij} + \eta \text{mean}(h_j - \hat{h}_j) \qquad (17.46)$$

There are no particular new surprises in the implementation of this pair of algorithms.

To see how well this works, we continue with the three characters from the Binary Alphadigits dataset that we used to demonstrate the RBM. Figure 17.14 shows the output for a DBN made up of three RBNs, each with 100 nodes in the hidden layer.

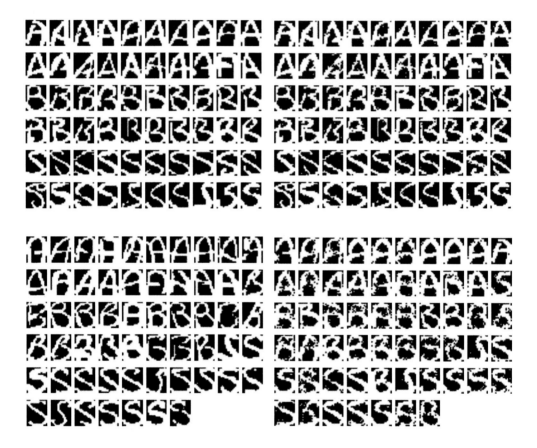

FIGURE 17.14 Training with the DBN. *Top left:* Training set, *top right:* reconstructed versions of the training set, *bottom left:* Test set, *bottom right:* reconstructed versions of the test set. The reconstructions are clearer than for the single RBN, although some errors are still visible such as the very last one.

FURTHER READING

The Hopfield network and some early work on Boltzmann Machines is covered in:

- D.J.C. MacKay. *Information Thoery, Inference and Learning Algorithms.* Cambridge University Press, Cambridge, UK, 2003.

For more up-to-date information, Hinton's papers are the best resource. If you are looking to make implementations of the RBM, then the following is definitely helpful:

- G. E. Hinton. A practical guide to training restricted Boltzmann machines. Technical Report UTML TR 2010-003, Department of Computer Science, University of Toronto, 2010.

For more on Deep Belief Networks, try:

- G. E. Hinton and R. R. Salakhutdinov. Reducing the dimensionality of data with neural networks. *Science*, 313(5786):504–507, 2006.

- Yoshua Bengio. Learning deep architectures for AI. Technical Report 1312, Dept. IRO, Universit'e de Montréal.

- Juergen Schmidhuber. Deep Learning in Neural Networks: An Overview `http://arxiv.org/abs/1404.7828`

PRACTICE QUESTIONS

Problem 17.1 In the Hopfield network the learning rate is not an important parameter. Work out why not, and justify the use of $\frac{1}{N}$.

Problem 17.2 Modify the Hopfield network code to make a continuous version of the network, using tanh() (which is available as `np.tanh()`) as the activation function. Produce a greyscale version of the digits problem and use it to recognise them.

Problem 17.3 The Travelling Salesman Problem (TSP) was discussed in Section 9.4. It can be solved using a Hopfield network by using an $N \times N$ network for N cities, with the columns representing the cities, and the rows representing the order in which they occur, so that there is exactly one active neuron in each row and column in a valid solution. The weights between adjacent columns encode -1 times the distance between the cities, and the weights between nodes in the same row or column should be set as a large negative value to stop more than one entry in each row and column being activated. Implement this and compare it to solving the TSP using the methods in Section 9.4.

Problem 17.4 Create a dataset that consists of horizontal and vertical stripes in a 2D array of size 4×4. Test whether or not an RBM can differentiate between the horizontal and vertically striped examples. Is the result what you expected?

Problem 17.5 In the RBM the probabilities for the nodes can be used, or actual activations based on random numbers. Hinton, in the practical guide referred to in the Further Reading section suggests that for the hidden nodes it is important to use activations for the hidden nodes (except for the final step of the CD learning), but probabilities are fine for the visible nodes. Modify the code to experiment with using both versions and compare the results on the AlphaDigits dataset.

Problem 17.6 Hinton also suggests that it can be very effective to use minibatches of between 10 and 100 examples (as was discussed in Section 4.2.7 for the MLP) in order to estimate the gradient. Implement this and investigate how many cases work best for different datasets. Make sure that you randomise the order to the data at each iteration.

Problem 17.7 Apply the Deep Belief Network to the MNIST dataset. Compare to just using a single RBM.

## CHAPTER 18

Gaussian Processes

The supervised machine learning algorithms that we have seen have generally tried to fit a parametrised function to a set of training data in order to minimise an error function. This function is then used to generalise to previously unseen data. Some of the differences between the methods have been the set of model functions that the algorithm can use to represent the data; for example, the linear models of Chapter 3 and the piecewise constant splines of Chapter 5. However, if we do not know anything about the underlying process that generated the data, then choosing an appropriate model is often a trial-and-error process.

As a very simple example, Figure 18.1 shows a few datapoints. If we assumed that these were drawn from a single Gaussian distribution then we would have two parameters to fit (the mean and standard deviation) in order to get the best match that we could, as shown in the middle figure. However, choosing a different distribution (here, a Weibull distribution, which also has two parameters):

$$f(x; k, \lambda) = \begin{cases} \frac{k}{\lambda} \left(\frac{x}{\lambda}^{k-1} e^{-\left(\frac{x}{\lambda}\right)^k} \right), & x \geq 0 \\ 0 & x < 0 \end{cases} \tag{18.1}$$

gives a better fit, as shown on the right (where the dashed line is the Weibull distribution and the solid line is the Gaussian). For the Gaussian $\mu = 0.7$ and $\sigma^2 = 0.25$, while for the Weibull $k = 2$ and $\lambda = 1$.

One possible solution to this problem is to let the optimisation process search over

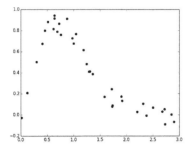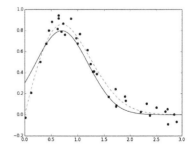

FIGURE 18.1 *Left:* a set of datapoints, *right:* two possible fits to that data, using a Gaussian (solid line) and Weibull distribution (dashed line). It can be seen that the Weibull distribution fits the data better, although both are a fairly good fit.

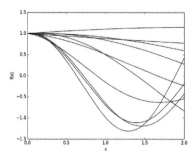 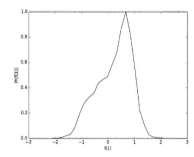

FIGURE 18.2 *Left:* 10 samples from the stochastic process $f(x) = \exp(ax)\cos(bx)$ with a and b drawn from Gaussian distributions. *Right:* The probability distribution of $f(1)$ based on 10,000 samples of $f(x)$.

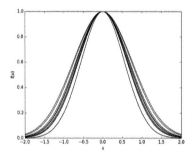 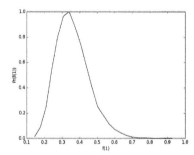

FIGURE 18.3 *Left:* 10 samples from the stochastic process $f(x) = \exp(-ax^2)$ with $a > 0$ drawn from a Gaussian distribution. *Right:* The probability distribution of $f(1)$ based on 10,000 samples of $f(x)$.

different models as well as the parameters of the model. To do this, we need to generalise the idea of a probability distribution to something that we can optimise over. This is known as a **stochastic process**, and it is simply a collection of random variables put together: instead of having a set of parameters that specify a probability distribution (such as the mean and covariance matrix for a multivariate Gaussian), we have a set of functions and a distribution over that set of functions. Figure 18.2 shows an example of a set of samples from the stochastic process $f(x) = \exp(ax)\cos(bx)$ with a drawn from a Gaussian with mean 0 and variance 0.25, and b from a Gaussian with mean 1 and variance 1, together with the probability distribution of $f(1)$ (computed from a set of 10,000 samples of $f(x)$).

Dealing with general stochastic processes is very difficult because combining the random variables is generally hard. However, if we restrict the process in such a way that all of the random variables have a Gaussian distribution, and the joint distribution over any (finite) subset of the variables is also Gaussian, then this **Gaussian process** (GP) is much easier to deal with. In order to see that it is still very powerful, Figure 18.3 shows a set of samples from $f(x) = \exp(-ax^2)$ with a drawn from a Gaussian distribution with mean 1 and standard deviation 0.25. It can be seen that the probability distribution of $f(1)$ is not a Gaussian.

The way to think about modelling with a Gaussian process is that we put a probability distribution over the space of functions and sample from that. A function is a mapping from some (possibly multi-dimensional) input $\mathbf{x}$ to $f(\mathbf{x})$, so to specify the function we could just list the value of $f(x)$ for every value of x, which would be an infinitely long vector. One sample would consist of a specification of this vector. However, because everything is Gaussian, just as we specify a Gaussian distribution with the mean and covariance matrix, we can specify a Gaussian process by the mean function and a covariance function.

A complete specification of a particular function would, as has already been remarked, require an infinitely long vector. However, it turns out that Gaussian processes are very well behaved, so that considering only finite sets of points gives exactly the same inference result as would the compete integral (for more on this, see the references in the Further Reading section).

There have been various versions of Gaussian processes around for a very long time, known as **kriging** after one inventor, and **Kolmogorov–Wiener prediction** after two more. In more than one dimension it is technically a **Gaussian random field**, which was the focus of Section 16.2.

In fact, Gaussian processes are just smoothers, fitting a smooth curve through a set of datapoints. It seems amazing that such a simple process can be so powerful, but regression problems do all pretty much boil down to finding a smooth function that passes through the data. More surprisingly, we will see later in the chapter that Gaussian processes can also solve classification problems, which are harder to view in this way. Regardless of how it is viewed, it is time to start working out how to use one.

18.1 GAUSSIAN PROCESS REGRESSION

As was mentioned previously, the GP is specified by the mean and covariance functions. In fact, it is usual to subtract off the mean first, so that the mean function is identically zero. In this case, the GP is completely described as a function $G(k(\mathbf{x}, \mathbf{x}'))$ that models some underlying function $f(\mathbf{x})$, where covariance function $k(\mathbf{x}, \mathbf{x}')$ gives us the expected covariance matrix between the values of f at $\mathbf{x}$ and $\mathbf{x}'$. The random variables that define the GP are used to provide an estimate of $f(\mathbf{x})$ for each input $\mathbf{x}$.

This is where we have to put some prior work in: the covariance function needs to be specified, and this is what provides the expressive power of the GP. This covariance function is the same thing as the **kernel**, which we explored in Chapter 8, and there are strong links between SVMs and GPs; for more details see the references in the Further Reading section.

Taking a hint from SVMs, then, we will start with a covariance matrix that has the form of the RBF kernel:

$$k(\mathbf{x}, \mathbf{x}') = \sigma_f^2 \exp\left(-\frac{1}{2l^2}|\mathbf{x} - \mathbf{x}'|^2\right). \tag{18.2}$$

In GPs, for some reason, this is normally known as the **squared exponential** covariance matrix rather than the RBF. For a set of input vectors it enables us to specify a matrix of covariances $\mathbf{K}$ where the element at place (i, j) in the matrix is $K_{ij} = k(\mathbf{x}^{(i)}, \mathbf{x}^{(j)})$.

There are two parameters in this covariance function: σ_f and l, and we shall consider them shortly. First, though, we will work out how to use the GP to predict the value of $f^* = f(\mathbf{x}^*)$ for some values of $\mathbf{x}^*$ based on a training set of values $f(\mathbf{x})$.

As is usual for supervised learning, the training set consists of a set of N labelled examples $(\mathbf{x}_i, t_i), i = 1..N$. Since this is a GP, the joint density $P(t^*, \mathbf{t}_N)$ is a Gaussian (where the notation is meant to imply that t^* is a single test point, while $\mathbf{t}_N$ is the whole set of training target labels) and so is this conditional distribution:

$$P(t^*|\mathbf{t}_N) = P(t^*, \mathbf{t}_N)/P(\mathbf{t}_N). \tag{18.3}$$

The covariance matrix for the joint distribution is $\mathbf{K}_{N+1}$, which has size $(N{+}1){\times}(N{+}1)$, and can be partitioned in the following way:

$$\mathbf{K}_{N+1} = \left(\begin{bmatrix} \mathbf{K}_N \end{bmatrix} \begin{bmatrix} \mathbf{k}^* \end{bmatrix} \atop \begin{bmatrix} \mathbf{k}^{*T} \end{bmatrix} \begin{bmatrix} k^{**} \end{bmatrix} \right) \tag{18.4}$$

where $\mathbf{K}_N$ is the covariance matrix for the training data, $\mathbf{k}^*$ is the covariance matrix between the test points $\mathbf{x}^*$ and the training data (which also appears in transposed form), and k^{**} is the covariance between the points in the test set (which will be a single scalar value when building $\mathbf{K}_{N+1}$ from $\mathbf{K}_N$). If there are N pieces of training data and n test points, then the sizes of these parts are $N \times N$, $N \times n$, and $n \times n$, respectively. We will drop the size subscript from $\mathbf{K}$ from now on, and use it to denote the covariance matrix of the training data ($\mathbf{K}_N$) and use the notation introduced in Equation (18.4).

The joint distribution of the training and test data ($p(\mathbf{t}, t^*)$ is the Gaussian distribution with zero mean and the extended covariance matrix shown in Equation (18.4). We know the values of the observations for the test data, so we only want to produce samples that match the observables at these points. We could do this by choosing random samples and throwing them away if they don't match, but this would be very slow, since very few of the samples would match.

Fortunately, we can condition the joint distribution on the training data, which gives us the posterior distribution as:

$$P(t^*|\mathbf{t}, \mathbf{x}, \mathbf{x}^*) \propto \mathcal{N} \left(\mathbf{k}^{*T}\mathbf{K}^{-1}\mathbf{t}, k^{**} - \mathbf{k}^{*T}\mathbf{K}^{-1}\mathbf{k}^* \right), \tag{18.5}$$

where $\mathcal{N}(m, \Sigma)$ denotes a Gaussian distribution with mean m and covariance Σ.

There is one important thing to notice, which is the requirement to invert the $N \times N$ matrix $\mathbf{K}$, which is an expensive operation, and not necessarily a numerically stable one. The good news is that only the covariance matrix of the training data needs to be inverted, and so this only has to be done once. However, if there is a lot of training data then this is still an expensive $\mathcal{O}(N^3)$ operation, and it requires that the matrix is (numerically) invertible.

18.1.1 Adding Noise

The top-left plot in Figure 18.4 shows the mean and plus/minus two standard deviations of the posterior distribution for the squared exponential kernel with the five datapoints marked as the training data. In that plot, you can see that the variance at the training data is zero, which is fine if you don't believe that your training data has any noise. However, this is, of course, very unlikely. The usual way to add noise into any GP is to assume that it is independent, identically distributed Gaussian noise and so include an extra parameter into the covariance matrix, so that instead of using $\mathbf{K}$ we use $\mathbf{K} + \sigma_n^2 \mathbf{I}$, where $\mathbf{I}$ is the $N \times N$ identity matrix. Noise is only added to the covariance for the training data. Together, the parameters of the kernel, including σ_n, are known as hyperparameters.

The posterior distribution is then:

$$P(t^*|\mathbf{t}, \mathbf{x}, \mathbf{x}^*) \propto \mathcal{N} \left(\mathbf{k}^{*T}(\mathbf{K} + \sigma_n \mathbf{I})^{-1}\mathbf{t}, k^{**} - \mathbf{k}^{*T}(\mathbf{K} + \sigma_n \mathbf{I})^{-1}\mathbf{k}^* \right). \tag{18.6}$$

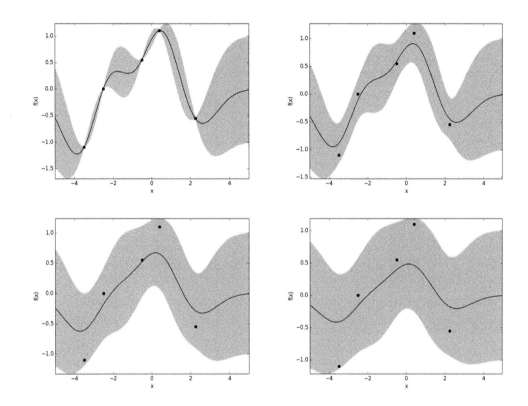

FIGURE 18.4 The effects of adding noise to the estimate of the covariance in the training data with the squared exponential kernel. Each plot shows the mean and 2 standard deviation error bars for a Gaussian process fitted to the five datapoints marked with dots. *Top left:* $\sigma_n = 0.0$, *top right:* $\sigma_n = 0.2$, *bottom left:* $\sigma_n = 0.4$, *bottom right:* $\sigma_n = 0.6$

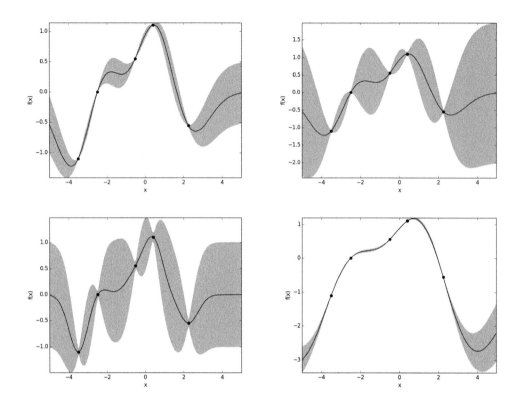

FIGURE 18.5 The effects of the other two parameters in the squared exponential kernel (compare to the top-left plot of Figure 18.4). Each plot shows the mean and 2 standard deviation error bars for a Gaussian process fitted to the five datapoints marked with dots. The parameters of the kernels were: *Top left:* $\sigma_f = 0.25, l = 1.0, \sigma_n = 0.0$, *top right:* $\sigma_f = 1.0, l = 1.0, \sigma_n = 0.0$, *bottom left:* $\sigma_f = 0.5, l = 0.5, \sigma_n = 0.0$, *bottom right:* $\sigma_f = 0.5, l = 2.0, \sigma_n = 0.0$.

The other three plots in Figure 18.4 show the effect that adding increasing amounts of observation noise makes.

Since we have considered the role of one of the hyperparameters, this is also a good place to consider the role of σ_f and l. Figure 18.5 shows the effects of changing these parameters for the same data as in Figure 18.4. It can be seen that modifying the signal variance σ_f^2 simply controls the overall variance of the function, while the length scale l changes the degree of smoothing, trading it off against how well the curve matches the training data.

Of the two parameters it is the l factor that is of most interest. It acts as a length scale, which says something about how quickly the function changes as the inputs vary. Figure 18.6 shows GP regression with similar data, except that in the plots on the second row, the x values of the points have been brought closer together. On the left, $l = 1.0$, while on the right $l = 0.5$. It can be seen that the top left and bottom right plots, where the length scale 'matches' the distances in the data, the fit looks smoother.

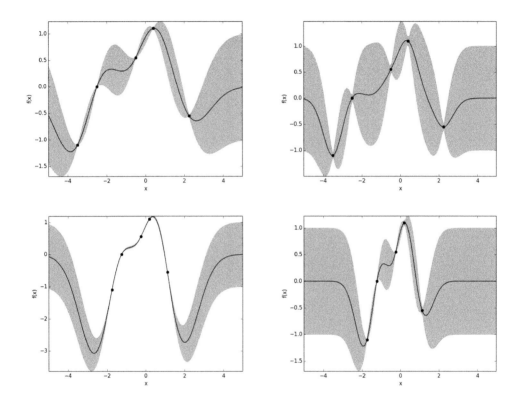

FIGURE 18.6 The effects of changing the length scale in GP regression. The top row shows one dataset, while the second row shows the same dataset, but with the points brought closer together. The length scale is the same for the plots above each other, being $l = 1.0$ on the left and $l = 0.5$ on the right.

18.1.2 Implementation

We have seen everything that we need to compute a basic Gaussian process regression program: we compute the covariance matrix of the training data, and also the covariances between the training and test data, and the test data alone. Then we compute the mean and covariance of the posterior distribution and sample from it. This results in the following algorithm:

Gaussian Process Regression

- For given training data $(\mathbf{X}, \mathbf{t})$, test data $\mathbf{x}^*$, covariance function $k()$, and hyperparameters $\boldsymbol{\theta} = (\sigma_f^2, l\sigma_n^2)$:

    - compute the covariance matrix $\mathbf{K} = k(\mathbf{X}, \mathbf{X}) + \sigma_n \mathbf{I}$ for hyperparameters $\boldsymbol{\theta}$
    - compute the covariance matrix $\mathbf{k}^* = k(\mathbf{X}, \mathbf{x}^*)$
    - compute the covariance matrix $k^{**} = k(\mathbf{x}^*, \mathbf{x}^*)$
    - the mean of the process is $\mathbf{k}^{*T}\mathbf{K}^{-1}\mathbf{t}$
    - the covariance is $k^{**} - \mathbf{k}^{*T}\mathbf{K}^{-1}\mathbf{k}^*$

However, before implementing it, there are a few numerical problems that need to be dealt with, as inverting the matrix $(\mathbf{K} + \sigma_n \mathbf{I})$ is not always stable, as it can have eigenvalues that are very close to 0.

Since we know that $\mathbf{K}$ is symmetric and positive definite, there are more stable ways to perform the inversion. The key is what is known as the Cholesky decomposition, which decomposes a real-valued matrix $\mathbf{K}$ into the product $\mathbf{L}\mathbf{L}^T$, where $\mathbf{L}$ is a lower triangular matrix that only has non-zeros entries on and below the leading diagonal. There are two benefits to this, first that it is relatively cheap to calculate the inverse of a lower triangular matrix (and the inverse of the original matrix is $\mathbf{K}^{-1} = \mathbf{L}^{-T}\mathbf{L}^{-1}$, where $\mathbf{L}^{-T} = (\mathbf{L}^{-1})^T$), and secondly that it provides a very quick and easy way to solve linear systems $\mathbf{Ax} = \mathbf{b}$.

In fact, these two benefits are both parts of the same thing, since the inverse of a matrix $\mathbf{A}$ is the matrix $\mathbf{B}$ for which $\mathbf{AB} = \mathbf{I}$, and we can solve this column-by-column as $\mathbf{AB}_i = \mathbf{I}_i$ (where the subscript is an index for the ith column of the matrix).

To solve $\mathbf{L}\mathbf{L}^T\mathbf{x} = \mathbf{t}$ it is simply a matter of forward substitution to find the $\mathbf{z}$ that solves $\mathbf{Lz} = \mathbf{t}$ followed by back-substitution to find the $\mathbf{x}$ that solves $\mathbf{L}^T\mathbf{x} = \mathbf{z}$.

The cost of these operations is $\mathcal{O}(n^3)$ for the Cholesky decomposition and $\mathcal{O}(n^2)$ for the solve, and the whole thing is numerically very stable. NumPy provides implementations of both of these computations in the `np.linalg` module, and so the whole computation of the mean (`f`) and covariance (`V`) can be written as:

```
L = np.linalg.cholesky(k)
beta = np.linalg.solve(L.transpose(), np.linalg.solve(L,t))
kstar = kernel(data,xstar,theta,wantderiv=False,measnoise=0)
f = np.dot(kstar.transpose(), beta)
v = np.linalg.solve(L,kstar)
V =                    kernel(xstar,xstar,theta,wantderiv=False,measnoise=0)-
np.dot(v.transpose(⌒
),v)
```

The computation of `V` uses $\mathbf{v}^T\mathbf{v}$, where $\mathbf{L}\mathbf{v} = \mathbf{k}^*$ and to see that this does indeed match the covariance in Equation (18.6) requires a little bit of algebra:

$$
\begin{aligned}
\mathbf{k}^{*T}\mathbf{K}^{-1}\mathbf{k}^* &= (\mathbf{L}\mathbf{v})^T\mathbf{K}^{-1}\mathbf{L}\mathbf{v} \\
&= \mathbf{v}^T\mathbf{L}^T(\mathbf{L}\mathbf{L}^T)^{-1}\mathbf{L}\mathbf{v} \\
&= \mathbf{v}^T\mathbf{L}^T\mathbf{L}^{-T}\mathbf{L}^{-1}\mathbf{L}\mathbf{v} \\
&= \mathbf{v}^T\mathbf{v}
\end{aligned}
$$

Comparing the code to Equation (18.6) you might also notice that the mean can be written in a slightly different way as:

$$
m(\mathbf{x}, \mathbf{x}^*) = \sum_i \beta_i k(\mathbf{x}_i, \mathbf{x}^*), \tag{18.7}
$$

where β_i is the ith part of $\beta = (\mathbf{K} + \sigma_n^2\mathbf{I})^{-1}\mathbf{t}$. This suggests that we can consider GP regression as the sum of a set of basis functions positioned on the training data; indeed for the squared exponential covariance matrix, we have produced precisely an RBF method; see Chapter 5. In that chapter we could modify the weights that specified the locations of the RBFs, but here we can't, but we can modify the weights that connect them to the outputs. Seen in this way, this GP is basically a linear neural network.

So providing that the hyperparameters are chosen to match the data, using a GP for regression is very simple. Now we are ready to do some learning to modify the parameters based on the data in order to improve the fit of the GP.

18.1.3 Learning the Parameters

The squared exponential covariance matrix (Equation (18.2)) has three hyperparameters (σ_f, σ_n, l) that need to be selected, and we have already seen that they can have a significant effect on the shape of the resulting output curve, so that finding the correct values is very important. In the next section we will also see that with more complex covariance matrices there are many more hyperparameters to choose, and so finding an automatic method of choosing the hyperparameters is clearly important if GPs are going to be useful.

If the set of hyperparameters are labelled as $\boldsymbol{\theta}$ then the ideal solution to this problem would be to set up some kind of prior distribution over the hyperparameters and then integrate them out in order to maximise the probability of the output targets:

$$
P(t^*|\mathbf{x}, \mathbf{t}, \mathbf{x}^*) = \int P(t^*|\mathbf{x}, \mathbf{t}, \mathbf{x}^*, \boldsymbol{\theta}) P(\boldsymbol{\theta}|\mathbf{x}, \mathbf{t}) d\boldsymbol{\theta}. \tag{18.8}
$$

This integral is very rarely tractable, but we can compute the posterior probability of $\boldsymbol{\theta}$ (which is the marginal likelihood times $P(\boldsymbol{\theta})$). The log of the marginal likelihood (also known as the evidence for the hyperparameters, which marginalises over the function values) is:

$$
\log P(\mathbf{t}|\mathbf{x}, \boldsymbol{\theta}) = -\frac{1}{2}\mathbf{t}^T(\mathbf{K} + \sigma_n^2\mathbf{I})^{-1}\mathbf{t} - \frac{1}{2}\log|\mathbf{K} + \sigma_n^2\mathbf{I}| - \frac{N}{2}\log 2\pi. \tag{18.9}
$$

In order to derive this equation you need to remember that the product of two Gaussians is also Gaussian (up to normalisation) and then write out the equation of a multivariate Gaussian and take the logarithm.

We now want to minimise this log likelihood, which we can do by using our favourite gradient descent solver from Chapter 9 (for example, conjugate gradients from Section 9.3), providing that we first compute the gradient of it with respect to each of the hyperparameters. We will write $\mathbf{Q} = (\mathbf{K} + \sigma_n^2 \mathbf{I})$ and then recall that $\mathbf{Q}$ is a function of all of the hyperparameters $\boldsymbol{\theta}_i$. Amazingly, these derivatives have a very nice form, as can be seen with the use of two matrix identities (where $\frac{\partial Q}{\partial \theta}$ is simply the element-by-element derivative of the matrix):

$$\frac{\partial \mathbf{Q}^{-1}}{\partial \boldsymbol{\theta}} = -\mathbf{Q}^{-1} \frac{\partial \mathbf{Q}}{\partial \boldsymbol{\theta}} \mathbf{Q}^{-1} \tag{18.10}$$

$$\frac{\partial \log |\mathbf{Q}|}{\partial \boldsymbol{\theta}} = \operatorname{trace} \left(\mathbf{Q}^{-1} \frac{\partial \mathbf{Q}}{\partial \boldsymbol{\theta}} \right). \tag{18.11}$$

Then:

$$\frac{\partial}{\partial \boldsymbol{\theta}} \log P(\mathbf{t}|\mathbf{x}, \boldsymbol{\theta}) = \frac{1}{2} \mathbf{t}^T \mathbf{Q}^{-1} \frac{\partial Q}{\partial \boldsymbol{\theta}} \mathbf{Q}^{-1} \mathbf{t} - \frac{1}{2} \operatorname{trace} \left(\mathbf{Q}^{-1} \frac{\partial \mathbf{Q}}{\partial \boldsymbol{\theta}} \right). \tag{18.12}$$

Now, all that is required is to actually perform the computations of the derivatives of the covariance with respect to each hyperparameter, and then optimise the log likelihood using the conjugate gradient solver.

It will make things slightly easier if we change the way that the hyperparameters are presented a little bit. Note that all of the hyperparameters are positive numbers (since they are all squared in Equation (18.2). We can also make them positive by taking the exponential of each of them, and since the derivative of an exponential is just the exponential, this can make things a little clearer. Further, we will effectively work with $1/\sigma_l$ since it also makes the computation easier.

For the squared exponential kernel (where there is a slight notation abuse in the use of the identity matrix $\mathbf{I}$ in the last term):

$$k(\mathbf{x}, \mathbf{x}') = \exp(\sigma_f) \exp\left(-\frac{1}{2} \exp(\sigma_l) |\mathbf{x} - \mathbf{x}'|^2 \right) + \exp(\sigma_n) \mathbf{I} \tag{18.13}$$

$$= k' + \exp(\sigma_n) \mathbf{I} \tag{18.14}$$

these are nice and easy to compute:

$$\frac{\partial k}{\partial \sigma_f} = k' \tag{18.15}$$

$$\frac{\partial k}{\partial \sigma l} = k' \times \left(-\frac{1}{2} \exp(\sigma_l) |\mathbf{x} - \mathbf{x}'|^2 \right) \tag{18.16}$$

$$\frac{\partial k}{\partial \sigma_n} = \exp(\sigma_n) \mathbf{I} \tag{18.17}$$

Note that the term inside the bracket in $\frac{\partial k}{\partial \sigma l}$ is precisely the one that has already been computed for the exponential calculation.

18.1.4 Implementation

The basic algorithm is very simple again, which is to call the conjugate gradient optimiser to minimise the log likelihood, providing it with the computations of the gradients with respect to the parameters. The SciPy optimiser was used in Section 9.3 and the syntax is no different here:

```
result =    so.fmin_cg(logPosterior,    theta,    fprime=gradLogPosterior,
args=[(X,y)↲
], gtol=1e-4,maxiter=5,disp=1)
```

where possible implementations of the log likelihood and gradient functions are:

```
def logPosterior(theta,args):
            data,t = args
            k = kernel2(data,data,theta,wantderiv=False)
            L = np.linalg.cholesky(k)
            beta = np.linalg.solve(L.transpose(), np.linalg.solve(L,t))
            logp = -0.5*np.dot(t.transpose(),beta) - np.sum(np.log(np.↲
            diag(L))) - np.shape(data)[0] /2. * np.log(2*np.pi)
            return -logp

def gradLogPosterior(theta,args):
            data,t = args
            theta = np.squeeze(theta)
            d = len(theta)
            K = kernel2(data,data,theta,wantderiv=True)

            L = np.linalg.cholesky(np.squeeze(K[:,:,0]))
            invk = np.linalg.solve(L.transpose(),np.linalg.solve(L,np.↲
            eye(np.shape(data)[0])))

            dlogpdtheta = np.zeros(d)
            for d in range(1,len(theta)+1):
                    dlogpdtheta[d-1] = 0.5*np.dot(t.transpose(), np.dot(↲
                    invk, np.dot(np.squeeze(K[:,:,d]), np.dot(invk,t)))) ↲
                    - 0.5*np.trace(np.dot(invk,np.squee
ze(K[:,:,d])))

            return -dlogpdtheta
```

In terms of implementation, the only thing that we have not covered yet is how to compute the covariance matrix, but there is nothing complex about that: the function takes in two sets of datapoints and returns the covariance matrix, and possibly the gradients as well (which is the wantd switch). One possible way to do this for the squared exponential kernel is:

```
def kernel(data1,data2,theta,wantderiv=True,measnoise=1.):
        # Squared exponential
        theta = np.squeeze(theta)
        theta = np.exp(theta)
        if np.ndim(data1) == 1:
                d1 = np.shape(data1)[0]
                n = 1
        else:
                (d1,n) = np.shape(data1)

        d2 = np.shape(data2)[0]
        sumxy = np.zeros((d1,d2))
        for d in range(n):
                D1 = np.transpose([data1[:,d]]) * np.ones((d1,d2))
                D2 = [data2[:,d]] * np.ones((d1,d2))
                sumxy += (D1-D2)**2*theta[d+1]

        k = theta[0] * np.exp(-0.5*sumxy)

        if wantderiv:
                K = np.zeros((d1,d2,len(theta)+1))
                K[:,:,0] = k + measnoise*theta[2]*np.eye(d1,d2)
                K[:,:,1] = k
                K[:,:,2] = -0.5*k*sumxy
                K[:,:,3] = theta[2]*np.eye(d1,d2)
                return K
        else:
                return k + measnoise*theta[2]*np.eye(d1,d2)
```

Figure 18.7 shows an example of a Gaussian process before and after optimisation, with initially random hyperparameters. Before the optimisation process the log likelihood of the data under the model, based on random initialisation of the hyperparameters, was around 60, whereas afterwards it was around 16. It can be seen that the model fits the data much better after the optimisation process.

18.1.5 Choosing a (set of) Covariance Functions

Like any other kernel, the choice of covariance function is crucial to successful prediction. This is the modelling part of GP learning, and it is entirely human-dependent: you choose appropriate covariance functions and then the algorithm learns their parameters. All that is required is that the functions must generate positive-definite (or actually, non-negative definite) covariance matrices. There is a fairly large choice of typical kernels for GPs, but given that our only restriction is that they must be positive-definite, it is possible to add and multiply kernels as we saw in Section 8.2 using Mercer's theorem. The upshot of this is that you can string together a whole set of covariance functions that represent different parts of what you believe the data is doing. So for example, if you think that there are two different squared exponential processes, but with different length scales, you could include two versions of the kernel, and optimise the two different length scales.

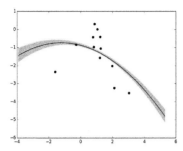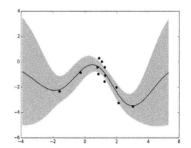

FIGURE 18.7 *Left:* the data and the model based on random parameters, *right:* the fitted model.

A few commonly used covariance functions are:

Constant $k(\mathbf{x}, \mathbf{x}') = e^{\sigma}$

Linear $k(\mathbf{x}, \mathbf{x}') = \sum_{d=1}^{D} e^{\sigma_d} \mathbf{x}_d \mathbf{x}_d'$

Squared Exponential $k(\mathbf{x}, \mathbf{x}') = e^{\sigma_f} \exp\left(-\frac{1}{2} \exp(\sigma_l)(\mathbf{x} - \mathbf{x}')^2\right)$

Ornstein–Uhlenbeck $k(\mathbf{x}, \mathbf{x}') = \exp\left(-\exp(\sigma_l)|\mathbf{x} - \mathbf{x}'|\right)$

Matérn $k(\mathbf{x}, \mathbf{x}') = \frac{1}{2^{\sigma_\nu - 1}\Gamma(\sigma_\nu)} \left(\frac{\sqrt{2\sigma_\nu}}{l}(\mathbf{x} - \mathbf{x}')\right)^\nu K_\nu\left(\frac{\sqrt{2\sigma_\nu}}{l}(\mathbf{x} - \mathbf{x}')\right),$
    where K_{σ_ν} is a modified Bessel function and Γ is the **gamma** function.

Periodic $k(\mathbf{x}, \mathbf{x}') = \exp\left(-2 \exp(\sigma_l) \sin^2(\sigma_\nu \pi (\mathbf{x} - \mathbf{x}'))\right)$

Rational Quadratic $k(\mathbf{x}, \mathbf{x}') = \left(1 + \frac{1}{2\sigma_\alpha} \exp(\sigma_l)(\mathbf{x} - \mathbf{x}')^2\right)^{-\sigma_\alpha}$

18.2 GAUSSIAN PROCESS CLASSIFICATION

While it is possible to perform multi-class classification with a Gaussian process, we will consider only two classes, labelled as +1 and -1. The task of the process is then to model the probability that input $\mathbf{x}$ belongs to class 1, which means that the output should be a value between 0 and 1 (inclusive) like all good probabilities. We will arrange this in the same way that we did it for neurons: by squashing it using the logistic function $P(t^* = 1|a) = \sigma(a) = 1/(1 + \exp(-a))$, where a is the output of the regression GP, and a little care is needed since we are now using $\sigma(\cdot)$ to denote the logistic function, as well as σ_n to denote a hyperparameter and even σ^2 as the variance. Since there are two classes $P(t^* = -1|a) = 1 - P(t^* = 1|a)$, and so we can write $p(t^*|a) = \sigma(t^* f(x^*))$. So GP classification consists of finding a GP prior over $f(\mathbf{x})$ (known as the latent function) and then putting this through the logistic function to find a prior on the predicted class, which is:

$$p(t^* = 1|\mathbf{x}, \mathbf{t}, \mathbf{x}^*) = \int \sigma(f(\mathbf{x}^*)) p(f(\mathbf{x}^*)|\mathbf{x}, \mathbf{t}, \mathbf{x}^*) df(\mathbf{x}^*). \qquad (18.18)$$

This is a 1D integral, and so it can be computed numerically, but unfortunately the likelihood function $p(f(\mathbf{x}^*)|\mathbf{x}, \mathbf{t}, \mathbf{x}^*)$ is not a Gaussian function and so computing that term is intractable. This means that some form of approximation is needed. There are several methods of doing these approximations, including using MCMC, but we will consider only the simplest version, which is known as Laplace's approximation. The references at the end of the chapter provide a list of places with more information about more advanced approximation methods.

18.2.1 The Laplace Approximation

Laplace's approximation is a way to approximate any integral of the form $\int \exp(f(\mathbf{x}))d\mathbf{x}$, which, of course, includes Gaussians. The basic idea is to find the global maximum of the function $f(\mathbf{x})$, which occurs at some $\mathbf{x}_0$. At this point the gradient of $f(\mathbf{x})$ (which is $\nabla f(\mathbf{x})$) is 0, and so the second-order Taylor expansion around $\mathbf{x}_0$ is (where $\nabla\nabla f(\cdot)$ is the Hessian matrix):

$$f(\mathbf{x}) \approx f(\mathbf{x}_0) + \frac{1}{2}(\mathbf{x} - \mathbf{x}_0)^T \nabla\nabla f(\mathbf{x})(\mathbf{x} - \mathbf{x}_0). \tag{18.19}$$

Since the logarithm of a Gaussian is a quadratic function, this has a unique maximum, and so we replace $f(\mathbf{x})$ by $\log f(\mathbf{x})$ and then compute the exponential of this, which tells us that:

$$f(\mathbf{x}) \approx f(\mathbf{x}_0) \exp\left(\frac{1}{2}(\mathbf{x} - \mathbf{x}_0)^T \nabla\nabla \log f(\mathbf{x})(\mathbf{x} - \mathbf{x}_0)\right). \tag{18.20}$$

Normalising this to make it a Gaussian distribution tells us that:

$$
\begin{aligned}
q(f(\mathbf{x})|\mathbf{x}, \mathbf{t}) &\propto \exp\left(-\frac{1}{2}(f(\mathbf{x}) - \hat{f}(\mathbf{x}))^T \mathbf{W}(f(\mathbf{x}) - \hat{f}(\mathbf{x}))\right) \\
&= \mathcal{N}(f(\mathbf{x})|f(\mathbf{x}_0, \mathbf{W}^{-1})),
\end{aligned}
\tag{18.21}
$$

where $\mathbf{W} = -\nabla\nabla \log f(\mathbf{x})$.

In order to compute the Laplace approximation we need to find the value of $\mathbf{x}_0$ and then evaluate the Hessian matrix at that point. Identifying $\mathbf{x}_0$ can be done using the Newton–Raphson iteration, which finds an approximation to solutions of $f(x) = 0$ (in fact, here we want to find $f'(x) = 0$, but this doesn't change things much) by iterating the computation:

$$x_{n+1} = x_n - \frac{f(x_n)}{f'(x_n)} \tag{18.22}$$

until the changes are sufficiently small for the required accuracy.

18.2.2 Computing the Posterior

Returning to the actual computations that we need for the GP, we had reached the stage of approximating $p(f(\mathbf{x}^*)|\mathbf{x}, \mathbf{t}, \mathbf{x}^*)$. Using Bayes' rule we get that:

$$p(f(\mathbf{x})|\mathbf{x}, \mathbf{t}) = \frac{p(\mathbf{t}|f(\mathbf{x}))p(f(\mathbf{x})|\mathbf{x})}{p(\mathbf{t}|\mathbf{x})}. \tag{18.23}$$

We are in the lucky situation that the denominator is independent of $f()$, and so can be ignored for the optimisation. The first term in the numerator is:

$$p(\mathbf{t}|f(\mathbf{x})) = \prod_{i=1}^{N} \sigma(f(\mathbf{x}_i))^{t_n}(1 - \sigma(f(\mathbf{x}_i)))^{1-t_n}. \tag{18.24}$$

We will need to differentiate the log of this expression twice in order to use Equation (18.21):

$$\nabla \log p(\mathbf{t}|f(\mathbf{x})) = \mathbf{t} - \sigma(f(\mathbf{x})) - \mathbf{K}^{-1}f(\mathbf{x}) \tag{18.25}$$
$$\nabla\nabla \log p(\mathbf{t}|f(\mathbf{x})) = -\mathrm{diag}(\sigma(f(\mathbf{x}))(1 - \sigma(f(\mathbf{x})))) - \mathbf{K}^{-1}, \tag{18.26}$$

where diag() puts the values along the diagonal of a zero matrix, and this term is the $\mathbf{W}$ matrix in Equation (18.21).

We now need to find the maximum of $\log p(\mathbf{t}|f(\mathbf{x}))$, for which we construct the Newton–Raphson iteration:

$$\begin{aligned}
f(\mathbf{x})^{\mathrm{new}} &= f(\mathbf{x}) - \nabla\nabla \log p(\mathbf{t}|f(\mathbf{x})) \\
&= f(\mathbf{x}) + (\mathbf{K}^{-1} + \mathbf{W})^{-1}(\nabla \log p(\mathbf{t}|f(\mathbf{x})) - \mathbf{K}^{-1}f(\mathbf{x})) \\
&= (\mathbf{K}^{-1} + \mathbf{W})^{-1}(\mathbf{W}f((x)) + \nabla \log p(\mathbf{t}|f(\mathbf{x}))). \tag{18.27}
\end{aligned}$$

Thus, the Laplace approximation to the posterior probability is:

$$q(f(\mathbf{x})|\mathbf{x}, \mathbf{t}) = \mathcal{N}(\hat{f}, (\mathbf{K}^{-1} + \mathbf{W})^{-1}). \tag{18.28}$$

Based on this, we can estimate the posterior mean and variance. For the mean, we need to use the fact that at the maximum of $\log p(\mathbf{t}|f(\mathbf{x}))$:

$$\hat{f}(\mathbf{x}) = \mathbf{K}(\nabla \log p(\mathbf{t}|\hat{f}(\mathbf{x}))), \tag{18.29}$$

and then the expressions for the mean and variance of the GP regression give us posterior distribution:

$$P(t^*|\mathbf{t}, \mathbf{x}, \mathbf{x}^*) \propto \mathcal{N}\left(\mathbf{k}^{*T}(\mathbf{t} - \sigma(f(\mathbf{x}))), k^{**} - \mathbf{k}^{*T}(\mathbf{K} + \mathbf{W}^{-1})^{-1}\mathbf{k}^*\right) \tag{18.30}$$

For the optimisation we will also need to calculate the log likelihood and the gradient of it with respect to each hyperparameter, just as we did for GP regression.

The log likelihood is:

$$\log p(\mathbf{t}|\mathbf{x}, \boldsymbol{\theta}) = \int p(\mathbf{t}|f(\mathbf{x})p(f(\mathbf{x})|\boldsymbol{\theta})df(\mathbf{x}), \tag{18.31}$$

and so we again use the Laplace approximation to get:

$$\begin{aligned}
\log p(\mathbf{t}|\mathbf{x}, \boldsymbol{\theta}) &\approx \log q(\mathbf{t}|\mathbf{x}, \boldsymbol{\theta}) \\
&= \log p(\hat{f}(\mathbf{x})|\boldsymbol{\theta}) + \log p(\mathbf{t}|\hat{f}(\mathbf{x}) - \frac{1}{2}\log|\mathbf{W} + \mathbf{K}^{-1}| + \frac{N}{2}\log(2\pi).
\end{aligned} \tag{18.32}$$

Differentiating this with respect to each of the hyperparameters will lead to two terms, since both $\hat{f}()$ and $\mathbf{K}$ depend on $\boldsymbol{\theta}$. The same matrix identities as for the regression case are useful, and the first part, which is the explicit dependence upon any element of $\boldsymbol{\theta}$ is fairly similar to the regression case:

$$\frac{\partial}{\partial \boldsymbol{\theta}_j} \log p(\mathbf{t}|\boldsymbol{\theta})\Bigg|_{\text{explicit}} = \frac{1}{2}\hat{f}(\mathbf{x})^T \mathbf{K}^{-1} \frac{\partial \mathbf{K}}{\partial \boldsymbol{\theta}_j} \mathbf{K}^{-1} \hat{f}(\mathbf{x}) - \frac{1}{2}\text{trace}\left((\mathbf{I}+\mathbf{KW})^{-1}\mathbf{W}\frac{\partial \mathbf{K}}{\partial \boldsymbol{\theta}_j}\right)$$

(18.33)

We can then use the chain rule to get the other parts: $\frac{\partial}{\partial \boldsymbol{\theta}_j} = \frac{\partial}{\partial \hat{f}}\frac{\partial \hat{f}}{\partial \boldsymbol{\theta}_j}$, where:

$$\frac{\partial \hat{f}}{\partial \boldsymbol{\theta}_j} = (\mathbf{I}+\mathbf{WK})^{-1}\frac{\partial \mathbf{K}}{\partial \boldsymbol{\theta}_j}(\mathbf{t}-\sigma(\hat{f}(\mathbf{x}))),$$

(18.34)

and so we just need to compute:

$$\frac{\partial}{\partial \hat{f}(\mathbf{x}_i)} \log|\mathbf{W}+\mathbf{K}^{-1}|$$

$$= \left((\mathbf{I}+\mathbf{WK})^{-1}\mathbf{K}\right)_{ii} \sigma(\hat{f}(\mathbf{x}_i))(1-\sigma(\hat{f}(\mathbf{x}_i)))(1-2\sigma(\hat{f}(\mathbf{x}_i)))\frac{\partial \hat{f}(\mathbf{x}_i)}{\partial \boldsymbol{\theta}_j}$$

(18.35)

Note that this includes the third derivative of the $\sigma(\cdot)$ term!

Putting these three terms together gives us the whole gradient, ready for the conjugate gradient solver.

18.2.3 Implementation

The algorithm can be written out from the previous discussion, but as with the regression case, there are some tricks that can be used to improve the computational time and stability. The main one is that the matrix $(\mathbf{K}+\mathbf{W}^{-1})$ can be inverted using another matrix identity:

$$(\mathbf{K}+\mathbf{W}^{-1})^{-1} = \mathbf{K} - \mathbf{KW}^{\frac{1}{2}}\mathbf{B}^{-1}\mathbf{W}^{\frac{1}{2}}\mathbf{K},$$

(18.36)

where $\cdot^{\frac{1}{2}}$ means the element-wise square root and $\mathbf{B}$ is the symmetric positive definite matrix

$$B = \mathbf{I}+\mathbf{W}^{\frac{1}{2}}\mathbf{KW}^{\frac{1}{2}}.$$

(18.37)

To make implementation easier, the algorithm is written out here in these computationally efficient terms:

Gaussian Process Classification

- **To find the maximum by Newton–Raphson iteration:**

    - compute the covariance matrix $\mathbf{K} = k(\mathbf{X}, \mathbf{X}) + \sigma_n \mathbf{I}$ for hyperparameters $\boldsymbol{\theta}$
    - repeat until change < tolerance:
        * $W = -\nabla\nabla \log p(f(\mathbf{x}))$
        * $L = \text{cholesky}(\mathbf{I}+\mathbf{W}^{\frac{1}{2}}\mathbf{KW}^{\frac{1}{2}})$
        * update f using Equation (18.27), with Equation (18.36) giving the form of the inverse matrix
        * change = oldf - f

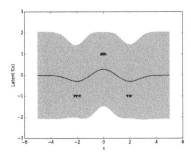 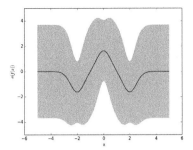

FIGURE 18.8 Gaussian process classification for a very simple dataset (shown plotted in the figure on the left). The latent function can be seen on the left, and the output of the logistic function on the right.

- **To make a prediction:**
    - compute the covariance matrix $\mathbf{k}^* = k(\mathbf{x}^*, \mathbf{X})$
    - compute the covariance matrix $k^{**} = k(\mathbf{x}^*, \mathbf{x}^*)$
    - compute the maximum f^* using the Newton–Raphson iteration algorithm
    - the mean of the process is $\mathbf{k}^* \nabla \log p(f(\mathbf{x}))$
    - solve $\mathbf{L}\mathbf{v} = \mathbf{W}^{\frac{1}{2}} \mathbf{k}^*$ for $\mathbf{v}$
    - the variance is $k^{**} - \mathbf{v}^T \mathbf{v}$

- **To compute the log likelihood and gradient:**
    - compute log likelihood using Equation (18.31)
    - compute $\mathbf{R} = \mathbf{W}^{\frac{1}{2}} \mathbf{B}^{-1} \mathbf{W}^{\frac{1}{2}}$, where $\mathbf{B}$ is defined in Equation (18.37).
    - compute $\mathbf{s}_2 = \frac{\partial}{\partial \hat{f}(\mathbf{x})} \log q$ using Equation (18.35)
    - for each hyperparameter $\boldsymbol{\theta}_j$:
        * compute gradients of covariance matrix with respect to $\boldsymbol{\theta}_j$
        * compute explicit gradient $s_1 = \frac{\partial}{\partial \boldsymbol{\theta}_j} \log p(\mathbf{t}|\boldsymbol{\theta})$ using Equation (18.33)
        * compute $\mathbf{s}_2 = \frac{\partial \hat{f}}{\partial \boldsymbol{\theta}_j}$ using Equation (18.34)
        * full gradient of log likelihood for $\boldsymbol{\theta}_j$ is $s_1 + \mathbf{s}_2^T \mathbf{s}_3$

Figure 18.8 shows a very simple example of Gaussian process classification. The data consists of a few points at around $x = -2$ and $x = +2$ that belong to one class and a few at around $x = 0$ that belong to the other class.

It is possible to do multi-class classification with GPs. The basic idea is to use a separate latent function for each class (so that the function $f(\mathbf{x})$ gets c times longer for c classes), looking like:

$$(f_1^{C_1}, f_2^{C_1}, \ldots f_n^{C_1}, f_1^{C_2}, f_2^{C_2}, \ldots f_n^{C_2}, \ldots f_1^{C_c}, f_2^{C_c}, \ldots f_n^{C_c}). \tag{18.38}$$

The target vector has to be the same dimension, so it will contain a row of n 1s where the

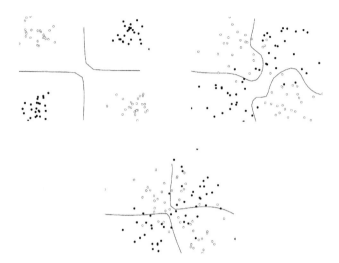

FIGURE 18.9 Gaussian process classification on the modified XOR dataset, with standard deviations $\sigma = 0.1$ *(left)*, $\sigma = 0.3$ *(middle)*, $\sigma = 0.4$ *(right)*. *The line gives the* $p = 0.5$ *decision boundary.*

f_i for the correct target class are, and 0 everywhere else. The covariance function will then be represented by a set of blocks of the individual covariance matrices. It is also necessary to use soft-max instead of the logistic function to do the 'squashing' of the regression output, which changes the derivatives in the computation of the log likelihood and its gradients. For further details on this, see the references in the Further Reading section.

There has been a lot more work on Gaussian processes over the past 10 years, including far more sophisticated optimisation methods, better ways to perform multi-class classification, and a better understanding of the links between Gaussian processes and neural networks, splines, and many other topics, but they are beyond our scope here: for more information, consult the references in the Further Reading section.

For a fairly simple idea, Gaussian processes do tend to work very well on a wide range of topics, and the way that the covariance function explicitly encodes the correlations that can be seen in the data means that the user has a lot of control. Even in the simple treatment here we have put quite a lot of effort into making the computations numerically stable and relatively fast. However, there is much more that can be done, including methods for approximation to speed things up significantly. Again, the Further Reading section provides more detail.

FURTHER READING

There is a very readable book dedicated solely to Gaussian Processes, which is:

- Carl Edward Rasmussen and Christopher K.I. Williams. *Gaussian Processes for Machine Learning*. MIT Press, Cambridge, MA, USA, 2006.

Another summary that may be useful is:

- D. MacKay. Neural networks and machine learning. *NATO ASI Series, Series F, Computer and Systems Sciences*, 168:133–166, 1998.

and GPs are also covered in:

- D.J.C. MacKay. (Chapter 45) *Information Theory, Inference and Learning Algorithms.* Cambridge University Press, Cambridge, UK, 2003.

- C.M. Bishop. (Section 6.4) *Pattern Recognition and Machine Learning.* Springer, Berlin, Germany, 2006.

PRACTICE QUESTIONS

Problem 18.1 The current implementation only has the squared exponential kernel in. Implement some more of those listed in Section 18.1.5 and experiment with them, particularly with the Palmerston North ozone layer dataset that we saw in Section 4.4.4. You might find the example in Section 5.4.3 of Rasmussen and Williams helpful.

Problem 18.2 Compare the optimisation results with using other optimisers, such as BFGS.

Problem 18.3 A simple version of multiclass classification uses one-against-all classifiers as we did with the SVM. Implement that and see how well it works on the iris dataset.

Python

The examples in this book are all written in Python, and the various graphs and results were also created in that language, using the code available via the book website. The purpose of this chapter is to give a brief introduction to using Python, and particularly NumPy, the numerical library for Python.

A.1   INSTALLING PYTHON AND OTHER PACKAGES

The Python language is very compact, but there are huge numbers of extensions and libraries available to make it more suited to a wide variety of tasks. Almost all of the examples in the book use NumPy, a set of numerical libraries, and the figures are produced using Matplotlib. Both of these packages have syntax that is similar to MATLAB®. There are a few places where examples also use SciPy, the scientific programming libraries.

An Internet search will turn up working distributions as self-extracting zip files for the major operating systems, which will include the Python interpreter and all of the packages that are used in the book, amongst others. If you download individual packages, then they generally come with a setup script (`setup.py`) that can be run from a shell. Package webpages generally give instructions.

A.2   GETTING STARTED

There are two ways that Python is commonly used. The first is as an interactive command environment, such as *iPython* or *IDLE*, which are commonly bundled with the Python interpreter. Starting Python with one of these (using Start/IPython in Windows, or by typing `python` at a command prompt in other operating systems) results in a script window with a command prompt (which will be shown as `>>>`). Unlike with C or Java, you can type commands at this prompt and the interpreter will run the commands and display the results, if any, on the screen. You can write functions in a text editor and run them from the command prompt by calling them by name. We'll see more about functions in Section A.3.

As well as iPython there are several other Python IDEs and code editors available for various operating systems. Two nice possibilities are the Java-based IDE *Eclipse* using the extension for Python called *PyDev*, and *Spyder*, which is aimed at exactly the kind of scientific Python that we are doing in this book. Both of these are freely available on the Internet and include all of the usual syntax highlighting and development help. In addition, you can run programs directly, and you can also set up an interactive Python environment so that you can test small pieces of code to see how they work.

The best way to get used to any language is, of course, to write programs in it. There is lots of code in the book and practical programming assignments along the way, but if you haven't used Python before, then it will help if you get used to the language prior to working on the code examples in the book. Section A.3 describes how to get started writing Python programs, but here we will begin by using the command line to see how things work. This can be in iPython or IDLE, by typing `python` at the command prompt, or within the console in the PyDev Eclipse extension or Spyder.

Creating a variable in Python is easy: you give it a name and assign a value. While Python is **strongly typed** (so that variables that contain integers don't suddenly change to holding strings or floats without being told to) it performs all the declaration and creation of variables for you, unlike lower level languages like C. So typing `>>> a = 3` at the command prompt (note that the `>>>` is the command prompt, so you only actually type `a = 3`) defines `a` as an integer variable and gives it value 3. To see the effect of the integer typing, type `>>> a/2`, and you will see that the answer is `1`. What Python actually does is compute the answer in the most accurate of the types that are included in the calculation, but since `a` is an integer, and so is 2, it returns the answer as an integer. You can see this using the `type()` function; `type(3/2)` returns `<type 'int'>`. So `>>> a/2.0` will work perfectly well, since the type of 2.0 is a float (`type(3/2.0) = <type 'float'>`. When writing floats, you can abbreviate them to `2.` without the zero if you really want to save typing one character. To see the value of a variable you can just type its name at the command prompt, or use `>>> print a`, or whatever the name of the variable is.

You can perform all of the usual arithmetic operators on numbers, adding them up, etc. Raising numbers to a power is performed by `a**2` or `pow(a,2)`. In fact, you can use Python as a perfectly good calculator at the command line.

Just like in many other languages, comparison is performed using the double equals (`==`). It returns Boolean values `True` (1) and `False` (0) to tests like `>>> 3 < 4` and `>>> 3 == 4`. The other arithmetic comparisons are also available: `<`, `<=`, `>`, `>=` and these can be chained (so `3<x<6` performs the two tests and only returns `True` if both are true). The not-equal-to test is `!=` or `<>`, and there is another useful comparison: `is` checks if two variables point to the same object. This might not seem important, but Python works **by reference**, which means that the command `>>> a = b` does not put a copy of the value of b into a, but rather assigns to a a reference to the variable b. This can be a trap for the unwary, as will be discussed more shortly. The normal logical operators are slightly unusual in Python, with the normal logical operators using the words **and, or,** and **not**; the symbols **&, |** perform bit-wise and/or. These bit-wise operators are actually quite useful, as we'll see later.

In addition to integer and floating point representations of numbers, Python also deals with strings, which are described by using single or double quotes (' or ") to surround them: `>>> b = 'hello'`. For strings, the + operator is **overloaded** (given a new meaning), which is concatenation: merging the strings. So `>>> 'a' + 'd'` returns the new string `'ad'`.

Having made the basic data types, Python then allows you to combine them into three different basic data structures:

Lists A list is a combination of basic data types, surrounded by square brackets. So `>>> mylist = [0, 3, 2, 'hi']` is a perfectly good list that contains integers and a string. This ability to store different types inside a list gives you a hint that Python handles lists differently to the way other languages handle arrays. This comes about because Python is inherently **object-oriented**, so that every variable that you make is simply an object, and so a list is just a collection of objects. This is why the type of the object does not matter. It also means that you can have lists of lists without a problem: `>>> newlist = [3, 2, [5, 4, 3], [2, 3, 2]]`.

Accessing particular elements of a list simply requires giving it an index. Like C, but unlike MATLAB®, Python indices start at 0, so `>>> newlist[0]` returns the first element (3). You can also index from the end using a minus sign, so `>>> newlist[-1]` returns the last element, `>>> newlist[-2]` the last-but-one, etc. The length of a list is given by `len`, so `>>> len(newlist)` returns 4. Note that `>>> newlist[3]` returns the list in the 4th location of `newlist` (i.e., `[2, 3, 2]`). To access an element of that list you need an extra index: `>>> newlist[3][1]` returns 3.

A useful feature of Python is the slice operator. This is written as a colon (:) and enables you to access sections of a list easily, such as `>>> newlist[2:4]` which returns the elements of `newlist` in positions 2 and 3 (the arguments you use in a slice are inclusive at the start and exclusive at the end, so the second parameter is the first index that is excluded). In fact, the slice can take three operators, which are [start:stop:step], the third element saying what stepsize to use. So `>>> newlist[0:4:2]` returns the elements in locations 0 and 2, and you can use this to reverse the order of a list: `>>> newlist[::-1]`. This last example shows a couple of other refinements of the slice operator: if you don't put a value in for the first number (so it looks like `[:3]`) then the value is taken as 0, and if you don't put a value for the second operator (`[1:]`) then it is taken as running to the end of the list. These can be very useful, especially the second one, since it avoids having to calculate the length of the list every time you want to run through it. `>>> newlist[:]` returns the whole string.

This last use of the slice operator, returning the whole string, might seem useless. However, because Python is object-oriented, all variable names are simply references to objects. This means that copying a variable of type `list` isn't as obvious as it could be. Consider the following command: `>>> alist = mylist`. You might expect that this has made a copy of `mylist`, but it hasn't. To see this, use the following command `>>> alist[3] = 100` and then have a look at the contents of `mylist`. You will see that the 3rd element is now 100. So if you want to copy things you need to be careful. The slice operator lets you make actual copies using: `>>> alist = mylist[:]`. Unfortunately, there is an extra wrinkle in this if you have lists of lists. Remember that lists work as references to objects. We've just used the slice operator to return the values of the objects, but this only works for one level. In location 2 of `newlist` is another list, and the slice operator just copied the reference to that embedded list. To see this, perform `>>> blist = newlist[:]` and then `>>> blist[2][2] = 100` and have a look at `newlist` again. What we've done is called a shallow copy, to copy everything (known as a deep copy) requires a bit more effort. There is a `deepcopy` command, but to get to it we need to `import` the `copy` module using `>>> import copy` (we will see more about importing in Section A.3.1). Now we can call `>>> clist = copy.deepcopy(newlist)` and we finally have a copy of a complete list.

There are a variety of functions that can be applied to lists, but there is another interesting feature of the fact that they are objects. The functions (methods) that can be used are part of the object class, so they modify the list itself and do not return a new list (this is known as working in place). To see this, make a new list `>>> list = [3, 2, 4, 1]` and suppose that you want to print out a list of the numbers sorted into order. There is a function `sort()` for this, but the obvious `>>> print list.sort()` produces the output `None`, meaning that no value was returned. However, the two commands `>>> list.sort()` followed by `>>> print list` do exactly what is required. So functions on lists modify the list, and any future operations will be applied to this modified list.

Some other functions that are available to operate on lists are:

append(x) adds x to the end of the list

count(x) counts how many times x appears in the list

extend(L) adds the elements in list L to the end of the original list

index(x) returns the index of the first element of the list to match x

insert(i, x) inserts element x at location i in the list, moving everything else along

pop(i) removes the item at index i

remove(x) deletes the first element that matches x

reverse() reverses the order of the list

sort() we've already seen

You can compare lists using `>>> a==b`, which works elementwise through the list, comparing each element against the matching one in the second list, returning True if the test is true for each pair (and the two lists are the same length), and False otherwise.

Tuples A tuple is an immutable list, meaning that it is read-only and doesn't change. Tuples are defined using round brackets, e.g., `>>> mytuple = (0, 3, 2, 'h')`. It might seem odd to have them in the language, but they are useful if you want to create lists that cannot be modified, especially by mistake.

Dictionaries In the list that we saw above we indexed elements by their position within the list. In a dictionary you assign a key to each entry that you can use to access it. So suppose you want to make a list of the number of days in each month. You could use a dictionary (shown by the curly braces): `>>> months = {'Jan': 31, 'Feb': 28, 'Mar': 31}` and then you access elements of the dictionary using their key, so `>>> months['Jan']` returns 31. Giving an incorrect key results in an exception error.

The function `months.keys()` returns a list of all the keys in the dictionary, which is useful for looping over all elements in a dictionary. The `months.values()` function returns a list of values instead, while `months.items()` gives a list of tuples containing everything. There are lots of other things you can do with dictionaries, and we shall see some of them when we use the dictionary in Chapter 12.

There is one more data type that is built directly into Python, and that is the `file`. This makes reading from and writing to files very simple in Python: files are opened using `>>> input = open('filename')`, closed using `>>> input.close()` and reading and writing are performed using `readlines()` (and `read()`, and `writelines()` and `write()`). There are also `readline()` and `writeline()` functions, that read and write one line at a time.

A.2.1 Python for MATLAB® and R users

With the NumPy package that we are using there are a great many similarities between MATLAB® or R and Python. There are useful comparison websites for both MATLAB® and R, but the main thing that you need to be aware of is that indexing starts at 0 instead of 1 and elements of arrays are accessed with square brackets instead of round ones. After that, while there are differences, the similarity between the three languages is striking.

A.3 CODE BASICS

Python has a fairly small set of commands and is designed to be fairly small and simple to use. In this section we'll go over the basic commands and other programming details. There are lots of good resources available for getting started with Python; a few books are listed at the end of the chapter, and an Internet search will provide plenty of other resources.

A.3.1 Writing and Importing Code

Python is a **scripting** language, meaning that everything can be run interactively from the command line. However, when writing any reasonable sized piece of code it is better to write it in a text editor or IDE and then run it. The programming GUIs provide their own code writing editors, but you can also use any text editor available on your machine. It is a good idea to use one that is consistent in its tabbing, since the white space indentation is how Python blocks code together.

The file can contain a script, which is simply a series of commands, or a set of functions and classes. In either case it should be saved with a `.py` extension, which Python will compile into a `.pyc` file when you first load it. Any set of commands or functions is known as a module in Python, and to load it you use the `import` command. The most basic form of the command is `import name`. If you import a script file then Python will run it immediately, but if it is a set of functions then it will not run anything.

To run a function you use `>>> name.functionname()`, where `name` is the name of the module and `functionname` the relevant function. Arguments can be passed as required in the brackets, but even if no arguments are passed, then the brackets are still needed. Some names get quite long, so it can be useful to use `import x as y`, which means that you can then use `>>> y.functionname()` instead.

When developing code at a command line there is one slightly irritating feature of Python, which is that `import` only works once for a module. Once a module has been imported, if you change the code and want Python to work on the new version, then you need to use `>>> reload(name)`. Using `import` will not give any error messages, but it will not work, either.

Many modules contain several subsets, so when importing you may need to be more specific. You can import particular parts of a module in this way using `from x import y`, or to import everything use `from x import *`, although this is rarely a good idea as some of the modules are very large. Finally, you can specify the name that you want to import the module as, by using `from x import y as z`.

Program code also needs to import any modules that it uses, and these are usually declared at the top of the file (although they don't need to be, but can be added anywhere). There is one other thing that might be confusing, which is that Python uses the `pythonpath` variable to tell it where to look for code. Eclipse doesn't include other packages in your current project on the path, and so if you want it to find those packages, you have to add them to the path using the Properties menu item while Spyder has it in the 'Spyder' menu. If you are not using either or these, then you will need to add modules to the path. This can be done using something like:

```
import sys
sys.path.append('mypath')
```

A.3.2 Control Flow

The most obviously strange thing about Python for those who are used to other programming languages is that the indentation means something: white space is the way that blocks of code are shown. So if you have a loop or other construct, then the equivalent of **begin** ... **end** or the braces { } in other languages is a colon (:) after the keyword and indented commands following on. This looks quite strange at first, but is actually quite nice once you get used to it. The other thing that is unusual is that you can have an (optional) **else** clause on loops. This clause runs when the loop terminates normally. If you break out of a loop using the **break** command, then the **else** clause does not run.

The control structures that are available are **if**, **for**, and **while**. The **if** statement syntax is:

```
if statement:
    commands
elif:
    commands
else:
    commands
```

The most common loop is the **for** loop, which differs slightly from other languages in that it iterates over a list of values:

```
for var in set:
    commands
else:
    commands
```

There is one very useful command that goes with this **for** loop, which is the **range** command, which produces a list output. Its most basic form is simply >>> range(4), which produces the list [0, 1, 2, 3]. However, it can also take 2 or 3 arguments, and works in the same way as in the slice command, but with commas between them instead of colons: >>> range(start,stop,step). This can include going down instead of up a list, so >>> range(5,-3,-2) produces [5, 3, 1, -1] as output.

Finally, there is a **while** loop:

```
while condition:
    commands
else:
    commands
```

A.3.3 Functions

Functions are defined by:

```
def name(args):
    commands
    return value
```

The `return value` line is optional, but enables you to return values from the function (otherwise it returns `None`). You can list several things to return in the line with commas between them, and they will all be returned. Once you have defined a function you can call it from the command line and from within other functions. Python is case sensitive, so with both function names and variable names, `Name` is different to `name`.

As an example, here is a function that computes the hypotenuse of a triangle given the other two distances (`x` and `y`). Note the use of '`#`' to denote a comment:

```
def pythagoras(x,y):
    """ Computes the hypotenuse of two arguments"""
    h = pow(x**2+y**2,0.5)
    # pow(x,0.5) is the square root
    return h
```

Now calling `pythagoras(3,4)` gets the expected answer of `5.0`. You can also call the function with the parameters in any order provided that you specify which is which, so `pythagoras(y=4,x=3)` is perfectly valid. When you make functions you can allow for default values, which means that if fewer arguments are presented the default values are given. To do this, modify the function definition line: `def pythagoras(x=3,y=4):`

A.3.4 The doc String

The help facilities within Python are accessed by using `help()`. For help on a particular module, use `help('modulename')`. (So using `help(pythagorus)` in the previous example would return the description of the function that is given there). A useful resource for most code is the `doc` string, which is the first thing defined within the function, and is a text string enclosed in three sets of double quotes (`"""`). It is intended to act as the documentation for the function or class. It can be accessed using `>>> print functionname.__doc__`. The Python documentation generator `pydoc` uses these strings to automatically generate documentation for functions, in the same way that `javadoc` does.

A.3.5 `map` and `lambda`

Python has a special way of performing repeated function calls. If you want to apply the same function to every element of a list you don't need to loop over the elements of the list, but can instead use the `map` command, which looks like `map(function,list)`. This applies the function to every element of the list. There is one extra tweak, which is the fact that the function can be *anonymous* (created just for this job without needing a name) by using the `lambda` command, which looks like `lambda args : command`. A `lambda` function can only execute one command, but it enables you to write very short code to do relatively complicated things. As an example, the following instruction takes a list and cubes each number in it and adds 7:

```
map(lambda x:pow(x,3)+7,list)
```

Another way that `lambda` can be used is in conjunction with the `filter` command. This returns elements of a list that evaluate to `True`, so:

```
filter(lambda x:x>=2,list)
```

returns those elements of the list that are greater than or equal to 2. NumPy provides simpler ways to do these things for arrays of numbers, as we shall see.

A.3.6 Exceptions

Like other modern languages, Python allows for the trapping of exceptions. This is done through the `try ... except ... else` and `try... finally` constructions. This example shows the use of the most common version. For more details, including the types of exceptions that are defined, see a Python programming book.

```
try:
    x/y
except ZeroDivisonError:
    print "Divisor must not be 0"
except TypeError:
    print "They must be numbers"
except:
    print "Something unspecified went wrong"
else:
    print "Everything worked"
```

A.3.7 Classes

For those that wish to use it in this way, Python is fully object-oriented, and classes are defined (with their constructor) by:

```
class myclass(superclass):

    def ___init___(self,args):

    def functionname(self,args):
```

If a superclass is not specified, then the class does not inherit from elsewhere. The `__init__(self,args)` function is the constructor for the class. There can also be a destructor `__del__(self)`, although they are rarely used. Accessing methods from the class uses the `classname.functionname()` syntax. The `self` argument can be ignored in all function calls, since Python fills it in for you, but it does need to be specified in the function definition. Many of the examples in the book are based on classes provided on the book website. You need to be aware that you have to create an instance of the class before you can run it. There is one extra thing that can catch the unwary. If you have imported a module within a program and then you change the code of the module that you have imported, reloading the program won't reload the module. So to import and run the changed module you need to use:

```
import myclass
var = myclass.myclass()
var.function()
```

and if there is a module within there that you expect to change (for example, during testing or further development, you modify it a little to include:

```
import myclass
reload(myclass)
var = myclass.myclass()
var.function()
```

A.4 USING NUMPY AND MATPLOTLIB

Most of the commands that are used in this book actually come from the NumPy and Matplotlib packages, rather than the basic Python language. More specialised commands are described thoughout the book in the places where they become relevant. There are lots of examples of performing tasks using the various functions within NumPy on its website. Getting information about functions within NumPy is generally done using `help(np.functionname)` such as `help(np.dot)`.

NumPy has a base collection of functions and then additional packages that have to be imported as well if you want to use them. To import the NumPy base library and get started you use:

```
>>> import numpy as np
```

A.4.1 Arrays

The basic data structure that is used for numerical work, and by far the most important one for the programming in this book, is the **array**. This is exactly like multi-dimensional arrays (or matrices) in any other language; it consists of one or more dimensions of numbers or chars. Unlike Python lists, the elements of the array all have the same type, which can be Boolean, integer, real, or complex numbers.

Arrays are made using a function call, and the values are passed in as a list, or set of lists for higher dimensions. Here are one-dimensional and two-dimensional arrays (which are effectively arrays of arrays) being made. Arrays can have as many dimensions as you like up to a language limit of 40 dimensions, which is more than enough for this book.

```
>>> myarray = np.array([4,3,2])
>>> mybigarray = np.array([[3, 2, 4], [3, 3, 2], [4, 5, 2]])
>>> print myarray
[4 3 2]
>>> print mybigarray
[[3 2 4]
 [3 3 2]
 [4 5 2]]
```

Making arrays like this is fine for small arrays where the numbers aren't regular, but there are several cases where this is not true. There are nice ways to make a set of the more interesting arrays, such as those shown next.

Array Creation Functions

`np.arange()` Produces an array containing the specified values, acting as an array version of `range()`. For example, `np.arange(5)` = `array([0, 1, 2, 3, 4])` and `np.arange(3,7,2)` = `array([3, 5])`.

`np.ones()` Produces an array containing all ones. For both `np.ones()` and `np.zeros()` you need two sets of brackets when making arrays of more than one dimension. `np.ones(3)` = `array([ 1., 1., 1.])` and `np.ones((3,4))` =

```
array([[ 1.,   1.,   1., 1,]
 [ 1.,   1.,   1., 1.]
 [ 1.,   1.,   1., 1.]])
```

You can specify the type of arrays using `a = np.ones((3,4),dtype=float)`. This can be useful to ensure that you don't run into problems with integer casting, although NumPy is fairly good at casting things as floats.

`np.zeros()` Similar to `np.ones()`, except that all elements of the matrix are zero.

`np.eye()` Produces the identity matrix, i.e., the 2D matrix that is zero everywhere except down the leading diagonal, where it is one. Given one argument it produces the square identity: `np.eye(3)` =

```
[[ 1.   0.   0.]
 [ 0.   1.   0.]
 [ 0.   0.   1.]]
```

while with two arguments it fills spare rows or columns with zeros: `np.eye(3,4)` =

```
[[ 1.   0.   0.   0.]
 [ 0.   1.   0.   0.]
 [ 0.   0.   1.   0.]]
```

`np.linspace(start,stop,npoints)` Produces a matrix with linearly spaced elements. The nice thing is that you specify the number of elements, not the spacing. `np.linspace(3,7,3)` = `array([ 3., 5., 7.])`

np.r_[] and **np.c_[]** Perform row and column concatenation, including the use of the slice operator: np.r_[1:4,0,4] = array([1, 2, 3, 0, 4]). There is also a variation on np.linspace() using a j in the last entry: np.r_[2,1:7:3j] = array([2. , 1. , 4. , 7.]). This is another nice feature of NumPy that can be used with np.arange() and np.meshgrid() as well. The j on the last value specifies that you want 3 equally spaced points starting at 0 and running up to (and including) 7, and the function works out the locations of these points for you. The column version is similar.

The array a used in the next set of examples was made using >>> a = np.arange(6).reshape(3,2), which produces:
```
array([[0, 1],
       [2, 3],
       [4, 5]])
```
Indexing elements of an array is performed using square brackets '[' and ']', remembering that indices start from 0. So a[2,1] returns 5 and a[:,1] returns array([1, 3, 5]). We can also get various pieces of information about an array and change it in a variety of different ways, as follows.

Getting information about arrays, changing their shape, copying them

np.ndim(a) Returns the number of dimensions (here 2).

np.size(a) Returns the number of elements (here 6).

np.shape(a) Returns the size of the array in each dimension (here (3, 2)). You can access the first element of the result using shape(a)[0].

np.reshape(a,(2,3)) Reshapes the array as specified. Note that the new dimensions are in brackets. One nice thing about np.reshape() is that you can use '-1' for 1 dimension within the reshape command to mean 'as many as is required'. This saves you doing the multiplication yourself. For this example, you could use np.reshape(a,(2,-1)) or np.reshape(a,(-1,2)).

np.ravel(a) Makes the array one-dimensional (here array([0, 1, 2, 3, 4, 5])).

np.transpose(a) Compute the matrix transpose. For the example:
```
[[0 2 4]
 [1 3 5]]
```

a[::-1] Reverse the elements of each dimension.

np.min(), **np.max(a)**, **np.sum(a)** Returns the smallest or largest element of the matrix, or the sum of the elements. Often used to sum the rows or columns using the axis option: np.sum(axis=0) for columns and np.sum(axis=1) for rows.

np.copy() Makes a deep copy of a matrix.

Many of these functions have an alternative form that like a.min() which returns the minimum of array a. This can be useful when you are dealing with single matrices. In particular, the shorter version of the transpose operator, a.T, can save a lot of typing.

Just like the rest of Python, NumPy generally deals with references to objects, rather than the objects themselves. So to make a copy of an array you need to use c = a.copy().

Once you have defined matrices, you need to be able to add and multiply them in different ways. As well as the array a used above, for the following set of examples two other arrays b and c are needed. They have to have sizes relating to array a. Array b is the same size as a and is made by `>>> b = np.arange(3,9).reshape(3,2)`, while c needs to have the same inner dimension; that is, if the size of a is (x, 2) then the size of c needs to be (2, y) where the values of x and y don't matter. For the examples `>>> c = np.transpose(b)`. Here are some of the operations you can perform on arrays and matrices:

Operations on arrays

---

a+b Matrix addition. Output for the example is:
```
array([[ 3,  5],
       [ 7,  9],
       [11, 13]])
```

a*b Element-wise multiplication. Output:
```
array([[ 0,  4],
       [10, 18],
       [28, 40]])
```

np.dot(a,c) Matrix multiplication. Output:
```
array([[ 4,  6,  8],
       [18, 28, 38],
       [32, 50, 68]])
```

pow(a,2) Compute exponentials of elements of matrix (a Python function, not a NumPy one). Output:
```
array([[ 0,  1],
       [ 4,  9],
       [16, 25]])
```

pow(2,a) Compute number raised to matrix elements (a Python function, not a NumPy one). Output:
```
array([[ 1,  2],
       [ 4,  8],
       [16, 32]])
```

Matrix subtraction and element-wise division are also defined, but the same trap that we saw earlier can occur with division, namely that a/3 returns an integer not a float if a is an array of integers.

There is one more very useful command on arrays, which is the `np.where()` command. This has two forms: `x = np.where(a>2)` returns the indices where the logical expression is true in the variable x, while `x = np.where(a>2,0,1)` returns a matrix the same size as a that contains 0 in those places where the expression was true in a and 1 everywhere else. To chain these conditions together you have to use the bitwise logical operations, so that `indices = np.where((a[:,0]>3) | (a[:,1]<3))` returns a list of the indices where either of these statements is true.

A.4.2 Random Numbers

There are some good random number features within NumPy, which you access in `np.random` after importing NumPy. To find out about the functions use `help(np.random)` once NumPy has been imported, but the more useful functions are:

`np.random.rand(matsize)` produces uniformly distributed random numbers between 0 and 1 in an array of size `matsize`

`np.random.randn(matsize)` produces zero mean, unit variance Gaussian random numbers

`np.random.normal(mean,stdev,matsize)` produces Gaussian random numbers with specifed mean and standard deviation

`np.random.uniform(low,high,matsize)` produces uniform random numbers between low and high

`np.random.randint(low,high,matsize)` produces random integer values between low and high

A.4.3 Linear Algebra

NumPy has a reasonable linear algebra package that performs standard linear algebra functions. The functions are available as `np.linalg.inv(a)`, etc., where `a` is an array and possible functions are (if you don't know what they all are, don't worry: they will be defined where they are used in the book):

`np.linalg.inv(a)` Compute the inverse of (square) array `a`

`np.linalg.pinv(a)` Compute the pseudo-inverse, which is defined even if `a` is not square

`np.linalg.det(a)` Compute the determinant of `a`

`np.linalg.eig(a)` Compute the eigenvalues and eigenvectors of `a`

A.4.4 Plotting

The plotting functions that we will be using are in the Matplotlib package (also known as pylab, and which we will import as `import pylab as pl`). These are designed to look exactly like the MATLAB® plotting functions. The entire set of functions, with examples, are given on the Matplotlib webpage, but the two most important ones that we will need are `pl.plot` and `pl.hist`. When producing plots they sometimes do not appear. This is usually because you need to specify the command `>>> pl.ion()` which turns interactive plotting on. If you are using Matplotlib within Eclipse it has a nasty habit of closing all of the display windows when the program finishes. To get around this, issue a `show()` command at the end of your function.

The basic plotting commands of Matplotlib are demonstrated here, for more advanced plotting facilities see the package webpage.

The following code (best typed into a file and executed as a script) computes a Gaussian function for values -2 to 2.5 in steps of 0.01 and plots it, then labels the axes and gives the figure a title. The output of running it is shown in Figure A.1.

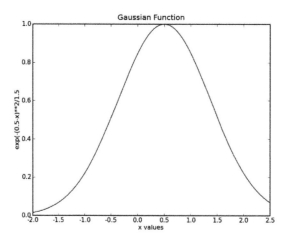

FIGURE A.1 The Matplotlib package produces useful graphical output, such as this plot of the Gaussian function.

```
import pylab as pl
import numpy as np

gaussian = lambda x: exp(-(0.5-x)**2/1.5)
x = np.arange(-2,2.5,0.01)
y = gaussian(x)
pl.ion()
pl.figure()
pl.plot(x,y)
pl.xlabel('x values')
pl.ylabel('exp(-(0.5-x)**2/1.5')
pl.title('Gaussian Function')
pl.show()
```

There is another very useful way to make arrays in NumPy, which is `np.meshgrid()`. It can be used to make a set of indices for a grid, so that you can quickly and easily access all the points within the grid. This has many uses for us, not least of which is to find a classifier line, which can be done using `np.meshgrid()` and then drawn using `pl.contour()`:

```
pl.figure()
step=0.1
f0,f1 = np.meshgrid(np.arange(-2,2,step), np.arange(-2,2,step))

# Run a classifier algorithm
out = classifier(np.c_[np.ravel(f0), np.ravel(f1)],soft=True).T
out = out.reshape(f0.shape)
```

```
pl.contourf(f0, f1, out)
```

A.4.5 One Thing to Be Aware of

NumPy is mostly great to use, and extremely powerful. However, there is one thing that I still find annoying on occasion, and that is the two different types of vector. The following set of commands typed at the command line and the output produced show the problem:

```
>>> a = np.ones((3,3))
>>> a
array([[ 1.,   1.,   1.],
       [ 1.,   1.,   1.],
       [ 1.,   1.,   1.]])
>>> np.shape(a)
(3, 3)
>>> b = a[:,1]
>>> b
array([ 1.,   1.,   1.])
>>> np.shape(b)
(3,)
>>> c = a[1,:]
>>> np.shape(c)
(3,)
>>> print c.T
>>> c
array([ 1.,   1.,   1.])
>>> c.T
array([ 1.,   1.,   1.])
```

When we use a slice operator and only index a single row or column, NumPy seems to turn it into a list, so that it stops being either a row or a column. This means that the transpose operator doesn't do anything to it, and also means that some of the other behaviour can be a little odd. It's a real trap for the unwary, and can make for some interesting bugs that are hard to find in programs. There are a few ways around the problem, of which the two simplest are shown below: either listing a start and end for the slice even for a single row or column, or explicitly reshaping it afterwards.

```
>>> c = a[0:1,:]
>>> np.shape(c)
(1, 3)
>>> c = a[0,:].reshape(1,len(a))
>>> np.shape(c)
(1, 3)
```

FURTHER READING

Python has become incredibly popular for both general computing and scientific computing. Because writing extension packages for Python is simple (it does not require any special programming commands: any Python module can be imported as a package, as can packages written in C), many people have done so, and made their code available on the Internet. Any search engine will find many of these, but a good place to start is the Python Cookbook website.

If you are looking for more complete introductions to Python, some of the following may be useful:

- M.L. Hetland. *Beginning Python: From Novice to Professional*, 2nd edition, Apress Inc., Berkeley, CA, USA, 2008.

- G. van Rossum and F.L. Drake Jr., editors. *An Introduction to Python*. Network Theory Ltd, Bristol, UK, 2006.

- W.J. Chun. *Core Python Programming*. Prentice-Hall, New Jersey, USA, 2006.

- B. Eckel. *Thinking in Python*. Mindview, La Mesa, CA, USA, 2001.

- T. Oliphant. Guide to NumPy, e-book, 2006. The official guide to NumPy by its creator.

PRACTICE QUESTIONS

Problem A.1 Make an array `a` of size 6×4 where every element is a 2.

Problem A.2 Make an array `b` of size 6×4 that has 3 on the leading diagonal and 1 everywhere else. (You can do this without loops.)

Problem A.3 Can you multiply these two matrices together? Why does `a * b` work, but not `dot(a,b)`?

Problem A.4 Compute `dot(a.transpose(),b)` and `dot(a,b.transpose())`. Why are the results different shapes?

Problem A.5 Write a function that prints some output on the screen and make sure you can run it in the programming environment that you are using.

Problem A.6 Now write one that makes some random arrays and prints out their sums, the mean value, etc.

Problem A.7 Write a function that consists of a set of loops that run through an array and count the number of ones in it. Do the same thing using the `where()` function (use `info(where)` to find out how to use it).

Index